LAURA WOOD ROPER

A Biography of FREDERICK
LAW
OLMSTED

The JOHNS HOPKINS UNIVERSITY PRESS
Baltimore and London

Frontispiece: portrait by Fanny Perkins, after photograph
by James Notman; modern photograph by X. de Gery,
photographer

The Johns Hopkins University Press, Baltimore, Maryland 21218
The Johns Hopkins University Press Ltd., London

Library of Congress Catalog Card Number 73-8125
ISBN 0-8018-1508-8

Library of Congress Cataloging in Publication data
will be found on the last printed page of this book.

To W. C. R., Jr., L. E. R., and C. N. R.

CONTENTS

ILLUSTRATIONS

ACKNOWLEDGMENTS

IN preparing this book, I drew heavily on the aid of a number of people. My largest debt, affectionately acknowledged, is to the late Frederick Law Olmsted, son of the subject of this biography, whose initial encouragement made the project possible and whose sympathetic, frank, and thoroughly informed discussions of his father's work and personality were invaluable. During my visits with him his wife, Sarah Sharples Olmsted, not only made interesting contributions to the interviews but also offered a warm and unaffected hospitality that made each visit a happy occasion.

Their daughter Charlotte Olmsted Kursh, Mrs. Kursh's son Dr. Stephen P. Gill, John Charles Olmsted's daughter Miss Carolyn Olmsted, Albert Henry Olmsted's grandsons Frederick Olmsted and the late Julian Olmsted, and Mrs. Julian Olmsted are other members of the family to whom I am indebted for encouragement, information, and the generous loan of photographs and other memorabilia.

The late Miss Stella D. Obst, secretary of the younger Frederick Law Olmsted, was thoroughly efficient and tirelessly kind in aiding my research at the Olmsted Brothers office. Mrs. Marion Vaux Hendrickson, granddaughter of Calvert Vaux, and Miss Marguerite Weidenmann, daughter of Jacob Weidenmann, kindly produced manuscripts and personal recollections that contributed materially to my knowledge of those two associates of Olmsted.

I am indebted, further, to the indefatigable staffs of the Manuscripts Division and the Prints and Photographs Division of the Library of Congress; of the Houghton Library, Harvard University; and of the Manuscripts Division and the Prints Division of the New York Public Library. Among the scholars and friends who have forwarded my research are Miss Caroline Shillaber, librarian, Frances Loeb Library, Graduate School of Design at Harvard University; Professor James Howard, editor of the 1962 edition of Olmsted's *Journey through Texas*; Dr. George Mazaraki, author of a valuable dissertation on Andrew Haswell Green; Mrs. Margaret Boyle-Cullen, authority on the history of Olmsted's Staten Island home; Miss Elizabeth Duval, bibliographer, Smith College Library; and Dr. J. N. Bowman, historian, California State Archives.

Special thanks are due Mrs. Helen Duprey Bullock, formerly of the Manuscripts Division, Library of Congress, whose help in dealing with the mass of manuscripts in the Olmsted Collection there made the rough places smooth at the beginning of this enterprise; to Mr. Frederick A. Gutheim, chairman of the

Olmsted Sesquicentennial Committee, whose timely and effective interest toward the end of the work was of critical importance to a successful culmination; and to Professor Dana F. White, of Atlanta and Emory universities, whose thoughtful editorial comments were a welcome guide to me in the revision of an overlong manuscript.

I cannot adequately thank the two foremost Olmsted scholars, Professor Albert Fein, of Long Island University, and Professor Charles C. McLaughlin, of American University, for their support and proven friendship. Mr. McLaughlin cheerfully and often placed his files and his encyclopedic knowledge of all things Olmsted-related at my disposal. Mr. Fein freely and enthusiastically shared his discoveries and his stimulating insights with me. Finally, I am infinitely grateful to my husband, W. Crosby Roper, Jr., not only for his sound criticism and incisive editing, but also for other less direct contributions, some subtle and some substantial, that he has made to this work over a long period.

The reader will perhaps notice that, in the course of handling more than two thousand citations, I have mislaid half a dozen. The fact should not surprise anyone, although the admission may. In quoted passages, spelling and punctuation have been regularized where literal transcription might have been confusing or distracting.

L.W.R.

FOREWORD

FREDERICK Law Olmsted set out early and deliberately to make himself a man of influence on his time and on his country. His course, erratic to begin with, found its true direction only after several false starts. Extricating himself from the backwater, farming, that was his first enthusiasm, he embarked on journalism and publishing and entered directly into the mainstream of contemporary American life.

As a journalist he explored the agitating questions of the day with candor and intelligence and in the space of a decade produced a body of work that was something of a revelation to his pre-Civil War readers, and that offers readers today a clear and credible view of a disputed past. Dropping his literary career to work on the construction of Central Park, Olmsted turned his mind to the problems, already acute, of big-city living. His connection with the United States Sanitary Commission during the war then carried him into the area of the social sciences, the concerns of which dovetailed nicely with those of the work that was his passion and finally his profession, landscape architecture. Thus his early ventures, any one of which might have become a satisfactory life work to a less searching spirit, helped to prepare him for his later career.

America's great pioneer landscape architect, Olmsted during his own long day was recognized as a prophet by a few and held in simple gratitude by multitudes. At his death, he was praised from one end of the nation to the other. Within a quarter of a century he was half-forgotten; his name became a feature of footnotes, and his great landscape works were let lapse toward ruin or, worse, cobbled and botched.

It is a provocative question why Olmsted's career, which spanned forty years of superb creativity, should have fallen upon neglect. With his partner, the English-born architect Calvert Vaux, Olmsted originated the rural park movement in the United States; he was the theoretician and director of the successful drive to set aside areas of unusual scenic beauty for popular enjoyment; with Vaux and other associates he designed parks, parkways, and suburban developments and the grounds of public buildings, expositions, institutions, railroad stations, military installations, and private estates and homes, east and west, north and south. Under the impact of Olmsted's thought and practice, landscape design shifted its sights from decorative to social aims; land was to be arranged not only for scenic effect but also to serve the health, comfort, convenience, and good cheer of everyone who used it. In a country rapidly being urbanized,

Olmsted's far-sighted moves to humanize the physical environment of cities and to secure precious scenic regions for the use and enjoyment of all the people constituted a heroic undertaking.

Yet Olmsted has no standing as an American hero. He fits no generally accepted heroic mold. He was not a courageous soldier, a towering statesman, an intrepid explorer; he was not even an underdog triumphant over odds. He was, instead, something not at all glamorous: a well-bred intellectual, a determined patriot, a practical and foresighted artist, a brilliant executive, and a man of multifarious interests and enormous industry. Nor was he self-aggrandizing: he believed that the function of the fine arts, especially the one he practiced, was to uplift and refresh the spirit of others, not to express the personality of the artist.

The peculiar ideal that motivated his work was not a catchy one, appealing as it did to impulses too lofty to be comfortably, or often, indulged. He called it "communicativeness," and by it he distinguished the civilized man from the barbarian. Communicativeness involved recognizing, and acting consistently on the recognition, that one had an essential community of interest with other human beings, regardless of regional, class, economic, color, religious, or whatever differences. Barbarism, conversely, assumed that those not distinctly allied to one's self by some clearly identifiable bond were alien, contemptible, and fair game. Communicativeness had no room for narrowly selfish interests, whether of individuals or groups or classes. As an ideal, it was Christian, democratic, and utopian, something between a will-o'-the-wisp and the last, best hope of earth.

Translated into political terms, communicativeness was the essence of democracy, and Olmsted was democratic to the marrow. No common man himself, he was guided the length of his career by the perception that it was the tone of the commonality, not of the elite, that determined the health of political bodies. "Men of literary taste or clerical habit," he wrote as a young man,

> are always apt to overlook the working-classes, and to confine the records
> they make of their own times, in a great degree, to the habits and fortunes of
> their own associates or to those of people of superior rank to themselves.
> The dumb masses have often been so lost in this shadow of egotism, that,
> in later days, it has been impossible to discern the very real influence their
> character and condition has [sic] had on the fortune and the fate of nations.[1]

Olmsted's lifelong concern for the character and condition of the masses of his countrymen and for the fate of his country was expressed most happily in his great public works. Yet despite their continuing presence—usually mutilated —their creator is too little known. There was nothing flamboyant in his personality nor facile in his ideal. The reserve of the one and the elusiveness of the other, combined with Olmsted's self-effacement in his work, tend to account for his fading from the public mind, especially since his works, originally sources of excitement and admiration, literally merged into the familiar scene and with the passage of time came to be taken for granted.

At the peak of Olmsted's contemporary fame, just after the opening of the Chicago fair, *Garden and Forest*, then the only publication in the country seriously and regularly to discuss landscape architecture, predicted his eclipse and philosophically took the long view of it.

> The foremost artist which the New World has yet produced, Mr. Olmsted, has been singularly fortunate in impressing himself during his own lifetime upon his time and people, in living to see with his own eyes the development and perfection of his greatest conceptions. The memory of his name and personality may be dimmed in the passage of years, for it is the fate of architects to be lost in their work, but millions of people now unborn will find rest and refreshment in the contemplation of smiling landscapes which he has made, and will enjoy the shade of trees which he has planted. No American has been more useful in his time or has made a more valuable and lasting contribution to civilization in this country.[2]

This biography attempts to rediscover and introduce the architect long lost in the work. Olmsted emerges from the shadow of neglect as a man extraordinarily effective in a range of socially creative undertakings and as one dedicated passionately and intelligently—even, sometimes, successfully—to conserving the beautiful and healthy and to remedying the ugly and harmful in the American scene a full hundred years before the environment (a word that, to the best of my recollection, occurs nowhere in his writings) became a matter of popular concern.

L.W.R.

A NOTE ON THE CITATIONS

Most of the manuscripts used in the preparation of this biography are in the Frederick Law Olmsted Collection, Library of Congress, Washington, D.C. All the manuscripts cited without mention of their location are in that collection; and unless it is otherwise indicated (by noting box number, or letterbook) those cited are in the chronological file.

The location of manuscript materials not in the Olmsted Collection is given with the citation.

KEY TO CORRESPONDENTS

CLB	Charles Loring Brace
HWB	Henry Whitney Bellows
GWC	George William Curtis
HWSC	Horace William Shaler Cleveland
AHG	Andrew Haswell Green
ELG	Edwin Lawrence Godkin
FJK	Frederick John Kingsbury
FNK	Frederick Newman Knapp
CEN	Charles Eliot Norton
O	Frederick Law Olmsted (1822–1903)
FLO (son)	Frederick Law Olmsted (1870–1957)
JCO	John Charles Olmsted
JHO	John Hull Olmsted
JO	John Olmsted
MAO	Mary Ann (Bull) Olmsted
MCO	Mary Cleveland Bryant (Perkins) Olmsted
HHR	Henry Hobson Richardson
LWR	Laura Wood Roper
GTS	George Templeton Strong
MGVR	Mariana Griswold Van Rensselaer
CV	Calvert Vaux
GEW	George Edwin Waring, Jr.
KPW	Katherine Prescott Wormeley

A Biography of FREDERICK LAW OLMSTED

I
YOUTH AND SCHOOLING

1822–1840

FREDERICK Law Olmsted was born the twenty-sixth of April 1822 in Hartford, Connecticut, into a secure place, his by right, in the city founded by his ancestors and in the community formed and sustained by seven generations of his family.

In the larger world, the Olmsted family had had a secure place at least since the time of the Norman Conquest. The name is recorded, as "Almestede," in the Domesday Book for the county of Essex, England. In the northern part of the Essex parish of Bumsted-Helion, Olmsted Hall, a small stone farmhouse, moated around, was the family homestead until some time about the beginning of the fifteenth century, when it passed out of Olmsted hands and eventually became part of the endowment of Queens' College, Cambridge.

Rooted in Essex, the family prospered through the Wars of the Roses, the reigns of the Tudor sovereigns, and into the era of the Stuart kings. The Olmsted to turn his back on the civil and religious turmoil of his ancient homeland was James, landed gentleman and Puritan. Perhaps life in England became flavorless to him after the death of his wife and four of his seven children; certainly the suppression of nonconformity made it uneasy. His friend and neighbor, the redoubtable preacher Thomas Hooker, was silenced for nonconformity and fled to Holland in 1630. In the summer of 1632, James Olmsted, fifty-two years of age, with his sons Nicholas and Nehemiah, his nephews John and Richard, and his niece Rebecca, sailed from Braintree on the ship *Lyon*, Captain Pierce commanding, to renew their lives and launch their family in a new world that might be theirs to order.

The *Lyon*, carrying one hundred twenty-three passengers, fifty of them children, reached the Massachusetts colony on Sunday, September 16, 1632, after a voyage of twelve weeks. The Braintree colonists settled first at Mount Wollaston, now Quincy, and soon after moved to Newtown, now Cambridge. At their invitation Thomas Hooker, with his ministerial assistant Samuel Stone, joined them as their pastor in September 1633.

Dissatisfied in Massachusetts, the Braintree contingent in the summer of 1634 sent a dozen men, one of whom is thought to have been James Olmsted, to explore the Connecticut Valley. The following year about sixty of Hooker's flock migrated to the site of Hartford, arriving early in November, in time to be caught by a winter of deadly severity. Many of the group, fearing starvation, made their painful way back to Massachusetts overland or by water along the coast. The few who remained ate even acorns to say alive.

Hooker and his congregation set out from Newtown to join the faltering remnant on May 31, 1636. For two weeks they traveled through the wilderness to reach the outpost little more than a hundred miles away. Their arrival revivified it, and the colony took firm root.[1]

Having endured the hardships of settlement, James Olmsted shared the rewards. In the land distribution of 1639 he, an original proprietor of Hartford, was assigned seventy acres on the highway that later became Front Street. There his son Nicholas built a house that stood until the 1830s.

Toward the end of 1640, James "slept sweetly in the Lord," so his grieving pastor Hooker wrote, "having carried himself gratiously in his sickness." In his short term in the new world James had accumulated an estate worth almost four hundred pounds, which he bequeathed to Nicholas and Nehemiah. Nehemiah died in 1657, leaving no sons; Nicholas, who died in 1684, left three, from whom descended legions.[2]

Nicholas served the colony well as an officer in the wars against the Indians, and as surveyor of highways, list maker, rate maker, and deputy to the General Court. He served himself well too and died in possession of considerable land on either side of the Connecticut River.[3]

Nicholas's son Joseph, who settled on the farm his father left him on the east side of the river, and Joseph's son Joseph both were deacons of the First Congregational Church of Hartford. The second Joseph's son, Jonathan, enjoyed a measure of wealth as a farmer and the satisfaction, unusual for the time, of seeing eight of his ten children grow up. He died in 1770 at the age of sixty-four, leaving six sons.[4]

These were farmers, seafaring men, and patriots. The oldest, Jonathan, born in 1740, kept moving westward; his final migration took him, when he was ninety-six years old, from Marietta, Ohio, to Danville, Illinois. His five brothers all bore arms during the Revolution. One of them, Ezekiel, sailed against the British in a privateer, was captured, and died at the age of twenty-seven on a prison ship in New York Harbor. Gideon, master of another privateer, was luckier; captured off Cuba and placed with three of his shipmates aboard a sloop to be transported to New York, he seized the little ship from her surprised crew and brought her with cargo intact and crew captive into Philadelphia. The remaining brothers, Benjamin, Epaphras, and Aaron, acquitted themselves respectably as soldiers. After the Revolution, Aaron became a shipmaster in the China trade; he died in 1806, a rich and cultivated man. Benjamin, who had been furloughed in November 1775 to marry Content Pitkin, followed with less success in Aaron's wake in the China trade. Over the years, Benjamin fathered seven children. John, the fifth of them, became the father of Frederick Law Olmsted.[5]

When Frederick was born in 1822, Hartford had grown from a struggling settlement into a thriving little city, with a population of almost seven thousand.

Capital of the state, home of an arms manufacturing plant, center of the infant insurance business, it supported twenty-two dry-goods stores, four brokers, a museum, ten milliners and mantua makers, thirteen physicians and surgeons, twenty-two lawyers, a dozen churches, and fourteen taverns and hotels.[6] Set in charming countryside watered by streams full of salmon and trout, it was surrounded by rural villages, low wooded hills, and thrifty farms that produced corn, tobacco, fruit, hay, grain, and livestock. Although inland, it had become one of the most important ports and distributing centers in New England. Stage and coastwise shipping lines connected it with the rest of the nation, and the Connecticut River, navigable to ocean-going ships, linked it with the world beyond the seas.

Warehouses and shops crowded the waterfront. The wholesale houses on Commerce, Ferry, Kilbourne, and Morgan streets unloaded at their own wharves ships laden with goods from remote ports. The Front Street merchants dealt in groceries, dry goods, West Indian wares, lumber, soap, rope, jewelry, and nautical gear. Substantial homes, some of them almost two hundred years old, lined the shady streets, and a few, more pretentious, stood in carefully tended "ornamental grounds." City and country still mingled harmoniously: house lots were large enough for vegetable gardens and barns, many families kept a cow, and pleasant countryside lay within walking distance.

The churches, their steeples topping the surrounding buildings, were the city's most prominent feature, architecturally and morally. They dominated the urban scene, and they still went far toward dominating the lives spent there. Their bells tolled for the dead, marked the hour each day at noon, and every evening at nine rang curfew, by which time respectable citizens were, supposedly, within doors, and the streets were abandoned to the night watch, stray animals, and reprobates. The Congregational Church, although it had to contend for souls with the Baptist, Episcopalian, Roman Catholic, and other later arrivals, was the prevalent religious force in the community. Its ministers, relying on frequent revivals, and on long sermons, the alternating terror and tedium of which some listeners remembered from childhood into old age, guided their parishioners along the narrow path of righteousness.

The citizens of Hartford were on the whole, however, so respectable that clergymen and church members were almost equally in awe of each other. The Reverend Dr. Joel Hawes, who held the pulpit of the First Congregational Church from 1818 to 1862, had been almost overwhelmed when he first addressed its congregation. "I seemed to be in the midst of an assembly of Roman senators," he recalled, "so thickly scattered in every part of the house were . . . grave and venerable men. . . . Their heads, hoary with age and with honor, their upturned countenances, so intelligent, so dignified, so devout and thoughtful, filled me with awe as I beheld them."[7]

One of the least awe-inspiring of Dr. Hawes's auditors on that memorable Sunday may well have been young John Olmsted, merchant, son of Benjamin, belonging to the sixth generation of descendants from the original proprietor, James.

John Olmsted was born September 27, 1791, in East Hartford, the third of Benjamin's four sons.[8] He is said to have had no more than a common school education and to have picked up a little French somewhere.[9] Not until 1825, when he began to keep a daybook and to come under the awakening observation of his son Frederick, can much be said with certainty about him. By then he was a member of the Hartford fire department, aide-de-camp to the general of militia, and part owner of Olmsted and King, a large dry-goods store at the corner of Main and Pearl streets.[10] He was civic-minded, moderately prosperous, and more than moderately generous. He contributed regularly to missions, churches, prison society, and orphanage, and his yearly donations to charities sometimes came to more than his expenses for travel, his prime recreation.[11] Toward the building of the Hartford Retreat for the Insane, a pioneer institution in this country in the humane treatment of the mentally ill, he gave first, fifty dollars, and later one hundred in five yearly installments.[12] He became a director of the Retreat[13] and a benefactor and trustee of the Wadsworth Atheneum as well,[14] but he never became a prominent, or public, figure. While his strong sense of duty drove him to accept civic responsibilities, his insuperable modesty prevented him from thrusting himself forward to court recognition for ably discharging them; and it served, in fact, to mask his merit. ". . . His real qualities had so little of brilliance," his son Frederick wrote, "that he passed with others, even with many of his friends, for a man of much less worth, ability and attainment than he was."[15]

Nor did John Olmsted obtrude himself in the daybook that he kept from 1825 until his death in 1873. Not his deep love of nature, nor his warmth of family feeling, nor his devotion to country, nor the range of his ideas and opinions show through its entries; instead, he meticulously recorded such matters of fact as the weather; the date the first shad came up the river; the price and quantity of domestic purchases like meat, sugar, tea, rum, wine, Poughkeepsie ale, and shoes; his occasional transactions in real estate; the wages of his household help; the cost of rent and insurance; each child's first tooth, first step, diseases, and dosages; and visitors, lectures, deaths, and local and national events—hundreds of details, trivial and important, that made up the mosaic of daily life. The record he kept is laconic; the only emotion is implied. On September 2, 1825, he recorded the birth of his second son, John Hull (Frederick Law had been born before he started his daybook), and on March 12, 1826, he wrote in his usual well-formed, unwavering hand, "No a/c kept of expenses from Feb 24 to March 12. Tues Feb 28 at ½ past 5 p.m. my dr wife died & was buried on Sunday following." He did not even record the cause of her death: an overdose of laudanum taken, by mistake, for cough medicine.[16]

John's "dr wife" was Charlotte Law (Hull) Olmsted. Born September 9, 1800, she was sixth of the nine children of Samuel Hull and his wife Abigail Ann (Doolittle) Hull, of Cheshire, Connecticut. Charlotte's oldest sister, Stella, fourteen years her senior, was married to Jonathan Law, who was like a father to his little sister-in-law and is said to have adopted her, although her parents were living. Charlotte married John Olmsted on June 5, 1821, had two sons, named the older for his uncle Law, and died at the age of twenty-five.[17] She is a shadow.

To Frederick Law Olmsted she was even fainter than that; she was the shadow of a shadow: he did not remember her, he only recalled once having done so. He believed he had had, in earliest childhood, a vague memory of her sitting under a tree sewing, while he played at her feet. Vague as it was, it was strangely poignant, and it always moved him in later life to see such a tableau.[18]

Another early memory, oppressive, and not less so for being indistinct, haunted his recollection: he was present, a very small child, ignored and frightened, in a room full of distraught grown people where some domestic tragedy was coming to a climax. Perhaps it was his mother's death bed; whatever it was, it was the stuff of troubled dreams.[19]

A little more than a year after Charlotte's death, on April 25, 1827, John Olmsted made the terse entry in his daybook, "married $10⁰⁰." The events of the months before his marriage to Mary Ann Bull he had indicated sketchily: baby John had had his first tooth at the age of seven and a half months (Fred had been six months old when he got his); Fred had started to Mrs. Jeffry's dame school, at a tuition of two dollars a quarter; on December 11, John began to walk, and Fred got chicken pox; Fred gave it to his brother, who fell ill a few days after Christmas. Early in January 1827 John, senior, paid a dollar for a sled for Fred and called Dr. Terry to vaccinate his younger son. Then, on April 19, he "moved from Dodd house (5½ years, 180 a yr) to Wadsworth house" in preparation for his marriage, which took place the day before Fred's fifth birthday.[20]

John Olmsted's second wife was, like himself, of Puritan stock native to Hartford. She was born there April 11, 1801, the daughter of Isaac D. and Mary (Watson) Bull.[21] A friend of Charlotte Olmsted's, she carried a guilty memory of her death. The dying woman, past caring for the others in the sick room, had implored, "Pray with me, Mary Ann!" And Mary Ann, ashamed to pray in the presence of observers, had pretended to misunderstand and had answered, "Yes, I will pray for you."

She never forgave herself for withholding, out of cowardly and misplaced shame, the comfort Charlotte had asked in her extremity. Remorsefully, she made herself practice "social prayer" and, as her stepsons were growing up, recommended it to them zealously. Her first effort for their spiritual welfare, however, was to see that they were baptized. The sacrament, strangely delayed, was performed on June 3, 1827.[22]

Mary Ann Olmsted was efficient, dutiful, and pious. Her rather chilling merit was enhanced, happily, by a quality of spirit shared with her husband. Both were quietly, joyously responsive to the gentle rural scenery that lay about them. Their delight in it was reticent, and if they analyzed it at all, they did not talk about it. Yet their manner of life was governed to an unusual degree by their concern to indulge their innocent enjoyment. Leisurely drives about the Connecticut Valley, and longer journeys during vacations and holidays were their chosen recreation. John Olmsted, who would not or could not discuss the quasi-religious emotion that charm of landscape awoke within him, spent more time and thought to secure such enjoyment than on all other luxuries. The little boys, accompanying John and Mary Ann on their journeys, were steeped from childhood in regional scenery and in the silent happiness that it evoked.[23]

Fred was only six when he made his first long trip. After the birth of Charlotte, Mary Ann's first child, on March 18, 1828, he was sent to spend several months with his father's younger brother, Owen Pitkin Olmsted, in Geneseo, New York. His memory of the visit was faint and fragmented: he recalled seeing Indians weave baskets, visiting a house where a fawn grazed in the front yard and a beautiful woman gave him candy, and "being sometimes driven rapidly and silently over the turf of bottom lands among great trees."[24]

When John Olmsted went to fetch his son in July, he took him to Buffalo, Niagara Falls, Lockport, Rochester, back to Geneseo, on to Geneva, Syracuse and Albany, and so home. Laconic as usual, he noted the itinerary in his day-book, remarking that the distance both ways had been twelve hundred miles, the expenses $153.50.[25]

Fred claimed later that, before he was twelve, he had been driven

over the most charming roads of the Connecticut Valley and its confluents, through the White Hills and along most of the New England coast from the Kennebeck to the Naugatuck. We were our own servants, my father seldom fully trusting strangers in these journeys with the feeding, cleaning or harnessing of his horses. We rested long in pleasant places; and when at noon we took the nags out and fed them by the roadside, my father, brother and I would often wander far looking for a bathing place and an addition of fresh wild berries for the picnic dinner which my mother would have set out in some well-selected place.

I had also before I was twelve traveled much with my father and mother by stage coach, canal and steamboat, visiting West Point, Trenton Falls, Niagara, Quebec, Lake George.[26]

These early excursions Fred preserved in happy, sometimes inaccurate, memory. His recollections of his schooling were, overall, less agreeable.

It began happily enough when he was just four at Mrs. Jeffry's dame school, where he learned to read. The little brown schoolhouse stood beside a brook in a wood of birch and alder and chestnut trees. The children dammed the brook and caught with their hands little trout and frogs, which they put in a pool where, too, they filled the school's pail of drinking water. When the teacher heard wheels approaching on the narrow road that ran past the school, she

6

would stop the lesson and exclaim, "Your elders are coming. Make your manners! Make your manners!" The children would line up along the road, the little girls to curtsy, the little boys to bow.[27]

Fred attended Mrs. Jeffry's school for three terms, then he went to Mrs. Smith's, and in August 1828, after his return from Geneseo, he started at Miss Rockwell's.[28] Miss Rockwell's pupils studied Webster's speller, the New Testament, Olney's *Geography* and *Atlas*, *Jack Halyard*, and the popular Peter Parley's *Tales* and *Geography*, the author of which may already have been known to Fred as his fellow citizen Samuel G. Goodrich.[29] A little girl half-a-dozen years older than Fred used to lead him to school by the hand; she was Anne Charlotte Lynch. Fred was then, Miss Lynch revealed in later years when her former schoolmate had become an occasional visitor to her popular literary salon in New York, a beautiful little boy, with light blue eyes and golden curls, dressed in short-sleeved frocks that showed his chubby neck and dimpled arms.[30]

Fred's schooling with Miss Rockwell came to a shocking end six months after it began. On February 8, 1829, John Olmsted wrote in his journal: "Sunday rain. Miss Naomi Rockwell buried—died Friday Eve from burns by clothes taking fire. (Frederick's teacher)."

After the dame schools, Fred was farmed out to a succession of clergymen for further education. John Olmsted's diffidence would seem to have dictated the arrangement. Brought up in unquestioning faith in the efficacy of preaching and didactic instruction and knowing how poorly fitted he himself was to impart anything by such means, he sought to have Fred educated by men trained in those approved methods.[31]

The ministers with whom Fred lived seem, however, not to have been selected specifically as schoolmasters; three of them, he later said, sent him out to day school, and only one of them personally gave him regular instruction. Even his religious education, he recalled, was delegated to Sunday school teachers, "that is to say, vain, ignorant and conceited big boys and girls,—parrots and quacks at the business."[32]

The first of his ministerial caretakers was the Reverend Zolua Whitmore, of North Guilford, with whom Fred boarded for twelve shillings a week from November 1829 to September 1830. Three days after he emerged from Mr. Whitmore's control, he started the Hartford Grammar School, where the fee for the term, payable in advance, was eight dollars. There he stayed for two terms; then on May 18, 1831, John Olmsted wrote in his daybook, "carried Frederick to Ellington high school." Apparently that school was unsatisfactory, since the following October 8 Fred was sent to school and board at three dollars a week with the Reverend Joab Brace, in Newington, Connecticut. Mr. Brace was to prepare him for Yale, and Fred remained with him, except for vacations, until the end of May 1836, when he was fourteen years old.[33]

Brace in 1831 was a black-eyed man of fifty, six feet tall, commanding and demanding. He was never sick; he never took a vacation. He was a Latin and Greek scholar, he read the Bible in Hebrew, and he was considered a spiritual leader.[34] Fred regarded him with lasting resentment:[35] the discipline at his school was primitive, and the discomfort barbarous.

An early by-product of Fred's discontinuous education was his permanent, smoldering sense of outrage, well fueled by Brace, at the cruel treatment Christian tutors visited on their small charges. Brace, when he surprised his students in delinquency, was likely to rush among them and beat them with random fury over head and shoulders with broomstick, firewood, ruler, or whatever came to hand, shouting as he did so, "Oh! the depravity of human nature!"[36]

Brace housed the four students he was preparing for college in an old, small country store that he had bought and moved alongside the parsonage. He kept root vegetables in the cellar, used its ground floor as a workshop and harness room, and assigned the second floor to his pupils as schoolroom and living quarters. The clapboard of the building was warped and loose, and in winter freezing drafts filtered freely through, to be modified to a point well short of comfort by a sheet-iron stove built by Brace himself.

The minister had to take part of his salary in kind in his poor parish, and some of his flock hauled firewood, usually in logs, to him when the sledding was good. From his first term Fred, not yet ten and small for his age, had to keep up the schoolhouse fire one day out of four, splitting whole logs with wedge and beetle, carrying wood upstairs during his playtime, and getting up before daylight to start the fire. In winter all the boys arose in the dark and dressed by candlelight, then went to the parsonage kitchen, sometimes through deep snow, to wash faces and hands with homemade soft soap in cold water. All their meals were served in the kitchen; there they knelt on the bare floor twice daily in prayer; and there each received his ration of hot water for the limited bathing that took place Saturday nights.[37] What Brace's rigorous academy lacked in comfort, however, it made up in godliness. The parson prided himself on the frequency of revivals in it and piously hoped that his graduates "never learned anything of me but what might lead them to 'Jesus Christ and Him crucified.' "[38]

Young John, who had been trailing his older brother through dame school and grammar school, joined him at Brace's school late in 1835. The next June, their father removed them.[39] Perhaps the severe case of sumach poisoning, which seriously affected Fred's eyes, accounted for his deliverance from Brace's Spartan oversight. It certainly accounted for his desultory drift between tutors and schools for the next year and a half. For a time during the summer of 1836, Fred was with the Reverend G. C. Eastman at Saybrook. In September he was again sent to the Hartford Grammar School, where he lasted only three months; by early December he was attending Mr. E. Perkins's school in East Hartford. The following summer, he reverted to Mr. Eastman's hands; finally, on November 20, 1837, he was sent to study engineering at Andover, Massachusetts, with Mr. F. A. Barton, a clergyman who was also a civil engineer formerly with the Coast Survey.[40]

Because his sight was thought still to be in jeopardy, Fred was kept from serious study. The prospect of Yale faded from consideration. For two and a half years, while his contemporaries were toiling in college, Fred gave himself over without hindrance "to a decently restrained vagabond life, generally pursued under the guise of an angler, a fowler or a dabbler on the shallowest shores of the deep sea of the natural sciences."[41] Sometimes he amused himself with what he called "play practice," or imaginative topographical work laying out towns, but principally, his occupation and his pleasure were rambling over hills, woods, and meadows and laying away, not at all consciously or deliberately, countless impressions of characteristic New England scenery.[42]

Little academically constructive came of Fred's intermittent schooling under clergymen. It neither taught him to think nor encouraged him to learn; it permanently incensed him against particular ministers; and it may well have been the fount of his profound distaste as an adult for organized religion and its practitioners, lay and clerical. On the other hand, it allowed him considerable liberty to roam the countryside in idle and contemplative enjoyment, and it permitted, mostly by default, his natural curiosity to flourish. If it failed to encourage his tastes, which were intellectual and creative, at least it did not stultify them, and the influences that developed them were steadily at work independently of it. Certain relatives; the books, quite unchildish, that he discovered and read; and above all the excursions, really trips in search of the picturesque with his parents—all had, in his own opinion, a far more important role in forming his taste and character and in educating him than the drilled-in Latin grammar, the Euclid learned by rote, and the physical abuse in the guise of discipline that he experienced at schools.

Fred's propensity for wandering showed itself early, and it was encouraged rather than curbed from childhood. Even when he lived with Mr. Whitmore, at the age of seven and eight, in the farming community of North Guilford, he was under no more constraint, as he remembered it, than a man. In the year he was there, he became familiar with every road and lane, and with every house, barn, stable, and shop in the neighborhood. Everywhere he was recognized and kindly welcomed. "With all their hardworking habits," he said of these early neighbors, "no one seemed to begrudge a little time to make life happy for such a bothering little chap as I must have been. Such a thing as my running into danger even from bad company would seem not to have been thought of."[43]

What he best remembered was not what he studied but what he did. The greater part of the time he was busy and happy outdoors. He did chores on the parson's small farm; with other little boys he smoked woodchucks out of their burrows and trapped mink and rabbits and quail; he took rye to the gristmill, riding on the sacks behind a bigger boy; went with apples to the cider mill and with yarn to the weaver; beat a pan when the bees swarmed; and helped pick the geese, wash the sheep, make soap, dip candles, and set up the martin house. He was on affectionate terms with Mr. Whitmore, whom he called "Uncle," and sometimes rode out on pastoral calls with him.[44]

At home, Fred often went far afield. The region for thirty miles around

9

Hartford was sprinkled with Olmsteds, Olmsted relatives and Olmsted friends, and he was sure of a kindly reception in almost any household where he might stop.[45] As he familiarized himself with his part of the world and with his family that had settled it, fought for it, and farmed it for two centuries, he came to feel a sense of belonging that verged on patriotism. When he and John were respectively nine and six, they confidently walked sixteen miles over country new to them to visit their own mother's sister and brother-in-law, Linda and David Brooks, at Cheshire; they were two days on the road and spent the night in a rural inn.[46] Several times before he was twelve, Fred got lost on a ramble and stayed overnight with strangers. His parents assumed that he was safe in some familiar or friendly household; they did nothing to discourage his adventurous bent.[47]

If the Puritan strain in Fred was weakened by contact with his heavy-handed Congregational tutors, the patriotic was fortified by association with his grandfather Benjamin and his great-uncles Gideon and Epaphras. When Fred knew them, they were aged, and infirm with rheumatism and old wounds.[48] Gnarled relics of a time fading into history, they injected a flavor of the stirring past into the tamer present. Gideon wrote, and Fred read, an account of his audacious exploit at sea.[49] Benjamin told him about the march through the Maine wilderness to lay siege to Quebec and heartily laughed when Fred asked if he had really had to cook and eat his boot tops. Benjamin's very clothes brought the Revolutionary period within easy reach of the boy's imagination: he wore knee breeches and stockings, ruffled shirt bosoms and wrist bands, and a high-crowned hat of real beaver. He dressed his hair in a queue and carried a tall Malacca staff that he had cut himself on the "pepper coast" when he was a ship's captain.[50]

Awed though he was by his grandfather's patriotic past, Fred was as much struck by the long consequence of a simple act of his childhood: as a boy, Benjamin had dug up in the swamp and transplanted to his father's yard a small sapling; as an old man, leaning totteringly on his Malacca stick, he pointed out to his little grandson the great elm it had become.[51]

Almost as familiar in many of the neighborhood households as if he lived in them, Fred poked about in their gardens, libraries, and attics as naturally as in his own. His uncle Jonathan Law, a scholar and a friend of John Greenleaf Whittier's, gave Fred beds in his garden to cultivate and read aloud to him from the Latin poets. Another elderly man with whom Fred had an early friendship had a fine house with an old garden, a natural history collection, and an excellent small library. He was shy and kind, and let Fred study and handle his treasures. It was in his library that Fred discovered Izaak Walton.[52] His grandfather's house, too, where he lived for a few months while he attended school nearby, was full of delightful finds—not only the cocked hat, the charts of distant seas, and the quadrant he dug out of a closet but also old novels, plays, and books of travel. His grandmother, Content Olmsted, a nice old lady who told him she had danced with French officers passing through Hartford on their way from Newport to join General Washington, let him browse at will through the books he found. He read, among others, Sterne's *Sentimental Journey*, Goldsmith's *Vicar of Wakefield*, and much of Zimmermann's *On Solitude*.[53] Somewhere he came upon a portfolio of prints of English park scenery, and the developing taste that led him to pore, fascinated, over them led him, too, to read Sir Uvedale Price's *The Picturesque* and William Gilpin's *Forest Scenery*, which he discovered in the six thousand-volume library of the Hartford Young Men's Institute, of which his father was a life member.[54]

In his own home were more books to feed his eclectic taste, and current publications to keep him abreast of the outside world. John Olmsted's journal mentions a few besides the Testaments, the Latin, German, and Spanish grammars, and the mathematics books the boys needed for school: Webster's recently published *Dictionary*, the thirteen-volume *Encyclopaedia Americana*, Moore's *Life of Byron*, Boswell's *Johnson*, Miss Sedgwick's novels, Charles Lamb's works, Lamartine's *Pilgrimage in the Holy Land*, and Prince Maximillian of Weid's *Travels in North America*. John Olmsted especially enjoyed the travel books of Miss Martineau and of President Timothy Dwight and Professor Benjamin Silliman, Sr., of Yale, and read them aloud to his assembled family. He subscribed to half a dozen New York papers—among them the *Journal of Commerce*, the *Observer*, the *Mirror*, and the *Weekly Courier*—in addition to the *Hartford Courant*; he was the Hartford agent for the *Cultivator*, a popular magazine on farming and gardening; and at various times he took, among other magazines, the *Watchman*, *Abbott's*, the *Knickerbocker*, the *Congregationalist*, the *Missionary Herald*, the *New England Weekly Review*, and the *Connecticut Observer*.[55]

Factors besides wide and random reading contributed to the spontaneous education that Fred picked up at home. Shy but not reclusive, John Olmsted liked social gatherings if he could remain inconspicuous. Sometimes the family enjoyed a "musical evening" with friends around the piano. Occasionally John Olmsted took them to a concert.[56] They attended the lectures at the Young Men's Institute, where they heard some of the most prominent public figures of the day, including Leonard Bacon, Horace Bushnell, Alonzo Potter, and Charles Upham, ministers; the Benjamin Sillimans, father and son, and John Olmsted's cousin, Denison Olmsted, scientists from the Yale community; Horace Mann, Henry Barnard, and Mark Hopkins, educators; George Bancroft, historian; Samuel G. Goodrich, the elder Richard Henry Dana, and Park Benjamin, literary men; John Quincy Adams, George P. Marsh, and Caleb Cushing, diplomats and politicians; and of course the unique Ralph Waldo Emerson.[57]

Perhaps because his own shyness made him uncomfortable in company, John Olmsted was at pains to have his boys develop skills that would help them become cultivated and confident men. Fred took drawing lessons and young John, German and Spanish.[58] Horseback riding, sailing, sleighing, and skating hardly fell in the category of sports—they were normal means of getting about —but poise, prestige, and fun were the rewards of skill. A fine horseman, John

Olmsted took Fred on a pillow in front of him before he was big enough to sit a pony, bought him his first sled before he was five, got him skates at intervals, saw that he learned to handle a sailboat and, when he had become practiced with a gun, gave him one of his own.[59] Angling and hunting were still less sports than means, pleasurable and accessible, of supplementing the table. John Olmsted, for instance, was past fifty before ever he bought a fresh salmon. (It weighed nine pounds and cost him $2.25.)[60]

There was in John Olmsted's household not luxury but a sort of humane worldliness, or urbanity, not quite consistent with the idea of Puritanism, and symbolized by the piano, the light reading, the wine and spirits and good table, the frequent travel for pleasure, and the quiet emphasis on physical skills and social grace. And John Olmsted was, in his unassuming way, an urbane man: he moved easily, like one at home, in both the physical world beyond his native habitat and the intellectual beyond his Puritan heritage. The force of his example would seem to have affected definitively the attitudes and later style of life of his oldest son; and their fortunate relationship surely influenced Fred's with his own son: in each case the boy respected the father, confided in him with unusual freedom, and dearly loved him. Not even Fred's resentment of his wretched education spilled over onto the father who had subjected him to it; Fred knew that John Olmsted had always tried to do his best for him and afterward spoke with affectionate understanding of the sense of duty that had so misled him in the particular instance.[61]

With his brother John, Fred's friendship was close; they were affectionately disposed toward the half-brothers and half-sisters who came after them, and devoted absolutely to each other. As children, both were small for their age, and Fred naturally fell into the habit of looking after his younger brother. He never quite outgrew it, although John, no dependent, became an equal force in the brotherly combination. John, growing up, was handsome, witty, and inclined to be languid; Fred was good-natured and straightforward, and there was no trace of languor in either his quick mind or his wiry frame. The brothers complemented each other, and they never conceived of themselves as having separate or conflicting interests.

By the time they were in their teens, their father's home sheltered a large family. Aunt Jerusha Watson, a relative of Mary Ann's, and Aunt Maria Olmsted, John Olmsted's plain and devoted younger sister, were occasionally in residence. Charlotte, born in 1828, was followed by Mary, born March 29, 1832; Bertha was born three and a half years later, on September 16, 1835; Owen not quite a year after, on September 10, 1836; and Ada Theodosia on April 3, 1839.[62]

Where there are children, there are children's diseases. John Olmsted kept a scrupulous record in his daybook of the mumps, measles, whooping cough, chicken pox, and scarlet fever that afflicted his little brood and of the remedies that afflicted them, too. Treatment in that day was drastic, survival chancy. It was accepted practice to dose a small child with nine grains of calomel in a six-hour period.[63] Sweet spirits of nitre, a febrifuge; spirits of antimony, an emetic and expectorant of lethal potential; ipecac, an emetic; laudanum, a derivative of opium; Dover's powder, an anodyne composed of laudanum and ipecac; and castor oil, all were standard medications. When four-year-old Charlotte became ill with measles on May 24, 1832, she was given an emetic, a cathartic, a foot bath, and forty drops of sweet spirits of nitre. As she worsened, her chest was blistered, and two grains of calomel were administered every three hours until she had taken six grains, after which she was given Dover's powder. Her breathing became labored, and she was bled; her limbs were "fomented" to induce sweating; she was dosed with digitalis and more calomel. Ten days after the onset of her illness, she died.[64] She was probably a victim equally of measles and of the drastic medication of the two reputable doctors who attended her with desperate solicitude throughout her sickness.

Fred was ten, a student at Mr. Brace's school, when Charlotte died. Death was to become a commonplace of his youth; and it may have been more rather than less frightening for its familiarity. The capriciousness with which it struck was unnerving. It successively laid low old Benjamin on Christmas Day in 1832, the same year as little Charlotte; Uncle Owen's baby boy and seventy-year-old Grandmother Hull within two months of each other in 1836; and Fred's two-year-old half-brother Owen in the fall of 1838, almost a year before his eighty-seven-year-old grandmother Olmsted.[65]

Life was uncertain; far worse, so was the afterlife. If death was to be apprehended, how much more to be feared was the possibility of hell throughout eternity. "Your dear little brother Owen," John Olmsted had written Fred on the sad September evening the child died, ". . . is now we trust an angell of light in heaven his home."[66]

He trusted, but his church allowed him no grounds for confidence: according to its dogma, Owen might just as well be damned as saved, even though he died an infant hardly capable of either faith or works, or of knowing the saving grace of conversion. In the Congregational faith, which was the religious ambience of generations of Olmsteds and of Fred's home, the possibility of damnation loomed to aggravate the apprehension of death. If there is any validity in the theory that the insomniac's resistance to sleep, a temporary simulation of death, is an unconscious expression of his fear of the real thing, an explanation of the insomnia that undermined Fred's health as an adult might perhaps be found in the Puritan dogmas—accepted in his youth, traumatically rejected later —fixed fast during childhood in his impressionable mind.

John Olmsted's prosperity kept pace with his growing family. In April 1836 he paid eleven thousand dollars, seven thousand in cash, for a house and lot at 34 Ann Street. He equipped his new home in part with furniture bought at an estate auction, including a dozen mahogany chairs and a double bedstead, and in June he moved in.[67] One of young John's intimates, speaking years afterward of John Olmsted's cultivated taste, remembered the house, newly fitted out by its owner, as the finest thing he had seen up to that time.[68]

Fred was not at home much that summer, the season of his sumach poisoning. Having been advised that sea bathing would be good for his eyes, he was most of the time with Mr. Eastman at Saybrook, except for a few days in August that he spent with his father, John, and little Mary at Sachem's Head.[69]

Besides treating his family to frequent visits to nearby seaside inns and to a long trip to Geneseo and Niagara Falls in the late summer of 1834,[70] John Olmsted went once a year or oftener to New York, presumably to buy for his store. The nation was still young and informal enough for the highly placed and the relatively obscure to mingle with few restraints: on his return from New York on June 16, 1833, the self-effacing merchant had found himself on the New Haven boat with President Andrew Jackson, who was making a triumphal progress through New England with an entourage that included Vice President Martin Van Buren, Secretary of War Lewis Cass, Secretary of the Navy Levi Woodbury, the former Minister to Mexico Joel Poinsett, and Governor William L. Marcy of New York.[71] Usually he traveled in less exalted company. Once or twice he took his wife, and on June 14, 1837, he took Fred.[72]

The New York that the young tourist saw for the first time was a city of about a quarter of a million people, growing fast and already metropolitan. Its great port sheltered ships carrying cargoes from Europe and the Orient and from the hinterland by way of the Erie Canal and Hudson River. Wharves hemmed its lower end, and around them the water bristled with masts. Its narrow streets, laid out on a rigid and uniform grid, were gaslit by night, and by day were thronged with horsecars, drays, carriages, carts, pedestrians, and pigs on whom fell much of the responsibility for keeping them clear of garbage. Fashionable houses still clustered around the Battery, up Greenwich Street, which had been the shore road to Greenwich Village in colonial times, and along Broadway, which, with the elegant City Hall set in its park on one side and the splendid new Astor House on the other, was a focus of city life. Not far downtown, around the Tombs prison and the Five Points, existed slums of horrifying squalor. There were few architectural remains of the period of Dutch ascendancy: a disastrous fire less than a year and a half earlier had consumed some six hundred buildings, at a loss of about twenty million dollars, in the close-packed old district around Pearl and Front streets and Exchange Place. Some of the streets in the devastated area had been widened, and new buildings, crowded as closely as those they replaced, had gone up on the burned-over sites. To the north, Manhattan's shores still were green with farms and woodlands running down to the rivers, and the Boston Post Road ran through open country and past interior hamlets linked by country roads. The far north end, too rugged for farming, was wooded and sparsely occupied. Over the great island, moored snugly in its rivers, perceptible change was moving. The residential district was pushing northward, red brick houses were sprouting on side streets around

Washington Square, and lots as far north as Eleventh Street were bringing good prices, although financial activity was seriously interrupted by the panic that had caused New York banks to suspend specie payment early in May.

What Fred saw or did, other than visit a dentist and an eye doctor, in the four days he spent in New York is not known.[73] He left no record of the first impression made on him by the city on which he was, himself, to leave a lasting mark.

Of his next extended journey, Fred left a bare memorandum. On Wednesday, August 8, 1838, he, his parents, and his brother John left in the double carriage for a trip to the White Mountains. Traveling along the Connecticut River valley and eastward after Haverhill, they arrived after a week at Franconia Notch.[74] There the craggy profile of the Old Man of the Mountain was already much remarked by tourists. Fred's youthful impression of the curious formation is not on record; as an adult, he disliked it as a gratuitous stunt of nature's, a frivolous distraction from the scenery.[75]

Leaving the Notch on the sixteenth, the travelers turned eastward to reach the coast at Portsmouth and went on to Boston. John was sent home from there on the twenty-third by boat, Fred was dispatched to Mr. Barton at nearby Andover, and John Olmsted and his wife started for Hartford, arriving the twenty-fifth. They had been gone eighteen days, driven five hundred seventy-five miles, and spent one hundred twenty dollars, John Olmsted recorded in his daybook. Little Owen was sick when they arrived; John Olmsted's next entries noted the progress of his fatal illness.[76]

In Andover Fred found himself unsettled about his studies, and he was probably unsettled further by the sudden death of his small half-brother on September 4. When he asked his father to permit him to drop engineering and concentrate on rhetoric, John Olmsted reacted with characteristic mildness and concern. He regretted that Fred was unhappy with his studies, allowed him to make the change he proposed, and offered him some serious advice: "Be desirous of pursuing such studies as will most tend to your intellectual and moral improvement and to fit you for usefulness and enjoyment when you take your place in the great theatre of life and throw everything from you that tends to distract your mind from this pursuit."[77]

Fred must have responded satisfactorily: within two weeks John Olmsted wrote of his pleasure that Fred was at last getting interested in his studies.[78]

Fred's next long trip was not scenic in motive. On Monday, December 9, 1839, his father set out with him to Washington. They were five days on the way, stopping in New York until Friday morning, spending the night in Baltimore, and arriving in Washington on Saturday.[79]

The capital of the United States must have struck the boy brought up in the long-settled, well-groomed capital of Connecticut as a shabby affair indeed. It scarcely hinted yet at the spacious elegance that its designer, Major Charles

Pierre L'Enfant, intended for it. Its broad straight avenues ran past fields and vacant lots, to peter out in farther fields. Along its streets at gaping intervals stood scattered buildings, a few of them fine. The Capitol, with its short wings and modest wooden dome, commanded from its low hill a westward view toward the White House along Pennsylvania Avenue, which was supposed to afford a reciprocal vista between the city's two most significant buildings. The imposing Greek Revival mass of the Treasury Building, however, was rising directly east of the White House, to obstruct the vista and thwart an important element of L'Enfant's design.

A few more buildings in the Greek mode held out some hope for the federal city's future dignity: the finely proportioned City Hall, only its center section and east wing finished two decades after the groundbreaking, overlooked the swampy waste of the Mall from Judiciary Square; on F Street between Seventh and Eighth streets, the middle section of the stately Patent Office, its main portico a replica of the Parthenon, had been building for three years and was nearly completed; and on the square south of it, work had begun on the new Post Office, the two sections of which would be twenty-seven years under construction. There was a sprinkling, too, of fine private houses at the Navy Yard, near the Capitol, around Lafayette Square, immediately west of the White House, and along Pennsylvania Avenue.

The avenue itself, although it was the main axis of the city and of the government that was the city's reason for being, was unpaved. So were most avenues and streets. Sidewalks, where they existed, were poorly maintained. The city's leading newspaper, the *National Intelligencer*, was warning its readers at the time of the Olmsteds' visit about the flagged pavement along D Street between Ninth and Tenth, where the walk was bordered by a deep ditch and so broken as to be dangerous, especially at night. The paper considerately warned, too, against light-fingered rogues who were slipping into hotels and boarding-houses to snatch the cloaks and pocketbooks of visitors and temporary residents, who had been brought to the city by the reconvening of Congress.[80]

The population of Washington, exclusive of Georgetown and other outlying villages, was about twenty-three thousand, more than a quarter of it black; of the blacks, some forty-eight hundred were free, seventeen hundred slaves.[81] Surely Fred, who had not been in slave territory until he passed through Maryland, had never before seen so many Negroes as he saw in the capital. Of the impressions he got and the things he did, however, the record is scant. Certainly he attended Congress, and on Monday, the sixteenth, from a perch in the House gallery, he and his father observed the temporary presiding officer, the venerated John Quincy Adams, and watched the House elect at last, after three weeks of wrangling over seating some of the New Jersey delegates, Robert M. T. Hunter, of Virginia, as speaker. Perhaps they attended the next day's session to hear the new speaker express his thanks to the House and to hear the continuing debate on the admission of the New Jersey delegates; but well before the decision to exclude them was reached, the Olmsteds had left for Philadelphia.[82]

Philadelphia was a contrast in civic amenity to Washington. Miss Martineau, visiting it a few years earlier, had declared that she might have thought herself in an English city, so well built and urbane it was, had it not been for certain American peculiarities of speech she overheard. Fred and his father stayed only one night, and next day reached New York, where they heard that a fire of incendiary origin had wiped out the buildings and stocks of several large dry-goods importers and jobbers in Cedar Street at a loss of at least half a million dollars; and the fire insurance companies, reeling from repeated heavy losses, had just raised their rates thirty percent on stores over forty feet in height, the limit to which fire hoses could raise water. New York was also beset by cold so severe that ice formed in the Hudson River as far up as Poughkeepsie, and on Saturday night it began to snow heavily. By Monday the storm, the worst in many years, had swept over New England and as far south as Washington, in places burying roads and rails under a deep cover of impassable snow.[83] Weather notwithstanding, John Olmsted and Fred reached home on Tuesday, December 24, in good time to share in the preparations for the next day's observances.[84]

After Christmas, Fred returned to Mr. Barton, whose recent move from Amherst to Collinsville, near Hartford, made frequent visits with his family feasible. He was home for a few days early in February and again on February 21 for a two-week stay. After another month in Collinsville, he came home for good, on April 6, 1840.[85] Just short of eighteen, he was through with schools and schoolmasters, and with his schooling—such as it had been.

II
SEAFARING
May 1840–April 1844

JOHN Hull Olmsted, infused with the Olmsted passion for travel, sailed for Europe in May 1840 on the *Great Western* with Mr. C. P. Bordenave, his Spanish teacher.[1]

Fred wrote his brother frequent letters to keep him abreast of local news. "The Connecticut Abolition Society has separated from its parents; and the old folks are divorced & form 2 units in society, one in Boston at the head of whom is Garrison & Co. These are the ultra Non-resistance women's rights 'Barney for President' loafers. The other the old anti-slav. folks Tappan overseer."[2] A conservative temperament set him, even so young, against abolitionism. He was a Whig himself and an enthusiastic supporter of William Henry Harrison's candidacy.[3]

For Fred, the rather aimless pleasures of the summer came to an end in August. Mr. Barton had not made an engineer of him; his father decided to try to make a merchant of him. Obediently, Fred went to clerk at Benkard and Hutton, French dry-goods importers, at 53 Beaver Street, New York. John Olmsted, having escorted him to New York on August 18 and having secured him room, breakfast, and laundry for $3.50 a week in a boardinghouse at 120 Henry Street in Brooklyn, abandoned his son to learn the mysteries of commerce.[4]

Fred, a privileged apprentice, was allowed to go home from time to time. In November, a fortnight after John's return from France, Fred went to Hartford, where, for a whole week, he could enjoy his brother's company and such dignified entertainment as the Young Men's Institute lecture by John Quincy Adams on "Faith." His father spent some days in New York the following January and two weeks in March.[5] After that, Fred was lonely and for company lured a pair of doves into a coop outside his window, where they started laying.[6]

Competent and reliable, Fred was entrusted after a few months with handling the petty cash. He did not develop a taste for business, but he did find incidental satisfactions. He was learning French, which was spoken almost as much as English at Benkard and Hutton, and he was becoming familiar with the workings of the great port of New York.[7] From Brooklyn Heights, where he lived, he had a splendid view of the harbor over which swarmed all sorts of craft, from the wallowing ferries that connected Brooklyn, Manhattan, and Staten Island to the exquisite, swift clipper ships engaged in the China trade.

His work took him onto wharves and aboard ships to send off mail and to check consignments, so that he got a tar-flavored hint of the romance of distant places.

Compensations, however, could not reconcile him to trade; by March 1842 he was home to stay.[8] His eighteen months in New York had proved to him that dry goods was not in his blood; and they had probably suggested to him that the sea was.

At home Fred marked time, and his patient father seemed to indulge his sons' idleness when he engaged a fencing master for them and bought them, for nine dollars, a small sailboat; but it was less indulgence than anxiety about their poor health that motivated him. The first of August Fred and John sailed down the river in their boat and met their father at Sachem's Head. His hope that outdoor exercise would toughen them was disappointed when his younger son arrived at the inn sick after three unseasonably cold days on the water. A few days later when young John recovered, he sailed away with Fred to spend five weeks with friends at Falkner Island, a dot of land off Sachem's Head. John, senior, having seen them off, returned to his domestic circle, recently enlarged by the birth of his eighth child and fourth son, Albert Henry, and to his dry-goods store, which was prosperous enough to permit him to keep his family in comfort and to contribute five hundred dollars to the newly organized Wadsworth Atheneum.[9]

The boys came home from Falkner Island September 5. Three weeks later John entered the freshman class at Yale, leaving his brother to idle the winter away. In October Fred walked to Cheshire to visit his uncle and aunt, the David Brookses; went to Falkner Island for duck shooting;[10] and visited his brother at New Haven, where John was ameliorating the rigors of dormitory life with luxuries that made his roommate suppose he was a rich man's son.[11]

John's roommate was Charles Loring Brace, son of John P. Brace, principal of the Hartford Female Seminary. The elder Brace, a graduate of Williams College and a teacher by profession, was also a competent mineralogist, an occasional composer, the writer of poems, scientific articles, and novels, an ardent angler, a skillful woodsman, and a well-informed critic of politics.[12] Charles, whose training at the Hartford Grammar School had been liberally supplemented by his versatile father, was generally regarded by his classmates as the best-educated man among them. At sixteen, he was fair and strong and rather humorless, with a tedious tendency to religious exaltation. An accomplished sportsman and an earnest debater, he was, in whatever he undertook, single-minded and tireless, "simple, sturdy and resolute."[13]

John's and Charles's dormitory room, heated by a stove they had bought themselves for $5.74,[14] was furnished simply enough, but John bought fencing foils, boxing gloves, and dumbbells and had, it seemed to Charley, a great deal of money, which he spent freely to treat his friends. Brace, almost touchily independent, saw no way to avoid sharing the amenities John so carelessly provided and was troubled lest, in enjoying them, he seem dependent. John had in him a devoted friend, and a moral watchdog. Having experienced religious conversion during his first term, Charley made a sustained effort to set his roommate a Christian example, for John, he thought, "notices very particularly and is influenced in his own conduct by what he sees in mine."[15]

Fred had an important matter to discuss with John and Charley: he had decided to go to China, not as a passenger or supercargo but as a seaman.[16] It was not a fad in the 1840s but it was not a rarity for young New Englanders from mercantile and professional families and comfortable homes to go to sea for a while. Richard Henry Dana, Jr., some eight years earlier had sailed before the mast to California, and the whole English-speaking world for the first time heard a "voice from the forecastle" give an unvarnished, authentic account of the tremendous hardships and trivial rewards of a seaman's life. *Two Years before the Mast*, however, had not discouraged young men like him from attempting adventures like his. Fred had read it and was not dissuaded by it,[17] and several of his friends were simultaneously hatching similar plans.

In Fred's case, it was no wonder. He was almost of age, yet he had not decided on a career. Restless, idle, inquisitive, and ill trained, he was at loose ends and susceptible to the lure of adventure; besides, a long sea voyage might strengthen his weak eyes and uncertain health. More than that, the seafaring tradition was strong in his family; his grandfather Benjamin, his great-uncle Aaron who as captain of the *Huntress* grew rich in the China trade, and the brave Gideon who, in his nineties, still lived in East Hartford, had been shipmasters.

Canton was a natural choice for Fred; Benjamin and Aaron had made it something of a family habit to go to China, and China had been for several years much in the news. The Opium War between the Chinese and English had ended, the English had wrung important trade concessions from the Chinese, and the American government, eager to secure similar advantages, was about to send Caleb Cushing as resident commissioner to China.[18]

These events were in the news while Fred was making his decision. Probably John Olmsted, who had always let his sons wander where they pleased, encouraged it. Perhaps, too, he was already troubled by the apprehension, which was to haunt him for another quarter century, that Fred was a drifter; he may have hoped that a long voyage would reveal to Fred that seamanship was his métier, as it had been that of other Olmsteds.

Ships taking the eastward route to China left their Atlantic coast ports so as to sail up the China Sea between the end of April and the end of September while the monsoon was favorable.[19] Thus Fred did not have to act immediately; he planned to leave the end of the winter.

Meanwhile the weather was cold and the sleighing fine. The Olmsteds entertained the glee club and heard their cousin, Professor Denison Olmsted, lecture on "Water."[20] "The venerable Audubon"—so Fred regarded the fifty-seven-year-old naturalist—dined with Mr. Ayres, a member of the Natural History Society, and spoke, to Fred's envy, of setting out in the spring for Council Bluffs, Yellowstone, and the Rockies.[21] John, at New Haven, caught scarlet fever the week before Christmas, and Aunt Maria and Fred had to fetch him home. It was the middle of January before he was well enough to return to college. A month later the entire family except the baby made a trip by sleigh to New Haven to visit him. Sunday, March 5, Allie, the youngest Olmsted, was christened by Dr. Hawes, and his sister Ada attended church for the first time. The following day John Olmsted purchased pew number two in the church of his ancestors, paying fifty-three dollars for it. So the idle winter passed. Finally, on March 27, 1843, Fred went to New York to find a berth on a Canton-bound ship.[22]

He was a week getting one. Never having been to sea before, he could qualify only as a "green boy," worth anywhere from four to eight dollars a month,[23] and such hands were little in demand. On April 4 George A. Talbot, of Gordon and Talbot, one of the leading New York firms in the China trade, having satisfied himself that Fred's family was not sending him to sea to get rid of him, agreed without enthusiasm to accept him if the captain of their bark *Ronaldson* consented. "We always dislike to take a green hand," he said, "but somebody must now and then, & we may as well as anyone, I suppose."[24]

The *Ronaldson*, when Fred next day saw her, was lying in the East River at the *Great Western*'s dock at Peck Slip. She was of about three hundred thirty tons, a usual size for an American ship in the China trade,

> pretty good form, but nothing clipper. Rakish rigging, long block yards (main royal up) (by the way the only ship I saw out of the Navy Yard with a lightning rod) handsome cabin on deck—high bulwarks, to'glnt fokstle now building—had a long boat quarter boat & whale boat. Carries two bull dogs (6 lb cannonades or so), wheel of best construction under cover (when wanted) & is about two years old.[25]

She had returned about six weeks before from Apalachicola with a cargo of cotton[26] and was undergoing extensive alterations to equip her for her first China voyage.

Fred went aboard and sought out Captain Warren Fox, who was supervising the building of the new forecastle. The captain promised to talk to Mr. Talbot about him and told him to come back next day. Next day it poured, and the captain did not appear, but Fred hung about the ship getting acquainted with her and with the mate, who said she was "the best calculated for Canton of any ship he had ever seen except the 'Morrison.'" His zeal whetted, Fred waited until six in the evening, when Captain Fox came aboard. "The Captn told me in a very handsome manner he had concluded to take me," Fred wrote John, "& in the conversation that insued he believed he had got three *good* boys & now he hoped he had another." Fred was the only green one; the others had all been to sea. One of them, Jacob T. Braisted, the son of Jacob Braisted of the United States Hotel, where Fred had several times stayed when in New York, had shipped with Captain Fox before. "He said he should have us in the steerage going out," Fred continued. "In return he should build a house on deck for us as he could not have his boys for'd with the men. (He don't let his boys associate with the old hands.)"[27] Fred was greatly impressed by the captain's "handsome manner" and his fatherly watchfulness over "his boys." Later he realized that he had thus shown himself a very green boy indeed.

Preparations for the voyage followed. John came up from Yale to spend Fred's last week at home with him. Aunt Maria, in whom the nautical strain was not dominant, begged him to get a good life preserver and never go "way up on the tip top" without it. He provided himself with the recommended life preserver and with an almanac, a quadrant, an oil suit and hat, three flannel shirts, seven colored checked shirts, cloth pants and duck pants, two clothes bags, a sea chest, and a homeopathic remedy for seasickness. Joseph Mond, a local artist, drew his picture in his new sailor costume. On April 20, a week before his twenty-first birthday, Fred went to New York with his father and brother to begin his great adventure.[28]

The adventure began without incident the next Monday, April 24.[29] From the wharf, John Olmsted and young John watched the *Ronaldson* move into the stream and drop anchor to wait for the tide to change. Soon she stood out with a light breeze, in the company of the packet *Albany* bound for Le Havre, the bark *Pilot* for Batavia, and some thirty smaller craft, and the little fleet scattered down the bay.[30]

The adventure began without incident, but with an ominous hint of discomforts to come. Accommodations for the men in the forecastle were crowded. For the boys in the tiny steerage room they were worse; all their chests were stowed there, Fred's under two others where it could not possibly be reached, and there was just room at the back for two bunks to accommodate the four boys.[31] The *Ronaldson*, which was carrying a cargo of ginseng, baled goods, and notions, was dangerously overloaded—Plimsoll marks to indicate the safe load limit were not required on United States merchant ships for another eighty-seven years—so that she rode low in the water. Even her decks were lumbered with stores.[32] Fred could, however, expect the strangeness of his new life to be mitigated by the presence of a friend in the forecastle, Jim Goodwin, a young man from Hartford who had shipped on the *Ronaldson* as a seaman.

During his first night out, as he stood watch with Jim and paced back and forth among the hawsers, hen coops, and casks that cluttered the deck, he may well have thought of Dana on his first night out, aloft on the pitching topsail yard, vomiting helplessly into the black night. His own case was not so hard: he was only beginning to be seasick. Next day it was worse. Turned out before daybreak, he was set to work at the head pump. Nearly exhausted after an hour of pumping without pause and suffering increasingly from seasickness, he ventured to ask the carpenter, who was passing water out of the deck tub, if they were almost through washing the decks. "Most through!" roared the carpenter, with an explosion of oaths. "Well by ——, youngster, —— you a'nt' tired yet, are ye? You may think yourself d——d well off if you get through before 8 oclock. So look about ye, you bloody young ————." Taking the advice literally, the wretched green hand looked about him and saw passing close under their stern a brig bound in, bound for the land, the home, the friends he would not see for an everlasting year.

Although desperately seasick, Fred doggedly kept afoot until the evening of April 27. By then the wind had freshened to a small gale, the topsails had been double reefed, and the overloaded bark was charging sickeningly through heavy seas. Fred was wet to the skin and so sick he could hardly stand when the mate, recognizing his useless condition, ordered him below. Wanting dry clothes, he went to the steerage room and opened the door. "That was enough—Faugh!— over she goes—such a sickening stench, you can't image it." He crawled to the forecastle, which was considerably less smelly, and fell into Jim Goodwin's berth.[33]

There he stayed for ten days, barely able to eat or drink or think, while the ship plunged through the riotous Atlantic, most of the time under double-reefed topsails, and the homeopathic remedy for seasickness lay uselessly in his inaccessible sea chest. Jim not only shared his wide bunk with Fred but cared for him, and Dr. J. P. Green, who was going to Canton as a passenger, attended him kindly. It was no reflection on either that Fred longed for his aunt; and when Dr. Green at length recommended a little gruel for him, he at once had "visions of dear Aunt Maria (how often I thought of her) with a nice thick mess covered with grated nutmeg in a white bowl."

What Jim brought him—in a tin pot—was a sour-smelling mash, which he recommended highly. A taste of it, however, was enough, too much. It was too sour to eat. "Oh, no," Jim said encouragingly, "that's your mouth. It will taste better in a minute." Fred choked down another revolting mouthful. Could it have salt in it? Had it been cooked with sea water? No indeed; after getting the meal from the steward, Jim had himself got fresh water from the scuttlebutt and carried meal and water to the cook. Coaxed further, Fred forced a little more of it down. It really was inedible; he could touch no more. Jim tried it. "Why, there's something wrong!" he exclaimed. "I knew there was, I knew there was. 'Try a little more, perhaps it will taste better,'" Fred taunted him feebly.

The steward, they later found, had given Jim spoiled meal left over from the previous voyage—meal "which it was hoped the pigs would take off their hands (one of the pigs died that night)." Happily, Fred did not follow the pig's example. Gradually he felt better. The next thing he tried to eat was some beans Jim had saved out of the soup and baked for him; then he ate some codfish souse. It was another two weeks before he could eat the ship's allowance.[34]

On Sunday, May 7, weak, thin, and still somewhat seasick, Fred tottered out of the forecastle to attend religious services, conducted by the captain, and wash and change his clothes. The next day he was back on duty.[35] Too feeble to go aloft, he was set to work filing rust from tools and cleaning weapons. His performance so pleased the captain that he made him ship's armorer, and, until he was able to return to full duty, he was busy burnishing muskets, blunderbusses, pistols, and knives, which quite conceivably might have to be used against pirates in the Java Sea.

Captain and officers, Fred felt, had been forbearing toward him during his illness. In gratitude he resolved that when he got out he would not growl at them; he was determined to be contented. It took determination, on that unhappy ship. Her overloading made movement about the crowded deck difficult and in rough weather dangerous; below, the men had almost no room for their gear and slept in cramped misery; and the owners had skimped on the ship's stores to make room for freight, so that one month out, just about the time Fred could begin to eat the ship's allowance, all fresh foods were gone, and the water was rationed.[36]

The crew was naturally resentful. ". . . A more discontented, grumbling, growling set of mortals than our men are, you cannot imagine," Fred wrote.[37] Foremost among the growlers was old Davis, of whom Fred had formed an unfavorable opinion the first night out. While he was standing watch he had heard a noise forward and, investigating, had found an old sailor, very drunk, blundering about the congested deck looking for the scuttlebutt. The next morning, by a gross injustice, the old man was feeling quite well, while his temperate shipmate was queasy with rising nausea. Davis was in a vicious humor, however, and complained furiously that he had shipped while on a spree, hadn't known where the ship was bound, and wouldn't have gone on a long voyage, especially to Canton, on the best craft that ever sailed out of heaven, not even for fifty dollars a month.[38] Fred took a dislike to the pale, dirty old "rum-heaver" with his mashed nose—flattened, Fred uncharitably supposed, against some curbstone —and his "nasty outre knondescript dress," made of stout canvas, which he cut and sewed himself. His disapprobation was stiffened by Davis's incessant growling and his prophesies of misfortune, all calculated to make the discontented crew still more miserable. Fred began to soften toward him, however, when one Sunday about a month out he came upon the old man sitting in the shade of the foresail, smoking a clean pipe and earnestly reading a very old worn Bible; and he was converted finally to respect when he realized that Davis was a superb sailor whose woeful prophesies were based on sound judgment.[39]

While Davis went up in the esteem of the critical green hand, the captain went down. "The infernal, deceitful old liar!" Fred angrily exclaimed when he realized how he had been humbugged by the "handsome manner." The captain, his professions notwithstanding, did nothing to keep the boys apart from the crew, "some of whom were rough and reckless men such as sober, quiet people anywhere in the world are shy of." It would have been a pointless gesture anyway, in the case of two of the boys—"moral young men, the Captn called them" —who swore as foully as the men, did their wash on Sundays during religious services, and got drunk as opportunity offered.[40]

The captain himself did not use profanity, but he had a wonderful skill in abuse without it, relying on such insults as "infernal sojer," "old granny," and "oh, you marine!" He was a driver and a harsh disciplinarian, given to "the lingering deliberate, studiously contrived torture inflicted in what is called 'working up' the men"—hazing and punishing them with unnecessary tasks.[41] Fred, conscientious though he was, was a victim of his billingsgate, and an unprotesting one; like every man aboard, he was in fact if not in theory utterly at the captain's mercy.

The *Ronaldson* carried another passenger besides Dr. Green. She was Mrs. Charles Gutzlaff, wife of a Protestant missionary to China who was interpreter to the English consular authorities. Fred found her "a very disagreeable, notional old granny" but could be grateful to her, along with Dr. Green, for moderating a little, by their mere presence, the captain's abuse.[42]

The monotonous days passed with little incident, except that occasionally on the endless, agitated waste of ocean they sighted a ship and spoke her. Fred, although weak from seasickness, never missed a watch; but he was always tired, so tired that one morning when he was stationed at the head pump to catch the flow from it in a bucket, he again and again fell asleep while the bucket was filling and woke just in time to pass it and slip another under.[43] He had no time for writing, but he kept rough notes of any event that made one day different from the next. On May 28, the *Ronaldson* crossed the equator; on June 5 she met an American brig; five days later as she neared the latitude of the Cape of Good Hope, he observed some cape pigeons and an albatross. The weather by then was getting cold, and the ship was running close reefed in a heavy squall. For almost two months thereafter, she drove eastward through boisterous seas. The great waves burst constantly over her, and she never had a dry deck. The monotony became one of constant storm: the old India hands aboard agreed they had never had such a voyage for weather.[44]

On July 4 Fred jotted: "Procession formed before daybreak—proceeded to fore topsail yard, close reefed fore and main topsails. Off Cape Lagullas [Agulhas] at noon. Long 40° S. Very heavy sea. Put on short allowance of water. Killed a pig."[45] So much for the patriotic observance aboard the bark *Ronaldson*.

The cold storms off the cape made work aloft hard and dangerous. One bitter July afternoon, while Fred and Jacob Braisted were shortening sail, "Jacob was slap^d off the foretoglt yd. (I was in the lee main toglt.) Most providentially he fell between the sail (outside) & the foretack. If he had wetted, he would have been lost (no stop)." There was no question of lowering a boat into those tremendous seas: it was all the staggering *Ronaldson* could do to survive. For a time that same night, while the wind rose in fury, it seemed that she could not. Her double-reefed topsail was "crack cracking away," so that Fred momentarily expected to see "the bloody old sticks snap out of her." Exhilarated by the wild commotion of the storm, he was the first man out on the windward yardarm when the order came to close reef. Before it could be carried out, a fierce squall burst the sail to tatters, and the ship was nearly capsized. All sail was furled. That night and the next day she scudded under bare poles through mountainous seas and blinding snow.[46]

It was the worst storm captain or mate had ever experienced; had the wind held its peak violence for a few minutes longer, they said, it would have been the last. The green boy had relished the excitement and the approval of the old sailor who told him he had good pluck and had done a man's duty.[47]

For the next month the *Ronaldson* was battered by a succession of gales. Wet, cold, tired, and ill fed, Fred must have wondered what had ever made him think that life before the mast was good for the health. He had suffered horribly from seasickness; during the bad weather off the Cape he had a severe fall; from constant exposure he developed rheumatism; and finally, one morning in the middle of July, he woke up with his right arm paralyzed. It was perfectly useless—and so was he—for a time, but by early August, as the ship neared Java, he was able to write his father, with weak, numb fingers, an account of the voyage so far.[48]

Dr. Green took a cheery view of the effects of hardship on the constitution, for he added a postscript to Fred's letter: "Your son is quite altered in appearance and I hope that the benefit he will derive from the voyage may be of permanent benefit to his health and with pleasure having learned that he is not addicted to the vices common among young men of today have little doubt that such may be the case."[49]

On August 8 the *Ronaldson* made Java Head; next day, a hundred and seven days out of New York, she dropped anchor at Anjer. Fred hoped dutifully that he was truly grateful to God still to be alive, after so perilous a voyage, to glimpse the oriental island. Glimpse it was all he did. He did not get shore leave or opportunity to obtain even a small exotic souvenir. Two of his bunkmates did and came back with a bottle of gin. Fred was more interested in the other supplies brought aboard—yams, sweet potatoes, plantains, bananas, coconuts, tamarinds, fowl, ducks, pumpkins, and, above all, fresh water. If he supposed feasts were in prospect, he misjudged Captain Fox: only the yams and water were for the crew; all the rest was for the captain's table. Even the two large green turtles, which the men combined to purchase for their own mess, did them little good. ". . . When the first one was killed the best part of it was taken for the captain's table & supplied it for some days while we had but one meal—the other was launched overboard, they called it *sick*, but the way it struck out for Cochin China was a caution to doctors."[50]

The *Ronaldson* left Anjer August 10. The wind was favorable, the pirates never appeared, and she proceeded through the Gaspar Straits and into the China Sea almost as buoyantly as the liberated turtle. There she was overtaken by more bad weather—calms alternating with heavy squalls and light breezes, with waterspouts and a typhoon in the distance. It was "weather to kill sailors"; they shortened and made sail hourly and were often kept at work with scarcely a moment's rest all the night watch.[51]

With his arm still disabled Fred could not fly about aloft; the captain set him instead to making an eight-times enlarged chart of the entrance to the Pearl, or Canton, River, including Macao and Hong Kong, the Portuguese and British colonies, respectively, on either side of its mouth. When they reached Hong Kong on September 2, after being in sight of it for three days and unable to approach because of adverse winds, the captain appointed Fred his clerk.[52]

The ship remained at Hong Kong only four days. There was no market for their notions, and the place was fever ridden. The redcoats there, a sailor told Fred, were "dying off like rotten sheep, not like men at all, at all"; and "young Morrison had just died, universally lamented," of malaria.[53] He was John Robert Morrison, son of John Morrison, a noted English Presbyterian missionary to China. Born in Macao, he was widely known as the author of the *Chinese Commercial Guide*, a valuable handbook on foreign trade in China and on the rigid system of conducting business that the Chinese imposed on the "foreign devils" at Canton.[54]

Presumably the *Ronaldson* followed the routine described in the *Guide*. It was customary for a foreign ship to take on a river pilot at Macao, who guided her upstream through the *chowchow* water, the turbulent eddies and undertows of the Pearl River that made the channels between its crowded islands difficult to navigate.[55] Arriving at Whampoa Reach, the anchorage a dozen miles below Canton beyond which the river was not passable to large vessels, the ship anchored, and her captain paid port charges—for American ships usually about four thousand dollars. There the captain secured a linguist and a *comprador*, if he had not already done so at Macao, and a hong merchant.[56] The comprador acted as steward for the ship, supplying her provisions, hiring the coolies and stevedores and workmen she needed, and taking care of all her housekeeping needs while she lay in the Reach.[57] The hong merchant and the linguist, according to the system then in effect, took entire charge of the ship's business.

The system was very simple and, to the foreigner, very galling: it delivered him helpless into the hands of the Chinese. The hong merchant, dealer in import and export goods and security for the good behavior of the foreigners, came aboard at Whampoa Reach and had the ship's cargo transferred to smaller craft and taken to Canton. There he sold it or bartered it for the return cargo, paying all the duties in and out.[58] The linguist was an interpreter for the Chinese government and handled all dealings between customs officers and foreign merchants. ". . . Under such a system the foreigner is entirely at their mercy; and owing to the poverty of the wretched medium of communication, Canton-English," young Morrison had observed, "even with good intentions the linguists were liable to misunderstand and misrepresent the subject they were to write on."[59] The ship's master had little to do but control his crew; and the supercargo, if there was one, had only to indicate his choice of return goods and take care that he got what he selected.*

In Canton foreigners were as a rule confined to the fifteen-acre area in the

---

*The *Ronaldson* probably did not carry one; by 1840 American commerce with China was so concentrated in the hands of a few large firms with representatives in Canton that the supercargo's function was disappearing.

west suburb outside the city wall, where the hongs stood. Trading places rather than factories, the hongs were long narrow buildings two or three stories high, extending back to the wall and facing on the park ground that bordered the river and the docks. Their lower floors held storage rooms and offices, and the upper, living quarters for commission agents, supercargoes, and guests, who were rarely permitted to penetrate the city or the surrounding country.[60]

The *Ronaldson* reached Whampoa September 9, but it was a month before Fred touched land. Confined to a ship moored between a rice paddy and a cemetery, he was frustratingly tethered just out of reach of the country and the adventure he had gone so far to seek. His letters of introduction from Dr. Hawes and the Reverend Mr. Thomas Hopkins Gallaudet (presumably to the Massachusetts born medical missionary, Dr. Peter Parker, in Canton) were no use to him; he could not collect specimens for the Natural History Society; he could not see the Chinese in their homes and places of business.[61] The river, however, brought some of the Chinese to him.

He noticed that they deeply respected their own queues: the sampan man, an intelligent young fellow who ran errands for the ship, convinced Fred that he would not part with his for five hundred dollars; and the punishment inflicted by some of the crew of the United States frigate *Congress* on thieves they had caught was regarded as frightful—they had lopped off their queues with cutlasses. He also noticed the Chinese were great tea drinkers; when the ginseng merchant came aboard with thirty or forty coolies to sift and sort the cargo of ginseng, two of the men did nothing but make tea and carry it to the rest.[62] And the Chinese were very polite. Having inquiringly raised his eyebrows at a sailor on the yacht of a rich hong merchant who had been dealing for part of the *Ronaldson*'s cargo, Fred was invited aboard, escorted to the cabin where two stately gentlemen were playing chess, and treated to tea and cigarettes with as much courtesy as if he had been an admiral.[63] Still, it was hardly worthwhile to go all the way to the edge of China to confirm a few truisms, and it irked Fred to be detained there.

There were some sixty sail anchored in the Reach, most of them British, a half dozen of them American, and the visiting back and forth among the crews opened Fred's eyes. In two weeks he was writing his father:

> I have tried with all my heart to think well of the bark in which my lot is cast—To believe that these evils which we have felt, & which have produced so much ill feeling in others, in *all* my shipmates, were the result of accident, negligence & necessity. . . . In this I succeeded pretty well, and as I wrote you from Anjer—there was not so contented a person on board. Since our arrival, however, I am convinced of necessity, that our men not only are more discontented but have much more cause for complaint than the crew of other vessels here—our neighbors. We are worked much longer if not harder & have many less privileges than are customarily allowed.[64]

After being shipbound a month, on October 8 Fred was unexpectedly ordered to take the boat and go with the other boys to Boston Jack's, the comprador at Whampoa. Unable to beat up the narrow passage against the tide, they landed lower down, where the shore was lined by low wooden houses, some with verandas and tile roofs, and by shops with gaudy little signs. In his next letter home Fred said little of this first excursion ashore, except that he had made a visit to a joss house;[65] perhaps it was the incident he described much later:

> Following some other sailors at a little distance, I once entered a building which, though no idols were to be seen, I took to be a place of worship of some sort. It was dark and overhead and in recesses on the right and left rafters, wainscot and tile were to be dimly made out through a thin veil of smoke. A table or altar stood opposite the door upon which joss sticks were burning. There were numerous inscriptions on the walls and on paper and silk, lanthorns, banners and tags hung from them and from the ceiling; there were also several quaint bells and gongs. The sailors had made their way through a little crowd of Chinese who stood before the altar and some of them had gone behind it and were lifting the banners and shaking the lanthorns; others were striking the bells and gongs with their fists and knives. As I stood peering in at the door and gradually making out what I have described a sailor called out to me with an oath: "What are you keeping your hat on for in a heathen temple?" Presently as my eyes became accustomed to the gloom, I saw an old gentleman observing me from a side door. As our eyes met he bowed and directly came forward and beckoning me to follow him, led the way into a little room where there were piles of books and manuscripts. He laid open one of them which appeared very ancient and showed me that it contained plans of the building and tried in a gentle, patient way to make me understand something of its origin and purposes. He could use a very few words of Pidgin-English and, rightly or wrongly, I made out that the object of the structure was to keep the memory green and preserve the sayings of some good man who lived many generations ago. Afterwards the old gentleman took me through the main room calling my attention to the decorations of the bells and other things which he thought admirable and when I left he gave me several printed papers which I presumed to be religious tracts.[66]

In the bizarre circumstances, Fred fastened upon an element as familiar as sunshine—the courtesy of the old man. It was the element he found everywhere in his dealings with the Chinese people.

When Captain Fox discovered that he could pull an oar, Fred at last had a chance to get to Canton.[67] Rowing the captain upstream through the boats and junks that thronged the river, he must have glimpsed from a distance the two lofty pagodas within the city walls, the reddish housetops, many of them surmounted by frames for drying and dyeing clothes, the tall red flagpoles and,

29

lying beyond, the White Cloud Hills, their slopes to the north of the city covered for miles with the graves and tombs of a vast necropolis. Strangely, however, Fred never mentioned in his letters the appearance either of the Chinese city or countryside.

It was late October, just a few days after a frightful fire that had laid in ashes two hongs, a street of shops, and a thousand dwellings.[68] Fred gave up the idea of buying gifts to take home, since prices had gone up so that the same articles could be had as cheaply in New York.[69] Nor had he any taste for visiting Hog Lane for samshu, the terrible triple-distilled liquor that the shopmen in that notorious and dirty alley adulterated with narcotics for their foreign trade.[70] Instead, he purchased a pair of bright brown grass cloth pants and, cleanly dressed, went to call on Dr. Parker and his pretty young wife, the former Harriet Colby Webster of Washington, a relative of Daniel Webster's and the first foreign woman permitted to live in Canton.[71]

Peter Parker was the first Protestant medical missionary in China; he could tell Fred, if any American could, how to behave and what to see. He had been a resident since 1834, and the following year, with the help of the British and American merchants of Canton, he had established the Ophthalmic Hospital, where he treated eye diseases of patients from all over the empire and gave medical instruction to Chinese students. The Parkers had suffered a fright but no loss in the fire, having had to flee their home, which, however, the flames had not reached. When Fred met them, Parker was in poor health, overworked, and suffering from a diminution of his "religious enjoyment"; yet his distress did not strike his young visitor, who reported "a most agreeable call."[72]

Dr. Parker's modern techniques for treating eye diseases had not displaced certain traditional ones, Fred observed when he explored Canton. "Canton is a queer place," he wrote his brother.

> ... 'Twould look rather odd down our way I guess, to see Dr. Beresford go to work on an old man in the middle of Main St—take his eye out, so that it hangs half down his cheek, scrape & clean it with his instruments, swab out the socket & slip it back again as good as new—that's the celestial way of doing business & by the way the old cove, he's operating on, takes it very cooly without a cringe or a sign as if 'twas an every day performance to him as well as the leech. But the prettiest sight (say in front of the Phoenix Bank) is a couple of incendiaries sitting in stocks, with their tongues cut out, undergoing the pleasant operation of starving to death.[73]

Fred's first visit to Canton was short, and he did not return soon. About the first of November he became very sick with a fever, which he then called typhus and later referred to as typhoid.[74] He lay wretchedly in the forecastle, unable to touch food for two weeks, and wished for Aunt Maria. Jim this time could not substitute for her because he too was ill, as were several other crew members. At the end of three weeks Fred could eat a weak broth and dictate a letter—"Oh Aunt Maria, to be sick in a ship's forecastle is the extent of human misery"— and on Thanksgiving he was strong enough to undertake one in his own hand.[75]

It was not a festive holiday for the homesick convalescent; but as he sipped his broth and watched his shipmates scoop tough fresh buffalo meat and taro (a kind of yam) out of wooden tubs and eat them with sheath knives and fingers from tin pans,[76] he could at least be confident that his family, at their very different kind of dinner, had missed him. "Thanksgiving Dr. Bull & family & Miss Brush here, cloudy & lt snow in Morning, clear cold P.M.," John Olmsted remarked in his diary. "*Fred⁸ company* much wanted."[77]

Dr. Green, although he had left the ship, maintained his interest in Fred. He visited him during his illness, warned him sternly against a relapse ("but the mate tells the men they must not mind what the doctor says but get to work as soon as they are able"), and about a week after Thanksgiving called for him in a sampan and took him ashore.[78]

Walking about Whampoa with a Chinese escort supplied by Boston Jack, Fred was interested in everything he saw and was charmed by the little boys he met. Dressed precisely like their fathers, they wore long rich robes to their feet, silken cords woven into their little queues, and small black satin skull caps. They appeared to differ from their elders only in size and gravity; the men bowed politely, murmuring *"Chinchin"* in answer to greetings, but the little fellows were full of smiles and fun. The few women he saw were less charming. They had elaborate headdresses of false hair—"as much as you'd care to lift on a pitchfork"—wore plain blue nankeen jackets and trousers, and hobbled along on their bound feet "exactly as if on wooden legs."

With their escort Fred and Dr. Green visited a few shops, a preserve factory, and a schoolroom, where the drone of the little Chinese boys reciting their lessons struck familiarly on Fred's Yankee ears. It was almost sunset when they returned to the comprador's to find Boston Jack and his two partners at tea on a platform overlooking the water in front of the store. They had finished the dishes of vegetables, lobster, crab, shrimp, and rice. Jack's partners were enjoying their tea, wines, and liqueurs, of which there were several choice kinds, while he himself "smuggled 'samshew'—(a wretched firey Chinese spirit, which has killed more English soldiers than any of their weapons) out of a tea pot, drinking from a cup the size of a thimble."

Invited to join them, Fred sat down at the table with his hosts. Jack had been to Boston as a young man and, returning to Whampoa, had made a fortune supplying foreign ships there with everything they needed from masts and anchors to duck eggs. The conversation, conducted in Canton-English, disclosed that he had known Fred's great-uncle Aaron ("Ah, he no come long time— suppose him catchee die"), and he asked with interest about Fred's family.[79] Such civilized treatment was tonic to Fred's spirits, which, oppressed by illness and forecastle life, had recently flagged.

It was a tonic he enjoyed several times more before his ship left. His impression that the Chinese were almost always kind and courteous to foreigners, notwithstanding their reputation for xenophobia and in spite of the provocations of the recent war, was confirmed by later trips ashore.

"We roamed wherever inclination led us," he afterward wrote:

> hardly ever saying by your leave but taking that for granted, much as I have since seen a band of saucy Comanches do in a Mexican border village. Thus we made our way, often interrupting men and women at their work, into shops and factories, boatbuilding yards and potteries, gardens, cemeteries and houses of worship, even into private houses; seldom receiving the rebuffs and rebukes which I am sure that we deserved, often invited and assisted to gratify our curiosity.
>
> This good-natured disposition was, as far as I can remember, universal. We met, to be sure, few but the poor and lowly, yet we occasionally encountered some of the more fortunate classes.
>
> I suppose that civilization is to be tested as much by civility as anything else, and I have recalled these incidents as illustrations of a personal experience which made a strong impression upon me, tending to a higher estimate of the social condition of the masses of the Chinese people than, I think, generally prevails.[80]

The *Ronaldson*'s departure, originally scheduled for early December, was several times delayed. The wait was a dreary one. In the course of it, all the boys and most of the men were sick; and the captain, who was living at the factory, was rumored to be "pretty sick" and to have a "very consumptive cough." Fred, emaciated first by fever and then by an intestinal complaint, had a face "sharp as a Malay proa" and skeletal arms, and he reminded the *Ronaldson*'s literate old sail-maker of Cruikshank's drawings of Smike. The house which, according to his promise, the captain had had built for the boys contributed nothing to their comfort. Rain and wind poured through its cracks. By the middle of December Fred was in misery with rheumatic pains.[81]

Abuse and punishment, now that the passengers were out of the way, were lavishly distributed. All of the boys except Fred were rope's-ended for various shortcomings, "one 'at the wheel' (particularly forbidden by law) pretty severely."[82] Fred, unlike Dana, neither described the punishment nor mentioned his own reaction to it. Its effect on him—indeed the cumulative effect of all the harsh and arbitrary treatment he witnessed—is apparent from the bitterness with which he later publicly and repeatedly denounced the absolutism granted ships' officers in matters of discipline. Being conscientious and perhaps lucky, he escaped the indignity of a flogging, but he received his full share of abuse which was "unavoidable . . . by any course of conduct."[83]

By December he had had enough experience of forecastle life, with its homesickness hardly to be borne, its hardships doggedly to be endured, and its injustices never to be resisted, to conclude feelingly that it was not for him. "Oh Jack," he burst out in a letter to his brother, "if you & I were passengers oh! The old sea is glorious (sublime) after all, but the focstle is—no—it's too grave to be ridiculous. Dear brother Jack—God bless you. I'm crying like a baby. Your loving brother Fred all the world over."[84]

On Saturday, December 30, the *Ronaldson*, with a cargo of tea, cassia, and silk, at last weighed anchor; the rice paddies, the pagodas, the grave-covered hills —all the exotic scenery that had grown familiar during four months—fell behind as the ship dropped down the river and made her way along the tortuous channel to the mouth. Arriving at Macao, she anchored briefly, then set sail for New York on January 1, 1844.[85]

The voyage home was punishing. Meal and flour were spoiled; even the beans, which had been the best dish, had a "confounded queer taste"; and the salt beef almost brought tears to the eyes at a distance of twelve feet.[86] The ship was shorthanded; the crew was scurvy, cruelly overworked and almost mutinous.*

Fred was habitually dog-tired. On watch one night in the South Atlantic, standing up and looking vigilantly ahead, he fell asleep and was awakened when he toppled over on the deck. To keep awake he decided that he must keep moving and he began pacing five steps one way, then five steps the other. This time when he dropped asleep he almost walked overboard. Then he sat on a spar where the heavy bolt rope forming the bottom of the foresail would hit him first from behind when the ship rolled and rake his head compelling him to crouch, then strike him from the front and oblige him to stoop again. From this strained position he thought he saw a light and, staring intently into the darkness to see if it would reappear, he lost consciousness. Whether a few minutes or a half-hour later he never knew, he became aware of the stroke of the sail and of eyes peering into his. They were the captain's. Having hailed Fred three times, first from the quarterdeck, then from the waist, and finally from a distance of three feet, Fox had supposed he was asleep on watch until, looking directly into his eyes, he saw they were wide open.[87]

---

*One day, three weeks from New York, the captain held and kicked, while the mate flogged, one of the boys for a trifling misdemeanor, which he truthfully denied having committed. "We are no men if we stand it longer!" exclaimed one of the sailors, after twenty-five lashes had been laid on. Almost to a man, the rest of the crew grasped handspikes and sheathknives and moved ominously forward. Almost to a man—one, an experienced old sailor, stopped them with the rough reminder that they were running their heads into a noose, when instead they could take legal action against the captain as soon as they reached port. The sequel vindicated their reliance on shore justice: Captain Fox was brought to trial; his crew members—one of whom had himself locked up in the Sailors' Home to be sure that he would be sober enough to give evidence—testified against him; and the captain was compelled to pay the boy substantial damages to atone for the flogging and other abuse. "But what can atone for, what can retain, what can restore the manliness degraded to brutality under the lash of a despised tyrant?" Fred bitterly demand ([Frederick Law Olmsted], "A Voice from the Sea," *American Whig Review* 14 [December 1851]: 525–35).

This episode, which forty-seven years later so interested William James that Olmsted wrote a full account of it for him, was eloquent of life in the *Ronaldson*'s forecastle. So, when he landed, was Fred's appearance. John Olmsted, meeting him on April 16 in New York, literally did not recognize the yellow, scurvy, skeleton who hailed him as father.[88] Perhaps young John would have, but that tireless traveler had left the end of January on eighteen hours' notice for a three-month trip to the West Indies with Denison's son, Dr. Francis A. Olmsted.[89]

III
SCATTERED ENTHUSIASMS
April 1844–November 1846

WHATEVER interest Fred took in public events in the year after his return is not reflected in his surviving letters. He idled and recuperated.

He enjoyed the company of his best friend and brother, home the end of April from the West Indies;[1] and he attended the meetings of the Natural History Society, where the aspiring savants sometimes forgot their scientific interests in a zestful exchange of anecdotes about the nude in art, brought on by the prospect of the Atheneum's purchasing a statue by Hiram Powers.[2] There were hunting and camping trips with friends and the usual short vacation at Sachem's Head in July, followed by a visit to Savin Rock in August. Fred was unsympathetic to his stepmother's lament that the hotel there was not run on temperance principles, and he was careless about going to church.[3]

In the course of the summer he was developing two enthusiasms: farming and girls. His stepmother observed the romantic phenomenon: "Freddy seems head over ears in love with Frances Condit. . . . I know not whether the admiration is mutual."[4] If it was, the romance left no perceptible trace, being swamped by a quick succession of light-hearted infatuations.

In October 1844 Fred went to live for a few months with the David Brookses in Cheshire to learn what he could about farming. The scenery of that hilly part of Connecticut enchanted him, especially the region around nearby Wolcott, where his father owned land commanding an extensive and beautiful view of the hills, river, and sound. There was a shack on it where Fred spent several cold days, cutting wood and exploring by day, reading Zimmermann's *On Solitude* (". . . one of the best books ever written. I wish everyone would read it") in front of an open fire by night. Another of Cheshire's attractions was the girls, and Fred was transparently pleased with the reputation he was getting as a beau. When he learned that he was rumored engaged to a girl to whom he had been attentive on a sleighing party, he jauntily wrote his father, "I wish you'd order me home or else send me some money & a ream of light blue note paper."[5]

When writing his father, Fred referred to his interest in girls with protective irony, but he exposed his real feelings to Charley Brace.

> It is a good world . . . and God be thanked, I do believe I am as happy as anybody in it—I don't know hardly anything I want, unless it is, of course, the welfare of my friends, besides a wife—Yes! that's what I want,

35

somebody that'l love me as much as I want to love her—Oh dear! I wish she was here now that I might tell everything to her. . . . I am desperately in love—now, and no mistake, only for the life of me I can't tell who it's with—the whole of 'em, I believe. . . . I wonder if every young man—& every young woman too, has these sort of troubles. . . .[6]

Fred went home about the middle of March to a father whose prosperity, and whose patience with his drifting son, remained constant. John Olmsted for several years previous to 1844 had been spending about three thousand dollars a year on his family expenses. That year he spent five thousand four hundred, which covered such extra expenses as painting the house inside and out and buying a piano at Christmas for John, whose deficiency in social graces troubled him. He was also about to tear down his store building and to erect a new one. He seems to have bought Fred an old sloop when he came home, for Fred spent part of April making one seaworthy—caulking her, making a gaff out of an old mast, getting new sails, and rerigging and painting her.[7]

Looking for another farm where he might like to work, Fred, through the good offices of John's classmate, Frederick J. Kingsbury, found what he wanted and was established by the middle of May on Joseph Welton's place, near Waterbury. His new situation appealed to the sentimentalist as well as the farmer in Fred. Welton was not only a good and successful farmer, but he openly loved his wife. He was also, Fred wrote Brace, "a *churchman*, and when he reads prayers you would think that he was trying to read so as to show the Examining Committee that he did not have to *spell* the *hard ones*."[*, 8]

Fred approached the farm work enthusiastically. Hauling stone made him so stiff and sore that he positively looked forward to hoeing; ploughing, he was soon able to keep up with Welton. In his spare time he boxed with Welton and wrote letters home asking about his fleeting flames. His brother tried to wet-blanket his ardors, and his father, mildly alarmed by his diffuse amorous interests, wrote him a stern lecture on rash and early marriages.[9]

Late in May young John became ill and had to leave college. Fred went home and, when John recovered in early June, the two boys sailed their sloop to New Haven.[10] The temperature was in the high nineties, and Fred, instead of immediately taking the stage to Waterbury, spent several hot days swimming, sailing, attending Benjamin Silliman's lectures, and seeing John's friends. Although John was one of the most popular men in his class, Fred found that "a very general regret was expressed at his return, for they say he cannot be induced to study in a rational manner. . . . I hope you will give John a good lecture about it," Fred urged their father.[11]

If John received the lecture, it did him no good: within ten days after

*Half a century later, on hearing of Welton's death, Olmsted wrote Kingsbury that he had hardly ever known so good a man: not one of his teachers had been more conscientious, or of a more simple, healthy, moral character (O to FJK, 18 May 1894).

Fred's return to Waterbury he fell sick again and had to go home.[12] Discouraged, he thought of giving up college altogether. "I'd rather be a healthy Irishman than a sickly professor," he said.[13] But, without professional training, what was he to do with himself?

Fred was led, for John's benefit, to write down the advantages he saw in an agricultural life. Emerson was not yet an influence on him, and it did not occur to him to see the farmer, as the transcendentalist did, as an archetypal figure standing at the door of the breadroom of the household of Nature, the creator who had for his handmaidens the ages, the seasons, the air, the earth, the worm in the earth, and the waters under the earth. To Fred a farmer was, simply, a professional man pursuing a respectable and skilled calling that required, both for its advancement and its practice, scientific knowledge. Agriculture, because it applied the principles of the chemist, the naturalist, the geologist, and the mechanic, kept the farmer's mind active, his ideas expanding.[14]

It was also a singularly peaceful occupation. The farmer's motives—to furnish food to his fellow beings and a livelihood for his family—were innocent, praiseworthy, and never suspect. Success did not expose him to envy and rivalry as it did in some other professions where, "the more you rise in distinction, the more you are marked by the shafts of malice." Farmers made a living, too.

> . . . They live and bring up their families in what they consider comfortable circumstances, with the usual system and management. I should think by the use of the proper tools and machinery which a man of intelligence and information would procure and invent, at least half of the most disagreeable and hard labor of our old-fashioned farmers might be dispensed with to advantage.

Fred might have added another point that appealed to him about farming: it was the only congenial work not barred to him by his inadequate education. Physically and temperamentally, he was unfit to be a seaman or a merchant; educationally he was unequipped for the scholarly professions. Farming seemed to offer a happy solution to his peculiar problem. Whether it would to John, Fred would not say.

> . . . If you could, however, and of this you are the best judge, become interested in its operations for a year or two and connect yourself with the present rapid advance as an honorable and learned profession, you would not only find it a sufficient means of support, but an agreeable and healthful pursuit.[15]

It was to take a decade of hard experience for him to modify this sanguine generalization.

John, in no hurry to determine his future, left early in July with a couple of friends on a memorably scenic trip through the White Mountains and into

Canada.* He wound up his journey at Saratoga, where he took the water cure until college opened late in September.[16] The water-cure fad was one he pursued less from gullibility than desperation: he would try anything to improve his frail health.

Fred, intending to go to college with him and audit, for one term, lectures useful to a prospective farmer, left Welton's in mid-August to do some preliminary study at home. He did little work, however, because he had too much fun sailing, picnicking, and distractedly flirting with the local charmers.[17] His studies, having proceeded unsatisfactorily among the social temptations of Hartford, went better that fall in New Haven. "F. I am rejoiced," John Olmsted wrote early in October,

> that you seem to feel the necessity of making the most of your time, as it
> must necessarily be short, by all means seek the society of those older & wiser
> than yourself & do not spend minutes (for they make hours) in light &
> foolish conversation & in no case keep company with smokers & drinkers,
> it is sometimes & perhaps frequently the case that those who feel
> most strong in their integrity are most easily overcome.[18]

Fred hardly needed to be warned away from fast company; he had no taste for it. More to the point was John Olmsted's advice concerning young John's health. Because of his frequent illnesses and absences, John had fallen back a class and was not to graduate with Brace and the class of 1846. He was sick frequently enough during the term to keep his father chronically worried, so that he wrote Fred half-apologetically, "As to your health, I seldom think to inquire, for John's seems paramount." Any confidence he may have had in Fred's, however, was dissipated the end of December by word that Fred had had an "alarming attack."[19]

It is not clear what the attack was. It was the third of its sort he had had in a few months according to his father, and it was preceded by a violent throbbing of the head. That John Olmsted thought and hoped it was not apoplexy suggests that it resembled apoplexy. Whatever it was, it was not grave enough to make Fred leave college before the end of the term; yet it was serious enough to make his father implore him to "consider himself a vulnerable man & in danger of his life," and write him insistently about the need for moderate, regular habits, especially in regard to food and sleep.[20] Fortunately, the term was almost over and John Olmsted could personally supervise Fred after his return home January 8, 1846.

What did Fred get out of his semester at Yale? One can but speculate. Even in the absence of any record of the lectures he attended, it may be assumed that

---

*A letter written during this excursion (3 August 1845), which contains an effective description of a landscape, has been mistakenly attributed to Fred (F. L. Olmsted, Jr., and T. Kimball, *Forty Years*, 1: 64–65). Internal evidence—the writer refers to having recently been in the West Indies—indicates it was written by John.

John Olmsted

F.L.O., circa 1850

Above: Olmsted Hall, Essex.
Sketch by John Charles
Olmsted, 1877.

Left: Friends at Yale:
front row, Charles L. Brace,
F.L.O. *back row,* Charles
Trask, Frederick J. Kingsbury,
John Hull Olmsted.

he learned something of chemistry, mineralogy, and geology from Benjamin Silliman and of "natural philosophy," which included biology and astronomy, from Denison Olmsted. He sharpened his skill in debate in long discussions of religion and politics with John's friends, some of whom, being southerners, upheld slavery. And Fred, exposed steadily for three months to the fervid piety of the converted Brace and to the pervasive religiosity of the Yale community, could hardly have helped concerning himself with the problem, then so awful and so pressing, of salvation.

But the telling experience of his Yale interlude was a girl. She was Elizabeth Wooster Baldwin, daughter of Roger Sherman Baldwin, lawyer, antislavery man, and recent governor of Connecticut. How Fred met her is not recorded, but he seems to have been an occasional caller at the Baldwins' house during his three months in New Haven. Lizzie had her father's earnestness and intelligence, and a charm that both captivated and reassured Fred. Knowing he was ill educated, he fancied he was a bumpkin. This misapprehension she corrected. She drew him out of his shyness, aroused in him "a sort of scatter-brained pride," and made him realize that his lack of formal education need not prevent him from becoming a cultured man. In short, she suggested to him possibilities in himself that he had been too diffident to consider. Through her influence he came to read Emerson, Lowell, Ruskin, and "other real prophets," and they, he told her half a century later, "gave me the needed respect for my own constitutional tastes and an inclination to poetic refinement in the cultivation of them that afterwards determined my profession." He had often listened while his father real aloud the travel books of President Dwight, Professor Silliman, and Miss Martineau, and his new reading strengthened the impression he got from them that "the love of nature, not simply as a naturalist but as a poet loves it, was respectable."[21] This was no small gain for a young man whose decision to be a farmer was predicated in large part on a deep love for rural scenery.

There must have been a strong sympathy between Lizzie and Fred: she always understood what he meant, he said, even when he could not express himself.[22] Yet close friendship seems never to have developed between them; Fred was perhaps too overawed by the perfection he imputed to her to seek a footing in that equalitarian relationship. Instead, he worshipped her and wondered if he was in love with her; and he always called her "Miss Baldwin."

Theoretically, Fred continued his studies when he returned home, but a new health regime, which involved a cold shower and a long ride, took up most of the morning;[23] and he was, as his father indulgently put it, "a good deal with the ladies." He attended the Reading Society's weekly meetings, which usually finished with a dance ("I was not the worst dancer," he remarked complacently after one of them), and most of all, he hovered over Lizzie Baldwin, who spent January with the Thomas C. Perkinses* in Hartford. After she left for New

*Mrs. Perkins was Mary Foote Beecher, a sister of Harriet Beecher Stowe and Henry Ward Beecher.

Haven, "on those cruel cars that have carried off so many good people," Fred lost his taste for female society. Temporarily, that is: a few days later he was writing Charley Brace about "Sarah Cook—nice girl—half love her."[24]

There followed a long spell of "abominable dirty weather"; the sun did not shine for two weeks, and the clay roads, rutted deeply, were frozen "hard as a Loco-Foco's head." Fred applied himself to his agricultural studies and his health, and with his cousin Lucius, Denison's son, and several other young men took dancing lessons and attended such sober entertainments as Dr. Hawes's lecture on George Washington and John Jay as model statesmen.[25]

This quiet routine was broken on Thursday, February 10, when little Ada, who was frequently ailing, had "one of her turns . . . something like the bilious colic." She rapidly became very ill. The doctor attended her constantly, and helplessly: the following Monday, at four in the morning, she died. Fred, shaken and resigned, notified John: "She had been in agony almost constantly since Saturday morning. . . . Nothing seemed to alleviate her pain . . . and we were prepared to consider death a mercy. Her moans and cries of distress have been heartrending."[26] A blizzard, blanketing the countryside in eighteen inches of snow that drifted deeply, prevented her funeral from taking place until February 18.

Whether in consequence of Ada's death, or merely subsequent to it, Fred's dormant piety stirred. His rather conventional acceptance of the Congregational faith had been infused, paradoxically, with both skepticism and fervor at Yale, where, in theological discussions, he had made a reputation as a keen man in an argument. Salvation, its achievement, its manifestations, and their chances of it, had been a staple subject of conversation among Fred and his circle, since at that time and in that place the state of one's soul was not a private matter or even a family affair but the urgent concern of friends and even of well-disposed acquaintances. After Fred left Yale there occurred one of those periodic awakenings of religious interest that characterized the university then, and from a distance he was drawn into it. Brace, capable of writing a ten-page effusion on the atonement to a young woman acquaintance,[27] wrote similarly to Fred. Kingsbury and Charles Trask, who were working up to conversion, wrote him in the same vein.

At the beginning of March, Fred took his father's cutter and drove to New Haven, drawn there, possibly, as much by hope of seeing Lizzie Baldwin as by interest in his friends' religious experiences. His relationship with her can have been little advanced during the visit, for afterward he stiffly directed John: "Offer my *regards* to Miss B *whenever* she *enquires* for me," and spoke warmly of an evening spent at the Braces' with Mary Warburton, who "sings very well . . . and calls me Fred."[28] Girls, however, were on the decline; religion was in the ascendancy. Fred's interest was focused on the revival at Yale; he began to pray for his friends' conversion and wrote them long letters about the condition of his soul.

He felt it something short of satisfactory, but it was not his skepticism that

41

made it so. He had little respect for blind faith: a good Christian, he thought, ought to question the tenets of his religion and decide on the basis of evidence to accept, if he could, Christian dogmas. That salvation was only for those who had faith was a theory repugnant to Fred. His humane spirit was repelled by the thought that a conscientious seeker after truth—pre-Christian, infidel, Unitarian, Roman Catholic, any non-Congregationalist—should suffer through eternity in Hell, while others who never bothered to think about the validity of their beliefs should effortlessly attain salvation through "blind faith in a *mystery.*" Agitated by doubts, he did not yet have any as to the truth of the Bible. He read it daily, and he earnestly recommended the habit to his brother,[29] who had weathered unconverted one season of religious interest at Yale and showed a distressing imperviousness to the current revival. In fact, John was taking dancing lessons.

His father approved: dancing was "good exercise & very desirable for every gentleman who goes into genteel young society at the present day"; but Mary Ann Olmsted, "exceedingly grieved" by his light-mindedness, begged young John to drop his lessons at once "and attend to that which is *far more ennobling* and *elevating* to you as a *man,* and of far greater consequence to you as an immortal and accountable being. . . ."[32] Fred approved the dancing but deplored the flippancy with which John asserted that he "never could perceive any good effects or great advantage" from daily Bible reading. He was scarcely in a position to judge, Fred thought: "Why, I did not see him read it but once, and then in French, all last term."[30]

The revival at Yale, although a minor one, was harvesting souls, and Fred and Brace prayed busily that Lizzie Baldwin's should be among them. Fred had tried to engage her in a correspondence, but she had refused on the elusive ground that it would be "neither right nor best." The rest of her letter had been "religious—most delightful" and had almost persuaded her thwarted admirer that he was "right smack & square on dead in love with her—beached and broken back^d."[31] When word reached him that she and Trask and Kingsbury were converted, he was ecstatic. "Thank God for Miss Baldwin and all the rest. What an angel she will make! How glad I am!" To Brace he confided: "I begin to think I *do* love Miss B. really. . . . If I never did before, I do now. What a blessed thing she must be—Pshaw! I am going to be a Clodpole—I should be a scamp to think of making her Mrs. Clodpole."[32] It was easier for him to think of her as an angel than as a wife.

John, fragilely armored in flippancy, was still withstanding the prayerful intervention of his friends and his brother, but he was one against many. Probably his father, so reticent and so modest—and unconverted himself—did not urge him to profess, but his stepmother wrote him pressingly. Miss Baldwin, with a convert's zeal, joined in the campaign for his soul. Fred panted for bulletins on his brother's spiritual state. "My heart has been with you so much for 2–3 days," he wrote John the beginning of April, "that I have given myself up to it entirely almost."[33] Finally overborne, John gave up and declared himself converted.

"Glory to God!—I am happier than ever," Fred exclaimed; and Mary Ann Olmsted rejoiced: "O, *wonderful* mercy! . . . How happy your circle must be, and how bless'd has Miss Baldwin been in her efforts for the good of others." Uncle Owen, almost weeping with joy, joined the chorus of congratulations, injecting, however, a lament for his exemplary brother, the elder John: ". . . Doubtless he thinks that his morality, and charity in giving to all benevolent institutions, and doing good to others in various ways will commend him to the mercy of God, being too proud to accept of Salvation as a free gift. It is a dreadful situation to be in," he observed darkly.[34]

Fred hurried to New Haven, where he had earnest and sympathetic talks with all the new converts—and was swept overboard himself. Mary Ann Olmsted, in a transport of thankfulness, wrote young John,

> I think I realize in some degree the unspeakably rich blessing which has been bestowed on me, in this great mercy conferred on you and F—— and I feel also that God in some measure prepared me to receive it, by the removal of our dear Ada, thus calling off my thoughts from this world and leading me more deeply to contemplate the things of eternity.[35]

Although converted, Fred still hung back from joining the church. He already had a fixed aversion to sectarianism and dogmatic Christianity. The thought that truth was the exclusive possession of any group whatever and that all outsiders—Carlyle, Jefferson, Voltaire, Socrates, his tirelessly good and loving father—were destined to eternal torment outraged justice and common sense; and his sense of his relationship to his fellow men precluded his identifying himself with the elect and the rest of humanity with the damned.

In later years he was to look back on this period of religious excitement, with its overstimulated emotionalism and its meddlesome intimacies, with revulsion; but his attitude shifted only gradually. On his return from New Haven, he was exalted, almost as much by having shared his recent experience with his brother and friends as by having had it. "Next to the bread of Life, I live by Sympathy," he wrote John.[36]

Meanwhile, the problem of his future had not become any less pressing: he had to put himself in the way of eventually earning his living. John Olmsted neither wished nor expected to leave his sons much money and had told them so. Contemplating his retirement, he had taken two of his assistants into the business in the middle of March, and the sign over the doorway of the new store now read, in gilt block letters, "Olmsted, Thatcher & Goodrich, Dry Goods & Carpeting." Thus his income from the store was declining and could be expected to decline further, and he was investing his money in, among other things, real estate.[37]

Wishing to work on a model farm in central New York state, Fred, with letters of introduction from Denison Olmsted, went to New York on April 10.[38] There he saw his former employers, and James A. Benkard, who "was very kind

—for him," gave him a letter to his father-in-law, Captain Henry Robinson, "a fancy farmer" at Newburgh. At the Sailors' Home Fred asked about his old shipmates and got news of several of them—none of it gratifying. And in Park Place he watched troops drill and was critical of the officers' shabby mounts, the soldiers' absurd busbies, and everyone's manifest ignorance of elementary maneuvers.[39] There is nothing to indicate that he was exercised by the imminence of war.

On April 16, spruced up by a haircut and shampoo, he took the Hudson River steamer *Santa Claus* as far as Newburgh; next day he went to Albany,[40] where he called on Luther Tucker, editor of the *Cultivator*, at his office. He found Tucker talking to a slender, dark man with melancholy eyes and an air of mild hauteur, whom he introduced as Andrew Jackson Downing.[41] Fred knew of Downing; so did most of literate America. Five years before, at the age of twenty-six, Downing, a nurseryman and landscape gardener at Newburgh, had published *A Treatise on the Theory and Practice of Landscape Gardening Adapted to North America.* The first book in this country to discuss domestic architecture in connection with the arrangement of grounds, it had made its author a celebrity overnight and the recognized arbiter of rural taste. Downing had quickly buttressed his reputation with *Cottage Residences,* "an important source for the new architectural styles which in the 1840s were everywhere supplanting the earlier Classical Revival for private dwellings," and with *Fruits and Fruit Trees of America.*[42] Downing and Tucker, when Fred met them, were discussing a new monthly periodical, the *Horticulturist,* which Tucker had invited Downing to edit.[43]

Two benefits accrued to Fred from the meeting: Downing took friendly note of him, and Tucker gave him a letter for George Geddes of Onondaga County, New York. Within ten days Fred was settled as an apprentice at Geddes's farm, "Fairmont."'

Geddes, then thirty-seven, was the son of James Geddes, engineer of the Erie Canal. He had three professions at his fingers' ends: law, engineering, and farming. He was best known as an agriculturist. Of his five hundred acres, he had made a model farm noted for its productiveness and general excellence. Twice entered for competition in the state fair, it twice won first prize. Geddes was president of the State Agricultural Society in its early years and a member of its board later, and the articles he contributed to agricultural magazines and the *New York Tribune* were authoritative.[44]

Married to the former Maria Porter, of Skaneateles, Geddes had two children, Mary and James. A Methodist, he had not had them baptized because he took an unorthodox view of the sacrament: it was, he held, intended only for proselytes, not for born Christians. Fred quickly came to suspect that his religious views were unsound and questioned whether he was a truly pious man.[45]

Although the farm was admirable and the family pleasant, Fred felt keenly the abrupt change he had made. Having intensely shared the highly personal experiences of conversion and frustrated love with a half-dozen intimates, he was famished for sympathy in this new situation, where the state of his soul was exclusively his own business and no one knew Miss Lizzie Baldwin. He was slowly recovering from his infatuation with her—"the whole affair was so *tapered* that it did not hurt me much"[46]—but she still remained the standard against which he measured other young women.

Letters from Kingsbury, Brace, and John were the principal solace of his loneliness during his first weeks at "Fairmont." Lonely or not, he felt himself well situated and soon gained confidence in his ability as a farmer. By the middle of June he could cultivate and hoe corn, plough and plant, and wash and shear sheep as well as most farmers. The garden was his special charge, and he constructed a canal to carry a mixture of water and manure into it from a pool of barnyard drainings. Unfortunately, his engineering skill was not equal to the work, and the first heavy rain carried away the gate to the canal so that the pond burst through and gullied out the garden it was to irriga e.[47]

Satisfactory as the farm and beautiful as the country were, Fred was disinclined to settle in the neighborhood. There was a little farm at Sachem's Head, the next property to the Head House, in which he was interested, and he thought the Akerly place, one hundred thirty acres on the south shore of Staten Island, was worth considering. He might have gone to Geddes for advice, but hesitated because Geddes, an intense local patriot, was "for sending any man to Bedlam, who would go out of Onondaga County for a farm."[48]

Although always busy and often tired, Fred tried to keep active mentally and socially. In the half hour he had to himself daily, he wrote in his journal. Sometime during each day he skimmed a chapter of Thomas Cogswell Upham's *Principles of the Interior or Hidden Life*, a tract recommended by his stepmother, and at bedtime he reread and pondered it. He memorized the Twenty-third Psalm, read the Bible regularly, intoxicated himself with *Sartor Resartus* —"I do think Carlisle [sic] is the greatest genius in the world. . . . I perfectly wonder and stand awe-struck as I would at a Hurricane"—and planned a course of history reading, beginning with de Tocqueville, which was to take him years.[49] Conscientiously, he made a point of being cheerful. Fredrika Bremer's exposition of cheerfulness as a Christian duty in *The Neighbours* impressed him, and he explained to Kingsbury: "With a gloomy disposition a man cannot prepare himself for immortality—because he does not understand and can not make himself worthy of it. A true Christian will already be happy on Earth. Man's only *actual* misfortune is the want of the friendship of God. Now I think there's a great deal of truth in that."[50] The conviction of the duty of cheerfulness was one he never gave up, although it came to rest at length on a social rather than a religious basis.

Fred was soon able to withdraw his complaint that there was "nobody to sympathize with me or for me to sympathize with or love—except the lady of an officer of the Army of Occupation," Mrs. Kirby Smith. In addition to Mrs.

Smith, there were her three sisters, "very pretty specimens. . . . They are always inviting me to call but I haven't yet. . . . I must attend to them before long."[51] And Mrs. Geddes had attractive nieces who came occasionally to "Fairmont." Fred's favorite was Sarah Porter, a tall, handsome girl with a "pleasing healthy face" and no airs. Their first meeting caught him at a disadvantage: she arrived while he was helping with the shearing, "and the first [she] saw of me I was 'all in a sweat' and smock frock, pretty considerably dirty and rum looking . . . on the barn floor laying across a sheep's belly." Geddes humanely gave him the rest of the day off, and after freshening up, Fred took Sarah to call on some nearby Geddes relatives, the Jerome girls, where they spent a happy afternoon taking turns, three at a time, in the swing.[52]

That evening Sarah Porter disclosed an unexpected faculty. In conversation with Geddes after dinner, Fred found that he was not only unsound on baptism, he did not grasp the meaning of the mediation of Christ. At first reluctantly, because he did not want to exclude Sarah, and finally quite forgetting her, Fred engaged Geddes in a long argument. Turning at length to Sarah, he was enchanted that she expressed entire agreement with him and took up the discussion herself very ably. Next morning, when she left, she gave him "a real Baldwin squeeze or shake," significant of special sympathy. Pulchritude, theological soundness, a suggestion of Lizzie—the combination overpowered Fred. For some days he was half in love with Sarah Porter.[53]

Although he continued to dally with thoughts of Sarah, political events by this time were preempting his attention. Zachary Taylor's army, sent to occupy the territory in dispute between Texas and Mexico, was pushing up the Rio Grande, capturing forts and villages on its drive toward Monterey. In June the Oregon boundary question was settled by treaty with Great Britain, and American settlers could at last enter, with confidence in its permanence as a part of the United States, the disputed northwest. The vast golden realm of California was being detached from Mexico and was gravitating into the orbit of the expanding United States. Inextricably mingled with the problems of territorial acquisition, so facilely solved when one opponent was too weak to resist and the other was unwilling to fight, was the far more ominous problem of slavery.

In spite of reservations about the Mexican War, its motives and its conduct, Fred thought that the entry of Texas, as a slave state, into the union would result in the admission of California and Oregon as free states.[54] An antislavery Whig, he hoped to see the presidency secured in 1848 by someone of his own party who would check the slave power's extension. Henry Clay was his first choice; his second was Cassius Clay, editor of the *True American*, which he admired as "a real *good* paper." The triumphant Taylor also might make a good president. "The skillful disposition, management and partisan diplomacy of a frontier army is prima facie evidence of a talent for Government—governing." He had no similar confidence in General Winfield Scott, "a vain, ambitious though talented man."[55] His views of the possible military candidates were certainly influenced by the "handsome, modest, interesting, informative" Captain

Kirby Smith, who, on furlough from Taylor's army, spent July with his wife on Geddes's farm.*,56

Opposed though he was to slavery, Fred could not think of it as the worst evil on earth, or of slaveowners as a wicked, hostile, or alien group. The abolitionists he believed had taken hold of the wrong end of the stick.

> I believe we can do a great deal more for deluded men—Catholics—or Unitarians, drunkards & Slaveholders—by praying *for* them than by . . . blackguarding them through the newspapers, and exasperating them— acting as if we hated them as much as their doctrines. . . . Men are oftener drawn to truth and Christ—I believe than driven.57

This was the instinct of a temperate disposition, the counsel of a mind that even in youth emphasized the community rather than the disparity of interest among fellow citizens.

After the harvest, Geddes released Fred to take, for the first time in many years, one of those long journeys in search of the picturesque that had been the joy of his childhood. With his father and John he spent two and a half weeks covering some sixteen hundred miles in upper New York State and southern Ontario and Quebec. Although they spent two days at Niagara Falls, which Fred had last seen when he was twelve, there was no time to linger over scenery, however majestic.58 Fred was due back at "Fairmont" before the middle of September, to accompany Geddes to the agricultural fair at Auburn.

At the fair he was appointed to fill a vacancy on the committee on farming utensils, and he found everyone flatteringly eager to demonstrate and explain the various implements to him. After a day of examining and trying them, he wrote the committee's report, which Geddes delivered. At the same time, he conducted an inquiry on his own account, and wrote his father, "All the folks I spoke to about the S. H. farm, thought well of it, only guessed I would not be contented there over winter."59

The Sachem's Head farm had, in fact, been a good deal on Fred's mind, and John Olmsted, shortly before their Canadian tour, had gone to examine it.60 In spite of its location, directly on the coast in the midst of the beautiful rural country familiar and dear to him, Fred recognized that it had two drawbacks: it was small and, in winter, bleak and exposed. Only about forty of its seventy acres could be in tillage at a time, he estimated, and there was no fruit on it. Nevertheless he was much tempted by it and was hoping to induce Geddes to inspect it with him "though I most know that his opinion of the place will be

*This was Ephraim Kirby Smith, a graduate of the United States Military Academy in the class of 1826. He died September 11, 1847, of wounds received a few days earlier at the battle of Molina del Rey. His younger brother, Edmund Kirby-Smith, who hyphenated the name, also was a graduate of West Point and became the well-known Confederate general.

unfavorable, for he has been getting mad that I should prefer it to this country."[61]

Geddes's displeasure could not have been serious, since early in October, about a week after Fred finished work at "Fairmont," he visited the Olmsteds in Hartford and went with Fred to look at the Sachem's Head farm. Nor could his advice have been emphatically discouraging, although he saw it in a fierce and destructive southeast storm, the expiring fury of a hurricane originating off Key West: a month later the place belonged to Fred.[62]

IV
FARMING AT SACHEM'S HEAD
December 1846–March 1848

PLANNING to move to Sachem's Head early in the new year, Fred continued to study geometry, natural philosophy, and agriculture at home. He also took singing lessons, practiced the guitar with passionate, short-lived enthusiasm, and enjoyed a number of little dancing parties, at which it began to dawn on him that Emily Perkins, the daughter of Thomas C. Perkins, was acquiring "a confirmed habit of being pretty and entertaining."[1] To the anxiety of his friends, he still had not joined any church. It occurred to his stepmother that he never would: "If he waits to find a pure church, a perfect rule of faith, or form of government, he will wait in vain."[2]

Fred took possession of his farm the beginning of February. After his departure, his father lamented to young John: "We miss Fred a good deal—the idea that he has gone to a new home & perhaps to be with us no more permanently, is rather gloomy, this dispersion of children is to a parent fond & devoted to the domestic circle one of the most melancholy circumstances in life."[3]

Fred, at Guilford, was too busy obtaining tools, a hired man, and stock to be melancholy over leaving home. The only thing that depressed him in the least was the run-down condition of his farm, and that not for long. "It does look real nasty and forlorn about the house," he admitted, but he now rejected the charge of bleakness. "There's nothing bleak at Sachem's Head—that is on my point," he asserted with proprietary pride.[4]

Only an enthusiast could have spoken so. The farm had been miserably handled and showed it. Some of the arable ground had not been broken for ten years. The barn was falling down, and the little brown gabled house was in disrepair. Moist from poor drainage, the ground was cold, and the crops were backward in the spring. At the end of winter, there was "a swamp for several acres about the house: real juicy," and "a stream from the barnyard empties itself near the front door—into the sea."[5]

To Fred, none of these drawbacks seemed incurable, and he was well pleased with his property: its excessive moisture could be corrected by drainage; its wood was better and more valuable than he had supposed and had a ready market at two local shipyards; its house and barn he planned to replace, and his quick imagination visualized the simple changes by which the grounds about the house could be redeemed. "The lawn is to be the grand feature of my gardening. The ground is naturally graded and finely adapted for a broad smooth green plat broken only by a few trees or clumps[;] along the rear edge of it and so circling towards the shore, some low thick shrubbery is wanted." Moreover, the view across the sound was wide and interesting, especially when the little harbor was full of sail. The fishing close offshore was excellent; and rockweed, to be had for the gathering, provided abundant and luxuriously clean fertilizer.[6]

When he went home for a few days to fetch furniture and tools, his brother found him almost impossible to communicate with: he talked, and would hear, of nothing but his farm. John, having left college because his eyes were failing, was suffering from an oppressive ennui. He dully marveled at Fred's zest and hoped "the present object of his affections i.e. his farm will not be as ephemeral as most of them seem to have been."[7]

John's implied criticism notwithstanding, there was a certain obscure coherence behind Fred's successive enthusiasms: he was feeling his way toward his place in the world, the place in which he could assume a responsible role as a Christian and a citizen. Farming meant something more to him than a means of livelihood: it meant an accountable position in the social order. Whereas an eccentric young transcendentalist, with joy not duty as his object, had withdrawn from a society too complex for his tolerance and retired to Walden Pond to simplify his life and seek the nature of reality, Fred went to the lonely coast farm to assume his duty to society and contribute to the upkeep of its intricate machinery. Drifter though he appeared to be, he was not the man to evade what he took to be his duty.

Visiting Sachem's Head for a few days early in May, John was struck by the narrowness rather than the direction of his brother's life. Fred had no near neighbors, and his most sympathetic companion was Nep, his Newfoundland puppy. He lived in one downstairs room of his farmhouse, while the hired man, Davis, and his wife and baby had the rest of the floor, and an Irishman and a hired girl lived upstairs. Mrs. Davis provided the meals—"horrid," John called the cold pork and cold potatoes she served—and the household ate together. All conversation, all ideas, were on planting, pruning, and fertilizing. At night, Fred was so tired that he went to bed directly after supper. John dreaded the idea of sharing such a life even for a few weeks in the summer and thought it would surely condemn his brother to respectable mediocrity at best.

> I presume it will be all the better for me—tho' all the worse for Fred. I'm sorry he didn't have the College Education as well as I, or rather than me. He has fine capabilities naturally, I think, but they want training now most shockingly. Still he'll make a good farmer, a good citizen & a good husband, one of these days.[8]

Kingsbury, more optimistic, thought experience would adequately train Fred's faculties and that the world needed enthusiasts like him.

> . . . One thing is curious, disappointments never seem to trouble them. They must in the nature of things meet with them often and yet they go

right on in the same old way, just as if it had not happened. They never get disheartened. I think Fred will be one of that sort. Many of his favorite schemes will go to naught but he'll throw it aside and try another and spoil that and forget them both while you or I might have been blubbering over the ruins of the first.[9]

John could neither share nor understand Fred's buoyancy. He was himself too often ill and too dispirited by illness for ambition or enthusiasm. Zeal had not dictated his choice of a profession: he had lately decided on medicine, less, it was suspected, because it interested him than because, unlike the law and the ministry, it did not require public speaking. Prevented, for the time, from studying it or anything else by his eyes, he was leading "a stupid life," inactive and desultory. During most of June, which he spent on the farm, he suffered not only from his eyes but from headaches and dysentery; still, he had a better time than he had expected.[10]

Fred by then had made repairs on the house, graded the grounds in front, and set out prairie rose and woodbine by the steps. His own room, which he shared with John and the cat, Minna, and her kittens, kidnapped from Hartford, had been freshly papered. He and his men had planted the garden in corn, potatoes, tobacco, lettuce, tomatoes, peas, and beans and the fields in onions, rutabagas, corn, hay, barley, and potatoes.[11] Most of the hard work was finished, and Davis, "a very decent man," pretty much managed the farming operations; so the brothers had leisure to sit on the breezy piazza reading Charles Dickens, Hannah More, and the *Weekly Tribune*. Sailing, swimming, and fishing were glorious. The Sachem's Head hotel was full of guests from Hartford, and Fred often took them out fishing and harpooning sharks. John, claiming he was looking for an heiress for Fred to marry, visited the hotel occasionally; almost every evening Fred put on his best coat and went over to lead the dance.[12]

Sundays, Fred and John went three miles to the Congregational Church in Guilford to hear Mr. E. Edwin Hall. A fierce Whig, Mr. Hall had but one Democrat in his church; and most of his congregation would rather die and be damned, he said stoutly, than be treated by a "heretic Loco" doctor. Such witless partisanship, whether in religion or politics, antagonized Fred, but he tried to like Mr. Hall. In time he succeeded, at least to the extent of taking him out for a morning's fishing and sitting through his sermons.[13]

Leisure was the only luxury on the farm. Business was bad that season at the store, and John Olmsted's frequent letters of advice to Fred were heavily laced with admonitions to be frugal; and he was insistent, too, on businesslike management. When Fred's accounts, which John Olmsted commanded him to keep balanced regularly, fell into disorder, his father inquired:

> Had I not better send you a treatise on Book keeping forms etc. You seem
> singularly deficient. . . . I am very glad John has got yr room to rights
> & hope he will keep it so, everybody agrees that you are much wanting

in that respect & some fear is expressed that your barns, out houses, tools etc etc may suffer in the same way. Pray reform.[*],[14]

John Olmsted inspected the Sachem's Head farm himself the middle of July. He brought with him Uncle Owen, his daughter Fanny, and all his own children including John, who, in spite of his eye ailment, had just successfully taken his final examinations at Yale, where, also, he had been initiated into Skull and Bones.[15] It must have been in the course of this stay at the hotel that John Olmsted met Samuel Bowne of New York. Bowne's wife was the daughter of Dr. Samuel Akerly and on Akerly's death had inherited the Staten Island farm that had attracted Fred's attention the previous summer. John Olmsted, dubious of Fred's prospect of success on the little Sachem's Head place, was interested in Bowne's account of the larger farm. Fred's interest in it was no more than moderate; he was satisfied that his barn was full of hay, that his crops promised well, and that his livestock were thriving.[16] Besides, congenial society, ever necessary to him, was within easy reach, at least until the beginning of September, when the Head House closed for the season.

Before it closed, Judge Greene C. Bronson, Chief Justice of the Supreme Court of the State of New York ("that clever old fellow . . . and the beau ideal of that character," Fred called him), and Dr. Horace Bushnell, whose heterodoxy was agitating the Congregational Church, stayed there, and Fred played ninepins with them. Geddes, visiting at the same time, was fascinated to hear that Bushnell bowled; they would "kill" a preacher for such frivolity in his part of the world, he said; and he wanted nothing so much as to go home and astound his neighbors with the boast that he had played ninepins with the controversial Yankee Doctor of Divinity and the distinguished judge. Fred willingly got up a game, pairing himself with Bushnell and Geddes with Bronson— Connecticut against New York.

New York was confident of victory; Connecticut's champions took off their coats and played to win. Connecticut won handily. Bushnell got the highest string, Fred the next, and poor Geddes, humiliatingly, the lowest. Bushnell,

---

*John Olmsted's letters were not always admonitory. One brought a touch of worldly excitement to the seaside farm. President James K. Polk and his suite passed through Hartford on their way to Springfield one hot day late in June, and John Olmsted and his wife watched the parade as it went down High Street from the porch of their neighbor, the popular poetess, Lydia Huntley Sigourney. To the consternation of the little gathering on the piazza, "the Pres[t] very unexpectedly to her stop[d] to pay his respects she shook hands with him he beg[d] a glass of water (for he was almost exhausted poor man). . . ." ". . . Mary hid behind a pillar & Mrs. S. look[d] as if she would like to. It was a beautiful compliment however to literature & poetry & handsomely done." An hour after the presidential parade had passed, Mrs. Sigourney discovered that, under cover of the excitement, thieves had entered and rifled her dressing room. She rushed across the street to John Olmsted, who hurried to the police, "& one of the Rogues was taken in a few minutes at the cars, the three others the next morning at S[pringfield] with all her missing jewelry" (JO to O, 29 June, 1847; JO to JHO, 2 July 1847).

pleased as a boy with the triumph, crowed so unmercifully over Geddes that the defeated farmer swore he would never again bowl against a D.D. "He has mistaken his profession," he protested to Fred, "he was cut out for a gambler."[17]

If Fred had any serious political talk with Bronson, he probably found it unsatisfactory: the judge was a states'-rights, proslavery Democrat. Conversation with Bushnell was a different matter. A poet and mystic, Bushnell rejected Congregational orthodoxy, which posited a dichotomy between natural, which was evil, and supernatural, which was good. To him, God was immanent in all His works and was the spiritual reality made manifest in man and nature. He contended that conversion, a supernatural intervention as his church understood it, was not necessary; a child born into a Christian household should grow up a Christian, be trained in the Christian faith, and at the proper time be received into the church without experiencing dramatic conversion.[18]

However appealing this idea was to Fred, he was not entirely pleased with Bushnell's exposition of it: "There seemed to be too much want of respect to his opponents." On another matter, he was more in sympathy with the minister: Bushnell was inclined to think that anyone who considered himself a follower of Christ should not be excluded from the sacraments because he was not a member of a particular denomination. "He was very glad indeed I had joined his church in communion although I had not profess'd to join it in faith," Fred reported. This exchange of ideas took place in the course of a wonderful two-hour sail, before a spanking breeze, from Falkner Island lighthouse to the Head. Bushnell declared he had rarely had so fine a time. "You would have imagined he was born for a sailor," Fred said admiringly.[19]

Bushnell's attitude confirmed Fred in his unorthodox religious course; but he wanted to do more than get his thinking straight. He wanted to give it a practical turn. Faith without works was a dangerous principle; Christ Himself had done more than pray and exhort men to prepare for the next world—he had given them bread and, very significantly, wine to make them merry, in this.[20]

Deeply patriotic, Fred knew he wanted to do something for his country and his countrymen, but what to do, how to do it, was the question. Religious principles were no sure guide: there were sincerely religious men among abolitionists, Quakers, and slaveholders, all in impassioned controversy about what course of political action was best for the country. The only thing at the moment clear to Fred was that sincere and intelligent men—including John C. Calhoun, apostle of slavery—should have a thoughtful hearing no matter how repugnant their doctrines: anyone *might* be right. "I wish I could keep out of politics altogether till I have a little more judgment," he concluded.[21]

John viewed his brother's grapplings with slippery problems of religion and politics with detached amusement. "Fred Olmsted still continues thinking big thoughts & growing daily more transcendental & perplexed," he wrote a friend. "His head is much fuller of Carlyle than it is of farming: perhaps still fuller of house plans—for he is going to build in the spring."[22]

He was going to build in the spring, he was increasing his herd, and he was

53

going to set an orchard. These do not sound like the plans of a man intending to sell his farm. At the beginning of October, he went to the Waterbury fair, where he met Joseph Welton and bought two fine heifers from him.[23] In the middle of the month he went to New York. If he visited the Staten Island farm, he did not say so in his letters to his brother and father, although he reported his side trip to Newburgh to buy apple and quince trees from Andrew Jackson Downing. Returning to New York, he called on Downing's friend, the popular architect Alexander Jackson Davis, who, sharing Downing's ideas on rural taste, was to become in 1852 one of the creators of the prototypical romantic suburb, Llewelyn Park, near Orange, New Jersey. Fred's business with him was to consult about house plans. Davis was not much pleased with those Fred had drawn —they wanted character—and made a rough draft himself. "His whole bill— drafts, specifications, etc. he says will be from $30 to $50.00," Fred reported.[24]

Fred's conduct of his trip was something short of satisfactory to his father: he had left his trunk to be forwarded with inadequate directions and his purse locked inside it; he had stayed away longer than he had intended; and he had managed to have a carriage accident on the way back. "He ought to have a *conservator* put over him if he ever attempts to journey again," John Olmsted testily remarked.[25]

With the Head House closed, the summer people gone, his brother and friends scattered, and not even a sail in the harbor, Fred suffered from loneliness. He tried to dissipate it by believing that he would be engaged by spring— although "I cannot think well of marrying any girl I am acquainted with now" —and by reading Georges Sand's *Devil's Pool*, "an interesting (and excellent moral) tale," the *Apochrypha*, *Tales from the Talmud*, an English translation of Schiller's *William Tell*, and his *Tribune* and *Cultivator*.[26] From the distance of Hartford, kind-hearted Aunt Maria fretted about him: "I am sorry he is not more comfortably situated. . . . I hope he will stay at home, this winter, at least long enough to look him up a wife . . . ,"[27] she wrote John.

Fred spent Thanksgiving with his family in Hartford, and it was probably at this time that consideration of the Akerly farm on Staten Island took a more serious turn. The middle of December Fred, accompanied by John, who was going to try a water-cure establishment in New York, went to the island to inspect the place. His father's distrust of his practical sense was implicit in the advice he gave him: to carry no baggage but comb, brushes, and two pairs of stockings; to take—and not lose—his rubbers; to find out if stock and tools and hay were included in the price of the farm; to inspect the foundations of all its buildings; to make sure there was good water on the land; and to determine, if possible, the real reason that Bowne was pressing the sale. "12,500 Dolls is a great deal of money to pay for a farm"; perhaps it would be put up at auction, and could be bought in for considerably less, he suggested.[28]

Fred returned to Hartford with a favorable report the day before Christmas. On December 28, with his father and Bertha, who was going to school in New

York, he went back to make the purchase. The deed was signed January 1. "Bot Fred the Ackerly [sic] farm 125 acres $13,000.00," John Olmsted entered in his daybook. It might be "a great deal of money," but he felt solvent enough to spend another $150 at Coleman's, the art dealer, for views of Belgium, Germany, and Afghanistan.[29]

V

FARMING ON STATEN ISLAND

March 1848–April 1850

T HIS farm," the *New York Tribune* advertisement had stated of Fred's new property,

> contains 125 acres, about 100 of which are in a high state of cultivation, and the rest woodland. It is beautifully situated on Raritan Bay, near the mouth of the Great Kills, with a wide front on the water, in which there is a great abundance of fish and clams. . . . The prospect from the house and the whole farm is one of unsurpassed beauty, taking in not only Raritan Bay, but the whole of the lower bay of New York, and the lighthouses on Sandy Hook, Neversink Highlands and Prince's Bay, together with the west end of Long Island, and every vessel which enters or departs the bay of New York can be seen from almost every part of this farm. The farm is well fenced, there are a large number of fruit trees on the premises, and two excellent gardens, with profusely bearing grape vines.
>
> The mansion house is new & large; the barns, of which there are two, are also new. The situation . . . is uncommonly healthy. . . .[1]

The beginning of March Fred, with Nep and Minna, fowls and furniture, and all his marketable produce, survived an agonizing move by sloop, through snow and sleet and storm, to his new domain.[2] One might have thought that, finally there, the young man who loved farming and views would be content to enjoy both for the rest of his life in such a spot. John Olmsted knew his restless son too well to hope so. "As you are at present situated," he admonished Fred a few months after his move, "I think your farm will require your *close & undivided personal* attention at all times & I hope no extraneous or unimportant matters . . . will take up your mind & time."[3] This reasonable expectation Fred succeeded in fulfilling for a while: during his first two years on Staten Island, he was away from home only about nine weeks in all; afterward he was hardly ever there.

There was, to begin with, "a *thundering* sight to be done," not only the spring planting, but repairs to the house and farm buildings and improvement of the unsightly grounds around the house.[4] The main part of the house, notwithstanding the allegation in the advertisement, was about a century and a half old. A Flemish-style farmhouse forty-eight feet long and twenty wide, part of it above unexcavated ground, it had originally been a story and a half high, with stone walls three feet thick and roof rafters projecting through them and extending over a porch that ran the length of the east side of the house.

House and farm had been in the Poillon family, early Staten Island settlers of French Huguenot origin, through three generations from 1696 until 1802. The last of the name to own it—according to a pleasing, and unauthenticated, legend—entertained George Washington there when he inspected the Staten Island fortifications.

After Poillon's death, house and property passed through several hands, and in 1837 came into those of Dr. Samuel Akerly. Akerly, retired as superintendent of the New York Institution for the Instruction of the Deaf and Dumb, built a full story onto the old house to accommodate himself and his wife, three of his children, and nine grandchildren. The additional story, built with wide clapboard, made the building disproportionately tall for its width. To offset its height, Akerly ran a narrow porch around three sides of the house. The kitchen ell, also clapboard, was probably added at the same time.[5]

The farm ran from the highway to the ocean, and the approach to the house from the road was by a drive, three quarters of a mile long, which led through a pretty grove of oak, maple, sassafras, and holly trees. The drive emerged into a clearing where the old stone house, covered over with plaster, stood on a gentle slope.[6] A rather artless sketch of the place, believed to have been done by Fred soon after he bought it, shows the surrounding grounds quite bare of ornamental planting and indicates a sweeping sea view to the south and east.

The grounds were worse than bald; they were shabby. The barns crowded unpleasantly upon the house, and behind it lay a little pond, some twenty feet across, with muddy, spongy banks, which was used for watering stock and washing wagons. "The whole place," Kingsbury recalled, "was as dirty and disorderly as the most bucolic person could desire."[7]

Fred transfigured his new home with a few simple improvements. He moved the barns and outhouses out of sight behind a knoll; he brought the drive in so that it approached the house by a graceful curve; he turfed the border of the pond, set water plants, and shielded the water from contamination; and by the time he had lived there three years, he had planted a variety of ornamental and forest trees—ginkgo, black walnut, mulberry, English and American elm, English beech, cedars of Lebanon, several varieties of linden, and a hedge of Osage orange, which was then becoming popular for barrier planting.[8]

Many of Fred's near neighbors were of the French Huguenot and Dutch stock of the island's original settlers, still living in the "old stone Dutchicofrancais cottages, *fixed up*," of their ancestors, and bearing the names Latourette, Poillon, Bodine, Winant, Van Pell, Garrettson, Seguin, Guyon, and Vanderbilt.[9] The nearest representative of the Vanderbilt family was William H., son of Cornelius, who lived as a farmer not far from New Dorp, his railroad career still ahead of him.

Fred's neighbors, genial and kindly, freely gave him information and advice, brought him his mail, sent over their newspapers, took him to church, entertained him in their homes, and called on him in his. His, pending the arrival of Aunt Maria, who was to come in April to keep house for him, was dismal. His furniture was not unpacked, his walls were bare, and he did his own cooking, subsisting, with Minna, largely on clam pies, for which he dug the clams himself on his beach. Nep, no fancier of sea food, ate lights.[10]

The family with whom Fred developed the closest friendship was that of Dr. Cyrus Perkins, who lived at nearby Holly Hill with his wife and orphan granddaughter, Mary Cleveland Bryant Perkins. The doctor was a fine-looking man of sixty-eight, bespectacled and bearded. He had been professor of anatomy and surgery at Dartmouth and had practiced in New York, traveled in Italy, and retired to run the Staten Island farm of his son, Frank, who was secretary of the Board of Pilots. The first time Fred dined with Dr. Perkins, one night in the middle of March, he was frankly impressed with his home; it had a large medical library, an original Salvator Rosa, and a portrait by James Frothingham of Daniel Webster, the doctor's close friend.[11] If Fred was impressed as well by Perkins's seventeen-year-old granddaughter, Mary, he neglected to say so.

Yet Mary was not a negligible girl. She was tiny, less than five feet tall, with a slight and trim figure, light blue eyes, an animated face, and a darting wit that sometimes amused even those it stung. Toward bores she was not charitable. She had precocious savoir-faire, which she insisted masked a consuming shyness. Born in Oswego, New York, on March 26, 1830, she was the daughter of Dr. Henry Perkins and his wife Sarah (Jones) Perkins.* Her father had died within a year of her birth; since her mother's death in 1837, she had lived with her paternal grandparents. As a child in their New York home, she had sat on the knee of the indulgent Webster, reciting Greek poetry to him. William Cullen Bryant, whose wife was her godmother and whose daughter Julia was her best friend, was amused by her cleverness and made a pet of her.[12] Growing up pampered by eminences, Mary never doubted her natural right to their regard.

This was the girl the susceptible Fred failed to mention when he first cataloged the attractions of Dr. Perkins's home. He, however, had made a strong impression on her a few days before her eighteenth birthday when, greatly

---

*Mary's mother, born in 1807, was a child of Horatio Jones, a farmer in Livingston County, New York. Son of a Chester County, Pennsylvania, gunsmith, Horatio enlisted during the Revolution in a body of minutemen called the Bedford Rangers, was captured in 1781 at the age of seventeen by Seneca Indians allied with the British, and was held by them for about four years. During his captivity, he mastered their language and customs, acquired influence among them as translator and counselor, and married Sarah Whitemore, also a captive. After his release and the death of his wife sometime before 1798, he married Elizabeth Starr. Until his death in 1836 he lived at "Sweetbiar," his farm near Geneseo. His granddaughter Mary remembered him as an old man with gold earrings, who rode bareback and was a fatherly counselor to all the Indians in the vicinity (George H. Harris, "The Life of Horatio Jones," *Publications of the Buffalo Historical Society* 6 [1903]: 383–526).

elated, he had rushed to Holly Hill to give Dr. Perkins the news, just received in New York, of Louis Philippe's abdication. Blazing with democratic sympathy and reckless of possible armed conflict in Europe, he had exclaimed, "I really revel in a *righteous* war."[13]

Aunt Maria, installed as housekeeper and aided by two Irish girls, soon made Fred's house comfortable.[14] Furniture was unpacked and arranged; some books were borrowed from John Olmsted, some bought; and pictures, also borrowed from John Olmsted, were hung. With his home in order and his crops planted—timothy, oats, corn and wheat (although "the Akerly books indicate the farm is very poor for grain"), and such garden truck as cabbages, turnips, tomatoes, potatoes, and lima beans[15]—Fred was ready to give some time to his nonfarming interests, especially to entertaining and arguing with his friends.

Trask and George Hill, both theological students, were among his first visitors, and Brace, who was living in New York, frequently came down for the weekend. That Brace was getting "settled," as he put it, in his faith, becoming convinced of the rightness of his own beliefs and the wrongness of those who disagreed, irritated Fred, who was getting more and more unsettled in his. Having tried to believe the Bible categorically, he was now hanged if he could. His own reason, however finite and imperfect, was the most reliable guide he could find toward belief. Increasingly tolerant of heterodoxy, he was increasingly impatient with the intolerance of his orthodox friends. He thought he knew not a single theological school graduate with "ordinary *charity* in his heart," and Brace was no exception.[16]

Their sharp disagreements did not alienate the two friends; rather, they increased their respect for each other. After one weekend, when a torrent of fierce argument had poured from six to midnight Saturday and all day Sunday, Brace admiringly told Kingsbury: "I must say Fred is getting to argue with the utmost keenness—a regular Dr. Taylor* mind in its analytic power! . . . I shouldn't be surprised if he turned out something remarkable among men yet." Fred considered Charley an "inestimable" influence for good on him. He thought, too, that Charley was inclined to overrate him. "—You may as well consider that you are—I am pretty good authority—as I do not think anybody else esteems me high enough."[17] He exempted Charley, but few others, from the complaint he was repeatedly to make: his opinions were given less weight than they deserved.

Soon after the middle of July the Hartford Olmsteds migrated to Staten Island to spend the rest of the summer in Fred's nine-bedroom house.[18] Driving, riding, and taking long walks about the island, which had charming inland views, the family indulged their taste for scenery; or rocking on the cool piazza, they watched sail coming up and dropping away on the busy ocean thoroughfare spread out before them. They saw a great deal of Dr. Perkins's family, and John, in his indolent way, was sufficiently attentive to Mary to incur a certain amount of teasing.[19]

*Dr. Nathaniel W. Taylor (1786–1858), Yale theologian.

Fred was getting his farm work systemized. Strict order was expected of the hired men: chores had to be done at set times, tools and implements returned to their appointed places at the close of work, and the foreman had to report on the day's progress and receive instructions for the next day before going in to supper. No gentleman farmer, Fred worked alongside his men, except when, having laid out tasks for them, he went driving or sailing or calling with his guests. Mary, recalling that happy season many years later, spoke of the simplicity, order, and thrift of Fred's operations.[20]

Fred sometimes took a very long view of thrift. In this he was upheld by Dr. Perkins, who had advised him the first evening Fred dined with him to avoid his own mistake: the gradual making of improvements. It was false economy, the old doctor had said; had he made his promptly, he would have saved money in the long run. Fred, he thought, had bought the farm cheaply, and the sooner he put it into top condition, the sooner he would begin to draw a profit from it.[21] Such advice recommended itself seductively to Fred; to John Olmsted, source of Fred's funds, it was less beguiling.

Disappointed at having been unable to sell his peaches in the glutted New York market, Fred was thinking of setting out a pear orchard. Dr. Perkins, who raised several fancy varieties of pears, assured him that the supply of choice ones never equaled the demand. "I think pears will probably occupy the land more profitably than anything else," he told his father, "though it will be some years before they begin to pay."[22]

John Olmsted's reaction to Fred's expensive scheme looking to distant profit was characteristically mild. "I have a letter from him today full of enthusiasm on tree planting & nurseries," he told John. "He goes it strong when he gets hold of a new project. . . . I trust his regular farming is not neglected in the meantime."[23]

The fact was that John, as usual, gave him so much anxiety that he hardly took time to worry about Fred. John continued to be ailing; he had developed a hollow-chested stoop that suggested to every eye "a consumptive tendency";[24] and studying medicine since early October with Dr. Willard Parker in New York, he persisted in his listless unsociability. His father implored him to board "in some social circle where you will form new acquaintance & get new ideas. As it is you will only associate with Charles, the same old story over again. A very proper & very good companion no doubt, but it is time you was forming new acquaintance, & enlarging your ideas. . . . You never," he concluded with a touch of exasperation, "will make a social & conversable being unless circumstances force you to it."[25]

Fred set out part of his pear orchard the end of October, under the eye of his father, who came down to the island to spend a week. Returning, John Olmsted took with him Mary Perkins, who was to spend Christmas in Hartford with her new friends. Young John, Fred, and Aunt Maria were home for Christmas and for the big New Year's party at the Olmsteds', after which young John and

Mary returned to New York. Fred, who had been home only once since moving to the island, stayed on. Again, he was a good deal with the ladies, so charmed with each that he could not tell which he was in love with. He rather inclined toward Emily Perkins, who "saw into things beautifully and showed that she valued friendship more than attention," he ingenuously told John.[26]

He returned to his farm in mid-January to sell his hay, potatoes, and turnips; back in Hartford on February 6, he resumed his sleighing, flirting, and reading of Macaulay and Ruskin with the Hartford enchantresses.[27] Too dazzled for decision, he was "dead in love, but with all his acquaintances. Now, if we could manage to carefully pull all but one out from under him," his brother suggested to Kingsbury, "he would have to cave in & get married at once." John was concentrating leisurely on Mary Perkins, with whom he was reading Dr. Bushnell's "Unconscious Influence."[28]

When Fred at last returned to the island on March 8, he was in such an emotional state that, John noted, "the consequence is his physical system is somewhat relaxed—his face pale & anxious & he is unable to sleep nights." Then in May he came down with measles.[29]

By the time he was well again, cholera had broken out, as it regularly did each hot season in New York and on the island. The epidemic persisted throughout the summer, not severely enough to keep the older Olmsted and his family from spending two months with Fred, but enough to make everyone worry about the disposal of the garden truck. "Ask your father," young John begged Kingsbury, "what Fred can do with 35,000 cabbages & 3 acres of turnips, if the cholera don't stop before fall. Can you make *sour kraut* that will keep over a year?"[30]

John, at the farm during July, was dyspeptic. Too listless to work or study, he hung about Mary and read *Modern Painters* aloud to her. He was struck by Ruskin's definition of the end of man, an end that could as well be achieved in a short life as a long one: "Man's use and function . . . is to be the witness of the glory of God, and to advance that glory by his reasonable obedience and resultant happiness." And he appeared to be smitten by Mary; his friends began to suspect that he was in love with her. When he visited Hartford and New Haven in August, he was amused to notice that everyone, with glaring tact, avoided mentioning her name to him "even when it was most naturally suggested in the conversation—except Miss Lizzie Baldwin & she only with her eyes—hang her—a great deal harder to bear than tongues any time. . . ." He professed neither to know nor care whether he was in love with Mary. "We are neighbors together on the jolliest terms & enjoy one another's society—*Fred's* included—with no sort of compunction of conscience or looking forward. That's all I know about it."[31]

Fred, as unwell as his brother, tried the water cure at Northampton late in August. When he returned to his farm, on September 11, the house was still full of visiting family, who left in time to make way for more guests—his cousin

Fanny, Charles Brace, and young Jim Geddes, who was going to stay till spring, to learn about farming from Fred, as Fred had learned from the elder Geddes. Jim's table manners were sloppy, he was "very self-conceited," and his efforts to make himself agreeable to Fanny and Mary Perkins were so fatuous that Fred and Aunt Maria were in a constant panic lest the girls laugh openly at him.[32] Fred professed, however, to see some excellent and rare qualities in him.[33]

In spite of the faintly discordant note introduced by Jim, the winter passed pleasantly. Fred made elaborate plans for his orchards; he had masons and carpenters at work to improve his cellar and to build stanchions in the stalls for his oxen and cows; and he wanted to erect a cottage, like that recommended by Downing in the *Horticulturist*, for about two hundred fifty dollars to house six Irishmen, so that he would not have to hire men living at a distance.[34]

He was convinced that the farm had to be intensively worked to pay; as it was, prices fell while he, short-handed, labored to get in his crops; he had no hands to spare to make labor-saving and money-saving improvements and so had to hire outside workmen. Defensively he explained to his father:

> I won't say I have done the best I could—for I do not think I have—but I think I ought to remind you that I have shown no want of economy or regard for the money making character of the farm. I spend nothing for luxuries—my board costs less now than any man's on the farm. I am clothed as cheaply and I work pretty constantly. Not an hour's work even of trowel or plane any more than plow or spade has been done for ornament or mere appearance this fall but every minute to contrivances to save labor or other items of cost or waste or in planting or harvesting.[35]

Mary Perkins, an established intimate, was frequently at the farm, especially when John, who had inertly chosen to board with the worthy Brace on West Washington Place, came down for weekends. Charley, busy that winter spreading the gospel on Blackwell's Island, occasionally came with him and fascinated his friends with accounts of his experiences in the prison and hospital there and in New York's slums. They read Emerson aloud to each other and got "many thoughts from him & by his aid from ourselves. Of course he is a humbug when you come to argue about him or almost any idea of his," John said deprecatingly, "but an immense amount of deep truth is scattered in his works too."[36]

Fred enjoyed discussions with sympathetic people, hearing about their work, ideas, and ideals, and reaching conclusions, however tentative, on the duties and purpose of life. Conventional social gatherings, on the other hand, tended to bore him. In New York on New Year's day with Charley, who wanted to call on "some stuck up people in Union Sq.," Fred foresaw vapid conversations and pointless exchanges of pleasantries and stiffly declined to go. "Acquaintances that had to grow with such manuvring were not worth cultivation and . . . friendships were nonsense that had to be fostered with ceremonies," he haughtily declared. Instead, he dropped in on the Jared Flaggs, watched Flagg at work on his painting, "Paul before Felix," and admired the handsome young girl from Maine who was modeling for him. Later, he stopped by the rooms of John Priestly, editor of the *American Whig Review,* and discussed the President's message with him. Finally, he went to see the Willard Parkers, whom Emily Perkins was visiting, had tea, and spent the evening. Very content with his New Year's observances, he reached home about ten to find Charley and John, both low-spirited, sitting up for him. John was suffering from blue pills, Charley from a squandered day. Charley could at least console himself, Fred cheerfully remarked, that he had experienced something of the world—"more inane talk, more dolls & parrots & more drunken gentlemen than ever he saw before."[37]

A man of some consideration in his community by this time, Fred was a trustee of the school board, served on the grand jury—and was scandalized sometimes to hear conflicting testimony given under oath—and helped form a small club among some of the more prominent farmers as a preliminary to organizing a county agricultural society. In this movement he was a dominant, perhaps a domineering, spirit. He drew up the constitution and maneuvered the election of officers. He was himself elected corresponding secretary and prepared an "Appeal to the Citizens of Staten Island by the Board of Managers of the Richmond County Agricultural Society," urging support for the new society.[38] He first represented the practical advantages it would bring to the island—the diffusion of scientific knowledge, introduction of modern agricultural methods, improvement in the breeds of horses and cattle, new and better varieties of fruits, vegetables, and flowers, and even an improvement in domestic architecture and rural taste. Then he shifted to higher ground and in effect made membership in the society a moral issue:

> It is not in its effect on mere physical comforts that this subject rests
> its claim upon your serious consideration. The benefits of our support to
> this society, we warmly trust, will not end here. With the Farmer must rise
> the Man. The mysteries of God are ever opening to his observation.
> Give us to read aright their unwritten word, and our hearts shall hear his
> voice. With increased knowledge of the operations of nature, with our
> eyes opened to a thousand wonders thitherto unseen, our sensibility to the
> Beautiful will be awakened. We shall mutually cultivate true taste, and
> its fruits will ripen not only to gladden our eyes by the adornment of our
> Island, but to nourish in our hearts all that is true and good.
> We ask you then, Fellow Citizens, one and all, to associate with this
> Society. We entreat you to support it. We believe it will increase the
> profit of our labor—enhance the value of our lands—throw a garment of
> beauty around our homes, and above all, and before all, materially promote
> Moral and Intellectual Improvement—instructing us in the language of
> Nature, from whose preaching, while we pursue our grateful labors, we

shall learn to receive her Fruits as the bounty and her beauty as the manifestation of her Creator.*,39

The Emersonian overtones of this statement reverberate so clearly that it is no surprise to find Fred, at about the same time, enthusiastically recommending *Nature: Addresses and Lectures* to his Hartford friends.[40]

Full as his life was, Fred desperately wanted a wife to make it complete. The most promising candidate in sight was Emily Perkins, and while she was visiting in New York, Fred hovered around her. One January day he went to call on her at nine in the morning. "I have not seen him since—perhaps they have eloped," John wrote Kingsbury, not very hopefully. "I am very sorry he is not married & that his prospects for it seem so dim."[41]

That many of his friends were marrying made Fred the more restive in his single state. In November Fanny had married Henry Coit in circumstances that amused her cousin John: "Fanny settled down at home the next day—Mr. Bunce was sick so Coit had to stay—he was in the bank till 6 oclock—then went up and got married & went back to the bank next morning. Real Yankee?" Trask was about to marry and go to Europe for two years. Rumors were afloat that Kingsbury was engaged. Tom Beecher, the admired young friend who was principal of the Hartford Grammar School, proposed to Livy Day "Friday night Dec 28th at 9 o'clock, was in an agony of doubt till Wednesday Jan 2nd & was then made happy."[42] Finally, John himself decided he really was in love, and his engagement to Mary Perkins became known late in February.[43]

Fred, who looked on his brother as his alter ego, and dearly loved Mary, was filled with happiness at the prospect of their marriage; John's more immediate plan, however—to take a walking trip through England with Brace—caused him simple anguish. In Hartford for a few days in February, he managed to conceal his feelings, but once back on the farm, he wrote his father with undisguised emotion: "John thought I did wrong not to let you know how it tries my whole *manliness* to have such a trip as this brought close to me. . . ."[44]

For at least seventeen years, he went on, ever since reading Silliman's *Journal of Travels in England, Holland and Scotland*, he had had a barely controllable passion to do just what John and Charley were planning. So strong had it grown in the past winter that only filial gratitude had restrained him from indulging it at whatever cost. Could he not be permitted to go with them?

Cannily, he marshaled his arguments. The experience he would gain from observing English and Scottish agricultural methods would be worth money in his pocket. His health, still feeble after his summer illnesses, would benefit from

---

*Among the immediate practical objects of the society were the purchase of a good bull and a Morgan stallion colt to improve the stock of the society's members and the encouragement of members in useful hobbies. Toward the latter end, one of its officers offered five dollars for the best hundred oysters; another, five dollars for the best bouquet of roses; "& Vanderbilt $5 for the best game cock!!"—a hobby, Fred obviously thought, hardly consistent with moral and intellectual improvement (O to JO, 26 January 1850).

the sea voyage and outdoor life. Shrewdly, he laid heavy emphasis on the help he would be to his frailer brother: "My experience and aptitude for *Roughing it*, his diffidence and Charley's awkwardness in obtaining information and services of men, would make my confidence and sympathy and experience with common and rough men of great assistance—to his comfort, his health, & his purse."

A little wistfully, he concluded his long and urgent letter: "I did not mean to argue the matter so much, but I hope you won't consider my opinions as if they were those of a mere child."[45]

John Olmsted answered in a less discouraging vein than his son had dared to hope. Without further ado, Fred decided to go. His brother was delighted. His only reservation he expressed to Kingsbury: "Won't it add to the preconceived notions people have of his *stability*."[46]

Preparations for the trip occupied much of the next few weeks. The young men planned to make two hundred dollars apiece last them through a tour of the British Isles and a short excursion to France and Germany. "The economy is of course mostly on Charley's acct," John explained. "I should hardly care to go in the 2nd cabin for my health. The passage is $12—bunks between decks, only separated fr the steerage by a bulk head. Jolly."[47]

With the help of Alfred Field, an Englishman living on Staten Island as American representative of his family's hardware business, they worked out a careful itinerary. Field provided Fred with letters of introduction to English farmers and manufacturers. Fred secured introductions to several Scottish farmers from an old acquaintance, John Pitkin Norton, professor of agricultural chemistry at Yale, and to Irish farmers from Thomas Antisell, the young Irish chemist and doctor who, since his exile for political activity two years before, had been practicing medicine in New York. Samuel Parsons, the nurseryman at Flushing, Long Island, from whom he had bought fruit trees, gave him letters to English and French nurserymen, from whom Fred intended to buy trees for import. His new friend and neighbor, Judge William Emerson, brother of Ralph Waldo, gave him introductions to "the lions of London," whom he could meet, also, through Henry Stevens, the young New England bibliophile who had been at Yale with John and who was then living in London.[48]

John Olmsted, having committed himself to supervising the farm in Fred's absence, concerned himself little with his sons' preparations. He was busy with plans of his own. On April first he left with his wife and daughter Mary for a journey by rail, stage, river, and canal to Cincinnati, St. Louis, Keokuk, Peoria, Chicago, Detroit, Buffalo, and Niagara. By May 20, when he finally reached Hartford and made the usual entry in his journal—this time it recorded fifty days, four hundred and thirty dollars, and about three thousand, seven hundred miles—his sons and Brace had already been three weeks at sea and were suffering a low-grade *mal de mer* about a hundred and fifty miles west of Cape Clear.[49]

VI

ENGLAND

April–October 1850

T HE ship on which the three friends took passage was the sailing packet *Henry Clay* of the Dramatic Line.[1] Having resisted the blandishments of several ships' agents, the young men were finally taken in by "the perfect impudence and utter simplicity in falsehood" of the line's agent, who sold them, exclusively for themselves, a large cabin that, on boarding ship, they found half full of baled cotton and ship's stores and in process of being further crowded with steerage passengers. Appeals to the captain, to the agents, and finally to the owners resulted in a compromise: they settled for one roommate, a young Irish surgeon who, on sight, promised well.

The *Henry Clay*, advertised to sail April 26, anchored off the Battery and stayed there for three days, without explanation or apparent reason. While she lay idle, other large ships put to sea. Her passengers fumed at the delay, and her crew took advantage of it to stage a near mutiny.

As the ship lay in the stream, with the captain ashore and the first mate in charge, most of the men refused to go on duty. Seeing that the officers, although armed with pistols, were not inclined to enforce their orders with them, Fred offered to talk to the crew. All that he could learn from the soberest of them was that she was an unlucky ship and, more credibly, that they had engaged to ship in her when they were too drunk to know what they were doing. The commonplace complaint called for a commonplace remedy. A fiddle to set them dancing, Fred told the mate, would get their minds off their grievance. No fiddle could be found, but supper, a substitute pacifier, was sent to them. They fell on it gladly and, having finished, spent the rest of the evening in horseplay. Fred, no friend to defiance of properly constituted authority, observed with interest that the steerage passengers were: before they had any notion of the grounds of the revolt, they sided almost to a man with the crew.

He was no friend to arrogant abuse of authority either. When the captain came aboard next morning and found most of the crew sulking below, he seized a hatchet and sprang into the forecastle, where he knocked down and kicked about a few men, broke open sea chests, confiscated half-a-dozen bottles of grog, and drove everyone out on deck.

"A handsome Napoleonic performance of the captain's," Fred remarked:

> the more need that I should say that in my mind he disgraced himself
> by it; because while we lay almost within hail of the properly constituted

66

officers of the law, and under the guns of a United States fortress, such dashing violence was unnecessary and lawless; only at sea had he the right, or could he be justified in using it.[2]

The *Henry Clay* was a large, handsome ship, with wide decks and plenty of room to move about. Her tall masts and narrow hull led John to expect "a steamer's passage of not more than 16 days"[3]—an expectation frustrated by the late start and adverse winds. She did not reach Liverpool until May 27, after a voyage so dull and uneventful that the young men positively enjoyed the three-day storm they ran into off Ireland. They diverted themselves by playing chess, reading aloud, and arguing about religion, and they enjoyed "a few staggering hops with the ladies on the quarter deck." The captain, who took the Olmsteds and Brace to be somewhat more gentlemanly than the rest of the second-class passengers—"say about two dollars apiece more," Fred estimated—invited them to use the first-class quarters. He also ordered the cook to serve their meals, so that instead of using their stores of cured meat and hard bread they were able to distribute them among the worst provided of the steerage passengers.[4]

On Sunday, May 26, the coast of Ireland loomed vaguely through the fog. The *Henry Clay*, running smoothly before a hard wind, entered St. George's Channel, and early next day when the fog opened, her passengers were thrilled to see land—"a great, sublime mountain, its base in the water, its head in the clouds," Holyhead. The channel was thick with big and little vessels, strangely rigged to Yankee eyes. By noon the *Liver*, of Liverpool, a black, efficient little steam tug, took hold of the big ship and towed her up the Mersey through the steamers, liners, East Indiamen, and smaller craft that crowded the river toward the heavy, low-lying black cloud that was all that could be distinguished of the great port.[5]

As the ship penetrated the smoke pall, her passengers could see, on the left, chimneys, steeples, and masts; and on the right, the spring countryside lying back of the beach, along which women and children, pleasure-bent, were driving pony carts and swimming from horse-drawn bathing wagons standing in three or four feet of water. Soon the ship reached the great enclosed docks of the city, and looking up, Fred could see floating in them, fifteen or twenty feet above the level of the river traffic, the ships that had entered them at high tide. The *Henry Clay*, unable to haul into her dock until the midnight tide, dropped anchor in the river at five in the evening. The accommodating tug took ashore those passengers impatient to go, among them the Olmsteds and Brace.[6]

The young men debarked at Liverpool the evening of May 27; by June 21 they were in London. They had passed through Birkenhead and Chester into Wales; through Shrewsbury and Ludlow and Leominster to Hereford; on to Monmouth and along the banks of the Wye to Tintern Abbey; across the Severn to Bristol, Bath, Warminster, Salisbury, Winchester, and Portsmouth; and across to the Isle of Wight, back to Portsmouth, and so up to London. They had covered more than three hundred miles, most of it on foot, in twenty-three days at the cost of seventy-one cents a day per man.[7]

Primarily a farmer—for the time being—Fred closely observed the agricultural practices in the regions through which he passed. Especially attentive to the drainage of arable land and its effects, he became convinced that thorough underdrainage was the technique by which to increase the productivity of cold, clayey soil. On the whole, however, he found that an American farmer—at least, one like himself, familiar with the best American agricultural writers—had little to learn from English farmers and orchardists, and of that little, much was not applicable under American conditions.[8]

He was more than a farmer, however; he was an ambitious young man conscientiously working to overcome the handicap of haphazard education, to round it out by observation and study, and to acquire knowledge, polish, and cultivation. He observed, therefore, with the eye not only of a farmer but of a student of society, alert, intelligent, critical, and enthusiastic. His first enthusiasm, spontaneous and lasting, was for the enchanting English countryside.

By background and tradition, he was an Englishman; love of England was a rooted, almost an instinctive, sentiment with him. After his first night in a rural inn near Chester, he rose at dawn and looked out of his latticed, woodbine-curtained window onto a cluster of thatched cottages, a flowering hawthorne hedge enclosing a field of grass and clover that sparkled with dew, some haystacks, a farther field spotted with sheep and trees, and beyond, low hills behind which the rising sun was rosily lighting quiet clouds in a gray sky. It was not a remarkable view; yet he experienced a flood of emotion. "Such a scene I had never looked upon before, and yet it was in all its parts as familiar to me as my native valley. Land of our poets! Home of our fathers! Dear old mother England! It would be strange if I were not affected at meeting thee at last face to face."[9] Almost at first sight of England a sense of familiarity, of having returned to his ancestral home, rushed over him, bathing him with comfort and happiness. It was a feeling that persisted throughout his trip and in modified form all his life.

It pleased him, too, to discover with what respect and appreciation Americans were almost universally regarded in England, notwithstanding the "atrocious caricatures" circulated by Mrs. Trollope and Dickens among a large public. In the course of his five months in the country, during which he met and talked freely with every class except the aristocratic, he found not a single man who thought America had been wrong in maintaining her independence and only a few who were hostile to her principles of government. American heroes—Washington, Jefferson, Franklin—were venerated; prominent contemporaries like Bushnell, whose picture Fred noticed in the study of a Congregational minister at Ludlow, were respected;[10] and English kindliness extended to the three obscure young foot travelers, who were habitually treated not as foreigners but as friends.

Yet Fred was not an uncritical Anglophile. His aesthetic sensibilities were charmed, his moral scandalized, by the luxurious trappings of aristocracy. Inspecting a splendidly maintained Welsh castle set in a beautiful park, he was enraptured by the elegance and taste of the life it typified. But his immediate second thought was: "Is it right and best that this should be for the few, the very few of us, when for many of the rest of us there must be but bare walls, tile floors, and every thing besides harshly screaming, scrabble for life?" And his third thought was:

> Whether, in this nineteenth century of the carpenter's son, and first of vulgar, whistling, snorting, rattling, roaring locomotives, new-world steamers, and submarine telegraphs; penny newspapers, free schools, and working-men's lyceums, this still, soft atmosphere of elegant age was exactly the most favorable for the production of thorough, sound, influential manhood, and especially for the growth of the right sort of legislators and lawgivers for the people.[11]

The poverty, the nearly brute circumstances, of some of the peasantry contrasted horribly with the ease of the well-to-do and shocked him deeply; not in France, in Germany, even in poor Ireland, or among American Indians or Negroes did he ever see "men whose tastes were such mere instincts or whose purpose of life and mode of life was so low, so like that of domestic animals altogether," as some of the farm laborers he met and talked with in the western counties. He was no less shocked—and he felt a sort of patriotic shame—that so few Englishmen "seemed to feel that any one but God, with His laws of population and trade, was at all accountable for it."[12]

Fred had no use, then or later, for the doctrine of laissez faire. The idea that depressed classes should be left undisturbed in their "degradation and supine misery"—whether because God or their own shortcomings had got them in such a fix—was repugnant to him. Paupers, lunatics, slaves, criminals, children—all had, he contended, the same natural rights and the same natural duties attached to those rights as the president of the United States, the queen of England, and responsible men and women generally. When they failed to perform their duties, for whatever reason, responsible people justly deprived them of their rights.

> But in taking upon ourselves to govern them . . . our first duty is that which is the first duty of every man for himself—improvement, restoration, regeneration. . . . We are bound to make it our highest duty and chiefest object to restore them, not the liberty first, but the capacity for liberty—for exercising the duties of liberty—which is their natural right. And so much of the liberty as they are able to use to their own as well as our advantage, we are bound constantly to allow them—nay, more than they show absolute evidence of their ability to use to advantage. . . . As faith is necessary to self-improvement, trust is necessary to education or restoration of another: as necessary with the slave, the savage, the maniac, the criminal, and the peasant. . . as with the child.

The principal undertakings of Fred's future life were guided by this conviction; and his belief was already explicitly stated that it was the duty of American slaveholders, not immediately to manumit their slaves as the abolitionists demanded, but to educate them for the eventual use and enjoyment of freedom.[13]

Fred saw much poverty and misery between Liverpool and London—the quiet prostitutes who met the ship when it docked; the city slum dwellers existing in "a dead mass of pure poverty" worse than anything that could be found around New York's Five Points;[14] the debased rural laborers; prisoners in a "model prison" in Hereford whose physical needs—for ventilation, cleanliness, food, and exercise—were scrupulously met and whose mental and moral needs were ignored as completely as if they had been cattle in a model barn.[15] But he saw as well public bath houses and wash houses, model lodging houses for the homeless, and "ragged schools" for poor children and learned of a functioning prison system that stressed rehabilitation rather than punishment[16]—all evidences that at least some responsible and powerful people shared his view of the duty of the fortunate toward the unfortunate.

The scenery of rural England was a constant delight, and his observation of it was acute and studious. On his trip to China his letters had contained not a word about the landscape; on this trip he referred to it frequently and specifically. He found the chief peculiarity of the English landscape in the long, graceful lines of deep green hedge rows crossing hill, valley, and plain in every direction; in the occasional large cottages and in the clean, careful cultivation and general tidiness of agriculture. He was struck by certain peculiarities, such as the sunken lanes near Hereford, "narrow, deep and shady, often not wider than the cart-track, and so deep that the grassy banks on each side were higher than our heads."[17] They were not, as he supposed, roadways washed deep by centuries of rain but ancient boundary ditches dating back to Anglo-Saxon times.[18]

Altogether, he found a fascination in what he called "the commonplace scenery" of midland rural England that he did not quite understand: it had no particular and striking features; yet in later years he was still able to say that, though he had visited many places celebrated for grandeur and had lived for months in Texas in perhaps the finest natural pastoral scenery in the world, he had nowhere else been "so charmed as I was continually while walking through those parts of England least distinguished and commonly least remarked upon by travelers as beautiful."[19] Yet he had already formulated a theory to which he adhered for the rest of his life:

> Beauty, grandeur, impressiveness in any way, from scenery, is not often
> to be found in a few prominent, distinguishable features, but in the manner
> and the unobserved materials with which these are connected and com-
> bined. Clouds, lights, states of the atmosphere, and circumstances that
> we cannot always detect, affect all landscapes, and especially landscapes
> in which the vicinity of a body of water is an element.[20]

70

Although he seems hardly yet to have realized it, two absorbing interests—the one in landscape, the other in means of elevating the character and condition of the poorer classes—were beginning to converge to produce in him a compelling enthusiasm for public parks in cities. The park at Birkenhead, across the river from Liverpool, was the first he had ever seen, and it broke on him like a revelation. There Joseph Paxton, former head gardener of the duke of Devonshire's magnificent estate, Chatsworth, and future designer of the revolutionary Crystal Palace, had in 1844 laid out one hundred twenty acres of flat, clay farmland as a rural park. He had dug a lake and, with the earth taken from it, varied the level surface with artful naturalness; he had created shady glens, open meadows dotted with trees, rock gardens, cricket and archery grounds, ornamental buildings, avenues of trees; and he had made the whole accessible by good hard roads and footpaths. Birkenhead citizens of every class flocked there to pass leisure hours in restful surroundings—invalids, nurses and mothers with children, whole families on holidays—freely enjoying their own park, paid for out of their own tax money "in the same way that the New Yorkers pay for 'the Tombs,' the Hospital, and the *cleaning* (as they say) of their streets." Nor was Fred indifferent to the financial acumen that had reserved sixty acres of the original farm on the periphery of the park for building lots. They had been graded and landscaped, streets had been laid, several fine houses with private entrances onto the park had already been built, and local land values had, accordingly, soared.

Certainly as a reader of Downing's *Horticulturist* and Bryant's *New York Evening Post*, Fred was already familiar with both editors' efforts to induce New York to appropriate land for a public park. The Birkenhead park must have stimulated his sympathy with the attempt; and the parks and promenades he saw in other English cities must have encouraged the conviction that such public pleasure grounds were a necessity to civilized urban living. America had nothing of the sort to offer: cemeteries and scraggly commons were the makeshift, and the only, places of public resort. "Not a town have I seen in England," Fred remarked at the end of his trip, "but has a better garden-republic than any town I know of in the United States."[21]

Fred was less impressed by the private parks he saw than by such public recreation grounds as the Birkenhead park, the Chester promenade, and the London parks. To be sure, it was Eaton Park near Chester, seat of the marquess of Westminster, that provoked his apostrophe to the creator of park scenery:

> What artist, so noble, has often been my thought, as he who, with far-reaching conception of beauty and designing power, sketches the outline, writes the colors, and directs the shadows of a picture so great that Nature shall be employed upon it for generations, before the work he has arranged for her shall realize his intentions.[22]

Yet he had little to say of Eaton Park itself; that little was not ecstatic; and he did not mention, if indeed he knew, that "Capability" Brown was, reputedly, the artist he was extolling in that instance. Nor did he mention Brown's supposed responsibility for Wynstay Park, estate of Sir Watkin Wyn, which he saw when he was in Wales.[23] The exclusive character of such parks, their reservation to the use of the owner and his friends only, and the debarring of the public who could have taken pleasure and benefit from them made them much less interesting to Fred socially, however interesting they may have been artistically, than public pleasure grounds. Beauty, for him as for his mentor Ruskin, could not be dissociated from social utility.

In London, the three young men took a furnished room with parlor privileges in the Strand near a church with "very queer chimes—starts off like Yankee Doodle & slides into Old Hundred." The chimes, which operated by clockwork, rang for ten minutes every three hours and sometimes stunned auditors with a Double Bob Major—"ringing all the tunes there are, one running into another without a moment's interval & keeping it up for two *hours* without stopping."[24]

The Olmsteds and Brace could have been little disturbed by the din: they left their lodgings early in the morning and returned only to change their clothes or to sleep. Meals they took at coffee houses, thriftily confining themselves to bread and meat, since vegetables were scarce and fruits expensive. The self-denial did not trouble them, but the un-iced water did—when they could prevail on a waiter to substitute it for the usual tea or ale. "And such stuff when you do get it," John exclaimed in disgust, "warm & soapy—or mouldy."[25]

With their assiduous interest in the poor, they visited ragged schools, model lodging houses, and bathing establishments; but London had other and, to John, more attractive features—"the best pictures, best buildings, even the best gardens and parks, and not only these things but the best *men*." Having found the poorer classes both ignorant and opinionated, he was glad to consort once again with more intelligent and educated men than those they had met, on an average, in the country. One of their first calls was on Abbott Lawrence, the Massachusetts manufacturer who was then American minister to Great Britain. They were a little taken aback to find the servants at his fine Hyde Park house in livery, but it was "a quiet & inoffensive one—all one color—so that your democracy is not much shocked"; and the minister himself was so kind and hearty that he immediately put them at ease.[26]

Bancroft Davis, the young secretary to the legation, and Henry Stevens, with whom he boarded, were pleasantly attentive to the American visitors. They entertained them at dinner in their rooms and obtained invitations for them to the Fourth-of-July dinner party given by "Mr. Peabody, a Baltimore merchant," as John naïvely called the prominent and popular George Peabody. Merchant, philanthropist, and financier, Peabody, since taking up permanent residence in London in 1837 and founding a successful banking house, had become a sort of unofficial American ambassador to Great Britain. His constant care was to use his great influence and wealth to strengthen Anglo-American friendship. His

Fourth-of-July dinners, a social device for doing so, were a highlight of the London season. They were said to cost twenty-five dollars a plate, and John, rather ungraciously, wished that their share might be applied instead to the ragged school they had just visited.[27]

This scruple notwithstanding, he enjoyed himself. The dinner was held at the Star and Garter in Richmond in a dining room that gave a wide view over the Thames valley. Mr. Lawrence, guest of honor, sat at Peabody's right; Neill Brown, former governor of Tennessee and newly appointed minister to Russia, at his left. Among the others present were Edward Hitchcock, president of Amherst; William Brown, member of Parliament and founder of the Liverpool branch of Brown Brothers; and Charles Astor Bristed, grandson of John Jacob Astor II and a rising young literary man. An "unknown lot" filled in between head and foot, where Davis and Stevens presided. The dinner was superb. The speeches, "mostly either bombast or nonsense," disappointed the critical young American, but they had at least the merit of expressing good feeling between the United States and England. The American minister spoke no better than the rest, with "some common sense, much absurdity, & curious grammar. . . . Father wd make a much better speech than Lawrence," said John witheringly.[28]

The young men also saw a private collection of early Turners;[29] they visited Kew Gardens with Asa Gray and his wife, who was a cousin of Brace's[30]—an occasion that was probably the beginning of Fred's cordial life-long connection with the Harvard botanist; Fred had several valuable talks with Kew's superintendent, Robert Thompson, who had been to Paris that spring and told him what to see there;[31] and one day the three Americans saw Queen Victoria passing in the street. To John's staunchly democratic eye she appeared "plain coarse & even vulgar—haughty in expression, not the least like her portraits, nor Queen like."[32]

Through the kindness of Lawrence, the Olmsteds and Brace received cards to the Speaker's Gallery of the House of Commons[33] and had the considerable thrill of hearing on June 28 the most important debate held in four years, subjecting to complete review the foreign policy of Lord John Russell's ministry.[34] Having tried unsuccessfully to intervene in the affairs of Spain and Germany, Lord John had been subjected to growing criticism at home and had answered it with the panicky charge that his critics, among them Sir Robert Peel, were conspiring against his ministry with foreign powers. For eight hours, too fascinated to move from their seats, the young Americans hung upon the speakers—Cockburn, Gladstone, Walpole, Monckton Milnes, Cobden, Sir Robert Peel ("a fine, tall and venerable man"), Lord John himself, and finally, Disraeli, who finished speaking at three in the morning.[35] By the time the vote was taken and the government sustained by a majority "just sufficient to enable Ministers to retain office without disgrace,"[36] the thrill was probably attenuated by fatigue and hunger, but it was rendered retroactively more solemn by the fact that they had witnessed Peel's last parliamentary appearance. "Whilst every cabinet and crowned head in Europe was listening to him, he was called from the stage of history to appear before the King of Kings."[37] In other words, he was next day thrown from his horse and fatally injured.

The grandiloquent expression is Fred's. It occurs in the account of the debate he sent Brace's father, then editor of the *Hartford Courant*. His Americanism sticks out all over it. The traditional black dress and white wigs of the three clerks seated in front of the speaker impaired rather than enhanced their dignity, he thought, but he liked the looks of the members of Commons very well. "There was no more aristocratic *air* about them than in our own Representatives. It seemed to me that those qualities which make a man most valued among his equals, such as generosity, frankness, tact, and good fellowship, had been found of more importance at the hustings than all the influences of wealth and family importance." He thought he detected in all the speakers, both Whig and Conservative, "a recognition of the most liberal ideas and principles of government," and carried away by this discovery, he was led to a rash speculation on the throne: "Possibly when the present notable housewife leaves it, its empty honors may be resigned peaceably and happily to inevitable fate."[38]

John, with brotherly disdain for Fred's literary effort, doubted that Mr. Brace would care to publish "all his lucubrations";[39] Mr. Brace, on the contrary, gave them two columns on the editorial page of the July 25 issue of the *Courant*.

The travelers planned to leave London on July 9 for Paris, where Fred intended to see nurseries, John hospitals, and Charley people.[40] Of their month on the continent, during which they saw, as well, parts of Holland, Belgium, and Germany, little record remains. They spent most of their time in Germany, where they approved the custom, common among the middle classes, of taking meals in garden or summerhouse.[41] Early in August they were back in London for a few days and on the tenth resumed their English tour. Their first stop was Windsor, but nothing connected with royalty could truly appeal to the taste trained in democracy. Fred could report only "some fine trees, and a great overgrown castle—palace—which looked anything but comfortable & homely."[42]

Olmsted Hall, the ancestral manor of the Olmsted family, was a different matter. Fred searched it out next day, in the northernmost part of the parish of Bumsted-Helion and not far from the village of Saffron-Walden in Essex. Approaching by narrow parish roads and farm lanes, he came upon a low stone farmhouse in the midst of level wheat land. It was surrounded by a moat, dry and filled in front to allow the lane to come up to the house, and shaded by a yew tree several hundred years old. The tenant, whose family had for generations leased it from its current owner, Queens' College, Cambridge, on hearing Fred's name, received him with respect and some excitement and showed him around the house. It was in no way imposing: its main feature, the "old hall," was a low-ceilinged room about twenty feet by twenty, with a single window taking up most of one wall and an immense fireplace, bricked up for a coal grate, occupying another. Although the unpretentious manor had passed out of the Olmsted family two centuries before the Puritan migration, it appealed romantically to Fred's ancestral piety. "I don't know whether this diminutive *Hall* will much gratify your family pride," he wrote his father.

> I rather think it does mine, quite as much as to have found the arms of some big murdering baron over a dunjon door. At all events as I imagined the simple country life that had probably been enjoyed there, the narrow moat that sufficed to defend the home of the peaceful family and the kind lord of the secluded manor, the little hall and the great hospitable fireplace, I enjoyed in a considerable degree the pleasure of a sympathetic relationship and the good influence of a worthy ancestry.[43]

The rest of the tour is ill documented. Fred returned to London and walked with John and Charley to Reading, whence they went by rail to Oxford. The university town, in the middle of the long vacation, was dusty and disappointing, and they pressed on to Stratford-on-Avon.[44] Passing through Sheffield, John obtained from the secretary of the People's College there a copy of the first annual report of the institution, which had been established "to improve the condition of the labouring classes" by offering them courses in reading, writing, arithmetic, elocution, French and Latin, bookkeeping, geography, and singing.[45] Folded away in the same envelope as the report is a momento of a "ragged dormitory" they visited in Westminster, a form "to be *correctly Filled* up by *Every Candidate* for Admission." The censorious tone of the questions put to the applicants—samples: "How long have you been a thief or a beggar?" and "How long have you been tired of the miserable life you are leading?"—can have offered small inducement to unfortunates to take advantage of the benevolent facility.

After Sheffield, the pedestrians went to Bradford, and by early September they were in Ireland, where they stopped at Banbridge, Dundalk, and Belfast. John was shocked by the conspicuous poverty and the cheerful slovenliness of the poor and disarmed by their jolly and hospitable amiability. He was also sick of traveling and of monotonous food.[46] A letter of introduction to Robert Neill, of Belfast, a strong antislavery man, probably resulted in at least one good dinner in Ireland. Brace, anyway, got something more than a meal out of it: a wife. After ardent correspondence, he married Neill's daughter Letitia on August 21, 1854.[47]

At Edinburgh the Olmsteds parted from Brace, who was sailing for Hamburg to travel alone through Germany and Austria. They themselves sailed for home from Glasgow Sunday October 6 on the *City of Glasgow*, a low, sharp, three-masted steamer with a single screw that could drive her through smooth water at the rate of ten miles an hour.[48] They did not, however, have much smooth water. Sunday night a fierce storm broke, and on Monday, when the wind became so furious that it tore the jib away, Captain Matthews, veteran of ninety-six Atlantic crossings and former master of the *Great Western*, for the first time in his nautical life put his ship about and ran for port. She lay over for twenty-four hours in Belfast Bay to wait out the storm; and her hundred and sixty passengers, grateful to have been spared its worst rigors, offered the captain a signed testimonial approving his action.[49]

As it was, they endured enough bad weather. After six fair days, the ship began to buck gales and headwinds that made fellow passengers, who might otherwise have seemed first-rate traveling companions to the brothers, "nauseous." The numerous Scotch and Irish Presbyterians on board sought to minimize their discomfort by frequent recourse to religious exercises and hot toddies. Fred and John evaded illness by keeping as much as possible on deck: their second-class cabin, which they shared with six others, afforded just enough air to "support a small kitten in uninterrupted life & health for ten minutes." They might have taken some pleasure in the company of their old acquaintance, the Reverend Mr. Hall of Guilford, who, transfigured by a new set of whiskers and a new Swiss wife, was one of the dozen ministers on board, but he also was "nauseous," too seasick for any social use.[50]

The *City of Glasgow* reached New York on October 23;[51] by then that phenomenon familiar to travelers was already well advanced: particulars of the trip had become confused in their minds. They held "a regular chaos of men, monuments, bad eggs & grateful sleeps—weary legs & tough steaks—lots of remembrances of chambermaids & waiters, lots of milestones & lots of names down in a small book . . .—the faces belonging to the names getting dimmer & dimmer every day."[52] It was to require reference to his letters and journal, and work on his book, *Walks and Talks of an American Farmer in England*, to restore some order and clarity to Fred's recollections.

VII
FARMER INTO WRITER
November 1850–November 1852

HOME was almost hateful to Fred on his return. He had lived for five months so intensely, so joyously, that now he felt burnt out. Nothing stimulated, everything depressed, his exhausted spirits. He resented the hard farm routine and the demands it made on his time and his thoughts. How could he attend to constant and pressing chores and at the same time attend to making himself the man he wanted to be? "The best *farmer* may not be the *best* farmer," as John put it. Fred was inclined to think he was already too good a *farmer*.[1]

He felt that the trip had greatly improved him—given him more independence, faith in himself, "dignity of MIND"—but again he voiced his chronic complaint:

> I am disappointed in the increased power I have over others as yet. The mere fact of having been to Europe is worth nothing—to me in looking at another it always was an expectation of an increased value to the man—rightly so. But I have now this impression that here people do not *respect* anyone sincerely. . . . They, in the closet, think nothing of you except as you have something to buy or sell.[2]

Scenting materialism everywhere, he was less surprised than disgusted by the temperance of northern reaction to the passage of the Fugitive Slave Act. Scornfully he wrote Brace that "the free principle of the North can not stand the danger of losing Southern trade." All the saints were dead—almost all of them, anyway: Dr. Henry Ward Beecher and Dr. Richard Storrs,* alone of all the ministers Fred knew, had come out strongly against the law.[3]

Listening to Beecher, Fred felt his misanthropy lift slightly, and he and John made several trips to Brooklyn during the winter to hear him preach.[4] Other circumstances gradually mitigated Fred's spiritual jaundice. His old friend Henry Barnes paid him a visit, which he enjoyed, although it enhanced his contempt for the run of the clergy to hear the petty ways in which a young minister was hedged about by his conventional elders: Henry, preaching in Princeton,

---

*Storrs, a Congregationalist, was minister of the Church of the Pilgrims in Brooklyn and a founder and editor of the *Independent*.

had been sharply rebuked for quoting Byron from the pulpit.[5] The visit from Kingsbury and his fiancée, Althea Scoville, Fred enjoyed less. He found the girl "nothing but an old fashioned sub half man. . . . Good enough for a wife or a servant—no equal friend. Is it impossible, must equality make rivalry, must unity depend on submission?" he asked Brace.[6]

The agricultural society Fred had helped start held a successful fair in November at which some of his produce made a fine showing. In December, he learned with the satisfaction of a vindicated prophet that a plank road was to be undertaken from Southside to Northside on the island, at just the sum per mile that he had estimated in an article he had written for the *Staten Islander* the previous spring. Through winter and spring, both brothers corresponded argumentatively with Brace, who, having become a passionate abolitionist, was pouring torrents of wrath upon "that damnable thing going on at home . . . that black injustice and wrong crying for vengeance . . . this outrageous inhuman law" and upon Fred and John for being less vehement about it than he.[7]

Brace was paying the expenses of his protracted European tour by sending travel letters to New York and Philadelphia papers, correspondence most of which John arranged for him. Encouraged by his mentors safe on Staten Island, he entered Hungary to report on its revolution and its hero Kossuth.[8] The Austrian authorities, rightly suspecting that he sympathized with Hungary's aspirations to independence, threw him into prison in Gros Wardheim. Word, but no particulars, of his plight filtered out to alarm the friends who had helped get him into it. John emotionally wrote him to be firm and true and a martyr if necessary; and Fred lost some sleep wondering whether he might hang.[9] Fred did not, however, regard his imprisonment as particularly outrageous: Brace had known Hungary was under martial law and had gone there against the express wishes of the Austrian authorities. After his release at the end of a month, Fred could even declare, with sang-froid, that he and John were "not much pleased with his cry for justice—it seems boyish."[10]

The fever to write had meanwhile attacked Fred. Even more than a supplementary income, he wanted the influence he did not command and thought he deserved. Having collected the letters he had written home from England, he was beginning by the end of 1850 to put a book together from them. He was encouraged by the interest of his Stapleton neighbor George Palmer Putnam, considered the most honest and liberal of the New York publishers.[11] More encouragement came from Downing, who accepted the sections on Birkenhead Park and on English apple orchards and "A Note on the True Soldat Laboreur Pear" for the *Horticulturist*, where they eventually appeared, respectively, in May 1851 and in January and December 1852.

By late March 1851 the trees Fred had ordered abroad had come. Their cost on arrival was one thousand thirty dollars, and he promptly sold five hundred dollars worth at a profit of seventy-five percent. Perhaps he offered some to Downing; in any case he made him a visit in midsummer, but he reported nothing of the occasion except that he liked Downing and Newburgh.*,[12] Between his new literary interest and his new nursery business, Fred's farming must have suffered some neglect; and he was further distracted by the growing seriousness of his affair with Emily Perkins. Fred and Emily, John wickedly remarked, had been "at work at one another for near three years, off & on, with a vigorous & noble correspondence (wh. I can't refrain from hoping may one day be given to the world for its benefit!)." Fred was not quite sure he was in love with her but pronounced her "certainly the noblest and most sensible woman I ever saw. I never imagined such a union of Faith and Courage—Religion & Freedom." By August, John thought Fred was at last, notwithstanding his somewhat impersonal and exalted view of Emily, in a fair way to marry her.[13]

John's plans for marriage were suddenly jeopardized by a shattering reverse: early in August he had a lung hemorrhage, and the long-held suspicion that he had tuberculosis was confirmed. He was working during the summer at the Seamen's Retreat, a hospital for sailors at Stapleton, and he had seen too much of tuberculosis among the patients there to be optimistic about his own case. A horde of problems immediately beset him. Should he marry? Should he abandon his proposed European medical study? Should he give up medicine entirely? Where should he live to prolong his threatened life? These "and a thousand other things tumultuously crowd in your mind when you once get sentence of death," he told Kingsbury. "Yet we all have it upon us—& how absurd it is to get worried when the particular mode of death is indicated." Dr. Parker's expressed hope, however, that with good care John might live to old age encouraged him and Mary to go ahead with their plans to marry.[14]

Fred's meanwhile quietly accelerated. In August he and Emily at last became engaged, but no announcement was immediately made nor date set. Perhaps the practical farmer was deficient in ardor—he had to attend to selling his cabbages before he could attend to marrying;[15] more likely it was Emily who was. She soon announced the engagement, then stunned Fred by having her mother write begging him to release her. He hurried to Hartford to enlist the help of her aunt Mrs. Stowe and to plead his case, but it was no good; Emily had recently met a handsome young minister, Edward Everett Hale, and she had no further thought of Fred.[16] Thus the high-minded liaison finally collapsed, leaving Fred reeling in its wreckage.

But was he properly heartbroken? He presented so good a face to the world that even his closely devoted father was puzzled. "Pray tell me," John Olmsted wrote an intimate, "what it is makes Fred so happy since his *disappointment*, as it is call'd? He seems like a man who has thrown off a tremendous weight. Can it be that he brot it about purposely?"[17] It is a curious question and unanswerable.

John was married on schedule. Having passed his medical examinations the

*It was probably on this visit that he met for the first time Downing's young architectural associate, Calvert Vaux.

week before, he married Mary on October 16, and they sailed the twenty-second on the *Asia* for Liverpool,[18] whence they intended to go by easy stages to Rome. Fred, with his expectation of marriage shattered and his dearest friend an ocean-breadth away, had further cause for dejection: a severe northeast storm late in November wrecked his boat and washed out a big section of his bank; and a few days later a sudden cold snap froze half his cabbages in the ground so that his return from the crop was some six hundred dollars less than he had expected. ". . . Poor Fred," Aunt Maria wrote his father, "he meets with so many losses I wonder he is not discouraged, I am."[19]

Still, life was not consistently gloomy. Fred's nursery business was developing satisfactorily; his health was unusually good, and he was putting on weight; and Kossuth's arrival at Staten Island to begin his tour of the United States provided grand excitement. The cause of Hungarian freedom had aroused generous and enthusiastic sympathy in America, and the island, elated to be the port by which he should enter the land of the free, seethed with preparations for his arrival. When the steamship *Humboldt*, bearing him and his entourage—and, incidentally, Lola Montez, who was quite eclipsed by the greater blaze of his popularity—reached quarantine at one in the morning of Friday, December 5, a military guard and a large crowd, which included Fred, were on hand to greet him and escort him to his island headquarters, the home of the health officer Dr. A. Sidney Doane. There he was officially made welcome in a grandiloquent speech by Major Hagedorn, commander of the guard, and, replying to it, made his first address to an American audience.[20]

Standing in the crowd beneath the balcony from which Kossuth spoke, Fred saw a man "younger and less *distingué*" than his portraits suggested, whose broad forehead, fine eyes, and animated expression reminded him of Daniel Webster. He was wearing a black coat with small jet buttons to the collar, a black velvet cloak trimmed with lamb's wool, and the low steeple-crowned hat with broad band, buckle, and small black plume that was soon to become the fashion in New York. Speaking at first slowly and with long pauses, he gradually gained confidence and finally spoke freely and quickly with frequent small grammatical errors.[21]

Although fatigued from seasickness and two or three sleepless nights, Kossuth was given little rest by his island hosts. He spent the morning receiving the committees—press, national groups, patriotic societies—that swarmed to thrust invitations and resolutions upon him and at noon was guest of honor at a great parade and reception. The cortege, a half-mile long and composed of the military in marching order and citizens in whatever order they could assume, formed at the gate of the quarantine grounds. Marching to the music of Dodsworth's Cornet Band, imported for the occasion from Manhattan, it moved through Tompkinsville and out Richmond Road to a large field where a tent capable of holding three thousand people had been erected to house the reception. The procession, the *Tribune* conceded, "was a very imposing affair, considering it took place on Staten Island."[22]

Fred, although pitying the hero for having to endure on the island what he would immediately have to endure again on a grander scale in New York, as a member of the committee on reception took part in the ceremonies. Following directly behind the four-horse carriage in which Kossuth rode, he carried the Hungarian flag. As the parade was forming, Kossuth turned and took his hand. "I had some conversation with him—about the harbor and fortifications," he wrote his father. "Mentioned Charley, he didn't seem to know anything about it."[23]

Probably Fred's most satisfying activity during this dispiriting time was his foray into the literary world. Still burning with anger at the vicious treatment of sailors, he wrote a long article called "A Voice from the Sea"—a clear echo of Dana's "voice from the forecastle"—which appeared in the *American Whig Review* for December 1851.[24]

In it he ascribed the almost universal barbarity of captains toward their crews to the fact that captains usually rose from the forecastle and, having been trained to submit to the customary brutality, were trained as well to regard it as the routine, and only, way to maintain discipline.

> It is the direct, irresistible, unconquerable effect of CUSTOM, to which in that educating forecastle, they were obliged to surrender all manly trust in the reward of honest purpose; all hopes of avoiding cruelty by simple performance of duty, all hopes of kindness, or even justice, from those having power to those who make themselves subject to it. There and then was formed that habit of mind that makes it impossible for them to expect a sailor will obey from any but a sordid or despicable motive, or that he can respond with any confidence to a kind, just, and reasonable authority. . . . So, and only so, can it be explained that our brave, generous, courteous, and affectionate packet captains should be indifferent, reckless savages to their crews. . . .

Sailors, of course, were not, as a rule, persecuted saints; often they were suspicious, dishonest, and hard-hearted, and the captain was quite right in supposing that they would not respond to humane command. "Trained like brutes, they must yet be driven like brutes. The old wrong has produced the evil, and the evil excuses the present wrong; and thus here, as often elsewhere, both are perpetuated."

Fred suggested some minor changes in the laws regulating the equipment of ships and protecting the rights of sailors; but to break through the vicious circle effectively he proposed the establishment of mercantile naval training schools, on land and free from the brutalizing influence of the forecastle, for educating a body of seafaring young men in the arts of seamanship and in habits of order and discipline. Boys so prepared would be far more valuable than the usual green hands, and unusual regard for their care and comfort could be exacted from masters. Schooled themselves under a humane and reasonable discipline, these young men would know its effectiveness and, as officers, would enforce the same kind themselves. Slowly an entirely new spirit would be infused into the merchant marine, and savagery would at length become archaic. Such schools should be organized by shipowners, shipfitters, and merchants, with state assistance, Fred thought. He cared little for any particular plan but much that the public should awake from its apathy.

The article is of some interest, but not because Fred was unique in trying to stir the public conscience; Dana and Melville both had stronger voices, raised to the same purpose. It is interesting because it relates incidents of his China voyage that do not appear elsewhere but particularly because it indicates, although incidentally, his already firm belief in the beneficent value of healthy recreation, including the sort that could be provided by public parks. In suggesting how the sailor's lot might be improved while he was ashore, Fred wrote:

> With the improvement of our cities; with the formation of free public parks
> and gardens, and rational and healthy places of exercise and amusement;
> with the cleansing of such sinks as the Points and the Hook in New York,
> and Ann street in Boston; with the establishment of liberal, honest,
> pleasant and suitable habitations for them, like the Sailors' Home; with
> reputable employment and a comfortable living for honest labor, plainly
> opened and assured to the poor, ignorant, homeless, abandoned, and, by
> all but sailors, scorned and unfriended girls of our streets, the grasp of vice
> and recklessness may be slackened on them while they are on shore.

These are the words of a man who not only cared for parks as scenery but saw them in the context of a social plan.

Consistently trying to harness literature to social ends, Fred wanted to make his book on England, which he was fast completing, "attractive to Farmers and men of small means and ordinary information, and work in with it some suggestions and ideas of good taste and an improving tendency that more directly put, would not take their attention."[25] His aim was abetted by the form in which Putnam intended to publish the book: he was just launching one of the earliest American experiments in the publication of good books at a very low price. He had conceived of a semimonthly series of paperbound books, of travel, biography, history, poetry, and social philosophy, to sell for twenty-five cents each or five dollars for a year's subscription. Worth reading and keeping, they were to be small in size to fit into a traveler's coat pocket, and well printed on good paper to be bound later for his library if he wished. Popularity was the prerequisite of profit: only a very large sale could make the undertaking pay.[26]

The opening book of the series, which was published at the beginning of 1852, was *Home and Social Philosophy*, a selection of essays from Dickens's popular magazine, *Household Words*; the second was *Whimsicalities*, by Thomas Hood; the third was the first volume of Olmsted's *Walks and Talks of an American Farmer in England*, due for publication on February 14, "the cheapest original book ever published," the happy author told his father. Then another selection of essays from *Household Words* and another from Hood's writings were scheduled. Fred's book was to have a dozen woodcuts by Orr, the popular engraver, most of them from Fred's own sketches "worked up artistically by Marryat Field," since Fred was but an indifferent artist. He had no expectation of making any money on the book, unless it was well enough received to induce Putnam to bring out an edition in hard covers at a higher price. Little concerned about profit, Fred was content to think that it would "do much to improve taste."[27]

Volume one of *Walks and Talks*, dedicated to Geddes, appeared on February 18, 1852. Its style was often boyish and awkward; characterization, with some animated exceptions, was perfunctory; and it was admittedly pieced together from letters and a journal. Nevertheless, it was very cordially reviewed in the *Horticulturist*, the *American Whig Review*, the *Philadelphia Bulletin*, and a few other publications; Fred, however, was a little disappointed that the reviewers did not "recognize me as writing for a particular audience as much as I would like."[28]

To the modern reader, its interest lies not in the account of English farming practices that recommended it to its contemporary critics but in the acute social observations that adumbrated the mature Olmsted. Some of the great problems that were to be his deepest concern in his socially creative years—the elimination of slavery, the creation of a humane urban environment, the definition and enforcement of the duty of government to the governed and of the privileged to the poorly endowed—already engaged his earnest thought. The effect of his thought was to be gradual and cumulative; *Walks and Talks* made no great impact.

If neither much influence nor much money flowed from it, it served at least to secure Fred's foothold in a new society, which acquaintance with Putnam had opened to him, that of literary men and women. During 1851 he had begun to frequent Putnam's Stapleton home. There one evening, in an amateur production of *The Rivals* made memorable less by the acting than by the fact that the house was discovered to be on fire as the curtain fell, he had appropriately played the role of Bob Acres while Parke Godwin, Bryant's son-in-law and associate on the *Evening Post*, had played Sir Lucius O'Trigger. In 1852, after Putnam moved from the island to Manhattan, Fred continued to visit him at his East Sixteenth Street home where, on Tuesday evenings, the publisher held informal receptions, which were attended by some of the foremost literary and intellectual people in the East. There the aspiring writer could meet the editors Bryant and Godwin and George Ripley; Bayard Taylor and George William Curtis, both authors of popular travel books; Asa Gray and Benjamin Silliman; Downing; Anne Charlotte Lynch, whose poems Fred thought as bad as Mrs. Sigourney's and whose *salons* were a feature of New York intellectual society; Katherine Prescott Wormeley, translator of Balzac, Molière, and other French writers, with whom Fred in a few years was to be thrown into platonic intimacy; the aging lion of American letters, Washington Irving; and even the mysterious Eleazar Williams, who moved in the aura of the delightful suspicion that he was, in fact, the Dauphin.[29] Fred's articles* and book were small productions compared to those of most of the other guests, but by the time his second volume appeared in October 1852,† he was already entertaining the scheme of a more important work that would earn him wider recognition. He was planning to go South and send back to the one-year-old *New York Daily Times* a series of articles on southern agriculture and economy as affected by slavery. Earlier in the year his friend Mrs. Stowe had tapped gushers of emotion in her readers with her novel *Uncle Tom's Cabin*. Fred proposed to offer his readers unsentimental data on the economic aspect of slavery—"matter of fact after the deluge of spoony fancy pictures now at its height shall be spent."[30]

The idea of the series originated with Henry Jarvis Raymond, cofounder and editor of the *Times*. Seeking a suitable correspondent to undertake the tour, he consulted Brace, who recommended Olmsted.[31] Editor and farmer had never met; they knew each other only by reputation. Nevertheless they consummated their business in five minutes at their first meeting. Raymond did not question Olmsted on his views of slavery, and Olmsted did not haggle over terms of payment. Olmsted came away from the interview with a single injunction—that he was to confine his reports to matters that fell under his personal observation—and with the assurance that he was not to be constrained by the paper's editorial position on slavery.[32]

Unexpected though the assignment was, Olmsted was not without some useful, if negative, preparation for it: sharp arguments with abolitionists like Brace and Theodore Parker and William Lloyd Garrison, whom Brace had brought to the farm, had convinced him that in the North there was little reliable information on slavery as a system of labor, too little in fact, for constructive discussion of the question. He therefore had no opinion on its economic merit and, without preconceptions, was without temptation to arrange his findings in the form of special pleading.

On its morality, however, he had a firm opinion, which he had stated at least once in print[33] and repeatedly in his letters. He believed it was utterly, but not uniquely, evil. The bondage in which priests and churches held men's spirits was as bad;[34] and the lot of American merchant seamen, English rural laborers,

---

*In addition to the articles already mentioned, Fred, as "An Outsider," published in the *New York Daily Tribune* of 29 July 1852 a long article on "The Phalanstery and Phalansterians" at Red Bank, New Jersey, where he had recently visited.

†The book was at the printer's in July and should have been issued in August, but since Putnam had others advertised in advance of it, it had to wait its turn. While it was waiting, Downing was killed in one of those "melancholy accidents" so frequent in the period: the Hudson River steamer *Henry Clay*, on which he was a passenger, engaged in a race with the *Armenia* and blew up on July 28. Downing, a strong swimmer, was drowned, apparently while trying to rescue someone else. Only thirty-seven, yet immensely influential, he was widely lamented by a large circle of friends among the intelligentsia. Fred dedicated the second volume of *Walks and Talks* to him.

Irish tenant farmers, and slum dwellers North, South, and abroad was as cruel and helpless and degraded as that of slaves. He considered the South not wicked, slaveholders not necessarily bad; slavery was the entailed misfortune of the section, and a slave's master could be as good a Christian as a Yankee. Olmsted's attitude toward abolitionists had grown increasingly unsympathetic: at eighteen he had poked fun at them; at thirty he believed they were uncharitable, provocative, and impractical.[35] A long educational process would be required to fit slaves, unaccustomed either to think or to act for themselves, for freedom; immediate freedom would cast them without preparation on their own resources that had been stultified in slavery and would create for them worse problems than it solved.[36]

These were not the attitudes of an observer hostile to the South; and Olmsted's inclination to be both sympathetic and fair was reinforced by determination to be so. Neither was to save him from much abuse.

VIII

TRAVELS IN THE SOUTH

December 1852–April 1854

FRED started south on December 11. He went first to Washington, then to Richmond and Petersburg, whence he proceeded to Norfolk, Raleigh, and Fayetteville. Reaching the coast at Wilmington, he made a detour inland and came to it again at Charleston. From there his journey took him to Savannah and westward across Georgia through Macon and Columbus to Montgomery, Alabama, and south to Mobile and New Orleans. After a short excursion up the Red River, he returned to the Mississippi and ascended it to Vicksburg and Memphis. Following the eastern face of the Appalachians through upper Mississippi, Alabama, and Georgia, he finally made his way home through Virginia, arriving on April 6, 1853.[1]

During the four months he was on the road, he traveled by rail, stage, and boat, and wherever he stayed any length of time, he took horseback excursions in the region. In the neighborhood of Richmond and Petersburg he lingered for two weeks, at Norfolk for one; he spent a few days at Raleigh, a few in and near Charleston, a few at Columbus, a week at Montgomery, and some days in and about New Orleans. Although he covered some of the principal cities of the South, he had little to say of them; it was agriculture, the leading occupation of the section, and especially cotton culture, that was his main interest.

His method of reporting was the same that he had used in *Walks and Talks*: he presented a profusion of concrete, specific details from which the reader could draw conclusions, and he offered his own. A tireless observer, he described the dress and manner of people he talked to; the construction and furnishings and upkeep of houses and hotels where he stopped; the management of plantations, from marginal to model; methods of agriculture, backward and modern; the roads, railways, and boats by which he traveled; and the appearance of the country through which he passed. From slaves, barroom acquaintances, traveling companions, overseers, poor farmers, rich planters, housewives of all classes, he gleaned information on a multitude of subjects: the price and productivity of land, methods of cultivation, population changes in a given locality over a period of years, the character of the nonslaveholding whites, the discipline and punishment of slaves, their abilities, the cost of their labor, the amount of work they did per day, their food and housing, their religion and morals, their amusements, and their relationship to their own families and to their owners. When he could, without giving offense or arousing hostility, he even asked his interlocutors their opinion of slavery. Throughout, he sought to determine the typical fact and condition, while recognizing the exceptional.

His considered conclusion about slavery as a labor system was consistent with his first impression. Visiting, at the outset of his tour, a fine Maryland farm known widely for its excellent management and its owner's hospitality, he cordially sympathized with the harassed proprietor, who had to direct such exasperatingly slow and incompetent workmen.[2] By the time he reached Richmond, where he visited a farm owned by a Quaker who employed free labor, he thought he was going to be able to demonstrate that slave labor was costlier than free. Finally, at the end of his tour, he was convinced that it was not only a maddening nuisance to its managers but that it was more expensive than free and an economic handicap to southern agricultural and industrial progress sufficient in itself to account for the discrepancy between the prosperity of South and North.[3]

In estimating cost, there had to be considered the original purchase price of a slave or the expense of rearing him; the expense of his maintenance in good health and bad; the loss from tying up capital in him that could have been otherwise employed; and especially the loss from waste. The waste arose from the fact that slaves worked, except in unusual cases, slowly and carelessly, as mindlessly as mules. They took two to four times the length of time for a given task as an Irish or German hired man; they broke and neglected implements; they abused and maimed animals; they could not be trusted with complicated tools or on operations requiring skill or judgment; they scamped critical work if any lapse of supervision permitted; they malingered; sometimes they ran away, or deliberately hurt themselves, thus obliterating at a stroke not only their owner's anticipated profit but a part of his capital as well.[4]

It did not follow that slave labor was necessarily unprofitable. Olmsted visited and described a number of plantations, some very large, some of moderate size, which operated at a profit at least when the price of their principal product —cotton, rice, or sugar—was high. He concluded, however, that profitable ones would have shown a larger profit, and others that teetered from year to year between profit and loss would consistently have made a better showing, had free labor been employed.

Olmsted's business was to investigate the economic implications of slavery, but an inquiry into *why* it should be expensive and wasteful necessarily led into its moral aspects. Up to the time he went south, he had been reticent about the characteristics and natural capacities of Negroes. Frequent observation there of their poor workmanship and unreliability might have tempted another man to conclude that they were, indeed, inferior beings; but it was offset by significant exceptions that led Olmsted to conclude that these shortcomings were not innate. They were due to the fact that Negroes were not an inferior race, but an enslaved race. Deprived of liberty, they were deprived also of incentive. Whether they worked well or ill, fast or slowly, whatever profit their work produced accrued to their owners; whether they worked well or ill, fast or slowly, their minimum physical wants were supplied by their owners. Neither the expectation of gain nor the fear of want operated on them—only fear of punishment and the hope of avoiding it. In the occasional instances when some of the reward of their labor was granted slaves in the form of money or indulgences, Olmsted noticed that they worked with a will and cheerfully. A few he saw, intelligent and fortunate in their masters, had developed skills that compared favorably with those of free white workmen and held positions of privilege and trust. The great mass, however, systematically poisoned by ignorance and by the witholding of responsibility, had as little care for their work as the farm animals.[5]

The fault therefore lay not in the Negro but in his slave status. To treat a man as a slave was to reduce him to "the body of a man, moved only by outward force; a mind, acted on only by fear; a soul, without responsibility."[6] It was to deprive him of the attributes that distinguish a man from a beast. To Olmsted, this was axiomatically immoral. He rejected the justification that it was an inferior race, deservedly so treated, and with it the argument, bolstered by citing the shiftlessness of many free Negroes, that Negroes could not take care of themselves when free and were not fit for freedom. It was as wrong to deprive a human being of the responsibility of managing his own life as it would be to blindfold him and lead him through it. And,

> As the eye would suffer and be rendered nearly unfit to perform its natural functions by such usurpation, so I believe the mind and soul suffer in Slavery. And as the tyrant who was guilty of such cruelty would not be justified by showing that the man when freed from his tyranny was but poorly able to make his way over a mountain, so I think the conditions of negroes at the North is no justification of permanent Slavery at the South.[7]

The only justification he could accept was the possibility that, in slavery, slaves were being educated for freedom, prepared to fulfill their capacities as men rather than as working cattle.

Was there any scheme of management of the slaves in the South to encourage the belief that such an educative process was going on or was contemplated? Olmsted could find none.[8]

The physical treatment of slaves, to be sure, was better than he would have thought possible, especially considering what provoking workmen they were. Almost universally, they were adequately provided with food, clothing, and shelter. Although they were frequently and harshly disciplined, even though one was occasionally killed by savage punishment, still they were not killed one-tenth as often as sailors were by the cruelty and carelessness of their masters. Nor, he thought, were they often more cruelly and wantonly punished than he had seen a New England schoolmaster punish boys entrusted to him for education. On the whole, he found, whites treated slaves with remarkable indulgence, although it was indulgence, such as one might show to a dog or a child, that sprang from a sense of complete superiority.[9]

Nothing, however, was done to stimulate those abilities or satisfy those wants that distinguished them from brutes. Maintained in enforced ignorance, they were deliberately stunted mentally and morally. They were not encouraged to learn anything, to think, to read, to provide for the future. They were not led to regard as binding their family relationships, which could be and often were disrupted at the convenience of their masters. Their religious instruction, emphasizing the duty of submissiveness, left them in a state of almost primitive superstition. While house servants might be favorably influenced by association with a cultivated family, the field hands, whose only contact with the white race was through overseers, generally a class of rascals, were remote from civilizing influences.[10]

Not only was slavery doing nothing to elevate the Negro race, Olmsted believed, but it was demoralizing the white. A man could not have absolute power over others without its impairing his sense of justice. Moreover, where the laborer was held in contempt, labor necessarily was also. Five-sevenths of the southern whites were not slaveholders; as a class they were unambitious and indolent, willing to work only enough to produce their own necessities. Even conscientious and energetic workmen lost heart where work was habitually ill done and the standard of workmanship was low.[11] The bad roads, the shabbiness and discomfort of the houses, the monotonous and poorly prepared food, the wretched means of transportation, the ill-cultivated and meager crops, the dearth of schools, churches, lyceums, community enterprises and interests—the overall frontier character of much of the long-settled region through which he passed—amply testified that the dominant race was indifferent, "superior," to the thoughtful, painstaking labor that produced those far-reaching and hard-won results that could be summed up as civilization.[12]

Scrupulously, Olmsted noted exceptions unfavorable to his thesis, but reasoning from the preponderance of his findings, he reached the categorical conclusion that slavery was an economic liability, a moral wrong, and a disastrous handicap to both black and white.[13]

He did not arrive lightly at it. His assignment was a hard one to execute thoughtfully and fairly. It took him much more time to study and to write than he had expected, much more than to observe, and southerners' reticence toward a northerner was an impediment. From Louisiana he wrote Brace: "You can't imagine how hard it is to get hold of a conversable man—and when you find [one] he will talk about anything else but Slavery. . . . They are jealous of observation of things that would tell against slavery."[14]

Although he was entertained cordially in a few southern homes, on the whole he saw little of southern society or domestic life. Most of the hospitality he met with was from northerners and Englishmen settled in the South.

Obstacles notwithstanding, Olmsted had eight letters in print by the time he reached home in April and material for more than forty more. Raymond displayed them prominently and launched the series, which began on February 6, 1853, with a flattering editorial introduction of their pseudonymous author "Yeoman." Stressing "Yeoman's" freedom from preconceived ideas about slave economy, Raymond stated that his letters were intended "to contribute somewhat to that general and reliable public knowledge of the actual condition and character of the Southern States, upon which public sentiment concerning them ought to rest."[15]

The southern press, however, accepted at face value neither this declaration of motive nor Olmsted's conciliatory statement that he hoped to show the North that it was only in the justice, good sense, and Christian feeling of the people of the South that the evils of slavery were to be ended. Shortly after the series began, the *Savannah Republican* declared editorially that, since neither a northerner nor a southerner could be unprejudiced about slavery, neither was qualified to discuss it. The *Times* replied that the *Republican* apparently wished to preclude any discussion of slavery whatever, and that the great evil was not that it had been discussed but that it had not been factually and reasonably discussed.[16]

Other southern papers took hostile note of the letters, but not all southern reaction was unfriendly. The *New Orleans Delta*, defending Olmsted from the charge of dishonesty and unfairness, called him "prejudiced, but manly and honest"; and "A Native Southerner," upholding slavery on economic and moral grounds in the *Times*, expressed pleasure in "Yeoman's" "candor and intelligence."[17]

Although disappointed in the condition of the southern people, both citizens and slaves, and resentful of the southern press's insinuations of venality, Olmsted nevertheless tried conscientiously to be just in his reports. Further, genuine appreciation of the difficulties that faced the South in connection with slavery led him into such expressions of sympathy that, Raymond said, the abolition press accused him of conducting a whitewash. He urged the North to realize that slavery was a matter beyond its control, to correct the injustices of its own labor system, and to abandon denunciation—in which case, he thought, "hosts" of talented and selfless men would arise, in Virginia, at least, to attack the problem; and he had found enough antislavery sentiment in other parts of the South to make it seem not improbable that Virginians' efforts would be abetted in other states. Contrasting the physical well-being of free and slave laborers, he reminded his readers that no slave ever killed her child in cool calculation of saving money, like English free women, or froze to death for lack of shelter and fuel, like free men in Boston. He offered without comment a résumé of one standard southern defense of slavery: that the Negro race was an inferior one expressly designed by Providence for servitude.[18]

Even his last letter, which concluded that slavery was economically ruinous and morally indefensible, was placating in tone. Wrong as slavery was, Olmsted said, slaveholding itself was not necessarily evil: the term "property" conveys the idea of stewardship over things that God has placed, under the state, in our hands. "I am willing, for the present, to look upon the relation of the master and the negro as that of stewardship, and am willing that the law should allow the master a reasonable use of the labor of the negro, as the wages of his steward-ship."

As to the duty of the North in regard to slavery, it was to discuss it and to work for its ultimate disappearance—but not by direct action, which would in his opinion justify the South in leaving the Union. Olmsted's fundamental con-servatism was implicit in the policy he recommended to the North: to make

> the best possible use of free labor, by demonstrating that the condition of the laborer is *not* necessarily a servile one; that the occupation of the laborer does *not* necessarily prevent a high intellectual and moral develop-ment. . . .
>
> Yet mainly, the North must demolish the bulwarks of this stronghold of evil by demonstrating that the negro is endowed with the natural capacities to make a good use of the blessing of freedom; by letting the negro have a fair chance to prove his own case, to prove himself a man entitled to the inalienable rights of man. Let all who do not think Slavery right, or who do not desire to assist in perpetuating it, whether right or wrong, demand first of their own minds, and then of their neighbors, FAIR PLAY FOR THE NEGRO.[19]

Thus, Olmsted ended his first series of letters with a ringing admonition, not to the South but to the North.

Olmsted's series, having begun in February 1853, ended the following Feb-ruary. For the rest of the year after his return in April, therefore, he had not only to run his farm but to work up his notes to supply the *Times* with two letters a week. A farmer's life increasingly palled on him, and a writer's increasingly attracted him. He attended to his planting, fretted over his fruit trees, spoke hopefully of clearing perhaps a thousand dollars on the farm that year; but his letters were full of his literary affairs. He was in splendid writing trim. Raymond wanted him to name his price for editorials on agricultural subjects. His series was being read with great interest in the South. The London *Spectator* had run a long complimentary review of *Walks and Talks*; but J. A. Dix, a clerk at Put-nam's, told him the second volume had not paid the cost of publication. Miss Lynch, who knew "all the distinguished people," had visited him at the farm. Although he managed to produce for *Putnam's Magazine* a moral anecdote, "Gold under Gilt," about a rich man and his wife who selflessly nursed their servants through a contagious illness, Fred lamented that he had no time to do the editorials Raymond wanted. "If only I had health it seems as if I might make a decent living writing," he said wistfully.[20]

Never one to resist the lure of travel, Fred took a junket in June with Alfred Field and his wife to Syracuse, Utica, and Trenton Falls. He was back in New York by the twenty-first to meet the *Humboldt*, carrying John and Mary and their son, John Charles, who had been born September 14, 1852, in Geneva.[21]

It was not long before the reunited brothers had laid out an ambitious itinerary that was to take them, by way of Texas, across the continent to California.

The purpose of the long journey was threefold: Fred was going to send letters to the *Times* "further to promote the mutual acquaintance of the North and South"; both brothers hoped that a winter spent on horseback in the open air would help their chronic dyspepsia;[22] and they had some thought of finding a place to settle in a mild climate where John's tuberculosis, which had responded disappointingly to Switzerland and Italy, might be overcome. A free labor community was of course the first desideratum, and California, admitted as a free state under the compromises of 1850, therefore recommended itself. Their decision to get there by way of Texas seems to have been motivated by the wish to see slave labor's effect on the development of a frontier, as compared with its effect in the longer-settled parts of the South.

On November 10, 1853, the Olmsted brothers started west. They went to Baltimore and then took the Baltimore and Ohio Railroad as far as Wheeling. Embarking there on the *David L. White*, they steamed down the Ohio River to thriving Cincinnati, where the only quiet thing they found amid the city's tumultuous bustle was "the residence of Mr. Longworth—a delicious bit of rural verdure, lying not far from the heart of the town, like a tender locket heaving on a blacksmith's breast." From Cincinnati they set out by stage for Lexington and, having ferried the Ohio to Covington, rolled over a fine macadam road through the wooded parklike country of northern Kentucky and pronounced it "landscape gardening on the largest scale." Lexington itself, quiet, neat, and pleasant, made an impression of "irresistible dullness"; and they sensed there, as elsewhere in the South, in the tone of the men they met—"these fine fellows, these otherwise true gentlemen"—"a devilish, undisguised and recognized contempt for all humbler classes." It sprang, they believed, from "their relations with slaves, 'poor whites,' and tradespeople," and was simply incurable.[23] This automatic arrogance of southern men and the other characteristics that distinguished them from northerners gave Fred the subject for one of the most interesting letters of his first series.

A main point that emerged in his lengthy reflections was that the southern gentleman, gallant, brave, forthright, and otherwise admirable as he was in many ways, was governed by a sense of honor dictated by a conventional and external standard rather than by an "enlightened conscience." The "habitual contemplation of a relation so essentially wrong as that of slavery, as a permanent and necessary one, not in progress of removal or abolition, destroys or prevents the development of his sense of any standard of right and wrong above a mere code of laws or conventional rules." The "moral law," to which the most sensitive Yankee conscience sought to atune itself, meant nothing to the southern gentleman.

Yet his good qualities—the dignity of character, the generosity of impulse, the manly courtesy that distinguished him in society, in his family, even in his business—were sadly rare in the North, much rarer than in the South. Southerners and aristocratic foreigners blamed the democracy of northern society for its inadequacy in this respect. Olmsted contended that more democracy, not less, would rectify it.

Almost incidentally, he tossed off the most striking observation in this long letter: the bold, strange theory "that the simple protection to capital and letting-alone to native genius is not the whole duty of Government. . . . That the aesthetic faculties need to be educated—drawn out; that taste and refinement need to be encouraged as well as the useful arts. . . ." Government should encourage and sustain,

> at points so frequent and convenient that they would exert an elevating influence upon all the people, public parks and gardens, galleries of art and instruction in art, music, athletic sports and healthful recreations, and other means of cultivating taste and lessening the excessive materialism of purpose in which we are, as a people so cursedly absorbed, that even the natural capacity for domestic happiness and . . . for the enjoyment of simple and sensible social life in our community, seems likely to be entirely destroyed. The enemies of Democracy could bring no charge more severe against it, than that such is its tendency, and that it has no means of counteracting it.

Olmsted's last word on the southern gentleman was that he was unfortunately outnumbered two to one by a class of men, well dressed, free spending, drinking, chewing, gambling, who were absorbed in such exciting schemes as filibusters and projects of disunion and war.

> They are invariably politicians, and they generally rule in all political conventions and caucuses. . . . If they were not dependent on the price of cotton for the means of their idleness, they would keep the country incessantly at war. Being so, however, they are as conservative in the policy they favor towards any powerful nation as the cotton lords of England or the land lords of Austria. They hate and despise the Democrats of Europe as much as *Francis Joseph* himself. They glorify *Napoleon,* and they boast of the contempt with which they were able to treat the humbug *Kossuth.* They call themselves Democrats, and sometimes Democratic Whigs. Call them what you will, they are a mischievous class—the dangerous class at present of the United States. They are not the legitimate offspring of Democracy, thanks to God, but of slavery under a Democracy.[24]

In Nashville, the brothers pursued the subject of southern and northern characteristics and social institutions with Samuel Perkins Allison, a young lawyer and classmate of John's, who entertained them. Fred, having already conceded that there were more gentlemen South than North, had to concede the "lack of elevation" of the northern farming and laboring classes. He refused, however, to draw his host's conclusion that slavery, which deliberately and permanently degraded the workman and allowed the development of a small class of uniquely superior quality, was justified over democracy, which negligently permitted the workman's degradation and produced fewer of the superior class. Between the representatives of the aristocratic and the democratic viewpoints, the differences were irreconcilable: they had no common idea of what constituted a good society. They could not even greatly respect each other's opinions. Fred thought the view of slavery held by Allison and his friends was dictated by their own material interests, that considerations of sectional and individual, not national and common, good counted with them. For their part, they could not conceive of a disinterested view and did not believe his was.[25]

This collision of opinion provoked Fred to urge Brace, who was organizing his life work, the Children's Aid Society: "Go ahead with the Children's Aid and get up parks, gardens, music, dancing schools, reunions which will be so attractive as to force into contact the good and bad, the gentlemanly and the rowdy. And the state ought to assist these sort of things as it does *Schools* and Agricultural Societies. . . ." The young man who saw literature as a social force added, "We ought to have that Commentator as our organ of a higher democracy and a higher religion than the popular . . ." to cure the polarity of democratic society, to elevate the lowest class to approximate the best. "A cross between Westminster Review and the Tribune is my idea. Weekly, I think, to give it variety and scope enough for this great country and this cursed little people. Keep it before you!"[26] It was under the influence of these ideas that he wrote the final letter of his first series, urging on the North the duty of elevating its own working classes.

By the time the last letter of the first series appeared, the brothers had finished the long river trip from Nashville to New Orleans, gone up the Red River to Natchitoches, Louisiana, and on horseback, penetrated into Texas as far as San Antonio, where they intended to await the formation of a larger group for the comparatively perilous trip to California. By then, too, the uneasy balance between North and South sought by the compromises of 1850 had been wrecked by the introduction in the Senate of the Kansas–Nebraska bill. The storm of anger let loose in the North by this assault on the Missouri Compromise provoked, Fred reported to the *Times*, only a tepid response among the planters he and his brother met on the way to San Antonio: although in principle gratified by the proposal, they felt it would be of doubtful value to them because the territory, if slavery was to be established in it, would then come into competition with their own. Their reaction gave him another occasion to observe that, in the South, attitudes on slavery questions were determined by local and personal interests quite untainted by any consideration of the national or the common good.[27]

This manner of thinking was no surprise to the brothers, nor was the manner of living that went with it: the unglazed or broken-paned windows, the doors without latches, the log houses with chinks through which one could thrust a hand, the eternal fried pork and cornbread and bad coffee, the shared soiled beds, the common drinking cup and towel, the crude furniture, the coarse manners, the carelessness and discomfort to be expected where work was done by slaves, and the lack of even those simple conveniences and ornaments that might have been expected in a land settled a few years. The surprise, stunning and delightful, came when they encountered, between Austin and San Antonio, the German settlements, seedlings of European civilization flourishing on the barbarous American frontier. Prior to entering Texas, they had known nothing of them.[28]

The migration had begun in the 1820s, and during the next two decades many Germans had settled between the Brazos and Colorado rivers, coming in increasing numbers as more stringent political repression and worse living conditions developed at home. While an educated minority of the colonists, who founded the so-called Latin settlements along the Texas frontier, were politically motivated, the large majority wanted only to get to a place where they could make a living in peace. During the 1830s and after, some of the emigration had been organized by societies, among which was the Mainzer Adelsverein. Founded in 1842 and supported by several German princes, its objects were to reduce pauperism at home by affording protection and help to emigrants and to concentrate emigrants in one place apparently with the idea, encouraged by certain English politicians, of placing a German dependency across the path of American expansion. In 1844 the association had sent over a group of one hundred fifty families, led by Prince Carl of Solms-Braunfels, a close friend of Queen Victoria's consort. Finding on arrival that the "paradise" they had bought, sight unseen, from land speculators in Germany was in fact a desolate wilderness hundreds of miles beyond the farthest settlement, the swindled colonists stopped when they reached the confluence of the Comal and the Guadalupe and laid out the town of Neu Braunfels.

The association mismanaged its second venture not ludicrously like the first but tragically: the following year it dumped, without supplies, shelter, or money, more than five thousand emigrants at Indian Point, in the midst of a country stripped of provisions and transportation by the United States Army in preparation for the war with Mexico. Survivors of the winter's ghastly suffering eventually straggled inland, some of them reaching the German villages, some settling as laborers in American towns, a few pushing beyond Neu Braunfels to found the town of Fredericksburg. Details of the horrible fiasco, reaching Germany, ruined the association and all but halted emigration to Texas. The events of 1848, however, gave it fresh impetus. The post-1848 colonists in Texas, exiles rather than voluntary emigrants, were for the most part educated and intellectual and more radical politically than their predecessors. Some of them became Latin farmers at Sisterdale, while others entered teaching, journalism, and the law in and around San Antonio.[29]

The Texas Germans, especially the forty-eighters, were suspect in the eyes of their American neighbors, who saw evidences of depravity in their beer and wine drinking, their Sunday picnics, their anticlericalism, and above all in their aversion to slavery. The Olmsteds, as they neared Neu Braunfels, heard various hostile reports of them.[30]

At the hotel in Neu Braunfels, the first German hotel where they passed a night, they felt they had been transported, magically and instantaneously, to one of those charming little inns that had delighted them on their walking trip through the Rhine Valley. The prompt and cheerful landlady; the fresh white table cloth; the variety of well-prepared meats and vegetables; the white bread, fresh milk, and sweet butter; the genial and cultivated Germans smoking their pipes by the stove; the plain clean bedroom with glazed and curtained windows and, luxuriously, a bed for each of them; a German encyclopedia and the thick clean towels laid out on the dresser—all these were unlike anything they had previously met in Texas. So, too, were the evidences of civilized living throughout the community. The houses, though low and plain, had verandas and gardens, and most of them were either painted or stuccoed. The town supported dozens of mechanics—carpenters, wagon-makers, smiths, bakers, tailors—and the outlying farms, small and carefully cultivated by free labor, produced not only cotton but a variety of crops rarely attempted by the Americans nearby.[31]

Intrigued by his first impressions of the Texas Germans, Fred communicated them to the *Times*, which then editorially informed its readers that there was an element in western Texas, the Germans, who rejected slavery, worked better and cheaper than slaves, and by example and influence, was "uprooting. the system more than all the ranting attacks of Abolitionists for the last twenty years."[32]

Events did not bear out the *Times*'s estimate of the Germans' effectiveness; yet their presence suggested at the time an interesting possibility for western Texas. The Joint Treaty of Annexation had contemplated that Texas, when its population increase justified, should break up into five states. Western Texas, an ill-defined region extending from the Mexican border northward to the Guadalupe or Colorado rivers, was one candidate for statehood. In 1854 only one-quarter of its fifty thousand white American inhabitants were slaveholders, although four-fifths of them originated in slave states; its twenty-five thousand Mexicans were unequivocally hostile to slavery; and its eleven thousand Germans, of whom only a tiny handful owned slaves, were generally opposed to it, although they were equally opposed to antagonizing their suspicious American neighbors by making any decided move against it. Thus there was some prospect that western Texas might in time enter the union as a free state by the choice of its inhabitants.[33]

One German quietly dedicated to promoting the free-soil movement there was Adolf Douai, "a man of great strength and beauty of character and of perfect integrity," who was editor of the *San Antonio Zeitung*. Born in Altenburg, Thuringia, in 1819, of a French refugee family, Douai had attended the University of Leipzig, tutored in Russia for five years, and returned in 1846 to become principal of the Altenburg Gymnasium. Active in the revolutionary movement, he was three times imprisoned and released. The experience persuaded him to emigrate. Arriving with his large family and his aged father in Texas in 1852, he established a school in Sisterdale but gave it up the next year to move to San Antonio as editor of the *Zeitung*, a German-language paper.[34] The *Zeitung* was the second largest of the fifty-seven newspapers then published in Texas; the Olmsteds, who first saw it in Bastrop on their way to Austin, found it carried more news of general interest than any other paper they had seen since entering the state.[35] Eager to get accurate information on the Texas Germans, they called on the editor when they reached San Antonio and were at once captivated by "the force and gentleness of his character."[36]

Douai did more than tell them about the Germans. He escorted them to Sisterdale, the recent Latin settlement of perhaps ten farms some forty miles north of San Antonio, and introduced them to the forty-eighters living there. The brothers were enraptured with them. Men and women of education and formerly of position, stripped of wealth and exiled forever from friends and home, they lived by hard manual labor, yet were happy, and remained civilized.

Edward Degener and his family were typical. Born in 1809, the son of a wealthy Brauschitz banker, Degener had been educated in England and Germany and had married the daughter of a titled general. He had not found being a banker incompatible with being a popular leader and had twice been elected to the Frankfurt parliament. When the reaction came, he lost estate and position; so in 1850 he took his family to the United States, settling the next year at Sisterdale.[37] There he lived in a comfortable and well-furnished log house with his wife and his young sons Hugo and Hilmer, who helped him raise cotton, corn, wheat, and tobacco on his nearby fields. His one serious regret was that he could not give his sons as good an education as he had had; for the rest, he considered himself a fortunate man. His neighbors were like him. After an evening party at his home, where there had been good conversation, piano playing, waltzing, and singing of Mozart airs and student songs, the brothers thought that they could have found no better or more cheerful company in Germany than they had found among the exiles. Living independently by their own labor, relishing the social and political freedom they had vainly sought at home, enjoying the intellectual pleasures accessible to well-cultivated minds even at the edge of the wilderness, they were a happy group of men and women. "But how much of their cheerfulness," John moralized, "may arise from having gained, during this otherwise losing struggle to themselves, the certain consciousness of being courageously loyal to their intellectual determinations—their private convictions of right, justice and truth."[38]

The Germans, the rich country, the wonderful scenery, the possibility that western Texas might be secured for freedom, all induced Fred and John to think of settling there. They finally, however, had to abandon their California plan since they could not get a large enough band together to undertake the journey in safety. They made, instead, a somewhat risky trip, with only a guide, through the sparsely settled, Indian-haunted border country into Mexico.[39] Dozens of times in Texas taverns they heard it said, as a standing joke, that in Mexico a

Negro fancied himself as good as a white man: if you didn't treat him civilly, he'd have you hauled before the alcalde and fined. It did not displease the brothers to find that, south of the border, the "poor yellow-faced, priest-ridden heathen, actually hold, in earnest, the ideas on this subject put forth in that good old joke of our fathers—the Declaration of American Independence."*,[40]

Fred and John made another long trip, through the coastal region of eastern Texas, before leaving San Antonio for good. On April 24 they started homeward, going through Neu Braunfels again and Houston to Beaumont. There they sold two of the animals they had bought on entering Texas—Fanny, the high-strung, haughty mare, and Mr. Brown, the comedian of the party, a dun-colored, short-legged pack mule—and bought a cheerful, sturdy American stallion, Bel. A few days later, when they reached the Mississippi, they parted almost tearfully with the Creole pony Nack, a robust, playful, and intelligent little animal, and then with each other. John took the steamer to New Orleans, and Fred started on the long ride to Richmond with Judy, the faithful, footsore terrier who had shared their Texas adventure, for company.[41]

*From March 6 to June 7, 1854, the *Times* ran fifteen of Fred's letters, and it used two more editorially. The series stopped abruptly with the letter describing the first leg of the excursion from San Antonio to Mexico.

IX

JOURNALISM AND FREE-SOIL

June 1854–April 1855

JOHN reached home early in June, well ahead of Fred, to find the farm suffering from the failing interest of its owner. The pear orchard had not been pruned for two years; the peach trees were not bearing; the house needed paint, the fences and outhouses repair. The garden was poor, tools were rotting away, Nep and the other Newfoundland had turned chicken killers. John, trying to fill his brother's place, found he could not handle the men; they failed to show up for work and alleged illness or did not bother to allege anything. Burdened by duties for which he had no taste and no talent, he became depressed; he was sick, too, from months of exposure and bad food. His single wish was to live alone with his wife and his child, and it seemed to him unlikely of fulfillment.[1]

Fred returned in August with Bel and the terrier Judy and was host throughout the month to his Hartford family.[2] Like John, he was in worse health than when he had set out, but nothing could distract him from his new passion for journalism. The columns of the *Times* were by then open to him whenever he wanted to write on a public question, and he had much to say on several, first among them a frightful disaster at sea, the loss of the Collins Line steamer *Arctic*.

On September 27, 1854, the wooden-hulled steamer, homeward bound from Liverpool, collided in a patchy fog off Cape Race with the small iron-hulled propeller *Vestris* and went to the bottom in a few hours. News of her loss reached New York October 11, while hope was still held that she was merely overdue. The appalling particulars rocked the city. The survivors' report that the crew had rushed the lifeboats, that the engineers had fled the engine room, that passengers had had to man the abandoned pumps, that the captain had been unable to exercise the least control over the crew, that panic and pandemonium had reigned may have been exaggerated in some particulars; but the facts spoke for themselves: there were boats to accommodate at least two hundred and twenty of the four hundred souls aboard, and there was time between collision and sinking to launch them and a large raft; yet only seventy-seven were saved, and of those, only twenty were passengers. The owner's wife, Mrs. E. K. Collins, was lost with two of her children; so were two daughters, a son, a daughter-in-law, and two grandchildren of James Brown, of Brown Brothers. The captain's little boy drowned along with the duc de Grammont of the French Embassy. But it was not the prominence of some of the victims or even the extent of the disaster that shook the public. It was "the devilish cowardice of the wretched crew." With a few heroic exceptions, the conduct of officers and men alike had been despicable.[3]

To the chorus of editorial outrage that burst forth, Olmsted, horrified but rational, contributed a realistic note. In a three-column letter, which the *Times* published and noticed editorially on October 18, he proposed that vessels running in fog should be absolutely required by law to give frequently repeated notice of their course by firing the signal gun or sounding a steam whistle or steam trumpet; that the safeguards, especially boat drill, already required of passenger ships be rigorously enforced; and most important, that a radical reform of discipline in the merchant marine be set afoot immediately.

"Discipline," Olmsted emphasized, "does not mean forced and frightened obedience, discipline means system." To the ferocious and degrading treatment that passed for discipline on American ships, only "the meanest, most reckless, dastardly and despicable class" would subject themselves; and only by a constant, brutalizing "working up" could the officers make the "desperados and sots" who predominated most crews do ship's duty. It was no wonder that such men, treated worse than slaves, became "slavish and even diabolical" in character and behaved, in a crisis, like devils. To attract a better class of men and make better seamen of them, discipline should be made not more severe but more educational. Reiterating the thesis of "A Voice from the Sea," he proposed that young men be trained for the sea, just as they were trained for other skilled and respectable callings, and that crews be kept in the service of the lines instead of being scraped together at need from bars and boardinghouses. Only then would the demoralization of the merchant marine be overcome, and only then could seamen reasonably be expected to know their duties and perform them conscientiously always.

Fred's suggestions met all but unanimous approval, to judge from the correspondence in the *Times*. His one hostile critic, however, the superintendent of a hotel for seamen run by a benevolent society, blasted his letter in every particular, extolled the character and treatment of American crews, and wondered if such "utterly and shamefully" false and ignorant assertions as "F. L. O's" could have been made by an American.[4] Fred retorted a few days later by expanding and documenting his statements and tartly assured his detractor that he was indeed an American, "though as far as possible from being a Know-Nothing. Neither am I so anxious to deny and hide from myself and others what is wrong in my country as to [neglect to] contribute to make it right."[5]

Another public matter on which Olmsted wrote was unemployment in New York. In the spring of 1854, while he was still away, Peter Cooper, Horace Greeley, and others disturbed by the plight of thousands of immigrants stagnating and starving in the city had formed the American and Foreign Emigrant Protective and Employment Society. Its object was to funnel both native born and foreign out of the huge reservoir of the unemployed in the port of entry into suitable jobs in other parts of the country.[6] Olmsted, almost as concerned for immigrants as for sailors and sympathetic to the aims of the society, published in the late summer a questionnaire in the *Weekly Times,* the *Tribune,* and the *Agriculturist* asking farmers for information on the wages and conditions of hired farm workers in various regions. Eighty-eight replies came in from nineteen states ranging from Maine to Mississippi and from Texas to Wisconsin.[7]

While the number was not impressive, the consensus was. According to a large majority of the answers, there was a decided shortage of help, male and female, on farms throughout the nation; and a fair possibility existed that an able and provident hired man could become, in a few years, the owner of land and the employer of labor.[8] By February 1855, when Olmsted's three-column article, "Work and Wages," which John prepared for publication,[9] appeared in the *Times,* there was such distress among the New York jobless that it would have been murder to close the soup kitchens; Fred suggested, however, that the city could more usefully spend a part of its relief money by furnishing immigrants with railroad tickets to the interior, where the new society was finding jobs and opportunities for them, than by sustaining them indefinitely in almost hopeless circumstances with doles of food or in the poorhouses and prisons where many of them necessarily landed.*,[10]

Olmsted's suggestion was prompted by a philanthropic concern for the unemployed; conceivably, too, a political *arrière-pensée* entered into it. The principle of squatter sovereignty had been established with the passage of the Kansas–Nebraska Act in May 1854, and the New England Emigrant Aid Society was already sending bands of settlers to the territory in an effort to secure it against slavery. At the same time Douai, from western Texas, was soliciting help for his free-soil efforts there. It may well have occurred to Olmsted that they could be advanced by directing some of the New York unemployed into the section that, in time, was expected to decide by a vote of its inhabitants whether to be slave or free. In any case, he entered actively into Douai's design.

---

*Olmsted's proposal, backed editorially by the *Times,* embroiled him in a somewhat uncivil argument, conducted in the columns of the paper, with one William West, who described himself as a working man. West said that Olmsted, in making public his returns, must have suppressed answers unfavorable to his proposal: there was no demand in the rest of the country for labor nor would there be so long as protection and land monopoly were tolerated (*New York Daily Times,* 9 February 1855).

Peter Cooper, on the contrary, was impressed by Olmsted's investigation and asked him to become a member of the board of governors of the emigrant protective association; and the *Times,* having editorialized on his suggestion when it appeared, pressed it again in the early summer. Whether or not Olmsted accepted Cooper's invitation is not clear, although he met Cooper to discuss it at least once. If he refused, he was spared connection with a dubious success. The society by the end of its first year had spent $7,882, only $482 of it on transportation, the rest on the salaries of its agents and expenses; and coming under sharp criticism by October 1855, it had to close one of its two offices and restrict its activities (JHO to JO, 9 February 1855; *New York Daily Times,* 21 February, 15 June 1855; O to JO, [?] February 1855; *New York Daily Times,* 12 October 1855).

Douai's immediate object was to buy the *Zeitung* and rid himself of the restraint of a faction of its stockholders who were fearful of antagonizing the local slaveowners. Although the paper, as a matter of strategy, had not yet declared against slavery, Douai's views were well known, and the stockholders, divided and alarmed by them, were willing to sell him the paper at cost and on credit. Early in September 1854, Douai wrote the Olmsteds asking for a loan of three hundred fifty dollars to help him swing the purchase and buy English type so that he could reach Americans as well as Germans.[11]

Fred and John, ever dependent on their father for funds, had no money to give away, but they appealed to such friends of their own and of freedom's as Brace, Henry Ward Beecher, Henry H. Elliott, and the merchants Bowen and McNamee. By the end of October they had raised and sent most of the requested loan, ordered the English type, got subscriptions among their friends for the *Zeitung*, and purchased newsprint for it.[*,12]

It was as well that Douai had friends at a distance, for those at hand were few and, mostly, fainthearted. An exception was Charles N. Riotte, a refugee German lawyer in San Antonio. Riotte urged Fred to place in northern journals articles, silent on the slavery issue, describing the advantages of western Texas. Thus they might attract bona-fide settlers without at the same time provoking an invasion of border ruffians. Reprinted in newspapers in Germany, such articles could be expected to stimulate further migration from there.[13]

Accordingly, Fred supplied material drawn from the *Zeitung* and his friends' letters to Raymond, who several times used it editorially during January 1855. Fred himself reviewed a book on slavery in the United States by Friedrich Kapp, an influential refugee lawyer who lived in New York;[14] he had met Kapp's uncle, one of the Sisterdale farmers, on his Texas trip and had lately become friendly with the nephew. The long report in the *Tribune*, also in January, on Kapp's lecture, "The History of Texas," which the speaker concluded by urging Free-Soilers to take up land in Texas, was perhaps another product of Olmsted's little newspaper campaign to promote immigration.[15] Ironically, he could not promote it at home: John decided not to settle there because of the hot summers, the lack of educational facilities, and slavery. Degener, urging him to reconsider, spoiled his argument with the admission that feeling against the Germans was steadily mounting and that Sisterdale in particular had been denounced as having "secret understandings with the abolitionists of the north," of whom the suspected agents were—the Olmsted brothers.[16]

While he was hardly the agent of an abolitionist conspiracy, Fred was indeed active in the free-soil interest. For the *Zeitung* he wrote an article, which

---

*Douai, who sometimes had to get his newsprint from the *Western Texan,* was doubly happy to obtain it through the Olmsteds: he was relieved, at a stroke, of his partial dependence on his proslavery rival and of the humiliating necessity to treat with some politeness the paper that maliciously twitted him with "plump, gross, ridiculous invectives" on his English-language articles (Douai to O, 28 October, 7 December 1854).

Andrew Jackson Downing

F.L.O.,
circa 1859

Site of lake at south end
of Central Park in 1857
(*above*) and Olmsted's
proposed effect with
lake (*left*).

The Staten Island
Farmhouse, circa 1848,
from a sketch attributed
to F.L.O.

was published also in the *Hartford Courant*, on Know-Nothingism.[17] When
Victor Considérant, the French Fourierist, passed through New York on his way
to found a colony in Texas, Fred arranged to meet him to advise him on locating
it.* Fred also got in touch with Emigrant Aid Society members to discuss various possibilities of cooperation between the Kansas and the Texas Free-Soilers.
Douai, kept abreast of his activities, constantly urged the need to soft-pedal the
free-soil angle of the immigration they were seeking to stimulate.[18]

But the difficulties of developing a concerted movement and at the same
time maintaining secrecy as to its motive were overwhelming, especially after
Kapp, whose lecture was fully reported in the *Tribune*, had let the cat out of
the bag. Forced into the open, the editor of the *Zeitung* published an article in
the issue of February 9, 1855, that declared that western Texas must be free.

From that time on, attacks on him were unremitting. The local newspapers
blackguarded him editorially. The big San Antonio merchants withdrew their
advertising from his paper. Subscribers by the score canceled. The rumor flew
that he was "sold" to the Yankee abolitionists and on the verge of bankruptcy.
The campaign of harassment was so far successful by August that Douai realized
that nothing lay ahead but bankruptcy unless he sold the paper. Determined to
retain his means of influencing opinion to the last possible moment, he let his
compositor go to save money and, with no help but that of his old father and
fourteen-year-old son, continued to publish the *Zeitung*.[19]

Between inflamed proslavery and mounting Know-Nothing feeling, all the
Texas Germans, whatever their politics, were in an uneasy position. Some,
frightened, ostentatiously discountenanced free-soil sentiment. Many considered
abandoning their homes and their hopes once again and migrating to Mexico.
Others, like Riotte, planned to sell farms and town lots at the depressed prices
brought about by the increased lawlessness and go North poor men rather than
live out their lives under slavery.[20]

All during 1855 Olmsted followed Texas affairs intently. What he could do
to sustain his Texas friends from afar, he did. He used their letters to try to
raise money from the "peace people," whose consciences would not allow them
to send arms to Kansas, to keep the *Zeitung* solvent. Although he said he was
still unable, three years after being jilted by Emily Perkins, to write his successful rival without "much emotion," he begged Edward Everett Hale to try to
make something for publication out of Douai's interesting and touching letters;
and he probably inspired the *Times* to lament editorially the proposed German
exodus to Mexico. But it was all no good. No matter what its good will in New
York and New England, without local support the Texas free-soil paper could
not survive; and by the beginning of 1856 the Free-Soil party there was crushed,
and crushed beyond hope, Riotte wrote Olmsted, because of treason, meanness,

---

*That Considérant established his phalanstery, *La Réunion*, at San Antonio suggests
that he may have been influenced in his choice of a place by Olmsted.

and self-seeking among the Germans. Douai clung to his newspaper until the spring of 1856; compelled finally to sell it—and to the opposition—he turned his back forever on Texas.[21] Degener elected to remain and so invited calamity.

During the same period that he was supporting the Texas Free-Soilers in their unequal and little-noticed campaign, Olmsted was quietly trying to influence the course of the dangerous and dramatic events in Kansas. The Lecompton legislature, elected in March 1855, when bands of armed Missourians entered Kansas to vote illegally, was about to be challenged by the antislavery settlers who were rallying to set up a rival government at Lawrence. Anticipating a fight, the Free-Soilers dispatched an agent, Major James B. Abbott, east in the late summer to raise money for arms. Among the men Abbott approached was Olmsted, in whom he found "a prompt and energetic friend of Kansas."[22]

Abbott met Olmsted early in September, when he reached New York on his fund-raising tour, and before returning to Kansas he delegated him to collect money and buy arms. The evening of September 17 Olmsted assembled a small company: Horace Greeley, editor of the *Tribune*; David Dudley Field, brother of Cyrus and a leading New York lawyer; John Priestly, lately editor of the *American Whig Review*, which had expired a bit ahead of its party at the end of 1852; Frederick Beecher Perkins, Emily's brother, formerly an editor of *Putnam's* and currently one of the editors of the *Tribune*; and Charles Wyllis Elliott, who supported his versatile interests in landscape gardening, literature, and philanthropy with the proceeds of the iron business he operated with his brother Henry. The little gathering drew up a list of potential contributors and arranged that they should be called on next day by solicitors.[23] "I hope in a week," Olmsted discreetly reported to Abbott, "to have funds to purchase you 100 ——. It is thought best that the way in which the money is to be used should not be mentioned. It is for the Kansas settlers, with whom I am in correspondence, to direct that, and I keep my own counsel."[24]

By October 4, when he next wrote Abbott, Olmsted had raised almost three hundred fifty dollars, intended to wait until he had four hundred dollars to purchase arms, and had changed his mind about buying rifles.* A "veteran officer," unidentified, "who, under Garibaldi and others had had part in a good deal of guerrilla defensive warfare in Europe," confirmed his theory that the Kansans

---

*Contributors to the fund were John Bigelow, B. F. Butler, John E. Devlin, Abijah Mann, George S. Robbins, Seth B. Hunt, E. S. Miller, E. A. Stansbury, B. F. Seaver, J. S. Whiting, William Cullen Bryant, S. T. Gordon, Charles King, W. S. Aspinwall, Cyrus Field, David Dudley Field, Horace Greeley, Hiram Barney, R. Carrigan, F. B. Perkins, Samuel B. Ruggles, C. L. Brace, John Priestly, Thomas Fessenden, Minthorne Tompkins, Paul Babcock, James Freeland, John E. Williams, Watt Sherman, Jonah Coddington, Shephard Knapp, A. G. Philips, H. Gray, Alfred Pell, Benedict Hall, Robert Gilchrist, F. A. Conklin, Simeon Draper, F. S. Berry, Thaddeus Hyatt, and E. D. Morgan (*Topeka Daily Capitol*, 8 January 1884).

by then had as many Sharp's rifles as they could advantageously use.[25] "For the bulk of your arms," he wrote Abbott, "the old-fashioned pieces would really be better than S's. . . . I shall, therefore, probably either send you an H or M's. . . ."[26]

A few days later he decided on a howitzer in preference to muskets, having found a twelve-pound brass mountain howitzer, privately owned, in the New York State Arsenal. "One discharge of it at musket range," he explained to Abbott, "is considered equally effective with a simultaneous fire of one hundred muskets, while its moral effect in producing consternation and panic upon an enemy, especially of undisciplined men, is far greater. . . ."[27]

On October 24 he notified Abbott that he had shipped it, by the underground, to a consignee in St. Louis.[28]

"It was supposed by the seller," he explained long afterward,

> that the goods were going on board ship and had been so packed with a view to landing in boats on some foreign coast. Care was taken to favor this presumption and to prevent their actual destination from being ascertained. It is of interest that the only man to whom I confided the arrangement for this purpose, and who personated the shipmaster supposed to receive the goods from me was afterwards an officer of high rank in the southern confederacy.[29]

This officer, too, he left tantalizingly unidentified.

"The goods" consisted of the howitzer and its carriage, twenty-four shells, and twenty-four cannister cartridges. Powder, too dangerous to ship, was to be purchased in St. Louis with the thirty or forty dollars left over.* The shipment was forwarded from St. Louis to Kansas City, whence Abbott's emissaries conveyed it to Lawrence early in December. It arrived just as the Free-Soilers, fortifying the town, and the proslavery force, surrounding it, were on the brink of outright warfare. Negotiations averted bloodshed, for the moment; and the twelve-pounder was retired, peaceably and anticlimactically, to the cellar of its Lawrence consignee.[30]

At the same time that he was participating in the Texas and Kansas schemes, Fred was busy expanding his first series of articles into book form. Wanting background material in Virginia history, he did some of his research at the Astor Library in spite of considering it an "immense humbug," merely a collection to the glory of Dr. Joseph Green Cogswell, who treated the books like curiosities.†,[31] When he was not working at the library, he found other reasons

---

*Olmsted's later recollection was that he also shipped five hand grenades, fifty rockets, and six swords (*Topeka Daily Capital*, 8 January 1884).

†Several editorials and letters complaining of the superciliousness of an attendant had appeared in the *Times* by July 1855. One was signed "Rusticus," and there is reason to suppose that the rustic was Olmsted. Having twice been rudely received by an attendant,

for being away from the farm, which he was leaving more and more to the re-luctant John's management. He spent a weekend with Brace, whose charitable work had put him "hand in glove with all the best people," at Mrs. George Schuyler's, dined with her father, Colonel James A. Hamilton, son of Alexander, and found them "most capital people—the most finished people I ever saw." An evening at the theater, where he enjoyed "a good crying spell" over a pathetic play about a newsboy, a dinner party with Kapp and his German friends, visits to Miss Lynch's salon, calls on Raymond, engagements business and social, kept him often away from home.[32] Already looking ahead to the time when his book should be finished, he proposed to Raymond that the *Times* send him to England for two years as its correspondent. When Raymond pointed out that the strug-gling newspaper might die a dozen times in that period, Fred cast about for some other literary connection.[33] Farm affairs impinged less and less on the interest of the owner who, having decided that his career lay elsewhere, let it be known that he would sell if he could get two hundred dollars an acre.[34]

It was quite otherwise with John. The farm was being palmed off on him just as everything on it was going wrong. Bel had been unmanageable since the end of 1854, when he ran away with Fred and smashed up the carriage. Mary, pregnant and ill that winter, was unable to walk and dared not take carriage exercise. Irrevocably committed to their criminal careers, the Newfoundlands had progressed from chicken killers to sheep killers and had slaughtered nine lambs and five sheep in a single night. The sow littered, and all the little pigs were born dead. The cabbages, having several times frozen and thawed in the ground, were expected to be a total loss, and the hay crop was poor. Repairs to house and outbuildings could no longer be put off and cost more than estimated. John had constantly to fall back on his wife's small income and to ask his father for loans that he could see no prospect of repaying.[35]

Wretched with dyspepsia and nerves but fancying his tuberculosis better, he described himself as "miserable but calm."[36] After he began to spit blood again in February, he wished simply to die and have done.[37] Worry about his finances and his health was slowly crushing all capacity for enjoyment out of him. Not even the birth of his second baby, Charlotte, on March 15, 1855, could lift his spirits for long. He saw himself as a man without a future, marking time, at his father's expense, until he should die. "I have always before supposed," he

---

"Rusticus" said, he mentioned the incidents to a literary friend who said, "Oh, they don't know you; you must let me introduce you to Dr. Cogswell."

"I have since observed that there is a great difference in the manner of the young gentleman to different people. I once saw two threadbare Germans—evidently scholars, but starving poor—so rudely repulsed in asking for some information that I was moved to offer them an apology myself for the country; and on calling at the library when dressed for a dinner party, I found myself very differently treated from what I was when I came in my traveling clothes.

"I am a rather small and modest looking fellow, over thirty years of age, and don't wear spectacles" (*New York Daily Times*, 23 July 1855).

gloomily wrote John Olmsted soon after the baby's birth, "I should stop drawing on you some time or other—but now I despair of it and draw perpetually as little as I can, with no particular object in view for the future. I hope your investment in Fred won't prove as great a failure."[38]

That investment had just been substantially increased: Fred required fresh funds to enable him to embark on an entirely new course. He was about to join the staff of *Putnam's Magazine.* John was to assume full management of the farm. "I regret to be left in the lurch," the younger brother said with muted bitterness.[39]

He regretted to be left in the lurch; yet he did nothing to avoid it. It was almost as though, despairing of making anything of his life for himself, he had determined to use what was left of it for Fred. By the end of April he had taken title to the farm, and Fred was establishing himself in rooms in town. For seven years Fred had called on his father for a thousand dollars or more a year to keep the place, himself, and Aunt Maria going; now John was going to try to run the farm with only Mary's seven hundred dollars a year, and with a wife, two babies, and a nurse to support instead of a maiden aunt.[40] He could hardly have anticipated success, but he could know that he was releasing his restless brother from a wearisome failure and enabling him to turn his talents in a more promising direction.

X

THE "LITERARY REPUBLIC"

May 1855–August 1857

P UTNAM'S *Magazine*, a rival and a reproach to the piratical *Harper's New Monthly Magazine*, had begun publication in January 1853. *Harper's*, in the absence of an international copyright agreement, looted English magazines and books for its material and paid the authors not a cent; *Putnam's* printed, and paid for, original work by American writers. Owned by George Palmer Putnam and edited by Charles Frederick Briggs, George William Curtis, and Parke Godwin, the journal had published Lowell, Longfellow, Hawthorne, Whittier, Melville, Agassiz, Lydia Maria Child, Edward Everett Hale, Bayard Taylor, and Henry James, Sr., and was an authentic expression of American culture. Early in 1855 Putnam, in debt, sold the magazine to the firm of Dix & Edwards, publishers of the American edition of Dickens's *Household Words*.[1] Joshua Augustus Dix, twenty-four years old, was a friend of Brace's and an acquaintance of Fred's. He had earlier been in charge of Putnam's retailing and importing department and was popular and respected in the publishing trade.[2] His partner, Arthur T. Edwards, a former dry-goods clerk, was supposed to be a man of unusual financial ability. Fred, learning that Dix & Edwards had purchased *Putnam's*, thought he recognized an opportunity to get into a literary position that would give him both influence and a living.[3]

Dix was eager to have him in the firm, Edwards reluctant.[4] They finally agreed to take him if he would bring five thousand dollars capital with him.[5] Once again, Fred asked his father to finance him. Once again, that generous and patient man did so.[6]

Putnam's, in changing owners, changed editors. Briggs dropped out; Curtis declined the editorship but agreed to help with advice and pen as much as his other literary commitments would let him; Godwin promised to do book reviews and notices of foreign affairs; and Charles Anderson Dana, too busy on the *Tribune* to do much outside writing, consented to give editorial advice. "I am just at this moment inclined," Fred wrote his father the middle of March 1855, "to take the responsibility of editing the Magazine myself with the stated assistance of these three men."[7]

In the end, Olmsted became not editor but a sort of front man. John wrote Bertha, who was touring Europe with friends, that Fred "acts as publisher, i.e. editing publisher, answers letters, receives literary men, and conducts the literary side of the business. Above him is an editor whose name is unknown, to decide upon manuscripts and furnish articles but Fred's influence though subordinate is large. . . ."[8]

The mysterious editor was, in fact, Curtis, who had reconsidered his earlier refusal. While Olmsted worked in the outer office, Curtis, often with Dana, was at work on manuscripts in the inner room. His incognito was carefully preserved, at least for some months; and Dana's connection with the magazine was so effectively concealed that information about it was discredited after his death by close associates, both of his and of the magazine's.[9]

With such backing, Fred was not seriously handicapped by his inexperience. The handsome and popular Curtis was one of the most practiced literary men in New York. Born in Providence, he had come to New York at the age of fifteen, later had spent two years at Brook Farm, where he became comfortably immunized to transcendentalism, and then had traveled in Europe, Egypt, and Syria from 1846 to 1850. He had sent letters to the *Tribune* and had come home to enjoy a considerable success with *Nile Notes of a Howadji*, published in 1851. He had followed the one popular book with others, and simultaneously with being *Putnam's* editor, he was editor of "The Easy Chair" in *Harper's*. The scholarly Parke Godwin, also an alumnus of Brook Farm, had become William Cullen Bryant's assistant on the *Evening Post* at the age of twenty, almost two decades before; his articles in *Putnam's* assaulting the slave power and the president had drawn national attention. Dana, too, had been seasoned by Brook Farm and newspaper work: after five years among the transcendentalists, he had joined the *Tribune* in 1847, where he became managing editor within two years. Thus there was no lack of editorial judgment to correct Olmsted's, should his be at fault.

Olmsted's, though inexperienced, was sound. It was, as well, so confidently emphatic that Curtis fell into the habit of referring to him as "Mr. Law." "Mr. Law" was well satisfied with the May issue, the first under the new management, except for the art, music, and drama notices turned out by Richard Grant White and Clarence Cook. Curtis, concurring, insisted that White and Cook be fired and, still concealing his true relation with the magazine, got William Henry Hurlbert* to take over the fine arts notes.[10]

Under its new editors the magazine's literary quality remained high, and it continued to attract distinguished writers. The *Times*, which often reviewed it, called it "the most original magazine published in this country"; and Thackeray, it was reported, declared "that 'Putnam' was much the best Mag. in the world . . . better than Blackwood is or ever was."[11]

On moving to town in April 1855 to begin his new career, Olmsted rented two rooms for two hundred dollars a year in the Moffet Building on Broadway at the corner of Anthony Street[12] and within easy reach of *Putnam's* office at 10 Park Place; and since his twelve hundred dollars-a-year salary permitted him

---

*Hurlbert was an antislavery South Carolinian. Brilliant and erratic, he had graduated from Harvard at the age of twenty in 1847 and from Harvard Divinity School two years later. For a short time he was a Unitarian minister, then attended Harvard Law School for two years before turning, more or less permanently, to journalism. He was on the staff, successively, of *Putnam's*, the *New York Times*, and the *New York World*. He bore a somewhat tarnished reputation, being prone to getting into amorous and financial scrapes.

no extravagances,[13] he furnished them at second-hand dealers' shops.[14] Frugally, he made his own breakfast of tea and toast on a gas cooker in his rooms, lunched on soup and crackers at the Astor House, and dined at six, usually with Dana, at a French ordinary in Barclay Street.[15] Evenings he spent on his book.

If the financial return of his new life was slight, the moral was considerable. It was immensely gratifying to him to rub elbows with literary men and women well advanced up the slope of Parnassus, at the foot of which he toiled. He was often at Miss Lynch's salon; elected a member of the Press Club, he attended a dinner honoring Thackeray with Washington Irving and some thirty other literary men;[16] for Lowell, who was about to go abroad, he gave a luncheon to which came Dana, Curtis, Godwin, "and others of the generation of serious literary men of somewhat earnest semi-political disposition antagonistic to the growing war spirit of the slave states."[17] He made sorties into New England to see Emerson, Longfellow, Asa Gray, Theodore Parker, Mrs. Stowe, and other contributors whose continued support was important to the magazine;[18] and in his office he could regularly fraternize with visiting literati.

The disadvantages of his new position did not yet obtrude themselves, but he was aware of them. For one thing, he did not perfectly trust Edwards, the partner responsible for the financial management of the firm. Perhaps Edwards's reluctance to take him as a partner disposed Olmsted to be cool toward him; certainly Edwards's view of their obligation to the English authors reprinted in *Household Words* confirmed Olmsted's coldness. Edwards held it a courtesy, not a duty, to pay them. Olmsted thought it a clear duty: to print a foreign author's work without his permission and without paying him was simple thievery, and it was not to be condoned because the practice was standard and no law forbade it in the United States. The statement of their conflicting views in an exchange of letters, pious on Edwards's side, polite and unyielding on Olmsted's, cannot have left them better friends, but it clarified for Olmsted his partner's business ethics.[19] Olmsted concluded that Edwards would not do anything "which all the world would without reserve stigmatize as dishonest. But his standard of morality is purely conventional, not interior or philosophical & is the standard of a very bad school. . . ."[20]

Edwards's entirely legal sharp practice was traceable to something besides unscrupulousness: the firm was terribly hard up. Olmsted had been in the partnership only a month when he began to fear that their entire capital would be consumed by their heavy expenses before any returns began; within another six months he had to borrow substantial sums twice from Godwin and Howard Potter* for his own living expenses because the company could not pay his

---

*Howard Potter (1826–97), son of Bishop Alonzo Potter of Pennsylvania, was a member of the New York bar, but by this time had quit practice to become secretary and treasurer of the Novelty Iron Company in which his father-in-law, James Brown, of Brown Brothers, had the controlling interest. Later he joined Brown Brothers and became a partner in 1861. Throughout the thirty years of their association, Potter was one of Olmsted's most dependable friends.

salary.[21] During that period, however, the publishing business began to emerge from the doldrums, and *Putnam's* publishers, encouraged by a rising circulation and by the favorable notice the magazine was receiving throughout the East, hopefully proposed to branch out into book publishing.[22] They immediately tried to secure *Prue and I*, their popular editor's sketches that had run serially in *Putnam's*. Failing, since Putnam stood on his right to publish Curtis's work in book form, they went after smaller game and readily bagged the subordinate editor's observations on the slave states, which he had almost completed by early November.[23]

The firm agreed that Olmsted should own his book and pay Dix & Edwards a percentage on sales for bringing it out; it agreed also, at first, to advance the money for the publishing costs, charging Olmsted interest on it. Edwards, however, said they could not afford the loan and insisted on canceling the arrangement. Olmsted, left to raise the necessary money himself, with a heavy heart asked his father for one thousand dollars. The elder Olmsted was hesitant; the younger was chagrined. It began to dawn on him that his entry into publishing had been a mistake. "I wonder how I could have been swerved from my repeated resolution not to be a business man, knowing so well my inaptness for it . . . ," he exclaimed.[24]

There was a personal loan, however, for which Fred felt justified in asking, since it would help him to establish his literary position. "There is a sort of literary republic," he explained to his father,

> which it is not merely pleasant and gratifying to my ambition to be
> recognized in, but also profitable. It would, for example, if I am so recog-
> nized & considered, be easy for me, in case of the non success of this
> partnership, to get employment in the newspaper offices or other literary
> enterprises at good wages. . . . To take & keep a position as a recognized
> literateur, as a man of influence in literary matters, I need at the time
> of the publication of my book to be able to spend a little more than I like to
> draw out of our partnership bank, and I hate as Edwards expects of me,
> to be running in debt to tailors & coblers & cooks.[25]

The indulgent father again overcame the careful businessman; John Olmsted agreed to finance the publication of Fred's book. *Journey in the Seaboard Slave States*, a fat volume selling for $1.25, appeared in a printing of two thousand on January 16, 1856. Forewarned by George Ripley, who had read the book in proof, Fred rightly expected a critical, not a commercial, success. At first it had no sale at all in a market overcrowded with books on slavery. As reviews drew attention to it, it began slowly to sell. By April 30 five thousand copies had been printed, but ten weeks later probably two thousand of them were still heavy on the hands of Dix & Edwards. Critical reaction as well as sales bore out Ripley's prediction. Except in the South, *Slave States* was received with acclaim and with interest sharpened by the fact that the author had looked at slavery from an economic, not a humanitarian, standpoint. Metropolitan dailies, and magazines such as the *Christian Examiner*, the *North American Review*, and of course *Putnam's* reviewed and praised it. Mrs. Stowe, in the *Independent*, called it "the most thorough *exposé* of the economical view of this subject which has ever appeared." Even the abolitionists, as a rule contemptuous of gradualists, were cordial: John Greenleaf Whittier, to whom Olmsted had sent advance proofs, wrote warmly, and the *National Era* and the *Liberator* recommended it heartily.

Articulate southern reaction, on the whole, was hostile, and more intemperate than Olmsted had anticipated. The comment of the *Southern Literary Messenger* was representative. Avoiding mention of the book by name, it complained that "the literary workshops of the North are even now resounding with the noisy and fanatical labors of those who, with Mrs. Stowe as their model, are forging calumnies, and hammering falsehood into the semblance of truth."[26]

Southern resentment was understandable. Olmsted had been dangerously persuasive on the rottenness of the slave economy; he had outlined a sensible plan by which, under a system of charges for goods consumed and credits for goods produced and work accomplished, the slaves could eventually buy their freedom; and he had exposed a widespread determination in the South to cling to slavery at any cost, notwithstanding its uneconomic operation and notwithstanding practicable suggestions for gradual and compensated emancipation. In short, he had raised a powerful new voice against slavery, and he was winning a respectful audience not only at home but in England, the South's vital market. Moreover, the olive branches he had offered the South in the *Times* letters— the admonitions to the North to correct the evils of its own labor system, the presentation of proslavery arguments, the warnings that emancipation must come on the South's initiative—he pointedly failed to offer in his book. Two years had passed between the original observation and the final writing; during them, reflection, study, and events in Kansas and Texas had stiffened his attitude and suggested to him that conciliation was futile.

Even though the South withheld its approval, the appearance of *Slave States* made Olmsted what he wanted to be: "a recognized literateur, a man of influence in literary matters."[27] It was as one fully entitled to represent America's literary republic that, a month after the appearance of his book, he sailed for England on the firm's business.

With his half-sister, Mary, who was going abroad to join Bertha, Fred sailed from Boston Wednesday, February 13, 1856, on the *Arabia*.[28] His principal business was to persuade English publishers to consign books to Dix & Edwards to be sold on commission,[29] and he probably wondered, as Captain Stone drove his ship at full speed through the iceberg-haunted, fog-shrouded waters off the Grand Banks, if he would live to undertake it. Still, a year and a half after the loss of the *Arctic*, the ship used no fog signals and posted, on the edge of an ice field, only the usual night lookout. As she slackened speed and plunged into it, Fred saw the most terrifying sight he had ever seen in fifty thousand miles of sea travel: *"right abreast of us, and not a hundred yards distant, yet spectral in the fog, a dead, ghastly and unblemished white iceberg, just about as large above water as the City Hall in New York."* Fred, who admired the captain's seamanship almost as much as he deplored his recklessness, refused to sign the passengers' testimonial to him and wrote the *Times* a letter, ambivalent in its attitude toward him, describing the crossing.[30]

In London by the end of the month, he and Mary stayed with Henry Stevens, who was helping the British Museum build its collection of books on the New World and who knew most of the prominent literary people in town. During the day Fred called on publishers and editors or on the American minister, James Buchanan; evenings, he enjoyed long dinners and sleepy late conversations with his host.[31] After some three weeks, during which his principal success was to make a satisfactory arrangement with Bradbury and Evans, owners of *Punch* and publishers of Dickens and Thackeray,[32] he took Mary to Paris, where he delivered to the American legation dispatches entrusted to him by Buchanan.[33] Gathering up Bertha, he set out with his sisters on a whirlwind tour that took them by rail through Lyon to Marseilles, by boat to Toulon, Genoa, Leghorn, and Civita Vecchia, and thence by diligence to Rome, where they arrived in time for Easter.[34]

After Rome, the little party hastened through Naples, Amalfi, Pompei, Florence, Venice, Trieste, and Prague to Leipzig, where Fred tried in vain to get consignments from Tauschnitz, who, more fortunate than Putnam, had made a tremendous success of their well-printed, cheap classics.[35] In Dresden, Fred left the girls in the home of an art professor to await the arrival of John Olmsted, who was planning to rent his Hartford house for a year and come to Europe with the rest of his family in the summer.[36] Fred then returned by way of Paris to London, where he arrived the middle of May. "I was born for a traveller," he wrote happily. "I do enjoy it exceedingly and I had no idea I could get so much out of such a hasty journey."[37]

His most lasting impressions of the trip were not of the superiority of French railroads over American; or of the elegance of the French emperor's big steam yacht, plunging at anchor close to leeward of them in a storm in Toulon harbor; or of the dazzling gaiety of the Easter fireworks in Rome.[38] They were of the landscape and gardens of Italy, which were much finer than he had expected and were interestingly clothed in vegetation and laid out on principles novel to him. At a time when he had "no more thought of becoming a landscape architect than a cardinal," he studied them with an eye and a mind that retained for the rest of his working life the impressions and information he gleaned then.[39]

In London during May, Fred engaged Stevens to act as his shipping agent and persuaded John William Parker, publisher of *Fraser's Magazine* and of Mill, Buckle, Lewes, Kingsley, and Froude, to consign books to Dix & Edwards.[40] The following month, he went to Edinburgh for a few days to try to interest Scottish publishers in his scheme. It was in Edinburgh, about the middle of June, that the bad news from home reached him.

All in the month of May, Representative Philemon T. Herbert, of California, had shot an Irish waiter dead in a Washington hotel for addressing him with insufficient deference; Lawrence, the free-soil stronghold, had been sacked by a proslavery mob; and Representative Preston Brooks of South Carolina had beaten Senator Charles Sumner of Massachusetts unconscious with a heavy cane in the almost empty Senate chamber in reprisal for his vitriolic speech, "The Crime Against Kansas," in which he had vilified Brooks's kinsman, Senator Andrew F. Butler of South Carolina.

At word of these violent episodes Olmsted, as "Yeoman," promptly wrote a letter to the *Times*. Such occurrences, he said, were making the position of Americans in Europe very painful; even the friends of republicanism were silent and abashed, while its enemies said that such atrocities were its necessary consequences. The *North British Daily Mail*, he added, displayed a rarely friendly spirit in arguing that such outrages were the result not of republicanism but of slavery.[41]

Opportunely, his own book, which tended to document the friendly paper's thesis, was just beginning to attract attention in England. An early review of it appeared on June 28 in the *Athenaeum*, which, despite its reputation for being unusually hard on American authors, offered Olmsted rather condescending congratulations. In July, *Fraser's Magazine* and the *Examiner* noticed it at length and favorably; and the *Daily News's* glowing criticism, which Olmsted thought was written by Miss Martineau, appeared in two installments before the end of the month. In August, the English edition of *Household Words* carried a lengthy article on it; and in October the *Edinburgh Review* published a long piece, "Political Crisis in the United States," based on *Slave States* and half a dozen other current American books.* Finally, in November, the *Saturday Review* ran a flattering article on it; and the August London *Times*, which in those days noticed no more than a hundred books a year, recommended it as a work that would throw "new light on the workings of the slave system in retarding the legitimate progress of the south."[42]

How much influence Olmsted had on opinion in England would be hard to estimate. Through these journals, however, his ideas were spread before a considerable, and thoughtful, public; besides that, men were admittedly influenced by him in their view of the contention between North and South who were themselves greatly influential, among them John Stuart Mill, Charles Darwin, and John Eliot Cairnes. Nor can it be doubted that Olmsted expounded his

---

*Like most magazine journalism of the day, the article was anonymous. Any number of people knew, however, that its author was Hurlbert, Olmsted's associate on *Putnam's*; but probably nobody but Olmsted and his father knew how close the manuscript, committed to Olmsted's careless custody, had come to being forever lost before he personally delivered it to the editor of the *Edinburgh Review* (O to JO, 28 February 1856).

views often and well among the literary men he met, although that he did not always expound them persuasively is indicated by *Punch's* even-handed contempt for both sides during the ensuing war.

London that summer was the rendezvous of a number of Americans. The Bostonian Tom Appleton, a mediocre poet but a brilliant dinner guest, was sharing a house at Walton-on-Thames with William Wetmore Story, the successful lawyer and writer on legal subjects who was on the point of deserting his assured career for the uncertain rewards of sculpture. Bayard Taylor, the popular travel writer, was in town, and so was the engaging cad, Hurlbert. Richard Henry Dana, Jr., whose voice was now heard from the bar instead of the forecastle, was also in London, as, briefly, was Lowell. Olmsted, not neglected in favor of his better-known compatriots, had reason to be satisfied with his reception in the English republic of letters. The serious magazines paid serious attention to him; prominent publishers made consignments to his firm; William Henry Wills, intimate of Dickens and assistant editor of *Household Words*, asked him to contribute; and Thackeray invited him to dine.[43]

It was Thackeray's custom to have an informal dinner party for *Punch* at his home once a year. On the night in early August when Olmsted attended the annual celebration, there were present Mark Lemon, Tom Taylor, Shirley Brooks, John Leech, Percival Leigh, and Horace Mayhew, all contributors; Messrs. Bradbury and Evans, its financial supporters; and Story, Bayard Taylor, and Hurlbert. The Americans, with Tom Taylor and Thackeray, did all the talking; the others were rather slow, thought Bayard Taylor, who considered the affair genial but deficient in brilliance.[44] Olmsted, on the contrary, happily found his companions not only good men but jolly fellows and was especially gratified that the two publishers were "markedly polite" to him.[45] His keenest recollection of the occasion, however, was of his entering, correctly arrayed in the stiff white choker that was *de rigeur* for evening, Thackeray's drawing room, to find it full of informally black-cravated gentlemen and to hear his host exclaim: "Here comes Olmsted, in a *white* stock!"[46]

Olmsted met his family at Liverpool the end of July and escorted them on a leisurely eight-day journey to London. He entertained them there with sightseeing and opera and then piloted them to Dresden. By the middle of August he had deposited them there, having acted as their interpreter on the way—"the blind leading the blind," John Olmsted, not much impressed, commented—and he probably had had some fun out of his father's reaction to things German: the old gentleman was astonished to have seen not one double bed in Germany; "& what do you think a beefsteak is here? Why, it is *mince meat* made into the form of a *pancake* & then *fried*."[47]

But by the middle of August nothing could amuse Fred for long; he was consumed with worry over his firm's financial situation. When he left New York, it had seemed fair enough; Edwards had said that they had on hand some five thousand dollars that could be drawn on without inconvenience to the business.[48] Soon after Olmsted's arrival in England, he had been surprised to hear from his brother that the partners, pressed for funds, were seeking fresh capital. They had offered first John Olmsted and then John Hull Olmsted a special partnership in the firm for ten thousand dollars.[49] Both had declined. Curtis, next approached, was considering the offer.[50] At almost the same time, Olmsted, who had purchased some woodcuts on the firm's account and had them shipped to New York, received a brusque letter from Edwards telling him that the woodcuts were useless and had been sold at a loss and ordering him, in language a calm or sensitive man would not have used to his partner—or to his lackey—to make no more purchases on Dix & Edwards's account without their express permission.[51] Later placating notes from Edwards saying that Curtis had joined the partnership with ten thousand dollars capital, urging Olmsted to spend at least a year abroad to build up the foreign business, and telling him to forget about the woodcuts, there were no hard feelings, did nothing to mollify Olmsted.[52] Baffled and furious, he wrote Dix a stinging letter in early August, demanding to know why, if they had on hand the firm's five thousand dollars and Curtis's ten, they should be short of funds and upbraiding him for keeping him in the dark about their finances and for permitting Edwards to write him, over the firm's signature and as its spokesman, as if he were a very silly, junior, irresponsible clerk.[53]

Meanwhile, more disquieting news was coming from John. Fred's book was selling only slowly; *Putnam's* had fallen off alarmingly both in circulation and in merit; Edwards's arrogance had antagonized everyone in the office and only Dix's tact kept it going; and there was no demand for such English books as had arrived.[54] Worse news was to come.

At Dresden, Olmsted received two letters that made him literally sick with alarm. John's, written July 27, said that Dix had become suspicious of Edwards, who kept the firm's financial affairs close in his own hands; Fred should come home at once to support Dix in a showdown with Edwards.[55] Dix's letter, dated two days later, urged him to return but not to worry.[56]

Having already lost thirteen pounds from worry, Olmsted rushed back to London, arriving sleepless and agitated, "after a damned nasty 60 hours passage from Hamburg," on August 29. He found waiting at his hotel a letter from Dix —"confidential"—saying that Edwards had explained everything satisfactorily and canceling the summons home.[57] In a fury Fred dashed off an almost apoplectic note—". . . Write me in a fever of fear & trembling & what not one week —all going to the devil & no hot pitch to be had at any price unless I come home in my shirt tail to help you heat it & then next day—all as smooth & jolly [as] a summer's sea of champagne with icebreezes. Damn you for a high pressure hypochondriac . . ."[58]—before he could settle down to calm himself.

A few days later Fred received from Dix a long, lame explanation in answer to his angry letter of early August. Within a month of Olmsted's departure, Dix wrote, he had been amazed to find the firm was almost out of money and had learned from Edwards that a note of fifteen hundred or two thousand dollars "was lost sight of at the time and was not recorded in the right place and that all the money we had was gone." The matter had not seemed of "sufficient importance" to report to Olmsted, since Dix supposed the embarrassment was temporary. It was just then, when there was no money to pay for them, that the woodcuts had arrived from England, and Edwards had insisted on selling them and writing Olmsted the insolent letter that had so angered him. Far from condoning its tone, Dix protested, he had quarreled with Edwards and forced him to alter it. With the infusion of Curtis's capital, Dix had believed there was clear sailing, until Edwards fell ill and went to the country, and Dix found "another money blunder was made—same as before and *hence* my letter to you so full of trouble and sorrow and calling you home, but on Edwards' return he made all straight again." Dix nevertheless had had a "talk" with him, as a result of which Edwards "gave up everything to me except mere money matters and it remains to be seen if I succeed." Finally, Dix urged Olmsted to destroy his letter and suggested that, if Olmsted wished to write him confidentially, he place two letters in the envelope, one that Dix could show Edwards, the other the confidential one.[59]

In the same mail arrived an apparently open and friendly note from Edwards explaining some of the firm's transactions—none of them the ones Olmsted questioned—and again strongly urging him to stay a year in London.[60]

This time in sober anger, Olmsted answered Dix's feckless letter. Edwards, he said, had either cooked his accounts or made a gross, almost ruinous error— and, incredibly, repeated it within six months. How could Dix allow him continued control of their financial affairs? And how could the firm still be strapped when, so far as he could tell, Curtis's capital remained untouched? Moreover, when Edwards had written Olmsted abusive letters to draw attention away from his own mistakes, Dix had weakly let him get away with the maneuver, only preventing him from being as insulting as he might have been. Cowardly, too, was Dix's conduct in imparting his suspicions in "confidence"; refusing to do his duty himself, he prevented Olmsted from doing his, which was to insist on an explanation of Edwards's transactions and to warn Curtis. Demanding a complete, authenticated statement of their finances, Olmsted threatened that if it was not forthcoming he would report what he had heard of them to Edwards and Curtis.

"I can tell you one thing," he warned heatedly,

> I am not going to burn your letters. When our concern busts up as its likely to do right soon, if there is half the foul gas in it your letter would indicate, what other evidence have I that I have been imposed upon so shamefully? how can I else justify myself from the charge of obtaining property on false pretenses? . . .
> There is another reason why I cannot burn your letter. How could I ever justify myself to Edwards in case it should turn out someday that

it was you were the imposter & that you had led him into this position towards me, for purposes of your own, to conceal some mistake or knavery of your own instead of his having got you by the nose and making you make an ass of yourself?

Making a letter-press copy of his letter to Dix, he sealed it up with his letters from Dix and from Edwards. In case of the worst, he would have evidence in hand that his involvement in any hanky-panky was innocent. And he half expected the worst. "I do not see any reason to apprehend that we are at present near bankruptcy but I know nothing, absolutely nothing about it and I can not but look upon it as a very eminent possibility that we shall stand before the world as a pack of rascals," was his gloomy summation.[61]

There was nothing to keep him longer in England. In the circumstances, he could no longer solicit consignments from publishers; indeed, he could hardly look them in the face. Worse than the specter of bankruptcy, the prospect of failing to meet the obligations he had undertaken on the firm's account—obligations that he felt involved his honor—oppressed him.[62] Miserable and ashamed, he sailed for home the end of October, resolved to force a showdown with his partners and to resign from the firm.

By the time Olmsted reached New York, James Buchanan was president of the United States. He had been put forward by the Democrats largely because, absent in England, he had not had to take a public stand on the Kansas–Nebraska issue and so was not unacceptable either to northern or southern Democrats. He had, however, secured only a minority of the popular vote. The majority had been divided between Fillmore and Frémont in a proportion that indicated that the Democrats had nothing further to fear from the old Whig party and had a formidable rival in the new Republican party, which had carried New England, New York, and most of the Middle West. In New York City, however, the Democrats were still firm in the saddle; Fernando Wood had been elected by a comfortable majority to his second term as mayor. It was a majority procured, of course, by the various effective devices of Tammany, of which one was the promise of jobs to deserving Democrats on the new Central Park, where, after long delay, a little grubbing and clearing had got under way.

How his native land seemed to Olmsted on his second return from Europe he did not say; but to an intelligent young Irishman newly arrived it seemed, despite slavery and political corruption, full of hopeful, high-minded purpose. "I am far from pretending that the politics were all pure and the politicians all patriots," wrote Edwin Lawrence Godkin of that time. ". . . But the air was full of the real 'Americanism,' the American gospel was on people's lips, and was preached with fervor. Force was worshipped, but it was moral force; it was the force of reason, of humanity, of human equality, of a good example." The young journalist-lawyer met Olmsted soon after his arrival in the United States; for a time, while he studied law in Dudley Field's office, he studied American customs and institutions at Olmsted's knee and found him "a delightful expositor of nearly everything that puzzled me in American manners and politics."[63] Olmsted was living then, for the last time, at the farm. It was an anxious period for him; during it his satisfactions were few, his troubles heavy. He was trapped in Dix & Edwards, and John was failing.*

On his arrival home, Olmsted must have found the firm in less bad shape than he feared; he was persuaded to rescind the resignation he had drafted before he left England.[64] As the year neared its end, however, he again tried, vainly, to withdraw. Various writing assignments beckoned;[65] and he was sick of hearing Edwards, at the biweekly partnership meetings at which he was required to make a full financial report, ritualistically assure his associates that solvency was just around the corner: this, or that, or something else unexpected, had given them a temporary setback, but if they could just keep afloat past the first of the month, they would be safe and prosperous. Disgusted with the rickety business, Olmsted wanted only to stand from under.[66]

Not having enough to keep him busy in the office, he wrote a long introduction to Thomas Gladstone's *Englishman in Kansas*, which Dix & Edwards expected to publish in June; worked on a new book of his southern travels, *Journey in the Back Country*, installments of which, unsigned and without special notice, appeared in the *Tribune* from June through September under the heading "The Southerner at Home"; and indulged in the debilitating habit of late night work that was to undermine his health and make a desperate insomniac of him.[67]

John wanted to stand from under, too. He had no more heart for life on the farm, which he had never wanted to run in the first place. He had not been able to make it pay, even after his father had canceled all debts between them and made him a fresh loan. His hope of selling off lots, after a railway company was

---

*Olmsted was not too bowed down with care to enjoy occasional high-jinx and in March took part in an episode that in later years made him blush for his boyishness. Charming, shady Hurlbert, "really clever and alas! very peculiar, to say the least, in his view of the meum and the teum," borrowed for a particular social occasion the new pants of a young man who lived in his boardinghouse, Jim Carter, a brilliant lawyer whose total absorption in his profession precluded any tolerance of levity and destined him for the first rank of the New York bar. Hurlbert wore the pants not once but several times, and Carter, neglecting to mention that he had lent them in the first place, complained of his bereavement to some of his friends, among them Joe Choate, who was then at the threshhold of his legal career. It turned out that others, including Curtis, had similar complaints of Hurlbert. Olmsted, hearing of the charges, suggested that a Court of Honor be convoked to sit in the matter of Carter's pants. The Court, after a solemn hearing, handed down the opinion that Hurlbert had been justified in wearing the trousers once but at fault in wearing them again. All the young men involved were sufficiently prominent for the incident to gain some small notoriety. Hurlbert was more easily amused than abashed; but Carter, feeling that he had been made to look ridiculous and seeing nothing funny in a spoof on the law, never forgave its instigator. According to Mary Cleveland Olmsted, he was in after years "often heard to say that never would he shake hands with Olmsted" (MCO to "My dear boy," undated memo).

organized to serve the south side of the island, was encouraged when Brace bought about six acres for three hundred dollars an acre; it was soon dashed, however, by the prospective establishment of a new quarantine station at Seguin's Point. Finally, unable either to sell or to mortgage the place, John threw in his hand. He accepted five hundred dollars from Uncle Owen, gave Fred his power of attorney, and in the forlorn hope of recovering his health, left for Italy with his wife and children early in January.[68] Of his parting from his brother, Fred could only say bleakly, "I much fear that I shall never see him again."[69]

John's last year, however disappointing, had not been empty of accomplishment: while Fred was in England, he had worked Fred's Texas notes into book form,[70] and by the time he left the United States, *A Journey through Texas* was in proof. Fred, still keenly interested in Texas free-soil prospects, thought he saw in *Texas* a possible means of reestablishing the routed Free-Soilers. The book, without directly propagandizing for immigration to Texas, said much to promote interest in it; and it was Olmsted's hope that settlers would be lured by it from Kansas, from northern states, and from England, where factories were dependent on the southern cotton supply and statesmen and manufacturers were alarmed by impending shortages. He did not ignore the possibility of further immigration from Germany—*Texas*, translated into German, came out in 1857 and, according to the *Times*, received good notices—but he bent his principal efforts to stimulating it from England, playing down its antislavery implications and emphasizing its cotton supply aspect.

Although the *Times* abetted him editorially, Olmsted's scheme came to nothing. His several feelers—to Lord Goderich, member of Parliament for the West Riding of Yorkshire, to Delane, editor of the London *Times*, and to the recently formed cotton supply associations—were rejected and for good reason: English colonists going to Texas to form free-labor communities would be exposed not only to the usual hardships of pioneers but to border ruffianism; and for England to encourage, officially or unofficially, such a migration would create the impression that she was meddling in America's internal affairs.[71]

Although *Texas* was a failure as a stimulus to immigration, it was a critical success and within a month of its publication, in January 1857, it had even cleared three hundred dollars for the Olmsted brothers.* The numerous northern journals that reviewed it were almost unanimous in its praise; a rare dissent came from the proslavery *New York Commercial*, which said it was cleverly tailored to maintain its author's views. Another measure of its success was the hostility it provoked in the South. Middleton and McMasters, booksellers of Mobile, having innocently ordered a dozen copies, begged to return seven, pro-

---

*Fred and John had agreed that John, having done most of the work on the book, should receive two-thirds of the royalties (Laura Wood Roper, "Frederick Law Olmsted in the 'Literary Republic,' " *Mississippi Valley Historical Review* 39 (December 1952): 475).

testing they had had no idea it was abolitionist in sentiment and saying that there was "considerable objection made here" to it. *DeBow's Review*, while relying on it for some of the data for its lead article on Texas in its August issue, spitefully assailed Olmsted himself. Another extravagant personal attack came later from David R. Hundley, who, in his *Social Relations in Our Southern States*, ferociously castigated a "certain literary Peripatetic of New York, who has been in the habit of taking a jaunt through some portions of the South every few years and afterward putting in book-form an account of what he saw and heard." The *Southern Literary Messenger* disdained to notice *Texas*; it and *Russell's Magazine*, however, reverting to *Slave States*, took bitter exception to the *Edinburgh Review*'s "Political Crisis in the United States" and denounced both its sources and its anonymous writer, whom *Russell's* correctly identified as Hurlbert.

Texas enhanced Olmsted's reputation in England as well as in the United States. *Household Words*, the London *Times*, the *Westminster Review*, and the *New Quarterly Review* endorsed it, and the *Athenaeum* dropped its severity toward American writers long enough to say of Olmsted, "He has not only right on his side, but ever-blessed reason also, with happy common-sense enabling him to support both."[72]

While *Texas* was achieving a *succès d'estime*, Dix & Edwards was muddling its way toward bankruptcy. The books showed a margin of safety of eleven thousand dollars; but Olmsted stated the stock was overvalued by ten thousand dollars; and the firm was losing money, Edwards admitted to Curtis, at the rate of one thousand dollars a month.[73] "The terrible Nemesis of hap-hazard business comes daily nearer & at length begins to be recognized by other eyes than mine," Olmsted wrote his father a month after the publication of *Texas*.[74] The other eyes, presumably, were Curtis's; Dix was cheerfully making expensive plans on the assumption that someone would be green enough to lend them twenty-five thousand dollars, and Edwards intended to ask Francis George Shaw, Curtis's wealthy father-in-law, for the money. Scandalized at the thought of inviting Shaw to risk such a sum in a failing venture, Olmsted tried to block Edwards. Shaw, however, was a hard-headed philanthropist not given to unproductive benevolence; after a look at the books, he refused. "I am glad of it," declared Olmsted, who preferred a prompt to a protracted failure.[75]

The time was an uneasy one not only for the Dix & Edwards partners but for the whole business community, and the effects of overexpansion, speculation, and European war were beginning to be felt widely. Bankruptcy was becoming less a calamity than a commonplace, as the *Times*'s list, "Failures in the Country," grew gradually longer throughout the spring. To keep off it, Dix & Edwards underwent a metamorphosis: late in April, the two original partners resigned, leaving Curtis and Olmsted to form a new partnership with their printer, J. W. Miller, to whom Dix & Edwards owed a considerable amount of money. The new firm, Miller & Company, acquired all the assets and assumed all the obligations of its predecessor. In June, Olmsted was at length permitted to retire, and the firm became Miller & Curtis.[76] Shaw, in an effort to salvage Curtis's investment, entered it as a special partner with ten thousand dollars capital; and the partnership, thus reorganized and fortified, braced itself for the rough economic going ahead.[77]

Its prospects were not dazzling. Although the Dix & Edwards list, which it took over, contained Melville, R. H. Stoddard, and Greeley, it was Olmsted's opinion that his books and Curtis's were the only ones in the house worth a dollar.[78] The English imports included works of such dubious appeal to American interest as full sets of *Punch* and Chambers's *Cyclopaedia of English Literature*.[79] *Putnam's Magazine* continued to be profitable, but hard times had reduced its circulation from a peak of eighteen thousand seven hundred in April 1856 to fourteen thousand by the spring of 1857, and its earnings had declined accordingly.[80] It continued, however, valiantly to maintain its position as the most stimulating magazine in the country and spoke with vigor and good sense on controversial topics. But however stimulating, it could not sustain its tottering publishers. They would have had to be dogged by good fortune to stand firm while substantial houses crashed all around them, and good fortune did not dog them. On August 6, just three weeks after George Palmer Putnam failed, Miller & Curtis declared itself insolvent. "We have lost everything—but we have not made a misstep," Curtis, taking what comfort he could, wrote Olmsted. A fortnight later he gave Olmsted further particulars of the failure; and he concluded: "My dear copartner in the General Book Publishing business, I hope you are less & less bothered about it—that you keep comfortably, & hear the sea under your windows."[81]

Olmsted could indeed hear the sea under his windows, but its sound could not soothe a man so beset with troubles. He had again been disappointed in the farm: an offer of thirty thousand dollars, recently made for it, was abruptly withdrawn when the new quarantine station, built in June at Seguin's Point, was burnt down in July by its irate neighbors.[82] He was deeply chagrined by the publishing failure, so deeply that for the rest of his life he shrank from discussing it. And he was heartbroken by his brother's slow dying.

John had gone from New York to Havana, to St. Thomas in the British West Indies, to Southampton, thence to Paris, and on by mid-March to Sorrento, where his father anxiously awaited him. Together they went to Rome. After several months there, he followed his father, who was conscientiously sightseeing, to Geneva, where he arrived the end of June to settle down for some two months. All this travel had demonstrated that no sea voyage, no Swiss or Italian air, could arrest the course of his illness. His lung hemorrhages were more frequent; he weighed a scant hundred pounds; action, to which he forced himself, exhausted him; and depression sapped his spirit as much as disease. These melancholy developments, reflected in John's letters, which were alternately sad and wry, wrung Fred's heart.[83]

Yet, in the midst of distracting troubles, he found at hand the grand opportunity of his life and vigorously seized it.

XI
OPPORTUNITY SEIZED
August–November 1857

C HANCE lay in wait for Olmsted at a seaside inn at Morris Cove, Connecticut, to which he retreated early in August 1857 to work on *Back Country*. At tea one day, he sat beside a commissioner of the new Central Park, on which work had recently begun, who happened to mention that at their next meeting the commissioners intended to elect a superintendent; there were no candidates, he said, with whom he was much pleased.* Olmsted asked what the superintendent's duties were to be.

The commissioner explained that he would be director of labor and police under the engineer and would be responsible for enforcing the rules governing public use of the park. They were looking for a Republican but not a politician; the Republicans could do little without the aid of the reform Democrats and were ready to agree that the park should be managed free of politics.

Olmsted observed that a park so managed would be an excellent thing for New York. "I wish we had you on the Commission," said his friend, "but, as we have not, why not take the superintendency yourself? Come, now." Although the idea had not crossed Olmsted's mind, he caught at it. "I take it? I'm not sure that I wouldn't if it were offered me. Nothing interested me in London like the parks, and yet I thought a great deal more might be made of them." "Well," replied the commissioner, "it will not be offered you; that's not the way we do business; but if you'll go to work I believe you may get it. . . . Go to New York and file an application; see the Commissioners and get your friends to back you." "I'll take the boat tonight and think it out as I go," Olmsted told him. "If no serious objection occurs to me before morning, I'll do it." None did. When he reached New York next day, Olmsted set to work canvassing his friends.[1]

In 1857 not a city in the United States had a rural, spacious public park. Any city dweller who wanted to lie down on a bit of grass and look at the sky through the branches of a tree or to stroll on something other than a city street had to go into the country or to the town common, public square, or cemetery. The popularity of the newly developed rural cemeteries—Mount Auburn near Boston, Laurel Hill in Philadelphia, and Greenwood near New York—as places

---

*It was the impression of Olmsted's son, Frederick Law Olmsted, that the commissioner was Charles Wyllis Elliott, secretary of the first Board of Commissioners of Central Park, and Olmsted's friend of some years' standing (interview with FLO [son]).

of public recreation suggested that, by the middle of the nineteenth century, there was a keenly felt want in this country for public parks and gardens such as Londoners, Parisians, and some Germans had long and freely enjoyed. Many of the European parks had developed in historic circumstances foreign to the new country: originally the hunting preserves and gardens of royalty, they had gradually come to be open to the public for recreation so that the public's use of them had slowly evolved from a privilege to a recognized right. Others had developed when it began to be realized around the beginning of the nineteenth century that commercial advantage lay in reserving space for a park in the midst of building lots. In London, Regent's Park was an example of this latter class; Green, St. James, and Hyde parks, and Kensington Gardens, of the former.

A strong feeling, too, was manifest in England as early as the 1830s that cities lacking parks should have the lack remedied, and a Select Committee was appointed by Parliament "to consider the best means of securing Open Spaces in the vicinity of populous Towns, as Public Walks and Places of Exercise, calculated to promote the Health and Comfort of the Inhabitants." Birkenhead Park, near Liverpool, was a landmark in this movement. New cities in the colonies, too, such as Wellington and Adelaide, were laid out with special provision for public walks and parks.[2]

In Germany, the conscious movement to create municipal parks antedated the English by a decade or so; and the Bois de Boulogne in Paris was undertaken soon after Central Park. Olmsted, trying in 1880 to account for the rise of the park movement in different countries at about the same time, concluded rather lamely:

> Parks have plainly not come as the direct result of any of the great inventions or discoveries of the century. They are not, with us, simply an improvement on what we had before, growing out of a general advance of the arts applicable to them. It is not evident that the movement was taken up in any country from any other, however it may have been influenced or accelerated. It did not run like a fashion. It would seem rather to have been a common spontaneous movement of that sort which we conveniently refer to the "Genius of Civilization."[3]

Midcentury New York was ill endowed with open space for recreation, although there had been agitation for an adequate park at least since 1785, when someone signing himself "Veritas" addressed a letter to the mayor and aldermen suggesting that the Battery be improved and the Fields, formerly a common and by then a public nuisance, be reclaimed for a park. In 1853, sixty-eight years after Veritas's proposal, the Battery, the City Hall Park on the site of the Fields, the dozen or so squares, and the few little downtown triangles on Manhattan island contained, among them, merely one hundred seventeen acres. This meager acreage represented not an advance but a shrinkage: the street plan of 1811 had provided for four hundred fifty acres of parade ground and squares, and although the parade ground proposal had been dropped, there had been in 1838 a total of one hundred seventy acres in planted open spaces. Even before that date, William Cullen Bryant, the first influential advocate of a large public park for New York, had been privately discussing the desirability of securing one while there was still open land to be had; and on July 3, 1844, he published in the *Post* his first editorial on the subject, "A New Park." A visit to London the next year whetted his enthusiasm, and from then on the *Post* repeatedly labored the topic. Downing, in the *Horticulturist*, became a constant, able advocate of a large rural park comparable to those he had admired in Germany and England.[4]

Partly because of the *Post*'s persistence, the park question was injected into local politics, and in 1850 both candidates for mayor, Ambrose C. Kingsland and Fernando Wood, advocated the project. On April 15, 1851, the victor, Mayor Kingsland, addressed a message to the Common Council urging them to take prompt action to secure a park while suitable land at reasonable prices was yet available and cannily assuring them that such a park would be "a lasting monument to the wisdom, sagacity and forethought of its founders." Thus lured, the Common Council's Committee on Lands and Places recommended the taking of Jones' Wood, a fine wooded tract of one hundred fifty acres on the East River stretching from Sixty-fourth Street to Seventy-fifth Street and west to Third Avenue. After the New York legislature authorized taking the wood on July 11, 1851, opposition to the proposed park quickly developed; the most telling point was that the selected tract was too small. Downing contended that five hundred acres was the smallest acreage that should be considered; Bryant, who had first proposed the Jones' Wood site in 1844, argued that not only it but an additional tract near the center of the island should be taken.[5]

In early August, the Board of Aldermen appointed a committee of two to study the suitability of the Jones' Wood site and to determine if another might be more appropriate. The committee strongly urged a more central site, and the aldermen accepted its report. On July 21, 1853, the New York State legislature finally authorized the city to acquire the central site, now Central Park, and at the same time again passed the act for taking Jones' Wood. Opposition to two parks was so powerful, however, that the following year the Jones' Wood Act was repealed; the waterside woodland, ideal and irreplaceable for park purposes, was lost to the city as a recreation ground and was condemned to obliteration under pavement and buildings. When the New York Supreme Court, however, on November 17, 1853, appointed five respected New Yorkers as commissioners of Estimate and Assessment to take land for Central Park, their fellow citizens could rightly feel that a long step forward had been made toward providing them with the first fine rural park in the United States.[6]

For more than two years the commissioners labored; their report, confirmed by the Supreme Court on February 5, 1856, awarded the owners of city lots taken for the park $5,069,694. And for more than two years, the park's enemies tried to whittle down its area. In 1854, the Committee of Public Lands of the Common Council, and a year later the Board of Aldermen, adopted a measure to cut off its lower end and to reserve a strip four hundred feet wide along Fifth Avenue and Eighth Avenue for residence sites. By then Fernando Wood, a Tammany man, had again achieved the mayorality; disreputable or not, he is to be recalled with gratitude for vetoing this move. Thanks to him, the park entered upon its development with its territory intact.[7]

Its development, however, was inhibited by political frictions and lack of funds. The state legislature failed to provide for the management of the park; the Common Council, therefore, on May 19, 1856, named the mayor and his street commissioner, Joseph H. Taylor, commissioners of the Central Park, with full authority to plan and improve it. The commissioners, committed to Tammany, could not command public confidence; to secure it, they named seven reputable citizens—Washington Irving, George Bancroft, James E. Cooley, Charles F. Briggs, James Phalen, Charles A. Dana, and Stewart Brown—as a consulting board to attend their meetings and to help them decide on a plan. A plan, in fact, with the topographical survey on which it was based, was already at hand, the work of Egbert L. Viele, a West Point graduate of the class of 1847 and a veteran of the Mexican War. Viele, since resigning from the army as a first lieutenant of infantry in 1850, had been in the practice of civil engineering in New York City; he had undertaken the park survey and plan in 1853 without pay and on his own initiative on the chance that he would be suitably compensated eventually. His reward seemed at hand when the commissioners adopted his plan early in June 1856 and appointed him engineer-in-chief at a salary of twenty-five hundred dollars a year.[8]

Viele had the job and the salary, but he had only a miserly amount of money to do the work: the legislature struck the Central Park appropriation from the tax bill, and the Common Council appropriated only one hundred thousand dollars for the use of the commissioners and whatever money the rent or sale of buildings on the park site might bring. His hands tied by insufficient funds, Viele was able to do little for the year after his appointment but clear. The conspicuous lack of progress did not enhance public confidence in Tammany's handling of park affairs; so the legislature, which was dominated by Republicans, on April 17, 1857, removed the park's management from the Democratic mayor and the city government and confided it to a board of commissioners supposedly nonpartisan, independent, and willing to supervise the work for the love of the thing.[9] The skepticism that this move aroused was reflected in the *Times*'s comment: "The Central Park is to be laid out by Commissioners, who are not to receive compensation (except what they steal), and to be completed as speedily as possible."[10]

The new board was composed of eleven members: Tammany Democrats, reform Democrats, and Republicans, who had a majority of one. For its supplies, it had to appeal to the Common Council, which, dominated by Wood's partisans, was disposed to be obstructive. Obstruction, however, was a politically dangerous indulgence: citizens were eager to see some progress made on the park that had already absorbed more than five million dollars of their tax money; and the working population, as failures spread and unemployment grew, was avid for the jobs that construction of the park would throw open. While the Democrats fulminated against the tyrannical usurpation of power at Albany by which the Republicans had seized control of the park with the intention of plundering the city against the will of the local majority, the new board of commissioners deflected their charges by electing James E. Cooley and Andrew H. Green, both reform Democrats, president and treasurer, respectively, and reappointing Wood's whole engineer corps, headed by Viele.[11] It was at this point, when compromise and accommodation among factions were imperative if work was to be started and voters were to be placated, that Olmsted decided to apply for the superintendency.

When he got back to New York from Morris Cove, he moved from the island up to town and devoted himself to canvassing for the job.[12] Since his activities in recent years had brought him into contact with men of prominent and various affairs, he had no difficulty in collecting a number of imposing sponsors. Asa Gray wrote a letter for him. James Hamilton drew up a brief petition and got Dudley Field, Peter Cooper, and Washington Irving, among others, to sign it. Greeley and Russell Sturgis were among a half-dozen men to set their names to another appeal. Olmsted's own petition had a list of almost two hundred signatures, among them those of William Cullen Bryant, Albert Bierstadt, Whitelaw Reid, Willard Parker, August Belmont, James Brown, George S. Schuyler, Bayard Taylor, Hiram Barney, and Morris K. Jesup. In it, Olmsted emphasized that he was skilled in the management of agricultural labor, that he had been engaged in the direction of farm laborers and gardeners for the past ten years, that he had studied most of the large British, French, German, and Italian public grounds, and that he had given special attention to the policing of parks and to the economical employment of labor on them.[13] Notwithstanding these facts, the commissioners and the engineer knew him best as a literary man; they wanted a "practical" man, and they were doubtful that a man existed so gifted as to combine in himself a literary and a practical faculty.

The outcome of Olmsted's application appears to have been entirely in doubt when the commissioners held their meeting to select the superintendent on September 11. A city surveyor, a builder of Fifth Avenue houses, a son of President Nott, of Union College, a son of Audubon, and Olmsted were contenders. During the long meeting Olmsted waited nearby in Kapp's law office and passed the anxious time in writing a letter about the state of his affairs to his brother. When the good news was brought to him, he scribbled:

> After a very long session and much debate, I am elected: on the final vote, 8 of those present voting for me, one against me.* Elliott and Green

---

*Thomas C. Fields, a Tammany man whom the diarist George Templeton Strong characterized as "that wretched pickpocket."

128

(Pres. Bd. Education) being my determined advocates. The strongest objection to me, that I am a literary man, not active; yet if I had not been a "literary man" so far, I certainly should not have stood a chance. [14]

Anomalously, it had been the endorsement of Washington Irving, then America's most venerated literary figure, that overcame the commissioners' apprehension that Olmsted was rather too literary to be practical.[15] His salary was set at fifteen hundred dollars a year.[16]

Doubt of the literary man's ability to direct gangs of laborers may have been put to rest on the commission; certainly it was not in the park. When Olmsted went there to report for orders to Viele, Viele summoned a Mr. Hawkin— "he is what I called a practical man," the engineer said ominously—to show him the work in progress. Hawkin appeared coatless, with his trousers tucked into the legs of a pair of heavy, muddy boots and seemed surprised when Viele told him to escort Mr. Olmsted, the new superintendent, over the park. "Now?" he asked. Viele looked at Olmsted, who said, "I am quite ready, sir." "Yes, now," Viele answered. "In truth," Olmsted later wrote, "as I had intended this to be rather a call of ceremony or preliminary report to my superior officer, I was not quite so well prepared as I could have wished to be for what followed."[17]

What followed was, simply, a hazing. Hawkin led his neatly dressed victim through the nastiest bogs on the site. Since they were full of the overflow from pigpens, slaughterhouses, and bone-boiling works, they stank horribly in the muggy September heat and were very nasty indeed. During the long course of the afternoon, Hawkin uttered only one remark not strictly required by his assignment. Pausing as they waded out of a knee-deep slough to watch Olmsted scrape the smelly, unctuous slime off his legs against a stump, he remarked: "Suppose you are used to this sort of business?"

"I believe," Olmsted observed,

> that he was some years my junior, and it is probable that I had been through fifty miles of swamp to his one. There was not one operation in progress in the park in which I had not considerable personal experience, and he spoke with apparent gravity; nevertheless I felt very deeply that he was laughing in his sleeve, and that I was still a very young man.

He had the impression that not only his conductor but the foremen and workmen he met were almost openly amused by the idea of being directed by him. One foreman, to whom he was introduced as the new superintendent, remarked: "Oh, that's the man, is it? Expect we shall be pushed up now." He laughed, and his gang, who had stopped work to stare at the newcomer, grinned. There were then more than five hundred men, in perhaps fifteen gangs, working on the park. Almost all were Democrats and had been appointed by a Democrat, Viele, who owed his original appointment to Wood. Most of the workmen had been recommended to Viele by Democratic members of the Common Council, and each knew that his patron had recommended him, not because of any special fitness he had to serve the city on the park, but because of services that he was expected to render at the coming election. In the circumstances, it was clear that when the foreman pleasantly remarked that he supposed they should be pushed up now and his men smiled at the suggestion, it was because the idea that the new superintendent might expect a day's work from them for a day's pay seemed a good joke. "For several days," Olmsted observed, "there continued to be something that stimulated good humor in my appearance, and in the inquiries and suggestions which I made as I walked from gang to gang, feeling my way to an intelligent command of the business. It was as if we were all engaged in playing a practical joke."

Olmsted's amused subordinates could hardly have discerned in the slight young man whose orders they expected to flout an unfledged but formidable executive. Perhaps no one could have. Nothing in his record—a farmer who had not made his farms pay, a writer who had made nothing but reputation, a publisher who had gone bankrupt—suggested his capacities. They had usually gone unsuspected, except perhaps by Brace and his brother John, who, loving and fathoming him, thought he held a promise of greatness; and they had had, so far, little more than routine challenges to evoke them. A thoughtful reader of Olmsted's books, however, might have suspected their writer of the vision to grasp complex problems, the acuity to analyze them, the balance to see the whole and the parts in proportion, and the discipline and imagination to devise solutions; but his park associates had no reason to suppose that the unassuming little man who was the new superintendent would quickly convert the anarchic and sometimes turbulent work force into a model of discipline and efficiency.

Olmsted's achievement was the more striking since, when he took charge of the largest public work in New York, public order there was in dark eclipse. It had been declining all through the 1840s, when a million and a half European immigrants had poured into the city, many of them to crowd and stagnate in its sordid and degrading slums. There gangs, native and foreign born, fought and slaughtered each other; in better neighborhoods footpads, pickpockets, prostitutes, and beggars operated busily; at fires, companies of volunteer firemen brawled with rival companies and other rowdies. Gang members, firemen, criminals, each with his vote to sell, had palpable influence in the political organizations of the city, especially Tammany Hall, and were little disturbed by the police. The state government, moving finally in June 1857 to curb some of the local administration's much-abused powers, sought to replace the corrupt police with a new force under five commissioners appointed by the governor; and the governor appointed a new street commissioner. Lawlessness for a time increased: Wood and his police defied the new police commissioners and threw the new street commissioner out of City Hall. Even after the authority of the new police was established, order was not: on July 4 the Dead Rabbits, an east-side gang, attacked a Bowery saloon and precipitated two days of murdering violence in which other gangs and members of the old police enthusiastically joined; and less than two weeks later an armed mob, alleged to have been mostly recent Irish immigrants, attacked the police. In both instances the militia had to be called.

These disturbances pointed to grievous conditions of dense ignorance, cruel poverty, reckless despair—conditions that were then aggravated by a far-reaching catastrophe, which had been slowly building, the panic of 1857. It struck Wall Street the end of August with the failure of the Ohio Life Insurance and Trust Company of Cincinnati, which had a New York branch, and promptly and painfully made itself felt throughout the economy among the wealthy along with the poor.

"You can scarcely have a conception of the ridiculous straits of men who are ordinarily flush," Olmsted wrote his father soon after he became super-intendent. "I heard a fellow yesterday offering 6 pct. a month for a hundred dollars." Olmsted's own straits were worse than ridiculous; in debt for his horse, his horse's board, and his own lodgings, he had to borrow from Elliott, Godkin, and Uncle Owen and was, even so, "confoundedly bothered" for lack of a hat, shoes, and a coat for outdoor work.[18] The unemployed, carrying placards reading "Bread or Blood," demonstrated by the thousands in Tompkins Square, at City Hall, and in the park, where they presented Olmsted with a list of ten thousand men alleged to have starving families and demanded immediate employment for them. Mayor Wood, in a tight race for reelection after a glaringly scandalous term, allowed them to believe that, if elected, he would distribute park jobs like alms among them. After his defeat, the park commissioners, in a serious effort to stretch the park work as far as possible, several times during the desperate winter ordered the entire labor force discharged and a new one taken on. This tactic rotated employment and had the incidental benefit of freeing Olmsted, to a limited extent, to select workmen on the basis of competence instead of political pull.[19]

Olmsted was for several months too busy with his new duties—ditching, draining, grubbing, tearing down fences and squatters' shacks, removing stone— to give much thought to his late failure. Curtis, however, was angrily threshing in the toils of the law and writing indignant letters, signed "Justice," to the New York papers on the iniquity of the legal proceedings brought against Miller and Curtis by their largest creditor, the Boston paper manufacturers Rice, Kendall and Company: they were trying to hold Mr. Shaw on a technicality, not as a special partner liable only to the extent of his investment in the firm, but as a general partner responsible for the full extent of its indebtedness.[20] Olmsted took little part and only reluctant interest in the matter. He got William Emerson to represent him and resignedly awaited the outcome.[21]

To his father, who protested that he did not understand the process and the grounds of the failure, he admitted that he did not really understand them him-self.[22] John Olmsted was just becoming aware of the serious character of the financial crisis. Before realizing its gravity, he had breezed about Europe, run-ning into globe-trotting friends wherever he went—Bayard Taylor in Frankfort,

Mrs. Stowe and her sister Mrs. Perkins in Marseilles and Rome, the Aspinwalls in Sorrento—and had traveled, with an alert curiosity and an easy mind, from Switzerland to Germany to Holland to England to Scotland. By the time he reached Edinburgh, however, at the end of September, he was becoming alarmed about the panic and thinking of cutting his tour short. Traveling with his wife and keeping the children in pensions and schools were costly; he was bearing young John's heavy expenses, which had been augmented when, on August 10, a new baby, Owen Frederick, "slid into the world, without apparent means of support, shouting like a well-to-do Irishman at a fair";[23] and by the first of the year he would be six thousand dollars in debt to Peabody's, with, unexpectedly, little money to pay it and little hope of raising any. "I think had I heard in London that things were continuing so bad in America I should have given up Scotland and journeying any more," he anxiously wrote Fred. Fred's successful application, of which he learned September 28 when he picked up a *New York Evening Post* in a Glasgow coffee room, was a comfort in the midst of worries and elicited a typical admonition: "You will, of course, be cautious not to give offense in your new position and particularly careful in your accounts if there are any to keep."[24]

Over both father and son, however, there hung a threat far more oppressive than financial reverses—John's sinking health. The ailing doctor, not having improved in Switzerland, was en route to the Riviera for the winter and at the beginning of October was resting in Paris. He knew it was in vain that he dragged himself about Europe searching for a restorative climate, he hated his transient's life, and he wanted above everything to go home; nevertheless, he scarcely knew why, he was on his weary way to Nice. His father's nearness had buoyed and consoled him for months, but that comfort was about to flee: John Olmsted had decided to sail on the *Commodore Vanderbilt* November 14 from Le Havre. Young John was desolated when his father wrote him not to wait in Paris to say good-by but to go south at once. "It seems a thousand pities we are so near each other not to meet," the sick man mourned. "I wanted to cry a bit about it."[25]

If this wistful complaint shook John Olmsted's resolution to return home promptly to his neglected affairs, his son's succeeding letters steadily eroded it. The trip to Nice had been a horror, John reported, his exhaustion so overwhelming that he had had to stay in the carriage and let Mary deal with customs. "It was a real blow to me, to give up my natural duties—it seems next to getting bedridden."[26] And from Nice Mary wrote of a wretched hotel full of fleas; of the new English doctor who said it was the worst possible climate they could have sought out; of wet, cold, dreary weather; of John's helpless, hopeless longing for home. Her last letter to her father-in-law as he was about to sail told of John's sudden, shocking decline: his breathlessness, his constant cramps in back and legs and sides, his painful palpitations, his prostrating weakness. "This is but sorry news for a good-bye, but so it is," stoically concluded the young woman who was prepared to find herself, within days, a widow.[27]

John Olmsted could not bear it for a good-by; he canceled his sailing and hastened to Nice, arriving late the night of November 17. Young John by then was bedridden, wasted, and resigned to die. A few days earlier he had written, in a hand tremulous with weakness, his farewell letter to Fred.

> Dear dear Fred
>
> It appears we are not to see one another any more—I have not many days, the Dr says.
>
> Well so be it since God wills it so. I never have known a better friendship than ours has been & there can't be a greater happiness than to think of that—how dear we have been & how long we have held out such tenderness.
>
> I am kept wild with opium & am so weak that I suffer from many little things. I cannot comprehend this suddenness—but I see it. I can hardly be got out of bed & have no breath.
>
> Give my love to the boys. I want you to keep something of mine—my watch or cane or something & give something to C. & . . .* of some sort.
>
> Don't let Mary suffer while you are alive.
>
> God bless you
>
> John H. O.[28]

All their lives each had been the other's dearest friend; each had considered his interests, his joys, his problems, his duties as interchangeable with his brother's. Now, John, with his clear last injunction, "Don't let Mary suffer while you are alive," transferred to Fred his dearest responsibility.

At seven o'clock in the evening of November 24, after a day during which he had been utterly weak but free from pain, John died. He was buried two days later in the Protestant Cemetery on Castle Hill. To Fred his grieving father wrote: "In his death I have lost not only a son but a very dear friend. You almost your only friend."[29]

In John's death Fred lost something more, and more intimate, than his father realized: his youthful self. The ardent, open-hearted young man who had frankly longed for a wife to love, who had eagerly shared his amatory and religious emotions with a dozen friends, who had lavished affection and advice on the girls and boys he cared for, who had embraced one calling after another with fresh, headlong enthusiasm—who had, in fact, been very slow in growing up—this young man, who depended for his exuberant existence on the perfect sympathy of the brother who was his confidant and alter ego, under the burden of heavy sorrow was crushed out. After John's death, Fred's boyish high spirits

---

*Possibly "Clt," which might be an abbreviation for "Clint." Clinton Collins was a classmate and close friend of John's.

were transmuted into a rational even temper. His open-heartedness gave way to a reserve bordering on remoteness. His hasty ardors came to be replaced by a permanent, dedicated enthusiasm for his new work; and the sometimes elusive inner light by which he always tried to guide himself took on the steady, unmistakable glow of duty. Bowed down by grief, he so immersed himself in his work for a time that it threatened to become his life until a curious but comprehensible turn of events restored a normal balance between his professional and his personal life.

XII

THE COMPETITION AND THE PRIZE

December 1857–June 1859

ORK on Central Park threw Olmsted into close association with the man who was to exert the determining influence on his professional life: Calvert Vaux. Born in London in 1824, Vaux had been graduated from the Merchant-Tailors School and apprenticed to George Truefitt, a prominent London architect. His talent, promise, and enthusiasm won an almost fatherly interest from Truefitt so that he supplemented his young assistant's office training with trips about England to study fine examples of architecture. Vaux, enthusiastic from childhood about the parks of London, became interested in the public recreation grounds he observed in other English cities; and at the age of twenty-one he went to the continent to study some of the great examples of royal parks and gardens there.[1]

In the summer of 1850, when Downing was in London, Vaux met him. One of Downing's motives in visiting England was to find a well-trained architectural assistant, and he found the young man he wanted in Vaux. Vaux accompanied him to America in the fall and was installed as his assistant in his Newburgh office. Within a few months he became his partner. Taking root, Vaux in 1854 married Mary McEntee, sister of Jarvis McEntee, a painter of the Hudson River School. After Downing's death in the summer of 1852, Vaux, as the youthful inheritor of his practice if not quite of his mantle, carried on the work of Downing's office until he moved to New York in 1857. He was intensely interested in the progress of the park for which his patron had agitated, but he thought that Viele's plan for it, marred by "manifest defects," could result only in a work that would disgrace both the city and Downing's memory.[2]

He was in a position to make his views felt, since he was well acquainted with two members of the board of commissioners of Central Park. He had known Charles Wyllis Elliott, who had been a friend of Downing's, for half a dozen years; and he had built a large house on Fifth Avenue for John A. C. Gray, a prosperous New York merchant, who had been so pleased with his architect that he secured for him the commission to design the building of the Bank of New York, of which Gray was a director.[3] Conceivably, Vaux influenced the decision of the commissioners, made at the same meeting at which they appointed Olmsted superintendent, to lay aside Viele's plan and to hold a public competition for designs for the park.

Intending to enter the competition himself, Vaux invited Olmsted to join him in preparing a plan. The two men had first met at Newburgh during

Downing's lifetime,[4] and they had had some contact later in New York when Vaux considered buying a few acres of Fred's farm and building a villa;[5] the Seguin's Point quarantine troubles, however, had put him off, and he instead took a house on Eighteenth Street in New York. If he had any intimation of Olmsted's latent genius for landscape design, he did not record it, but he was admittedly influenced by the fact that Olmsted, as superintendent of the park, was daily on the ground and could provide "accurate observation in regard to the actual topography which was not clearly defined on the survey furnished to competitors by the Board."[6]

Olmsted at first hesitated to accept Vaux's invitation, feeling that his entry into the competition might be interpreted as a slight by his superior, Viele. When he consulted Viele, however, the engineer told him that he didn't care whether he entered or not, in terms so little friendly that Olmsted's scruples on his account vanished.[7] By the middle of January 1858, he was at work on a plan with Vaux. By that time, too, he had got his force of a thousand men into "a capital discipline"; and his standing with the commissioners was so good that they raised his salary to two thousand dollars.[8]

The rules of the competition specified that each plan should provide for certain features: at least four fairly direct east-west crossings between Fifty-ninth Street and One hundred sixth Street, a parade ground of twenty to forty acres, three playgrounds of three to ten acres each, a site for an exhibition or concert hall, a site for an ornamental fountain and one for a prospect tower, a flower garden of two or three acres and a design for it, and a place that could be flooded in winter for skating. Cost was to be held to the one and a half million dollars allowed by the legislature.[9] Given the fact that all the designers would be working with the same specifications and the same terrain, all the plans were bound to have many features in common; their differences would depend on how they solved the problems.

These were essentially two: artistic and social; and they were without any precedent in this country. First, the planners had to form a work of landscape art on an intractable piece of ground; this meant creating charming passages of scenery, varied yet coherent in theme, on a large and largely barren rectangle that featured few and scrubby trees, poor soil, numerous rocky outcroppings, and stagnant morasses. No natural feature of the site as it stood was beautiful; anything beautiful on it would have to be created, literally, from the ground up. They had, moreover, to adjust the whole work to the rest of the city, to order it in every particular to enhance the convenience of city living: to devise easy approaches to it and to control the circulation of traffic through it, to make accessible its scenic and recreational features, and to secure the comfort and safety of its visitors.

Second, the designers had to provide for judicious use of the park, inducing the public, including the so-called dangerous classes, to treat a work of art, delicate and perishable in many of its features, with a thoughtfulness that would preserve it from harm and its visitors from inconvenience. Since it was to be open and free to everyone, great tact and firmness would be required to enforce a desirable standard of behavior without resort to burdensome restrictions. Olmsted considered this social problem of equal importance to the artistic one.

The competition offered premiums of two thousand, one thousand, seven hundred fifty, and five hundred dollars for the four best plans; its closing date was April 1, 1858.[10] Vaux and Olmsted, who had to work nights on their design because their days were occupied with their professional work, presented their plan, "Greensward," on the last day.[11] The thirty-three competing and two non-competing plans were put on view in a room over the bookstore of Stanford and Delisse, at 637 Broadway.[12] According to the *Times*, the commissioners, unwilling to rely entirely on their own judgment, had invited Edward Kemp, who had worked with Paxton on Birkenhead, and "some person" connected with the Bois de Boulogne improvement to advise them. "Now with some dozens of American competitors for plans, and the advice of an English landscape gardener and a French engineer, we fear that there is small chance for the realization of that grand and simple ideal which the popular mind has so long fostered in connection with the Central Park," the paper brooded editorially;[13] and it predicted that the commissioners would not adopt any one plan in all its details but would take such features as they considered desirable from the four plans selected for premiums.[14]

The winning plans were announced on April 28: Olmsted and Vaux took first prize with Number Thirty-three; Samuel I. Gustin, superintendent of Central Park planting, second; Miller and McIntosh, two employees in the superintendent's office, third; and Howard Daniels, an architect, fourth. The *Times*, approving the winning design, wrote:

> There can be little doubt that in its essential features the plan of Messrs.
> Olmsted and Vaux embraces all the leading requisites of a great Park . . .
> adapted not only to the nature of the particular grounds in question, but
> to the prospective wants of our City also . . . we fortunately possess in
> Mr. Olmsted a Superintendent capable of carrying out our wishes, and
> honest enough to be safely entrusted with our interests.[15]

The descriptive report that Olmsted and Vaux submitted with their plan explained that their intention was to create contrasting and varying passages of scenery, all tending to suggest to the imagination a great range of rural conditions.[16] This style was dictated as much by the nature of the ground as by the popularity of the English school of landscape gardening. The northern end of the tract, between the reservoir and One hundred sixth Street, had slopes of a sweep and breadth suggesting pastoral treatment, "the highest ideal that can be aimed at for a park under any circumstances." The lower section, more heterogeneous, had as its most prominent feature a long, rocky, wooded hillside south of the reservoir. The central and western parts were irregular tableland; the eastern section had pleasing undulations adapted to lawn or gardenesque treatment; and the south end, generally rugged and having several bold rocky bluffs, had as well some agreeable flat meadows.

This varied surface lent itself admirably to the formation of a work of landscape design in the natural style. The great difficulty was to minimize or debar, in the finished product, discordant urban elements, especially the rushing commercial traffic that increasingly, as the city expanded, would have to cross the long narrow obstacle of the park to get from one side of town to the other.

In their report Olmsted and Vaux described the leading features of their plan and mentioned the basic consideration that had controlled it: that this public work, unlike the City Hall, the Customs House, even the Croton Aquaduct, should be adequate to the demands made on it not only presently, by a city of less than a million people, but years thence when, they daringly imagined, Manhattan Island might have a population of two million. With this prospective growth in mind, Olmsted and Vaux, alone among the contestants, dealt adequately, brilliantly, with the twofold problem of accommodating cross-park traffic and keeping it clear of pleasure traffic: the four transverse roads, required by the terms of the contest, they sank beneath the general level of the park; and they provided three more, less direct, surface roads across it. Thus business traffic, wanting the most direct passage from one side of the park to the other, would not interfere with the more leisurely pleasure traffic, which would pass over it on bridges; and its hurly-burly would not even impinge on the peaceful scenery. Thus, too, direct passage across the park would be provided for the hours after dark when the park itself would be "useless for any good purpose," since even in London, with its admirable police arrangements, experience had shown that safe transit could not be assured the public through large parks after nightfall.* Having kept cross-town traffic entirely separate from pleasure, the landscape architects applied the same principal of separation of ways to pleasure traffic itself: the carriage roads passed over bridle paths and footpaths on bridges, and footpaths and bridle paths did not cross each other.

Vaux and Olmsted, each equally responsible for the design, were appointed to carry it out. On May 17 Olmsted, in recognition of the fact that all duties were to fall to him that were not specifically those of the designers—that is, the duty of employing and directing labor and of policing the park—was named architect-in-chief at a salary of twenty-five hundred dollars a year.[17] His newly created office absorbed both the superintendent's and the chief engineer's. Viele,

---

*Neither Olmsted nor Vaux would claim credit for any individual feature of the plans on which they collaborated, including the sinking of the transverse roads. The sight of a fire engine dashing across the park is supposed to have suggested to them the need for some radical solution to the problem of nonpleasure traffic; and the solution may have been inspired by the underpass at the Regents Park Zoo, which, built before 1850, was surely known to both of them.

his plan superseded and his position abolished, was offended and angry and threateningly insisted that Olmsted and Vaux had plagiarized his plan and that the commissioners were legally obligated to pay him for it.[18] More immediate trouble, however, was the action of two new commissioners, August Belmont and Robert Dillon, who proposed a number of amendments to the winning plan that, in effect, would have superseded it. Foremost among them were the proposals to divide the park from north to south by two straight lines of trees, except where the reservoirs interfered, and to abolish the sunken transverse roads on the ground that never in the future would there be enough cross-town traffic to justify the expense of building them. All the amendments were carefully discussed by the board. Fortunately, their advocates were outvoted on the commission and not supported by the public. The designers were authorized to proceed according to their winning plan, and the *Times*'s forebodings that incoherence would be the leading quality of the park landscape were quieted.[19]

The collision with Belmont and Dillon was an early illustration of the third problem the designers of Central Park had to cope with: the problem, essentially political, of maintaining their own integrity and that of their plan under constant pressure to grant favors and to make changes not compatible with honest management or good design. While the artistic and social problems that faced them in creating the park were difficult, they were soluble; this third problem was Hydra-headed. For instance, the previous December the Board of Aldermen had threatened to cut off Central Park funds and had harrassed the commissioners and superintendent with an investigation because they had not honored the aldermen's promises of patronage—by which, of course, they were not at all bound;[20] and Belmont and Dillon, though defeated in the commission, carried their disagreement to the press, and Dillon published criticism of the winning design replete with misrepresentations in the *Tribune*.[21] The election of Daniel F. Tiemann, Wood's reform rival, at the end of 1857, did little to relieve routine political pressures: so many politicians still gave so many "deserving" henchmen recommendations for jobs that there were multitudes more applicants than positions; and Vaux and Olmsted had to steal out upon the ground by moonlight to discuss their plans free of importunate job hunters.[22] There was no end to the accommodations demanded and to the pressures invoked to force them by people both prominently placed and humbly. These fell more heavily on Olmsted, as the employer and director of labor, than on Vaux.

Notwithstanding harassments, the work progressed with speed and order. In June Olmsted had about a thousand men at work, in September twenty-three hundred, in October twenty-five hundred, and in November two thousand. By December, when rain and cold made it necessary to lay off most of the men, this large force had accomplished an impressive amount of work. A seven-mile stone wall enclosed the site. Thorough drainage of the section below the old reservoir was almost finished, under direction of the talented sanitary engineer, George E. Waring, Jr. The drive in the same area was graded; portions of it had been constructed by different methods to test their comparative cost and efficiency; and ground for the drive above the reservoir was being cleared. Bridle paths were in progress and several miles of footpaths had been completed. The promenade, paved and bordered by transplanted elms twenty years old, was nearly finished, and the fourteen-acre cricket and baseball ground west of it was graded and ready for turfing in the spring. Two bridges to carry the carriage road over the bridle paths were well advanced;[23] designed by Vaux and built of olive-colored stone from Nova Scotia and dark red Philadelphia brick, they were much admired. A great variety of planting had been set out and the effect in the Ramble, though unfinished, was already charming. The lake above Seventy-sixth Street was ready to be filled and awaited the first hard freeze to offer New Yorkers the unusual opportunity to ice-skate. Twenty to thirty barrels of powder were for a time used daily in blasting, and precautions to avoid injury in this operation were so nearly perfect that not a man had been hurt in a year. "Most admirable order prevails through the Park grounds," the *Times* reported. "The Police regulations are strictly enforced, and the whole work is so perfectly systematized that everything proceeds with the quiet regularity of a private establishment."[24]

This admired result owed much to a specific quality of Olmsted's. The strong habit of discipline and subordination, which got him, unflogged, through his grueling term as a seaman, led him not only to obey properly constituted authority even when it was vested in a man like Captain Fox who abused it; it led him, further, to require obedience when he was in authority. The exacting discipline and close supervision with which he directed his subordinates were allied, however, with calculated trustfulness; Olmsted thought that the way to cultivate responsibility in a man was to lay responsibility upon him: a man trusted was, usually, a man whose aroused pride stimulated his best efforts. Olmsted was aware that not everyone on the park would respond to such confidence; there were bound to be some inefficient, lazy, and disorderly men among them. Those he discharged.

So thorough was his respect for lawful authority that he could as little bear to have it infringed from above as ignored from below, but he was too realistic to stand four-square on his own every time a commissioner invaded it. He had a large work to advance under delicate political difficulties, and he would yield on nonessential points rather than antagonize a man whose resentment might hamper the park's progress. Alderman Brady's man may well have got a job after Olmsted received the following hint from his friend Commissioner Elliott:

June 6, 1859

My dear Sir:

I have had an interview with Alderman Brady respecting the placing of a man on the Park. He feels that other members of the Board have had more of this kind of patronage than he has; and he complains that his man has been put off in a troublesome way. I think he said he had not a single foreman or assistant on the Park while other members of the Board have three and four each.

Mr. Brady seems to be an influential and sagacious man, one whom it is hardly worth while to offend—unnecessarily. Will you try to see me on Monday about it? I think as the matter stands Brady deserves consideration.

Your truly
(Signed) Charles W. Elliott[25]

New York, during the summer of 1858, had several causes for bounding pride. Its park was arousing widespread interest; not only New Yorkers but visitors from distant parts of the country were coming to study and admire it. The rich in carriages, the poor on foot, equally enjoyed its emergent charm; Olmsted was proud of it as "the first real park made in this country—a democratic development of the highest significance. . . ."[26] In addition, Saint Patrick's Roman Catholic Cathedral, a huge white marble edifice with stained-glass windows from Chartres, designed to be the grandest essay of the Gothic Revival, was being built on Fifth Avenue. And some of the city's leading businessmen, among them Cyrus Field, Peter Cooper, and Moses Grinnell, had with the aid of similarly enterprising Englishmen triumphantly realized a brilliant, visionary scheme: after several years of tremendous efforts and staggering disappointments, they finally succeeded in linking the old world to the new with the Atlantic cable. When their success was announced on August 6, the city's rejoicing was exuberant; the news was on everyone's tongue, and the papers proclaimed the opening of a bright new era in international understanding. On August 16, Queen Victoria and President Buchanan exchanged messages to celebrate; a huge parade was held in New York, in which eleven hundred Central Park workmen with their eight hundred carts, marshaled by Olmsted and two foremen, were a conspicuous unit; and fireworks flew so thick and hot that the roof of City Hall caught fire.[27]

The official celebration on September 1, just before the cable broke down, to remain out of commission until after the Civil War, was the occasion, however, for a harsh reminder that barbarism, even at the break of that hopeful day, did not lag far behind progress: while the governor, the mayor, and the highest law-enforcement officers of the city toasted the cable at a banquet at the Metropolitan Hotel in Manhattan, a mob of Staten Islanders, incensed by a recent outbreak of yellow fever at Tompkinsville, burned down every building but the main hospital and the health officer's house at the principal quarantine station there. Next night they returned and finished the job.[28]

Barbarism did not lag far behind progress, and it lurked in other hearts than arsonists': the island's elite endorsed the crime. William and Cornelius Vanderbilt went bail for half a dozen of the accused incendiaries. Judge Emerson and Francis Shaw were on the committee that presented a report justifying the arson to a meeting called to discuss it. George William Curtis eloquently moved the report's acceptance, and the affirmative vote was unanimous. When a local judge discharged the confessed ringleaders six weeks later, he had the overwhelming weight of public opinion behind him.[29]

It took the health officer, who had lost his home, his hospitals, and some of his patients, to denounce the mobsters for "infuriated devils," and an off-islander, the diarist George Templeton Strong, to pinpoint their meanly mercenary motive:

> This riot, robbery, and arson, and murder, this outrageous assault on men and women struggling against smallpox and yellow fever, was in fact a mere operation in real estate, a movement which Staten Islanders consider justifiable for the sake of ten per cent increase in the market value of building lots.[30]

As an operation in real estate, the arson miscarried, if its effect on the Olmsted place is any indication. In April 1857, shortly after his brother left for Europe and six months before the panic, Fred had rented the farm for eight hundred dollars a year. In 1858, when it fell vacant, Mary Olmsted, having returned to the United States, moved with her three children into her old home. She stayed only until October; and when Olmsted rented the place in April 1860, he had to accept three hundred dollars plus one-quarter of the market price of the fruit for it.[31] The panic, of course, had much to do with the diminished rental; but a few touches of arson had done nothing to offset its effects, nor had they been any remedy for the island's real drawbacks—its wretched ferry sevice, its lack of central municipal organization, and the inadequacy of its inland transportation.

Olmsted left no record of his view of the "quarantine war." Indeed, he left little of his thoughts and hopes during his first two busy years on the park. The profuse correspondent was almost lost in the emergent artist and planner who had, at the very nadir of his fortunes, unexpectedly stumbled upon his métier. The only surviving hint of his personal plans was their consummation, unless one can regard as a hint Mary's move in October 1858 to a rented brownstone on Seventy-ninth Street between Third and Fourth avenues, an easy walk along the paved and lighted street from Olmsted's office in the park.[32] Perhaps the quarantine disorders drove her from the island; perhaps she was lonely and haunted in the old farmhouse; perhaps she wanted her children more closely under their uncle's affectionate supervision; perhaps she and Fred already shared a more personal reason. One is tempted to suppose they did, since eight months later on June 13, 1859, they were quietly married by Mayor Tiemann in the Bogardus House on Central Park.[33]

So came to an unexpected, happy end Fred's long and troubled search for a wife and love.

CENTRAL PARK, THE PUBLIC, AND POLITICS

June 1859–February 1861

W HEN Vaux led Olmsted into the practice of landscape architecture in 1858, the profession in this country was embryonic. Its tradition was small, and the term itself was not yet in use, "landscape gardening" being still the accepted one. Its practitioners concerned themselves with the "embellishment" of country seats and suburban residences, the laying out of grounds around public buildings, and the development of rural cemeteries. Many of the outstanding private places owed their charm to the taste and talent of their owners; professional landscape gardeners were few. The dean of them, Downing, in his classic *Treatise on the Theory and Practice of Landscape Gardening* first published in 1841, stated that the only practitioner of any note up until then had been André Parmentier, who emigrated about 1824 from his native Enghien to Brooklyn, where he opened a nursery.[1] Before dying six years later, Parmentier laid out a number of places along the Hudson River including Hyde Park, then the seat of Dr. David Hosack, and several in the South and in Canada.[2] ". . . We consider M. Parmentier's labors and examples as having effected, directly, far more for landscape gardening in America than those of any other individual whatever," Downing declared.[3]

Among the few landscape gardeners practicing when Vaux and Olmsted won the Central Park competition were Robert Morris Copeland, Horace W. S. Cleveland, and Charles Follen, of Boston,[4] and Alexander Jackson Davis, the New York architect who had been a friend of Downing's and who was one of the creators of Llewelyn Park. Follen and Copeland were unsuccessful entrants in the Central Park competition, along with Viele, who was a civil engineer rather than a landscape gardener. The winners of the second, third, and fourth premiums seem to have been little known or distinguished in the landscape field; and a noncompeting entrant, Ignatz A. Pilat, an Austrian who was supposed to have designed Prince Metternich's grounds, was engaged on a botanical survey of the Central Park site. In the Midwest, Adolf Strauch was gaining recognition for his work on Spring Grove Cemetery in Cincinnati; and while the art of landscape gardening was alleged by a contemporary writer, G. M. Kern, to be flourishing in the Mississippi region, most of the "many representatives" he refers to remain unidentified.[5]

Outside of Downing's contributions, the literature was scant. His writings, however, were greatly influential and his popular *Treatise* went through four editions before his death and six after, the last appearing in 1921. His friend and editor, Henry Winthrop Sargent—whose place "Wodenethe" on the Hudson Downing had termed a "bijou"[6]—remarked in the 1859 edition: "There has been no one since Mr. Downing's death who has exactly filled the niche he occupied in the public estimation. . . . There is no one, we think, whose judgment and opinions would have, at this moment, such decided and marked influence in all matters of rural taste, as the late Mr. Downing exercised at the time of his death."[7] Indeed, no one ever did fill Downing's "niche," certainly not Olmsted or Vaux: these two, between them, redefined the profession. They gave it a scope and stature far beyond the modest elegance of its standing in Downing's time, advancing it from a polite art oriented toward horticulture, which could be competently practiced by skilled and intelligent amateurs, to an exacting professional discipline embracing various aspects of the arrangement of land for human use and enjoyment. They came to occupy a position too commanding to be called a "niche."

With Central Park, Vaux and Olmsted stood at the beginning of the life work that was to raise them and their calling to recognized professional standing. Olmsted understood well that this first essay in the creation of beautiful and extensive landscape for public enjoyment was an important departure for the art in the United States, making its benefits available not to a privileged few but to citizens generally.[8] Whether or not it was generally so recognized, the park received wide and warm public appreciation from the first. The throngs who entered it at varying seasons to ride, drive, ice-skate or boat, attend the semiweekly band concerts, or roam about on its footpaths were evidence of its huge popular success and of its immediate influence on the habits of a large population that had never before had opportunity for such recreations.[9] Newspaper comment was overwhelmingly favorable, although carping or partisan pieces occasionally appeared. New York's professional, intellectual, and wealthy people used the park as much and with as much enjoyment as the less privileged. It would take forty years of slow growth before the park would realize its designers' vision; yet almost from the beginning it established itself in the consciousness and the hearts of New Yorkers. Appropriately, as it was doing so the word "park" appeared for the first time in an American encyclopedia: Olmsted wrote the article for the 1861 edition of Appleton's *New American Cyclopaedia* at the solicitation of his friend Dana, who was one of the editors.[10]

Promptly recognized for their Central Park work, Vaux and Olmsted moved at a single step to the forefront of their profession. Within two years of starting on the park they had a growing practice; they were engaged to furnish plans for laying out eighteen hundred acres of rugged terrain in upper Manhattan and designs for the grounds of the Hartford Retreat, the Bloomingdale Asylum, the New Rochelle residence of the unfortunate ship owner, E. K. Collins, and Parke Godwin's country place at Roslyn, Long Island.[11]

If Central Park was satisfactory to the public, it was immensely so to Olmsted. Of its design he confidently made the sweeping prediction "that the park will not only be more convenient for exercise than any existing metropolitan pleasure-ground, its details more studied, more varied and substantial in character, but that there will be greater unity of composition, details being subordinate to general effects, than in any other."[12] He considered his responsibility for the park's artistic success indivisible from Vaux's; other aspects he held to be almost exclusively his own. "As to the organization and management of the work," he wrote Brace, "I think it more creditable to me than anything I have done publicly."[13] It was his responsibility and his special pride that his skillful training of the public in the use of the park had confounded the prophets who had predicted it would be an immense bear garden, overrun with ruffians, and unfit for women, children, and gentlefolk. From the beginning he had clearly defined its limits and treated all the ground so that it could not escape notice that the park site even where unimproved was distinctly different from the surrounding open land and should be used differently. As the design came to take shape on the ground and one section after another was thrown open for use, the role of park keepers and police assumed great importance. Carefully selected and trained by Olmsted, they were required to perform all their duties scrupulously and courteously. The public was almost insensibly led from the beginning of Olmsted's tenure as architect-in-chief to treat the park with solicitude and each other while in it with respect.[14]

This beautiful success was achieved in spite of pressures so severe that Olmsted, weakened by a bout of typhoid in the spring, lapsed two months after his marriage into a serious illness largely induced by the acute fatigue and agitation to which his position—and it must be admitted, his disposition—exposed him. He was relentlessly pursued by demands for patronage impossible to grant and almost impossible to refuse without inviting reprisals; and Andrew Haswell Green, one of the two commissioners who had vigorously supported his candidacy for superintendent, was taking on the role of his *bête noire*.

Green, a handsome man whose Roman head was covered with close-cropped black hair, was a lawyer in Samuel Tilden's firm. Born in 1820 in Worcester, Massachusetts, he had early contracted a love of nature and a taste for landscape at Green Hill, his family's estate there.[15] After studying law in Tilden's office and being admitted to the New York bar in 1844, he had begun to interest himself in civic affairs. He had been a member of the board of education in 1854 and its president two years later. Named one of the eleven Central Park commissioners in 1857, he was treasurer of the original board, became president of it next year, and on September 15, 1858, became comptroller.[16] His new office gave him absolute control over all park expenditures, and he exercised it absolutely. He delegated none of it, put no confidence in his subordinates, and dominated in most instances the judgment of his co-commissioners through his superior knowledge of park affairs. He was devoted to the park, and he was rigidly honest. He was also rigidly stingy.[17] Well-to-do, presentable, prominent, still he was a bachelor. It was as well: if he had brought to bear on a family his strong constitutional distrust of all honesty and capacity but his own, he would have made life as miserable for his dependents as he did for his park subordinates.

He was not an ill-natured man, but an aura of grudgingness overcast even his good nature. When Olmsted, soon after his marriage, asked permission to move with his family into an unoccupied suite in the old convent at Mount St. Vincent on the park, Green replied that he saw no reason "sufficient to induce the Board to deny the use of such part of the house as might be necessary for your family to you. On the contrary it might be attended with advantages."[18] The tone of Green's notes to Olmsted was frequently worse than grudging: it was testy, peremptory, and slighting; and he scarcely masked his conviction that Olmsted was flighty and extravagant and required close watching. His distrust and his penuriousness bore excruciatingly on Olmsted, whose tendency always was to be liberal of confidence and money; small wonder that the yoke of this suspicious and miserly faultfinder galled increasingly.

Olmsted strove to behave toward Green with scrupulous subordination and paid for his smothered exasperation in sleeplessness, digestive upsets, and headaches. In September 1859, his exhaustion became so severe that he had to take a short vacation at Saratoga Springs. It did him little good; on his return he was incapacitated again for a week—"worn out, used up, fatigued beyond recovery," he lamented to his father. His domestic circumstances were not bracing either: Charlie's eyes were bad, Charlotte was suffering from a plague of boils, and Mary, who was pregnant, was half frantic with sick children, ailing husband, and "she-devils" for servants. Nevertheless, his new family was already a standing source of joy to him, and even in detailing their miseries Olmsted could add: "However we have a good deal of happiness between the drops: that's a fact."[19]

He was still ill when, on September 23, 1859, the park commission voted him a six-week holiday and five hundred dollars to go abroad and study European parks.[20] Five days later Olmsted sailed for England on the *Persia*. He was sped by a scolding from Vaux.

> Upon my word, Olmsted, I will not forgive you if you do not make a better show. Who will be tempted to a study of nature and the polite arts if the best paid and most popularly appreciated professors cut such a lugubrious, sallow, bloodless figure as you insist on doing? I consider that the only thing to be really regretted in our last two years' operations is the absence of jollity; because you see there are so many aspects of comicality in the whole affair.[21]

Green, whose aspect of comicality eluded Olmsted, surprisingly dispatched him with a kind word: "I think you will rather be able to give information to Parks than get it from Europe."[22]

The weather was fair, the *Persia* fast. Although Olmsted complained of having the worst stateroom on the ship, he still admitted it was the best steamer passage he had ever made.[23] Landing at Liverpool on Saturday, October 11,

Olmsted revisited Birkenhead Park, this time getting full particulars of its construction, maintenance, and management. The following Monday he was in Birmingham, inspecting the sewerage and filtering works with the engineer in charge, visiting Aston Park with its superintendent, and calling on the mayor to get data on the policing of the park. Next day he was at Chatsworth to see the duke of Devonshire's park and gardens and the private grounds of Sir Joseph Paxton, creator of Birkenhead Park and the Crystal Palace. Wednesday he went to Derby, where he studied the Arboretum; Thursday he returned to Birmingham to visit the Botanic Garden; and Friday he spent in the Royal Park and Forest of Windsor. Reaching London early Saturday morning, he passed the day in the west end parks. On Monday, he introduced himself at the Office of Works of Her Majesty's Palaces and Parks, where his reception was unexpectedly gratifying: orders were issued to all London park superintendents to place themselves at his disposal whenever he should call, and the documents and plans in the office were opened to him. With his way thus made easy, he studied London's public parks for the next two weeks.[24] During the same time he managed also to see some of his friends, to comb booksellers' shops for rare books and maps on landscape work, planting, and engineering, and to pay his respects at the American legation where he made the acquaintance of a United States army major named Irvin McDowell.[25]

The two weeks in London were followed by two in Paris, where he had useful conversations with Adolphe Alphand, director of the Department of Roads and Bridges, under which the suburban improvements of Paris were being carried on. He visited all the pleasure grounds and promenades in Paris and nearby including the parks at Versailles and St. Cloud and the Bois de Vincennes and went repeatedly to see the work in progress in the Bois de Boulogne, often with John Bigelow, vacationing editor of the *New York Evening Post*.[26]

On November 11 Olmsted was in Brussels, where he spent the day at the Horticultural and Zoological Gardens with the directors. The next day found him at Lille, inspecting the gardens, parade ground, and promenade. That night he set out for London, where he spent another crowded week. He presented a letter of introduction to Sir William Hooker, who was expecting his visit; he met Samuel Parsons, the Long Island nurseryman, who was abroad on a purchasing expedition, and helped him select trees and shrubs for shipment to Central Park in the spring; he obtained detailed instructions from Sir Richard Mayne, commissioner of police, on the recruitment and management of London's celebrated police force; and he revisited the London parks and went to several public and private grounds out of town. The following week he saw the park of Elvaston Castle, reputed to have the finest plantation of evergreens in Europe; Trentham, seat of the duke of Sutherland, which he thought had the best private garden in England; Biddulph Range, a private place noted for its rockwork; Stoneleigh Abbey, an ancient park; the Botanic Garden at Manchester; and several other less well-known parks and gardens in the Midlands. On December 2 he crossed to Ireland and next day reached Dublin, where he visited Phoenix Park and the Zoological Garden. On the fourth he went to Cork and on the fifth sailed from Queensland for home on the *America*.[27]

"Let health and repose be *the first thing*," Green, temporarily benevolent and unconsciously ironic, wrote the traveler.[28] Olmsted's repose hardly could be promoted by so hectic a tour or by the news that had reached him of Central Park developments. His good friend George E. Waring, the engineer responsible for the novel and important work of installing the park's drainage system, his assistant A. J. Dallas, Vaux, and Mary Olmsted all wrote him long letters; scarcely one but was critical of Green. He had ordered the planting done in an impossibly short time and was winding up the season too soon. He was pushing the roadways too fast for good construction. He was parsimoniously skimping final touches on the careful finish of which costly effects depended. His demand for a list of all those employed in Olmsted's office had left Olmsted's staff quaking, sure that it portended discharges; poor Dallas, "nervously looking forward every day to some unseen coup by Mr. Green," did not even dare offer his services to Mrs. Olmsted, his position was so unpleasant and doubtful. Green had attempted to get control of employment from Olmsted but had encountered one of his rare defeats on the board. He was likely to show up before 9:30 in any part of the park; after he left there was a "general unbuttoning," and the whole force from top to bottom did less work under his suspicious eye than under Olmsted's liberal policy of trusting something to the men's sense of honor and duty.[29] Waring's temperate summation was:

> Your successor at the helm does not know much of human nature. Of course he means well but he is so cross & crabbed that all with whom he comes in contact wish him to the devil a dozen times a week. This remark does not refer to me, of course, as I talk with him every day & see some good nature left in him; but he cracks his whip over good & bad indiscriminately, and is not generally beloved therefore. . . .[30]

Mary Olmsted was kept busy listening to the grievances of her husband's colleagues. "They are all they say shaking in their shoes—as they have been ever since you went away," she wrote Olmsted. "They come to me and complain in the most naïve manner as though it were a compliment to you." For Olmsted she had a realistic word: "If you feel you can trust Mr. Green's generosity, stay until you feel quite well—and do not work yourself up in the absurd manner to which you are given—I must confess he frets me with his manner of thinking himself so much more efficient than you or anyone else."[31]

Olmsted reached home the week before Christmas to find his family comfortably established in the convent suite the commissioners had allowed him. It was warm, with a glassed-in gallery where the children could play in bad weather, and had that comparatively novel luxury, a water closet. The rats displaced from the razed shanties on the park were kept under control by the dutiful ferocity of the cat and the dog. The children's health was better, and Mary, although she had been ill off and on, was in good spirits. The "she-devils" had been replaced by a good cook and a good maid, and Olmsted's office was about to be moved from the farmhouse at the end of Seventy-ninth Street to rooms in the convent. Olmsted himself was fairly well and able to work steadily. "Altogether as happy, all of us, as you can possibly imagine," he assured his father. "What they'll do at Albany I don't know," he added, referring to a current legislative investigation into the park management, "but have not much fear—at all events they can't destroy the present, which is ours."[32]

Within the next few months Olmsted was totally routed from this pathetically cheerful position. The vexatious inquiry, inspired by a disgruntled former park commissioner, dragged through the summer and cost him scores of weary hours he could ill spare preparing data to be presented at the hearings.[33] Green, his brief benevolence spent, kept a burning eye on every penny. He would not authorize the spending of a few dollars to caulk a new bridge; therefore it could not be opened to foot traffic, which, barred from crossing it, clustered at its approaches and trampled costly plantings. He complained that the draughtsmen were using too many pencils and cut off their supply so that they had to buy their own in order to continue working. He returned a bridge estimate to Olmsted's office "with four certificates of its correctness on its face. An examination here has detected an error in it which please have corrected and return here." The error was of one dollar. When he found that a laborer, despite the manifold precautions to prevent such errors, had been paid twelve dollars for time that had in fact been passed in jail, he offered Olmsted a ponderous rebuke and a succinct statement of the philosophy that guided his life: "Although an error is not a crime, yet in money matters it is a very serious affair."[34] Olmsted, the competent and honorable director of a great public work on which millions of dollars of tax money were being honestly and economically expended, seethed at being constantly nagged like a frivolous schoolboy. Asperity crept into his answers to Green's letters, and his health again began to suffer.[35]

His own finances, too, were a source of worry. He, Curtis, and Dix had liabilities of about twenty-four thousand dollars as a result of their publishing failure,[36] and Olmsted's share of eight thousand dollars looked immense to him now that he was supporting a wife and a growing family on a salary of four thousand dollars a year. Fortunately Shaw, a large creditor and a sympathetic one, had been buying up some of the other creditors' claims at a discount and was willing to estimate the partners' debt to him at their cost instead of their face value. Olmsted had to pay his debt out of savings from his salary, since the farm was the property of John's children, and Mary's small capital was in a trust fund; he was able to make a start on his indebtedness to Shaw by assigning to him all his rights, estimated by Judge Emerson as worth five hundred dollars, in

Journey in the Back Country, which he had somehow managed to finish. The book was to appear the beginning of August under the imprint of Mason Brothers.[37]

But his pestiferous worries all were joyously eclipsed on June 14, 1860, when at dawn while the birds were waking a son, John Theodore, was born to Mary.[38] Joy, however, was fast dispelled by disasters.

On August 6, Olmsted, trying a horse he was thinking of buying, drove Mary and his infant son in an open buggy to the north end of Manhattan. On the way home, on the west side in the neighborhood of One hundred fifty-fifth Street, the mare, tormented by flies, caught one rein under her tail and bolted. Olmsted stood up to free it. The mare dashed around a corner, catching and smashing a wheel on a lamp post. Olmsted was flung out against a rock, and Mary, clutching the baby, was spilled from the tipsy vehicle farther along the block and dragged by her skirt until it tore free. Still clasping the uninjured infant, she staggered to her feet and rushed to her husband. He was lying in the road unable to get up; the end of his shattered left thigh bone was sticking through the cloth of his trousers. As a crowd gathered, Mary hurried to the nearest house and begged permission to have her husband carried in. The lady of the house, quickly sympathetic, took charge of John Theodore and ordered a shutter taken down. Olmsted, fainting with pain and sure he was dying, was laid on it and carried to a bed. When he was conscious again, his wife told him where they were: they had been taken into the home of Charlie Trask, whom Olmsted had not seen in many years, and Mrs. Trask, whom he had never before met, was the woman so prompt to aid him.[39]

The next day Olmsted was taken home, ominously, on a bier. To the consulting doctors, among them Willard Parker, the conveyance seemed barely premature: they doubted that he would live. They talked of amputating his leg, with its knee damaged and its thigh broken in three places, but decided against the radical measure: Olmsted was so run down and weak that amputation would surely kill him; left alone, he might live a week.[40]

The rugged vitality that had carried Olmsted through near-fatal illness on the China coast again came to his rescue; instead of dying on schedule he began to mend. But little John Theodore, wonderfully unscathed in the carriage accident, suddenly fell victim to a common killer of young children: just a week after the accident he died of cholera infantum.[41]

Bereaved and crippled, Olmsted yet presented a stoic face to the world. He was no stranger to sorrow, and untimely death had been part of his experience since childhood. The sympathy, attentions, and delicacies showered on him and probably the enforced rest helped to sustain his morale. In a month he was scribbling penciled notes to friends; and in two, he was being driven by his wife about the park in a phaeton with a board across the seat and supervising the work.[42]

As his strength came back, so did his passion for his work. When the young prince of Wales, convoyed by Mayor Wood and other officials, drove through

Central Park on October 12, Olmsted made all the arrangements; no one thought to introduce him, but his efforts were pleasantly acknowledged when the royal visitor, whose courtesy was enchanting even the most rigidly republican of his hosts, made it a point to catch his eye and bow.[43] Soon afterward Olmsted, still splinted and bandaged, was hobbling about on crutches and entertaining guests. When Mary went away over Thanksgiving, he enjoyed a visit from George Schuyler, whom he found "an ardent and happily confident Republican,"[44] undisturbed that an ungainly Illinois lawyer named Lincoln had whisked the Republican nomination away from the favorite, William H. Seward. A couple of days later he entertained the actress Charlotte Cushman and the sculptress Emma Stebbins at lunch in the park. "C.C. offered me a private box whenever I could come to the theatre," he told his father. "Wife being away, I fall among the Bohemians. As she goes to Boston it averages right."[45] It was during Mary's absence, too, that he became well acquainted with a man who was soon to become a close associate, the popular Unitarian minister, Henry Whitney Bellows.[46]

Bellows was forty-six years old then. Born in Boston, he had studied at Round Hill under George Bancroft and had been graduated from Harvard at eighteen. After teaching school at Cooperstown, New York, and living in Louisiana as tutor to the son of a wealthy planter, he had returned to Harvard to attend Divinity School and had been ordained in 1837. Older churchmen of his denomination regarded him as immensely promising; and from his first church, in Mobile, Alabama, he had been called in 1839 to the First Unitarian Church in New York. Thus he found himself, in his midtwenties, minister to one of the largest and most affluent Unitarian congregations in the country, automatically a man of consequence in the religious life of New York; he quickly made himself prominent in its social and civic life as well. Success, having come to him early and easily, had given him a manner ebulliently confident and guilelessly self-satisfied; he enjoyed turning phrases, and his speech was mellifluous and elaborate. He was, however, by no means all façade; he was a man of driving energy, quick to turn it to useful social purposes and brilliantly successful in engaging others in them with him, although not businesslike in handling the routine of the enterprises he inspired.

Bellows, Olmsted knew, had been watching the park from its beginning. When James T. Fields, wanting an article on it for the *Atlantic Monthly*, asked Olmsted to recommend a writer, Bellows was one of several men Olmsted mentioned as fit to write the piece.[47] After Fields gave the assignment to Bellows, Olmsted invited him to spend a day with him in the park. There had been much ignorant puffing and ignorant denigration of the work; ever keen to have its social implications recognized, Olmsted hoped that Bellows would clearly emphasize "how strongly experience in the park argues against certain political and social fallacies commonly entertained of its moral influence."[48] Bellows replied that he had watched with interest and satisfaction the progress of the park "both as a work of art and as an experiment on the people and our democratic institutions" and thought he understood the "politico-moral aspects" of the work.[49]

Bellows's appreciation of the moral aim and success of Olmsted's park work* was matched by his appreciation of Olmsted's books. *Back Country*, he said, "cannot but have a marked influence on public opinion, and to contribute anything to the settlement of this vexatious national question, ought to satisfy the moral ambition of the best man."[50]

If *Back Country* had a "marked influence on public opinion," it was an indirect one. Its sale was small, exhausting only one edition; but its critical acclaim was considerable and the more warm for Olmsted's continued moderation in the climate of accelerating crisis. He still opposed immediate abolition, still favored the continued subjection of the Negroes in the South to the whites, still advocated gradual and compensated emancipation, and still wrote in a composed and reasonable tone.[51]

Curtis described *Back Country* as "the heaviest blow (being true and moderate) that has yet been dealt at the system. It shows conclusively what a blight it is, but at the same time how difficult and distant the remedy seems to be." Friedrich Kapp dedicated to Olmsted his new book on slavery in the United States, written to win the German-American vote to the Republican Party, and freely acknowledged he had borrowed his conclusions from Olmsted. James Russell Lowell told his readers in the *Atlantic Monthly* that no more valuable contribution to American history had been made than *Back Country* and the preceding volumes. Charles Eliot Norton, as yet unacquainted with Olmsted personally, called his books "the most important contribution to an exact acquaintance with the conditions and result of slavery in this country that have ever been published. They have permanent value, and will be chief material for our social history whenever it is written." Newspaper notices in the North were generally favorable, although not as numerous as for the previous books.[52]

Again, the South could take little satisfaction in English response. The *Westminster Review*, the *Athenaeum*, and the *Saturday Review* all treated *Back Country* with rare enthusiasm; Charles Darwin, a close student of Olmsted, called it "an admirable picture of man and society in the Southern States"; and the *Times* concluded from it that the South would be ill advised to attempt secession and suggested that "a new edition of the whole series would be an addition to our economic science, as well as a help to a better knowledge of the difficulties of our American kinsmen."[53]

The *Times*'s comment appeared on December 8, 1860; by then the American difficulties it referred to had moved past hope of peaceful settlement, Olmsted believed. "We intend to have two republics, peacefully if we can, fighting if we must, don't we?" he inquired of Brace that same day. "But my mind is made up for a fight. The sooner we get used to the idea the better, I think."[54]

---

*Bellows's article, "Cities and Parks; with special reference to the New York Central Park," appeared in the *Atlantic Monthly* for April 1861.

This realism, though not universal, was scarcely clairvoyant. After John Brown made his attempt on Harper's Ferry and Virginia made a martyr of him, North and South had become, finally, irreconcilable. As the presidential nominations approached, the southern radicals, who were vindictively determined to thwart the selection of the one widely popular Democratic candidate, Stephen A. Douglas, had virtually assured the election of whatever Republican should be nominated. When the Republicans nominated Abraham Lincoln, the southern fireeaters threatened to take their section out of the union if he was elected. Pledged to leave slavery undisturbed where it existed, Lincoln was also pledged to its containment, which meant its eventual extinction. When he was elected, the southerners moved to carry out their threat. South Carolina was already on the point of secession; and Mississippi, Florida, Alabama, Georgia, and Louisiana were preparing to follow her lead. The prospect of war was growing clearer almost hourly. Rumors of treasonable conspiracies to seize Washington and paralyze New York with riots were beginning to circulate. They reached Olmsted soon after the New Year. Preston King wrote him that the schemes of disloyal secret organizations in the capital had been frustrated by the new cabinet, purged at last of the disunionists who had long surrounded the president, and by the vigor of General Scott's preparations to defend the city with regular troops.[55] George Templeton Strong reported that William T. Browne, the Englishman who was editor of the just defunct *Washington Constitution*, was privy to a plot to raise a mob to loot the homes of prominent New York Republicans. Strong put enough faith in the charge to go out and buy a gun. If Olmsted believed it, it must have appalled him. He had known Browne when he was on the *New York Journal of Commerce* and had thought well enough of him to offer him a job on Central Park. Browne had declined it for the larger salary and influence he would have as editor of the administration's Washington organ. Although his paper so blatantly defended slavery and justified secession that the embarrassed president was obliged to disown it by the turn of the year, Browne had been, as lately as December, in ostensibly friendly correspondence with Olmsted.[56]

Olmsted probably did not rush out and buy a gun, but he gave thought to how he might serve his country in its crisis. With one leg two inches shorter than the other, he was unfit for active military duty; but his books gave him influence and he quickly grasped an opportunity to extend it. Sampson Low, Son and Company of London wanted to bring out the three volumes in condensed form in England and to send the plates free to Mason Brothers for American publication; publishing in America was in the doldrums, and Mason Brothers' consent to the proposal was half-hearted. Olmsted, nevertheless, promptly arranged with Daniel Reeves Goodloe, editor of the abolitionist *National Era* and an authoritative writer on the economics of slavery, to do the condensing for half the 12.5 percent royalties Mason Brothers agreed to pay him.[57]

He considered, too, resigning from the park and getting work more relevant to the nation's immediate needs, especially since his position there had become both precarious and false. Some of the commissioners were toying with the idea of relegating him to an advisory capacity, on the ground that the park was almost completed. Even if this penny-wise scheme could be defeated by such potent influences as he invoked against it, William Cullen Bryant and Samuel Tilden,[58] Olmsted's situation would still be false. As superintendent and architect-in-chief, he bore titles that implied specific and large responsibilities and the power to discharge them. Yet the comptroller had effectively stripped him of power: through his tenaciously held financial control, Green was the absolute czar of the park. Nothing was done on the board unless Green prepared it; no motion was carried unless Green approved it. No activity of Olmsted's, no appropriation enabling him to secure supplies or labor, was authorized without a clause "with the approval of the comptroller" or of a committee that redelegated the trust to Green. It had reached the point where Olmsted could not act in the smallest detail—order the lawn cut, or nurse-trees removed, or direct a matter involving the expenditure literally of a dime—without taking the trouble to see Green personally and perfectly satisfy him that the expense was not merely desirable but unavoidable.[59] "As Treasurer," Olmsted wrote bitterly to John Bigelow, "not a dollar, not a cent, is got from under his paw that it is not wet with his blood and sweat."[60]

The practical effects of the situation were several. Least important was the wear and tear of constant chagrin on one autocrat regularly overborne by another. More serious was the fact that Olmsted often found his hands tied just when it was most important that he should be able to act with an artist's freedom and imagination, especially in the finish of his work. Most serious of all, Olmsted finally came to feel that not only his standing as an artist and a manager of works was jeopardized but also his reputation as a man of honor and honesty.[61] Nobody else thought so, but chronic humiliation at Green's hands had made Olmsted morbidly sensitive. The matter came to a climax late in January when he realized that he had spent more money than he had estimated he would need for the previous year's work, that the work was far in arrears, and that nowhere near enough remained of the appropriation to complete it. The real horror of his fix lay, to his mind, in the fact that he did not know which jobs had cost too much and had no way of finding out. He felt that he stood convicted on prima facie evidence either of incompetence or of neglect of duty.

The facts were subject to a different interpretation. The board had ordered him in April 1860 to present at the earliest possible moment a detailed statement of the work proposed for the rest of the year, with full estimates of its cost and reasons for doing each piece. Knowing that his overtaxed office force was unequal to the extra duty, Olmsted nevertheless had made the mistake of undertaking it. He was obliged to rely more heavily than he should have on the judgment of the engineers, and the job took longer to do than the board had expected. To have it ready by the beginning of June, Olmsted drove himself and his engineers and clerks day and night so that for the last week they did two days work in one. When the calculations were complete, Olmsted had no time to review them adequately. After the board accepted the plan and estimates and ordered him to go ahead, Olmsted, to be sure of keeping within the estimates, should have kept a book account of each section of the work and compared it monthly or oftener with the estimates. The precaution was simply impossible without an increase in the office staff, but the board refused his request for two extra clerks at one dollar a day to be assigned to the chief bookkeeper. Thus it was that near the end of January 1861 he found himself in the mortifying position of not knowing how he had spent too much money on too little work. He felt that he had failed in his duty; and he knew that if his conditions of work remained unchanged, he would continue to fail in it; so without advance warning, he abruptly handed his resignation to the president of the board.[62]

The president's consternation may be inferred from his action: he refused to present the resignation to the board for a vote.[63] There was reason to keep the matter quiet. The bill was even then before the legislature to extend the limits of the park from One hundred sixth to One hundred tenth Street; it was meeting influential opposition, and any hint of mismanagement on the park would prejudice it.[64] Besides that, Olmsted by implication had just been emphatically endorsed by the Senate committee that had spent the summer investigating the park. Its report, dated January 25, 1861, approved every aspect of the park's management—its physical construction; the careful and accurate devices employed to prevent graft, payroll padding, waste, and chicanery; and the precautions taken to protect the workmen against political pressure and exploitation.[65] Olmsted had originated most of the measures; even if the board had been unjustly disposed, which it was not, it could hardly have let him go bearing the stigma of carelessness.

Instead the president invited him to attend an informal meeting of the commissioners and present his complaints. He did so, lengthily, specifically, and feelingly.[66] "They all, including Green," he wrote Bigelow on February 9, "acknowledged the justness of my statement of personal wrong and promised to remedy it as soon as possible."[67] Relying on their promise, Olmsted withdrew his resignation. Thus he retrieved his position and simultaneously scotched the move to displace him. But his success was reduced to inconsequence by the swift trend of events toward war.

XIV
CIVIL WAR AND THE SEARCH FOR A MISSION
February–July 1861

O N February 4, 1861, delegates of the seceding states met at Montgomery, Alabama, to organize a separate nation, the Confederate States of America. Hope of peace was expiring,* and the South quickened its preparations for war. Jefferson Davis, president of the new Confederacy, summoned General P. G. T. Beauregard to take command at Charleston, where Fort Sumter, still in Union hands, guarded the harbor. Beauregard, recently appointed superintendent of West Point, resigned after only five days in the post and started south. On his way he stopped in New York long enough to go to Central Park, not for the aesthetic experience, but to engage Miss Curtayne, the Olmsted children's governess, as teacher for his daughter. He and Mary had an interview.

"A stiff, tall, thin, gray-haired youngish man—precise and positive—took a fancy to me so I hope to be well treated when we are conquered," Mary wrote her father-in-law after Beauregard had left to assume his fateful post.[1]

Notwithstanding the plain portents of war, the North still seemed more apprehensive than resolute, as though not quite believing in the onrushing catastrophe. "Few were fully convinced," Olmsted was soon to write, "that the whole proceedings of the insurgents meant anything else than a more than usually bold and scandalous way of playing the game of brag, to which we had been so long used in our politics. . . ."[2]

While southern members withdrew from the Senate and the House, and while the seceded states, unchallenged, seized United States forts, arsenals, and customs houses, the new administration, swamped with office seekers, worked frantically filling offices and distributing patronage instead of dealing with the crisis. Contempt, rather than consternation, greeted its performance. The London Times's celebrated war correspondent, William Howard Russell, arrived in New York the middle of March carrying a letter of introduction from his editor John Delane to Olmsted.[3] He was astounded to find that the political and social

---

*Almost its last gasp was the scheme Charles Francis Adams, Jr., proposed to Olmsted late in March. He suggested starting a magazine in Washington to turn a northern light on southern questions and gradually persuade "the Union portion of the Southern people" away from their advocacy of slavery. Such a journal "might give us a fulcrum," Adams wrote, "but it would require immense judgment, tact, ability, wit & energy to carry it out." It would have required, in addition, a miracle; nothing came of the proposal but the beginning of friendship between Adams and Olmsted (C. F. Adams, Jr., to O, 21, 29 March 1861).

leaders he met, instead of rallying to support the sorely tried administration, had little respect and less sympathy for it and carped at its undistinguished composition. Even at a press breakfast, where he met Dana, Hurlbert, Bayard Taylor, and "Mr. Olmsted, the indefatigable, earnest and able writer," Russell found that some of the guests were more exercised over the Heenan–Sayres prizefight, which a year after its loss by the American champion, Heenan, could still inflame Americans, than over secession and Sumter.[4]

How much Olmsted tried to indoctrinate his new acquaintance is impossible to say, but he clearly made some effort, and Russell clearly paid some attention to him. He agreed with his "thoughtful and earnest friend, Olmsted," that, so long as an abolitionist was less safe to speak his mind in Charleston than in Boston or New York, the United States could not rightly call itself a free country.[5] He was unreceptive, however, to more complicated and basic ideas. Olmsted's almost religious belief in democracy eluded him; and while his unexceptionable antislavery sentiments aligned him on the northern side, Olmsted recognized in him a failure of sympathy, in fact a contempt, for the democratic idea.

Regarding it as a patriotic duty to present democracy's case forcefully to English opinion, Olmsted took great pains with the introduction to the new edition of his books. At the beginning of April he went to Washington to discuss it with the editor, Goodloe. He wanted, while there, to gain access to the still unreleased 1860 census returns to bring up to date the statistics he used on cotton production, but their analysis was incomplete, and he was denied their use.[*,6]

When Olmsted returned to New York, the city was humming with rumors. Troops were being moved, no one knew where; but it was suspected they were to go to Texas, where General David E. Twiggs, wearing his United States uniform, had traitorously surrendered the army posts he commanded to state authorities. Ships in the Brooklyn Navy Yard were being readied to sail under sealed orders; the heady suspicion was afloat that Fort Sumter and Fort Pickens, the only major strongholds in seceded territory still in United States possession, were not after all to be surrendered but relieved. Soothsayers were giving Virginia three more months in the Union. An assault on Washington was said to be impending.[7] On April 11, Russell wrote Olmsted from the capital that an attack was apprehended at any moment from Richmond.[8] Before the letter could arrive,

---

*Olmsted probably also did some lobbying for Kapp and Riotte, who were seeking diplomatic posts from the party they had energetically supported. (Douai, as deserving as either and needier, had just become director of the Hoboken Academy.) Kapp wanted the consulship at Frankfurt-am-Main, while he considered whether to take advantage of the King of Prussia's amnesty and return to Germany. Riotte simply needed a job. Olmsted requested letters urging their claims from Bryant, Dana, Raymond, and Bigelow; in Washington he could reach Seward's ear and advance their chances. Riotte's application was ultimately successful; he was appointed consul to Costa Rica. Kapp failed to get the Frankfurt post (Riotte to O, 4 April, 1, 10 June 1861; Kapp to O, 12 July 1861).

an attack came indeed, but not on Washington: at four-thirty on the morning of April 12 Olmsted's recent caller, Beauregard, opened fire on Fort Sumter and touched off four years of desolating civil war.

The fatal act galvanized the North; it responded with a vast surge of patriotism, steady, angry, and determined. One resolution was everywhere evident: to uphold at whatever cost the flag and the lately despised government. In New York, red-white-and-blue cockades suddenly flowered on men, women, children, and cart horses. Flags appeared in such profusion that the supply ran out. Men from early youth to late middle age flocked to answer the president's call for seventy-five thousand volunteers. Crowds demonstrated threateningly before the *Journal of Commerce,* the *Daily News,* and other prosouthern newspapers until they ran up the Stars and Stripes. An immense mass meeting overflowed Union Square; it cheered patriotic speeches, greeted Major Robert Anderson, Sumter's last loyal commander, with roars, thundered the "Star Spangled Banner," and appointed a committee of public safety. Mayor Wood, not one to let principle jeopardize popularity, quickly committed himself to the Union he lately had been undermining.[9] Other disloyal or half-loyal critics of the government became enthusiastic patriots overnight. Russell would not have recognized the New York he had described less than a month earlier. Another Englishman, landing the middle of May, found the country in "the most extraordinary political condition conceivable." Alfred Field, once Olmsted's Staten Island neighbor, wrote his wife Lottie, "There is generally spread through all this northern community a sentiment of *savage hostility and anger* against the South that is astounding together with a unanimity that is admirable." The assumption that the South could be quickly blockaded or fought to submission was already yielding to the grim conviction that the war would be long and dear. "Olmsted thinks it will last 2 or 3 years and cost the North 600 millions of dollars," Field reported home. "All our best friends high toned earnest men lean to this sort of view and think it will be the end of slavery."[10]

Olmsted did not at once find a satisfactory role in the national tragedy; but he held it a religious duty to support the government in every possible way and did whatever came to hand. He formed a home guard of the park police and made them drill on Sundays. He encouraged enlistment by park employees.[11] He and Goodloe, angered by official England's coolness to the antislavery cause and by its recognition of the belligerent status of the rebels, pushed their work so hard that by the middle of June the finished manuscript was on the way to England.[12] As one of the twenty-four directors of the Women's Central Relief Association, an organization embracing groups of women in and near New York who had banded together to furnish comforts and medical supplies and services to the army,[13] Olmsted launched inquiries about the condition and needs of the recruits, suddenly funneled by the thousands into a capital utterly unprepared to take care of them. But these activities were footling; they did not add up to a mission, and a mission was what he intensely wanted.[14]

There were many civilians in the same position; one of the striking features of the barely begun war was the passion to participate that infused the pacific, the disabled, the overage—and women. Citizens raised and equipped volunteer regiments; they swarmed on Washington to offer their services and advice; they toured camps; they collected food and clothing and medical supplies and rushed them to the capital; they made the war their business. Some were excited busybodies; many were sensible and energetic people who saw that there were areas in which official agencies, caught unprepared, needed the help and stimulus of organized civilians.

One government agency that from the outset glaringly demonstrated its unpreparedness was the Medical Department of the army. It was geared to the peace-time needs of an army of some fifteen thousand men, most of them scattered about frontier posts; its commander, Surgeon General Thomas Lawson, was too ill to function; and the Acting Surgeon General, Colonel Robert C. Wood, a loyal career officer, had been for so many years swaddled in red tape that he lacked the vision to break through old routines to meet the radically altered situation.* As thousands of raw recruits poured into Washington, chaos threatened. Many of the volunteers arrived exhausted and dirty after long trips in boxcars devoid of facilities for comfort or cleanliness; some had sickened en route with contagious diseases; their officers, ignorant of military hygiene, had no notion how to select healthful camp sites, order sanitary arrangements, or supervise the preparation of wholesome food. The quartermaster corps of the regular army failed to provide sanitary facilities and canteens to receive the men when they arrived at the station. The medical corps neglected to weed out those who arrived sick or to enforce standards of camp hygiene.[15] The plain lesson of the Crimea was lost on it: there less than five thousand soldiers had succumbed to enemy action, more than sixteen thousand to disease. The death rate had been two hundred ninety-three per thousand until the alarmed government had conferred broad powers upon the British Sanitary Commission; then it had dropped, in the course of a year and a half, to twenty-five per thousand.[16] The lesson, however, was not lost on alert American civilians banding together in relief associations.

The Women's Central, which Bellows had been instrumental in organizing, offered its cooperation to the army medical purveyor in New York, Dr. R. C. Satterlee, in supplying comforts and stores, training nurses, organizing the scattered efforts of women all over the country, and collecting and making known information on the wants of the army. Rebuffed with patronizing courtesy, the ladies joined forces with two other local relief associations and selected a committee of four men to go over Satterlee's head to Washington and determine how they could best cooperate. Bellows and Dr. Elisha Harris, a prominent sanitarian, represented the Women's Central; Dr. William H. Van Buren, once an army doctor and now a leading New York practitioner, represented the Associa-

---

*Wood's loyalty was not strained by his kinship to Jefferson Davis: he was Davis's brother-in-law and hated him (O to MCO, 8 December 1861).

tion of Physicians and Surgeons of the New York Hospitals; and Dr. Jacob Harsen represented the New York Medical Association for Furnishing Hospital Supplies.[17]

They set out on May 15 on the first through train to leave New York for Washington since April 19, when Baltimore mobs had stoned northern troops passing through on their way to the capital. During the thirteen-hour trip, they evolved a plan to form a civilian sanitary commission, on the order of the British, to advise and assist the overwhelmed medical corps.[18] To present it in such a guise that it would be acceptable to the military was the tactical problem; the officers of the medical corps could hardly be expected to yield any of their authority or to consent to be bound by advice from a group of civilians.

Arrived in Washington, the committee saw Dorothea Dix, superintendent of nurses, who told them that the sick lacked nurses and supplies and denounced the apathy of the Medical Bureau.[19] They called on General Winfield Scott, so old, portly, and ill that two aides had to boost him to his feet to greet them. He promised to issue an order that recruits unfit for duty should be weeded out by medical inspection.* They saw the acting head of the medical corps, Colonel Wood, who politely assured them that his bureau needed no outside help to discharge its expanded duties. They met with exalted officials, including President Lincoln, Secretary of State Seward, and Secretary of War Simon Cameron.[20] Almost everyone they saw in government doubted the usefulness of the proposed novelty.[21]

Colonel Wood, however, soon was persuaded that a fact-finding commission, especially one that would assume the laborious task of distributing the flood of accumulating stores, would strengthen his department. He agreed to countenance it—if it would confine its benevolence to volunteers and if its advice was not legally binding. Such limited endorsement was not what the committee wanted but, perforce, it settled for it.[22] On May 22 Wood endorsed its request to the secretary of war that a civilian commission be appointed to cooperate with the Medical Bureau, and next day the four New Yorkers sent Cameron a statement describing the proposed commission. Organized for purposes of inquiry and advice, they requested no legal powers, only the official recognition and moral countenance of the government; and they proposed to investigate everything bearing on the health and morale of the troops and to make recommendations in the light of the best current scientific knowledge.[23]

The committee hardly had time to congratulate itself on its impending success when it was jeopardized. The ailing surgeon general died, and Colonel Clement Alexander Finley, born in 1797, succeeded him by right of seniority. Finley had once been "the handsomest man in the army"; by 1861 he was one of

---

*Such an order was issued on May 20. The results of early examinations indicated that so large a proportion of the three-month recruits would have to be dismissed if the order was strictly applied that it was abandoned (Charles J. Stillé, *History of the United States Sanitary Commission, Being the General Report of Its Work during the War of the Rebellion* [Philadelphia: J. B. Lippincott & Co., 1866], p. 48).

the most rigid. He informed Cameron that he disapproved of the proposed Sanitary Commission and did not concur with Colonel Wood's endorsement. "Then followed a scene," wrote the official historian of the Sanitary Commission in accents of pained discretion, "into the details of which we do not propose to enter, between the Surgeon General and those who having toiled so painfully to induce the Government to permit the inauguration of this great work of mercy, suddenly found themselves checked in their humane endeavor." Up against Bellows, however, whose business was exhortation, Finley was talked around; but he forced a concession: the Sanitary Commission specifically, not by implication, had to confine its interference to volunteer troops.[24] The distressing interview salvaged the nascent commission; it established as well the pattern of the surgeon general's unremitting hostility.

On June 9, the secretary of war signed the document authorizing the commission; four days later President Lincoln, openly unenthusiastic, endorsed it; and the Sanitary Commission came, on paper, into existence.[25]

Olmsted, meanwhile, little imagining that his mission was about to seek him, was still seeking it. He thought he might have found it late in May, after General Benjamin F. Butler, commanding Fortress Monroe, refused to return to their owners three slaves who had escaped to his lines and stated: "The question is simply whether they shall be used for or against the Government of the United States. I shall hold these negroes as *contraband* of war."[26] Surely, Olmsted reasoned, slaves in increasing numbers would flock, in hope of freedom, into Union-held territory; and certainly the government would have to devise some scheme for employing them. His own study of slave management, his experience in handling large numbers of laborers, and especially the considerable thought he had given to the management of Negroes in the state of limbo between slavery and freedom all peculiarly qualified him, he thought, for the office of commissioner of contrabands. The first of June he wrote to Bellows, still dangling about Washington, and asked him to find out if his application for such a post might be favorably received. "I think, in fact, that I should find here my 'mission' which is something I am really pining to find, in this war."[27] Bellows promised that he would look into the matter. His own business was just about consummated, he confided. "I think I am on the eve of effecting the appointment of a Commission —but *guns* hang fire so in this damp official atmosphere that one cannot be certain of his aim, until he sees his game lying dead at his feet."[28] When his game at length lay dead at his feet, Bellows had a better job for Olmsted than boss of contraband labor.

While the Sanitary Commission was cajoling and clawing its way into existence, more pressing developments were occupying official Washington and the public mind. Virginia and Tennessee seceded, and the loyalty of Kentucky and Missouri wavered. On May 24 Union soldiers crossed the Potomac into Virginia and, with a bit of skirmishing, seized Alexandria and the Arlington heights. General Scott ordered a movement against Harper's Ferry, where rebels had captured the arsenal and government stores. It was recaptured on June 15, just two days before Unionists in Missouri won a battle at Booneville. Fighting had fairly begun, and men were beginning to die.

Many of Olmsted's closest associates in the park were setting aside families, careers, and ambitions to join the army. The Hungarian Alexander Asboth, who had fought under Kossuth and embraced exile, resigned his job as engineer to become an officer.[29] Dallas, a Democrat, was in Washington trying to wring a commission out of the Republicans who manned the War Department.[30] Waring had been commissioned major in the Garibaldi Guards, a mixed bag of foreign adventurers raised in New York. Known as the "organ grinders," they wore red blouses and Bersaglieri hats, a costume which Waring conceded, with embarrassment, to be a bit "outré."[31] Still, he was in uniform.

Given patriotism and able bodies, these men and thousands more had readily known where their duty lay. Olmsted, lame and in uncertain health, had a harder problem; but Bellows, who knew how to utilize other men's talents, had the solution: he wanted Olmsted as executive secretary of the Sanitary Commission to direct its business in Washington. He invited him to meet the officers of the commission and discuss the proposal.

The minister lived in comfortable elegance in a house on Stuyvesant Square. There, at noon on June 20, Olmsted met the commission members. Bellows was president. The vice-president was Professor Alexander Dallas Bache, a grandson of Benjamin Franklin, an influential educator, and superintendent of the United States Coast Survey. George Templeton Strong was treasurer; a successful and public-spirited New York lawyer, cultured and witty, he secretly kept a diary in which he shrewdly reviewed the current scene and skewered his contemporaries. Dr. Cornelius Rae Agnew was a specialist in diseases of the eye and ear and occupied a place in the front rank of New York medical men. Dr. Harris, the sanitarian, and Professor Wolcott Gibbs, the most distinguished chemist in the United States, were the other members present.* Unanimously, they urged Olmsted to take the post of executive secretary, and he, already assured of three months leave from the park, at once accepted.[32] So Olmsted found his mission and came, for the second time, to a great popular and democratic work.

A great popular and democratic work—but nobody engaged in it had any clear idea yet just what it was to be. Olmsted met with the commission almost daily and nightly for a week to discuss its organization and its ends, form committees, draft appeals for funds, prepare a questionnaire on camp sanitation, and enlist members, like old Dr. Valentine Mott, the authority on surgical anesthesia,

---

*Members not present at Olmsted's election were Colonel Wood, Colonel George W. Cullum, and Major Alexander E. Shiras, all of the Medical Department of the United States army; Dr. Van Buren; Dr. Samuel Gridley Howe, of Boston, and Dr. John S. Newberry, of Cleveland. Additional members before the end of the year were Rt. Rev. Thomas M. Clark, Protestant Episcopal Bishop of Rhode Island, Horace Binney, Jr., of Philadelphia, and the Hon. Mark Skinner of Chicago.

whose special knowledge would be useful.[33] At the end of a week, Olmsted was ready to start to Washington, to feel his way into his new work.

He was still not sure what his duties would be or even his salary. Something like two thousand dollars a year, he supposed; and since he had made no definite arrangement with the Central Park commissioners as to the time he should spend or the money he should receive as part-time landscape consultant, he thought the change might cost him two thousand dollars a year in lost wages.[34] His wife hoped that the work would satisfy his patriotism and so make him happy; if it did not, she warned him, she would consider herself swindled as well as impoverished.[35] His father heard of the change with mixed feelings: Fred, almost forty, was again rushing off on a new tack.

Olmsted left for Washington late on June 26. The dearth of signs of war, as the train puffed through placid countryside and busy towns, was almost eerie. He did not see troops until the approach to Havre de Grace, where a dozen or so volunteers in shirt sleeves and dirty havelocks guarded the bridge over the Susquehanna. They were lounging around a shanty with a charcoal sign reading "Bloody 11th. Camp C" and they looked quite unmilitary. Indeed most of the troops he saw from then on looked dirty, ill equipped, and unmilitary—willing and patriotic citizens, no doubt, but not yet components of an army.[36]

About six in the evening of June 27 Olmsted arrived in Washington. The capital had been planned by Major Charles Pierre L'Enfant on a grandiose and farsighted scale, but sprawling untidy and incomplete on the Potomac flats, it barely hinted at its designer's vision. Coming out of the station, Olmsted could see the Capitol squatting on its low hill, its unfinished marble wings palely glaring in the early evening light. Its original modest dome was gone, and the work of replacing it with an impressive high cast-iron dome was continuing despite the war. Pennsylvania Avenue, stretching northwesterly from the Capitol, was still unpaved and undrained, a treacherous and filthy slough in wet weather, a suffocating dust wallow in dry. Its south side was lined with shabby stores, cheap boardinghouses, livery stables, shacks, and markets, while on its north, where a ribbon of brick sidewalk provided pedestrians a welcome foothold, stood hotels, shops, and restaurants. In the several blocks north of it, where the city's main business district lay, were scattered among a mass of undistinguished offices and houses a few public buildings—the City Hall, city hospital, county jail, the United States Patent Office, and the General Post Office. Before the avenue disappeared into Georgetown, it was interrupted by the president's park, where the red brick buildings housing the State and War and Navy departments and the imposing Greek temple of the Treasury Department clustered around the unpretentious and pleasant White House. The park itself, democratically open to all comers, sloped down to the disused and stinking canal, which had once been a waterway connecting the Potomac and the Eastern Branch. South of the canal lay the Mall, the planting of which had been begun by Downing before he died. James Renwick's turreted red sandstone Smithsonian Institution was its lone respectable occupant; work had been stopped on the Washington Monument, which stood half-finished at its western end. The effluvia of the government abattoir, recently established alongside the monument, made the whole neighborhood noxious.

This much of the city Olmsted could observe on the drive from the station to Willard's Hotel on Pennsylvania Avenue just east of the president's park. There was little in it to flatter his rational patriotism. In its careless dirtiness he saw reflected a frontier society; in its slovenly indolence, a slave. The few porticoed government buildings, which might have been symbolic of the "moral grandeur of a great republic," seemed, rather, tastelessly showy in their shabby setting like "precious stones on dirty hands."[37] Washington, with its congeries of mean buildings huddled around a few fine ones, its unsewered streets, and its pestilential canal, was not yet a capital but the unrealized idea of one, much as the hordes of undisciplined, half-equipped volunteers were not yet an army but the potential of one.

Olmsted engaged a room at the Willard. It was the most popular hotel in town, although some of its more fastidious patrons professed to loathe it for its bar and public rooms swarming with politicians, office seekers, lobbyists, and idlers; its atmosphere dense with tobacco smoke and vibrant with clamorous voices; and its floors beyond description with tobacco juice and litter.[38] There Waring met him. Less conspicuously clad than Olmsted might have feared, Waring had on a blue flannel jacket with regulation buttons, an army regulation cap and drab pants strapped and spurred.[39] He had obtained a pass for Olmsted that permitted him to go over the bridges daily within the lines to inspect camps. It also superfluously warned him on its reverse side that if he took up arms against the Union or aided its enemies he might incur the death penalty.[40]

Olmsted's first assignment was to inspect the camps in and about Washington, and he began that evening with the Garibaldi Guards, a couple of miles east of the Capitol. When he drove into camp, which was made up of lines of tents flanked by brushwood shanties, he was immediately surrounded by a crowd of men talking half a dozen languages, "very polite and very stupid & uncomprehending." After having a drink of brandy with Waring and other officers, Olmsted went to bed in Waring's tent, where he spent a restless night disturbed by unfamiliar camp noises. An early morning visit to the regimental hospital was followed by breakfast with the colonel and his staff. No one was in full uniform except one officer newly arrived from New York, and the officers' slovenliness was reflected throughout the regiment. "The men on duty were more or less dressed according to individual caprice, but generally in caps with havelocks, & straw hats & red shirts, though some wore the full dress, dirty & slouched," Olmsted commented with distaste.[41]

For the next ten days Olmsted, accompanied by Dr. Harris, inspected the camps that had sprung up in the wastelands around Washington; and early in July Olmsted drew up a report of their findings. It was a disheartening document. Scarcely a camp had a complete system of drains such as should have been laid out and dug the very hour the tents were pitched. The tents were poor affairs, so hard to ventilate that some of the men preferred to go outside and roll up on the ground. Latrines were usually nothing but trenches thirty feet long without a pole or rail; their edges were filthy, their stench was sickening, the expedient of turning fresh earth into them daily was often neglected, and they were frequently too near the camps. The volunteers' clothing was usually shamefully dirty, they themselves were often lousy, and only in rare instances was it a part of camp routine to march them daily to running water to bathe. Obviously, neither officers nor men had the least idea of the imperative need to keep clean or of the perils they invited by neglecting it. Besides being dirty, the clothing of the volunteers was as a rule "inappropriate, unbecoming, uncomfortable, and not easily kept in a condition consonant with health" and perhaps should be replaced by regulation uniforms. Their arms certainly should be replaced, being already in many instances in bad condition. Many men were being needlessly exhausted by two hours of drill at daybreak before breakfast. Their food, as issued, was usually good, but it was atrociously cooked and wickedly wasted; fresh vegetables, which ought to have been regulation issue, were not provided, and outbreaks of scurvy and dysentery were likely. Sea cooks should be engaged and attached throughout the army, one to each company. The report concluded:

> The Secretary . . . is compelled to believe that it is now hardly possible to place the volunteer army in a good defensive position against the pestilential influences by which it must soon be surrounded. No general orders calculated to strengthen the guard against their approach can be immediately enforced with the necessary vigor. The captains, especially, have in general not the faintest comprehension of their proper responsibility; and if they could be made to understand, they could not be made to perform the part which properly belongs to them in any purely military effort to this end. To somewhat mitigate the result is all that the Commission can hope to do. If the Commission and its agents could be at once clothed with some administrative powers, as well as exercise advisory functions, far more could be done. . . .[42]

But the commission was not clothed with any such powers, and its recommendations were little heeded. In essence they were to enforce the same standard of military discipline on volunteer as on regular troops, not merely such forms as saluting officers, but the fundamentals of obedience and cleanliness on which the health, morale, and efficiency of armies always depended. Throughout government, however, the opinion prevailed that it could not be done; the average American volunteer, bred in the tradition that all men were created equal, was an individualistic fellow who would do both his camp housekeeping and his soldiering in his own wayward fashion and do them well enough. Even the regular army officers of the commission inclined to such a view and so undermined its effort to establish discipline. "They do nothing but discourage and obstruct," Olmsted growled early in July, "and so of all officials."[43]

Too many of the seventy regiments of infantry under canvas around Washington were neglected by their officers, who boozed at Willard's and bandied such coarse language that respectable guests shuddered as they passed in and out with their families. Unsupervised, restless, and idle, the volunteers were beginning to get out of hand. Few regiments were being systematically prepared for the rigors of active military life. If any policy controlled their being, it was not discernible. Olmsted began to wonder if there was one,[44] and he was not alone in his anxiety.

It was General Scott's announced strategy to blockade the South and, while its slow strangulation progressed, to whip his volunteers into shape to advance and administer the *coup de grace* to the weakened foe. He was, however, proceeding so deliberately that critics official and unofficial were stridently demanding immediate movement—and the terms of enlistment of some of the regiments were already expiring. Why should not the great army encamped around Washington sweep forward to Richmond, as Greeley's *Tribune* was loudly urging, instead of wasting time parading, pilfering, drinking, and brawling around the capital?

Irvin McDowell, Olmsted's London acquaintance, who was the general commanding the Union forces in Virginia, could have explained exactly why. Although he was even then planning a movement against Manassas Junction to capture Manassas Gap and trap General Joseph Johnston's force in the Shenandoah Valley, he was hamstrung by a miserable deficiency of artillery and cavalry, inadequate transport, and the indiscipline of some thirty thousand troops who were "grossly and utterly ignorant of what an army was or should be." Besides that, he could nowhere get a reliable map of Virginia, and he could obtain no information on the terrain ahead of him because Beauregard's army lay before him and he had not a single calvary officer capable of conducting a reconnaissance.[45]

Breakfasting the Sunday after the Fourth at Wormeley's, the free mulatto caterer's place on I Street, Olmsted heard some vehement criticism of the military leadership. John Bigelow, soon to go as consul general to France, was host; among his guests were Russell, just back from an excursion into the South; Senators Preston King and Henry Wilson of the Military Affairs Committee; and Nathaniel P. Willis, dandy, social lion, and owner of the *Home Journal*, who was covering Washington for his paper from the sanctuary of Mrs. Lincoln's inner circle. Wilson inveighed against the officers of the regular army— excepting only Quartermaster General Montgomery Meigs, the single one to display real administrative ability—assailed West Point, and denounced General Scott as obstructive, obstinate, and unfit.[46] When the chairman of the Senate Committee on Military Affairs, in his informed position, so criticized the government's military policy, it was small wonder that Olmsted, in his peripheral one, should be disquieted. "I feel that the whole business is exceedingly uncertain & should not be much surprised to get up & find Jeff Davis in the White House," he confessed. No leadership, of course, was to be expected from its current incumbent: he was a nonentity. Olmsted had lately passed President Lincoln, walking "with two or three other loafers" to the War Department. "He looked much younger than I had supposed, dressed in a cheap & nasty French black cloth suit just out of a tight carpet bag. Looked as if he would be an applicant for a Broadway squad policemanship, but a little too smart and careless. Turned and laughed familiarly at a joke upon himself which he overheard from my companion en passant."[47] Alert to the president's lack of dignity, Olmsted seems to have been curiously insensitive to his companion's.

The dearth of political leadership, the incompetence of military organization, the uncertainty of military planning, all persuaded Olmsted that the Sanitary Commission could do nothing truly constructive; it could only try to palliate some of the results of official bungling. The commission, less pessimistic, set vigorously to work when it met in Washington on Wednesday, July 10. The government had assigned it a grand room in the Treasury Building, where the members sat for three days from ten to four and from seven in the evening till eleven or later. They appointed inspectors, adopted Van Buren's code of sanitary rules to be distributed to volunteers and Strong's draft of instructions to agents, and drew up a set of recommendations for presentation to the War Department and Congress: that rest rooms be provided near the station for arriving and departing soldiers, that arrangements be made with the paymaster enabling soldiers to send home part of their pay, that a military police force be organized to keep soldiers out of bars and brothels and gambling dens, that stringent rules of camp sanitation be enforced, that fresh vegetables be supplied and good cooks attached to each regiment. In a ploy to secure the next best thing to enforcement powers, they appeared in a body before the Senate Military Affairs Committee to submit their bill, which required, among other things, that all officers comply with the recommendations of Sanitary Commission agents or submit in writing to their commanding officer their reasons for not doing so.[48]

About the middle of the month Olmsted, learning that his status on the park was again in hazard, wrote Bellows that he wanted to resume his full duties there "in the autumn, or when you no longer need me."[49] Bellows answered firmly: "I cannot hear of your leaving us under any circumstances for the present. The Commission would lose its chief hope of future usefulness."[50]

It still had scarcely an intimation of the scope of that usefulness. Bull Run was soon to give it an inkling.

XV
THE SANITARY COMMISSION LAUNCHED
July–October 1861

OLMSTED was in New York for a few days working on Central Park when, on Monday morning, July 22, word of Bull Run began to trickle into the city. Loyal spirits soared at early dispatches; they collapsed at later ones. Bull Run was not the victory it was first reported; it was not even a creditable defeat; it was a disgraceful rout.

The truth was not as bad as incomplete reports suggested, but it was bad enough. The Union attack, begun early Sunday the twenty-first, had been successful during its first hours. McDowell's green troops had encircled and crushed Beauregard's left wing, made up of soldiers similarly green; but in midafternoon General Thomas J. Jackson and his men had held a moderately elevated plateau like a stone wall, against which repeated Union assaults ineffectually broke. The ill-trained Union force had already been in confusion, with men and officers lost from each other, and the steady repulse confounded it. Then General Johnston, having slipped out of the Valley of Virginia through Manassas Gap, attacked from the rear; his assault had turned confusion into retreat and retreat into rout.

On the whole, the rout had been more dogged than panicky, as the disorganized mob of soldiers, mingled with civilians who had driven out from Washington in holiday spirits to see the rebels whipped, poured in sluggish flight along the clogged roads back toward the capital. By nightfall, the vanguard of the runaways had begun to straggle into Washington, and by daybreak Monday they were stumbling into town in droves, while the local secessionists openly rejoiced and loyal citizens quaked to think that Beauregard's victorious hordes might soon sweep upon the unnerved city.

The Confederate force, almost as badly mauled as the Union, was in no shape for pursuit, but the fact was not at once grasped. Russell, to be sure, quipped that the Union army "ran away just as its victory had been secured by the superior cowardice of the South";[1] but the general impression was that the capital might well be attacked.

Olmsted returned at once to Washington to see what the Sanitary Commission could do. On arriving, he was appalled to realize that the real disaster was not the defeat of the army; it was its demoralization. He found the city crawling with bands of dank and dirty soldiers, begging food from door to door and bivouacking in the streets around fires built of palings torn from fences. The bars were packed with volunteer officers who, indifferent to their men, their duty, and their disgrace, were making light of the catastrophe and drinking to an

168

early return to civilian life. Military organization had collapsed and many regiments were but mobs, "parts of a disintegrated herd of sick monomaniacs," who started and turned pale at the breaking of a stick or the crack of a percussion cap. "Some appeared ferocious, others only sick and dejected, all excessively weak, hungry and selfish."[2]

What could have reduced thousands of loyal men, who had willingly enlisted in the army and cheerfully gone into battle, to the "miserable collection of dejected wild animals" foraging forlornly through the city?[3] To find out, the Sanitary Commission, within four days of the battle, instituted what was probably the first prompt and thorough investigation ever made into the causes of a military defeat. It sent seven inspectors to the thirty regiments engaged at Bull Run to ask officers and men a set of seventy-five questions bearing on their health, discipline, and morale at the time of the battle.[4]

Even before the returns began to come in, Olmsted blamed the failure to inculcate discipline in the volunteer army for its flight and disintegration. Within a week of Bull Run he wrote his wife: "There is but one sanitary measure to be thought of now, and that is discipline."[5] On July 29 the commission took the same position officially in a resolution assuring General McClellan, who had succeeded to McDowell's command, that "the humane, the intelligent, the religious, the patriotic," would uphold him "in every endeavor to communicate a spirit of subordination, fidelity and obedience to the troops . . . believing that the health, comfort and efficiency of the army are all united in their dependence on a strict uniform and all-pervading military discipline."[6]

During the melancholy, anxious days after Bull Run, Olmsted was oppressed by the conviction that the government could not cope with the emergency.[7] Unfit recruits, still accepted by the hundreds by the states, had to be sent home when they got to Washington. The selection of officers was haphazard, and the city was full of military adventurers of all nationalities, pressing their claims on the War Department and badgering commissions out of it. Ill selected and ill officered, the troops were besides miserably armed and supplied, badly fed, and poorly trained. No high official seemed to have a firm grasp on the situation. Only McClellan, beginning to inaugurate something approximating military discipline throughout the army, appeared to understand what was needed. As for the president, Olmsted still shared in the widely held derogation of his abilities—which, indeed, had scarcely yet come into play.

"Lincoln has no element of dignity; no tact, not a spark of genius," he wrote his father one still, chokingly hot night in August when he could not sleep in the wretched cubicle Willard's had assigned to him. "This is almost true of all his cabinet. He is an amiable, honest, good fellow. His cabinet is not that. There is the greatest conceivable dearth of administrative talent."[8] The single thought that sustained Olmsted was that the Sanitary Commission, and he from his influential position on it, could do something to awaken public opinion to the urgent needs of the hour and to overcome in some details the prevailing inefficiency and misery.

In the weeks following Bull Run, the commission turned its versatile hand to a number of problems well outside the scope of its original plan. It extended its sanitary inspection to camps and hospitals throughout the army, selecting its agents for their diplomacy as well as their professional knowledge, since, without enforcement powers, they could get their recommendations carried out only by persuasion. It set up a statistical bureau in the main office, where its actuary, Ezekiel Brown Elliott, a Boston insurance man with a genius for making "all information systematically incomprehensible," reduced the returns from its scattered agents to tabular form. It inaugurated a burial register and secured permission to have its printing done by the Government Printing Office.[9] To aid surgeons in the field, out of reach of medical libraries and sometimes faced with illnesses and injuries with which they had little familiarity, it had specialists prepare a series of monographs on medicine, surgery, hygiene, and anesthesia.[10] In a spontaneous response to an emergency, one of its most effective agents, Frederick Newman Knapp,* improvised the Special Relief Service, which came in time to operate forty soldiers' homes and lodges throughout Union-held territory, where soldiers who were sick, but not sick enough to be hospitalized, and soldiers who were in difficulties that it was not the business of the army to resolve could secure free care and sympathetic assistance.[11]

Branching out, the commission decided to do something about the hospitals around Washington crowded with wounded from Bull Run. It was not enough to remedy, as it did, the deficiency of supplies and services—to provide such necessities as nursing, bedding, nightshirts, medicines, and invalid foods, which the Medical Bureau had inertly proposed and miserably failed to furnish after the need for them arose. The hospitals themselves were makeshifts—seminaries, hotels, warehouses—ill adapted to their new use, incapable of accommodating any great influx of wounded, and as often as not, badly run. Van Buren and Agnew undertook to inspect all the hospitals in the Washington area, preparatory to drawing up plans to replace them with new pavilion hospitals for fifteen thousand patients.[12] At about the same time, Olmsted began to organize storage depots in large cities, where specified supplemental hospital supplies, of a sort government did not furnish, could be collected for shipment to points where they were needed on order from the Washington headquarters.[13]

As the commission's business expanded, its policy of being both supplemental and national crystalized. It was not, to be sure, staying within its self-imposed limits as a supplement to the Medical Bureau; it was too often, because of the bureau's inertia, supplanting it. Yet the ideal and the hope lingered that the bureau might be aroused to a proper discharge of its duties, allowing the voluntary agency to subside into its preferred advisory role. The commission's

---

*A Unitarian minister like his friend and cousin Bellows, Knapp was a man of the utmost warmth and kindliness. As an old gentleman he offered a bit of advice to a little girl, who as an old lady, passed it on to the writer's informant: "Never resist a good impulse" (Gershom Bradford, interview).

emphasis on its national character was partly for a practical administrative reason: relief work could be more efficiently directed from a central office to which all information came than from a number of regional offices cognizant only of local requirements. But it was primarily for moral effect: to uphold national and catholic principles, as opposed to the local and divisive principles represented by the rebellious states and the provincial principle represented by those northern states whose relief agents were engaged to aid only their own soldiers.[14]

Olmsted, although swamped by office duties, joined in the hospital inspection work, often accompanied by Russell, whose Crimea experience made his judgment valuable. Sometimes, after a day's inspection tour, he returned for supper to Russell's rooms. There, with his host, members of the British legation, and visiting Englishmen, he drank champagne and discussed politics and recent wars into the early morning. Occasionally someone had to be carried home, but never Olmsted. "I was prudent as usual," he wrote his wife after one such evening, "& not a bit the worse for it."[15]

In spite of overwork, erratic hours, and the stresses of his proliferating duties, Olmsted's health was fair and he was no longer seriously hampered by his lameness. He was in despair, however, at the fumbling conduct of the war and desperately impatient for some strong intelligence to assume direction of the war effort. Perhaps McClellan, still moving in an aura of success and promise, might be the man; but unless he proved himself a genius as well as a general and set himself up as military dictator over the "imbecile government," there would have to be a revolution in the North before anything could be done with the South, Olmsted declared.[16] The emergence, under the cruel pressures of disappointment and despair, of the autocratic streak in the dedicated democrat bewildered at least one of Olmsted's New York friends, when he returned there the middle of August for a few days' work on the park. Mrs. George Schuyler, who had known him for a decade, wondered what the future held when such leading men of the younger generation as he and Brace were tending to advocate centralization, unconstitutional and despotic measures like a national act of emancipation, revolution, and dictatorship. "Is this merely the impatience of energetic natures seeing half round the circle," she inquired apprehensively of Bellows, "or that prophecy of the future that can be read in the rough by studying the tendencies of the new generation?" Sensibly she added: "Is this painful excitement the best thing for him [Olmsted]? I hope you are brought near enough now to act upon his lovely tho peculiar nature."[17]

Painful excitement was certainly not the best thing for Olmsted; yet he could not avoid it even in the fellowship of the Sanitary Commission. When the commission met the beginning of September, he read his report on the causes of the demoralization of the army and collided head-on with a bloc of its members. The report, based on the returns of the elaborate questionnaire sent to the troops just after Bull Run, amounted to a devastating criticism of the War Department. It disclosed that only eight regiments had gone into battle in good physical condition. All the others had suffered various degrees of exhaustion from causes against which responsible officers would have protected them: want of food and drink and sleep before the engagement; a long, hot march, part of it taken on the double by some regiments, just preceding it; and overtasking during it. The men's consequent debility and their lack of confidence in ignorant and indifferent officers and in the government that had neglected them during months in camp had been the real causes of the army's demoralization, which had been brought into the open rather than brought about by a repulse in battle. It was significant that a few well-officered regiments, like the Second Rhode Island, whose health and discipline had been properly maintained in camp, showed no trace of the general demoralization, while the New York Fire Zouaves, a group of men undoubtedly brave but entirely insubordinate in a military sense, went to pieces in the field.[18]

The commissioners were "somewhat startled" that their secretary had traced the causes of the demoralization to "the imbecility of the government"; and the government members—Professor Bache, Dr. Wood, Colonel Cullum, and Major Shiras—absolutely refused to permit publication of the report.[19] Even Strong, who thought it clever and able, opposed publishing it on the ground that it would retard recruiting.[20] Olmsted reluctantly revised it so that its strictures applied less to the incumbent government and more to the laws.[21] Even so, the government members threatened to resign if it was made public. After long and warm discussion the commissioners compromised on a private printing.[22] While it would not reach the general public and awaken it to the desperate needs of the hour, as Olmsted wished, still he could scarcely doubt that Strong's point was well taken.

With fortifications being raised around Washington and with the enemy in sight across the river digging entrenchments, it was certainly no time to frighten away recruits; but it was past time to insist that the Medical Bureau safeguard their health. Not all failures in their care were to be blamed on the bureau, to be sure: the Quartermaster Department was responsible for erecting, adapting and furnishing hospital buildings and for transporting the wounded, and the Subsistence Department was responsible for supplying the hospitals with food; neither department had any special knowledge of what was appropriate for sick and wounded soldiers, and each was, in any case, overwhelmed by the job of providing for ten times as large an army as ever before. But whereas other army departments were reorganizing to deal with war conditions, the Medical Bureau continued to do business as usual.[23] Although a great battle was apprehended daily, with perhaps five thousand to twenty thousand casualties, the bureau failed to lay in medicines or requisition beds or hospital facilities in advance. When the Sanitary Commission remonstrated, it was told that supplies could be ordered from New York and workmen employed to make beds after the battle— it had never been the usage of the bureau to accumulate large reserves of hospital stores. Neither, of course, had it been the usage of the government to assemble one hundred fifty thousand men in a single place in the face of an enemy.

By the end of the summer, the surgeon general's do-nothing policy had become so frustrating, and his obstinate hostility so hampering, that the commission during its September session debated whether to continue to cooperate with the Medical Bureau as it was then constituted or to expose its nonfeasance to the public and, backed by an aroused opinion, force a thorough reform.[24]

The commissioners also visited the camps in September and found signs of improvement that caused the stirring of guarded optimism. At Chain Bridge, which Olmsted visited the evening of Thursday, September 11, the fortification looked workmanlike. The bridge was well guarded, howitzers were trained on it, the footpath planks had been taken up, and a contrivance for breaking up its far end had been erected on it. A steep rocky road led from the bridge up the Virginia hillside to an earthworks fortification. Freshly cut trees lay all about for a mile, opening ranges for the guns that were mounted and trained into Virginia. The site teemed with wagons, stores, artillery, and dirty, half-uniformed volunteers. They had been in a slight skirmish that morning, and the regulars spoke well of them. The next day Olmsted for the first time met McClellan and found that he, too, was encouraged: the same volunteers had engaged in a reconnaissance in force and an artillery skirmish that morning and had acquitted themselves well.[25]

The general, so busy with his new military duties that he had broken several previous appointments with the Sanitary Commission, met twice that Friday to discuss the troops' health and discipline with Olmsted, Bellows, and a new commissioner, Bishop Thomas M. Clark of Rhode Island. Olmsted found the promising young hero

> a more refined and less extraordinary looking man than the published portraits would indicate. A very fine animal. Graceful form perfection of muscles. A good honest eye with the slightest possible tenderness; power without fierceness, unpoetic. A low forehead, compact brain, bulldog tenacity of life and strength of jaw. Reflection, decision, confidence, prudence, tenacity. Dressed carelessly & not in good taste; careless & western in style. . . . A good voice, without being very musical. . . . He soon took our measure and became as frank with us and commanded our frankness as fully as if we had been familiar friends.[26]

After their second meeting, which began at ten Friday evening, McClellan took his callers with him while he reported on the morning's engagement to Secretary Cameron. Olmsted observed that with the cabinet officer the soldier was "as direct, frank and familiar as if he never saw a politician or heard of rank." Olmsted did not discern, during this first encounter, the arrogance toward his civilian superiors that tainted the general's familiarity or the Messianism that underlay his self-confidence.

When the conversation veered to the Sanitary Commission, the gathering turned into a love feast. Pouring his guests a drink of Pennsylvania whiskey,

Cameron declared to Bellows, "You have never asked anything of me yet, that you have not got it—and you never will." McClellan promised Olmsted, "I will do anything you will ask for your Commission, anything that you say will increase your usefulness in this department." Olmsted was impressed with the general: "His strength lies in his abnegation of self—or rather in his consciousness that he is indispensable & everything must give way to his will, and in his faith."[27] His strength and his weakness, too, as Olmsted and more idolatrous admirers would soon find.

Exhilarated by the backing of the popular hero and the secretary of war, the commission resolved on a radical course that Bellows outlined in a paper for McClellan and Cameron: it sought the removal of Finley as surgeon general, the creation of an independent ambulance corps for the Army of the Potomac, the more extensive use of men and women nurses in the hospitals, the requirement that the surgeon general grant or deny Sanitary Commission requests in writing, and the conferring of enforcement powers on its inspectors.[28]

The commission became uneasy when several days passed without a sign from its exalted friends. "Put not your faith in princes, nor in the confidential pledges of secretaries and heads of departments," Strong grimly mused.[29] When McClellan at length replied to Bellows's paper, he ignored the recommendation to remove the surgeon general, disapproved the proposal to invest inspectors with enforcement powers, and endorsed all the rest.[30] Olmsted drew up another paper omitting the request for enforcement powers and entered upon a tedious round of waiting in parlors and anterooms to catch the great men and secure their approval for it. He wasted dozens of hours thus, but Cameron evaded him, and McClellan put him off with polite messages.[31] By the end of the month he had nothing to show for his pains but his disillusion and his frazzled nerves; the surgeon general remained as powerful and immobile as ever, and the reform of the Medical Bureau seemed to be stuck on dead center.[32]

The commission, however, was making some small headway in other directions. It submitted to the War Department its plans for five pavilion hospitals accommodating fifteen thousand patients to be built in Washington.[33] It opened discussions with Secretary of the Treasury Salmon P. Chase of a system by which soldiers could allot part of their pay to their families. And it began looking around for possible candidates for surgeon general, should it ever succeed in prying the bureau loose from Dr. Finley's petrified grasp. Dr. William A. Hammond, unanimously praised by commission agents who had inspected the hospitals he administered, caught their eye, and the commission began to examine his qualifications.[34]

Meanwhile, the basic problem of the Medical Bureau remained. Surgeons continued to appeal to the commission for urgently needed supplies, having been unable to get them after several requisitions on the bureau. Miss Dix angrily complained that, while the wounded lay neglected, the surgeon general spurned her nurses.[35] Malaria was abroad in the neighborhood, but the bureau was short of quinine, and the commission had to spend five hundred dollars to provide it for the worst affected regiments.[36] Smallpox cases were mingled with measles, over Sanitary protests, in the Kalorama hospital, so that patients cured of measles and incubating smallpox returned to their regiments to scatter smallpox in the army. The Medical Bureau promptly ran out of vaccine, and the commission had to supply it for some twenty thousand men.[37]

The surgeon general's know-nothing, do-nothing obduracy made Olmsted wild with frustration. "I really think I would die satisfied with my life, tomorrow, if I could put a live strong man with a big humane heart also—at the head of the Medical Bureau," he exploded to Bellows.[38]

As September passed, the overwrought tone of Olmsted's communications suggested to Strong that hard work and excitement, acting on a sensitive, nervous temperament, were making Olmsted morbid.[39] But more than overwork and excitement, despair at broken promises, pervasive inefficiency, and lack of earnestness in the prosecution of the war was wearing him out. He wrote Bellows at the end of the month:

> I am so well convinced that it is necessary to the safety of the country that the war should be popularized that I can hardly be loyal to the Commission, and the government, while it is required of us to let our soldiers freeze and our armies be conquered for the sake of maintaining a lie. Let the people know that we are desperately in want of arms, desperately in want of money, desperately in want of clothing, desperately in want of medicine and food for our sick, and I believe we should be relieved of our difficulties as a suffocating man is relieved by opening a window. . . . It is yet possible to stir the whole North by a confession that we need to put forth a revolutionary strength to resist a revolutionary strength. . . .[40]

To his wife he confessed that he looked forward to nothing but humiliation and the ruin of every patriotic hope, "except a miraculous man, such as does not show his head in the least, soon appear." Obviously, he had already counted out McClellan. "The chances of war are open to us and at the worst we may throw doublets, but the North certainly is not and never can be what we had hoped of it. Vulgarity and poverty of intellect rule. We have no greatness; no heroism; no art."[41] And, in the White House, no dignity.

Lounging one late September evening in the president's park, Olmsted was enjoying the music of the Marine band and the strollers grouped pleasingly on the lawn when he saw on the grand portico of the White House, looking down in a queenly way, "Mrs. Lincoln, with no other lady, and no man but that insufferable beast Wycoff [sic]." Chevalier Wikoff was an elderly adventurer with a wide and glittering European acquaintance, and a shabby reputation that had not prevented his gaining a foothold in Mrs. Lincoln's circle. "One could endure the want of tact & dignity of such an exposure," brooded Olmsted, "if there were any sign of talent or any success or thoroughness in any direction. But in fact Wm. K. Strong or Andrew H. Green"—naming his least favorite Central Park commissioners—"are in my judgment either of them better fitted to rule the land & would rule it with more dignity than those who now occupy the seat of Washington & Adams."[42]

Yet within two weeks of his outburst against the lack of dignity in the White House, Olmsted was beginning to revise his opinion of Lincoln. He met the president personally on October 11, when several commission members called on him to explain its workings and its aims. Olmsted admitted to his wife:

> He appeared older, more settled (or a man of more character) than I had before thought. He was very awkward & ill at ease in attitude, but spoke readily, with a good vocabulary, & with directness and point. Not elegantly. "I heerd of that" he said, but it did not seem very wrong from him, & his frankness & courageous directness overcame all critical disposition.[43]

Bellows, complacently reporting that he had done much of the talking during their audience, congratulated the commission on having gained an important position "when the President in this stately interview paid us such marked compliments."[44]

Bellows spoke of an important, not a unique, position: a rival on the western horizon aspired to a similar one. General John Charles Frémont, commander of the Western Department, had issued a special order early in September creating the Western Sanitary Commission, an autonomous relief agency with headquarters in St. Louis.[45] The original commission was irked that Frémont should have ignored the War Department order naming it the official agency to aid and advise the Medical Bureau; it was taken aback that a rival and duplicating agency should move into the field that Dr. John S. Newberry, its associate secretary for the West, was organizing; and it was truly dismayed that the symbol of union and nationality, which it sought to hold aloft both in its structure and in its operations, should be opposed, even from humane motives, by one of sectionalism.

Newberry had sought to persuade the Western Sanitary Commission, of which the organizing spirit was the Unitarian minister and educator William Greenleaf Eliot, to subordinate itself to the original agency. Eliot, instead, went east the middle of October to urge on Lincoln and Cameron the unwisdom of making the western organization subject to a distant central authority in view of the special conditions, especially the extent of disloyalty, in Missouri.[46] Invited to meet and treat with the members of the Sanitary Commission, he unfortunately raised the banner—to the commissioners, the bogey—of local pride, and he remained unmoved by their appeal to the symbolic importance of union in the relief efforts. He and Bellows, not quite openly quarreling, "clawed each other in an urbane, velvety, brotherly, professional Christian way"; Strong made several points that told; and Eliot left the meeting shaken and angry.[47] Yet in the end he won his way: Lincoln, within a day or two of offering his compliments to the United States Sanitary Commission, conferred his blessing on the Western. An appearance of sympathy, or at least of coordination, was with difficulty salvaged by making two of the older body's inspectors associate members of the new.[48]

Miss Dix, superintendent of nurses, reformer, and "philanthropic lunatic,"[49] was another independent operator who made a mockery of the Sanitary Commission's aspiration to be the single symbol of a unified nation's benevolence toward its soldiers. "Working on her own, she does good, but noone can cooperate with her," Strong remarked, "for she belongs to the class of comets and can be subdued into relations with no system whatever."[50] Nevertheless, the commission had authorized her to draw on its stores for hospital supplies.[51] When Olmsted prepared an appeal "To the Loyal Women of America" for blankets and other goods in short supply, directing that they be sent to the commission for distribution,[52] Miss Dix perceived in its wording a slight to the distributive system she operated and sharply upbraided him. Olmsted altered the offensive phrases to accommodate her feelings, but the incident left a bad taste in his mouth: he told her tartly that it had not occurred to the commission in addressing the public to distinguish between supplies sent to her and to it, since it had never supposed that she and it were competitors; "nor have you ever indicated that the existing arrangements in regard to hospital supplies did not entirely meet your approbation, although you have kindly called my attention to what you deemed defects in the operation of the Commission."[53]

The Women's Central's request in September to be designated a branch of the Sanitary Commission, and Dr. Newberry's success during the winter in founding branches and drawing established societies in the West into the Sanitary network heartened the commission bent on unity and union.[54] But the spirit of separatism was inextinguishable and burned in more bosoms than Dr. Eliot's and Miss Dix's.

XVI
SOME FAILURES, SOME SUCCESSES
October 1861–April 1862

THE Union repulse at Ball's Bluff on October 21 was the first defeat, but not the first cloud, to dim the radiance of McClellan's promise. All during the mild and beautiful fall, when the weather was ideal for campaigning, McClellan had constructed a system of forts around Washington and drilled his army, lending credence the while to exaggerated reports by Pinkerton's operatives of formidable numbers of the enemy across the river waiting to pounce.

The Confederate force, instead of pouncing, withdrew. On the heels of anticlimax came fiasco: a detachment of Union troops crossed the Potomac to make a demonstration near Leesburg and was pinned down under the cliff at Ball's Bluff, cut to pieces, and driven into the river. Scores drowned; ambulances could not reach the fallen on the field; rescuers removed the wounded slowly and with agonizing difficulty. The planning of the attack, the management of the retreat, both were bungled. No feature of the engagement could give any comfort to a people eager for an advance and a victory except the improved bearing of the soldiers: after this defeat, there was no demoralization.[1]

The Sanitary Commission, as soon as it received word of the engagement, sent two agents and a load of hospital stores in a rented wagon to Poolesville, opposite Leesburg. Olmsted, visiting the improvised hospitals within the week, was gratified to find the wounded decently provided with all necessities and in good spirits, eager to rejoin their regiments and go another round with the rebels.[2]

He was thoroughly incensed, however, that many of the commission's most obviously sensible recommendations continued to go unheeded. There was no sign of an ambulance corps. The ambulances supplied by the quartermaster corps were mostly wobbly two-wheelers, in which travel for wounded men was torment.[3] There was still a reckless shortage of medical stores and hospital beds. The commission's plan for five pavilion hospitals with fifteen thousand beds, submitted to the secretary of war in September, was sidetracked; McClellan and Dr. Charles S. Tripler, medical director of the Army of the Potomac, lacking surgeons to staff them and fearing the ambitious building program would attract dishonest contractors, had approved only two with five thousand beds.[4]

Government had more pressing preoccupations than the recasting of a minor cog in its hastily assembled war machine; and the commission's palliative devices were, ironically, effective enough to obscure for a time the need for reform of the Medical Bureau. Even Olmsted, cautiously disinclined to overestimate the commission's usefulness, did not know where the army would be without it. To Brace he wrote:

> You are greatly mistaken if you mean you think that the distribution of supplies is its 'great work.' It is a mere incident to its work and if it had left it alone entirely the army would not be perceptibly weaker than it is. I believe it is many brigades stronger for what it has done otherwise.[5]

Olmsted was briefly distracted from his Sanitary chores by an event in his submerged personal life: the birth, on October 28, of his second child, a girl. He reached New York a day or so later, to plunge at once into controversy over the baby's name. He favored "Content" in remembrance of his grandmother Content Pitkin Olmsted, but Vaux objected to it so strongly that he feared it would become "Contention." In recognition of prevailing political realities, he thought they might have her baptized, in water from the Potomac River, "ThankGodthingscantbemuchmeanerinmytimes." The eventual safe choice was Marion.[6]

Olmsted stayed in New York for more than two weeks. He tried to work on the park, but he was demoralized by the feeling that he might as well be nonexistent, so far as it was concerned. To be underestimated was always irritating to him, to be set completely at nought was intolerable; his bitterness against Green, the source from which flowed his inconsequence, erupted so violently one day in conversation with Charles H. Russell, a member of the finance and executive committees of the park commission, that Olmsted felt compelled to write Russell a letter accounting for his outburst.

From the day when Green started drawing a larger salary than the superintendent, Olmsted said, he had made "a constant effort not only to assume more important responsibilities and more valuable duties, but to include all other duties and responsibilities within his own, and to make those of the inferior office not only completely and servilely subordinate but to make them appear of a temporary value only and unimportant even temporarily." He had so successfully minimized the role of the superintendent that no one bothered any more to consult Olmsted when he was on the ground or to write him for advice when he was in Washington. "Conscious that my devotion to the park has forced me to patience," Olmsted accused, "he has continued to pursue a course toward me, of which no honest man could know himself to be subject without occasionally giving more or less articulate vent to his feelings such as I was so unfortunate as to betray to you."[7] The episode was significant only because it underscored Olmsted's sharpening dilemma: he could not work under Green, and he could not give up the park.

Nor could he brood long over a personal grievance; military developments riveted his attention. On November 7 a combined army and navy expeditionary force under General Thomas W. Sherman and Flag-Officer Samuel F. DuPont captured the Sea Islands in Port Royal Sound off South Carolina. The next day Senator Charles Sumner, happening to meet half a dozen Sanitarians at the Jersey ferry on their return from an organizing meeting in Philadelphia, told them that General Sherman's instructions for dealing with the ten thousand or so slaves abandoned by their masters on the Sea Islands plantations amounted to emancipation.[*,8] Olmsted could not hear such news with satisfaction: he had long held that abrupt emancipation would subject the slaves, untrained to take care of themselves, to cruel hardship.

His views on emancipation and slavery were, by coincidence, just receiving renewed attention: on the same day that Port Royal was captured, his *Cotton Kingdom* was published in New York. The literary blow hardly approximated the military; still, it stung. The English edition, published the previous month, was providing ammunition to northern sympathizers. While the *Saturday Review* dismissed it as a clever piece of special pleading and the London *Times* kept silence, the *Westminster Review* and the *Athenaeum* strongly recommended it; and John Stuart Mill, to whom Olmsted had dedicated the new edition, published a resounding article on "The Contest in America" in *Fraser's Magazine.* Acknowledging his reliance on "the calm and dispassionate Mr. Olmsted," Mill denounced the southern cause as a bald effort to perpetuate a villainous institution, denied the legality of secession, and warned that in case of a southern victory England would have to fight the Confederacy within five years.[9]

In America *Cotton Kingdom* was well received but not widely reviewed. Sumner, to whom Olmsted presented a copy, grandly but vaguely called it "a positive contribution to civilization." Lowell wrote that he was particularly impressed by the "compactness and the quiet power of the introduction to the new volumes."[10]

The introduction was a substantial addition to the original works. Otherwise, the new edition had been evolved principally by deleting sections of the three originals, mostly of *Texas*, and by effecting a certain amount of condensation and transposition. The most conspicuous deletion was the extended account of the free labor communities of the Texas Germans, sports in the southern social system that no longer seemed viable. No change in tone or temper distinguished the body of *Cotton Kingdom* from the earlier volumes, but the introduction revealed how far time and events had carried Olmsted since his first series of articles in the *Times* almost nine years before.

Olmsted had written articles and books when the nation's peace was threatened to illuminate a disputed question and to inform and moderate the

---

*Sherman's instructions were less radical than Sumner represented. Cameron, who had drafted them, had proposed that slaves who entered government lines should be used in government service, including, by implication, military service; and he had given assurance that those employed by the army would never be returned to slavery. Lincoln, solicitous of border sentiment, had eliminated the pledge that such slaves would not be handed back to their masters and specified that employment by the government was not to mean a general arming of them for military service (Allan Nevins, *The War for the Union*, 2 vols. [New York: Charles Scribner's Sons, 1959], 1: 398).

disputants. He wrote the introduction when the nation's life was threatened to deliver as heavy a blow as he could to its enemy. "Introductory: The Present Crisis" contained not one conciliatory expression. Flatly he stated that the North could make no peace with the South as a separate power; one or the other had to be subjugated and compelled to accept the labor system of the victor. In a persuasive argument, he marshaled facts and statistics—the statistics, taken from the 1850 census, had been prepared by James D. B. DeBow, champion of slavery, once head of the United States Census Bureau, and by then a leading secessionist—to demonstrate that the cotton monopoly was not a boon and a source of strength to the South but an economic and social drag more debilitating than she or her friends understood. In brief, this was war to the finish; and the southern cause was weak as well as wrong. English readers, to whom the introduction was specifically addressed, could judge which side deserved their support.[11]

But could they? Upper-class English sympathy, at least, lay with the South; the *Times*, long considered the spokesman of aristocratic liberalism, smiled on the rebellion; and the *Trent* affair was even then exciting dangerous irritation in England.

The United States sloop *San Jacinto* on November 8 had forcibly stopped the British mail ship *Trent* in the Bahama Channel, removed from her James Mason and John Slidell, Confederate commissioners on their way to Europe, and carried them off to Boston to be imprisoned. This exercise in tail twisting had enraged the British lion; in America, it had delighted the thoughtless, alarmed the sober. Olmsted, getting back to Washington from his New York sojourn soon after news of it reached the city, found his English acquaintances in "a precious stew";[12] before the commissioners were surrendered and war with England was safely skirted, he was in one himself. Russell offers a glimpse of him, one evening in December, the bearer of an alarming report that Lord Richard Lyons, the British minister, had had a violent quarrel with Seward, flown into a passion, and stamped out of the room. The idea that Lord Lyons might behave violently or passionately was laughable to Russell.

> I was enabled to assure Mr. Olmsted that there was not the smallest foundation for the story; but he seemed impressed with a sense of some great calamity, and told me there was a general belief that England only wanted a pretext for a quarrel with the United States; nor could I comfort him by the assurance that there were good reasons for thinking General Scott would soon annex Canada in case of war.[13]

Nothing—certainly not frivolous rumors about the conquest of Canada—could comfort Olmsted for England's failure of sympathy. Regarding her as the mother country, he had long had a reverence akin to patriotism for her, a feeling that was mocked and outraged by the comment of the London *Times*:

> A fearful uproar of words, screams and blows reaches the mother, who hastens to allay the tumult. When she arrives she finds all confusion,

and Master John and Master Tom each with a tale of outrages and provocations, each resolved to have the last word, and afraid of nothing so much
as that the other should get a hearing. The parent sees enough to be sure
that both were abundantly in the wrong, but that it is impossible to ad-
judicate between them. The general impression in this country is that both
sides in the States have acted as ill as could be, and that it is not for England to decide which of them bears the palm for insolence, treachery, and
folly.[14]

It was bad enough that such a sentiment was general and that a man in Russell's
position should foster it. "But when I know," Olmsted wrote his old friend Alfred
Field, "that a man for whom I have the respect and regard and something more
that I have for you, expressed no other than the popular view of the case, to
which the Times administers above, I must say that I am shocked and grieved,
and feel it is a more melancholy thing than all that occurs at home."[15]

At home Olmsted recognized melancholy things besides slavery and war. "I
don't really think the fact of slavery is nearly as degrading to the race as the fact
of Lynch's election,"* Olmsted wrote Brace. "I think the slaveholders stand
higher in the rank of civilization than English merchants or New York politicians. I declare that nothing in the progress of the war has been half so discouraging to me as the evidence of an insanity of meanness in England and of imbecility in the people of New York, which it has evoked."[16]

Thus disinclined to consider slaveholders uniquely sinful, Olmsted sharply
rebuked Brace as "savage" for suggesting that the slaves be stirred to rise against
them.[17] He believed that the slaves ought to be used against the rebellion but in
an orderly and disciplined way. Resurrecting his favorite pseudonym "Yeoman,"
he set forth a proposal in a letter to the New York Times late in November.

It was one of the leading delusions of the rebels, he wrote, that the slaves
were a source of military strength to their owners. The conduct of the Port Royal
slaves was the first clear evidence of the weakness of the proposition: they did
not flee with their fleeing masters; they stayed behind to pillage and without any
inducements or promises dropped into the hands of the Union army. As property, however, they were the sinews of the rebellion; and the government could
cut the sinews. Let it seize and fortify points at Wilmington, Hilton Head, Fer-
nandina, Pensacola, Galveston, San Antonio, and a few other places; control
strategic mountain passes in Kentucky and Tennessee, and offer them as harbor
for slaves. The prospect of escape would "set on foot a quiet and inactive method
of exhausting the effective resources of the rebellion, which will increase and
become more and more irresistible, the longer all other methods of attack are
incompletely successful." Olmsted also advocated arming the slaves, arguing that
to subject them to military discipline would reduce rather than increase the danger of servile insurrection.[18]

*James Lynch was elected sheriff of New York in November 1861.

The suggestion received no official recognition; nor was any comprehensive policy yet formulated for handling contrabands. Olmsted feared "that the slaves will get emancipated long before we are in a condition to deal with them decently in any other way than as slaves."[19] He, however, was elaborating a plan to get them dealt with decently as paid workmen.

It was his idea to show in the Sea Islands with contrabands that Negroes would work for wages, that slavery was not a necessary condition of their usefulness and good order, and that there was an alternative consistent with the peace and dignity of the southern white population. Such a demonstration would give pause to moderate southerners and weaken their attachment to slavery and the rebellion. The prerequisite to a successful demonstration was a workable policy.

Up to the end of the year, no policy but military expedience, leavened by incidental and faltering benevolence, had controlled the relations of the army to the Sea Islands contrabands. It had seized the cotton crop still standing in the fields and all other useful property, including mules and boats for transport and grain and cattle for the commissary, thus leaving the blacks, to whom the usual issue of winter clothing had not yet been made when their masters and overseers fled, unprovided as well with draft animals and food. The contrabands were put to work for wages to pick and gin the cotton for shipment north, where it was to be sold to the government's account—their wages to come eventually out of the proceeds of the sale. This was the only financial arrangement that occurred to the harried secretary of the treasury, who was saddled with collection and sale of the crop. It hardly seemed consistent with the blessings of freedom to the contrabands, who were resentful, suspicious, and reluctant to work.

To collect and sell the crop, Secretary Chase had appointed cotton agents under the direction of Lieutenant Colonel W. N. Reynolds of the First Rhode Island Artillery. To organize the contrabands' labor and plan for their future welfare, he sent to Port Royal his young friend Edward L. Pierce, a Harvard Law School graduate of abolitionist sympathies, who had had some experience in handling contrabands at Fortress Monroe. Pierce left for his assignment on January 13. At about the same time, Olmsted heard from the Sanitary Commission agent at Port Royal that no adequate policy was yet in operation there.

Disquieted, Olmsted called on Edwin M. Stanton, who had just replaced Cameron as secretary of war, and on Chase to urge them to set the blacks immediately to work listing the fields for the next season's crop, the proceeds of which ought to support them during the following year; failure to do so would certainly make paupers and objects of charity of them in the near future. Not satisfied with Chase's assurance that he had just employed "a person whom he believed to be fully competent to superintend the business and that he possessed all requisite authority of action," Olmsted went to see Senator Lafayette Sabine Foster of Connecticut. Foster asked him to draw up a bill outlining a plan of management for the estates and contrabands that he could introduce into the Senate.

Olmsted's bill expressed two basic purposes: one, to protect the blacks against the impending ravages of hunger and disease—simply to keep them

183

alive; the other, to train them in a few fundamental duties of free men: self-support without recourse to charity, regard for family obligations, and submission, now they were free of the despotic will of their masters, to the rightful authority of law.

The bill called, specifically, for the creation of a bureau under the War Department, directed by three appointive commissioners who would arrange with private citizens to rent the plantations and employ and support the Negroes on wages or, alternatively, who could take the business into their own hands and provide for its cost out of government funds at the rate of ten dollars an acre. For the plantations, the commissioners were like receivers in bankruptcy; toward the contrabands, they were in the position of guardians of the poor or of orphans, charged to encourage and enforce industry and vested with authority like that of a master over apprentices. Government funds, derived from the sale of the cotton crop, were to be spent only on operating the plantations; no money was allowed for charity, and none was allotted for educational or moral training. The commissioners, however, were empowered to help the contrabands help themselves to that end and to forward the work of benevolent societies. Foster, satisfied with Olmsted's draft, introduced it unchanged to the Senate the middle of February.

Pierce, meanwhile, proposed to Chase that superintendents be engaged at one thousand dollars a year to cultivate the plantations and supervise the education and moral training of the contrabands with the aid of missionaries and teachers. The operation was to be managed under Treasury jurisdiction by a director general of recognized ability and character. The weakness of Pierce's proposal was that Treasury authority derived only from an act that authorized the president to permit commercial intercourse with any part of the country declared to be in insurrection, under rules laid down by the secretary of the treasury.

When Pierce sought the required authorization from Lincoln, the president handed him a note requesting Chase to give Pierce "such instructions in regard to Port Royal contrabands as may seem judicious." Olmsted, wanting the experiment to be conducted under clearer authority than the Treasury Department seemed to have, continued to work to enlist popular and editorial support for Foster's bill; and he fumed at the "listlessness, indifference and utter childish cowardice" of "controlling minds at Washington," who neglected the priceless opportunity for proving to the South the economic mistake of slavery.

Controlling minds in Washington might be shirking the contraband problem, but minds elsewhere were earnestly engaged on it. Three philanthropic societies were formed in February and early March—the Education Committee in Boston, the Freedmen's Aid Organization in New York, and the Port Royal Relief Association in Philadelphia. To a leader of the Boston group, who had suggested starting savings banks for the contrabands, Olmsted pointed out the hazard of piecemeal benevolence. Something systematic and far-reaching was required. "Little can be done by philanthropy as philanthropy," he declared.

> The extension of civilized law & social polity so as to include the negro among other human beings is what is wanted & for any organized work there must be some few, distinct, large purposes clearly in view, and some central will & power to which all details must be subordinated in their proper order.

While Foster's bill hung fire in the Senate, Chase acted to forestall it. On February 20 he appointed Pierce a special agent of the Treasury Department with general supervision of all employees on the Sea Islands plantations. Less than two weeks later Pierce sailed for Port Royal to take up his new duties. He bore with him a far from compelling letter from Stanton to the military authorities at Port Royal; it recommended Pierce to their countenance and to such assistance as they might conveniently give him incidental to the operations of war. With him sailed forty-one men and twelve women, the first contingent of the force of missionaries and teachers that the relief societies had assembled and would pay until the government could assume some of the expense after the cotton crop was sold.

Thus, under a divided and dubious authority and supported by private philanthropy, began the Sea Islands experiment.

Olmsted, still hoping to get Congress to confer specific authority on the War Department, wrote a letter on March 8 to Lincoln stating the "few, distinct, large purposes" which should guide the government in dealing with the contrabands: to maintain their lives during the current emergency and to train them in the social duties of free men in a civilized society. He did not mention the Foster bill, but Lincoln could see for himself, if he came to read it, that the government's duties as Olmsted had outlined them could be satisfactorily carried out within its framework.

The bill, in fact, passed the Senate early in March, and Olmsted began to organize backing for it in the House. Chase thereupon sent for Olmsted, told him he did not want the bill to pass, and asked him to take entire charge of the Port Royal plantations and Negroes. A couple of days later, on March 13, he wrote Olmsted a hasty note asking if he had made up his mind to be designated Pierce's successor.

Olmsted had not. Out of courtesy to Chase, however, he asked his congressional supporters to let the Foster bill sleep while he considered the offer. Meanwhile the three Port Royal relief associations had combined into one organization and formed a sort of league with the government, somewhat on the order of the Sanitary Commission. On March 19 its representatives asked Olmsted to take the post of its general agent, charged with the direction of affairs at Port Royal and empowered to deal with the government on its behalf. With Chase and the relief society both urging him to accept top spot, Olmsted seemed surely destined for Port Royal and control of a unique and critical demonstration that might conceivably shorten the war. Pierce, who had all along wanted to be relieved in April, wrote Olmsted that he expected any day to welcome him as his successor.

Somehow the project collapsed. Olmsted's discretion veils the particulars, but he later referred to a disillusioning interview he had with Chase about the beginning of April. During it he learned that the secretary "had never read the Bill in question [Foster's]; that he entirely misapprehended its scope and purpose; and that he regards himself as having no power to confer any authority upon an agent which would have the slightest practical value." Olmsted bluntly told Chase that the business could never be conducted under such insufficient authority as his and that he would not take charge of it. He would accept the job only from Stanton.

Olmsted saw Stanton the evening of April 11. He read the secretary a paper outlining the government's possible courses toward the contrabands and eliminating all but one—that of saving them in the current crisis of beggary and training them in the responsibilities of free men; and he urged Stanton formally to assume the duty for the War Department. If he would do so, he, Olmsted, would be willing to accept the responsibility of executing it. He was authorized to pledge, too, the faith of leading citizens of Philadelphia, New York, and Boston that they would meet in a systematic and generous manner the requirements of education and moral training that ought to lie outside the government's sphere of activity.

Olmsted left Stanton with the satisfied feeling that he had won him over; and the president, he knew, was being pressed by members of the aid society who hoped to convince him that Chase's course was wrong, Olmsted's right. If both Stanton and Lincoln came around, Olmsted could expect to be nominated military governor of the Sea Islands within twenty-four hours.

The aid society delegates, however, found the president "much perplexed," favorably impressed with the plan they proposed but unable to grant their main point, the nomination of Olmsted as military governor, because "Mr. Chase had already offered the place to someone else." When they called on Chase, he professed to be delighted that the difficult question had engaged their attention; he was committed, however, by an offer to Pierce.*

One of the aid society men wondered how he could be committed by an offer to a man who had repeatedly said that he wanted to give up the post. Olmsted, however, was philosophical about the failure of his appointment and did not consider his three months of lobbying wasted: he had thoroughly impressed his views on the aid society members, and their agents on the spot could be expected to be influenced by them.[20] Of his Sea Islands agitation he said to his father: "I believe it paid, though the study and energy I gave to the matter did not accomplish the precise result, or anything like as good a result, as I meant it should."[21] Whether he recognized it or not, it was the kind of failure to which

*Perhaps it was Chase's ambiguous role in this matter that led Olmsted to revise his opinion of him. Not long before, he had said that Chase, with Stanton, was the nearest thing to a great man that there was in Washington; not long after, he wrote him off as "a ward politician with a clean face" (O to Bertha Olmsted, 28 January 1862, O to CLB, 30 September 1862).

he was constitutionally prone—the failure to get a philosophically based, carefully thought-out plan accepted by minds not necessarily lighter than his but constrained by considerations the urgency of which he saw in a different perspective.

While Olmsted's Port Royal scheme was tacking into oblivion, the Sanitary Commission's effort to bring about the reform of the Medical Bureau, in which Olmsted was simultaneously engaged, was nearing success. The first overt move to oust Surgeon General Finley had come when Dr. Agnew, acting independently of the commission, denounced his nonfeasance and called for his removal in the *New York World* of November 16. The *Times*, counterattacking, had defended Finley and severely criticized the commission.[22] The *World* had retorted with more charges against the surgeon general,[23] the *Tribune* had joined the fray on the side of the commission, and the *Washington Republican* had impugned Sanitary respectability.[24] Raymond, thitherto Olmsted's steady ally, allowed a Miss Powell, with whom he was cultivating "a silly Platonic friendship," access to the *Times* to air under the pseudonym of "Truth" horrendous charges against the commission and to reveal that its secretary was consumed by a passion for power and money.[25] Olmsted personally assured Raymond that his information was false and his informant an imposter, but the editor was unmoved;[26] he continued as though spellbound to uphold the surgeon general and denigrate the commission.

Meanwhile the commission, in December, had presented a damaging bill of particulars against Finley to McClellan and urged his dismissal;[27] and it had persuaded Senator Wilson, chairman of the Military Affairs Committee, to introduce its bill for the reform of the Medical Bureau. The bill provided, among other things, for the compulsory retirement of medical officers at the age of sixty-two, the selection of the surgeon general on grounds of competence, not seniority, and the independence of the bureau from the Subsistence and the Quartermaster departments.[28]

Finley, himself sixty-five, called all the medical officers in Washington to a meeting at which they went on record against the bill. Hammond, the Sanitary Commission's candidate for surgeon general, and Olmsted began to organize support for it among well-disposed senators. As both sides worked feverishly to rally backing, the infighting became bitter. Hammond, perhaps rightly, suspected Finley of ordering him and other dissidents to out-of-town posts so that the apparently united opposition of the medical corps to the bill might not be breached; and Miss Powell, probably wrongly, accused Olmsted of tipping off Mrs. Raymond that her husband's concern for the surgeon general was motivated less by friendly than by amorous considerations.[29]

The Sanitary Commission, finding itself in the course of the exchange of slurs under a cloud along with the Medical Bureau, had at hand the means to dissipate it: a document addressed to the secretary of war making full disclosure of its findings, recommendations, and accomplishments. Olmsted had begun writing it, with Strong's help, early in December, working in his usual suicidal way. "I have been up every morning at nine o'clock," he wrote his wife, "had tea in my bed-room & then read from memo to a stenographer, who is writing out my General Report. . . . This till the Board meet, & that till dinner time, then evening sessions & odds & ends till 2 o'ck. . . ."[30] By that time he was sometimes so tired that he fell fully dressed into bed. A couple of weeks of such work left Olmsted done up and Elliott no better. Toward the end, Olmsted did not dare leave the statistician alone, "as he topples asleep."[31]

The report appeared the end of December. Synthesizing the returns of nearly four hundred inspections of every branch of the army, it spoke specifically and authoritatively of campsites, tents, food, clothing, sanitary arrangements, discipline, recreation, diseases, ambulances, hospitals, surgeons, administration; everything affecting the health and efficiency of the volunteer troops was frankly and knowledgeably discussed. Dangerous conditions were exposed, remedies proposed, and the commission's palliatives described. Nowhere did personalities or polemics enter in, and the newspaper controversy was not mentioned. The motive of the report was plainly what Olmsted said it was: "A simple desire and resolute determination to secure for the men who have enlisted in this war that care which it is the duty and the will of the nation to give them."[32]

Sending an advance copy to Bellows shortly before Christmas, Olmsted advised him to organize "a grand simultaneous expression of confidence in the Commission" to counteract the *Times's* attacks.[33] When the report appeared, the *Tribune,* the *Herald,* and the *Post* joined with the *World* in a chorus of approbation; and the *Times,* with a few feeble face-saving expressions, reversed itself.[34] Perhaps Miss Powell's friendship had already palled on Raymond; perhaps the report converted him.

While the Sanitary Commission, having silenced the *Times,* lobbied high and low for the passage of the medical bill,[35] the surgeon general took the offensive. He attacked Hammond on the ground of health: Hammond had given heart strain as his reason for resigning from the medical corps of the regular army in 1859. And in March, Finley struck at the commission, refusing its agents, "irresponsible and ignorant pretenders," access to Medical Bureau records, which, he said, they misinterpreted to discredit him.[36]

The prohibition was conceivably a blunder, since the War Department order forming the commission had specified that all department employees were to forward its efforts. Finley then committed a worse one: he quarreled with Stanton. The irascible secretary accused him of handling an inquiry indiscreetly, Finley demanded a court martial, Stanton threatened to strike him summarily from the rolls, and Finley addressed a pathetic appeal to Lincoln for protection against "official injustice." Whether justice or mercy or somewhat tempered vengeance was the operative factor in his fate, Finley was assigned to duty in Boston, whereupon he asked to be retired. His request was granted, with a generous sop: he was breveted brigadier general.[37] Almost simultaneously, on April 18, 1862, the medical bill passed both houses of Congress and with Lincoln's signature became law.[38]

Effective reform of the bureau depended, finally, on the selection of a strong surgeon general. Dr. Hammond, the commission's choice, having reenlisted in the medical corps at the beginning of the war, was low on the roster of officers; nevertheless, his experience in and out of the army, his standing as a hospital administrator, and his knowledge of the Medical Bureau's needs all recommended him above any other medical officer to the commission.[39] It had obtained McClellan's cordial and Stanton's cool endorsement of him.[40] Bellows, designated to urge the appointment on Lincoln, called at the White House the evening of Friday, April 18, and was earnestly expounding Hammond's merits when the president amiably cut him short: "Shouldn't wonder if he was Surgeon General already," he remarked.[41]

"As to the Sanitary Commission," Olmsted exultantly wrote his father next day,

> our success is suddenly wonderfully complete. The Medical Bill after having been kicked about like a football . . . until it was so thoroughly flabbergasted that nobody knew where or what it was, and a new one had to be started—this process repeated several times—all of a sudden a bill which is just the thing we wanted quietly passes thro both houses the same day and before we know it is law, and this occurs the moment the Secy of War kicks the old Surgeon General out of his seat. . . . The President yesterday promised to nominate for Surgeon General, Hammond, the very man whom, eight months ago, we picked out as the best man in the corps for that office, and who, this having been discovered, has since been regarded as a rebel and rancorously hated accordingly. . . .[42]

The old officers were outraged that Hammond had been passed over so many venerable heads.[43] They could do no more, however, than bewail the "ruin" of the corps while Hammond set about the job of reorganizing the bureau.

XVII
HOSPITAL TRANSPORTS
March–July 1862

DURING the first months of 1862, the Sanitary Commission had had increasing difficulty in raising funds to continue its work; and it was so disheartened by official promises repeatedly broken that it had several times debated resigning in protest.[1] Olmsted had begun casting about for other work. Mayor George Opdyke of New York wanted him as street commissioner, and he was half-disposed to accept the nomination.[2] A bill, too, was before Congress creating a Bureau of Agriculture and Statistics, and Olmsted toyed with the idea of seeking appointment as its commissioner. The third possibility he considered was to return to landscape architecture and build up a private practice. Much as that course appealed to him, he feared that he was not likely to follow it very steadily, even at forty. " 'Wherever you see a head, hit it,' is my style of work," he admitted to his father, "and I have not yet sowed my wild oats altogether. . . ."[3]

After the middle of April, both the commission and its secretary dismissed the thought of quitting; the passage of the medical bill improved their position vis-à-vis the Medical Bureau, and the war had at last entered an aggressive phase. Lincoln, whose patience was exhausted by McClellan's reluctance to join battle, at the end of January ordered an attack on the Confederate army at Manassas. McClellan proposed instead to make a feint toward Manassas, then move the entire army by boat to Fortress Monroe, march up the peninsula between the James and York rivers to Richmond, and capture the Confederates' capital while their army was still distracted by the threat to Manassas. Lincoln refused to hear of the plan unless forty thousand men were left to cover Washington. After some debate, McClellan conceded the point, and the stage was set for a major military movement.

On March 10 the army began to advance on Manassas. General Johnston, who had been able to follow the Washington newspapers' accounts of the Lincoln-McClellan dispute, withdrew toward Richmond. McClellan encountered no enemy but only a drab countryside ravaged by foragers and at Manassas, a smoldering camp littered with wrecked equipment and dead horses. The Sanitary agents accompanying the army had nothing to do but pick up souvenirs.

The campaign on the peninsula, however, was to lay a heavy duty on the commission, and there was a useful precedent for discharging it. Earlier in the year, after the battles of Fort Donelson and Shiloh, distance and terrain had precluded setting up general hospitals near the lines, and the wounded were transported by river steamers to military hospitals in St. Louis, Cincinnati, and other port cities. The army's hospital ships, in charge of the Quartermaster Department, which was more than occupied in moving troops and military supplies, had been tragically inadequate. Western branches of the Sanitary Commission and other nongovernment relief agencies had hastily chartered, staffed and supplied steamers, and cared for thousands who might otherwise have perished. The commission proposed a similar arrangement for the care of the army about to embark on the peninsular campaign.[4]

The Army of the Potomac began to go ashore at Fortress Monroe on April 4. McClellan intended to attack Yorktown from the south with two corps under Generals Samuel P. Heintzelman and Erasmus D. Keyes, while a third corps, under McDowell, having moved up the north side of the river, attacked the city from the rear. The latter tactic was abandoned: Lincoln, learning that McClellan regarded the army in the Shenandoah Valley as the promised forty-thousand-man cover for Washington, complained that the commander had not kept his word and withheld McDowell's corps to defend the capital. Deprived of his flanking column and misled again by the egregious Pinkerton spies as to the enemy's strength, McClellan decided to take the position by siege, not by assault. For a month the army sat and occasionally skirmished in the mud around Yorktown, while fevers did heavier execution in its ranks than guns.

Meanwhile, Olmsted was equipping and staffing the few hospital ships the Sanitary Commission's limited funds would permit.[5] Again, the commission intended merely to supplement the work of the Medical Bureau by caring for the sick and wounded whom the bureau placed aboard its ships. After an unexpected delay—the first ship assigned by the quartermaster general was withdrawn after she was partly converted[6]—the *Daniel Webster*, with Olmsted commanding the Sanitary contingent aboard, weighed anchor at Alexandria at four P.M. on April 27 and steamed down the Potomac.[7]

She was an old ocean liner, formerly on the New York–Aspinwall run, and lately used as a troop transport. Turned over to the commission only two days before by General Meigs, she had been hurriedly stocked and staffed; cleaning and converting to hospital use were to take place en voyage. The Sanitary party included Olmsted, Knapp, Strong, and Agnew, several of their Philadelphia colleagues, four surgeons, half-a-dozen medical students to be used as dressers, a score or more of volunteer male nurses, and four New York women: Mrs. William Griffin, Mrs. David Lane, Mrs. Joseph Howland, and her sister Georgeanna Woolsey. Besides the Sanitary agents, the *Webster* carried a short ship's crew, some convalescent soldiers and officers returning to their regiments, a few carpenters and Quartermaster Department mechanics, and some contrabands and miscellaneous passengers.[8]

As the *Webster* dropped downstream on the bright Sunday afternoon, the ladies sat on deck sewing on a hospital flag and singing hymns. They thrilled to such warlike sights as the "stone fleet" ready for sinking in the channel should the *Merrimac* try to run up the Potomac and the little gunboat *Yankee* herding five rebel craft she had just seized in the Rappahannock. Olmsted busied himself dividing the Sanitary group into two watches and assigning the work of refitting the ship.[9]

All the *Webster's* transport arrangements were filthy, in addition to being unsuited to hospital use, and had to be torn out. She had to be scraped from stem to stern; the steerage had to be whitewashed, new bunks had to be installed and furnished, a new deckhouse had to be built forward, and an apothecary's shop had to be knocked together and fitted. Laboring around the clock, workmen and Sanitary people made the *Webster* into a shipshape floating hospital by Monday afternoon when they reached the broad mouth of the York River.[10]

Threading her way at sunset up the river, the *Webster* came to anchor at Cheeseman's Creek. On either shore the woods were studded with tents and alive with masses of men, and the stream was dense with hundreds of transports —steamers and sailing vessels, big and little—some of them packed with men who had been waiting days for the order to debark. As night came, the *Webster's* wondering passengers watched the ships about them light up, until the fleet sparkled in the harbor like a floating city. Campfires glowed from either shore, and huge bonfires, set to get rid of brush and small timber useless for road-building, reddened the night sky. The sound of singing, drums, and bugles arose from camp and fleet and floated across the water. Occasionally through the melodious martial clamor sounded the menacing voices of the big guns at the siege.

The first order of business next morning was to report the *Webster's* arrival to the medical director, Dr. Tripler. Up at dawn, Olmsted, accompanied by Strong, Agnew, and several other colleagues, took a small boat and went up the harbor. Navigating warily among the anchored transports and the shuttling tugs and lighters, they came to the shore of a big meadow and debarked upon a scene of purposeful commotion. Orderlies with horses, hurrying messengers, sentries, loungers, fatigue parties, quartermaster personnel black and white, and teams and heavy army wagons crowded the landing. Big guns and stacks of shot and shell cumbered the ground; wagons loaded with forage and biscuit boxes and ammunition lurched up the slope. Beyond, in the open field, stood a number of wall tents, one the quartermaster's office, another the post office, another the telegraph office, and another the harbormaster's office, and a stockade filled with rebel prisoners of war.[11]

Olmsted and his party penetrated the confusion to the tent of Colonel Rufus Ingalls, the quartermaster. Kind and prompt, he at once ordered horses for them, and they rode off toward McClellan's headquarters through the swamp forest. The roads, used up by heavy military traffic, were bottomless and sticky morasses, where wagons mired hopelessly and draft animals sank and occasionally drowned. Work parties of soldiers were felling trees, the crash and smell of which thickened the air, to make corduroy roads, along which drivers of sixteen- and twenty-mule teams navigated wagons carrying mortars, gun beds, and other heavy equipment to the siege. Riding through woods, open ground, and camps, Olmsted and his party came to the crest of a low rise and broke abruptly upon a grand open view of the valley, where the York, a full mile wide, rolled between wooded banks. On the slope before them, an open space of several hundred acres, lay a tent city for some thirty or forty thousand men alive with movement. The crash of artillery in the near distance enhanced the theatrically military effect.[12]

They found Dr. Tripler in his tent. His account of his preparations was disquieting. They were sketchy, and he had been unlucky as well. He had arranged for a thousand beds in hotels and other improvised hospitals at Fortress Monroe; closer to the siege at Ship Point, he had requisitioned three clusters of abandoned rebel huts, floorless and standing on swampy ground, for hospital use; and he had secured two hospital transports to carry the wounded north. Medicines and hospital equipment were almost entirely lacking; before the army was set in motion, Tripler had distributed what he thought were adequate supplies, but they had been left behind. The medical officers, he found, supposed that the medical purveyor would furnish them with fresh supplies at every change of position. New supplies had been arriving for the past couple of weeks, but they had been shipped in various vessels and mingled with other cargo so that it was taking days first to find them, then to unload them. Even then at the Ship Point hospital, men were lying on bare floors in their filthy uniforms, dying of typhoid; many might have been saved had they had a bed or a blanket, a clean nightshirt, stimulants, and appropriate food.[13]

The Sanitarians, dismayed, asked themselves what would happen when the siege became heavy and the wounded outmatched the sick in numbers. The question was not immediately put to a test. On the morning of May 5 the Sanitary people on the *Webster*, having listened through a disturbed night to heavy bombardment at Yorktown, learned that the enemy had evacuated the stronghold.[14]

Until then, the *Webster* had taken aboard only thirty-five patients, mostly fever cases, but as the Army of the Potomac prepared to shift its base farther up the York, the sick and wounded from the broken camps began to come in, some jostled cruelly in wagons that had bumped over miles of corduroy roads, others carried more comfortably on the *Wilson Small* and the *Elizabeth*, small shallow-draft boats the commission had secured to run up creeks and ferry patients to the transport.[15] When the *Webster* had almost two hundred seriously ill and wounded aboard—all of them dirty, neglected, and suffering terribly—she sailed for New York in charge of the Sanitary Commission's Dr. J. M. Grymes. Olmsted at once turned his attention to making the *Ocean Queen*, a fine large steamer just obtained from the quartermaster general, ready for hospital use.[16]

The *Queen* was lying-to in the channel off Cheeseman's Creek, one of the fleet of three hundred transports and a dozen men-of-war about to sail for Yorktown, when Olmsted boarded her with Knapp, Mrs. Howland, Miss Woolsey, some medical students, and two doctors. While the commission's agents stood on her deck in the rain watching the impressive advance of the fleet, the *Queen*, her hospital flag snapping at the mast, moved slowly through the squadron and steamed at its head up the river until she anchored off Yorktown with only a gun-boat as picket guard above her.[17]

Shortly after, two small sternwheelers loaded with sick men came alongside. The officer in charge intended to place them upon the *Queen*. They were mostly typhoid cases who had been sent by ambulance to the shore of Wormeley's Creek, dumped on the ground there, and left to lie for twenty-four hours in the rain without food or attendance. Some were delirious, all were miserable. Olmsted was sure several would die unless they promptly received food, medication, and warmth. Since nothing was yet available on the *Queen*, he refused to accept them. When the officer in charge insisted on transferring them, Olmsted posted ship's officers at the gangplanks with orders to let no one come aboard and went ashore to find a surgeon. Returning with a willing civilian doctor, he found his guards had given way and every man who could crawl had boarded the *Queen*. Dirty, shivering, and hungry, they huddled on the cabin floors in their wet uniforms, while the "glorious women," who had somehow dug up a barrel of Indian meal and made gruel, fed it to them out of the deck buckets with the only two spoons on the ship. "I never saw such misery or such gratitude," Olmsted reflected.[18]

Bribing and browbeating the "half-mutinous, superstitious, beastly Portuguese crew," Olmsted got them to work helping the helpless aboard, a painful and tedious process. Before it was over, Knapp and Dr. Robert Ware arrived on the well-stocked *Elizabeth* from Cheeseman's Creek, and the captain, with the medical students, from shore. Straw, bedsacks, medicines, and stimulants were hoisted onto the *Queen*. Knapp went ashore in search of meat. Displaying a cold-blooded efficiency that surprised Olmsted in so gentle a man, he shot and dressed a rebel cow he found at pasture and returned triumphant with the meat. By ten that evening, every sick man was in a warm bed and had had medical treatment, beef tea, and milk punch. Three had died.[19]

Next day, even before more supplies and personnel reached the *Queen*, the sternwheelers had put aboard her more than three hundred patients. Some were delirious, some comatose, some moribund; all were filthy and shattered by travel in springless carts, by rough handling, and by exposure, hunger, and thirst. Each had to be washed, changed, bedded, medicated, and fed—everything had to be done for everyone at once. To cope systematically with overwhelming confusion was the problem.[20]

Olmsted quickly organized the ship into six wards, five for the very sick, most of whom had typhoid, and one for those suffering from bronchitis, hernia, rheumatism, lameness, and exhaustion. He placed a surgeon in charge of each ward. To each surgeon he assigned two ward masters and four nurses, each with specific duties, who took watches. To help these, he assigned assistant nurses, contrabands, servants, and convalescent soldiers. The ladies, already in charge of the linen and household supplies, operated the special diet pantry, where meals were prepared for those too sick for the regular food.[21]

To get decent food, properly cooked and properly distributed, was the greatest immediate difficulty. The resourceful Knapp, pursuing his search-and-slaughter operations ashore, provided adequate beef. The women improvised chafing dishes, which wonderfully extended the possibilities of the ill-equipped galley. The captain, resolute and sympathetic, exacted extra duty from his sulky crew as waiters. Somehow, Olmsted scarcely understood how, everyone was cared for. "Just think of it for a moment," he wrote.

> Here were one hundred miserably sick and dying men, forced upon us before we had been an hour on board; and tug after tug swarming around the great ship, before we had a nail out of a box, and when there were but ten pounds of Indian meal and two spoons to feed them with. No account could do justice to the faithful industry of the medical students and young men: how we all got through with it, I hardly know; but one idea is distinct,—that every man had a good place to sleep in, and something hot to eat daily, and that the sickest had every essential that could have been given them in their own homes.[22]

When the *Ocean Queen* put to sea with her cargo of eleven hundred casualties, Olmsted finally realized that he was ill himself from exhaustion. "A few hours' rest and a quiet dinner brought me all right, however," he reported, "and at sunset I set out with Knapp to look after the sick ashore."[23]

The medical director's scant appreciation was expressed in his official report. Olmsted, Tripler said, had engaged to fit up the *Ocean Queen* as a hospital transport within forty-eight hours of getting possession of her.

> It took rather longer than that, however, and then she carried but three-fifths of the number she should have carried. Of course, in inaugurating a system of this kind, under our circumstances, some delays, some awkwardness and some confusion were to be expected. If I had had at my disposal a few medical officers of experience, these arrangements could have been made with more rapidity and precision. As it was, with the exception of the Surgeon General of Pennsylvania, I had no one on the water who had the faculty of rapid systemization; but all seemed disposed to do the best they could, and I believe the operations at Yorktown were fully as successful as could have been hoped for.[24]

This was the Sanitary Commission's comparatively simple—or so it seemed in retrospect—introduction to its role during the peninsular campaign. After the army moved its supply base upriver to West Point, and while it slogged and fought through the swamps, the commission, which had engaged to care only for the casualties placed by the medical director on Sanitary ships, instead found itself aiding them wherever they lay—in camps, in shore hospitals, on government-operated ships, on wharves, and on creekbanks. For a time early in the campaign, Olmsted claimed, it was actually distributing more food, medicine, stimulants, and hospital supplies than the government itself, much of them to surgeons under Dr. Tripler's jurisdiction.[25]

The commission's work was complicated by the fact that Olmsted rarely knew from day to day what transports he could command. It repeatedly happened that a ship assigned by the quartermaster to the commission, and readied by it for hospital use at considerable expense, was abruptly withdrawn. The *Ocean Queen* made but one trip to New York before she was taken away and replaced with the less desirable *Spaulding*.[26] The *Elm City* was suddenly requisitioned to transport troops; her Sanitary contingent, having put in an exhausting day transshipping wounded to the *Spaulding*, spent the whole of a very dark night stripping her of hospital gear and coaling her; next day, plans were changed, and she was reassigned to the commission, whose agents had another twenty-four hours' work to refit her, carrying back on board the same supplies they had just taken off. "It is an exercise of patience, but it must be done without delay," Knapp observed with forced resignation.[27]

A hazard the commission could avert was unsuitable volunteers. Olmsted was insistent "that whoever comes here on any business comes, not to do such work as he thinks himself fit for, but such as he will be assigned to, and under such authority as will be assigned him. He or she must come as distinctly under an obligation of duty in this respect as if under pay, and must expect to submit to the same discipline."[28] Many volunteers offered themselves on those terms. One was Katherine Prescott Wormeley. Daughter of a British rear admiral, she had spent the first eighteen of her thirty-two years in England and France, where she had a wide acquaintance in the upper ranks of society and among literary people. High-minded, humorless, and homely, Miss Wormeley was, as well, clever and cultivated; her executive capacity made her an outstanding lieutenant to Olmsted, and her literary skill made her an effective propagandist for the commission.

Between the Sanitary workers—those who passed the grueling test imposed by daily experience—and their chief a peculiar bond developed, intimate and respectful. Olmsted was more than the executive whose administrative genius was a constant source of assurance and comfort to them; he was also a fatherly protector who guarded their health, their time, their dignity with more zeal than he did his own. Familiarity bred mutual admiration. The women openly venerated him. The Woolsey sisters felt safe in his care even at the edge of a war;[29] and Miss Wormeley revered him with a dash of something very like ardor.[30] Young Edward Mitchell marveled at his tact: he had "as much as a woman. Also much shrewdness and a very quiet manner."[31] For his part, Olmsted could hardly write a letter or a report without some appreciative mention of the selflessness, ingenuity, sang-froid, discipline, cheerfulness of his coworkers. For all of them, in spite of the strain and frequent horror of their duties, their fellowship and their experience were rewarding, even happy. When Olmsted remarked to his weary crew, after an excruciatingly hard night's work, that all their hardships would be very satisfactory to recall by and by, one of the women exclaimed earnestly: "Recall! Why, I never had half the present satisfaction in any week of my life before!"[32] They all were daily witnessing heroism, caring for heroes, sharing with them in a small measure but worthily the immense burden of the nation.

Those who could stand the gaff had more than benevolence and sacrificial spirit: they had discipline and stamina. Otherwise, confusion, fatigue, and shock would have utterly nullified good intentions. After the skirmishes, the wounded poured into the hospital ships, torn, mutilated, dirty, half-crazy with pain and thirst. The Sanitary workers who stayed the course—or stayed until their hard-driving supervisor feared for their health and sent them away—providentially developed a sort of stoicism for each ghastly occasion and functioned in the face of appalling mass suffering simply as eyes to observe and hands to relieve it. Olmsted was so moved by the wonderful spirit—brave, patient, even cheerful—of the wounded that he was constantly drawn to the wards. Georgie Woolsey, going about her nursing duties late one night, surprised him seated on the floor by a dying man's pallet, his arm around his pillow, speaking gently to him. Olmsted came in only when the wards were quiet, she noticed, and he thought there was no one around to observe him.[33]

System and routine made each crisis manageable, but they had to be flexible to fit changing circumstances. Although certain workers were assigned to certain ships, doctors and dressers had no fixed quarters; they slept anyplace, afloat or ashore, where they could lie down, anytime they could snatch the chance. The *Wilson Small*'s staff sometimes slept on the open deck and took their meals on slices of bread because every foot of space under cover and the entire stock of china were required for the wounded. Watches were usually observed, but if word came in the middle of the night that a group of wounded had been left untended on some creek bank, the off-watch would turn out, with scarcely time to snatch a shawl or a jacket, board one of the shallow-draft boats, and grope up a tortuous stream to fetch them back to the saving care and comfort of a hospital ship.[34]

Olmsted could establish some sort of flexible system in the operations he directed; so much could hardly be said of Dr. Tripler. "He seems to be in a worse boggle than ever as to the disposition of his sick," Olmsted observed with disgust soon after the middle of May.[35] By then, the Army of the Potomac had advanced to within eight miles of Richmond, and its supply base was at White House on the Pamunkey River, a feeder of the York. Downstream from the White House, a pretty, tree-shaded cottage that had once been the home of Mrs. George Washington, the hospital fleet was assembled; and the Sanitary Commission had set up its headquarters nearby on the line of the railroad running to Richmond. Hard fighting had not yet begun, but some wounded and fever-stricken hundreds were being brought back to the base, where there were almost no facilities to care for them.

Dr. Tripler complained, Olmsted believed with justice, that he had tents but no details to pitch them and that he had ordered ample supplies but that they had not reached him. It was the old difficulty of having to rely on the Quartermaster Department. All he could do with his sick was leave them exposed to whatever weather on the wide lawn around the White House or place them on hospital transports. He about agreed one day to Olmsted's proposal to set up a large shore receiving hospital; there, the gravely sick and wounded, who needed to be sent away for a long convalescence, could be selected with deliberation and put aboard transports each of which should be equipped to carry special types of cases; and the less serious cases could be transferred to nearby hospitals from which they could be discharged within convenient reach of their regiments. When Olmsted ordered the *Webster* to White House, however, to take off the most seriously sick, he found that Dr. Tripler, who was superintending their embarkation, "seemed to have entirely lost sight of the plan about determined upon the day before, to establish the shore receiving hospital, and was only anxious to get the sick off his hands as rapidly as possible, being appalled by their accumulation and the entire absence of provision for them."[36]

Hospital tents were soon pitched on the White House lawn, but some twelve hundred patients still had nothing except shelter until the commission's energetic agents supplied blankets and mattresses, carted in fresh water in hogsheads, sent casks of ice from the *Webster*, provided medicine for all who needed it, set up five great pig kettles simmering with food, and even got some of the tents floored. "The greater part of the men are not very ill," Olmsted noted, "and, with nice nourishment, comfortable rest, and good nursing would be got ready to join their regiments in a week or two; but this is just what they are not likely to have."[37]

The weather was turning hot, the army faced the enemy in a malarious region, and it was probable that the base might soon be flooded with sick and wounded from the impending battle before Richmond. Olmsted dreaded to think what might happen unless the surgeon general, to whom he had appealed directly, promptly sent complete hospital equipment for six thousand.

> Those responsible for the care of the sick here—I mean the military administrative as well as medical officers—have made the presence of the transports near them an excuse for neglecting all proper local provision, and evidently have the idea that, in hurrying patients on board vessels, they relieve themselves of responsibility. I saw this danger from the first, and have (I wish the Surgeon General and our friends to be sure of this) constantly done all that I could to counteract it, not only by verbal protest, but by a habit of action which I know that Knapp, and other friends here, who have not had the duty of looking at the matter as comprehensively as I have, have not been able always to regard as justifiable. . . .[38]

Chaos, as Olmsted foresaw, prevailed after the battle of Fair Oaks. The wounded from it began arriving at White House the first night in June. They came by every train from the front, two hundred and more at a time unattended

Calvert Vaux

bove: F.L.O., in
he early 1860s.

Above: Bridge in
Central Park,
F.L.O. at right
(Stuart Collec-
tion, Rare Book
Division, The
New York Public
Library, Astor,
Lenox and Tilden
Foundations).

Right:
Owen Frederick
Olmsted, circa
1860.

Left:
John Charles
Olmsted, circa
1860.

or attended by a detail of two soldiers, at best. The less seriously injured rode the roofs of the cars, and the more gravely hurt were packed like herring inside without pallets, usually without even straw. The living, the dying, and the dead, some with horrible wounds infected or full of maggots, lay jumbled together in the sweltering boxcars, suffocating in a stench that sometimes made the Sanitary nurses, inured though they were to sick duty, vomit.

The shore hospital, not having been enlarged, could not accommodate such numbers, and the patients had to be put on hospital transports. Pending their embarkation, no one was in charge of them; no provision to care for them was made, except that made by the commission. The commission's Dr. Ware and his assistants met and examined them as they came off the cars. The commission women, busy in the tent kitchen Olmsted had had set up on the river bank by the railroad, distributed bread and butter, tea, coffee, hot soup, oranges, stimulants, and delicacies to the pitiful swarms waiting to get aboard the hospital ships.[39] Olmsted wrote the surgeon general later in the month:

> Nearly all of those with whom I conversed, of the first three thousand men who received aid at this point from the Sanitary Commission, assured me that they had been without shelter from sun or rain, and without nourishment, from the time they fell until the time they came into our hands. This would be a period of from one to four days. The men seemed sincere, and their appearance was such as to lead me to the conclusion that, in many cases at least, they asserted no more than the truth.[40]

The wounded taken aboard Sanitary Commission transports were fortunate; those ships were well stocked and well staffed. The government-operated transports were a different matter. The *Daniel Webster II* for a time just after Fair Oaks had no medical officer in charge; the *Vanderbilt*, which had lain idle at her wharf for a week before the battle with surgeons and a large detail of soldiers aboard, was disclosed, as soon as the wounded began to be carried aboard, to have neither commissary nor medical supplies.[41]

Altogether, Dr. Tripler's arrangements were so insufficient to provide for the Fair Oaks casualties that Olmsted wrote from White House the Tuesday after the battle: "Between two and three thousand wounded have been sent here this week, and at least nine tenths of them have been fed and cared for, as long as they remained, exclusively by the Commission."[42]

The pressure on the commission's workers was killing: one of its best men, after several days of sleepless exertion, broke into uncontrollable hysterics when he at last had a chance to rest; Knapp, prostrated by fever and exhaustion, had to be invalided home.[43] Everyone who kept going did so on sheer nerve during that exhausting week. By the beginning of the next, however, Eliza Howland could speak of "a delightfully quiet Sunday." A mere hundred fifty wounded had come in during the night; and Dr. John Foster Jenkins, one of the commission's devoted medical men, doubling as clergyman, held a service under the trees. "We have almost lost sight of Sunday lately in the press of work," Mrs. Howland commented.[44]

"Congressional picknickers," coming to observe the progress of the war, observed also the improvident handling of casualties and went home to raise an angry question in Congress: why, almost two months after the passage of the medical bill, had the secretary of war not yet named the medical inspectors who were to have been immediately appointed to keep the surgeon general informed of the medical necessities of the forces in the field?[45] Hammond had submitted his list of candidates to Stanton promptly on taking office. For half the list Stanton had substituted men of his own choice, selected, it was thought, for political reasons; and he had been unaccountably slow in moving to have the nominees confirmed. Bellows had clashed headlong with him over the delay as early as the middle of May; and the disharmony that had arisen between the secretary of war and the surgeon general was rapidly turning into frank enmity. Jogged finally by questions in Congress and by Lincoln's reputed dissatisfaction, Stanton presented his list of nominees, so that on June 17 Hammond was able to wire Olmsted that he had ordered Colonel Edward P. Vollum, a regular army officer and one of his own nominees for inspector, to White House to take charge of the army's hospital transports.[46]

Olmsted came a few days later to an agreement with Vollum by which, he hoped, government and Sanitary Commission would each have specified and distinct roles in the care of the ten thousand wounded who were expected to fall in the battle before Richmond; and Olmsted worked out with him a close schedule for the movements of the commission's transports to and from northern hospitals.[47] The careful scheme was rendered obsolete within the week, when McClellan had to abandon his White House base.

Olmsted had not foreseen the move. Although on the fringe of the fighting, the Sanitary Commission workers had no exact idea of what was going on. Predictions and hearsay reached them, but little precise information. When the rumor flew that Stonewall Jackson, fresh from his slashing campaign in the Valley of Virginia, was about to strike at McClellan's White House base, Olmsted was at first inclined to disregard it. Privately advised, however, by the post executive officer on the afternoon of June 26 that the camp had to be evacuated and all stores burned that could not be run down the river, Olmsted called in the Sanitary workers. Within a quarter of an hour the *Wilson Small*, the *Elizabeth*, and the *Wissahickon* started downstream, passing on the way the gunboats readied for action and the pretty White House shore line ravished of trees to allow a sweep to their guns. The *Small* anchored at West Point for repairs and next day steamed again for the last time up the Pamunkey, moving through scores of vessels making away from the former headquarters.

At White House, the *Small's* contingent found the post partially evacuated and the stores that remained readied for firing. The little ship proceeded to gather in the railroad men and northern stragglers; and the government hospital ships were called up and took aboard the fifteen hundred sick from the shore hospital. All departed in good order, the *Small* lingering to the last and leaving only when the telegraph was cut and the enemy announced by mounted messenger to be at Tunstall's Station, harried constantly in his advance by Stoneman's cavalry, which was covering the Union retreat. As she crept downstream in the darkness, her passengers watched the flash of the big guns to the west, the dull glare, and the heavy pall of smoke from millions of dollars worth of abandoned and burning stores and wondered with heavy hearts what was to be the fate of the Army of the Potomac.[48]

While the great army made its agonizing retreat toward the James River, through swamps and under sustained Confederate battering, the Sanitary Commission's boats recoaled at Norfolk. Olmsted still had no clear idea of what the army's movement signified; reports and opinions that he gathered from the wounded were so contradictory that he could form none;[49] but he had two clear ideas: that the army's most urgent necessity was reinforcements and that the "guillotining" of the secretary of war, whom he considered responsible for withholding them, was a service "to which a true patriot and Christian could as well devote his energies."[50]

"I have always thought Chase and Wadsworth and the Tribune & Post wrong in their policy with regard to McClellan," he wrote Brace the Sunday "after the skedaddle of the Pamunkey."

> I have done my best, in a humble way, to oppose it. Stanton I should say, I know is an infidel, infidel scoundrel—with the others it is simply an error of judgment. Because I respected those people individually—morally and common-sensically—I did not till lately feel much in opposition to them, lacking confidence in my own judgment, but lately, here, as I know the business better & better, I feel hotly and bitterly. I don't think McClellan a great man, certainly not a genius of a general. I think we might find a better one; I think he makes a great many mistakes and is altogether unworthy of the hero-worship which he commands from the army as a whole. But as between him and his enemies, I am a McClellan man to the backbone. Everything depended on him—to begin cutting the ground from under him, if it had been never so carefully and considerately, was desperate folly.[51]

After the battle of Malvern Hill on July 1, when the superb Union artillery, abetted by bad Confederate staff work, disintegrated the enemy assault with terrible slaughter and saved the Army of the Potomac, McClellan withdrew to Harrison's Landing, where the Union gunboats on the James could cover his encampment. There his battered army established its new base; and there the Sanitary Commission workers resumed their labors, operating again from headquarters aboard the *Wilson Small*.

By July 3, Olmsted realized how close the army had come to destruction, and his apprehension sharpened. He accepted the medical director's estimate that it had lost thirty thousand men during that ghastly, grueling week and currently mustered an effective force of only sixty thousand to oppose the enemy's one hundred fifty or two hundred thousand. Both estimates were exaggerated, the latter grossly: Lee had about ninety thousand men. But the Army of the Potomac was, undeniably, in terribly weakened condition. The majority of the men had lost tents, blankets, and knapsacks and retained only musket and cartridge box. Many were bareheaded and barefooted.[52] Officers as well as men, even those not positively ill with fever, dysentery, or scurvy, were feverish with six days and nights of frightful exertion, fatigue, hunger, and excitement. A major general told Olmsted he had not eaten or slept in five days and had kept going on coffee and cigars; most of the soldiers, Olmsted reported, had fought five battles in as many days against double their numbers, made a forced march each night to a new position, and had had but two days' uncooked rations during the whole time and but one night's sleep—and that on their arms in a torrential rain.[53] The gravely wounded had been left where they fell or at the Sanitary Commission's camp at Savage's Station. Those who could stumble along or had friends to help them were making their way to Harrison's Landing; the rest fell into Confederate hands.[54]

The army's sanitary condition had, of course, become precarious. Although the new base was on an elevated and airy tableland, there were swamps at no great distance, and the July sun, when it came out, would beat fiercely on the unsheltered thousands. The area was small and crowded. Officers, faced by an active enemy, were too busy with immediate military necessities to enforce sanitary regulations; and the men were too tired to expend the strength in digging latrines that they would need for combating a pertinacious foe.[55]

Yet the men's spirit was superb; they had an almost exultant confidence in themselves and in their commander, who could appear nowhere among them without being greeted with cheers. It was Olmsted's deep conviction—and he had talked to enough men and officers to have respectable ground for it—that the army believed, and lived on the belief, that its general, better than any other person, had recognized the military opportunity and had appreciated the resources and fanaticism of the enemy; that the government had failed to understand either the possibilities or the dangers of the situation and hence had refused, out of miscalculation and out of distrust of McClellan's motives, the reinforcements essential to his success; and that, driven from its base and hurled across the peninsula, the army had at frightful cost and with fabulous stamina and heroism salvaged the so nearly lost opportunity to strike at the Confederacy's heart.

> They believe the country appreciates this now and will throw everything else aside to avail of it. They cannot hold it long in their exhausted condition, and they believe that every hour will bring the beginning of the

stream which is to flow in to stay, and, in its turn, to set back and finally to overwhelm the foe who still desperately renews the effort on which his all is staked.[56]

On the Fourth of July Olmsted steamed up Chesapeake Bay toward Washington on the *Wilson Small*, the personal emissary of the new medical director of the Army of the Potomac, Jonathan Letterman, to the surgeon general.[57] Letterman had replaced Tripler only a few days before; dry, taciturn, and chary with his promises, he was nevertheless already beginning to make things happen that Tripler had found impossible.[58] One of his first acts was to send Olmsted to report to Hammond on the physical needs of the army in greater detail than he could himself write. As the *Small* moved higher and higher up the bay, Olmsted, scanning its broad sweep, was filled with bitter amazement to spy not a single ship bearing soldiers southward-bound. Why, he demanded, in the name of God, if the public servants in Washington knew their duty and the plight of the army, did they not send reinforcements to "the parched and haggard heroes" on the peninsula?[59]

In Washington, Olmsted dispatched his business with Hammond, secured hospital tents for six hundred men from General Meigs and the promise of others to shelter fifty thousand, and tried to see Lincoln to urge on him the absolute necessity for sending reinforcements to McClellan. Since the president could not receive him, Olmsted addressed a pressing letter to him. His attitude toward Lincoln had altered slowly but radically, and now he wrote:

> In the general gloom there are two points of consolation and hope which grow brighter and brighter—opening my eyes suddenly, as I seem to have done, in the point of view of Washington, I may see these and their value more clearly than those about you. One is the trustworthy, patriotic devotion of the solid, industrious, home-keeping people of the country; the other, the love and confidence constantly growing stronger, between these people and their President.
>
> Here is the key to a vast reserved strength, and in this rests our last hope for our country.
>
> Appeal personally to the people, Mr. President—Abraham Lincoln to the men and women who will believe him—and the North will surge with a new strength against which the enemy will not dare advance. Then, cannot fifty thousand men, now doing police and garrison duty, possibly be drawn off with safety and sent within a month to McClellan? Add these to his seven times tried force, and he can strike a blow which will destroy all hope of organized armed resistance to the Law. Without these, the best army the world ever saw must be idle, and in discouragement and dejection be wasted by disease.[60]

This letter he sent for delivery to Professor Bache, who in turn sent it to John Nicolay, for the young secretary to hand to the president or not, as he saw fit.

At the same time Olmsted wrote Senator Preston King a letter urging the advisability of a draft; King, concurring, laid it before Lincoln.[61]

Lincoln had already, at the end of June, called for three hundred thousand more volunteers, but he was not yet prepared to resort to conscription nor was he inclined to reinforce the army whose general, in spite of clear superiority in numbers and supplies, had fumbled his chance to trounce the enemy and had barely escaped a deathtrap. Yet Lincoln's concern for the Army of the Potomac was deep, and to show it he paid a surprise visit. "The President returned this A.M. from the *Army of the Potomac*," Bache ecstatically wrote Olmsted on July 11.

> How well might he say to us as a Master once said before: Oh! Ye of little faith. Who could have supposed from what we saw and heard on Saturday around the Executive Mansion, that within two days the President would have gone to hear and see and confer in person! with that glorious leader of his officers and men! . . .
>
> Is it not a lesson for us not to be down hearted? With such a man to guide the councils of the country?[62]

It is unlikely that Olmsted shared Bache's ecstacy: witnessing the army's terrible vicissitudes, he knew that, to the worn and depleted regiments, the inspiration of the presidential presence could be no substitute for an infusion of fresh troops into the ranks. The Army of the Potomac obviously had to be reinforced, or withdrawn, or let perish.[63] Olmsted passionately believed that it should be reinforced. The disillusion with McClellan, which by then infected the country, was not shared by most of those in his environs, certainly not by Olmsted; but he shared intensely their resentment of Stanton, which was based on the impression that he had withheld needed reinforcements and so frustrated the general's chance of victory for mean political motives.[64]

On his return to the peninsula, Olmsted came to the conclusion that the commission's work there ought to be terminated. Their transport service no longer paid what it cost, and their position was undignified. He did not really control the transports he was supposed to control: they often were removed from his jurisdiction and assigned to other work just when they were most needed for the care of casualties. If the medical director or his subordinates made any discrimination between them and the slipshod government transports, it never indicated a preference for them, Olmsted grimly noted, and it had become a constant struggle to make them useful. It was probably not practicable, Olmsted concluded, for government agents, in the tumult and occupation of war, to avail themselves of assistance and instruction offered by anyone to whom they were not officially responsible. Finally, in its main objective, the commission's transport service had been a decided failure: while it had evacuated some eight thousand sick and wounded, saved hundreds of lives, and eased incalculable suffering, it had not either by its advice or its example produced any improvement in the government's hospital transport service. On the contrary, by assuming some of the government's responsibility toward the sick and wounded, it had probably retarded the government's assumption of its own duty toward them. In this way it had perfectly demonstrated what the Sanitary Commission's function was not.[65]

Olmsted was the more willing to see the commission's transport service ended, since Dr. Letterman in his short tenure had already radically improved the medical service in the army. Sick and wounded were better fed and nursed and more smoothly evacuated; sanitary regulations were being enforced in camp; and an independent ambulance corps was being organized for the Army of the Potomac under his direction.[66] With the sanitary interests of the army in the hands of so competent a medical officer, the commission's function was dwindling away.

By the middle of July its crew on the York had little to do but distribute their remaining supplies, reminisce with each other, and wait around to carry back on their last trip north some of the wounded left behind in the retreat, whose return Lee had arranged under flag of truce. The letdown and the comparative idleness were, in a way, harder on them than their earlier ceaseless work. Miss Wormeley became "a fascinating wreck," and Olmsted, tired out, suffered from "excessive indolence of mind and body."[67]

The *Daniel Webster* returned Olmsted and some of his lieutenants to New York on July 25. Their last night out, he, Miss Wormeley, and Georgie Woolsey sat up most of the night, talking over their experiences. Miss Wormeley's reverential ardor for Olmsted burned ever brighter. "Every day I have understood and valued and trusted him more and more," she wrote at the close of her great adventure, and of her other associates,

> . . . we worked together under the deepest feelings, and to the extent of our powers, shoulder to shoulder, helping each other to the best of our ability. From first to last there has been perfect accord among us; and I can never look back on these months without feeling that God has been very good to let me share in them and see human nature under such aspects. The last I saw of Mr. Olmsted, he was disappearing down the side of the Webster, clad in the garb of a fashionable gentleman. I rubbed my eyes and felt that then it was indeed *all over*. I myself had risen to the occasion by putting on a black lace tablespoon [bonnet] in which I became at once conventional and duly civilized.[68]

XVIII
THE SECRETARY BESET
August 1862–February 1863

ALTHOUGH the transport service had but a limited success on the peninsula, it accomplished something in the North: it made known the work of the Sanitary Commission as nothing before had done. Its shipshape floating hospitals had become familiar sights in the big northern seaports; thousands saw in them dramatic evidence of its usefulness. Funds, consequently, were more easily raised. Contributions in June 1862 amounted to something more than seven thousand dollars; those in July and August, coming in response to an affecting appeal issued on July Fourth—the single tear-jerking one the commission permitted itself—came to almost fifty thousand dollars.[1] Although the commission's expenses increased sharply during the peninsula campaign, the nagging possibility that it might have to shut up shop for lack of money faded. Other hazards, however, were arising to replace the fear of insolvency. The secretary of war did not bother to mask his dislike; a spirit of localism in relief work, marked by an envious hostility toward the commission, could be widely sensed; and within the commission itself, a slighting of routine and a reorganization of operating procedures were causing confusion and conflict.

When Olmsted returned to Washington toward the end of August after a short visit with friends and family in New England,[2] the troubles within the commission broke upon him. He was "roasted most cruelly" when he could give the executive committee no definite information about the commission's work in the West, which was directed by Dr. Newberry, from Louisville. Olmsted had, of course, been away since April, and his duties had been discharged by deputies; moreover, his office had received no report from any western inspector since February 7—the reports were required weekly, and Newberry himself was supposed to send in occasional general reports—although Olmsted had repeatedly implored Newberry, officially his subordinate, to send reports regularly.[3]

Besides that, relations with the secretary of war were turning vicious. Stanton refused to sanction a Sanitary order for the printing of several thousand medical monographs on the ground that the commission had no authority to place orders with the Government Printing Office;[4] and he was blocking an independent ambulance corps. Bellows charged that he *allows himself to speak of our Commission with contempt, and of the Surgeon General as not having his confidence. In both respects he injures himself more than either of us,* he added loftily and mistakenly.[5] Olmsted had come to distrust Stanton as "a bad man, a coward, a bully and a swindler."[6] Besides, he had held out on McClellan. Olmsted was steadfast, though moderate, in his defense of the eclipsed general. He wrote Brace:

> McClellan is not a Napoleon and he has the great merit of not thinking himself a Napoleon. He has got to be successful, if at all, by wise and considerate action, not by audacity or strokes of genius. . . . We may hope, but we have no right to expect, to succeed by genius. What we want is conscientious, *industrious, studious* men, who will do their duty, carefully, thoroughly. . . . that is our great want, our most urgent want. . . . It is equally apparent in all departments. I see it most directly in surgeons and chaplains, but I also see it in sergeants and captains and colonels and generals. Men with great responsibilities are careless about them, will not take the trouble—apparently cannot study carefully and thoroughly how they can best be executed, but *get along somehow and guess it will do.* Damn them. *Guess it will do* when the life of the nation and much more may depend on it. . . .[7]

Olmsted wrote thus on August 25, a few days before the second Battle of Bull Run. By then, McClellan's army had been withdrawn from Harrison's Landing and returned to the environs of Washington, just where they had started months before. From there the peninsula veterans were being shipped as fast as the railroad could carry them toward Warrenton Junction to reinforce the newly formed Army of Virginia under General John Pope. Pope was a West Pointer, fresh from success at Island Number 10 in the Mississippi. His fellow officers, Olmsted heard, considered him a liar and an ass; Olmsted, slightly more charitable, thought he had a "very common" intellect.[8]

While Pope was assembling his army at Manassas, Lee was concentrating his forces to crush him before he could make a forward thrust. Surgeon General Hammond, visiting the Sanitary Commission's board room on August 20, told Olmsted he anticipated the greatest battle of the war within ten days between Richmond and Washington.[9] It came on schedule and resulted in the second defeat of the Union army at Bull Run.

Again, the battlefield relief work was anarchic. Out of the whole Union army, only two corps, coming from the Army of the Potomac where Letterman had been at work, had their own ambulance system. Three days after the battle, three thousand wounded still lay where they had fallen, most of them unfed and with wounds undressed; it was September 9 before the last of them were removed. Many of the wounded must have lingered in torment for days, finally dying, victims of shocking disorganization.[10] Hammond's critics blamed him; the Sanitary Commission blamed Stanton, who, having turned against Hammond, frustrated his desire for an ambulance corps.[11] Meanwhile, McClellan was hastily restored to command, and the victorious Lee hurried his tough and tattered army north to invade Maryland.

Olmsted took no part in these melancholy events. He had jaundice. Ever since his return from the peninsula, he had been decidedly unwell; by the end of August, when he was finally too sick to keep his post, he was so deeply yellow he could have passed for a dark mulatto, and the whites of his eyes were saffron. He itched furiously, and wherever he scratched he turned purple. He had to spend most of the day lying down, and a little exertion or excitement shook him so that his voice trembled.

In pitiable shape, he was loaded on the night train to New York, consigned to Dr. Agnew.[12] Agnew took him on to Saratoga and, after prescribing a course of treatment and rest, left him in charge of Dr. Willard Parker. Unable to sleep for itching or to walk for lameness, Olmsted had nothing to do but wait restlessly for the papers that progressively disclosed the extent of the latest Union disaster.[13]

Olmsted was well enough to return to work within two weeks. En route to Washington, he stopped in New York. There he found new troubles. Mason Brothers, his publishers, had just failed. They owed him about one hundred dollars, but they had managed to keep his plates and copyright out of the forced sale and hoped to pay him in full. Worse than that, Vaux was seriously ill with some sort of undiagnosed remittent fever. Irrational and sometimes violent, he chattered incessantly about glass and colors and draperies and, obsessed with the delusion that he could float, kept trying to repose on air.[14] Olmsted had lately insisted on a more just distribution of their joint annual fee from Central Park, of which he had thus far had the larger share: twenty-five hundred dollars for Vaux, who worked on the site; two thousand dollars for himself, who was consulted; now he borrowed three hundred dollars from his father so that Vaux's household should not lack for ready cash.[15]

Reassuringly, Olmsted found Bellows no longer critically disposed toward him. The commission president, fresh from a trip to Washington, confessed that what he had seen there convinced him that they had been unjust to Olmsted in fearing a breakdown of the central machinery in his absence; it had been admirably maintained. Better yet, after the mid-September meeting of the executive committee in Washington, Olmsted's report on his summer's work "carried their convictions and sympathies and regained their entire confidence."[16]

Olmsted had scarcely resumed his post when the Battle of Antietam took place. McClellan's army clashed with Lee's invading force at Sharpsburg on September 17 and, in the fiercest battle of the war so far, defeated it. The army field relief, again under Letterman, functioned better than it had at Second Bull Run: by the end of the day after the battle, the wounded had all been removed to some seventy hospitals improvised in nearby homes, churches, and barns, and from these they were systematically evacuated to hospitals in Frederick, Baltimore, Washington, and Philadelphia.[17]

Still, Strong and Agnew, who had been prompt to reach the scene, were thoroughly dissatisfied. Hammond, in spite of his energy, was paralyzed by continuing dependence on the Quartermaster Department; the Sanitary Commission, foreseeing a backup of railroad traffic, had sent supplies by wagon, which had beaten the Medical Bureau's to the field by two days.[18] Olmsted, reaching Sharpsburg on the twenty-fifth, was appalled by the enormity of the suffering. "It was very squalid," he wrote his wife, "but everywhere I saw the great value of our work."[19]

McClellan was bitterly censured for not having pursued and decisively crushed the Confederate army; instead he had allowed it to escape across the Potomac. The functioning of his invincible, his fatal, caution was seen in his inaction. Even before Antietam, Brace had written Olmsted that McClellan's honest, well-intentioned defects "have nearly broken the heart of this Nation"; and if reports were to be believed, he had acted "most disgracefully and wickedly" in not promptly reinforcing Pope at Second Bull Run and in forcing himself upon Lincoln "by military influence and power as Commander in Chief in the field."[20]

Olmsted sprang, this time angrily, to McClellan's defense. Brace's talk about him was "wild." He was better as a general than Lincoln as a president, Chase and Stanton as secretaries, or Dana, Greeley, Bryant, and Raymond as editors.

> He is a simple, stupid Christian, which is hardly the case with any other man of eminence. He is industrious, brave, patient. I cannot see that he has not accomplished all that could have been reasonably asked of him. I do not see where he has made a single great mistake. McClellan has from the first estimated the difficulties of overcoming the rebellion somewhat higher than most other men. . . .

Even Stanton, Olmsted said, had had to admit that, where McClellan had been allowed to take his time, he had formed soldiers who could be relied on to do their duty. At the same time, the other generals had been intriguing, and fighting intrigues, with "those infernal gamblers," the abolitionist politicians in Washington.

> . . . The damnedest fools and rascals out of asylums and prisons in this or any other country are our republican leaders. They are liars, pettifoggers and sneaks. . . . I mean, for instance, Chase—he is contemptible, a mere ward politician with a clean face. I mean Wilson—he lies and jumps the fence faster and more freely than any man I have known except one. . . . I have been on intimate terms with him and have seen a good deal of Chase. McDowell is Chase's nephew and Pope is the son-in-law of Chase's neighbor and friend [Valentine B.] Horton M. C. of Ohio. Chase six months ago at his own dinner table stated his purpose to depose McClellan and put McDowell in his place. If this had not been his purpose and if similar purposes had not ruled others, we should have been in Richmond, Raleigh and Charleston long before this. But of all the damned infernal

scoundrels that the Almighty for our sins' sake curses us with, Stanton is the hardest to bear. In all Dixie there is not so wicked a man. . . .

The Tribune and Post and Independent abound with the most outrageous lies. There is a great deal of carelessness in them . . . but there is also, I am sure, a great deal of intentional falsehood . . . whose is it? . . . Some of these damned rascals here in Washington who take advantage of the prejudices and strong desires for emancipation of those simple men to deceive them. The President is a poor whining broken-down idiot at such a time as this. . . .[21]

Brace, troubled by both tone and content of Olmsted's letter, conceded that Chase and Stanton might be as bad as Olmsted represented, defended Sumner among the abolitionists as a statesman and patriot, and detailed the case against McClellan. "His delays have cost hundreds of millions, the national honor and universal discouragement. His action (until Antietam) has brought only disgrace and disaster," he summed up; and he declared his "profound moral conviction that under General McClellan we shall not for two years drive the rebels from Virginia—and *never* conquer them."[22]

"I assert that 'his delays' have never been his delays," Olmsted retorted. "That interference and arrest of his operations in the interest of certain Presidential aspirants, and of John Pope, Fremont and McDowell, have occasioned and necessitated these delays." As for Brace's conviction that he would take two years to flush the rebels out of Virginia and would never conquer them, Olmsted fully shared it—"if Stanton and Chase rule and you and others who believe in their statements instead of asking for facts . . . continue to encourage them in their corner grocery strategy."[23]

However costly and limited a victory Antietam was, it encouraged Lincoln to issue, on September 22, the long-considered Emancipation Proclamation. Brace, in his lead editorial in the *Times* of the same date, predicted that it would knock the cornerstone out from under the Confederacy. He asked Olmsted if he thought the slaves would rise or run.[24] Olmsted replied, in the tone of one repeating a truism for the thousandth time, that the slaves couldn't rise because they couldn't combine. " 'Will they run?' Yes, when they have something to run to. But they will not run to starvation."[25]

The intemperate tone of Olmsted's letters reflected not only his terrible anxiety but his ill health. Barely over jaundice, he was suffering from frequent and alarming attacks of vertigo; and he was so taut emotionally that at least once, on learning that the executive committee had rejected some proposal of his, he burst into tears in the office.[26] Curtis, worried about him, begged him to get out of the "mephitic" atmosphere of Washington and into rural New England. He wrote:

You will find that this is the people's war; that the people control it; that every family has invested its blood and tears in it. . . . Besides, granting everything to the contrary, see how steadily we have gone *on* and not backward. . . . You are too near the machinery; you smell the grease and feel the thick air, and it makes you sick. No matter; that nasty smell and mess sends the ship forward. Come up on deck, and breathe the air that blows from the unseen shores ahead.[27]

The opportunity for Olmsted to escape Washington did, in fact, glimmer briefly when Mayor Opdyke of New York nominated him for street commissioner.[28] Bellows, however, cheerfully informed him that he had been "rejected by the dirty aldermen—who don't want either clean men or clean streets."[29] Olmsted was not sorry.[30]

Although the park and Vaux exercised a strong, continuing pull on him to return to New York, duty to the commission and gratitude toward the commissioners held him in Washington. They were "gentleman, liberal, generous, magnanimous,"[31] who relied on him to carry out their policies like an honorable and judicious man; he, in turn, treated his subordinates the same way.

It was a technique calculated both to minimize red tape and to elicit the best from men devoted to their duty and to their superiors; but it had an inherent hazard that assumed an alarming aspect as the commission's expenses and funds increased. Its large expenditures in September "frightened" the executive committee, Bellows wrote Olmsted.[32] Their fright was not allayed by California's two great gifts, totaling two hundred thousand dollars, in October. The committee feared careless spending or the appearance of it might result in loss of public confidence; therefore it proposed to assume some of the financial responsibility it had left to Olmsted. Olmsted dashed off several long and vehement letters protesting that the commission's affairs could not be conducted on the conventional business principles applicable to banking, railroading, or the usual sort of philanthropy, with the conventional safeguards against waste and peculation; hasty and lavish expenditures were frequently imperative and had to be made at the judgment of the executive secretary or his trusted delegates. To clear them with the executive committee would wreck the rapid and efficient system that had been established. The commissioners' "fright" suggested a lack of confidence in his management and left him uncertain as to how far they wanted him to rely on his judgment. He said he was willing to have his responsibility decreased as the commission's business expanded, but any redistribution of responsibilities should be made thoughtfully and systematically, not under the impulse of sudden alarm.[33]

Bellows capitulated. He conceded that he was unbusinesslike and that his efforts to appear otherwise were vain posturings; he could not forgive himself for drawing from Olmsted such a wasteful expenditure of thought and feeling.[34] But he was a weather vane, quickly talked around by other members of the executive committee. When the commission soon after passed a resolution requiring Olmsted to submit proposed salary increases to the executive committee for approval, Bellows answered Olmsted's protest by ordering him to do as he was told.[35]

Strong, less pliant than Bellows, wrote Olmsted a patient, cordial letter supporting the decision. Since the commission represented itself to the public as the responsible trustee of a public charity, it ought to know and control the cost of its operations; so far as it did not, it was not executing its trust with fidelity. In fact, the commissioners had very little idea of where the money went until Olmsted reported *faits accomplis*; this was a weak spot in their system that ought to be remedied. "I do not see how any practical inconvenience can grow out of this rule," he added conciliatingly. "Whenever you think an Inspector's salary ought to be increased, you have only to telegraph to New York. If the case is too urgent for even this delay . . . you are surely safe in telling him that his salary will be increased, for you know that we are always disposed to ratify your action."[36]

Although the difficulty was patched up temporarily, the divisive question of Olmsted's fiscal responsibility had driven a wedge between the secretary and the executive committee. Strong, who so admired Olmsted that he wished he were secretary of war, was pained by the "unhappy, sick, sore mental state" that made him seem to be trying to pick a quarrel with the committee and ascribed it to his "most insanitary habits of life. He works like a dog all day and sits up nearly all night, doesn't go home to his family (now established in Washington) for five days and nights altogether, works with steady, feverish intensity till four in the morning, sleeps on a sofa in his clothes, and breakfasts on *strong coffee and pickles*!!!!"[37]

While Olmsted was skirmishing with the executive committee, a row erupted between the commission and its Cincinnati branch, which threatened to secede and join the Western Sanitary Commission unless it was given a share of the California bonanza.[38] Correspondence and resolutions, ranging in tone from judicious to acrimonious, passed between the commission and its wayward branch. Olmsted's major contribution to the controversy was a pamphlet, one hundred thirty-eight pages long, explaining the philosophy and organization of the commission and its relationship with its branches.[39] Courteous, logical, doctrinaire, and elaborate, it was supposed to be an "irresistible battery" to crush the spirit of secession.[40] Not surprisingly, it failed. To preserve the fiction of unity and the remnant of a working basis with Cincinnati, the commission in the end allotted fifty thousand dollars to its western branches, of which Cincinnati received fifteen thousand. Already, against its secretary's urgent advice, the commission had given fifty thousand dollars to the Western Sanitary Commission in an unsuccessful effort to forestall its aggressive rival's move east to raise funds in its own well-cultivated field.[41]

Worried by Cincinnati's separatism and St. Louis's invasion of its fund-raising territory, the Sanitary Commission also was faced with disaffection in New England. Bellows, traveling there, complained that he "encountered a spirit of localism everywhere and never failed to put it to flight. But . . . it returns like a ghost the moment the Exorciser disappears and carries his daylight with him. The proper appreciation of our works, our views, our methods implies more candor, more sense, more patience than the people possess."[42] Connecticut was falling out of line and Olmsted's stepmother, squeezed between duty to the commission and the demands of the state aid society, asked him what to do. Olmsted advised her to share collections with the state society. Better that than have the Sanitary Commission's work injured by hostility and disparagement; yet at the same time she should urge "the true principles—the federal principle and the economic principle" in the hope of converting the local relief people.[43]

Increasingly strong in disaffected areas was the Christian Commission organized in November 1861. Representing Protestant ministers, the Young Men's Christian Association, and the American Tract Society, it conducted "exclusively, in spirit and aim, a religious work." Its ministerial agents visited camps and hospitals, conducted prayer meetings, and distributed Bibles, tracts, and material comforts. Its religious complexion gave it a clear advantage in communities where the Unitarianism of the Sanitary Commission's president was suspect; and the fact that it placed its offerings directly in the hands of soldiers, instead of distributing them through authorized army personnel as the Sanitary Commission did, gave it a touch appealingly personal. By the end of 1862 its solicitations were undermining the success of Sanitary appeals in some regions.[44]

Frontal assault on other relief agencies would have been unseemly on the part of the Sanitary Commission, which was always exhorting to unity. Accordingly, Olmsted instructed all Sanitary inspectors to accept "gratefully" any offers of assistance made by Christian Commission delegates during battlefield relief operations and to pay special heed to their reports on the wants of the hospitals.[45] The commission moved purposefully, however, to offset encroachments on its position. It engaged ministers friendly to it to travel as its agents, preaching the Sanitary gospel in sections where ears had turned deaf and purses dry.[46] Olmsted ordered Newberry to occupy the western field as fast as possible ahead of the Western Sanitary Commission and to elicit from the western military commanders commendations for the relief work that would apply exclusively to the Sanitary Commission. "This must be done," he warned, "before it is public knowledge that there is a quarrel on foot, or that the Western Sanitary Commission is trying to supplant us."[47]

The commission's incapacity to unite public feeling in support of its aims paralleled the government's failure to secure unqualified support for national policies, and the Sanitarians, who saw in their machine not only a humane instrument but an educational one designed to promote national and override sectional feeling, were aware of the fact. The strength of dissidence was revealed in the November elections, notably in New York, where Horatio Seymour won his second term as governor. He was a critic of the Lincoln administration and had rallied all the dissatisfied and disloyal elements in the state. Outraged by Seymour's election, Wolcott Gibbs, who had been incubating a scheme to organize a club that would propagate socially the same ideas that the Sanitary Commission was promoting in its field, consulted Olmsted, who was in New York on election day.

The following day, November 5, Olmsted wrote Gibbs a long letter suggesting the basis on which the club should be established. Loyalty to freedom and union was not enough to require of its members, he said; requisite, too, was loyalty to the democratic idea, and aversion to the structure of European society with its hereditary and legally recognized aristocracy. The club should be one of "true American aristocracy," men of worth and accomplishment, with no room in it for any who considered American society inferior because of the absence of a legally privileged class.

Starting with Gibbs and Agnew, a small nucleus should be selected, men of substance and position like Robert Minturn and James Brown, men of notably high character and reputation like George Templeton Strong and John Jay, and men who bore respectably old colonial names. Then should be chosen a number of "clever men," literary, artistic, and professional, like Friederich Kapp, George Waring, and George W. Curtis, who would be the most effective working members. Finally, there should be admitted promising young men, especially "those innocent rich young men . . . who don't understand what their place can be in American society, gentlemen, in the European sense, in a society which has no place for 'men of leisure.' The older and abler established men ought to fraternize with them, to welcome and hold every true man of them in fraternity—so soon they may govern us if they will." The club's dues should be moderate—many of Olmsted's "aristocrats" had to live on their pay—and its quarters modest. Members, joining from motives other than those which usually led gentlemen to join clubs, would expect to aid its purposes in more ways than by their fees and dues. Its structure and aims should be fully matured by a very small group before a canvass for members was begun.[48]

Thus was conceived New York's Union League Club, designed "to discountenance and rebuke by moral and social influences all disloyalty to the Federal Government" and "to concentrate and organize the sentiment of devotion to the Union and the Nation." Four of the Sanitary commissioners—Gibbs, Agnew, Bellows, and Strong—were of the organizing nucleus. The strong core of the club was soon assembled; on February 21, 1863, a scheme of organization was adopted and the club was fairly launched.[*,49] Influential as Olmsted's suggestions may have been in setting its character, he took no part in the preliminary meetings to organize it and little in its affairs during the two years he maintained his membership. His contribution to it in its germinal stage represented no more than an alert snatch at an opportunity to fortify Union sentiment.

---

*Very shortly before, a similar club had been started in Philadelphia. Both bore the same name and were formed for the same purposes, but they had been conceived independently.

THE SECRETARY AT THE SIEGE OF VICKSBURG
February–March 1863

I
N November Olmsted had rented a house, owned by the retired captain of a potato steamer and furnished with hideous objects left from her when she wore out, and had brought his family to Washington.[1] He still saw little of them, feeling that, if men didn't subordinate their family to their community duties, the social structure might be so altered that their children had better not have been born. "It is a day for heroes, and we must be heroes along with the rest," he grimly told his wife,[2] and in that spirit unhesitatingly sacrificed health, income, and domestic comforts.*

Austere personally, he could still be indulgent toward a friend. Miss Wormeley, at the army general hospital at Portsmouth Grove since August, had come to venerate its chief, Dr. Lewis A. Edwards, somewhat as she did Olmsted and, when Edwards was ordered to report to Washington, entreated Olmsted to persuade the surgeon general to cancel the transfer.[3] Able and glad to accommodate her, Olmsted told his wife, "I like to have the gratitude and friendship of such a high strung and thorough bred woman, even at small cost."[4] Her freighted regard was not yet a burden to him, and he sent her a picture of himself, which had, she thought, "his inspired look—with the sweetness of his nature added."[5]

In mid-December the Union disaster at Fredericksburg spread despondency through the loyal states. It was somewhat offset by General William S. Rosecrans's partial success just after Christmas at Murfreesboro, Tennessee, where he badly mauled the enemy in a fierce encounter, but Yankee spirits were heavily oppressed by news of the continuing failure of General Ulysses S. Grant's operations against Vicksburg.

Grant had first tried to take the strategic stronghold while based on Memphis. Failing, he moved downstream in January and camped along the west side of the Mississippi above the city. The banks there were low, the river was high, and continuous rain compelled some regiments to move daily to keep out of the rising water. Lamentable accounts of the troops' sanitary condition reached the commission. In February Olmsted was instructed to inspect the commission's operations with both Grant's and Rosecrans's armies.[6]

*His sacrifice was slight compared to that of his Texas German friends, of whom Kapp, the same month, sent him a detailed account. Some had been expelled from the state on twenty-four hours notice, and some jailed in San Antonio. Most unfortunate of all was Degener: he was in prison, and his two sons, young men in their early twenties whom Olmsted had known a few years before as high-spirited and promising boys, were dead, killed in a guerrilla ambush near the border.

Uneasy and unhappy in his newly restricted position,[7] he balked at the assignment and longed for his beloved park. The prospect of returning to it, however, was dim and becoming dimmer. Vaux wrote that it was only a question of time until the all-powerful comptroller, Green, should provoke him to resign for the two of them. Reconciled to do whatever Vaux thought best, Olmsted wrote him wistfully, "It will continue to be just beyond my highest hope of fortune to be allowed to superintend the park with a reasonable degree of freedom from Greenism."[8]

With his Sanitary Commission work less and less satisfying and the possibility of returning to the park increasingly remote, Olmsted thought of reverting to a literary career and began to make notes for a book on the social nature and institutions of Americans.[9]

On February 18 he reluctantly began his western tour with Knapp. Commission business kept them in Baltimore almost a week, after which they traveled to Philadelphia, Altoona, Pittsburgh, Xenia, and Cincinnati, meeting everywhere with local affiliates of the commission. Their conferences at Louisville with the Kentucky branch went amicably in spite of Olmsted's continued annoyance at the persistent failure of his egalitarian subordinate, Dr. Newberry, to submit regular reports to the central office. After two days of meetings, inspections, and tea parties, Olmsted and Knapp started for Nashville.[10]

Up at six, they left the hotel in an omnibus driven by a recklessly fast driver in good time to catch the train scheduled to leave at eight. It was late. Olmsted, who kept at hand a pocket notebook to record observations for his book, generalized from the incident: "This hurrying and waiting process, experienced at Louisville before, probably grows from steamboat customs. How much these must have injured the national character."[11] The journey resurrected, quite incidentally, the "honest growler" of *Slave States*; Olmsted did a good deal of virtuoso growling about trains that did not run on schedule, cars with floors slimy with tobacco juice, apple cores, and other muck, and "palatial" hotels ("the dreariest of all American humbugs") that offered drafty rooms, beefsteak tasting of tainted lard, and bad service.

The landscape, scarred by war from Louisville on, became progressively more dismal as they neared Murfreesboro, where Rosecrans had his headquarters. The countryside was pocked with burned farmhouses; no domestic animals were to be seen and few inhabitants, black or white. Where the track ran through the recent battlefield, clusters of graves marked the melancholy scene, and scores of dead horses lay still unburied.

At Murfreesboro, the Sanitarians met Rosecrans's chief of staff, General James A. Garfield, and spent a couple of hours in conversation with the commander himself.[12] Of his impression of Garfield, Olmsted left no record; of Rosecrans, he formed a moderately favorable opinion.[13] His interest and his heart were more with the men than with the officers. The officers he met on equal terms; the men he regarded with a sort of loving reverence. He noticed, in anxious particular, their clothing, their food, their shelter, their bearing for clues to their well-being; and he generally referred to them as "heroes." To his eye, Rose-crans's troops appeared on the whole "unkempt," but he was heartened by their "healthy, good natured and decent businesslike aspect";[14] and when the general escorting him unexpectedly maneuvered him into addressing a regiment of Indiana veterans, he was momentarily overawed. ". . . There I stood, when they had done cheering the general," wrote Olmsted, a bit awed still in retrospect, "on a little horse, with 350 heroes who had marched 5,000 miles since the war began and had fought three of the hardest battles of the war—Pea Ridge (Corinth), Perryville and Stone's River, waiting for me to talk to them. I waited a minute and then rose in my stirrups and said—just sixteen words."[15] The heroes rewarded him with three cheers, whether for his inspiration or his brevity.

Back in Louisville on March 10, Olmsted and Knapp spent two more days with the Kentucky members of the commission in a round of tea parties and meetings so congenial that Dr. Newberry was sure that his and Olmsted's long-standing differences would soon be reconciled. Their views diverged on means, not ends, he wrote Bellows, and were not "so different as to be inconsistent with the most sincere and earnest good will."[16]

Bellows himself, however, reached down *ex machina* to make sure that his two subordinates reached no meaningful agreement. He cut the ground from under Olmsted. To the Reverend John H. Heywood, one of Newberry's lieutenants, he wrote:

> I hope you will sustain Dr. Newberry under all the discouragements of feeling from which he may suffer. You understand . . . the glorious and invaluable qualities of our General Secretary, his integrity, disinterestedness and talent for organization, his patriotism and genius. You also understand his impracticable temper, his irritable brain, his unappreciation of human nature in its undivided form and his very imperfect sympathies to weak, mixed, inconsequent people (which are the main!). . . . He has an indomitable pride of opinion. . . . If he were a priest he would be worse than Hildebrand or Laud. . . . We don't intend he shall break Dr. Newberry down, nor take the reins out of the hands of the Board. . . . You . . . must sustain Newberry in any controversy with Olmsted and look to us to sustain your joint judgment.[17]

To Newberry himself Bellows wrote:

> Mr. Olmsted's views, most conscientiously entertained by him, are not in many particulars those of the Commission. Neither when he differs from the Board is it to be expected that his views will be allowed to prevail over ours. On the contrary, he must either abandon his opposition or surrender his place . . . and I very much fear it will come to the last. His paper on organization [the long pamphlet written during the controversy with Cincinnati] . . . although adopted temporarily by Prof. Bache, myself and the secretary . . . is not acceptable to the Board and will not, I think,

be confirmed. . . . I beg you, therefore, without quarreling with Olmsted or coming to any open breach, to preserve as much independence as you may require trusting to us to uphold you. . . .[18]

Olmsted, who had more sympathy with "weak, mixed, inconsequent people" than his weak, mixed, vacillating superior supposed, might have felt nothing harsher than surprise had he known of Bellows's double-dealing and probably not even surprise at the suggestion that his resignation would be acceptable. He had sensed the unspoken decline of confidence in him among the board members, and now it was being privately admitted and not by Bellows alone. On March 11 Strong wrote in the carefully guarded diary in which he spoke his secret mind:

> I fear Olmsted is mismanaging our Sanitary Commission affairs. He is an extraordinary fellow, decidedly the most remarkable specimen of human nature with whom I have every been brought into close relations. Talent and energy most rare; absolute purity and disinterestedness. Prominent defects, a monomania for system and organization on paper (elaborate, laboriously thought out, and generally impracticable), and appetite for power. He is a lay-Hildebrand. There will be a battle when the Commission meets, and incredible as it seems to myself, I think without horror of the possibility of our being obliged to appoint somebody else General Secretary.[19]

Bellows was wrong about Olmsted's pride of opinion, Strong about his appetite for power, but both were right about one thing: Olmsted would soon have to quit his post. His authority was circumscribed; Newberry was empowered to flaunt the regulations subordinating the Kentucky branch to the central; yet Olmsted's accountability remained undiminished. His position would soon be untenable.

Meanwhile, Olmsted and Knapp were proceeding toward Cairo, to catch a boat for Memphis. Somewhere in the middle of the flat, thinly wooded Illinois prairie ("one of the most tiresome landscapes I ever met with," Olmsted said) the trainload of travelers were left, "by a fracture of the promises of the Ohio and Mississippi Railroad," to wait twelve solid hours for a connection. A few of Olmsted's stranded companions swore fiercely at the railroad company for a minute or two; the rest shrugged off the delay as about what might have been expected. Growling impartially at offenders and offended, Olmsted jotted:

> It is a misfortune and a fault of our national character that we bear evils too patiently and carelessly. If every traveller was made crabbed for a day by every railroad company's or innkeeper's mismanagement that he suffered from, if some one of my twenty [companions] would write for the Times, or even, as I do, once in ten thousand cases, complain, in a book, of these things, our progress in civilization would be more sure.[20]

Reaching Cairo at dawn the fourteenth, Olmsted and Knapp transacted some Sanitary business and left on the *Belle of Memphis* at noon next day. Much of the way to Memphis, the scene was a watery desolation. Far out of its banks, the muddy river lapped over fields and around farmhouses and out-buildings. The surrounding country, although in Union hands, still sheltered guerrilla bands who harried river traffic, and the *Belle*'s progress was threatened toward evening, when some twenty men, presumably part of a band who had tried to capture her on her last trip up, appeared on the wooded shore and fired ineffectually at her as she churned deliberately downstream.

From Memphis down, Olmsted and Knapp were on the *Southwestern.* Iron shielded her pilothouse; freight covered her more vital parts. Sacks of oats piled around the cabin formed a breastwork for the protection of the passengers, while a consignment of cavalry horses, for which the oats were intended, took their chances in the open on the main deck. Some miles past Helena, a wretched town drowning behind its broken levee, the *Southwestern* landed at a narrow strip of wooded dry ground, barely above water, where a division of General James B. McPherson's corps was camped. The swamp, or backwater, was barely a hundred feet from the river bank, and the land between lay so low that the slight swell from the steamer's paddles washed into one of the tents creating, of all things, merriment among its occupants. "I wished the scene could be photographed," Olmsted scribbled,

> tall close trees with vines, water about their trunks from 100 feet away as far as the eye could penetrate glistening bright in the setting sun, low sandy island, river about the trees on shore, tents closely among the trees, pickets of horses, wagons, a battery of artillery, tarpaulin-covered heaps of commissary goods, smoke from many camp fires, ground thus thickly occupied each way up and down the river bank, and thousands of men gathering closely near us.[21]

Going ashore to call on McPherson, Olmsted found camp and troops in very fair condition. The grounds were clean; sides of tents, looped up for ventilation, disclosed bedsteads made of saplings; blankets and shirts were drying on poles. The hospital held not a single sick man. About the kitchens stood open boxes of hard bread, chunks of clean, sweet salt pork at which the men cut at will, boxes of sugar, cheese, onions, and butter, and open barrels of flour. Coffee was hot on the fires, loaves of bread were baking, and potatoes frying. The sutler was surrounded by a crowd of men buying dried beef, apples, tripe, tobacco, and wool socks.[22]

Even then, an expedition was trying to force its way from the northwest toward Vicksburg through the Yazoo cutoff, opposite but out of sight on the distant bank, and through the chain of streams and bayous connecting with the Yazoo River. It was "a desperate undertaking at best," and word was going about the camp that the boats were getting the worst of it. "One would expect to find them waiting here amphibious, very gloomy," Olmsted noted, "but they were as merry as crickets and as comfortable as possible. . . . It is this good feeding that keeps the men up."[23]

Certainly it was not the promise of the military operations, which seemed no closer to success than in December. Grant had kept his engineers busy digging various huge ditches, to by-pass the fortified heights, through which his troops might be carried on Admiral David D. Porter's boats to attack Vicksburg obliquely. These laborious efforts had failed, and the failures, provoking a clamor of angry disappointment in the North, had placed Grant in real danger of being removed from his command. Frustrated and puzzled, he nevertheless rejected advice from his subordinates to pull his army back to Memphis, march it down the railroad, and attack from the east. The country was in no humor for retreats; and he could not afford to admit to a false start.

It was during this stalemate in the campaign that Olmsted, on March 22, reached Grant's headquarters on the west side of the river above Vicksburg at Young's Point. General William T. Sherman's corps alone remained there in direct observation of the stronghold; General John McClernand's, drowned out, had recently moved a few miles upstream to Milliken's Bend. Some thirty thousand men were camped along the levee, some of them on terraces cut into its slope, for a couple of miles above the canal that had been dug through the peninsula formed by the sharp bend of the river at Vicksburg. Against the bank, bow up on the only dry land below Milliken's Bend, Olmsted saw Grant's headquarters boat, the *Magnolia*; in the stream rode a dozen large supply and transport steamers and a score of coal barges. Nearby were several ironclads and rams and, in the mouth of the Yazoo opposite headquarters, floated Admiral Porter's flagship and a navy hospital ship. Looking past the levee, here fourteen feet high, Olmsted could see the ground beyond under water, soaked with seepage where it was not flooded. The levee itself offered the only passable ground in the neighborhood, except for a single corduroy road. It offered, as well, the only ground dry enough for burials; two immensely long lines of graves, laid head to foot, flanked the road along its top. Dispiriting though the scene was, spring was beginning to grace the water-logged countryside. Roses and yellow jasmine were in flower, trees were leafing out, and mockingbirds were singing; less pleasingly, vultures coasted aloft.[24]

For several days Olmsted and Knapp inspected camps, hospital ships, and the naval squadron and called on the commanders. One fine morning, they rode with Grant's medical director, Dr. Henry S. Hewit, toward Vicksburg, approaching close enough to set their watches by the town clock and to observe Negroes working on the fortifications, under white superintendents. Later they lunched in a tent outside Sherman's headquarters, a planter's house in a little grove of willow oaks and Pride of China trees. In the absence of Sherman, who was on an expedition trying to thrust through Steele's Bayou to Vicksburg, his staff engineer, Captain William LeBaron Jenney, took them in charge. A Boston man educated at the *Ecole Polytechnique*, he was "warm on parks, pictures, architects, engineers and artists." Olmsted found "a peculiar zest" in his reminiscences of student life in Paris, recounted against the shouts of toiling contrabands, the clamor of drums and bugles sounding for evening parade, and the distant boom of Admiral David Farragut's big guns pitching shells into the rebel battery at Warrenton—which, for added piquancy, was commanded by General Richard Taylor, the Dick Taylor who, ten years earlier, had entertained Olmsted at "Fashion," his sugar plantation in St. Charles Parish, Louisiana.[25]

After talking to Jenney, who was in charge of building the Young's Point canal, both Olmsted and Knapp concluded that its function was merely diversionary. And from Grant, whom they met for the first time that same evening, Olmsted got the impression that neither it nor any of the canals had ever been expected to accomplish anything serious.

The general, who had invited them to tea, was in his living quarters in the ladies' cabin of the *Magnolia* when they arrived. A sentry at the boat's gangway passed them, as he did everyone, without hindrance; the commanding general was more accessible than many a businessman. This night Grant was too busy to give them much time: unfavorable reports of Sherman's expedition were arriving, and a Confederate deserter had come in with a bundle of Vicksburg papers. Grant spent most of the evening reading and writing, while his guests looked over the Vicksburg journals and talked to his staff. When they rose to leave, however, he said: "I wish you would be in as much as convenient while you stay. I am not always as much occupied as I am tonight, and whenever you see that I am not, understand that I shall be glad to talk with you."[26]

Olmsted's favorable first impression of Grant was transmuted to enthusiasm by a long interview with him the next night. "He is one of the most engaging men I ever met," he wrote.

> Small, quiet, gentle, modest—extremely, even uncomfortably modest—frank, confiding and of an exceedingly kind disposition. He gives you the impression of a man of strong will, however, and of capacity, underlying these feminine traits. As a general, I should think his quality was that of quick common-sense judgments, unobstructed by prejudices, and deep abiding quiet resolution. . . . The openness of mind, directness, simplicity, and rapidity of reasoning and clearness, with consequent confidence of conclusion, of General Grant is very delightful.[27]

Olmsted's enthusiasm for Grant derived in part from the general's attitude toward the Sanitary Commission; he seemed genuinely "benevolent and laborious in his desire to aid the fundamental purposes of the Commission, to clear the ground for it and to put us in the way of remedying mistakes." Impeded by rival relief agencies, its operations with his army were unsatisfactory to its two representatives. They detailed their complaints to Grant and won important concessions: he directed the quartermaster to turn over to it the steamer *Dunleith* for its exclusive use in transporting supplies; and he issued Order Number 86, which provided that the Sanitary Commission, alone of all the voluntary relief agencies, should be given free transportation, thus testifying to his approval of its methods and his belief that it was able single-handed to meet all the needs of the sick and wounded. "You cannot easily conceive what a host of enemies of the Commission this order is adapted to dispose of," Olmsted wrote Bellows.[28]

The one weakness Grant was alleged to have did not trouble Olmsted. A light drinker himself, he was charitable about the occasional excesses of others. Earlier, when a Sanitary Commission agent at Aquia Creek had been sent back to Washington for drunkenness, Olmsted instead of dismissing him had put him to work in the warehouse out of public view; he was a man of excellent qualities suffering from "a disease involving self-respect in its consequences," Olmsted declared, and needed not to be punished but to be "cautiously and delicately helped."[29] When his half-brother Allie had complained that his colonel was "a drunken loco-foco," Olmsted had sharply reminded him that Washington, Green, Putnam, Marion, Jackson, Taylor, and Scott all drank, "and the men got rather to like them."[30] And when he later learned that a lady with a petition, who had unexpectedly interrupted his and Knapp's interview with Grant, got the impression, and industriously spread it, that Grant was drinking with two cronies and had to cling to the back of his chair to hold himself upright while he talked to her, Olmsted made a public record of his opinion on the rank drunkenness held in relation to gossip in the hierarchy of vices: ". . . The zealous devotion with which I have often heard both men and women undermining the character of others for temperance on equally slight grounds, has often led me to question if there are not vices in our society more destructive to sound judgment and honest courses than that of habitual overdrinking."[31]

When the censorious lady appeared, Grant was, in fact, talking to Olmsted and Knapp about the repulse of Sherman's expedition and discussing, clearly and comprehensively, the grand military problem that faced him. If he had already hit on the solution, he did not tell his visitors. Olmsted left with the impression that he was disappointed, anxious, and entirely at a loss what to do next.[32]

As they started back toward Memphis March 29 on the *Dunleith*, Olmsted and Knapp observed the expedition's return, with stern-wheel transports "wonderfully knocked to pieces," stacks down, and black coal smoke pouring over the crowded decks. Both were convinced that Grant had made his last attempt against Vicksburg from the river.[33]

From the *Dunleith*, Olmsted wrote reports on the troops and the commission to Bellows and Newberry. The army, considering its unhealthy and depressing circumstances, was in amazingly good health and spirits, thanks to excellent sanitary care, an enlightened military administration, and the efficient distribution of good and varied food. Hospital accommodations were the best he had seen in the field. And the men seemed actually to be enjoying themselves. "There are trials and hardships enough and not more than enough to give an enjoyable nobility and overruling satisfaction of duty." The navy, in which commissary arrangements had broken down, was less well off, but prompt distribution by the commission of two hundred thirty barrels of potatoes and onions with ale and pickled cabbage, and more to come, insured that there would be no serious outbreak of scurvy.

Sanguine about the troops, Olmsted continued to be grim about the commission and his role in it. He had found Sanitary concerns "so mixed up, complicated and overlaid by various agents," he told Newberry, "the duties and rights of its agents so vague and uncertain, that any efficiency of management seemed to me to be hopeless unless upon a radically new base. . . . As it has been, I believe the Sanitary business did more harm to the Republic than good. I was thoroughly disheartened." And he warned Bellows, "I do not believe the difficulties in our affairs here are to be remedied by any temporary meddling, and you must not hold me responsible for the going wrong of matters with which I shall have happened to meddle, because I obey orders under protest, thrusting me in here." Only Grant's order handing over the *Dunleith* ameliorated the Sanitary outlook, in his opinion. "The great advantage of it is that it must establish the fact in the minds of our agents that they have specific duties and are responsibly connected with the army, and that they are not everybody's friends. More than half the time of all our force, at present, is spent in attending to business that does not belong to the Commission, and which, in *my* opinion, would be better left undone."[34]

For his friend Godkin, Olmsted summed up in a long letter his impressions of the armies and the generals he had seen. "Both armies are in the finest conceivable moral and physical condition," he wrote. "They are well-clothed, well-shod, well-armed. . . . Parts of them are really well-disciplined. The mass is not but is improving." Rosecrans he described as quick-witted, fertile, and rapid in expedients, not a deep planner but excellent in action. "He is ambitious, over-confident, enthusiastic, vain, religious and healthily patriotic and angry with rebels. He is the only general I have seen in the West who fights with this sort of religious enthusiasm in his cause." Sherman, whom he had not met, he suspected of having the most "genius." McPherson was dependable; Stephen A. Hurlbut, commander at Memphis and half-brother of the attractive scamp Hurlbert, promised better than he had expected; McClernand was "a miserable, squabbling, mean, intriguing politician; flay him alive at the first chance." As for Grant, he was *"par excellence, a gentleman,* a modest, good-hearted, self-sacrificing, resolute, common-sense gentleman. In whatever you write," he admonished, "treat Grant with great respect."[35]

Since Godkin contributed regularly to the *New York Times* and the London *Daily News*, which was a consistent champion of the Union, Olmsted's words had more than a private impact: Godkin copied the letter bodily and sent it to the *Daily News*, suppressing only the signature and details that would have identified its author.[36]

XX
BATTLES AND A NEW PROSPECT
March–August 1863

THE trip home took Olmsted to St. Louis, where, unexpectedly, members of the Western Sanitary Commission showed a cautious interest in combining with the United States Sanitary Commission. Such evidence of declining sectional spirit encouraged Olmsted to begin work on a scheme to bring the two relief agencies into a single organization. "If . . . an arrangement should become practicable for the union of the Western Sanitary Commission and that which I have the honor to serve, I shall regard it as by far the most satisfactory incident in my Western trip," he assured James Yeatman of the western agency.[1]

The start of Olmsted's tour had not been auspicious, nor was its end. He had not wanted to step out of his executive rank to "meddle" with his subordinates' duties; as soon as he was back, Agnew let him know that he was to keep on doing precisely that. On a recent visit to the Army of the Potomac at Aquia Creek, Agnew found that the Sanitary Commission had fallen into low esteem because of the misconduct of some of its agents. It was a grave mistake, he wrote Olmsted, to rely on the agents for reports of their own work: all men needed to be watched. "I believe, as I have always believed, that you should be a locomotive secretary, instead of spending so much time in office work upon theoretical plans of organization. While we are theorizing in Washington, our agencies in the Potomac Army are rotting from neglect."[2]

This was disconcerting word to a man even then engaged on a large scheme of consolidation and reorganization. Olmsted consulted Bache, the member of the executive committee who usually took his side; then he asked to be relieved of all responsibility for the general management of the commission.[3] Prevented from running its affairs as he thought they should be run, he refused to abandon his reputation as an executive "under the feet of the careless, good-natured, self-opinionated Executive Committee."[4]

If he left the commission, he wrote his father, he was not sure what he would do. His salary was twenty-five hundred dollars a year, his one hundred a month from the park was likely to be stopped any day, and the farm had gone to the dogs. He had, therefore, no accumulated capital to fall back on. No capital, except that of reputation. ". . . Business men regard me as a man of unusual capacity and good judgment in certain respects, and there are some matters which it is getting to be thought I can handle better than anybody else in the country."

Perhaps he could get the backing to launch a high-class weekly newspaper with Godkin; they had several times discussed the possibility.[5]

To John Olmsted, this suggestion was the last straw. His angry distress may be inferred from the surviving half, his son's, of the exchange of letters that followed. He apparently reproached Fred for giving up his park job because of conflict with his superiors and for proposing to quit his Sanitary Commission job for similar reasons. Stung, Fred retorted:

> You seem to give yourself unnecessary annoyance by adding to your regret that I was no longer able to keep the [park] post, regret for my incompetence, weakness and folly. I gained the post by my own wholly unaided exertions. . . . The same qualities, and judgment and skill in their use by which I gained it, I used with far greater effort and persistence to retain it. . . . It pains me that you should have the misfortune of supposing me to be so much less respectable a man than I am.[6]

John Olmsted's reply must have contained an affronted sort of apology, for Fred replied:

> I wanted the benefit of your judgment. I don't know what you mean by asking my pardon, but I know that I never gave you occasion to keep up this style of dealing with me. . . . Now I should like to know what you would advise me or what you wish me to do, fairly considering the facts I have laid before you. . . . You write as if you thought me wrong. If I am wrong, I want to be right. Why not give me a chance? . . .
>
> You characterize my letter as "unkind." I am sure that the intention was nothing but kindness—an effort to remove the grounds of false and uncomfortable suppositions which you had expressed about your son. . . . I deal with you as I hope my children will deal with me. I don't want them to be indifferent to my judgment of them or lazily let me set them down as unwise and obstinate in their unwisdom. However wanting in sagacity I may be, I am obstinate only in honest dutifulness. You ought to know that I will never quietly acquiesce in being put in an undutiful position.[7]

Pained though he was by his first serious rift with his father, he felt he could not stand the Sanitary Commission much longer. "The primary and essential conditions of sound administration are cut off square at the root, according to my notion of sound administration," he complained to Bellows. ". . . How the house stands with an underpinning of expedients, I don't know. It rocks too much for my head." He remarked incidentally, because it was not worth fresh emphasis, that he was not getting the promised monthly reports from Newberry. "Yet you pretend to hold this office 'responsible for our Western Department.' "[8]

Separated at last from Central Park when Vaux resigned for both of them the middle of May and half-decided to relinquish the commission,[9] Olmsted scouted more actively the possibility of establishing a weekly paper. As early as the beginning of April he had written Godkin from the Mississippi that he was prepared to go into one with him at a month's notice.[10] Since then, Godkin had satisfied himself that the project was practicable. Finally, on June 25, meeting at the Union League Club in New York with a group that included Bellows, Strong, George Griswold, Jr., Dr. Benjamin A. Gould of Cambridge, Howard Potter, and William J. Hoppin, Olmsted read a paper that he and Godkin had prepared.[11]

Presumably it covered the same points later covered in the prospectus soliciting stock subscriptions. The prospectus proposed an independent weekly newspaper, more thoughtful and authoritative than a daily could be and free of partisan political interests. Such a paper was needed because the time was past when "anyone" could administer public affairs. New and specialized problems faced the country: the future of a standing army and a large navy, complicated foreign relations, four million disaffected whites to bring to order, and slaves to be raised as citizens. A government confronting such questions needed to be supported by men more thoughtful and far-seeing than those who established the character of the daily press. Studious men now should take hold of public affairs; they should have some organization and a means of making their leadership felt. The editor of a weekly could draw on widely scattered and expert contributors and would not have to rely on men in the office writing without due reflection and thorough information against a daily deadline. The proposed journal would carry three or four pages of comment on legal, social, commercial, and political events; three or four careful articles on leading topics of the day; three or four pieces on social, economic, literary, and scientific subjects; critiques of books, paintings, theater, and music in leading cities; and correspondence from London and Paris on literary, scientific, and political matters. Research and accuracy were to distinguish the publication. It would be expensive, but it would have no rival; and the fact that Mill's *On Liberty* had sold two thousand copies in a few months in New York suggested that there was a growing class of readers for such a paper. Stock subscriptions in units of five hundred dollars were to be solicited, but no one was to be asked to subscribe for the purpose of making money.[12]

The statement was well received. Griswold immediately pledged a thousand dollars; Potter, Strong, and Hoppin were appointed trustees; and it was resolved to go ahead. "I can only say that, so far, the enterprise is initiated as I could wish in all respects," Olmsted wrote his wife, who was visiting in Connecticut. "We meet about it Tuesday night and shall then go ahead for subscriptions. The thing starts so favorably, I shall go into it strong, meaning to succeed."[13]

He had the more motive for concentrating on the paper since his plan for combining the United States and the Western Sanitary Commissions had run, after a promising start, into obstacles. Both the Louisville and the Chicago branches of the original commission were set against the merger; and Olmsted suspected that, if he turned his back, the executive committee would drop it. "I can manage the Executive Committee while here, very well," he told his wife, "but they would put the fat in the fire as soon as I left them."[14]

Quite overshadowing Olmsted's other interests, however, was the approaching crisis of the war. After defeating the Union force at Chancellorsville in May, Lee had determined to invade the North, and on June 15 he had put the first of his battle-hardened troops across the Potomac; ten days later his army was deep in Pennsylvania and advancing on Harrisburg. A strange indifference seemed to grip New York. "Our frivolous, self-indulgent apathy is marvelous," Strong exclaimed;[15] and Olmsted asked, "Are people as emotionless about this invasion, and the awful danger and hope before us, in the country as they are here, I wonder?" The import of Grant's beautifully bold movement below and to the rear of Vicksburg seems to have been eclipsed in Olmsted's mind by the peril at hand; and the unexpected promotion of Major General George Gordon Meade to command the Army of the Potomac aroused in him only muted optimism. "Meade, I have a good opinion of, as a gentleman of candid and receptive disposition. He has always been very good to the Commission."[16]

In anticipation of the decisive battle, the Sanitary Commission had been moving stores to the front. Olmsted was in Philadelphia on a purchasing mission when the battle of Gettysburg began; he snatched time while waiting for a train to New York to have some photographs taken, which did not please him: "I think I look like Ben Butler."[17] He was back in Philadelphia with Knapp on July 5, purchasing tons of fresh eggs, butter, mutton, chickens, fruit, and milk and chartering a refrigerator car. Skeptical of earlier good news from the front, he heard there "the first conclusive and circumstantial account of the victory of Meade"[18] and wired Bellows: "Private advices tend to confirm reports of capture of over fifteen thousand prisoners and one hundred guns. Lee retreating. Pleasanton holds Potomac fords." Strong took the wire and posted it on the bulletin board of the Union League Club. "Olmsted is wary, shrewd and never sanguine," he noted. "This dispatch was not sent without strong evidence to support it."[19]

On Sunday, the fifth, Olmsted and Knapp preceded the loaded refrigerator car to Baltimore, where they bought a carload of big camp-meeting tents and miscellaneous furniture; by Monday night they managed to get both cars attached to the first train through Gettysburg since the battle. Oliver Bullard, Henry Ward Beecher's brother-in-law, was in charge of a contingent that went with them to set up a soldiers' home and relief station; next evening Georgie Woolsey, veteran of the hospital transports, who had rushed to Baltimore with her mother under the mistaken impression that her brother had been wounded, was drafted by Olmsted to accompany another carload of supplies to the field. "We had fifteen men there before with wagons running from Westminster to Frederick. . . . Our regular wagon force was on the ground during the battle," Olmsted wrote his wife on Tuesday, "and the wagons visited all the field hospitals as fast as they were established and hours before they received supplies from other quarters. . . . I have arranged to receive and take care of about forty tons of supplies a day, for the present, if the people supply them, as I think they will."[20]

Staying at the Eutaw House in Baltimore with Olmsted were a score of slightly wounded officers, mostly from Massachusetts. From them he learned that the Army of the Potomac had "hardly a breath" left in it at the end of the carnage. "It was but a hair's breadth from a terrible defeat for fully half an hour. . . . But our men never behaved so well and I believe they fought better than the enemy—they were cool and steady and showed every good quality of veterans, and it was, I think, the best fought field of the war. Its moral effect is incalculable, taken with Vicksburg and Tullahoma, and what is better than all, if true, the report of the President's draft of 300,000. . . ."[21]

By July 9 Olmsted was in Frederick himself, directing Sanitary Commission operations. Thence he went to Meade's headquarters on Beaver Creek near Williamsport, where he had an intimate view of the fighting that continued as Lee withdrew his defeated but still viable army toward the Potomac. "I had two good days of campaigning," he wrote his wife on the fifteenth after his return to Frederick, "camping three nights and enjoying it. I went through our line of battle and crawled up among the trees and rocks to our most advanced skirmishers in the midst of the Indian fighting, our men advancing from tree to tree and driving the rebel skirmishers back from tree to tree. There was a good deal of sharp shooting but," he added soothingly, "the chances of a hit on either side were very small."[22]

After a brief meeting with the commander, Olmsted wrote his wife, "I liked General Meade very much. He is somewhat gaunt and stooping but very soldierly—veteran-like—in his whole aspect, much more so than any other general I have seen. His countenance is stern, dignified, oriental & yet Yankee."[23] His short talk with Meade and longer ones with Alfred Pleasanton and Ingalls, an acquaintance from the peninsula campaign, left Olmsted with the conviction that the commander had acted soundly on the basis of the information and advice available to him in allowing Lee's army to get away. Writing Godkin of his visit to the field, he said he thought he had earlier overestimated the Union force. "I had a hint that nobody was allowed to know how small it was, and I could see that those who knew best were not willing that I should believe some parts of the army to be as weak as I know they are."[24] The hint was broad enough: either Meade himself or Ingalls—later Olmsted was not sure which—said to him, "We are not as strong as we are supposed to be. I dare not say how weak we are."[25]

Lincoln's disappointment was intense that Lee had withdrawn uncrushed, and Olmsted heard that Henry Wager Halleck, the general-in-chief, sent Meade a wire, the tone of which Meade considered insolent, saying that he must make up by the energy of his pursuit of the rebel army for having allowed it to escape. Olmsted reported on the sequel to Godkin.

General Ingalls came into the tent as he was reading it and Meade said: "Ingalls don't you want to take command of this army?" "No I thank you, it's too big an elephant for me." "Well, it's too big for me, too, read that," and then he immediately wrote in reply that his resignation was at the service of the Department. Two hours afterwards he received for answer to his reply that neither the President nor the General in Chief wished to be understood as blaming General Meade for the escape of the rebel army. This I know to be true, but as I can't mention my authority it should not be made public except in general terms. I was at Hd Q at the time.[26]

Olmsted returned to Gettysburg from Frederick on the eighteenth. The wounded, originally packed into any shelter available, had by then been sorted out. The critically hurt remained in makeshift hospitals around Gettysburg; all the rest were being taken as rapidly as they could be moved to Hanover Station for shipment to hospitals elsewhere. There the commission had set up a lodge equipped with tents, beds, and kitchens, where its staff of nurses, surgeons, and dressers tirelessly cared for Union and Confederate casualties alike until their transfer.[27] Olmsted, having inspected the lodge, shared the traveling conditions of the wounded as far as Baltimore. They were not salubrious. He lay from eleven at night until three in the morning on the floor of a car that the day before had carried hogs and had not been cleaned, among a lot of wounded rebels and dead Pennsylvanians, "the whole producing the most sickening stench I ever endured." When he reached Baltimore at dawn, he limped into the Eutaw House, carrying his bag on his shoulder, to fall exhausted into his bed and rest, so far as the flies would let him, "after a pretty hard week's work."[28]

"The old army of the Potomac is in fine condition marches twenty or thirty miles a day and accepts what comes to it without hesitation," Olmsted had proudly observed at Gettysburg, "—its chief discouragement arises from the smallness of its regiments many being as low as 200 men."[29]

By this time, recruitment had become an acute problem; voluntary enlistment was not enough to keep the army up to strength. The Draft Act of March 1863, intended as a radical remedy for recruitment difficulties, was designed but poorly to solve them. In the eyes of many a prospective soldier, its most obnoxious feature was the provision that any unwilling draftee with three hundred dollars to spare could hire a substitute to go to war in his place. Criticism of the Draft Act was articulate and widespread; and on July 13 resistance to it rose to an atrocious climax when the Draft Riots broke out in New York.

The first drawing was held there on Saturday, July 11. The following Monday mobs of foreign-born laborers, largely Irish and Democratic, formed to give vent to their resentment of the draft and of Negroes, whose competition they were beginning to feel and to fear, in an uninhibited spree of arson, plunder, and murder. The city was prostrated and terrorized for four days before civil and military authorities could assemble the force to quell the mobs. They wrecked the draft office, sacked and burned the Colored Orphan Asylum and private homes, tried to fire the offices of loyal newspapers, looted stores, lynched blacks, threw up barricades in the cross streets, and fought pitched battles up and down the avenues with militia, police, armed bands of citizens, and regulars returned from fighting scarcely more savage at the front. By the time the tumult and the terror were exhausted, a million and a half dollars worth of private property had been destroyed. No one knew the number killed because the rioters were thought to have buried some of their dead secretly by night across the rivers; guesses ran as high as a thousand.

Although no good evidence later supported it, suspicion was abroad that the disorders had not been spontaneous but had been contrived by rebel agents. Olmsted blamed, rather, the city's Copperhead politicians who had created the climate in which insurrection dared to flaunt, and he angrily asserted he would like to see them all—Barlow, Bennett, Brooks, Belmont, Barnard, the Woods, even Seymour, whom he with less justice included—hanged and New York treated like such insurrectionary centers as Baltimore, Nashville, and New Orleans.[30]

The collusion of Copperheadism and mob rule, however, coinciding with resounding military successes at Gettysburg and Vicksburg, produced, Olmsted thought, a situation perfect for the launching of the new magazine. "Never was there so favorable a season for planting good seed, especially in New York," Olmsted wrote Bellows.[31] He was the more chagrined, therefore, that little was done throughout July to advance the business. The riots had knocked it out of the heads of the fund-raising committee, and most of the monied prospects were out of town. Bellows alone by the beginning of August had secured subscriptions from three of the gentlemen assigned to him. Olmsted fretted impatiently that nothing more would be accomplished until the vacationing wealth returned to the city.[32]

He, meanwhile, shuttling between New York and Washington, was wretched. The heat wilted and sickened him, he was queasy from the fatigue and the diet of poor ham and corn whiskey that he had had with the army,[33] and he was "oppressed beyond endurance" that the grand aims of the commission were being sacrificed "to little personal whims and good purposes of a narrow and ambiguous kind."[34] Finally, he was worried about his wife, who was suffering, like him, from occasional vertigo.[35]

His spirits were sustained by the prospect of a visit to Connecticut, where he would be reunited with his wife and, he hoped, reconciled with his father, about whom his conscience sorely troubled him.[36] To break the ice he wrote him, the beginning of August, an affectionate, conciliatory letter detailing his connection with the magazine and enclosing a prospectus for it and a copy of *Hospital Transports*, a newly published book put together from Sanitary Commission agents' letters about the commission's work on the peninsula.[37]

The first week in August Olmsted went to New England. Failing to locate his father either at Hartford or at Sachem's Head, he took his wife and Charlotte to visit Godkin at Salisbury and Bellows and Knapp at Walpole.[38] While he was still away, he received a letter from Charles A. Dana that abruptly revolutionized his prospects: Dana wrote that the new owners of the Mariposa Estate, a large gold-mining property in California, wanted Olmsted for superintendent.[39]

XXI
MARIPOSA: MODERATE EXPECTATIONS
August–October 1863

THE Mariposa Estate, a principality of seventy square miles, lay in the western foothills of the Sierra Nevada Mountains, within sight of the precipices rising out of the Yosemite Valley. Compact but irregular in shape, it stretched southward about eight miles from the Merced River and measured eleven miles along its greatest east–west axis.[1] It was connected with Stockton, the nearest large town, by a stage that crossed the eighty-five miles of intervening desert with mail and passengers three times a week.[2]

Within estate boundaries were a half-dozen villages, most of them no more than mining camps, of which the largest were Mariposa, the county seat, and Bear Valley, headquarters of the estate.[3] Gold mines were scattered over the property. One of them, Princeton, had an authentic reputation for tremendous productivity; and others—Mount Ophir, Pine Tree–Josephine, Green Gulch, Mariposa, and Agua Fria—had been worked either with profit or with tantalizing promise.[4] Gold-bearing quartz from the mines was crushed at the estate's stamp mills, amalgamated with quicksilver, melted and cast into thin bricks, and taken by Wells Fargo Express to the estate's San Francisco bankers, who had it assayed, delivered to the mint, and credited to the Mariposa account.[5] During the rainy season placer miners worked the streambeds on the property, sometimes in such numbers that substantial incidental income came to the estate from the sale of licenses.[6] The estate's population, floating and mostly men, was about seven thousand, a mixture of Americans, Mexicans, Chinese, Digger Indians, and Europeans.[7]

The business history of Mariposa had been characterized by sharp dealing, protracted law suits, insolvency, and reorganization. The boundaries of the estate had not been established when the adventurous soldier Frémont bought it in 1847, and his survey and claims to certain mines had been contested in the courts for eight years. He had heavily encumbered the property to secure loans, and in 1859 the sheriff of Mariposa County sold it to satisfy a large judgment against it. Mark Brumagim, a San Francisco banker, bought the purchaser's interest in the estate in February 1860 to protect loans his firm had made to Frémont.

Another large creditor, a Vermont lawyer named Trenor W. Park, was made manager of the estate in June 1860, with the agreement that he was to be entirely free of Frémont's supervision and that he was to work the mines for the payment of his loan.

Brumagim, meantime, had agreed to reconvey to Frémont seven-eighths of the property whenever Frémont could pay the estate's debts. In the hope of raising money to pay them and to get operating capital, Frémont and his lawyer, Frederick Billings, went to London and Paris in January 1861. Their glowing prospectus did not entice capitalists alarmed by the approach of war, the mission failed, and the county sheriff on October 31, 1861, gave Brumagim a deed to the estate.

Whether Brumagim actually owned it or merely had a lien against it and whether Frémont had anything more to sell than the right to redeem seven-eighths of it were problems on which respectable legal opinion later divided. Even after the sheriff's deed to Brumagim, Billings, Park, and Abia Selover, another of Frémont's creditors, each regarded himself as owner of one-eighth interest in Mariposa, and Frémont considered himself owner of the remaining five-eighths. Acting in this belief, they entered into a complicated transaction to sell the estate to a group of New York financiers that included some of the most prominent businessmen in the city: David Dudley Field, lawyer; George Opdyke, mayor; and Morris Ketchum, banker and confidant of Salmon P. Chase.[8]

Park went east to take a hand in arranging the sale. The New Yorkers, skeptical of his representations, sent one of their group, a banker named James Hoy, west to inspect the mines. Hoy arrived as Princeton's production was at a glorious peak, and his report was an important factor in inducing his associates to close the deal. On the twenty-fifth of June 1863, the Mariposa Company was organized.[9]

The new company had a nominal capital stock of ten million dollars, most of which went to Frémont and his colleagues. Bonds for one and a half million dollars were authorized to provide for discharging all encumbrances upon the property. Billings estimated them at no more than one million two hundred thousand dollars; three hundred thousand dollars could thus be counted on as working capital to pay interest on the debt, develop the estate, and meet other requirements.[10]

To the financiers who formed the company, a dazzling success must have appeared almost inevitable. In the six months preceding the sale, the mines had yielded almost half a million dollars in gold.[11] Production had overshot the hundred thousand mark in May, when Princeton alone yielded ninety thousand dollars.[12] Park alleged that the estate's profit just before the sale was sixty thousand dollars a month.[13] In addition to the mines already opened, the property held at least a score of prominent quartz veins, and Professor Josiah Dwight Whitney, director of the California State Geological Survey, declared that the gold the estate could produce was limited only by the time and capital spent on building mills and roads and opening mines.[14] With its substantial working capital and current profits, the company could begin development at once, and further and more fabulous profit should automatically follow.

Olmsted, on receiving Dana's letter, went to New York at once to see the estate's new owners.[15] Presumably they—all, he supposed, "reputable, steady, careful capitalists"[16]—told him what they knew of the past and current history of the business and of its outlook. Their expectations, he thought, were based on insufficient data; even so, the company's prospects looked temptingly good. So was the remuneration offered him: ten thousand dollars a year, a house, and five hundred shares of stock in the company, with a par value of fifty thousand dollars.[17]

In a quandary, Olmsted discussed the factors that would influence his decision in long letters to his wife, his father (with whom he had resumed his usual loving and confidential relations), and Bellows. He was not indifferent to the salary, especially now that he had no clear prospects in the East: his influence in the Sanitary Commission was spent—". . . I think it has been decided again & again that I am not wanted," he wrote Bellows, "not in so many words, not in the logical & distinctly conscious conclusions of *my friends*, but in the deliberate vetoing—obstructing, condemning, upsetting and disusing all that I regard to be of any value in my work of the last two years"—the door to Central Park had been slammed on him, the magazine was hanging fire, and he was twelve thousand dollars in debt and sliding a little farther in all the time. While he wanted to play some part on the national scene in the solution of postwar problems, his chance of doing so was at best doubtful. At Mariposa, there would be a certain and immediate prospect of exercising an influence "favorable to religion, good order & civilization." "As the clergymen say when a rich parish bids for them against a poorer," he reflected wryly, "I think the call to California is a *clear* one if not as loud as that to the battle here."[18]

Still, doubt paralyzed decision. Would it promote the ultimate welfare of his family to set them down on a wild frontier among uncouth miners and savages? Possibly, too, what the owners of the property really wanted of him was his name, to help the stock on the market. He shrank, besides, from running into difficulties he was unequipped to handle. "I am not a merchant, banker, bookkeeper or broker any more than miner or miller, and I am afraid of being swindled from my ignorance of these affairs."[19] A disquieting factor was the evident surprise among "the sound California men" at some of the claims made for the estate; if he found they were false, he wanted no part of the business. "As I am forty-two years old, I can't afford to go on board a rotten ship," he said. He decided to consult his old friend Howard Potter, a Brown Brothers partner, who was knowledgeable about California affairs, and to be guided by him.[20]

Bellows, who had contemplated without perturbation Olmsted's possible dismissal as executive secretary, was jolted out of his complacency. He had of course counted on Olmsted's staying with the commission until it wound up, he protested, and he feared it could neither end gracefully nor continue effectively without him. More than that, he gravely objected to Olmsted's removing himself "at this special juncture of our National life" from the center of affairs "and giving to Mariposa what belongs to your Country and mankind."[21] The political settlement with the South, now that victory was in sight, and the forging of a sense of nationality to overcome the rancorous error of sectionalism offered fields Olmsted was peculiarly suited to work. He wrote:

> I don't know a half dozen men in the whole North, whose influence in the next five years I should think more critically important to the Nation. I don't know how it is to come *in*—whether by means of the Newspaper (which I think can be made to go) or by means of public office—but I am sure it is to be largely felt. . . . I think the faith of many, already pinned unconsciously to you, would fail and grow cold, if you should quit the field under what would seem to be a pecuniary temptation.[22]

Olmsted pointed out in reply that Bellows's estimate of his character was hardly consistent with the suggestion that he was governed by a mercenary motive. He was not; but regard for his family weighed greatly with him, regard for his creditors even more. And if he believed that by going to California he would sacrifice any of his influence for good, he would unhesitating stay. He added:

> I do not think that I am as wise as you allege by a great deal, but I am less influential, my advice and my information are of less effect than I feel they deserve to be—very much. There is something wrong in this . . . and I hope by going to California to earn the means . . . of commanding more of the respect for my judgment, to which I think it is legitimately entitled. . . .[23]

Bellows was sure that Olmsted underestimated both the esteem in which he was held and his chance of exerting influence during the coming five years. "I cannot give you my reasons for thinking so," he admitted.

> I have the feeling—and I have a strong reluctance to your going so far away from the center of influence. . . . I feel as if we were losing one of our most reliable pieces of national stuff in your going. I hope you will not feel after a year in California that I was right in my judgment—that you will not wish yourself back among the friends . . . with whom no differences of opinion had ever been able to create any coldness, distance or doubt.[24]

Bellows's appeal won Olmsted's careful attention: he postponed his decision a week, while he reviewed his arguments.[25] Then, for the second and last time in his life, he made the mistake of committing himself to a commercial venture.

On August 20 he came to terms with the board of trustees of the Mariposa Company.[26]

Olmsted's resignation from the Sanitary Commission was greeted with consternation and gave his friends, some of them hitherto reticent, an irresistible excuse to express their regard. Strong wrote that he could ill be spared.[27] Gibbs was thunderstruck.[28] Louisa Lee Schuyler, a pillar of the Women's Central, found the verve and confidence suddenly gone from the work.[29] Miss Wormeley quoted friends who thought the commission would soon collapse for lack of public confidence in everyone on it except Olmsted.[30] Charles Eliot Norton, who had recently met Olmsted for the first time, regretted that he should have to exchange civilization for barbarism. "All the lines in his face," he declared, "imply sensibility and refinement to such a degree that it is not till one has looked through them to what is underneath, that the force of his will and the reserved power of his character become evident."[31] Knapp wrote touchingly of Olmsted's good influence on him.[32] The *Times* carried a long appreciative editorial, initialed by Godkin;[33] it did not satisfy Bache: only someone who loved Olmsted as greatly as *he* did could really understand him, he said.[34]

Sped by this surge of good will, Olmsted sailed out of New York harbor on the afternoon of September 14, on Commodore Vanderbilt's steamship *Champion*. With him he took a bookkeeper, Howard A. Martin; an engineer, J. H. Pieper, who had worked on Central Park, and Pieper's family; and a French valet called Charles. His own family was to follow when he had arranged living quarters for them at Bear Valley.[35]

The *Champion*'s single merit was that she was scheduled to make a close connection with the Pacific coast steamer on the other side of the Isthmus of Panama. She was, as a Russian passenger fitly put it, "very much little and very much nasty." Worse than that, her engine was weak and ailing, and her lifeboats were too few to accommodate even the crew. The more knowing of her passengers expected, if she met a bad storm in that hurricane season, to go to the bottom within minutes.

The *Champion*, however, did not go to the bottom. Instead she wallowed placidly through the smiling, swelling sea toward Aspinwall. Olmsted passed the dragging time by jotting down his impressions of voyage and voyagers,[36] and by writing long letters, full of good advice, to his wife.

On the evening of Thursday, September 24, the *Champion* sighted land. At 2:30 in the morning she tied up at Aspinwall, and her sleepy passengers made their way through the tropical dark to the large, dirty inn. Daybreak revealed a new, half-made, shabby shanty-town, leveed out of a swamp. Olmsted for a while prowled its outskirts, but the interest it held for him was soon exhausted, and he regretted that so miserable a place was named after a fellow countryman.

At nine o'clock he got on the train that was to carry him across the isthmus. As they pulled out of the town and passed into the swamp pressing close upon it, Olmsted's fatigue was suddenly dissipated by his absorption in the novel beauty of the scenery. It was lacking in grandeur, an element that in any case appealed to him little, and there was much muddy water; but the splendor of the vegetation was stunning.

Banana trees adorned with yellow and green fruit flourished among lofty cocoa, date, and sago palms, and delicate fan palms moved softly in the light air. Mahogany trees with fine trunks and handsome dark leaves rose like columns among the graceful bamboo. Brilliant flowers like the crimson hibiscus glowed in the lush greenery. The effect was so varied and glorious that even the finest foliage Olmsted had seen before now seemed tame and dull in comparison. Characteristically, he ascribed an ethical influence to the scenery. "I think it produces a very strong moral impression," he wrote his wife, "through an enlarged sense of the bounteousness of Nature."[37]

The train stopped every few miles at wooding stations and shortly after noon reached Panama. A steam tender promptly transferred the travelers to the Pacific Mail Steamship Company's *Constitution*, lying about a mile offshore. A delightful contrast to the *Champion*, she was the finest and largest ship Olmsted had ever traveled on, spacious, clean, and well equipped.

Olmsted, still enthralled by the scenery, studied it from the deck for hours. The little tile-roofed, white-walled Spanish town on the curve of the fine bay was surrounded by beautiful conical hills, while to the south of it the Andes faintly towered. Strange birds floated above the luminous green hills. Passing showers veiled the scene every hour or two; then the sun shafts darting forth made the foliage glisten gorgeously. Olmsted, after a day of pure delight, felt fully compensated for the past miseries of the trip.[38]

No misery attended the coastwise voyage except a dull sort of seasickness, and even that was minimized by the unusual steadiness of the *Constitution*. Nearly half the time she ran within sight of land, sometimes so close that her passengers could observe the shore landscape, which Olmsted found always noble and often very beautiful in detail; and sometimes her course lay farther out but still within sight of mountains wreathed in grand white clouds.

By October 10, when the ship had passed the Mexican coast and was off San Luis Obispo, the weather had become cold, with fog and chilling winds. The scene as well as the weather turned bleak. The coast approaching San Francisco was dreary, with bare, dry, brown, smooth hills, and low rocky cliffs against which heavy breakers crashed. Rolling for the first time, the *Constitution* next day crossed the dangerous bar twenty miles from San Francisco and entered the Golden Gate.[39]

Scores of large ships, flying the flags of nearly every maritime nation, lay in the perfect harbor. The town did not disappoint Olmsted, since he had expected little of it: around the waterfront it was Stapleton, Brooklyn, or Jersey City over again, and in the interior it was much like any western town with its plank sidewalks and its gridiron street pattern arbitrarily imposed on the unaccommodating terrain. The wharf, crowded with hackney coaches, teams and their shouting drivers, stevedores and travelers reminded him of New York. Indeed, the unmistakable familiarity of everything, except the arid scenery, made him know at once that he had come back to his own country. With yesterday's telegraphic news from New York, and the mails closing daily at three, he felt not a twenty-seven-day and ten-thousand-mile journey from his eastern home but as close to it as he had been in Washington.[40]

A superstitious man might have seen an omen in Olmsted's mishap immediately on landing: a draft horse kicked him on his lame leg at the pier. A second blow fell promptly. Billings, calling at the hotel where Olmsted was nursing his injury, warned him that the glowing promise of the estate might be an ignis fatuus: production had fallen from a hundred thousand dollars a month to twenty-five thousand and might well drop more, and the estate's account with its San Francisco bankers was overdrawn.[41]

A Vermonter like Park, Billings had been his senior partner in the foremost law firm in San Francisco; he was no longer friendly to him and blamed the startling decline of the estate on his bad management. Still, Billings believed in its ultimate value. "Your success," he told Olmsted, "will depend entirely on whether the company will sustain you in sufficiently radical and expensive operations. The estate is of no value unless they do, and if they do it is of enormous value."[42] He was wrong; but it was to be many years before further exploration would establish that the Mariposa mines were at the wrong end of the mother lode.[43]

On Tuesday evening, October 13, Olmsted, Billings, and Charles took the little bay steamer for Stockton. Landing next morning in the typically shabby, newly sprouted western town, they had a good breakfast in a dirty restaurant, hired a rockaway drawn by a pair of hackney coach horses, and set out for Bear Valley.[44]

The road ran through a dead-flat, dead-brown landscape marked only by scatterings of trees that grew scarcer and scarcer as the miles passed. Olmsted thought the journey across the plain was the most desolate, dreary, and tiresome one he had ever made. The dust rose in blinding billows from beneath the horses' hooves. The few trees were of a monotonous sameness; clustered on the rivers, which were dried to trails of red mud, they looked like overgrown, neglected apple trees with curled, leathery tags of leaves. They were live oaks, which to Olmsted's eye ever appeared cheerless and dull. As the Sierras began to rise from the plain to the east, and as the nearer mountains stood out with increasing distinctness, he could see that they were dotted to their tops with these somber trees and dotted so sparsely that the shade of one never touched that of another.[45]

By sunset the little party had reached more broken country, with rounded hills and outcroppings of rock thrusting out of the ground perpendicularly. Along the dried-up watercourses "the desolation was somewhat relieved by multitudes of children's graves"—so the tailings left by placer miners appeared to Olmsted's depressed imagination. The road mounted steadily into the foothills until a grand view could be had back across the darkening plain to the coastal range silhouetted in the red glow of sunset. Then it descended, by an easy grade, into Bear Valley. There, at the Oso Hotel, a flimsy, clean frame building, Olmsted and his party finished their long day with a good supper of omelette and vegetables.[46]

In the morning Olmsted had his first look at the little village where he was to spend the next two years. The wide street, rough with rocky outcroppings beneath its surface of thick red dust, ran between a score of shabby one-story buildings, some of which tried by means of false fronts to create an illusion of consequence. The shops—several bars, two inns, a billiard parlor, a bath house, two livery stables, a French restaurant and bakery, two laundries, the company store, and the Wells Fargo office—indicated the principal requirements of the floating population of miners. Off the main street was a small foundry, behind which were shanties and tents, while around the outskirts of the village clustered separate settlements for Chinese, Mexicans, and Indians. Behind one of the inns, the cemetery, unfenced, untended, and filled with men who had died the deaths "natural" in the region—by shooting, stabbing, or hanging—reinforced the suggestion of a rude and primitive society. Olmsted's first impression was: "It is just a miners' village—no women and everything as it must be where men don't live but merely camp."[47]

More striking than the crudeness of the village was the monotonous brown of the landscape. The region was gasping under the worst dry season in ten years, and the dusty live oaks and dried-up deciduous trees emphasized the appalling absence of greenery all about. Scanning the hills that flanked the valley, Olmsted thought he could detect some variety of foliage toward their tops, but at their feet he could see only live oak, thorny chapparal, and patches of dwarf buckeye. To the east, Mount Bullion, rising more than five thousand feet into the crystalline air, appeared to Olmsted to be better wooded; patches on its face looked, to his eager eye, actually green.[48] Yet, with its crest of glittering white quartz, its precipitous gullies, and its prevailing dead brownness, it too enhanced in his mind by its difference from the eastern mountains to which he was accustomed the alien quality of the parched, barren landscape. Olmsted's immediate reaction to the scenery was bewilderment. "It is—I really don't understand it & won't say whether it is beautiful or not. It is not—yet it may be, after you are used to the hot, dry summer. . . ."[49]

His doubts persisted several days. The grand style of the main feature of the landscape, its mountains, combined with the paltriness of the vegetation, were confusing and distasteful to the aesthetic sense responsive not to grandeur but to gentle rural scenery where much of the charm lay in the details, especially those of foliage. He could not at once assimilate it to his New England experience or to his ideal. Within a few days, however, he experienced a sort of revelation. Riding at twilight along the valley from the Mount Ophir mine to Bear Valley, he had a sudden intimation of beauty. In the merciful dusk the parched ground appeared as though turf covered, the dust-shrouded shrubs and trees took on the coloration of deep verdure, and the distant views reminded him, familiarly, of Italy.[50] He felt that he had never passed through a lovelier landscape; and from that time on his eye adapted itself to its strange beauty.

He was not, however, then or ever converted from his established standard of landscape beauty. The necessary elements of the scenery he loved and created were cheerfulness, grace, repose, a touch of mystery, to buoy and stimulate the spirit, not grandeur to paralyze the mind with a sense of its own inconsequence. The spectacular in nature never appealed to him strongly, however much it sometimes interested and impressed him; and it was no more than reasonable that vastness and impersonality should fail to touch or inspire a man who ascribed to scenery a moral function and who felt, like Wordsworth, that through it a moral influence mystically worked toward the betterment of man.

In his first few days on the estate, Olmsted traveled over its great extent, hastily familiarizing himself with its physical aspects and with its business. At the north end, the landscape was barren, rude, and grand; and across the valley of the Merced River the steep lower Sierras, almost bare of trees and covered with a furzelike shrub, resembled the heathery peaks of Scotland. The river at this season was only a muddy rill creeping through its steep ravine; from a mountain spur near the Josephine mine, one could look up its valley and see the bald gray cliff of El Capitan towering over the hidden Yosemite Valley.[51]

The southern part of the estate was scenically more congenial to Olmsted, with its rounded hills and deep dells and oaks scattered parklike everywhere. The withered vegetation and the heavy red dust, he began to realize, were phases rather than fixtures of the scene; the dry season would soon come to an end, and the estate would be beautiful in the spring and summer "when this brown is green & tinted with flowers as they describe it."[52] Even then, the weather was delightful, like the finest autumn weather in the East, and Olmsted thought he could already detect the bracing effect of the climate; otherwise he could not so well have withstood the hard journey and the exertions of the first few days,[53] or the repeated shocks of disappointment that, in spite of Billings's warning, they brought him.

With Billings as his constant companion, Olmsted inspected Benton Mills and all the mines. Candle in hand, he went down shafts and crawled and clambered over slippery wet crags, so fascinated by his new experience that he was unmindful of lameness and fatigue. He also looked at some twenty veins that had been more or less worked ("and know—as much as I did before")[54] and various abandoned mines and mills. He talked with mine superintendents and the collector of license fees from placer miners, examined the Bear Valley store and inquired into the storekeeping and boardinghouse system, and had talks with people who had lived for some years on the estate and with other residents of the county. The sources of his disappointment, itemized after a three-day survey for James Hoy, president of the company, made a staggering bill of particulars.[55]

Most disquieting to Olmsted, though hardest to define, were the tone and manner common to everyone who spoke of the estate that indicated a complete lack of respect for the interests of the company and a demoralized indifference to the welfare of the property. More definite was the huge falling-off of revenue. Moreover, the Pine Tree–Josephine mines at the north end of the property were, he found, not paying their way. The machinery in Princeton, the only other currently operating mine, was in such bad repair that it would probably have to be taken out; and most of the deadwork—timbering, ventilating, even exploring —absolutely essential to safe and economical mining, had been neglected for months. In addition, the management had neither prevented costly trespasses nor prosecuted trespassers; and the county authorities in charge of assessments were hostile to the estate. Finally Olmsted, who had understood that all claims against the estate had been settled, was at once called on to settle several of long standing, which, rightly or wrongly, were arousing bitterness against the new company.[56] "These facts, all new and entirely unexpected to me, coming to my knowledge mostly in one day, added to a landscape which for aridity, sterility, dust and desolation, neglect and slovenliness, I never saw anything approaching before, gave rise at first to a feeling of very great disappointment," Olmsted summed up with some restraint.[57]

Hasty though it was, Olmsted's tour of observation was enough to convince him that the paramount need of the estate was an adequate water supply.[58] The Mariposa River, the most important stream running through the property, was at its best only six inches deep and ten feet wide. This meager creek sustained not only immense—and in the landscape hideous—diggings but also the excellent fruit and vegetable gardens through which it was frequently diverted. Of the numerous other streams shown on the estate map only two, mere threads, were flowing.[59] Wherever Olmsted saw a rivulet, however small, or a puddle, however thick, he saw Chinese miners digging and washing; and wherever he found the streambed dry, he saw them constructing little ditches and dams and reservoirs in preparation for the rainy season.

> At first the importance given to every dribble of water seems almost ridiculous, but when Chinamen have been seen carefully forming the ground of every little puddle into a dish, guarding this around and using it again and again and again with the most painstaking frugality; when a hundred miles of dry water courses have been seen all deeply dug over and all now peopled with disconsolate men saving nothing, for want of water to make their labor useful, one becomes strongly inclined to think that half the gold on the estate might well be exchanged for a very small stream.[60]

Social conditions on the estate were no better than economic, Olmsted quickly learned. "A store has been robbed; two men have been killed with knives; another severely wounded in a fight; another has been stoned; and a plot of murder and highway robbery is reported to have been detected—all in the three days I have been on the estate," he reported to Hoy.[61] The first Sunday he passed in Bear Valley was typical of the rest; it was observed not by any religious exercise—there was not a church in the village—or by the sort of quiet recreation that he himself preferred to churchgoing but by a horse race, attended by enthusiastic betting, down the main street. The considerable Italian population spent it in noisy gambling, and the only token of respect for it he witnessed was made by a Chinese woman who had nicely tarred her hair and put on fresh sky-blue pantaloons. "Evening services," he told his wife, "consist of a dog-fight. . . ."[62]

Olmsted had justified to himself his acceptance of the Mariposa position on the ground that it held opportunities for a larger usefulness than making money for his employers and gaining security for his family. A frontier was there to be civilized, a crude society was to be refined, and the resources of a rich and remote region were to be brought into contact and cooperation with the forces—morality, art, education, commerce—conducive to progress. Now, having had his first view of the region and its people, he proposed to analyze their character and to lay plans for the accomplishment of his larger purpose.

XXII
BARBARISM AND CIVILIZATION

T HE business problem had to take precedence over the social, and Olmsted's first job was to get a grasp of Mariposa's tangled affairs. Billings, until his departure on October 19, briefed him on them intensively. Trenor Park then arrived and discussed them fully.[1] Olmsted's comprehension was further sharpened when he was served on October 28 with a demand by an assignee of Brumagim to be let into possession of his seven-eighths interest in the estate.[2] This incident, coming on top of other evidence that the legal consequences of Frémont's management were still unresolved, confirmed Olmsted's low opinion of the unlucky soldier. "He seems to have worn out the patience, after draining the purses, of all his friends in California," Olmsted wrote his father. "Whether he is more knave or fool is the only question. I am overrun with visits from his creditors, who all hope to get something from the new owners of the estate."[3]

Park's frank exposition of his managerial practice did much to account for the estate's deplorable condition and suggested more trouble ahead. He had left the management of nearly all essential business to the mine supervisors, and in the absence of a central executive, each supervisor did things his own way. Books were kept roughly and inaccurately; contracts were made orally and executed carelessly or dishonestly; makeshift methods of operating grew up which Park had made no effort to regularize since he expected from month to month that the sale of the estate would end his management.[4]

His mining, like his business practices, had been governed by his temporary status. Instead of spending capital to open new veins against the time when currently productive ones should be mined out, he had recently worked only Princeton and Pine Tree–Josephine, which required the least expense for their development. In them the workable portions were approaching exhaustion and no preparation for new work existed. He had not maintained the timbering; and in Princeton he had even mined out the columns, rich in ore-bearing quartz, which supported roofs and hanging walls and, through failure to replace them with timbers, had foreclosed further mining in these areas. In short, he had used every expedient to secure immediate profit.[5] As Olmsted had to admit, he was within his legal right to do so.

That Park had made a fine show of profit was due not only to his ruthless exploitation but also to a piece of perfect luck: several months before the sale he had hit a bonanza in Princeton. This vein had produced not only gold in quantity; it had produced as well the impression on Hoy that led to the sale of the estate. But by the time the sale was consummated the vein was exhausted.[6]

Olmsted's exploration of the company's books revealed in further particulars the workings and the effect of Park's policy. Some profits were fictitious. Some costs did not appear. Especially, expenses that had been systematically "saved" for the new owners did not show on the books but showed in inconvenience and damage to the estate. Guesswork entries were so common that it was impossible to determine accurately profit or loss on any specific estate operation, whether mine, company store, or boardinghouse. No allowance had been made for depreciation of improvements and personal property so that some items appeared at four times their current value.[7]

The analysis of the books and the inventory of estate property took Olmsted, even with the help of a bookkeeper sent by the San Francisco bankers, until early February. It took him only a few days, however, to understand that the books were not only chaotic but grossly misleading, that the business had been disastrously mismanaged, and that the Mariposa Company had naïvely bought a property that had been ravaged. "Things here are worse than I dare say to anyone but you," he told his wife within a week of his arrival;[8] and he wrote the company that his first examination of the books convinced him that the estate, far from making a monthly profit of sixty thousand dollars at the time of the sale, was not meeting expenses; that not a single mine on it was honestly paying its way when he took over; and that Princeton would take ten to twenty thousand dollars for deadwork before any profit could be expected from it.[9]

Olmsted, like others before and after him, wondered about Park's probity. He breathed his suspicions to Ketchum, who had cautioned him about dealing with Park, but he conceded that he was somewhat disarmed by Park's frankness. Olmsted was inclined to absolve him of outright dishonesty; he had probably not gone "beyond the bounds of legitimate artifice in trade." Yet, "I suspect Park thinks he has taken you in," he wrote Ketchum, adding, "The more important question is, has he?"[10]

It was a question that Olmsted himself saw some hope of answering in the negative. The recent productivity of the estate was beyond question; bankers' receipts confirmed Park's claim that in the last six months it had produced almost half a million dollars in gold. It was believed to hold practically limitless undeveloped reserves of ore under a great variety of circumstances. The scarcity and the high cost of labor, both major problems, would be relieved with the completion of the Union Pacific Railroad. By good management, Olmsted thought, the estate could be made to pay again.[11] He planned to regenerate the abused property by developing and diversifying its resources.

First of all he proposed to lead the South Fork of the Merced River by a canal through the estate.[12] The constant water supply would not only prolong mining operations into the dry season but would permit agriculture and sheepraising on a large scale. These occupations would draw newcomers and increase the rents collected by the company and the labor supply on the estate; and attracting permanent settlers, they would inject a stable element into a population that was shifting and shiftless. Olmsted also planned to tap the estate's neglected copper resources;[13] and he even conceived of washing all the gold out of the valley and creating a garden on the debris.[14]

Olmsted's routine for the first months was strenuous. He rose late in the morning, breakfasted about noon, and after attending to office business, spent the next six or seven hours riding about Mariposa, visiting mills and mines, taking the inventory of company property required by the New York office, and informing himself on estate business in conversations with miners, supervisors, storekeepers, and contractors. Between seven and eight he returned to Bear Valley and dined at his hotel with Peiper and Martin. He liked both men cordially but found the evening meal, at which the talk was constantly of mining, "not exhilerating." By eleven he was ready for the long night's work with the books.[15]

At the end of October, after he had reorganized the business procedure on the estate, he said confidently: "I have got pretty good command of the machinery and shall soon knock something out of it or burst the boilers."[16] Rather to his surprise, his reforms met little resistance, and he found it easy to assume control of operations. The reason was that no one else on the estate was exercising more than piecemeal authority.[17] By November 14 there was not a man left on it who had been on Park's staff of superintendents; Olmsted, who had discharged but one of them, suspected that they had all made arrangements to get away even before his arrival.[18] "This sojourning habit of the people who are here," he observed, "is shown in their want of interest in the fixed qualities of the place. Nobody knows what the trees and plants are."[19]

Since the nature of the society of this pioneer community was determined partly by the transient character of the population, Olmsted hoped to revolutionize the one by stabilizing the other. The first move, both in pursuit of his plan and in the commercial interest of the estate, was to determine the route of the proposed canal from South Fork and the probable volume of the streams to be turned into it. On November 9 Olmsted set out with an engineering party into the mountains to study the land about the head of the canal.

The eight-month drought was on the point of breaking, and winter was coming on. Snow had already fallen when the party reached the valley of the South Fork, and more fell while they were there. After a few days in camp Olmsted set out for Bear Valley and arrived back on November 13, sick and lame after his last day's ride of forty miles.[20] Fatigue notwithstanding, he wrote a long letter about his trip to the New York office the next day. The canal was feasible, it would bring even more advantage to the estate than he had earlier thought, it would cost about one million dollars, and it should be undertaken by the company itself as an estate improvement, he reported.[21] This businesslike communication hinted nothing of the delight he had had in his first venture into the Sierras.

The great experience of the trip had been seeing the Mariposa Big Tree Grove. The immense, ancient Sequoias, each standing distinct in the magnificent surrounding forest, had filled him with awe. "They don't strike you as monsters at all," he tried to explain to his wife, "but simply as the grandest tall trees you ever saw; . . . you recognize them as soon as your eye falls on them far away, not merely from the unusual size of the trunk but its remarkable color, a cinnamon color, very elegant. You feel that they are distinguished strangers, have come down to us from another world."[22]

Under the longed-for rain the mountains had at last been turning green; the smothering, enveloping dust had been laid; and the scenery had been fine "and at some points grand-terrible. One or two annual trips into it are the highest gratifications peculiar to the country that you have to look forward to," he declared.[23]

The social conditions Olmsted hoped to influence he described in an unfinished work on "the drift of human nature in America in the last fifty years."[24] Perhaps it was his study of the contrast between northern and southern society in the 1850s that had started him on this train of thought, or perhaps it was Bushnell's 1847 sermon, "Barbarism the First Peril," with which he was familiar. In any case, his desire to refute the criticisms of such popular English writers as Dickens, the Trollopes, Basil Hall, and Russell of the London *Times*, who as partisans of an aristocratic organization of society failed to understand or do justice to America's, induced him toward the end of his tenure on the Sanitary Commission to begin taking notes for a book examining and justifying American society and character.

In preparation for writing, he read extensively—François P. G. Guizot, Alexis de Tocqueville, Daniel Defoe, Sir Francis Bacon, Herbert Spencer, John Stuart Mill, Captain John Smith, Honoré de Balzac, Mrs. Elizabeth Gaskell, William Makepiece Thackeray, Johann Wolfgang von Goethe, Henry Mayhew, Francis Lieber, Washington Irving—scores of writers who, whether historians or sociologists or novelists, had something to say about the past and present state of society in America and Europe. A believer, like Henry Thomas Buckle, in collecting the facts of history scientifically as far as possible, Olmsted clipped hundreds of items referring to contemporary civilization from English and American journals; and to gather reliable information on the moral and social attitudes of Union soldiers and sailors—an index to their degree of civilization—he circulated, while he was with the Sanitary Commission, a list of questions to some seventy-seven hundred volunteers, with the intention of arriving at the typical and common opinions of this group of Americans by statistical analysis of the answers.* By the time he reached Bear Valley, Olmsted had a bulky accumula-

---

*This unique and irreplaceable raw material of our social history was destroyed through ignorance after Olmsted's death. Of the questions, one can certainly infer only that they covered the national origin of the volunteer, the length of time he had been established in the United States, and his reason for enlisting. Of the answers, just one

tion of material for his book, which he continued to supplement with clippings and memoranda.†

He worked on the book off and on at least until 1870 but never progressed beyond segregating his profuse memoranda under chapter headings and writing scraps of a first draft. From these fragmentary remains, however, a rough outline of the work may be deduced; in them may be clearly discerned the social features of the frontier he knew; and from them may be gained some insight into Olmsted's ideas on the nature and progress of civilized man.

It was Olmsted's theory that, contrary to the consensus of English critics, America's social and political structure was favorable to the advance of civilization and that the faults and crudities of American society that they attributed to democracy were concomitants not of democracy but of the pioneer conditions that still prevailed throughout a large part of the country. Progress in civilization could not be estimated from superficial facts hastily observed; as well try to judge the flow of a river by the motion of a few straws, some of them caught in its eddies and backwaters. Its true movement could be measured only by following the main current from its source. Dickens's fascinated emphasis on the prevalence of spitting in America and Mrs. Trollope's fastidious revulsion against the uncouthness of American manners took no account of the fact that American society was derived "largely from [the old world's] dangerous classes, mainly from its poorest classes and the more useless of its poor—little from the gentle and educated and highly civilized classes, and scarcely at all from what are called its upper and ruling classes, that is to say, the recognized leaders of civilization."

The predominance among the early immigrants of the depressed classes had been all but overlooked. Much was habitually made of such religious exiles as the Quakers, the Pilgrims, and the Maryland Roman Catholics, and of the enterprising poor who emigrated in search of opportunities lacking at home; little was said of the swarms of wastrels, jailbirds, failures, adventurers—all the socially undesirable who were cast by the old societies upon the new—compared with whom the more respectable element was numerically insignificant. The mainstream of American civilization, Olmsted contended, had its source not in the civilization of Europe but in its uncivilization. Most English travelers, neglecting this historic fact when they tried to estimate the progress of civilization in America, pointlessly asked, "How far beneath gentlemen are Americans?" and concluded that civilization had lost ground, when the relevant inquiry was, "How far above peasants are they?" Judging from his own observations in England, on the Continent, and in the United States, Olmsted confidently asserted that in

---

thing may be inferred from a statement of Olmsted's: the volunteers quite generally said they had joined the army or navy because they believed that by seceding the South had resorted to an illegal method of settling its dispute with the North. Respect for the slow, laborious, rational processes of law, and disapproval of schemes to circumvent them, Olmsted believed characteristic attitudes of Union volunteers.

†Olmsted thought so highly of these materials, even in their disconnected form, that he made them a bequest to Godkin in the will he made about the time he left New York.

manners, information, intelligence, and civilized disposition and habits, even in good nature, in which he saw a potent moral force, Americans not only of the upper classes but in all levels of society had considerably outstripped the classes of their origin in Europe.

How had human materials, on the whole so unpromising, failed to degenerate further when transplanted to a ruthless wilderness? How had they been able to produce leaders able to found, on a political principle novel in the modern world, a thriving nation and to develop into a citizenry capable of sustaining it? How, in short, had they progressed from their comparative barbarism toward civilization? Olmsted attempted to answer these questions by analyzing the frontier society he found on the Mariposa Estate, where he thought he saw repeated on a small scale the early steps in the irregular evolution of American society.

Bushnell had persuasively argued, with illustrations from ancient and modern history, that migrations to new settlements were always accompanied at first by social decline. At Mariposa Olmsted could see the decline accomplished and an opposite process setting in; paradoxically, the forces causing decline contained within themselves elements tending to reverse their effect—elements which could also function more freely and successfully within a democratic society than within an aristocratic society.

For instance, while men on the frontier, because they had to apply themselves to many tasks, lost their learning and special skills, they grew in versatility and ingenuity. They abandoned good manners and the refinements of life, but they gained strength. Out of loneliness they became asocial, but at the same time they developed independence and self-reliance. Suspicious and hostile toward strangers, they nevertheless came to realize from immediate personal experience the advantages of mutual helpfulness and of social organization for common purposes. Inclined to be each a law unto himself, the pioneers held law in contempt and had a careless, kindly disposition toward lawbreakers, but in this "greater instinctive charity—the impulse of good nature which says in a thousand ways 'Give the poor devil a chance'" Olmsted found "the chief *moral growth* of the pioneer state" and the element "at the bottom of many of our peculiarities."[25] Released from the disciplines of the society they had abandoned—its laws, its public opinion, all its impositions of duty—in self-protection they developed disciplines of their own. And unhampered by the restrictions of fixed classes, the fit among them—the strong, the ingenious, the enterprising, the adaptable—not only survived but moved into positions of leadership and tended to pass on to their children the qualities contributing to their success. The unfit gradually dropped out. Just as the immigrants developed their strength out of their shortcomings so the society they formed developed from its barbarism a new society infused with fresh energy and potentialities for progress.

This optimistic view of social evolution could be sustained, Olmsted believed, by examining the superficially discouraging facts of Bear Valley life against their historic setting. His notes, prepared in response to Norton's request for an article on life in the mining camps for the *North American Review*, were incomplete and suggest rather than demonstrate his thesis.

The Mariposa country had been open to white settlers only about fifteen years when Olmsted knew it; its entire population except the Indians were recent immigrants, many of them outcasts or refugees from older communities, in search of fortune at the mines. "The people," Olmsted later said of them, "would seem to have been almost completely emancipated from the operation of the ordinary laws by which civilized life is maintained."

Their routine resort to violence was one evidence of their barbarism. A normal cause of death in the region was murder, and where life was so lightly regarded, rights less valuable received even less consideration. Armed robbery, arson, and mayhem were standard hazards in the nearby mining towns. "There have been a great many robberies here lately," Olmsted remarked in a typical letter home, "and half a dozen men have been hung and two or three shot."

It was the rule to go armed; frequent brawls resulted in frequent killings. Mexicans, whose weapons were usually inferior, were victims of ferocious attacks. Negroes were generally believed to have no rights that a white man was bound to respect and were abused accordingly. The Digger Indians, of whom a few hundred still remained in a land now occupied by several thousand whites, were considered literally worthless. Eaters of grass, acorns, and insects, the apathetic and feeble remnants of the aborigines seemed less than human to the white settlers, who shot them without compunction and almost without provocation. Such murders, when they attracted any attention at all, were referred to in terms that would have been appropriate for the killing of a bear. Almost alone among his neighbors, Olmsted could detect distinctly human virtues in the dispirited savages—they were moderately industrious, pious in a primitive way, and kindly and loyal toward each other—and was revolted by the treatment they received.

He was revolted, too, by the treatment of the Chinese, whose cheap labor was intensely resented. They were lynched, robbed, burned out, systematically persecuted; and newspaper accounts of outrages against them were, in keeping with public sentiment, usually facetious or approving. Though heathen, they were in Olmsted's opinion the most respectable and civilized group in the community, being hard-working, peaceable, temperate, and in spite of provocation, patient. "There seems to be less essential vice in opium smoking than in our national excitements," Olmsted said. "If they have ever learned anything of white men except new forms of vice and wickedness, I can't think by what means it has been. I never heard of the slightest effort or purpose on the part of any white man, woman or child to do them good."

In this perilous society cliques and gangs—informal alliances formed for aggression or defense—were customary. They might be composed of two or three "chums" banded together to work a claim, rob Chinese, steal horses, or grow vegetables; or they might include everyone of a certain nationality or of certain religious or political views. "There is a strong tendency to come together in order to separate from and indulge in contempt and antagonism for others," Olmsted noted. Thus Yankees despised Southerners, Italians hated Mexicans, and Negroes looked down on Indians; every man had his "friends," often allied to him but loosely, and his "enemies," often antagonistic to him but vaguely. The churches were no exception: "As under this disintegrating management of the pastoral duty the pastor can have the hearty good will of but a few among any body of settlers, the members of his flock are generally widely scattered and incapable of effective cooperation and the organization is miserably weak, unreliable, disunited, stingy and poor."*

Hostility between groups was pursued with a ferocity and trickery conceivable only on a frontier; even men who were not especially ill natured committed acts against non-chums that would have been intolerable in the better disciplined and integrated communities of the East. No device, Olmsted found with horror, was too vile to use to put down an "enemy." One of his neighbors, "an amiable and estimable man," confessed to having taken part in the distribution of gifts to Indians, ostensibly as a peace offering, in which were deliberately included the soiled handkerchiefs of smallpox victims. Another had participated in the torture, in the Indian manner, of Indians in which some were finally killed and others mutilated and freed as a warning. Still another neighbor proposed lynching an Indian for the murder of a white man, although no evidence connected the Indian with the killing; Olmsted had some difficulty in dissuading him. No one, Olmsted remarked, made or acted on "the assumption which is the backbone of civilized society that others have a common interest with him or that he has a common interest with others."

Indeed, he concluded, a society composed of hostile factions devoid of any sense of reciprocal duties could not be called civilized at all.

> The foundation of civilized society is not a community . . . which is
> bound by arbitrary lines, or by lines which may be stretched or contracted
> by individuals according to their personal opinions and prejudices. These

*Olmsted allowed one exception to this judgment: "The only ecclesiastical organization which seems to be administered with any thorough system, constancy and steadiness is that of the Roman Catholic church. The official representative . . . is a French priest. He is well-bred and learned . . . withal a modest, zealous, heroic man. . . . I have met him but once when he called on me . . . & was induced to spend an hour or two with my family, who found him one of the most urbane, interesting and instructive visitors that ever came under our roof. But, after all, I think it would be hard to find a man who appeared to be more unsympathetic and outside of the whole ordinary life of the people, even those of his own creed, a man more incapable of entering into their minds and of influencing them, except as an authority and a dealer who as it might be had certain articles of clothing which they might need to sometimes wear and which they could get only of him and which he would supply as a duty delegated to him which his honor required him to fulfill to the uttermost and at whatever peril or actual suffering to himself. Twelve miles from us on one side and forty on the other are small wooden churches at one of which Mass is ordinarily celebrated every Sunday."

corruptions with regard to the Indian, the Negro and the Chinese cannot
exist without making other corruptions, and the man who has learned to
think that Negroes, Indians, Mexicans, Chinese, half-breeds may properly
enough be treated as . . . outlaws or on different principles of right and
duty from other men, does not require the inducement of a very strong
demand from his passions, his prejudices, his lusts, his covetousness or his
pride . . . to make him forget law and civilized customs in dealing with
any other man. . . . If there is such a thing as eloquence for modern
minds, it should not require much of it to make any intelligent man realize
that want of respect for a brute, want of respect for a "nigger" and want of
respect for the dearest individual rights of those nearest and dearest to him
all rest on one common criminal defect of judgment and will, and that he
cannot protect the virtue of his wife, prevent his children from being
brutally overridden or enforce the smallest benefit from his own industry
with any degree of manly energy unless he makes "common cause" with
all who are inconsiderately abused.

Olmsted devised a mental scale for rating the civilization of his neighbors.
Looking one day out of his office window, he placed near the bottom of it the
two men whom he happened to see.

One stands idle but erect, with the pose of a noble statue; his face is
streaked with vermillion, a quiver of undressed fox-skin, full of arrows,
hangs over one naked shoulder, a ragged blanket over the other; and there
is a bow in his hand, I saw him standing within six feet of where he is
now an hour ago, and with no difference of position except that his vacant
eyes were directed toward the other end of the village. He is a dull, silent,
stupid savage.

The other reclines near the tavern door. He has a cigar in his mouth, a
Colt revolver in one pocket, a Geneva watch in another, and scores of
machines and many hundreds of hands have been employed in preparing
his apparel. When freshly and mildly stimulated he has a very active mind
and a ready utterance. It is not unlikely that tomorrow morning, after he
has taken a warm bath, his Cognac and soda water, coffee and one or two
after breakfast drams, I may again hear him discoursing, as I did this
morning, with indignant eloquence, on "the mockery of justice, the
debasement of the ermine, the ignorance of law, the degrading
demagoguism, the abominable infidelity, by God!" of a recent decision of a
court with regard to the rights of colored people in public conveyances,
reported in a San Francisco paper. In twenty minutes he will have made
use of words primarily prepared for him by Saxon, Roman, Greek,
Sanskrit and I know not what other brains. Then again he will pass under
my window humming a hymn by Handel, or I shall find him at the post
office sitting in an armchair made for him in New Hampshire, and reading
a novel first written in France, translated in England and printed for him
in Boston. He will have been served before the day is over by your work

and mine, and by that of thousands of other men, and yet will think of nothing so often or so intensely as the "cursed luck" by which he is served no better. And what will he do for us? Play a game of billiards with you or take a hand at cards if you want amusement, and if he wins money in this or any other way of speculating, he will use it "generously." Within a year by pledging his word to drink no more he induced a poor hardworking widow to become his wife, having been previously the father of several children of different colors for whose maintenance or education he has never worked an hour or concerned himself a moment. He is a tall and large-framed white man of English stock, born (in Kentucky) in a state of society which he speaks of as "the highest reach of civilization."

Besides these two men there were, that day, out of sight but within earshot the German shoemaker, whose hammertaps carried through Olmsted's window, and the baker's Chinese helper, who could be heard chopping wood.

These two men again I at once range together very far above the Indian and the Fruit of Civilization—not perhaps more than half way to the higher notches yet not a majority of my neighbors stand higher than these two steady, plodding, short-sighted, frugal workers. But it is not industry, nor well-balanced supply and demand, nor sobriety and inoffensiveness only that I lay to the scale. There is some general quality . . . which I look for most and find feeble in the stolid German and the weazened Chinaman.

. . . I come to the conclusion that the highest point on my scale can only be met by the man who possesses a combination of qualities which fit him to serve others and to be served by others in the most intimate, complete and extended degree imaginable. Shall we call it communicativeness? Then I find not merely less of a community but less possibility of a community, or communicativeness, here among my neighbors of all kinds than in any other equal body of men I ever saw. And the white men, the Englishmen, the Germans and other civilized men do not possess it often in as high a degree as the Mexicans, Chinese and Negroes—nor do the good men always possess as much of it as the rogues, the wild fellows.

Not solitary or misanthropic, not incapable of love, generosity, fidelity toward family or friends, his neighbors yet were on the whole incapable of catholic relationships or of conceiving of a community of interest between themselves and anyone to whom they were not especially allied. Willing to have chums and submissive to family bonds, they could extend the chumming or family relationship to include their tribe or clan or race. "But aside from these ties, which are commonly very strong with the lowest savages, their instincts or intuitions toward other men seem to be those of beasts toward beasts, as if their only interest in them could be as toward objects of prey."

253

In spite of this severe judgment, Olmsted found many qualities, bred by the frontier, to respect in his neighbors—their manly habits of self-reliance and independence; the equalitarianism expressed in their calling him "Fred"; the trustfulness, possible in a sparse population where everyone knew the character borne by everyone else, with which business matters were arranged; and the gallantry and kindness with which women and children, creatures not frequently met around Mariposa, were treated.* Where such amiable characteristics already prevailed, a larger growth in sympathy, in "communicativeness"—in fact toward civilization—might be reasonably forecast.

Where the ideas of common cause and reciprocity of duties were without force, it followed naturally that ". . . of men who have any deep abiding faith in living by intelligent industry directed to the essential benefit of their fellow citizens," Olmsted saw almost none. Although there was little such industry, there was a great variety of occupations on the estate. Rather than being interdependent and mutually stimulating, however, these depended, every one, on gold mining for existence. The estate was spotted with tumble-down, burnt-out settlements, deserted by all but the frugal Chinese and a few Mexicans with the exhaustion of the nearby mine. Where the mines were productive, bakeries and bath houses, bars and billiard parlors, general stores and machine shops, lodges and dance halls, gardens and livery stables, and sawmills and express offices flourished.

Few men persisted long in a single occupation. The German baker, who made excellent bread, paid decreasing attention to his trade; he was also, in his bakeshop, selling beer, tobacco, and cigars and doing business as a gold broker, express agent, treasurer of two or three mining companies, and justice of the peace. The Mariposa surgeon, a Frenchman educated at the University of Paris, ran a whitesmith shop and an apothecary store and managed a mine; he had recently been admitted to the bar as well and was a candidate for the office of coroner. The common disposition to turn a hand from one thing to another and to hold to nothing was the most striking distinction, Olmsted thought, between the people of this district and any others he had ever observed. Accepting Spencer's theory that progress is measured by evolution from undifferentiated mass to differentiated individual forms and that a society evolves from barbarism to civilization by the development of specialization within it, Olmsted found in this abandonment of specialties further evidence of the barbarism of the Mariposa society.

The degeneration of masters into jacks-of-all-trades had as a corollary another phenomenon—the frequent moving in and out of the region of men seeking fortune in some way connected with the mines. With characteristic

---

*The women and children of Olmsted's household were in the habit of wandering unescorted about the estate. Only once were they accosted other than kindly and then by a helplessly drunk Indian.

thoroughness, Olmsted undertook to document the population turnover, and after two years he was able to write:

> Since I have been here, the District Attorney's office has been twice vacated by resignation and is now filled by the third incumbent. The two leading lawyers in the county have left it; four other lawyers have changed their residence. Three citizens previously engaged in other occupations have entered upon the practice of law. The principal capitalist, the largest merchant, and three other leading merchants have left the county; at least a dozen storekeepers have sold out and as many more come in. The men of my acquaintance who were running mills of various kinds (saw, grain and stamp) when I came here have left them. In one case a mill has changed hands three times, in several others twice. I know of not one which has not changed hands. The justice of the peace, the seven successive school committeemen, three out of four of the physicians, the five butchers, the five innkeepers, eight out of twelve tradesmen and their assistants, the blacksmith, the two iron founders, the two barbers, the daguerreotypist, the bathing house keeper, the seven livery stable keepers, the three principal farmers, the three school teachers and about seventy out of one hundred miners and laboring men who have lived nearest me or who have been most readily accessible and observable to me have moved from one house, office or shop to another, or have left the country within two years. I count in this village forty-seven separate places of residence and of business which have been occupied by eighty-seven persons, not including housewives and children. Of these eighty-seven, eighty-five have changed their residence or place of business within two years. This has not been on account of a destructive fire or any extraordinary occurrence; population on the whole has not decreased, and so far as I can ascertain the changes have not been markedly greater than at previous periods of the early history of the district.

Olmsted's conservatism is apparent in his analysis of the social effect of the tendency to turn facilely and frequently from one kind of work to another. Whereas in the older communities of Europe and the eastern states, he thought, public opinion operated with immense force to prevent men from behaving improperly—that is, inappropriately to the station in which they were expected to serve others and be served by others—here, because they passed rapidly from one station to another, public opinion could not classify and restrain them. For example: the blacksmith, after a hot piece of work, would go not to the pump but to the hotel and order not beer but champagne; and the widow who cleaned Olmsted's room for him, on hearing of a birth in a friend's family ten miles away, would hire a carriage and pair from the livery stable to take her on a call of congratulation. Such extravagance seemed to Olmsted significant not so much of frontier improvidence and thriftlessness as of the weakness of public opinion and the practical extinction of one of the great conservative forces of society. The precept and sense of propriety which directs that a man should carry himself as becomes his station in life assumes a continuity of occupation. . . . [Here] the habit of dealing with others or of expecting to be dealt with by others with reference to such a standard is impracticable and is rapidly eradicated. There is a rapid increase of freedom of thought, freedom of suggestion, . . . and a rapid weakening of each man's habit and disposition to follow any course which society seems to have laid out for him in a persistent or consistent way.

In a society where frequent change of occupation was the rule, respect for special training was naturally slight.

If a man who has shown ability in any direction, driving a stage coach or building a mill dam, chooses to give advice in a question of law or medicine or theology or political economy to which he has never given an hour's study, it is not unlikely to be taken with as much respect and confidence as that of men who have labored hard through a course of years to fit themselves to give such advice.

Professional advice, consequently, was likely to be extemporaneous and work inexpert or makeshift.

The condition about which centers all that there is here of peculiar conservatism and all that there is here of peculiar recklessness is, I finally conclude, that of Slipshod. Men love so dearly to be slipshod that they will even for a time be systematic and intense and far-reaching in their efforts to quench whatever tends to put them to shame, establish penalties or otherwise antagonize their contented following of slipshod ways. . . .

Lynch law itself, with all its outward show of thorough deliberation and system, is nothing but an intense form of the common effort to get along without real and prolonged deliberation and system. It is the darning together and inking over of the faded rags which the beggar would not if he could exchange for clean whole cloth. Just enough law, or show of law, to maintain the greatest degree of lawlessness under which men can have any use of neighbors.

The social situation thus roughly outlined presented a challenge and imposed a duty that Olmsted could not reject. However reasonable he found Spencer's theory of the inevitability of social progress through the working of natural selection, he withheld from its logical corollary of laissez faire the deference due to dogma. On the contrary, the conviction of his community of interest with all other members of society was an article of faith with him. Caring, out of humaneness and communicativeness, more for happier people in a better society immediately than for perfection millennia hence, he saw it as his obligation to help the unfit become better fit.

Miss Wormeley suggested to him that America, while offering vast opportunity to the lower classes to exercise their ability in the improvement of their condition, withheld from the upper classes opportunity to exercise their ability in the improvement of the common condition. Olmsted sternly replied:

> The difficulties and annoyances and embarrassments which gentlemen and gentlewomen of any talent have to meet in doing their duty with their talent are certainly very great, and talent is not to be exercised here with the preordained quiet, grace and decorum which may be associated with it in a country of thoroughly well established and congealed civilization. The greater the need, however, that it should be exercised courageously, resolutely and perseveringly.

His own duty with his talent on the Mariposa frontier Olmsted conceived to be nothing less than a grand and radical undertaking in social engineering: to transfigure a semiarid, barbarous principality into a well-watered, fertile garden; to turn its economy from dangerous dependence on a single industry to thrifty reliance on diversified enterprise; and to shape from its transient and semi-barbarous population a stable and civilized community in which should prevail "an all-embracing relationship based on the confidence, respect and interest of each citizen in all and all in each."

But, as he said realistically of his plan, "I can make nothing of it without water."[26]

THE MINES AND THE SCENERY

October 1863–September 1864

I N the alien surroundings, Olmsted was homesick. He pined for the Staten Island farm, and he longed for his wife and children, who were passing the months before their departure with their neighbor, Miss Errington,* on the island.[1] He filled his letters with plans and suggestions about the rustic house he hoped to build when the mines began to pay, and he selected the site for it on a knoll at the south end of the Princeton plateau, away from the village but not too distant.[2]

Eagerly, wistfully, he tried to recruit eastern friends for the community he hoped to form. He urged Jenkins and Godkin to consider joining him, and he applied to Bache to find if Trinity Church in New York could supply a good missionary to cultivate the "inert" moral soil of the community. Above all, he wanted Knapp. "I think a great deal of you and constantly comfort myself with the idea of your being here one of these days. . . ."[3] Everything, however, hung upon the canal. "If the company should refuse to let me get it in," he told Knapp, "—or if I should conclude it not feasible—I shall not advise you to come to Mariposa, but I think it will come and with it you and civilization."[4]

While he waited for a decision on the canal, Olmsted engaged William Ashburner, a geologist on the California State Geological Survey and one of the best-known mining engineers on the west coast, to advise on laying out new work in the mines, improving the metallurgic processes by which gold was recovered, and opening new veins.[5] Olmsted was not alone in recognizing that the firmest foundation of the region's general prosperity would be not gold but water. The *Mariposa Gazette*, published at the county seat, realized it, too, and rejoiced editorially that the canal "is now being projected under the superintendence of Frederick Law Olmsted." Brains, capital, and muscle, it said, had hitherto

---

*Harriet Errington (1812–96) was an Englishwoman who ran a locally celebrated school for young ladies on Staten Island. Mary Olmsted, as a girl, had been one of her pupils; and Harriet's sister Charlotte was the wife of Olmsted's friend and former neighbor, Alfred Field. Miss Errington was the oldest of the six children of George Errington, a well-to-do Northumberland merchant who migrated to America in 1832. When the Erringtons moved to Staten Island in 1843, Harriet opened her school, which drew its pupils from the most prominent families on the island. It suggests something of her flexible and adventurous disposition that, when she was past fifty, she left her secure, respected position in the well-ordered society of suburban New York to share the Olmsteds' primitive life on the California frontier (FLO [son] to Carl P. Russell, 30 June 1950 [copy], LWR Files).

been lacking for the successful operation of the estate, but "at last the project has fallen into the hands of a company which can command everything requisite to make that a success which is of such vital importance to our interests."[6]

On December 5, the very day when the *Gazette* was voicing its touching confidence in a group of speculators three thousand miles away, Morris Ketchum, by a melancholy coincidence, was writing Olmsted the letter that foreshadowed the end of the canal project and with it the end of his whole grand plan to kindle the beacon of civilization in the mining camps. The indebtedness of the estate, Ketchum wrote, had been underestimated at the time of the sale, and instead of having three hundred thousand dollars working capital left out of the sale of the bonds, "it now appears that the payment of liens will absorb nearly if not quite all the $1,500,000—while we shall be dependent upon *production* for the payment of interest, sinking fund $50,000 pr ann . . . and the development of the capacities of the estate." Mariposa stock had fallen, too, from fifty-five dollars to thirty-two as a result of Brumagim's claim for seven-eighths of the estate, but Ketchum added hardily, "I hope and *believe* that a day not distant will prove it worth a much higher price."[7] Even Park, he reported, in spite of his part in the scheme by which "the buyers were roundly and deliberately tricked," apparently had faith in the estate, since he was holding his stock.[8]

Olmsted's own faith in it was tentative: production, on which everything now depended, was not positively discouraging. By early December several of the mines that had been losing money were paying their way. A new Mariposa vein, which he believed would be the most valuable on the estate, had been opened and promised well. Losses on the mines, Olmsted thought, could be offset by profits from stores and boardinghouses and revenues from rents and placer miners' fees; and the estate would be able from December on to meet its outlays, including the debts "saved" for the new owners by Park.[9]

Olmsted was prepared for reverses, since the element of chance in mining was so great that it had "all the excitement of gambling."[10] It was as well, since setbacks were not infrequent during the winter. The drought, unexpectedly prolonged, interrupted work at Benton Mills; machinery broke down; veins petered out; Princeton's ore became deplorable; and explorations came to nothing.[11]

The project of bringing water power to the mills was for the time ruled out; substantial savings had been effected by the reorganization of the business and mining methods on the estate; the only considerable saving still feasible was the reduction of wages, which were three times what they were in New York. High as they were, labor was still scarce.[12]

Olmsted's first move to reduce labor costs was to engage Chinese, who worked for about half the wages of white miners, on the newly opened Mariposa vein, and by the first of the year he was employing enough of them to make a reduction of eight percent in the cost of work there.[13]

His second move was to reduce wages, and he notified the miners well in advance that a cut was impending. Thorough inquiry had satisfied him that the estate, with characteristic extravagance, for years had paid higher wages than any other mining property in California. Olmsted thought such extravagance could be justified only by higher living expenses on the estate, and he intended to compensate for the wage cut by reducing the cost of living. On February 27 he gave written notice to all superintendents that the daily wage of miners was to be reduced from $3.50 to $3.15, and that of other workmen proportionately, and that the charge at the company boardinghouses was to be cut from a dollar to eighty-five cents a day. The boardinghouses, he also stated, were no longer to make a profit for the estate; if they continued to show one, the charge would be lowered, but if they showed a loss it would be raised.[14] Olmsted's policy, fair enough in his own eyes, was naturally resisted by the miners, most of whom at once quit work. "I have a general strike to meet now, every mine stopped and some little rioting," Olmsted wrote Bellows early in March, "but as I am satisfied my demands are just it does not give me any trouble and I am personally rather enjoying the lull."[15]

He had small cause for anxiety. The strike had not the organization necessary to success. Labor unions were gathering force in San Francisco, but the idea of collective action had made no appreciable headway among the adventurous individualists who worked the mines on the estate, although the anti-Chinese sentiment, which was a factor in the formation of the coast unions, was sharp at Mariposa. Unused to cooperation and transient by habit, about half of the strikers demanded and received their back pay and drifted off the estate, as other workmen, attracted by the help-wanted advertisements Olmsted ran in the San Francisco papers, moved onto it.[16] Little violence occurred. The men, in spite of their "rioting," which must have been mild indeed, destroyed not five dollars worth of property, and the strike subsided quietly in its third week.[17]

While it lasted it gave Olmsted a much needed rest. For months he had been working through the night, and his health was suffering. Since early December he had been having attacks of indigestion, spells of vertigo like those that had troubled him on the Sanitary Commission, and violent palpitations, which made him suspect that his heart was out of order.[18]

It was the preparation of his general report to the company that had kept him up night after night throughout the winter. A document of one hundred twenty-four printed pages, it contained an analysis of the policy of the previous management, a persuasive explanation that the current failure of production was the necessary result of it, an exposition of the new policy, and a soberly optimistic forecast of its results, together with an inventory of the personal property on the estate and a statement of assets and liabilities.[19] A massive piece of work, it showed a thorough grasp of estate affairs; but it was a grasp that had been come by through killingly hard work. In mid-February, when he mailed the report to the company, Olmsted felt used up.[20]

"When a man is trying to navigate a big ship under jury masts, after a hurricane, in shoal water, you can't expect him to give much time to other things," he wrote a friend.[21] Yet, in spite of the demands of the estate, he had managed to keep up with the rest of the world during the winter. He took the California papers, the *New York Weekly Post* and *Tribune*, and *Harper's Weekly*; he often received from his father the *Living Age*, the *Home Journal*, and *Littell's Magazine*; and he occasionally saw the venerable *North American Review*, of which Norton and Lowell had recently become editors.[22] He followed the war and political developments closely and supported Lincoln firmly. There was no doubt in his mind that the president he had once despised should be reelected, and he said of Chase, "He is really a much more vulgar man than Lincoln. I am for Lincoln."[23]

He found time, too, to investigate stocks in California. Early in January he invested twenty-five hundred dollars—two thousand of it a loan from his father —in the telegraph company, the Pacific Steam Navigation Company, and the San Francisco city water corporation, all enterprises dependent on the general growth of the city and region.[24] "I think San Francisco is bound to be one of the greatest cities of the world," he prophesied, "from the position and advantages it has already gained."[25] Distrustful of investments in mines, he nevertheless speculated gingerly in Mariposa stock, accepting Ketchum's offer to buy the stock for him, hold it as security, and trade in it on his instructions.[26]

News of Sanitary Commission fund raising that winter was heartening. Fairs in Boston, Chicago, and Cincinnati brought in more than four hundred thousand dollars; California pledged another two hundred thousand; and even remote little Bear Valley raised $1,249 at a "Sanitary Ball" in January.[27] Private advice to Olmsted on the commission's internal affairs, however, were disquieting. All his Sanitary Commission correspondents, writing him confidentially, found fault with the recent management and with each other; they were united, however, in lamenting his departure.[28]

Olmsted anxiously followed Central Park affairs, too, especially Viele's suit against the city, which came to trial in January. In his complaint Viele claimed back salary as superintendent and payment of five thousand dollars for his plan accepted in 1856 and later discarded; he raised no question of the authorship of the plan then being executed. During the hearings, however, he asserted that the Olmsted and Vaux plan, along with several others in the competition, was nothing but a plagiarism of his own.[29] Although the requirements of the topography, the specifications of the commissioners, and the prevalence of the natural style were enough to make certain resemblances among the plans inevitable, it was Viele's claim, Vaux wrote Olmsted, "that we might as well have painted a pair of whiskers on a copy of the Greek Slave and called the statue ours."[30]

The jury's verdict, which awarded Viele a little more than nine thousand dollars, impugned the originality of the Olmsted and Vaux plan no more than had the complaint: it meant only that Viele had made surveys and a map for laying out the park; that the commissioners had adopted Viele's plan; that they had not paid him for it; and that on accepting it they had become liable to pay for it.[31] The *Herald* in announcing the verdict chose to interpret it to mean that the Olmsted and Vaux plan was a copy of Viele's; and Vaux, much concerned, consulted Richard Morris Hunt and Bellows as to the best way to vindicate the partnership's professional integrity and, incidentally, to emphasize the "art interest and the social status interest" of the park.[32]

Vaux's concern for the social implications of Central Park was of recent growth, the outcome of a painful controversy with Olmsted that had been running since November. He had asked Olmsted then to expound his view of what each had contributed to the park; and he had complained, as he was often to do again, that the public gave more credit to Olmsted than to him for its creation, and that Olmsted, instead of trying to redress this injustice, had appeared to acquiesce silently in it by clinging to the title of architect-in-chief until their resignation.[33] Olmsted was deeply agitated by the revelation of his partner's dissatisfaction.

In his answering letter, which was prompt, excited, and long, he declared that he and Vaux were equally and indivisibly responsible for the design of the park but that there was in addition to the design another element very dear to him for which Vaux had no responsibility and little respect: the management of the public's introduction to and use of the park. ". . . I have taken more interest in it, given more thought to it, had greater satisfaction in it, than in all else together. . . ." Had he not succeeded in developing the public's protective support and enthusiasm for the park, their design would have failed. Among the commissioners there was not enough sympathy, greatness of purpose, good taste, or respect for the landscape architects to have sustained their plan "if it had not been for the fact that the heart of the people was with us and was kept with us."[34]

It was because the title architect-in-chief implied precisely this extra, managerial function that Olmsted had clung to it.

> There was no hope on earth that I would not have sacrificed to my desire to hold that position. . . . A great deal of disappointed love and unsatisfied romance and down-trodden pride fastened itself to that passion but there was in it at bottom a special instinctive passion of my nature also. . . . It existed essentially years before it attached itself to the Central Park as was shown by the fact that while others gravitated to pictures, architecture, Alps, libraries, high life and low life, when travelling I had gravitated to parks . . . and this with no purpose whatever except the gratification which came from sources which the Superintendence of the Park would have made easy and cheap to me. . . . What I wanted in London and in Paris and in Brussels and everywhere I went in Europe, what I wanted in New York in 1857, I want now *and this from no regard to Art or fame or money.* . . . You know what the most obvious and constant obstacles to the realization of this desire—habit—passion—folly or whatever you choose to call it—was. I mean Green and what he embodied. You know that matters had got so arranged . . . that relinquishment of the title of architect-in-chief would have been equivalent to a relinquishment of a great and obvious vantage ground for contending with that chief obstacle.[35]

The mere thought of Green still filled Olmsted with bitterness. "I turned over my letterbook lately," he told Vaux, "and it made me boil with indignation to see how cruelly and meanly Green had managed me—how entirely regardless he was of honor, generosity and truth, and what a systematic small tyranny, measured exactly by the limit of my endurance, he exercised over me. It was slow murder. It made my head swim to read my studied and pathetic remonstrances and entreaties." Still, he concluded, "I don't know that I regret my course because the object was worthy . . . whatever it may cost me."[36]

Out of friendship and loyalty more than conviction, Vaux accepted Olmsted's view, novel though it was to him, of their joint and individual responsibilities for the park.[37] The rift between them was closed, but a weak and sensitive spot had been exposed in the fabric of their friendship.

It was during the work stoppage, and in the midst of concern about the Sanitary Commission, the park, the continuing drought, and his health, that Olmsted made the long-anticipated trip to the coast to meet his family. They were due March 11 on the *St. Louis*, with Miss Errington, who had been persuaded to come out as the children's governess, Ruth Tompkins, a pupil at her school, and Mary Olmsted's young cousin Henry Perkins, who was to act as Olmsted's secretary.[38]

While he waited for them in San Francisco, Olmsted consulted Dr. W. O. Ayres, with whom he had shot woodcock and quail in the East Hartford swamps as a boy. His heart was enlarged, the doctor warned, and he might have to return east and lead a quiet life.[39] Also, while he waited, Olmsted was himself consulted as a landscape architect, for the first time in California, on the new Mountain View Cemetery at Oakland. His interest, captured by the problems and possibilities of the steep, treeless site, was the keener since he had for some time wanted to try his hand at a rural cemetery on the order of Spring Grove, at Cincinnati.[40]

When the eleventh came, the *St. Louis* tormented her passengers and their friends ashore by beating about all day outside the bay in a heavy swell and a thick, cold fog. Not until eleven at night, when the fog lifted, did she dare cross the bar. Within an hour she had docked, and by midnight Olmsted was reunited with his family.[41]

"There is a great dearth of incidents in our lives here," Mary Olmsted wrote after a few weeks in Bear Valley, "but strange as it may seem, time does not hang heavily on our hands."[42] Almost every afternoon they rode, Olmsted on his lively bay, Dash, Mary on one of the carriage horses, John on his pony, and the younger children on donkeys. Miss Errington, who found horses uncongenial, rode Toady, most staid of the eight mounts in the manager's stable. She followed her companions over mountain trails skirting sickening ravines and, quaking with fright she was too proud to show, identified the flowers and rocks along the way for the children's instruction.[43]

The roomy upper floor of the stone-and-stucco store building was converted to pleasant living quarters as soon as the oiled black walnut furniture, bought in San Francisco, arrived. The Frenchman, Charles, prepared excellent meals, and a German woman, Meta, did the housework and took care of the baby.[44] Through with bivouacking, Olmsted luxuriated in his well-run household and resolutely shrugged off the expense. "I don't allow myself to be worried about that—. . . we are all I think gaining health for it."[45]

Charlotte was turning into a "nice young woman, simple, straight-forward & self-possessed." John was growing fast, and Owen remained "a perfect cub—the climate seems only to make him more clumsy, imperturbable, ravenous and prone to fall anywhere but on his feet."[46] The baby, flourishing and observant, uttered her first full sentence: "I know what stage say—stage say God damn!"[47] The parents were satisfied, the children happy. Of her three youngest Mary wrote contentedly, "I saw them coming down the mountain all three on the donkey last evening, singing and shouting, with their hands full of flowers."[48]

Olmsted, still unwell, began to lead a less strenuous life. He stopped writing entirely and, lying on a couch in his office, dictated even his letters to his father to his wife or Henry Perkins.[49] His alarming symptoms subsided. He soon came to believe that, in the healthful climate and under his new regimen, his chance of recovery was encouraging. The prospect of health became so alluring that, when asked if he would return east to head the Freedmen's Bureau, he declined to be a candidate for the post.[50]

After the strike, production fluctuated from month to month and from mine to mine, but only the Mariposa vein gave ground for steady optimism.[51] The estate, in spite of economies, continued to consume over twenty thousand dollars a month more than it produced,[52] and Olmsted deferred his expectations of breaking even until August, and necessarily deferred, too, all thought of building the canal.[53] Perhaps he was beginning to suspect that the canal was to be deferred to death, together with all the plans that hinged on it, but he kept trying to benefit the company indirectly by stimulating the general welfare of the region.

He bought out the Princeton and Mariposa storekeepers early in the summer, explaining in the *Gazette* that his idea was not to monopolize trade but to supply the wants of the population cheaply and so encourage it; if the company's purchasing advantage allowed it to sell cheaper at retail than its competitors, it would be willing to sell at wholesale to competing retailers.[54]

He also established a coffee and reading room at Princeton for the miners and, through Godkin, subscribed to a score of American and English journals, explaining, "The reason for taking so much cheap English stuff is that we want to draw off a considerable number of Cornish miners from the dram shops and gambling booths."[55]

The lack of incident of which Mary Olmsted spoke was relieved in mid-May by a ten-day visit from Benjamin Silliman, Jr., whom Olmsted had invited to the estate to analyze its mineral possibilities. A respected mining authority, Silliman was astounded by its latent resources and wrote a glowing report that asserted that Olmsted's plans to develop them "will not fail to secure the early and permanent prosperity of the Mariposa Estate." Olmsted, however flattered, thought the report overestimated estate prospects. He nonetheless urged the company to print and distribute it to offset damaging rumors probably stimulated by Park's and Selover's recent sale of their stock.[56]

Another welcome visitor was Bellows. He had come to California in May to raise funds for the Sanitary Commission and to take temporarily the pulpit of the popular Unitarian minister Starr King, whose sudden death two months earlier had struck away an invaluable support to the Union cause. In spite of bygone exasperations, Olmsted held Bellows in unwavering affection. Unable to get to San Francisco to meet him, he sent him a letter of welcome, freely sprinkled with useful information about Californians and their ways,[57] which Bellows genially brushed aside with the remark that he did not want his judgment forestalled. "Enbosomed in friends" and buried in duties—"specially those of soothing, comforting and interpreting to his people Mr. King's prodigious loss"— Bellows nevertheless planned a trip to the Yosemite with his son and daughter and King's widow, and a short visit with the Olmsteds on the way back to San Francisco.[58]

When he and his party reached Bear Valley in the middle of June, the weather was still pleasant. Although the trees were withering and the dust was inches deep in the roads, the hills were green, the temperature was moderate, and an occasional rain refreshed the countryside. The ebullient minister was enthusiastic about California—the generosity of its people, the magnificence of its scenery, and above all, the beauty of the Yosemite Valley, which, as an experience in landscape, he thought surpassed even Niagara Falls.[59]

After his departure, the temperature in Bear Valley crept day after smothering day toward a hundred degrees, and in another two weeks the streams on the estate were too low either to run the mills or to supply adequate water for domestic use.[60] On the morning of July 14, Olmsted, his wife and children, Miss Errington, Meta, Mr. and Mrs. Ashburner, and Bell, the Negro guide and cook, in a caravan of eight mules, ten saddle horses, and two carriages, set out for Clark's Station, some forty miles away on the South Fork of the Merced.[61]

They drove through dusty, boulder-sprinkled hill country until rising ground brought them into a region of lofty conifers—sugar pines, ponderosa, Libocedrus, and Douglas fir—many of them from two to three hundred feet tall and twenty feet around, springing out of ground cushioned with fragrant pine needles and covered with beautiful white azaleas. At evening they camped in a granite glen near a small mountain stream and next day about noon reached the hostel of Galen Clark, where they were to camp for three weeks before going on to the Yosemite.[62]

Clark was a "genial anchorite" who passed the winters in Mariposa and in the summers lived alone except for the occasional travelers he accommodated. A handsome, bearded, middle-aged man, he "looked like the wandering Jew and talked like a professor of *belles-lettres.*"[63] He knew the Yosemite well, and his deep concern was the protection of the valley. His tiny frame cottage, with its kitchen and other outbuildings, stood at a little distance from the South Fork. All about towered the splendid forest, and all about reached the dust, relieved by the green of the delicate-looking, ill-smelling tar weed.[64]

The Olmsteds selected a campsite nearby, among tall pines on a little plain sloping down to the river. White azaleas grew among the granite boulders that bordered the stream; the pine forest to the north concealed the base of the great mountains whose gray peaks were veiled by the smoke of surrounding forest fires. Within a day the camp, with its four tents, its chairs and rugs scattered under the trees, and its busy population, looked like a little village; and Miss Errington, who had been warned by friends who underestimated her that a lady past fifty would not enjoy tent life, reported that they were all perfectly at home.[65]

During the next three weeks the campers made horseback excursions on cool days to the Mariposa Big Trees, then threatened by the encroaching fires, and an overnight trip to the more distant Fresno grove and rambled about collecting flowers and rocks and taking the measurements of trees. When it was hot they lolled in camp, sketching, reading, or bathing in the stream. But no matter how hot the day, a big fire had to be built every night to repel the mountain chill. Men and boys, wrapped in blankets, slept on the ground around it, while the women went to bed in the tents.

The stream was full of trout, Clark and passing hunters supplied venison and occasionally grizzly meat, and Bell prepared the meals and served them on a rough table in the dining tent. Company as well as food was good and varied. Henry Perkins came up from Bear Valley; Ruth Tompkins, who had traveled west with Mary Olmsted, appeared unexpectedly with Kinsley Twining, pastor of the First Congregational Church of San Francisco; and Clarence King, a recent graduate of the Yale scientific school and a member of the State Geological Survey, spent several days in camp squiring the ladies on rides and entertaining them with stories of his adventures.[66]

Other interesting visitors were the Digger Indians, who were holding a tribal gathering on the South Fork. For several days they arrived a few at a time, until about sixty of them, mostly women and children, were in camp nearby. The following morning Olmsted, disturbed at daybreak by the sound of howling exhortations, dreamed for a moment that he was at a camp meeting in Georgia. The high-pitched, cadenced, entreating yell created an illusion so strong that it was dispelled only when he opened his eyes to see his boys sleeping beside him and Bell building the fire.

The cook, who had lived among the Indians and knew something of their language, explained to Olmsted that it was a tradition of these Indians to congregate yearly at a certain phase of the moon on South Fork. They poisoned the stream with soap weed, and when the trout floated belly up, the women hauled them in, made a sort of mush of them, and cooked it in holes in the rocks. It was customary, before they began fishing, for the tribal leader to exhort them. "Dey must be good Injuns and stick by dere tribe and be mighty kerful dey don't do nothin that'll be any good to anybody dat don't belong to dar tribe," Bell explained and Olmsted transcribed in his ever-ready notebook, "an den dey get plenty fish allers, and when dey die a great wite bird wid his wings as long as from dat yr mounting to dat un'll come and take em up to a big meadow war de clover heads don't never dry up and dars lots of grasshoppers all the year roun."[67] Olmsted, an ethnologist *manqué*, questioned Clark at length on the Indians' habits and characteristics and learned by his own observation something about their nonacquisitiveness. "They supply us with trout," he wrote Godkin, "but are persuaded to do so with some difficulty, having already got more money from us than they care to lug about."[68]

Leaving his family in camp on South Fork, Olmsted spent the first week in August on the estate. Princeton, which had been closed because of bad ventilation, was again operating, thanks to a novel and successful exhaust machine of Pieper's devising.*,[69] "Our mines all look better than when you were here," he wrote Bellows, "& I think we have turned the corner."[70] Such optimism in the face of Mariposa's continuing troubles was an act of faith Olmsted could not constantly sustain, and to another correspondent he admitted about the same time that the estate had not been paying expenses for the past year and that California's refusal to accept greenbacks as legal tender and the consequent increasing premium on gold created a progressively acute problem.[71]

Olmsted returned to South Fork August 9 and on the twelfth, with his wife and children and Bell, started on horseback for the Yosemite. They spent the night at Ostrander's sheep ranch in the high meadows back of the Yosemite's southern rim; next morning they rode the short distance through the woods to Inspiration Point and viewed for the first time the fabulous valley.

Photographs, sketches, the accounts of other travelers, nothing had adequately prepared Olmsted for the awesome, peaceful abyss. Its great cliffs, almost a mile high and backed by the vast Sierras, showed chalky in the morning light softened by the smoke of forest fires and by thunderheads in the east. Down their granite faces threaded the cascades, graceful ornaments to their grandeur. Far below in the serene meadows the green tracery of leaves alternated with grass, and the wrinkling silver stream of the Merced rippled among ferns and rushes and willows. Olmsted thought he was seeing a glorious vision, too wonderful to be believed, a sort of scenic allegory in which the awfulness of the chasm was forgotten in the beauty in which it was clothed.[72]

---

*It was, Olmsted said, the only one in California; all the other ventilating machines blew in fresh air instead of drawing out foul.

Significantly, he was enraptured not by the valley's bold and grand individual features but by the scene as a whole. "There are falls of water elsewhere finer," he later wrote,

> there are more stupendous cliffs, there are deeper and more awful chasms, there may be as beautiful streams, as lovely meadows, there are larger trees. It is in no scene or scenes the charm consists, but in the miles of scenery where cliffs of awful height and rocks of vast magnitude and of varied and exquisite coloring are banked and fringed and draped and shadowed by the tender foliage of noble and lovely trees and bushes, reflected from the most placid pools, and associated with the most tranquil meadows, the most playful streams, and every variety of soft and peaceful pastoral beauty. The union of deepest sublimity with the deepest beauty of nature, not in one feature or another, not in one part or one scene or another, not in any landscape that can be framed by itself, but all around and wherever the visitor goes, constitutes the Yosemite the greatest glory of nature.[73]

It must have been a peculiar gratification to Olmsted to know that not only the unique beauty of the valley but also the obligation of a democratic government to preserve that kind of beauty for the enjoyment of all the people had just been recognized officially and for the first time by the government of the United States: on July 1, 1864, President Lincoln had signed the bill withdrawing the Yosemite Valley and the Mariposa Big Tree Grove from the public lands and ceding them to California to be held "for public use, resort and recreation . . . inalienable for all time";* and Olmsted himself had been designated one of the commissioners to administer, for the benefit of his millions of fellow citizens, the unprecedented and invaluable gift.†

The trail, which descended from Inspiration Point at the rate of about a thousand feet a mile, was not difficult for experienced riders, and by lunchtime the travelers were in the valley. Preferring to camp rather than patronize either

---

*The bill, according to Senator John Conness of California, who introduced it, was prepared by J. W. Edmonds, commissioner of the General Land Office (Hans Huth, "Yosemite, the Story of an Idea," *Sierra Club Bulletin* 33 [March 1948]: 66–68; Carl P. Russell, *One Hundred Years in Yosemite: The Story of a Great Park and Its Friends* [Berkeley and Los Angeles: The University of California Press, 1947], p. 149). The claim occasionally made that Olmsted had a hand in writing it would appear to rest on supposition. He could have, and he may have had something to do with preparing it; this writer has found no evidence that he did have.

†Bellows wrote to Olmsted in early August congratulating him on his appointment to the Yosemite Commission, but it was not until late September that Governor F. F. Low announced the names of the commissioners (HWB to O, 10 August 1864; F. F. Low to O, 28 September 1864). Besides Olmsted, who headed the list, they were Josiah Dwight Whitney, William Ashburner, I. W. Raymond, E. S. Holden, Alexander Deering, George Coulter, and Galen Clark (Huth, "Yosemite," pp. 68–69).

of the two primitive hotels, they put up their tents on the bank of the Merced opposite Yosemite Falls.

Olmsted, whose rapture increased with his familiarity with the valley, wrote his father a few days later:

> . . . The Merced . . . is here a stream meandering through a meadow, like
> . . . the Avon at Stratford—a trout stream with rushes and ferns, willows
> and poplars. The walls of the chasm are a quarter of a mile distant, each
> side, nearly a mile in height—half a mile of perpendicular or overhanging
> rock in some places. Of course it is awfully grand, but it is not frightful or
> fearful. It is sublimely beautiful, much more beautiful than I had supposed.
> The valley is as sweet and peaceful as the meadows of Avon, and the sides
> are in many parts lovely with foliage and color. There is little water in the
> cascades at this season but that is but a trifling circumstance. We have
> what is infinitely more valuable, a full moon and a soft hazy smoky
> atmosphere with rolling, towering, white fleecy clouds.[74]

Enjoyment of the scenery was the principal occupation, and the principal reward, of the next weeks. During the day the visitors explored the valley. Morning and evening, when the North and South Domes were lighted by sunrise or twilight glow and other cones seen through the gorge between them melted softly into mellow light, they watched from the sandy riverbank the miraculous effects of light and color on the mountains and the reflections of the nearby spires and peaks and buttresses in the clear shallow water.[75]

Olmsted undoubtedly made the acquaintance of the valley squatters and familiarized himself with the particulars of their claims.[76] Foremost among them were James C. Lamon and James M. Hutchings. Lamon had taken out a claim in 1860 and had lived on it, summer and winter, ever since.[77] Hutchings, formerly editor of *Hutchings' California Magazine*, since visiting the Yosemite with the first party of tourists in 1855 had tirelessly publicized its charms.[78] He had just bought out the previous claimants and operators of the Upper Hotel for a thousand dollars and this season was starting his career as its proprietor.[79] Other claims had been made in the valley, but they were for the most part clearly not valid since they were not accompanied by permanent residence. Lamon's and Hutchings's claims, too, were faulty since when they were made the valley had not been surveyed and brought into the market and so was not subject to preemption. It was, however, a common practice, and one tolerated by state and federal officials, for homesteaders to establish themselves in the unsurveyed mountain regions;[80] and Hutchings and Lamon were determined to enforce their claims, although private ownership of any of the land in the valley would stultify the intention of Congress, which set it aside for the enjoyment of the public.

The climax of the vacation for Olmsted was a week's journey into the high Sierras with William H. Brewer, a member of the Geological Survey who was just back from a formidable exploration in the mountains. Having made another

269

hasty trip to the estate, Olmsted met Brewer at Clark's Station on August 23 and returned with him to the Yosemite. After a few days' rest there, they set out toward the snow-capped mountains to the east, taking John and a guide.

The first day out of the valley they reached an elevation of nine thousand feet and hardly came below it again for a week. At such altitudes the daytime temperature was pleasant, but at night the cold penetrated blankets and made a mockery of fires. "[It] kept me awake more or less every night," Olmsted told his father. "Every morning I found the water in my canteen under my pillow frozen . . . one morning half an hour after sunrise [the temperature] stood at 14 F."[81]

Arriving on the morning of the third day at the head of Bloody Canyon (Mono Pass), the lowest pass known for several hundred miles across the high bridge of the Sierras, they turned north and began a difficult ascent up a high, unnamed mountain. John and Brewer walked. Olmsted, too lame, tacked his horse back and forth across the boulders and splinters of rock and quartz and observed, in the frequent pauses he had to allow the animal, beautiful Alpine flowers, which he believed were indistinguishable from those found in the Alps. When they reached the twelve-and-a-half-thousand-foot peak, Olmsted claimed the privilege of the first to ascend a mountain: he named it Mount Gibbs, for his old Sanitary Commission associate, the foremost chemist in America, thus giving him recognition equal to that of James Dwight Dana, the foremost geologist, for whom Mount Dana, the great peak a few miles northward, had been named.[82]

From the summit the explorers could see, stretching away from the precipitous eastern face of the mountains, the Mono desert with its great dead lake and cones and craters of volcanic ash. The vast Sierras ranged north and south, their granitic peaks like "snowdrifts after a very gusty storm, some being of grand simplicity, while others are pinnacled, columnar, castellated and fantastic." Among the peaks lay glacial valleys with moraines and small lakes and narrow grassy meadows threaded with streams plunging down to disappear in the shrubs and taller timber of the descending slopes. Snow covered some of the peaks, and on Mount Lyell to the south, "there was a snowbank six miles long in parts of which we could see the red snow described by Arctic travelers."[83]

At the end of the week Brewer, who found Olmsted "a very genial companion," pronounced the trip "charming."[84] Olmsted unequivocally declared the scenery of the high Sierras "the grandest I ever saw."[85]

XXIV
YOSEMITE RESERVED, MARIPOSA IN RUINS

September 1864–October 1865

OLMSTED returned to Bear Valley early in September to resume his stubborn contention with the estate's problems. The chronic, basic one was still water; another almost as acute, as long as expenses exceeded production of gold, was the discrepancy in value between the greenback and the gold dollar. Yet the estate seemed, at last, to be making headway despite these crippling disadvantages. The August yield of the mines was forty-five thousand dollars, an improvement of twenty thousand dollars over July. The new fifty-five–stamp mill at Mariposa mine had begun to operate August 29 and was expected to contribute heavily to the estate's production.[1] In the middle of September, Olmsted could say for the first time: "We have made no drafts on the Treasurer for a month or more."[2]

In New York the Mariposa Company's corporate spirits rose, and so did its stock. Hoy, slipping once more into the error of optimism, believed the company was out of the woods. ". . . I cannot conceive any such word as failure," he declared to Olmsted. "I am sure that is your position exactly."[3]

It was not, exactly. The winter of light rains and the dry season, unusually prolonged for the second consecutive year, induced wariness in the manager. The drought, disastrous through central and southern California, was worse even than the previous year's, which had been unprecedented. Work at the mills was hampered by low water, and Olmsted therefore warned the New York office to shelve its fine hopes and to brace itself for a sharp falling-off in production and for a draft on the treasurer later to meet large payments coming due in the next sixty days with the expiration of contracts and the purchase of winter supplies for the stores.[4]

To buy the supplies he went to San Francisco the end of September, carrying twenty-eight thousand dollars in gold bullion—and a gun to guard it, since Wells Fargo refused to transport more than ten thousand dollars at a time because of recent robberies.[5] In the city Olmsted learned that the Bank of California, which had been carrying the estate with a large adverse balance, was getting impatient. Its cashier, William Ralston, insisted on drawing on the company in New York for thirty-five thousand dollars, even though the estate had produced fifty-two thousand dollars in gold during September. Olmsted, who had hoped to cover the deficit out of the next melting, reluctantly consented to the draft and wired Hoy to expect it.[6] The reverse exasperated him. "As for your hopes of me, my dear fellow," he wrote Knapp, they had better be dried up. I purchased your high estimate of my abilities apparently by using myself up. . . . I am going to lay out a burying ground near here and it is a great comfort for me to have that object— other than the heart-sickening waiting on gold, which don't come. I am very well, so long as I don't think. . . . Pray keep on thinking of me for what I was (as unfortunate women say).[7]

Olmsted's next message to the company, sent after his return to Bear Valley a few days later, was really ominous: the Mariposa mine was a shocking disappointment. Repeated experimental assays, made by Ashburner and Silliman, had yielded twenty dollars to the ton; but its rock when crushed at its own mill was giving, incredibly, only ten dollars. The only explanation was that the tests, although conducted with great care to use average rock, had somehow been run on quartz containing hidden gold.[8]

Olmsted was disconcerted by the failure of this exploration on which, above all others, he most confidently relied for a good return; and he was fearful that the company, which had recently expressed unqualified satisfaction with his management, would ascribe the bad result to his lack of previous mining experience.[9]

He need not have worried—yet. In New York there appeared to be no disposition to find fault with him. On the contrary, a mild euphoria prevailed: Princeton suddenly had produced another bonanza late in October, and by November 4 it was yielding an unprecedented forty dollars a ton.[10] The starved hopes of officers and stockholders revived and flowered as October production exceeded sixty thousand dollars and a remittance of twenty thousand dollars—a delightful novelty after so many drafts—was received from the estate.[11] As hope flourished, stock rose; neither could be checked by Olmsted's persistent warnings that he might have to draw again if the water supply did not increase more rapidly, that discriminatory taxation threatened the estate, and that Princeton alone could never sustain the property.[12] Indeed, not even the manager was entirely immune to the effect of better production, and he assured Hoy the end of October that he never contemplated the possibility of failure.

With resolute optimism Olmsted entered November. He by then had something more important than the estate's production to occupy him: the election. Confident of carrying California by several thousand votes, the state Republican committee had neglected Mariposa County; secession was rampant there, an insurrectionary movement was brewing, and the Copperheads were working busily.[13] Just as Olmsted saw in the jealousy among sects and in the enmity among racial groups the religious and social effects of the lack of communicativeness on the frontier, so he interpreted as its political effect the hatred of the Federal government and the enthusiasm for secession and states' rights among the "snarling traitors" surrounding him. Although asserting that "their chief weapon is gasconade," he was not contemptuous of their strength or their capacity for mischief.[14]

In behalf of the county authorities, he had made a request to Governor Low and General McDowell for military protection while he was in San Francisco, and in response to it a company of cavalry had been sent to Bear Valley.[15] On the estate he not only protected loyal sentiment; he encouraged it by the formation of Union Clubs and by bringing in speakers whose influence on the workmen, he thought, was greater than that of articles in the loyal *Gazette* or the Copperhead *Mariposa Free Press*.[16] "I am much occupied in thinking what can be done, and in trying to make sure that it is done, to get all the Union votes practicable here secured before election," he wrote Clarence King late in October.[17]

Refusing speaking invitations, he worked quietly in the background until, in response to an accusation by James H. Lawrence, editor of the *Free Press*, that he was abusing his position of company manager to influence the workmen, he stated his policy in the rival *Gazette*. Any employee found to be in the rumored conspiracy to resist the authority of the government would of course be dismissed, and such a discharge was certainly not political persecution. Although himself wholeheartedly for Lincoln, he wished, he said, "to exercise no influence upon any voter except such as may be addressed to his self-respect and understanding"; and he asked the company's employees only to compare the claims to confidence and the platforms of the two candidates and to judge for themselves.[18]

On the estate, election day approached in a tense atmosphere and passed in a quiet one, although elsewhere in the county there was some rioting. Olmsted had reason to be satisfied with the result: despite the Copperheads' original strength, every town on the property except Mariposa gave Lincoln a majority. "The election here was really sublime," he wrote Godkin. "I went in actively at last, writing for the papers etc.—and am told I helped. We lost the county by 75. I have put myself at swords points with the Secessionists. There was no blood shed, because each party was too well prepared for thorough work if it began. I had a good supply of arms ready, and let them know it," grimly added the man who never, except when he was guarding bullion, carried a gun.[19]

Olmsted received the early returns in Stockton on his way to San Francisco and sent back to the estate the good news that Lincoln's reelection was assured and that California had made an honorable contribution to victory by giving him a twenty-thousand majority.[20] Then he proceeded to the city, where he remained almost two weeks, making more winter purchases for the stores, advising the Oakland people on the cemetery, and making a thorough investigation of a manganese mine in the bay region in which Morris Ketchum had been offered shares.[21]

Olmsted probably undertook this errand, extraneous though it was to the company's business, because of his personal obligation to Ketchum, who, on Olmsted's instructions, had sold part of the Mariposa stock he had bought for Olmsted for a profit of almost fifteen hundred dollars.[22] After Ketchum's resignation as treasurer of the company in September, Olmsted, to avoid correspondence on estate business with one no longer a director, had begun selling his stock in Ketchum's hands, and Ketchum had bought for him twenty-four thousand dollars worth of 5/20 United States government bonds of the third issue, holding the bonds and Olmsted's remaining Mariposa stock as security for the money he advanced to buy the bonds.[23]

When Olmsted got back to the estate on November 23, he found that its yield for the month was already sixty-seven thousand dollars. Princeton ore, however, had dropped to twenty dollars a ton; the rich vein recently hit apparently was giving out.[24] Mariposa stock was forty-five dollars, and Olmsted ordered Ketchum to sell all the rest he was holding in his name.[25]

Just after his return the drought broke in a cloudburst not much less ruinous than the dry season itself. It drowned cattle, washed out bridges, interrupted the mails, smashed wagonloads of supplies on the road to Bear Valley, flooded mines, and temporarily stopped the mills;[26] but the ample water supply enabled estate production for the month to reach the record, under Olmsted, of eighty-three thousand dollars and gave the company a small credit balance at the bank. Mariposa ore was slightly richer, too, and the new Pine Tree tunnel, which had been a fertile source of disappointment and confusion, had apparently at last struck the true vein.[27]

These good omens were immediately offset when Princeton ore declined to seventeen dollars a ton, the county supervisors refused to modify the excessive tax assessment against the estate, and its small credit balance shifted to a large adverse balance, as payments for store supplies fell due. When Hoy asked how much remittance the company could expect in December, Olmsted on December 12 repeated his October warning that he could not make a second remittance before January.[28] The midmonth cleanup at the five mills a few days later scotched even this expectation: it gave on an average only half as much as the corresponding one in November. To climax these reverses, the bank notified him on December 18 that it was drawing on New York for sixty thousand dollars. Olmsted at once communicated all these painful particulars to his employers.[29]

Mounting production had anesthetized the company's officers to Olmsted's insistent warnings; now the inescapable fact that the property was still not paying its way had to be recognized just when the interest on the bonds was falling due. Default would be especially damaging to the company's reputation because, as Godkin wrote Olmsted on Christmas day:

> There is a tremendous libel suit going on here between Weed (Thurlow) and Opdyke. Weed accuses Opdyke and Field and Ketchum and Co. of having swindled Frémont when getting up the Company, but does not make out anything worse than Field's having charged 2000 shares as counsel fees. The shares were then 25, and some time afterward he made an unfortunate client of his take them from him at par, when they were 50. I am sorry to say, I am perfectly satisfied that the leading Republican politicians are worse rogues than the Democrats, inasmuch as they are fully as corrupt while making far more pretensions to honesty. Opdyke is, I

consider, a consummate rascal, to whom politics is a branch of his trade and nothing more."[30]

Apparently the public concluded with Godkin that the company was run by scoundrels and was unprofitable to boot. Confidence dissolved and a complete panic in Mariposa stock followed. "It has fallen to 16 and is falling," Godkin reported January 5. ". . . I hope for your sake the matter is not so bad as it looks here."[31] But it was.

Olmsted did not at once realize that this crisis was other than routine. His first intimation that it was different came on January 6, when representatives of the company's commercial agent, Dodge Brothers, and of the Bank of California arrived at Bear Valley with the news that the New York office was not honoring his drafts and that they intended to attach the company's personal property to secure the estate's debts of sixty thousand dollars to them. They agreed, however, to delay action until Olmsted could telegraph New York.

That evening Olmsted collected four thousand dollars, almost the amount owed him in back salary, in rough bullion to which he gave himself a bill of sale, and the following day he set out for San Francisco to wire the company. Cheered and warmed by sherry during the cold journey, he was sure that "the Mariposa will float over this bar & that Ralston has been hasty and wrong."[32]

His reception in San Francisco by the bank's president and cashier modified his sanguine belief. He found Ogden Mills and Ralston, whom he met at once although he arrived late at night, disinclined to delay execution longer than required for him to hear from New York and suspicious that the company's refusal to honor their draft was a speculative gambit to depress the stock. "They anticipate and intend the worst. Think it a great Wall Street swindle," Olmsted wrote Godkin.[33]

In spite of the bankers' reassuring insistence on their confidence in him personally, Olmsted found the interview sufficiently distressing to give him a headache, keep him awake the rest of the night, and make him think of looking around for other work on the coast. The old notion of running a paper with Godkin revived: "If we break down suddenly . . . [a paper] is what I shall first look to, & I shall do so reckoning on being able to get you to come out. I have the highest anticipation of the future of San Francisco, & I shall be ashamed to show myself in New York."[34]

He could, however, show himself unashamed in San Francisco. Although the California papers voiced the suspicion that the company's difficulties might be "an operation on the part of the first mortgage bondholders to depreciate the stock," no one ascribed any part in such a manipulation to Olmsted.[35] His integrity and the wisdom of his management were considered above question, and the creditors gave him "every possible favor and mark of confidence."[36] Their friendly attitude made his trying position in the next months tolerable; but the evasiveness of the New York office hampered his efforts to induce the attaching creditors to delay action. The New Yorkers at first let him understand that money would be raised in the East to lift the attachments;[37] but when they allowed days and weeks to pass with no answer to his wires "except a sort of bunkum message from Mr. Hoy amounting simply to 'don't worry,' "[38] Olmsted began to feel that he was working in the dark and perhaps to the wrong end. "I don't want to turn my hand to save the company if it ought to fail," he said in mid-February,[39] after he had spent more than a month staving off forced sales and trying to arrange a fair distribution of the estate's diminished production among all the creditors, including the workmen whose interest no one else seemed much concerned to protect.

Under a makeshift arrangement, peace and some production were maintained at Mariposa. The sheriff supplied the mines out of the attached merchandise and held all the bullion produced to secure himself against liability on his bond; when the miners refused to continue this arrangement, he had to apply the bullion to their current wages and arrears. Many men were idle, and there was considerable distress among them. Some turned to placer mining, some sold their claims for back wages at discounts as high as sixty percent, and many left the estate. Those who sought Olmsted out in San Francisco confirmed the news he was receiving in letters that there was great depression on the estate, but little bitterness.[40] "I think the men have all been very lenient and forebearing and we should feel grateful and generous to them . . . ," he wrote his wife.[41] He sent her fifteen hundred dollars in gold so that she would have money to meet her needs and to help the office employees whose salaries, like his own, were stopped.[42]

His depression, unlike the miners', was stiffly laced with bitterness, and he sharply concluded a report to Hoy: "It is useless to discuss what can be done in the future until I hear more definitely from you. I presume you understand that with every day's interruption of business on the estate the difficulties in the way of economical management rapidly increase."[43]

Negotiations with the creditors trailed on and on. Olmsted became demoralized and sick with cold, fever, and migraine by turns. Drearily he divided his time among Ashburner, the bankers, and the Dodges and made an occasional foray into polite society, where his preoccupation and shyness, he ruefully reported, got him into several "bad scrapes of rudeness and embarrassment with women."[44]

In his frustration, he turned restlessly from one thing to another. During a sleepless night he wrote Bellows a long letter outlining a scheme for the wide and cheap distribution of good literature through the organization of an association of book-buyers in New York that would print or buy books in quantity, have distributing centers in big cities, and sell and lend to local reading clubs throughout the country. "I can't help thinking," he concluded, "that if I could think about it enough, I could find a plan by which philanthropy could be applied to literary brokerage with vast profit."[45]

In another long letter, he took issue with Godkin, who had urged a system of class representation in the *Post*. Not only was the proposal offensive to his instincts, Olmsted told him, but he thought Godkin overestimated the comparative badness of the men who ran the New York city government. With refreshing skepticism he wrote: "I have no faith that government by the Central Park Commissioners, the Sanitary Commission, Trinity Church, the Union League or the Century Clubs would on the whole accomplish as much of the proper purposes of government at as little cost and with as little demoralization of the people."[46]

He went repeatedly to see Charles Kean, whose acting he considered a great intellectual treat;[47] he attended a fashionable ball given by his "very good friend" General McDowell;[48] and he continued to find consolation in the cemetery—partly perhaps because the directors "yielded to all my suggestions."[49] For a group of Californians headed by Ralston he looked into the possibility of establishing a commercial vineyard near Buena Vista.[50]

During the three and a half months he had to remain on the coast, Olmsted made a number of trips to the Santa Cruz region to inspect oil properties for Ralston, who paid him for his trouble and advice with shares in a promising looking claim.[51] Olmsted through similar means had by that time acquired shares in eight companies, both inland and coastal, but he viewed their prospects realistically: the hard fact, he told Godkin, was that though "there must be thirty or forty millions of stock valuation of California Petroleum property now held in New York—yet not one paying oil well exists in California."[52] Oil was still only a tremendous, and a tremendously popular, gamble.*

More and more he was turning to landscape architecture; he was getting enough landscape work to support his family at least through the summer, should the company continue to default on his salary.[53] The directors of the Oakland cemetery accepted his plan ("a very elaborate & complicated pattern"), and he put an engineer to work upon the ground.[54] The College of California asked him to arrange its property ("which I propose to lay out on the Llewelyn plan") across the bay from San Francisco in campus, residential development, and park, thus giving him his first chance to plan the placement and development of a community from its very inception.[55] Ogden Mills and George P. Howard, both owners of large places south of San Francisco, invited him to landscape their grounds.[56]

Diffident about his horticultural knowledge, Olmsted invoked his wife's aid for Howard's planting: "I want you to prepare and insert a detail of planting the mounds. . . . You will see I have shirked it, partly because not competent, partly because I could not remember the names of what I think best."[57]

Perhaps it was the realization that he was imperfectly trained in his true métier that led him just then strongly to oppose the intention of his half-brother Albert Henry to shift from a banking to a scientific career. The boy would lose all the advantage of his education thus far, Olmsted wrote their father, and the

---

*At this time Olmsted had six thousand dollars gold in first class California investments and an equity of six thousand dollars gold in his bonds with Ketchum (O to JO, 12 January 1865; O to ELG, 22 January 1865, Godkin Papers).

alternatives he was considering were "but cloaks under which he hides from himself a truant disposition—just as I did. . . . Allie has the difficulty which seems to me to belong to all your descendants—of an unusual slowness or feebleness in the development of his natural propensities and faculties. He does not know his own mind, and grows irregularly."[58]

This judgment was a criticism of himself even more than of Allie—and it was the judgment that Olmsted had indignantly repelled when it was earlier made by his father. Its justice was becoming apparent to him now that, having tried without great moral or financial satisfaction to make a living at farming, writing, publishing, the Sanitary Commission, and mining, he at forty-three was almost ready to follow his natural propensities and recognize his own mind. He was carefully considering Vaux's proposal, made early in the year, that they work together on the great new pleasure ground proposed for Brooklyn.[59] Besides, Godkin balked at going West, and Olmsted's hope of operating a San Francisco paper with him lingeringly died.[60]

The Mariposa Company, too, was dying lingeringly, Olmsted believed. The enterprise was a failure, financially and socially: the stockholders had lost money, and he had not been able even to initiate his private plan for stimulating a civilized social order on the frontier. Both creditors and officers of the company admitted that he had conducted his end of the business soundly and skillfully, and since no blame for the failure could justly be laid to him, he felt it would be only a relief to drop the whole thing.

Toward the middle of March he became so depressed that his wife, leaving Miss Errington to look after the children, went to San Francisco to cheer him.[61] While she was with him military developments did as much as she: General William T. Sherman, having captured Columbia, South Carolina, in mid-February, was marching northward through country Olmsted had described in *Seaboard Slave States.* When the telegram was published announcing his sweep around Raleigh on his way to combine with Grant, Olmsted read it over and over, for the sheer pleasure of it.[62] Although he relapsed into homesickness after his wife's departure, his spirits rose again with the news of the occupation of Richmond;[63] and when word came of Lee's surrender, he was utterly overjoyed. He immediately wrote his wife:

> I want the children should be impressed with this great event. There is no history to compare with it for the value of its teachings. . . . Give them a holiday and make them thank God, if you can without leading them toward insincerity or superstition. I do think that those of us who have lived to see this day ought to feel and must feel that we have had a peculiar blessing.[64]

Just five days later, about nine o'clock on the morning of April 16, San Francisco received the appalling news of President Lincoln's assassination. Bells began to toll and tolled throughout the day. Buildings were quickly draped in black, and mourning bands and rosettes appeared on arms and in buttonholes. Business was suspended and throngs of people, "almost haggard," swarmed the streets.[65] Olmsted hurried to the bank, where he found the officers in consternation, fearing a revolution in the East, followed by anarchy and dictatorship. He reassured them. His own faith in the capacity of a democratic government to maintain its course even after such a convulsion was not disturbed, although he was afraid that there might be some brief violence.[66] "There is great and I fear dangerous excitement," he observed soberly. "Everything should be done to prevent the thought of retaliation, and to prevent the loss of the habit of waiting for the slow action of the law."[67] But the outraged crowds burned several buildings, and Olmsted saw the office of the Democratic paper "broken up by a quiet mob" before the militia was called out to check disorders.[68] "You had better hang the house with black," he instructed his wife. "I would do so simply to impress the event in the minds of the children."[69]

"The awful calamity of the country . . . , " Olmsted admitted, "almost disables me from thinking of anything else."[70] Fortunately, he did not have to: he was about to settle the company's affairs and return to Bear Valley. The temporary arrangement under which the sheriff had been running the estate was to be superseded. Dodge Brothers was to receive a bill of sale to all personal property and a lease of the real property, was to assume most of the current debts including back wages, and was to sell the personal property and work the estate to pay the debts. The company was to repossess when all debts were discharged; meanwhile Olmsted had the duty of observation, access to the books, and control of expenses.[71]

The arrangement was suggestively similar to the one Park had made with Frémont, and Olmsted, fearing it might be fraught with similar dangers, wrote Ketchum: "By good management Dodge Brothers can pay the company's California debts from the proceeds of the personal property. Before they have done this, however, the value of the real property will have been seriously injured and a large expenditure will be required to restore affairs to an economical working condition."[72]

By the end of April, when Olmsted returned from San Francisco, it was hot in Bear Valley, and the country roundabout was already seared. Until their summer trip to the mountains, the family satisfied their longing for the sight and sound of running water by spending Sundays at the spring on Mount Bullion. "It is a very pleasant clamber up," Miss Errington wrote,

> our horses treading among dark blue larkspurs or beautiful white tulips, while great clumps of . . . painted cups are nestled among the rocks, and under the shade of scattered oaks or pines . . . is a carpet of the richest purple made of a flower . . . we call the Mariposa, or butterfly. . . . When we reach the summit the great Sierra bursts upon us, stretching inter-

279

minably north, south and east, with a great cleft just opposite us, in which lies the lovely Yo Semite valley. Then we ride on, and [descend] a steep stony no-path to a mountain spring where under the shade of trees and in full view of the Sierra we . . . bivouack for the rest of the day.[73]

Miss Errington, moved to open joy by her surroundings, was troubled by her companions' "slight, too slight expression of enjoyment."[74] A fixed habit of reticence had indeed fastened itself on Olmsted since his open-hearted youth; but even if he did not say so, this was to him the right, the ideal, way to spend Sunday. Had there been a church in Bear Valley, he probably would not have attended it. The half-literate ministers, the jealous and quarrelsome sects, the dilapidated church buildings, and the indifferent congregations—there was nothing about any of them that was dignified, reverent, or, to his mind, Christian. It was not the poverty and ignorance of the organizations that repelled him; he felt a similar distaste for wealthy and educated congregations in the East. It was their exclusiveness, their hostile contempt for each other, and their cozy, self-congratulatory air that made them unacceptable to Olmsted, who held his duty and his happiness to lie in communicativeness.

On the day in early June when the news arrived from Godkin that his weekly magazine was fairly launched, the Olmsteds naturally resorted to the spring. There in good Rhine wine they toasted the *Nation* and its editor and rejoiced that the long cherished idea was about to be realized.[75] The *Nation*, as Godkin visualized it, was to be something unique in American journalism. "Our leading political aim," he wrote Olmsted, "is to secure equality before the law in all parts of the Union; all others are open questions, but I seek to have everything discussed more temperately and accurately than is usual."[76]

Under "everything" Godkin included financial, economic, commercial, political, social, scientific, educational, literary, artistic, and legal matters; all were to be discussed in a spirit as little partisan as the rather Olympian editor could enforce. The magazine was to represent no special interest: it had no friends who must not be offended, no enemies who had to be pilloried, and Godkin himself had no political interest to be advanced. Every question was to be discussed by a well-informed writer on its merits and from the point of view of the public or national interest; and every subject was to be treated with brevity, lucidity, and ease of style. "It is in fact very difficult," Godkin complained, "to get men of education in America to handle any subject with a light touch. They all want to write ponderous essays, if they write at all."[77]

Olmsted, full of ideas how the paper should be conducted, made haste to communicate them to Godkin. It should advocate measures and tendencies that were "federal and civilizing" and so educate Americans slowly from the brutal condition of pioneers.

Your paper needs to be, peculiarly, a substitute to thousands of men situated as I am, as my lawyer twelve miles away is, as numerous clergymen are, for a cultivated companion, for cultivated society,—for drawing out their own more cultivated process of reflection—dying of torpor for want of something to draw them. . . . Do recollect that except at a very few points there is no cultivated *society* in America, but a great many intelligent men and women to whom a newspaper may well be the only substitute for whatever, in a society more elaborately civilized, keeps a man's commonplace civilization alive.[78]

Olmsted's own was kept alive largely by visitors. John Bowne, a former statistician of the Sanitary Commission, stopped at Bear Valley on his way to the Yosemite in June. "I can never forget the eager manner of Mr. Olmsted's questions respecting the Commission, its work & personal welfare of the employees, and of his utterance of the expression, 'It is the place where my affections lie,'" he later reported.[79] Another visitor who arrived about the same time as Bowne and with the same destination was Carleton E. Watkins, the San Francisco photographer whose extraordinary views of the Yosemite were then being exhibited and acclaimed at Goupil's gallery in New York.[80]

Professor John Torrey, the botanist, after a visit to the Yosemite, stayed in Bear Valley for a few days. Torrey, who had given names to hundreds of California plants, told Olmsted that on a few acres of Yosemite meadow he had found three hundred species, and in sight of the trail descending into the valley, at least six hundred, most of them small and delicate flowering plants—a wonderful variety attributable to the great variation in altitude. Olmsted, already planning how the valley's natural features might be protected and preserved and at the same time be made more easily accessible to the public, noted the information for use in the report he was preparing.[81]

Early in July, Olmsted had to make another trip to the coast. His family was about to go into camp at Clark's; his cook, suddenly rich when a copper mine in which he owned shares became valuable, was leaving; and Olmsted, surrounded by the bustle of packing and departure, felt a conviction that he would not again go to housekeeping in Bear Valley.[82] All around he saw change and decay: Dodge, as manager, was gutting the Mariposa Estate to pay himself and the other creditors as fast as possible, and the property was deteriorating daily; and in New York a new set of trustees, men of whom Olmsted knew nothing, had replaced his original employers. His function was gone, his policy was reversed, and the New York office had ignored him since March 3.[83]

During his two weeks in the city he dutifully averted another forced sale of company property[84] and, more gratifyingly, worked on a preliminary study of the placement of buildings for the College of California.[85] After a frightful return trip through 106-degree heat and dust so thick that the horses sometimes could not be seen from the stage they drew, he reached Bear Valley on July 22, to find a letter from the new president of the Mariposa Company saying that the New York office would not pay his salary: he would have to get it out of the estate.[86] Obviously, he could not: Dodge, who received all the gold produced, had no interest in paying him. It was clear to Olmsted that the new trustees did not intend to honor the company's obligations to him. He felt that his duty to it was effectually at an end.

What to do next was no longer a problem: on July 26 Olmsted and Vaux were reappointed landscape architects to Central Park, at the salary of five thousand dollars a year.[87] At last the way was open for Olmsted to resume a productive collaboration and to return to the park and the work that he loved.

That hazards lurked in the collaboration he realized. He and Vaux did not see eye-to-eye on the function of the art they practiced. Olmsted regarded himself less as an artist than as a sort of social engineer, an educator of hearts, a refiner of minds, one whose function was to civilize men, to develop in them communicativeness, and to raise the general level of American society by exerting a beneficent influence on environment and by modifying unfavorable surroundings through art. Vaux, on the other hand, saw himself as an artist, practicing and winning recognition for an important, yet little appreciated, art. Notwithstanding the divergence of their views, the basis for successful collaboration seemed to exist, and Olmsted accepted the invitation to renew their partnership.

Though he expected to be free of Mariposa almost daily after the first of August, Olmsted did not want to leave for the East until October. His West Coast investments—he had just borrowed five thousand dollars to increase them —needed watching and reorganizing. More than that, he had the cemetery and the college plans to complete; backed by the *San Francisco Bulletin*, he was making some progress in persuading San Franciscans to undertake a great rural park;* and above all he wanted to work for the acceptance of his Yosemite report, completed early in August.[88]

How the movement first arose to make a public reservation of the Yosemite Valley and the Mariposa Big Tree Grove is not clear. Senator John Conness, of California, when he introduced the bill to the Senate ceding the valley and the grove to California for use as a public park on March 28, 1864, said the scheme had been presented to him by several California gentlemen "of fortune, of taste and of refinement."[89] He did not identify them. They probably included Israel Ward Raymond, western representative of the Central American Steamship Transit Company, who the previous February 20 had sent Conness photographs of the valley and urged that the grant be made and that a number of commissioners, including Olmsted, Whitney, and George Coulter of Coulterville, be named to administer it.[90] Another early proponent may well have been Starr King, who at the time of his death was planning a book on the Sierras and the

---

*The *Bulletin* for August 4, 1865, printed a long letter from Olmsted (signed "Rusticus in Urbe"), referring to San Franciscans' current interest in a rural park, describing the advantages New York had derived from Central Park and urging San Francisco to launch a similar undertaking promptly.

Yosemite.[91] Still another was very likely Olmsted, whose interests would have drawn him into such a movement.

No matter who had originally promoted the grant, once it was made Olmsted had taken charge of the affair. In October 1864, soon after receiving his appointment as a commissioner, he had sent Clarence King and James T. Gardiner out to survey and map the territory and to plan roads to and through it according to his detailed instructions; and he had advanced five hundred dollars for the map work himself, since the state had no appropriation to cover such expenditures. It was natural, too, that he should assume the task of formulating the administrative policy for the grant and of making the recommendations for carrying it out.[92] Certainly there was no one on the commission, or in the country, better equipped for this unprecedented task than he, who had been since early childhood a loving analyst of natural scenery, for fifteen years a close student of park administration, and codesigner and administrator of one of the world's most beautiful and successful rural parks.

Olmsted's report was the first systematic exposition of the right and duty of a democracy to take the action that Congress had taken in reserving the Yosemite Valley and the Mariposa Big Tree Grove from private preemption for the enjoyment of all the people.[93] Only the most urgent considerations, he stated, could have diverted Congress, in the midst of war, from other pressing duties to dedicate forever to public enjoyment Yosemite Valley and the Mariposa Big Trees. One consideration was the obvious financial benefit to a commonwealth derived from possessing celebrated scenic attractions. As the Alps lured tourists and wealth to Switzerland, as the English Garden, created at vast expense, attracted them to Munich, so the valley and the giant sequoias, when accessible, would draw them to California. The more important consideration, however, was

> a political duty of grave importance to which seldom if ever before has proper respect been paid by any government in the world. . . . It is the main duty of government, if it is not the sole duty of government, to provide means of protection for all its citizens in the pursuit of happiness against the obstacles, otherwise insurmountable, which the selfishness of individuals or combinations of individuals is liable to interpose to that pursuit.

The benefits, physical and mental, which flow from "the contemplation of natural scenes of an impressive character, especially if the contemplation occurs in connection with relief from ordinary cares [and] change of air and habits," had been recognized from earliest historical times; wealthy men had always provided themselves with luxurious rural retreats. In the British Isles there were more than a thousand privately owned parks and notable grounds devoted to recreation, the value of which amounted to many millions of dollars and the upkeep of which was greater than that of the national schools. Yet their only advantage to the commonwealth was in the recreation they afforded their owners and their owners' guests; and these owners, together with their families, numbered less than one in six thousand of the whole population.

> The enjoyment of the choicest natural scenes in the country and the means of recreation connected with them is thus a monopoly. . . . of a very few, very rich people. . . . Thus without means are taken by government to withhold them from the grasp of individuals, all places favorable in scenery to the recreation of the mind and body will be closed against the great body of the people. For the same reason that the water of rivers should be guarded against private appropriation and the use of it for the purpose of navigation and otherwise protected against obstruction, portions of natural scenery may therefore properly be guarded and cared for by government. To simply reserve them from monopoly by individuals, however, it will be obvious, is not all that is necessary. It is necessary that they should be laid open to the use of the body of the people. The establishment by government of great public grounds is thus justified and enforced as a public duty.

In the old world the governing classes assumed that the greater part of the population should spend their lives in almost constant labor and that the capacity to enjoy beauty either in nature or in art required higher cultivation than they were capable of. Of this repugnant class philosophy Olmsted wrote:

> It is unquestionably true that excessive and persistent devotion to sordid interests cramps and distorts the power of appreciating natural beauty and destroys the love of it which the Almighty has implanted in every human being, and which is so intimately and mysteriously associated with the moral perceptions and intuition, but it is not true that exemption from toil, much leisure, much study, much wealth, are necessary to the exercise of the esthetic and contemplative faculties. It is the folly of laws which have permitted and favored the monopoly by privileged classes of many of the means supplied in nature for the gratification, exercise and education of the esthetic faculties that has caused the appearance of dullness and weakness and disease of these faculties in the mass of the subjects of kings. And it is against the limitation of the means of such education to the rich that the wise legislation of free governments must be directed.

It was therefore the main duty of the commissioners "to give every advantage practicable to the mass of the people to benefit by that which is peculiar to this ground and which has caused Congress to treat it differently from other parts of the public domain. This peculiarity consists wholly in its natural scenery."

The problems of the commissioners were to maintain the scenery as nearly as possible in its pristine state; to draw up regulations to prevent careless or wanton damage; and to make the grant readily accessible. Olmsted recommended a good road into the valley; another road, as inconspicuous as possible, circling the valley and connecting across it by several roads and bridges; a road to the Mariposa grove that should entirely encircle it and act as a protection against the frequent fires that threatened the magnificent trees; five cabins to be rented to tenants who should keep one or two rooms for visitors and keep on hand certain necessary camping supplies for sale at moderate prices; and a superintendent to live in the valley and oversee its use. Olmsted ended his report by requesting thirty-seven thousand dollars, twenty-five thousand of it designated for roads, for the execution of his recommendations.[94]

In this document Olmsted elaborated, for the first time in America, the policy underlying the reservation by government to the public of a particular, and fine, scenic area; and he gave it a general application. In short, he formulated the philosophic base for the establishment of state and national parks.

The idea that a democratic government ought to preserve regions of peculiar scenic beauty for the enjoyment of all its citizens was not one that originated with Olmsted. Hints and suggestions looking toward it had been made in the United States at least as early as 1815. In that year Thomas Jefferson, refusing to sell land around the Natural Bridge in Virginia, wrote, "I view it in some degree as a public trust and would on no consideration permit the bridge to be injured, defaced or masked from the public view."[95] In 1833 George Catlin, explorer and painter who had traveled up the Missouri River into Indian country, proposed in the *New York Daily Commercial Advertiser* that certain western regions "might in future be seen (by some great protecting policy of government) preserved in their pristine beauty and wildness, in a magnificent park. . . . A *nation's Park*, containing man and beast, in all the wild and freshness of their nature's beauty." And in 1844 Emerson was reported by the *Dial* to have said in a lecture, "The forests should become graceful parks, for use and delight."[96]

Such scattered suggestions had fallen on a soil increasingly receptive to them. The pioneer's hostility to the awful wilderness around him was yielding, as the wilderness became tamed, to less primitive feelings; and Americans, educated by the accounts of such travelers as M. G. J. de Crèvecoeur and Catlin, by writers like Irving, James Fenimore Cooper, Bryant, and Thoreau, by painters like Thomas Cole, Albert Bierstadt, and Frederick Church, and by photographers like Watkins, were by the middle of the nineteenth century becoming not only appreciative of the peculiar beauties of their country's natural scenery but aware that measures to conserve it would soon be necessary. The demand for rural parks in cities and the interest in natural scenery were both growing stronger just when the knowledge of the extraordinary scenic qualities of the Sierras and especially of the Yosemite Valley was becoming diffused through the works of painters, photographers, travelers, and writers. It was not remarkable that the two trends should combine to precipitate the idea that regions of unusual beauty should be set aside as public parks. Nor was it remarkable that it was in Olmsted's mind that the idea should crystallize in its clearest form. Yet he recognized

Yosemite Valley as Olmsted saw it in 1863; Yosemite Domes, by Carleton E. Watkins (Prints and Photographs Division, Library of Congress).

that the national park concept could not be traced to his report: quietly suppressed, it gained no currency whatever. He attributed the concept, rather, to "the workings of the national genius."[97]

Olmsted read his report in the Yosemite Valley on August 9, 1865, before a meeting of the Yosemite Commission attended by Alexander Deering, Coulter, Galen Clark, and Ashburner.[98] He had arrived there two days earlier with a party of seventeen, the largest so far to enter the valley. Besides the Yosemite commissioners and several San Franciscans, it included Schuyler Colfax, Speaker of the House of Representatives, Samuel Bowles, editor of the *Springfield* (Mass.) *Republican*, Albert D. Richardson of the *New York Tribune*, William Bross, lieutenant governor of Illinois, and Charles Allen, attorney general of Massachusetts, who were making a well-publicized trip across the continent.*[,99] The response to Olmsted's report must be inferred; no criticism of it was reported in the minutes.[100] Ashburner's antagonism to it also must be inferred from the part he later took, with Whitney, in suppressing it for fear that the California Legislature might grant the Yosemite's funds at the expense of the Geological Survey's.[101] Olmsted, probably unaware of Ashburner's reservations, undoubtedly discussed the report freely with other members of the party whose support would be valuable to the valley plan and to the novel theory he had propounded. That he brought the influential editor of the *Republican* to see eye-to-eye with him is apparent from Bowles's proposal, made in the book he published about his journey, that reservations on the same plan as the Yosemite and Mariposa Big Trees be established at Niagara Falls, in sections of the Adirondacks, and in certain lake-and-woods regions of Maine.[102]

Bowles and Olmsted quickly became sympathetic friends; they had not only ideas in common but ailments. Like Olmsted a compulsive worker, Bowles suffered from dyspepsia, insomnia, and other concomitants of overwork. Having undertaken the arduous trip across the continent with some notion of improving his health, he found himself instead worn out by exertion and fatigue. Olmsted, too, in spite of the restorative calm of the valley, was sick. He and Bowles compared symptoms and fell into the way of scolding each other solicitously, and with negligible effect, for working too hard and keeping inhuman hours.[103]

Mary Olmsted, still in camp at Clark's, missed the reading of the report but brought her children and Miss Errington to the valley to join the larger party the next day. With the peculiar combination of recklessness and nerve that her husband found so disquieting, she decided to make the hard thirty-five-mile ride in a single day, without any male escort but two men whose full attention was occupied by the pack mules. Miss Errington refrained from protest because she knew "it was no use to oppose what Mrs. O—was bent on." Her apprehensions were borne out: donkeys were stubborn; there was nothing to eat after the three o'clock lunch; the party reached Inspiration Point at sunset, groped down the

---

*It was said to be the first transcontinental trip made purely for observation and pleasure.

stony trail in thickening night, waited two hours at the bottom for the moon to rise, and arrived at camp at one in the morning. Anticipating some unusual strains on her fortitude, Miss Errington had provided against them. "I fortunately," she told a confidante, "had a tiny bottle of *whiskey* to which I applied my lips occasionally to prevent complete exhaustion."

Sustained by judicious tippling, the English lady reached the end of the long day in good condition and could afterward report, with pardonable complacency: "After I had something to eat, I was all right." Mary Olmsted fared worse. "[She] was very unwell at night, Mr. O—said, and I think he was not at all pleased at the exploit, for, poor man, he had had an attack of neuralgia all day and was just composing himself to sleep when he had word of our approach and mounted his horse to meet us."[104]

Olmsted did not permit his indisposition to interfere with the Yosemite Commission's business. He wrote a letter—intended, he told Vaux, principally as a recognition of the artist's function in society—to Watkins and the painters of California scenes, Virgil Williams and Thomas Hill, inviting them to advise the commission on its work.[105] At the same time Deering, the lawyer member of the commission, was finding out from the valley settlers the terms on which they held their land;[106] and Miss Errington, troubled by Watkins's diffidence in pushing the sale of his photographs and charmed by the studies of trees he was making in the valley, did her bit to promote both valley and photographer by urging her English correspondents to order sets of his pictures.[*,107]

On August 12 Olmsted went out of the valley with Colfax's party, leaving his family to follow later. Although sick on the way and subsisting on cholera medicine and scalded milk, he reached Bear Valley the following midnight and next day wrote Potter, who held his power of attorney and dealt with the officers of the Mariposa Company in his name, to "bring me *to an end* with the company" the best way he could. At nine the same evening he set out with Martin for San Francisco, where he had company and landscape business.[108]

On the boat from Stockton to San Francisco, Olmsted was taken violently sick with what he called cholera morbus. A doctor and Ashburner, summoned to the boat when it reached San Francisco, carried him to the Brevoort, where, for four or five days, he improved, relapsed, and improved again under the care of a professional nurse and a doctor who visited him several times a day.[109]

By the twenty-third Olmsted was convalescent and able to attend to his business. He collected one thousand dollars in cash from the cemetery trustees. He considered, and declined, an offer of seven thousand dollars a year to become

---

*A widely circulated picture of a bearded man on horse back in front of a waterfall in the Yosemite Valley, alleged to be Olmsted about 1864 or 1865, is a case of mistaken identity. Olmsted never reentered the valley after this visit of July–August 1865; he did not wear a beard until the early 1880s; and the photograph in question, according to internal evidence, was taken in or shortly before 1898.

executive secretary of the American Freedmen's Aid Union, a new organization composed of the principal freedmen's associations.[110] He read in the papers of the enormous Ketchum defalcation* and ascertained, with the sensation of going "in and out of a cold bath," that his draft for six thousand dollars on Ketchum had been paid in San Francisco only the day before. "So that instead of $6,000 U.S. bonds with *Ketchum*, I have $6,000 in Navigation, Water and Gas. Rather *you* have." he wrote his wife.[111]

Toward the end of the month he made a careful study of the ground of the College of California, spending several nights on it to determine whether the alleged difference in climate between it and San Francisco across the bay in fact existed. At least while he was on the site, the chilling fog and searching wind that made San Franciscans shiver even in summer with the approach of evening were absent, and the sky remained starry and the air mild throughout the August nights. The equable climate of the spot encouraged him to visualize the sparsely shaded, pathless hills, bronze under the glaring sun, as transformed with shrubs and trees, shaded roads, and pleasant homes around the collegiate center.[112]

At the beginning of September, when the plan for the grounds was well matured in his mind, Olmsted invited Samuel Hopkins Willey, vice-president of the institution, and some of the trustees to meet him and explained it to them on the site. He was so persuasive that, three weeks later, Willey had located his house and dug his well, and several other trustees were waiting to start theirs only until the engineer should have completed the section of the map covering their lots.[113]

The name of the community was a question to which Olmsted gave much laborious, and uninspired, thought; and he drew up a long list of names, some descriptive, some commemorative of distinguished men.[114] The trustees, lukewarm about all his suggestions, left the tract unnamed until early the next year, when Billings proposed that Bishop George Berkeley should be commemorated in the westernmost seat of learning in the new world.[115]

By September 7 Olmsted was back in Bear Valley. In the ensuing weeks the company sent him neither salary nor instructions, only questions. His position was both helpless and useless; the stockholders' interests would not be affected whether he stayed or left. He finally decided to sail for home by the Nicaraguan steamer of October 13, leaving Martin to observe in his stead the progress of the estate's decay.[116]

He was the more willing to go because epidemic fevers were rampant,

---

*Morris Ketchum, a man of spotless reputation, was highly respected in banking and brokerage circles. His son Edward Ketchum, in an embezzlement that rocked the financial world, disappeared on August 14 with a suitcase containing more than half a million dollars in negotiable securities. It was a strangely lackadaisical crime: Edward never left New York, showed himself freely in public places like Central Park, and was picked up, unresisting, in a room he had taken in West Twentieth Street on the evening of August 25. He was sentenced to Sing Sing. Morris Ketchum, forced into bankruptcy, eventually paid the full amount of the claims against him.

"typhoid on the highlands, congestive and remittent below."[117] The country, withered and dry, was "in the best possible condition to be left with satisfaction."[118] The desolation of the property, reflecting the forlorn condition of the company, opposed a painful reality to every hope he had held for the estate and the community. Most of the mills were stopped, crime of all sorts was increasing, and the villages were becoming depopulated as all but the most dispirited of their inhabitants left. It was all, Sam Bowles mourned, "a sad, vast ruin . . . a sort of grand land and mine Micawber."[119]

By October 9 Olmsted and his household were in San Francisco. And by then the Digger Indians, with their winter supply of acorns, were moving into the abandoned houses in the villages on the Mariposa Estate.[120]

XXV
POLITICS AND THE *NATION*
December 1865–November 1866

URING and after the Civil War, the United States developed a
sharpened consciousness of their unity as a nation. Symptoms of it
were various. Undertakings of national scope came into being, and certain ideas
spread, as though by contagion, nationally. National banks were superseding
state banks; national securities were a favorite investment. A railroad was being
constructed to bind one end of the sprawling nation to the other, and eastern
capital poured into the development of western resources. A National Academy
of Sciences was founded, a National Commissioner of Agriculture appointed,
and a National Department of Education established. For the promotion of industrial and agricultural education on a national scale, Congress appropriated a
vast domain from the public lands. The magazine called the *Nation* was winning
critical approval East and West. The national park idea was anticipated in the
reservation of the Yosemite Valley, and the idea of rural parks for cities was taking hold across the country from New York to San Francisco.[1]

Even in California Olmsted had not been entirely out of the mainstream of
this tendency toward nationality. His participation in the Mariposa venture had
connected him with an enterprise that was typical of certain national tendencies
—typical in its span of the country no less than in its fabulous promise, its
fraudulence, and its failure. More than that, he had been a prime mover in setting aside the Yosemite Valley as a public pleasure ground for the benefit of all
the nation. Back once more in the East, he was to take part, for a time, in national movements. Landscape work, however, was to become increasingly the
channel through which he satisfied that urge for social usefulness which had
made dedicated men of others of his background and generation and that strong
and disciplined artistic impulse which helped to raise landscape architecture
from the level of a trade to the status of a fine art and a profession.

"I hope you will not fail to do justice to Vaux," Olmsted once told an admirer, "and to consider that he and I were one. I should have been nowhere but
for his professional training."[2] He may have somewhat overstated his debt to his
partner, but he owed much to the guidance and goading of Vaux. It was Vaux
who had induced him to enter the Central Park competition, Vaux who with
patient craftiness maneuvered Green into returning Central Park to the control
of the landscape architects, and Vaux who secured the Brooklyn park work.[3] It
was also Vaux who persuaded Olmsted to return East, and finally, it was Vaux

who insisted that Olmsted recognize himself not only as a social engineer but as an artist.

Since the early days of the Central Park collaboration, it had been Vaux's idea that the partnership should concentrate on developing the profession of landscape architecture in America. "For us to be the means of elevating an unaccredited but important pursuit seems to me a direct contribution to the best interests of humanity," he wrote Olmsted.[4] While each believed with almost religious ardor in the value of their work, Vaux placed the larger emphasis on its art element, Olmsted on its social element. Vaux was pained by Olmsted's emphasis. "I wish you could have seen your destiny in our art," he wrote Olmsted. "God meant you should."[5]

Olmsted replied: "I think you are a little idolatrous and in danger of losing sight of the end in devotion to the means." Besides, he felt quite humbly "rather as if it was sacrilegious of me to post myself in the portals of art." At the same time, he was not so humble as to underestimate himself: he knew that, with proper assistance and enough money, he could do in landscape architecture anything that any man could do. "I can combine means to ends better than most," he said, "and I love beautiful landscapes and rural recreations, and people in rural recreations, better than anybody else I know. But I don't feel strong on the art side. I don't feel myself an artist."[6]

Vaux insisted that in justice to artists generally and to Central Park as "the big art work of the Republic" it should be presented by its creators as an artistic success, not an organizational and executive success. "I have always felt that it would be mean on the part of its makers to let the success be an administration success. It would seem as if they were ashamed of their work. You approaching this thing from the other side and not being except instinctively an artist failed to see this. . . ."[7]

Vaux was insistent, too, on the use of the term "landscape architecture," which Olmsted thought unsatisfactory and accepted only for lack of a better one. "I think it is *the* art title we want to set art out ahead," Vaux explained, "& make it *command* its position—administration, management, funds . . . and everything else. Then we have a tangible something to stand on: as administration with art attached the thing is in wrong shape."[8]

Vaux, in fact, had some misgivings about Olmsted's administrative capacity. Olmsted had engaged in a contest with Green on managerial ground and had lost. His administration had not been comprehensive, calm, or statesmanlike, and his diplomacy had been "very defective and impatient." But throughout, his art had been "pure . . . and far reaching and sound," and Vaux believed that, despite the autocratic habit of mind fostered by his executive function, he was animated by "the humble modest artist spirit."[9] Feeling his own incapacity to deal with Central Park and the Brooklyn park alone and believing Olmsted's contribution as an artist was indispensable to "the translation of the republican art idea in its highest form to the acres we want to control,"[10] Vaux had insisted that the work be offered not to him alone but to the partnership. The Brooklyn park commissioners had readily accepted his proposal; and even Green, who had at first balked at "countenancing the return of that overwhelming personality, F.L.O.," had come around.[11]

It was with this obligation to Vaux, and with a clear realization of his difference of opinion with him, that Olmsted returned to New York to resume the practice of landscape architecture in partnership with him.

When he reached New York, after a wretched six-week journey, Olmsted first of all attended to his business with the Mariposa Company. It was quickly dispatched: the company had no funds, and the trustees intended to treat the former manager precisely like any other creditor. They gave Olmsted no reason to suppose that he could collect either the eleven thousand dollars carried to his credit on the company's books or compensation for releasing the company from its contract with him. They were willing, he half suspected, to make him scapegoat for the failure. He worried about its effect on his reputation and prospects, but he knew he could rely on energetic friends—Mills, Silliman, Ashburner, King, Potter—to testify that he had managed the estate prudently and abandoned it only when in effect starved out.[12]

While his wife settled the family in an expensive boardinghouse run by a Mrs. Elizabeth Neely at 167 East Fourteenth Street,[12] Olmsted set to work with Vaux on the Brooklyn park. The site originally taken for it included almost three hundred twenty acres of pleasantly diversified meadow, woodland, and water and afforded several fine views of bay and ocean. Its great drawback was its division into two unequal pieces by Flatbush Avenue, a broad thoroughfare that, however indispensable to public convenience, was fatal to those impressions of spaciousness and repose that were the essence of a rural park. The reservoir, besides, occupied so much of the smaller section that it in effect divided it into two bits of land too small for successful incorporation into a rural park scheme.[14]

Viele, invited before the war to present a plan, in his report of January 1861 to the Brooklyn park commissioners had professed complete satisfaction with the site: its natural features required "but little aid from art to fit it for all the purposes of health and recreation." Taste as well as economy demanded that it be treated in the natural style because nature "conveys in all its phases and through all its changes no emotions which are not in harmony with the highest refinement of the soul." Notwithstanding this genuflexion toward nature, Viele saw no fault but a positive advantage in the location of Flatbush Avenue athwart the site: it obviated the need for any other direct road through the park to accommodate traffic between the city and its suburbs; and planted on either side with a double row of trees through which should run a promenade, it would form a main feature of the improvement, a sort of *grande allée* carrying the eye from one end all the way to the bay and from the other to the ocean.[15]

Because of the outbreak of war, no work had been started under Viele's plan. In any case James S. T. Stranahan, chairman of the park commission, was dissatisfied with it. Toward the end of the war he consulted Vaux, who urged a material change in the boundaries of the park. While Olmsted was still in California, Vaux drew up a plan for a park of about five hundred twenty-six acres lying entirely on the west side of Flatbush Avenue.[16] Olmsted on his return acquiesced in Vaux's design, and the park commission adopted it. In the report they submitted with the plan on January 24, 1866, the partners pointed out that the division of the site by Flatbush Avenue could not fail to frustrate a sound plan and remarked that even the one sizable open space, which Viele had pronounced adequate, was tantalizingly small, since with all its limits visible at a glance, it made no suggestion to the imagination of any reach of rural scenery beyond itself. They proposed abandoning the smaller piece of land east of Flatbush Avenue for the purposes of the park and greatly extending the larger to the south and west. By shifting its boundaries, low ground suitable for a large lake would be obtained and space would be insured both for the extensive, peaceful rural scenery that offered the most agreeable contrast to the restless town and for the safe and comfortable accommodation of large crowds. The report also incorporated the unfamiliar concept of a system of parks:

> . . . We regard Brooklyn as an integral part of what today is the
> metropolis of the nation, and in the future will be the centre of exchanges
> for the world, and the park in Brooklyn, as part of a system of grounds, of
> which the Central Park is a single feature, designed for the recreation of
> the whole people of the metropolis and their customers and guests from
> all parts of the world for centuries to come.[17]

While work on the Brooklyn park waited on the winter weather and the purchase of the additional land, Olmsted busied himself with the *Nation*, spending considerable time at its office and taking responsibility equally with Godkin for everything in it.[18] For twenty years he had been saying that he was less influential than he deserved to be; now his arrangement with Godkin gave him a gratifying opportunity to make his views known through the magazine's columns.

More than that, he gave Godkin valuable support in the tense situation existing between him and some of the magazine's Boston stockholders. The *Nation* had derived from two sources: the project for a weekly, to be edited by Olmsted and Godkin, for which Olmsted had prepared the prospectus in 1863; and a paper, to be called the *Nation*, dedicated to the freedmen's interest, which J. Miller McKim was trying to launch in 1865. After the editorship of the proposed *Nation* had been declined by Curtis and Whitelaw Reid, it had been offered to Godkin by McKim, Norton, and Major George L. Stearns, wartime organizer of Negro troops and tireless advocate of the freedmen. Opposed to an organ dedicated exclusively to any special interest, Godkin had suggested instead such a magazine as he and Olmsted had contemplated, in which all the important issues of the day, the freedmen's rights among them, should be treated. Norton and Stearns had agreed to Godkin's proposal. Godkin engaged to raise one-quarter of the capital, twenty-five thousand dollars, in New York, McKim one-quarter in Philadelphia, and Norton and Stearns one-half in Boston.

Without informing Godkin of its source, Norton and Stearns contributed sixteen thousand dollars from the Recruiting Fund, of which they were trustees. This fund, established during the war for the benefit of Negro soldiers, at war's end contained a considerable amount of money that its subscribers had consented to leave in the hands of the trustees to be expended "in the line of the original object."[19]

Stearns, having invested not only Recruiting Fund money but twelve thousand dollars of his own in *Nation* stock, fell foul of Godkin with the appearance of the first issue. He interpreted a short squib in it on the freedmen as a cynical slight to them and to all their supporters.[20] He learned, too, that Godkin was not an Englishman as he had supposed but an Irishman.[21] His resentment, compounded by anti-Irish prejudice, developed into a sharp dislike of the editor. Soon after the publication of the third issue, he charged Godkin in a public circular with bad faith in not making the *Nation* an organ of the freedmen's interest after accepting Recruiting Fund money pledged to that interest.[22]

Norton, hotly supporting Godkin, declared that Stearns's circular was plainly the production of an angry and unscrupulous man adept at distortion.[23] Sam Bowles, who regretted Stearns's eccentricities and admired his devoted work for the Negroes, took a kinder view: Stearns was neither unscrupulous nor a liar but a man capable of great self-deception. He had understood and agreed to the *Nation*'s program, was disappointed that the magazine did not give as much space as he wished to freedmen's affairs, and concluded that he had been imposed on. Bowles, in fact, thought Stearns and Norton had shown poor judgment in giving money earmarked for use in the freedmen's interest to a publication that was no more an organ for their advancement than his own *Republican*.[24]

Relations between Stearns and Godkin simmered ominously for some six months, during which it was a relief to the beset editor to have Olmsted share his responsibility. Olmsted, for one thing, was on friendly terms with Stearns; for another, he was not open to attack, as Godkin was, with the lethal epithet "foreigner."

Although Stearns called at the *Nation*'s office in December 1865 and offered his hand to Godkin, who took it *"with a smile,"* as Olmsted reported breathlessly to Norton,[25] six weeks later he was telling McKim, who urged him to compose his differences with Godkin: "No compromise is possible with such a man as Mr. Godkin. . . . Either he must resign, or the Boston stockholders will claim their capital."[26]

At the close of the magazine's first year, Stearns carried out his threat and forced it to buy out stockholders desiring to withdraw for the amount that remained of their original subscriptions.[27] The Recruiting Fund withdrew its share; other stockholders took theirs; still others stood by the magazine. Godkin took over the property, and the proprietors, with the issue of August 23, 1866, became E. L. Godkin and Company instead of the Nation Association.[28]

Scale of Feet.

PLAN OF

PROSPECT PARK

BROOKLYN, N.Y.

OLMSTED VAUX & CO., LANDSCAPE ARCHITECTS
J. Y. CULYER, CHIEF ENGINEER & SUPERINTENDENT.

1874

Olmsted was one of those who stood by the *Nation*'s editor. It may have been at this time that he invested money in the magazine; certainly he invested much time in it. His prominence in its management during the months of crisis was such that Emerson got the impression that he was supplanting Godkin. Godkin did not care if it was generally supposed that Olmsted wrote every word of it.[29]

Actually Olmsted wrote but little for the paper. Composition for him was a time-consuming and joyless process to be shunned whenever possible. He wrote laboriously, in pencil on odd-sized scraps of paper, spacing his lines far apart and making frequent interlinear corrections, and corrections of the corrections, until the space between the lines, the margins, and even the back of the paper were crowded with his hasty and crabbed writing. His wife was often pressed into service to make a fair copy,[30] and in the end, he was rarely satisfied with the finished product. "He writes hard," Sam Bowles observed, "and it reads hard, but there is meat in his thought. . . . O's style of writing must have changed, or I can't understand the popularity of his books. It is very hard work to read him, —he is so formal and stiff in his style."[31] Such a stylist did not lightly assume the burden of writing, and such a style was not the thing for the *Nation*.

Olmsted's responsibility as an editor, however, was large and he carried it easily, the more easily because his editorial and his personal interests often coincided. Although he occasionally disagreed with the magazine's positions, its views on some of the most interesting questions of the day were his. Its concern to secure international copyright, its advocacy of the Freedmen's Bureau and of equal rights for all citizens, its support of women's suffrage, its detestation of General Benjamin F. Butler, its repeated criticisms of Richard Morris Hunt's "feeble" and "tasteless" designs for the Central Park gateways, its interest in the better training of army officers, its recommendations for the protection of merchant seamen against cruel and absolute officers, its opposition to the eight-hour day and to the impeachment of President Andrew Johnson, its specifications for the readmission of the seceded states, its attitude on the southern famine, its indignation at California's ceding parts of the Yosemite to squatters, its zeal to make the national capital a city that would be a source of national pride—the *Nation*'s opinions on these and many other matters were shared or shaped by Olmsted.[32]

There is no evidence that Olmsted was paid for his editorial services to the *Nation*, and there is some that he was short of cash during the first few months after his return. Then, as ever, considerations of health compelled the family to live comfortably rather than thriftily: all the children were sick during the winter, Mary was pregnant, and Olmsted was so unwell that he was uninsurable.[33] He could not collect the money owed him by Mountain View Cemetery or the College of California; but fortunately his California investments, left in Ashburner's hands, were worth almost fifteen thousand dollars,[34] and he was able, when he needed money in the spring, to raise twelve hundred dollars by selling some of his western stock.[35] The Staten Island farm, too, the property of his stepchildren, was in the process of being sold to the tenant and could be counted on to bring in fixed amounts from time to time.[36]

More irksome than temporary financial straits were his domestic arrangements, controlled by a landlady who objected to his friends. The special target of Mrs. Neely's disapproval was George Waring, then an enthusiastic advocate of the earth closet, the now all-but-forgotten rival of the water closet; he fatally affronted her refinement by facetiously calling himself a "privy councillor." When she included even the blameless Brace in her censure, Olmsted could endure no more. Late in April he took a house on Amos Street, in Clifton, Staten Island, from which he could conveniently commute to his park work in Brooklyn.[37]

The firm was reappointed by the Brooklyn park commission May 29, 1866, as landscape architects with the duty of supervision, at a salary of eight thousand dollars a year.[38] An adequate appropriation, based on their estimates, was passed,[39] all but a few blocks of the additional land recommended by the partners was acquired, and work began on Prospect Park on July 1. During the summer four hundred workmen were employed, and as the work progressed, Olmsted's enthusiasm for it grew until it came to seem almost inconvenient to him, since it elbowed other interests out of his mind. Although the hot weather and hard work tired him, he began to feel better than he had felt in several years. Taking a little time off, he showed his father, who spent a week with him in June, over the park site; and two or three evenings a week he got back to Clifton early enough to row a couple of miles down the bay with John and Owen to go swimming. By the middle of August the work was well enough organized to let him and his wife accept Norton's frequently repeated invitation to visit him at Ashfield.[40]

Curtis and Bowles were there, too, and the four men had long political discussions. Curtis, Norton, and Olmsted saw almost eye-to-eye, and one rainy day in Norton's study they formulated their ideas on the most pressing national problem, reconstruction.[41]

They agreed that the speediest restoration of the Union consistent with constitutional justice was necessary; and that the Union, being perpetual, could be dissolved neither by the federal government nor by any state. The federal government had a right to wage war and subject a rebel state, and the duty devolved on Congress, not the president, to determine when the subdued state, by establishing a republican form of government and returning to loyalty, might resume the exercise of the rights suspended by its own wrongdoing.

They favored the fourteenth constitutional amendment, then pending, in all particulars. Advocates of equal rights for Negroes, they thought its adoption would tend toward that equalization of political rights among all citizens on which the future peace and power of the Union would depend. As for President Johnson, he was usurping the power of Congress and his policy was encouraging a spirit, demonstrated in the scandalous New Orleans massacre of peaceably assembled Negroes, fatal to order and obstructive to the restoration of the Union.[42] These opinions were also the *Nation*'s and appeared in it frequently prior to the fall elections;[43] and they found expression the first week in September in the platform of the New York State Republican Convention, held at Syracuse, where Curtis was chairman of the resolutions committee.[44]

While Curtis was securing the adoption of a moderate platform at Syracuse, the Olmsteds were continuing their vacation trip. In the White Mountains the landscape architect whose first concern always was the effect of scenery on people was disconcerted to find the roads as crowded as those of suburban New York. "We felt a little cheated of our enjoyment of the mountains," he complained to Norton, "by the crowd of infidels—philistines—which occupied them."[45] Notwithstanding Philistines, he and his wife spent delightful hours in a ramble up the course of a mountain stream. Predictably, he found the special charm of the White Mountains' scenery not so much in what was grand as in the underwood, mass, and water. After a short excursion into Quebec they returned to New York the first week in September, to find it, as usual at the season, in the grip of an abating cholera epidemic.

The political discussion begun at Ashfield was resumed by letter and was paralleled in the editorial columns of the *Nation*. Norton wrote that Andrew Johnson's tour of the country was not strengthening his party and that the bitterness and coarseness of his style of stump oratory was unlikely to appeal to northern voters.[46] Olmsted agreed: as a representative of the better sort of poor men of the South, Johnson had

> by showing his own essential barbarism of character confirmed and established the apprehension that it would not be just, merciful, prudent, or economical hastily to adopt [his] policy. We cannot safely hand over the negroes, nor can we risk the national welfare by giving the degree of responsibility to the whole body of whites of the South which Mr. Johnson proposes to do. It is a question of risk and our estimate of the risk depends on our estimate of the character of the men.[47]

On the other hand, Olmsted felt "a profound want of confidence in the statesmanship of such men as Stevens and Greeley and Sumner,"[48] and feared that their extremism would alienate moderate voters from the Republican party in the coming election. Norton, minimizing the possibility, dropped an idea that the *Nation* expanded editorially soon after: such men as they were not leaders in any true sense; indeed, the party led itself. Although they had a group of noisy followers, they wearied the thoughtful. "It is," he wrote,

> one of the main excellencies of our political system that it accepts revolutionaries and violent talk as part of the natural order of society. Mr.

Johnson's speeches, . . . Butler's speeches, Brownlow's rant, Greeley's
malignant follies, Sumner's unwisdom, and Stevens' extravagancies, are
waste steam let off through the national whistle or calliope, not the steam
by which the great engine is driven. . . . We are getting beyond leaders in
America. A moral thoughtful community does not need them. Mr. Lincoln
has shown us the example of a great popular Statesman, not a leader.[49]

The northern elections, in which the Republicans polled a decisive majority,
showed the groundlessness of Olmsted's fear that moderate voters would be antagonized by the Republican radicals. The local elections, however, which made
John Morrissey and Fernando Wood, respectively, congressman and mayor, gave
Olmsted and like-minded New Yorkers less cause for satisfaction. Compared with
New York, Francis Leiber lamented to Olmsted, Athens had been fortunate: "It
would be a god's send to us to be ruled by a tanner, instead of a professional
malefactor, a prizefighter and gamester and an open traitor." The *Nation* was
scarcely more sparing in its remarks.[50]

On November 24, 1866, Mary Olmsted bore her sixth child, Olmsted's
third, a boy who died within six hours. Her recovery dragged, and Olmsted's
anxiety about her continued for many months.[51] A professional blow, too, which
he must have felt deeply, had occurred only a month earlier: the burking of the
Yosemite plan by the very commissioners on whom he had relied to guide it
through the California Legislature.

A few months after Olmsted's return east, Ashburner had written that only
he and Whitney were at all active in the Yosemite matter: the legislator who
had undertaken to steer Olmsted's bill to acceptance had done nothing, and the
governor was unwilling to ask for so large a sum of money until the debt already
incurred was paid and the grant was formally accepted by the state.[52] Ashburner
neglected to mention something else rather crucial: that this inactivity was
directly traceable to three members of the Yosemite Commission itself. He,
Whitney, and Raymond, meeting "informally" as the commission in November
1865, had strongly recommended to Governor Low that he withhold Olmsted's
report from the legislature on the ground that it was "not expedient" just then
to ask for thirty-seven thousand dollars. Accordingly Low, in his message to the
legislature, said that no Yosemite report had been made.[53] Bowles, when he
heard what had happened, indignantly wrote Olmsted, "That was shabby treatment of you by Whitney, & without explanation, too. I have done some profanity
on the subject. . . ."[54]

Alex Deering, angrily asserting "foul play," charged that "geological fossil
Ashburner" had suppressed the report for fear the Geological Survey would be
slighted in favor of the valley in the next appropriation, and Galen Clark supported the belief that the survey members of the Yosemite Commission had deliberately sacrificed the valley's interest.[55] Olmsted's opinion of the matter must
be inferred: on October 23, 1866, he resigned.[56]

Note: The effect of the minority's action was soon plain. Hutchings, prevented by the Yosemite Commission in 1866 from setting up a sawmill, by 1868 had felled four hundred trees in the valley.[57] With Lamon, he lobbied through the California Legislature of 1867 a bill granting each one hundred sixty acres and requesting Congress to confirm their claims.[58] While the *Nation* fumed at the sentimental good nature that would sacrifice the rights of the entire country to the not-very-substantial claims of two individuals, the House of Representatives amiably passed a bill confirming the give-away to the squatters.[59] Whitney, who had been motivated by zeal for the survey and not hostility to the Yosemite Valley,[60] with Olmsted and others organized an effective protest to the Senate, so that the bill was unfavorably reported out of committee. Undaunted, Hutchings had his claim surveyed in a long strip down the center of the valley to monopolize the best pasture and access to water,[61] and he and Lamon renewed their efforts to get their claims confirmed by Congress. In 1870 they again came dangerously close to success,[62] and it required legal action, carried through the Supreme Court of the United States, to defeat their attempts to fasten private ownership on the valley. Not until 1875 did the Yosemite Commission secure full control of the grant.[63] The squatters were compensated, as the commission had originally intended they should be, with cash payments for the value of the improvements they had put upon the land.[64]

T HE scuttling of his Yosemite report was not the only professional reverse that Olmsted suffered at this period. His proposal for a San Francisco park fell through, his Berkeley plan was shelved, and his advice, solicited by the trustees of the Massachusetts and the Maine agricultural colleges, was rejected. The only significant result of all his labor for these clients was the four pamphlets prepared for them, which not only suggested a plan for each but also set forth the principles on which Olmsted conceived his profession to rest. Although each report was written largely by Olmsted, some parts were composed by Vaux, who, Olmsted told Norton, "knows what it is he thinks better than I."[1]

The first, addressed to a committee of the board of supervisors of San Francisco, described a series of pleasure grounds for the city.[2] Urged by newspapers and memorialized by Ashburner, Billings, and other leading citizens, the board in November 1865 had invited Olmsted, for a fee of five hundred dollars gold, to prepare a plan and report on it.[3] The committee's request did not reach him until late the following February, but working from a rough sketch he had made before leaving San Francisco and from maps and photographs, he was able to submit in the firm's name his drawing and report by March 31.[4] The report demonstrated a thoroughness and foresight in providing for the city's expansion and for the citizens' needs that entitle Olmsted to be regarded as a pioneer city planner; and it applied for the first time his principles of landscape architecture to a rural park in a climate not adapted to the English landscape style.

Predicting that San Francisco was destined to evolve from a provincial town dependent on the local trade of the Pacific slope into a great city with world-wide trade relations, Olmsted recommended that its park be laid out not with reference to the needs of its present population or even of the next generation but of several millions of people.[5] Yet its construction should not be delayed: already an almost treeless cemetery, scourged by winds and designed only for the convenience of funerals, was thronged on pleasant holidays with picnickers; and San Francisco, with its restless and impermanent population, especially needed a park as a stable attraction and source of pride to its citizens.

> To offer inducements to men of wealth to remain, and to all citizens to pursue commerce less constantly, to acquire habits of living healthily and happily from day to day, and of regarding San Francisco as their home for life, . . . must be a primary purpose of all true municipal economy, and no

pleasure ground can be adequate to the requirements of the city, the design of which is not, to a considerable degree, controlled by this purpose.[6]

Neither turf nor shade trees, elements essential to the landscape effects of eastern and English parks, could be counted on to flourish on San Francisco's sand hills, but the city was full of pretty little gardens. This fact suggested to Olmsted that the ornamental parts of the pleasure ground should be compact, protected from the cold winds and fogs that flowed upon the city, and rich in detail.[7]

It should also be easy of access and equipped with sheltered resting places and an extensive system of drives and walks. Ground of no great value should be taken, but the entrance to the park should not be far from the part of town already build up and the park should extend in the direction of the city's probable growth. In an expanding city ill supplied with water, built up with frame structures, and periodically leveled by fires, the park should also form a firebreak; yet it should not obstruct communication or disturb existing sewers, street grades, water mains, and other services.[8]

To accommodate these special requirements, Olmsted proposed a brilliantly imaginative arrangement: an excavation at least twenty feet deep, two hundred eighty feet wide at the top, and one hundred fifty-eight wide at the bottom, running across the sea wind from southwest to northeast along Van Ness Avenue from the water's edge to Eddy Street. Walks and roadways for pleasure driving were to be made along its sheltered bed, and its banks were to be turfed and planted with shrubs and topped by hardy evergreens. Bridges were to carry the city streets across it at convenient intervals, and hydrants were to be set on the edges of the streets above and the roadways below for watering turf and keeping down dust.[9]

The promenade was to terminate at its inland end close to the Mission on Market Street, where some acres of low level ground afforded space for play-and-parade ground that might accommodate several thousand persons without danger of damage to plantations and art objects. This level space was to be overlooked from the west by a grand terrace, either elaborately architectural and decked with formal gardens or more thriftily finished with turf banks and wooden or iron railings, which was to accommodate carriages and pedestrians on different levels and to be furnished with stands for music, fireworks, and public speaking facing the parade ground.[10]

Beyond the terrace to the west, where the ground became steep and hilly, Olmsted planned a garden in a nook, open to the southwest, where a sturdy growth of shrubs and flowers even in the dry season indicated a moist and fertile soil. A grove of trees was to clothe the higher ground near the terrace, the intermediate slope was to be laid out with walks and planted closely with shrubs and vines, and the lower level was to be maintained as a lawn sloping down to a still pool, behind which should be a fine display of foliage.[11]

In addition to this connected series of grounds, which could be developed piece by piece over a number of years, Olmsted proposed a sort of sea gate to the city, suitable for brief ceremonies, in a comparatively sheltered place on the east side of the ridge of Point San Jose and a larger parade ground well beyond the current city limits.[12]

This comprehensive and practicable plan was vigorously supported by some on the basis of the city's need but vigorously opposed by others on the basis of expense.[13] Economy won a Pyrrhic victory: forty years later, along the line of Van Ness Avenue, which Olmsted had designated for the grand promenade-firebreak, the closely built city blocks were dynamited as a last desperate resort to stop the ruinous blaze that followed the earthquake of 1906.

Olmsted's report on the proposed improvement of the College of California's property at Berkeley was not only a plan for the campus itself but also his first effort to plan a community on an unoccupied site, to create a town where none had before existed.[14]

The college was the raison d'être of the community; the kind of community desired was one in which college life could be best pursued. Neither distractingly urban nor rustically isolated, it was to be composed of pleasant homes around the academic nucleus so that "scholars, at least during the period of life in which character is most easily moulded, should be surrounded by manifestations of re-fined domestic life, these being unquestionably the ripest and best fruits of civilization." Homes such as these would be, he foresaw, increasingly in demand around San Francisco, where many men would become wealthy and would re-quire pleasant suburban residences within easy reach of their businesses in the city.[15]

The Berkeley property was unsurpassed in the region for climate, soil, ex-posure, water, and views. How was it to be adapted to the requirements of such homes? What were their requirements? Struggling with the complexity of his ideas, Olmsted evolved a somewhat clumsy formula:

> The relative importance of the different provisions for human comfort that go to make up a residence is proportionate to the degree in which, ul-timately, the health of the inmates is likely to be favorably influenced by each, whether through the facility it offers to the cheerful occupation of time and a healthful exercise of the faculties, or through any more direct and constant action.

Specifically, the first requirement was shelter. Next came two that were fre-quently neglected even in the homes of the wealthy: fresh air and sunshine. Attractive outdoor apartments Olmsted thought indispensable to good health and good humor; conversely, the lack of them led, he believed, to "languor, dullness of perception, nervous debility or distinct nervous diseases."[16]

Important, too, were those services, usually unavailable in the country, furnished by grocers, teachers, workmen, and other persons outside the house-

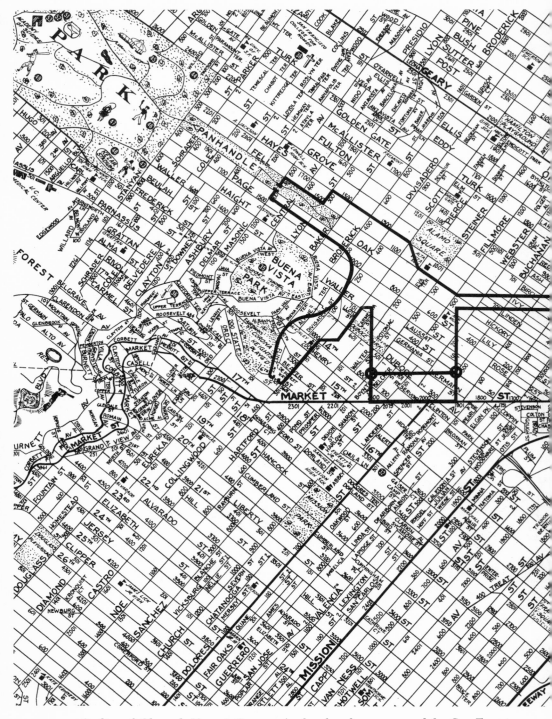

Outline of Olmsted, Vaux & Company's plan for pleasure ground for San Francisco, superimposed on modern street map. *Inset*: design showing sunken promenade, parade ground, terrace, and ways.

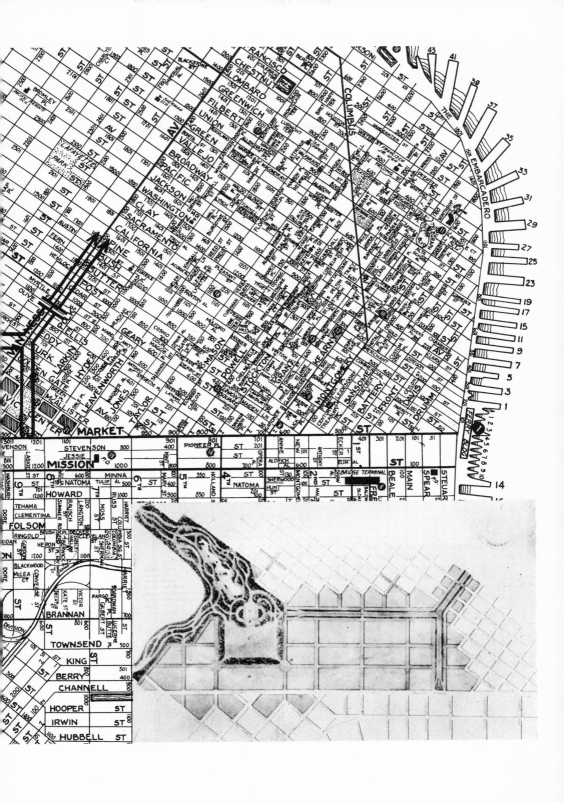

hold. Another necessity was good roads and walks, free from dirt, attractively bordered, and not so rough or so steep or so exposed to sun and wind as to discourage travel. They should open frequently upon pleasant scenes and have for objectives points commanding fine views so that women and children would be induced to leave their houses and gather there with their friends and benefit both by exercise and society.[17]

It was the custom, fixed by laziness, incompetence, and lack of imagination, to make the street plans of the new towns of the West on a gridiron pattern, regardless of whether such an arrangement was topographically convenient or socially serviceable. Olmsted planned the Berkeley streets otherwise. Being in a residential neighborhood, they were designed to discourage all commerce but that serving the neighborhood. Tradesmen and others having business on the other side of it would save time by going around instead of traversing the winding roads laid out to afford moderately direct routes only within it and to secure to property owners the best landscape effects from the largest number of viewpoints.[18]

While interesting views from individual houses were desirable, they were not so desirable that privacy should be sacrificed to them. The grounds about the house clearly should be private to it, and the distinction should be maintained between the foreground about the house and the middle ground of the neighborhood. This advice was inconsistent with the principle of "appropriation of ground" held by some landscape writers, but Olmsted explained with a touch of severity "that a man is going wrongly to work to make a home for himself when he begins by studying how he can make that appear to be a part of his home which is not so."[19] The estate was to be divided into lots of from one to five acres, each lot owner was to plant a proper foreground of trees and shrubs about his home, and these bodies of rich and well-tended foliage would from all points in the vicinity form a part of an artistic middle distance and would so frame the distant prospect that a strong graduation of aerial perspective would occur and the eye would rest on hills beautiful in both form and color under all atmospheric conditions.[20]

The main feature of the campus itself, which lay on the slope between two hills, was to be an artificial plateau at the head of the dell, with an unrestricted view westward over the ocean. Like the proposed terrace for the San Francisco park, it could have an architectural finish or a plain and economical one to be elaborated later.[21]

Two buildings—one for library, records, and scientific collection, the other for assembly hall and classrooms—were to be placed on the terrace, and two broad walks, between the lines of a formal avenue, were to lead from it to the head of the dell. Olmsted urged erecting not large dormitories for the students but houses looking like homes and consisting of drawing room, dining room, and small private rooms to accommodate twenty to forty students. In keeping with the atmosphere of scholarly and domestic quiet that he intended for the neighborhood, he advised that each college building be a detached structure, designed by itself and for its own exclusive purpose, and he proposed an informal rather than a symmetrical arrangement, both because it would harmonize with the character of the district and because it would more readily allow any modifications of the general plan of building that might later be found desirable.[22]

At the request of Billings the report was printed,[23] but little further action was taken on it. Water in iron pipes was introduced, and one or two houses went up on the property;[24] money was tight, however, and sales were few, and the college, far from being able to build, had to liquidate. In May 1870, the trustees voted to transfer all their assets to the University of California in return for the payment of the college's debts.[25] Olmsted's fee of two thousand dollars gold, with interest of one percent a month, was then paid,[26] but his plan was not carried out. The idea of selling lots on the college property was abandoned and the land devoted to college purposes; the gardener employed to lay out the campus departed from Olmsted's plan, and the plan itself disappeared by the end of 1872.[27]

Olmsted's proposal to replace the usual dormitories with homelike residential buildings was no caprice. It was a thought he developed more fully in his report, dated September 1866, to the trustees of Massachusetts Agricultural College.[28] This was one of the land-grant colleges organized under the Morrill Act of 1862, which provided that every state and territory should be granted thirty thousand acres of public lands for each of its senators and representatives, the proceeds of the sale of the land to be applied to colleges for mechanical and agricultural education. This vast proposed extension of the educational equipment of the country raised a number of questions. Should new colleges be founded or agricultural chairs endowed in old ones? If new colleges were to be founded, how were they to differ from established liberal arts colleges and professional schools? How were they to be organized, what should their curriculums include, what kind of instruction should be given, what degree of uniformity should prevail among them? These and related questions were being handled on an individual basis, with little comparison of views among educators and little public discussion. Each college was struggling into being in its own way, as best it could.[29]

The Massachusetts Agricultural College was no exception. The dispute whether to establish a new school or endow an old school was compromised: a new college was founded and received one-tenth of the proceeds of the sale of Massachusetts's share of public lands for its farm; the income from two-thirds of the remaining nine-tenths was earmarked for its endowment, and that from the other one-third was assigned to Massachusetts Institute of Technology. In sharp competition with several other towns, Amherst offered to contribute seventy-five thousand dollars to the college if it would build there and was selected as the site by the board of trustees.[30] The placement of the college's main building, an impressive stone affair designed for a site on the east side of the property by Vaux and the Boston architect Joseph R. Richards, was the next subject for disagreement. The building committee, contrary to the professional advice of Vaux

309

and Richards and to the common sense of the college president, Henry F. French, decided to place the building in the middle of the farm. The problem then arose of laying out an approach road to it. It was at this point that Olmsted was consulted.[31]

As adviser to the *Nation*, Olmsted had already given much thought to the problems of the new colleges. Charles Eliot, influenced by Germany's experience with agricultural schools, expressed the view in the magazine that land-grant money should be used to found chairs at already established institutions.[32] Olmsted disagreed with Eliot, doubting that an appropriate education for men who were to be engaged in nonprofessional, nonscholarly pursuits could be associated with a university. To draw a line between head-workers and hand-workers in the same school would go far to establish an undemocratic habit of mind, a habit that Clarence King and James Gardiner informed him already existed at Yale, where students of the liberal arts college did all they could to establish a social distinction favorable to themselves between it and the scientific school.[33]

The military training of civilians, required by the Morrill Act in the new colleges, was another subject on which Olmsted had done considerable thinking. He had been painfully impressed during the war by the widespread and disastrous ignorance of the volunteer officers of their administrative, or housekeeping, functions—especially the securing of food and shelter and sanitation for their men—and he had roughed out a scheme whereby carefully selected civilians should get some military education in special schools. When Henry Lee, Jr., of Boston, formerly a colonel of volunteers, criticized in the *Nation* the monastic seclusion of the training of professional officers at West Point, Olmsted wrote him a long letter expounding his plan for preparing civilians to become capable officers. He described a system for selecting students and for setting up polytechnical schools, opposite numbers to the agricultural schools, where young men would receive an education less exclusively military than that at West Point, be fitted as engineers, draughtsmen, architects, and the like, and be trained as well in campaigning and the administrative duties of officers.[34]

Thus when the invitation came to advise the trustees of Massachusetts Agricultural College, Olmsted was not dealing with an unfamiliar subject. He was prepared to give them not just a sketch of a roadway but an analysis of the philosophy that should govern the formation of the college and a method of training that would accord with the philosophy.

He went to Amherst May 23, 1866, stopping for a short visit with his father on the way,[35] and spent two days inspecting the college farm, which included three hundred ten acres and five sets of buildings. He attended a meeting of the building committee, which was beginning to have qualms, not about the placement of its grand edifice, but about its cost, which threatened to exceed the assigned fund. Olmsted, who was struck by the inappropriateness of such a building for an agricultural college, made an alternate proposal which the committee asked him to expand in his report. Calling it *A Few Things To Be*

Thought Of before Proceeding To Plan Buildings for the National Agricultural Colleges, he presented it a month later.[36] Typically, he began with certain basic considerations, completely scrapped the plan put forward by the trustees, and proposed one in keeping with fundamentals as he saw them.

First, he rejected the big building as unfit for the requirements of a college still undefined in character; something more flexible and easily modified was called for. Besides, a tall, massive building, however suitable to a city where ground rents were high, was unnecessary and inappropriate in open farming country. Olmsted suggested instead four small two-story buildings, each adapted to a special use. The first should have two lecture rooms and two private rooms for the use of the professors on each floor. The second, for scientific instruction, should have a chemistry laboratory and a lecture room on the ground floor and a museum on the second. The third should have a reading room for students on the first floor and a library above. The fourth was to contain a gymnasium and drill room with armory, washroom, and closets downstairs and a general assembly hall, offices, and boardroom upstairs.[37]

Discussing the ends that the college should promote, Olmsted reasoned that there were in the United States two opposing theories of the best means toward social progress. Both recognized the advantage of division of labor and of special training for special work. One attempted to secure not only the special training of each class in the occupation assigned to it but also distinctions of general condition and habits that did not necessarily follow from the occupation. The other regarded artificial distinctions between different classes of society, however distinct their work might be, as undesirable. The former was the policy of the late slave states; the latter was the drift of the New England states, where farmers and workmen, professional men, and merchants far more frequently than in the South wore similar clothes, read similar books and papers, had similar amusements, and lived in similar houses. A law providing for institutions to educate young men for farming, to be called "colleges" like those educating young men for the learned professions, clearly proceeded from the conviction that differences between social classes, not based on occupational necessity, were undesirable. This conviction ought to be consulted in all plans for the college, including the ground plan.

The ground plan thus ought to do more than provide convenient arrangements for instruction and demonstrations in farming; it ought also to influence the habits and inclinations of the students and to help equip them for the exercise of their rights and duties as citizens and householders. If farmers were to enjoy the same intellectual pleasures and have the same civic responsibilities as lawyers, ministers, and other professional men, they should be educated in many common and familiar things not peculiar to farming. Olmsted's question was: what can be done in the ground plan to forward this intention?[38]

If the much deplored tendency of young people to leave the farms for the cities was to be halted, their natural and healthy disposition to seek contrast and relaxation from the routine of farm labor had to be accommodated. The comparative isolation of farm homes or their grouping in small settlements naturally precluded them from the social pleasures open to residents of more densely populated neighborhoods. An agricultural college should furnish examples for mitigating the special disadvantage of farm life, its social seclusion. Its ground plan should provide not only for those educational requirements related to the special calling of a farmer but for those related to the social affairs of rural households and communities. Giving the educational requirements priority, Olmsted described how he would lay out the college land.[39]

His plan did not disturb the existing arrangement of the land on each side of the main road, which was already occupied by farmhouses and gardens. He suggested that the new college buildings be placed near the road at a point on the farm from which there was the easiest access to neighboring homes, meeting houses, post office, and railway station. The road itself took a graceful course and was planted with shade trees. The whole situation, already pleasing, could be improved, and the college buildings could be so arranged as to carry out the idea and the ideal of a rural neighborhood. It was not necessary that each college building represent a family house but only that they should be related to each other and to the highway in a way appropriate to the buildings of a rural community. Library, science building, chapel, classrooms, should be set like the public buildings of a village along the highway, in the midst of trees and shrubbery and along good walks. The drill ground, for the military training required by the Morrill Act, should be open to the public road and tree-bordered, and the assembly hall and drill room should open upon it, just as a country town hall or court house opens on the village green.

The things desirable in farm households were to be demonstrated in the president's and farm superintendent's houses. With their grounds, they were to be models of their kind, avoiding not only the farmer's too frequent disregard of taste and comfort but also displays of rural luxury, like complicated grounds and ornamental constructions, which usually degenerated into offensive shabbiness. Olmsted recommended for the students a number of homelike buildings, each accommodating twenty to thirty men. Sites should be selected at the beginning, and the buildings constructed as required. Each should have a small lawn, a few domestic additions such as birdhouses, croquet green, hedges, and icehouses; and inside perhaps a pet bird, inexpensive musical instruments, and a Wardian case full of plants—all real additions to the students' health and comfort and at the same time aids to their *"education in the art of making a farmer's home cheerful and attractive."*[40]

Having rejected throughout his report both the single large building and its proposed site, Olmsted closed with a brief description of the way in which, should the trustees persist in their original intention, he would modify his suggestions. But he warned: "It will be understood that I should regard these changes in the plan I have recommended as extremely undesirable."[41]

President French was delighted with Olmsted's report, but D. Waldo Lincoln, an important trustee and president of the Boston and Albany Railroad, was displeased that the landscape architect had not given the advice asked of him, taken his fee, and gone home. He wrote Olmsted asking for a plan of a road around the building site selected by the trustees, and Olmsted sent him one, pointing out again that the architects had not designed the building for that site and did not approve of placing it there.[42]

At this point the college's affairs were further confused when some reluctant taxpayers of Amherst obtained an injunction preventing the town from contributing the money it had pledged. Sam Bowles, a keenly interested observer, wrote in the *Republican* that the consequent delay was no loss, since no ground plan had yet been accepted and the trustees were at loggerheads not only over the building site but over the objects of the institution. The whole matter ought to be reconsidered from the beginning, and Olmsted's report would make a good starting point out of the confusion.[43]

Shortly before the trustees' quarterly meeting of August 1, 1866, French, still hoping that the building committee would accept Olmsted's plan, asked him for a rough sketch of a forty-building village.[44] The trustees, however, stung by an editorial in the *Boston Advertiser* criticizing their persistent rejection of expert advice, showed no disposition to consider Olmsted's plan. Passing a resolution beginning, "As there is nothing in the report of Mr. Olmsted to warrant the trustees in undoing or changing the action taken in regard to the general location of the collegiate building . . . ," they voted again to build in the middle of the farm.[45] French, thoroughly chagrined, apologized to Olmsted for their discourtesy, and a nonconforming member of the building committee, William B. Washburn, resigned.[46] Finally convinced that his frustration was irremediable, French himself resigned toward the end of September.[47] The *Nation*, under the caption "How Not To Establish an Agricultural College," recapitulated the institution's sorry history from its beginning four years before—years during which the trustees had bought a farm beyond their means, entered into an entangling alliance with the town of Amherst, spurned the best professional advice available on the arrangement of buildings and fields, resolved to erect an unsuitable edifice of which the estimated cost was larger than the entire building fund, forced the resignation of French, the only man who had advanced their business, and failed to mature a plan of instruction, appoint a single teacher, enroll a single student, or conduct a single agricultural experiment.[48]

Although the trustees scorned the report for which they had to pay Olmsted five hundred fifty dollars, the report made, when printed, a good impression in other quarters. Norton and Godkin both wanted to publish something about it and about the Berkeley and San Francisco pamphlets. Olmsted thought the reports had aroused too little general attention for any benefit to come of discussing them publicly; so both the *Nation* and the *North American Review* confined themselves to short favorable comments on the agricultural college report.[49] Several agricultural journals and daily papers commended it, and it was enthusiastically endorsed by proponents of independent land-grant colleges.[50] Olmsted's California friend, Brewer, by then professor of agriculture at Yale's Sheffield Scientific School, sustained Olmsted's position by asserting that costly buildings were a major cause of the failures of colleges—and made, incidentally, the pregnant suggestion that the Australian eucalyptus might grow well in the proposed San Francisco park.[51] Finally convinced, at least partially, the trustees of Massachusetts Agricultural College abandoned their massive building in favor of several small ones, although they persisted in ignoring Olmsted's advice as to both design and placement.[52] Several years later, French wrote Olmsted that the college had everything "but taste and agriculture" and that he would rather have failed with Olmsted than have built up a sham.[53]

The report made an impression, too, on the trustees of the proposed Maine Agricultural College, and in November 1866, Olmsted was invited to go to Orono, on the Penobscot River, and advise on laying out the college property.[54] The bill establishing the institution was the work of Phineas Barnes, of Portland, later its first president, a farmer and writer on agricultural matters who was familiar with the Nation's and Olmsted's contributions.[55] Barnes's bill specified not only that the students should receive industrial, agricultural, and military training but that the college should try to inculcate in them respect for morality and justice, sacred regard for truth, love of country and humanity, sobriety, industry, frugality, chastity, moderation, temperance, and "all the other virtues which are the ornaments of human society" and further recited that "to secure the best personal improvement of the students, the trustees shall provide, as fully as may be practicable, that the internal organization of the college shall be on the plan of one or more well-regulated households and families, so that the students may be brought into relations of domestic intimacy and confidence with their teachers."[56]

Olmsted agreed to look at the property and on the twenty-first of December 1866 arrived at Orono. With several of the trustees he tramped the snow-covered fields and woods of the college farm and suggested the main features of a plan for buildings and improvements. In another month he presented, for the firm, his formal report.[57] It included features familiar from the Massachusetts report: notably, separate buildings for specific purposes; houses for students, each accommodating from twenty to forty boys, simulating as far as possible the conditions of "healthy, cheerful, convenient family homes"; model domestic grounds around each; and a village-like arrangement of buildings tending to cultivate the tastes and form the habits of students under conditions roughly similar to the probable ones of their later life. In addition, he elaborated on the quasi-military plan he had suggested to Henry Lee, Jr. The students should be formed into companies of forty, with elected officers. A company fund should be established, and each company should have its own commissary officer, commissary storeroom and office, kitchen, and mess room. Each student in turn should perform for his company the duties of commissary officer, and none should be graduated with honor who could not undertake himself and instruct others in the duties of a regimental commissary officer. There was no doubt that, in the recent war, many men in the volunteer regiments had died because of the "imperfect provision for maintaining them in health and vigor which was at that time universal."[58] If Olmsted could prevent it, the country would not again be caught with a volunteer army in which the mass of officers were ignorant of their rudimentary housekeeping duties.

Olmsted's modest fee of one hundred ninety-six dollars was promptly paid— and a new board of trustees, elected in April 1867, decided that the plan laid too much emphasis on the military and followed his recommendations neither as to military organization nor as to buildings.[59]

These four reports, disparate though they were, had more in common than their rejection. Typical of each were the broad strokes of creative imagination like the sunken promenade and the grand terraces; the care that each feature of a plan serve a specific purpose, whether solitary or social, and the consequent exclusion of anything arbitrary, ambiguous, or superfluous; the concentration on general effect and the subordination to it of carefully worked-out details; and the insistence on cheerfulness and grace, no less than suitability, in plantations and architectural features.

The plans are alike, further, in their emphasis on appropriateness and adaptability. Since the English style of landscape design could not, in Olmsted's opinion, successfully be applied in San Francisco's climate, a style that could be had to be devised. Because a barrack-like dormitory would be out of keeping with a suburban neighborhood, homelike buildings for students were recommended. A heavy stone edifice, proper to a crowded city, was inappropriate both to the grounds and the aims of an agricultural college; so a village-like group of small buildings was suggested instead.

Each plan, moreover, began not where the client ordered but at the beginning, with an analysis of the ends it was to serve and with consideration of the relevant surrounding circumstances—climate, topography, probable population increase, kind of use, and so forth—and of the means in the circumstances best adapted to meet the ends. Only after laying his groundwork thus thoroughly did Olmsted make specific recommendations. If some of them now seem quaint, it is because we can look back on the developments of an era he was trying to foresee. But it is not the quaintness, which in any case derives largely from the nineteenth-century phraseology, it is the prophetic foreshadowing of principles we consider modern that strikes today's reader of these reports.

Morality, good health, good humor, well-ordered and civilized domestic life —these are the notes Olmsted harped on, and these are the real ends of each plan. Beauty, convenience, and appropriateness in landscape and architectural

315

arrangements were not ends in themselves but devices to secure moral aims. Implicit in each report was Olmsted's basic belief that man was a malleable creature who, by the favorable alteration of his surroundings, could himself be favorably changed. Implicit, too, was his view of the profession and the art of landscape architecture, a view fundamental and Ruskinian: it was not a means of self-expression; it was a means of manipulating human surroundings to promote human betterment, both physical and spiritual. Its purpose was no less moral for being practical. Indeed, to Olmsted the moral and the practical were the same: anything not moral was simply not practical.

XXVII
NEW PARKS, NEW SUBURBS
1868–1872

NOTHING in Olmsted's correspondence suggests that such failures of influence made him lose heart or doubt the eventual effectiveness of his work. A realist, he never expected unqualified success. An optimist, he viewed even partial success as a limited conquest for his ideas. A believer in progress, he could not doubt that as civilization evolved, there would also evolve a social climate favorable to the working and the ultimate triumph of his influence.

He had some reason to believe that such a climate—one of collective concern for the moral and physical welfare of all the members of the American community—was developing. A symptom of it had been the formation of the American Social Science Association, modeled after an English prototype, in the fall of 1865, "to guide the public mind to the best practical means of promoting"—among other things—"the Advancement of Education, the Prevention and Repression of Crime and the furtherance of Public Morality" and "to give attention to pauperism and the topics related thereto, including the responsibility of the well-endowed and successful, the wise and educated, the honest and respectable, for the failure of others."[1] It was no irrelevance that Olmsted early became an officer of this society.

Another symptom was the spread of the idea, especially among the well endowed and wise, that a city not only made a good financial investment in creating a rural park but had a duty to create one, since "a beautiful and healthful pleasure ground . . . must soon prove as conspicuous for its moral as for its material effects . . ." and because "if we seek to wean [others] from debasing pursuits and brutalizing pleasures, we can only hope to do so by opening freely to them new sources of rational enjoyment."[2]

By the end of 1869 city officials and civic leaders not only in Brooklyn and New York and San Francisco but also in Baltimore, Boston, Buffalo, Philadelphia, Washington, Cleveland, Cincinnati, Hartford, Chicago, Newark, New Britain, Albany, and Providence had made moves toward creating new rural parks. To be sure, the motives inspiring action in behalf of parks were mixed. Philadelphia, for instance, considered Fairmont Park and its proposed extensions across and up the Schuylkill River and along Wissahickon Creek primarily as a protection to the city's water supply;[3] and Paul Cornell, the Chicago lawyer who owned large tracts of South Side real estate and worked assiduously for the passage of the South Park bill,[4] could not have been indifferent to the fact that a park in the neighborhood would enhance the value of his own holdings. Still, it would appear that an enlightened concern for the public well-being was one motive, among others not at all altruistic, that led prominent citizens like Cornell to press for parks and that led city after city to act to secure them.

Olmsted, trying some years later to explain the accelerating strength of the American park movement at this time, thought he detected another, more basic, motive: society's instinct of self-preservation.

> Parks have plainly not come as the direct result of any of the great inventions or discoveries of the century. They are not, with us, simply an improvement on what we had before, growing out of a general advance of the arts applicable to them. It is not evident that the movement was taken up in any country from any other, however it may have been influenced or accelerated. It did not run like a fashion. It would seem rather to have been a common, spontaneous movement of that sort which we conveniently refer to the "Genius of Civilization." . . .
>
> Why this great development of interest in natural landscape and all that pertains to it; to the art of it and the literature of it?

The final answer, he thought, lay in the first and strongest of instincts: "Considering that it has occurred simultaneously with a great enlargement of towns and development of urban habits, is it not reasonable to regard it as a self-preserving instinct of civilization?"[5]

Olmsted did not hate cities or think them fatal to civilization; he hated barbarism. It was principally in cities and well-regulated suburbs, he recognized, that many of the graces of civilization could be enjoyed: effective and effortless sanitary arrangements; goods and physical comforts, obtainable in the country only by hard work; services to match every need; and leisure, society, recreation, and intellectual pleasures. But cities, growing ever larger, becoming ever more crowded, were also hotbeds of misery, vice, crime, and disease. Moreover they tended, Olmsted believed, to breed among their inhabitants not only physical ills but a callous habit of mind. One could not walk down a crowded street without constantly having to watch, to foresee, and to guard against the movements of others. "This involves a consideration of their intentions, a calculation of their strength and weakness, which is not so much for their benefit as our own. Our minds are thus brought into close dealing with other minds without any friendly flowing toward them." City dwellers, every day of their lives, "have seen thousands of their fellow-men, have met them face to face, and yet have had no experience of anything in common with them."[6] This lack of communicativeness, as he had earlier called it, was to Olmsted the very essence of barbarism.

A park had a powerful countervailing influence. It not only helped to offset the physical ill effects of the city's congestion, hurry, and noise; it not only exerted on the minds of individual beholders a soothing and edifying effect; it also gave to people of all classes the opportunity to meet and mingle in casual

318

friendliness, to enjoy the same circumstances side by side, yet independently, and to come together "with a common purpose, not at all intellectual, competitive with none, disposing to jealousy and spiritual or intellectual pride toward none, each individual adding by his mere presence to the pleasure of all others, all helping to the greater happiness of each."[7] Parks stimulated, he thought, that sense of communicativeness that was the intrinsic quality of civilization; and American society, in an instinctive effort of self-preservation, was cultivating in its urban soil their civilizing influence to counteract the barbarizing tendencies indigenous to the same soil.

Hartford had begun work on Bushnell Park, named for Horace Bushnell, the clergyman who had inspired it, not long after New York had begun Central Park. In 1866 Baltimore opened Druid Hill Park; and the same year William Bross, William Dorsheimer, and General Montgomery Meigs first approached Olmsted, Vaux & Company on the subject of rural parks for Chicago, Buffalo, and the District of Columbia.[8] In 1867 the partners were consulted for the first time about Philadelphia's Fairmont Park, and they submitted reports for new parks in New Britain, Connecticut, and Newark.[9] The next year they made recommendations for a park to a group of Albany citizens, in 1869 they were recommended to lay out land appropriated for a maritime park in Providence,[10] and they were following the course of Boston's park agitation.[11]

They were not uniformly successful during these years in their park recommendations. Albany's commissioners selected another design in preference to theirs.[12] The New Jersey Legislature, frightened by the prospect of paying one million dollars, the amount the partners estimated would be required to take and improve the land desired for Newark's park, refused to act, and economy chalked up another Pyrrhic victory: not quite thirty years later, two-and-a-half times that amount was needed to create the much smaller Branch Brook Park on the same site.[13] New Britain's town meeting was bolder than the New Jersey Legislature: in 1869 it voted to purchase land about the reservoir on Walnut Hill, which had been bought for a park in 1856 by a group of private citizens, and to add to it, as Olmsted and Vaux advised, the seventy-five acres of meadow land at the foot of the hill.[14]

Philadelphia, having consulted Olmsted, Vaux & Company and Robert Morris Copeland, of Boston, from time to time for several years, finally in 1871 selected a general plan for the improvement and extension of Fairmont Park offered by the engineer H. J. Schwarzmann in preference to "a very beautiful design for study, prepared by professional landscape artists, of well known skill and large experience."[15] Providence did not employ the partnership on its seaside park; and the District of Columbia plan came, for the time, to nothing.

Before starting, in the late 1860s and 1870s, the series of major projects— notably the Chicago, Buffalo, Boston, and Montreal parks and the Riverside suburban development near Chicago—that made Olmsted, Vaux & Company the most prominent firm of landscape architects in the country, the partners were building a diversified practice; and Olmsted, who when he returned east in 1865 had feared for his personal reputation, was receiving convincing evidence that it was unimpaired.

Within the first three years after his return he was offered a number of opportunities to go into several different kinds of endeavor: Waring wanted him connected, for the prestige of his name, with his earth-closet company; Robert Dale Owen and his associates offered him ten thousand dollars a year to head a photosculpture company in which they were interested; Henry Janin, a reputable mining engineer, proposed forming a permanent connection with him if he would interest eastern capital in the Keystone gold mine—a proposal singularly devoid of temptation to the exmanager of the Mariposa Estate.[16] He was asked if he would accept the presidency of Iowa's agricultural college; he was mentioned as a candidate for the presidency of the College of California; and Amherst conferred an honorary M.A. on him.*[17] Downing's widow, who had married Judge John J. Monell, asked him to edit a new edition of Downing's *Cottage Residences*; Charles Scribner tried to persuade him to prepare a book on agriculture; and the *Watchman and Reflector* wanted him to contribute articles on practical subjects related to farming—all requests on which Olmsted did not act, whether from lack of time or interest.[18]

Dozens of persons, many of them unknown to him, appealed for loans, jobs, information, advice he was well qualified to give (how obtain an education in landscape architecture?), and advice he could hardly have been less qualified to offer (how overcome a craving for strong drink?). He was invited to join half a dozen social clubs and professional associations, and he accepted an honorary membership in the American Institute of Architects and a directorship in the American Social Science Association.[19] He was called on for help in winding up the affairs of the Sanitary Commission, the expiration of which was symbolically pointed up by the sinking of the commission's one-time headquarters boat, the *Wilson Small*, in Chesapeake Bay in August 1867.[20] He was appointed to select a design for a memorial to Professor Bache, who had died in 1867, and in the course of doing so, sometime in 1868 consulted, apparently for the first time, the Staten Island neighbor who was to become one of his best friends and most congenial architectural collaborators, Henry Hobson Richardson.[21] He continued to carry large responsibility for the *Nation*, helped raise money to make possible the distribution of free copies to Congress and western newspapers, and in 1870 persuasively influenced its editor against giving up the magazine to accept a Harvard professorship.[22]

Olmsted was drawn, too, into various undertakings of the sort that usually depend for their success on the volunteer work of public-spirited people: he was head of a committee in charge of exhibits for the Paris Exposition of 1867;[23] he worked throughout 1867 on the Southern Famine Relief Commission;[24] and he helped Louisa Lee Schuyler with her plans for reorganizing charitable work,[25]

*Harvard had given him one in 1864 (JO to O, 24 July 1864).

thus becoming associated in a minor role with the placement of philanthropy on a professional basis.

His professional work can scarcely have left him much time for these various incidental interests. Central and Prospect parks, and the smaller New York and Brooklyn parks and squares that were also assigned to the care of Olmsted, Vaux & Company, formed the backbone of the firm's business, but they had a variety of other jobs. In March 1866, Edward M. Gallaudet, recalling to Olmsted their childhood friendship, employed the firm to take charge of improving the grounds of the National Deaf Mute Institute in Washington. Knapp, who had started a boys' school at Eagleswood, New Jersey, at which Olmsted's stepson John was a pupil, asked Olmsted to advise him about the property and the curriculum during the summer.[26] Howard Potter, planning to start a cottage suburb at Long Branch, New Jersey, engaged the partnership to divide the hundred fifty-acre tract into building lots and seaside common and to lay out his grounds there.[27] Olmsted was asked in behalf of the Pennsylvania agricultural college to state the firm's terms, but the warning that the trustees were a group of "obstructive clodhoppers" may well have deterred him from visiting.[28] Abby Woolsey solicited his advice about the buildings for the new normal school for Negroes at Hampton, Virginia—advice that when furnished was completely ignored[29]—and Amherst consulted him about the placement of its new Walker Hall.[30] During the summer of 1867 Olmsted made several trips to Ithaca, New York, to study an arrangement for the grounds and building of the new Cornell University. The president, Andrew D. White, liked his ground plan but said that the college could not accept his advice to replace its big building with smaller ones because it had to open in October 1868 and time was lacking to reconsider its architectural plans. A cordial relationship, however, sprang up between the organizers of the college and Olmsted, and he continued to consult with them about grounds, buildings, and academic matters. In 1873, when allegations of fraud in connection with the sale of the college's land grant were made against Ezra Cornell, Olmsted became for a short time a trustee of the college, principally to indicate his confidence in it.[31]

While the great parks the firm was to undertake had to wait on legislative action and popular votes, suburban villages launched by private capital were not so hampered. Although the most prominent characteristic of contemporary civilization was, Olmsted remarked, "the strong tendency of people to flock together in great towns," by the late 1860s "a counter-tide of migration, especially affecting the more intelligent and more fortunate classes, although yet of but moderate strength, is clearly perceptible, and almost equally so in Paris, London, Vienna, Berlin, New York, Boston and Philadelphia."[32]

American suburbs were, generally speaking, of two kinds: there were old and distinct settlements within comfortable commuting distance of cities, like the Staten Island towns, to which people whose business was in the city migrated for the advantages they offered; and there were city outskirts, often pushing along the old country roads into the surrounding country over which the gridiron pattern of the city streets was being projected. In the first instance the suburb, already established, gradually adapted itself to its new role in relation to the city; in the second, it was a scarcely planned extension of the city, destined to lose its rural or suburban character as population increased and the city overflowed it and the country beyond. Only rarely was a suburb placed upon unoccupied land at a convenient distance from a city and designed specifically for suburban residence.

The first notable planned suburb had been Llewelyn Park, established in the decade before the Civil War on New Jersey's picturesque hills, where spacious house lots were laid out to face upon a common park with drives, ponds, streams, and woods.[33] Another one, abortive, had been Olmsted's own Berkeley Neighborhood. And in Chicago a land company with a speculative eye on the suburban movement, having purchased a sixteen-hundred-acre tract along the Des Plaines River nine miles west of the center of town, asked Olmsted, Vaux & Company in 1868 to plan, fresh and entire, a residential suburb on the site.[34]

Olmsted received the invitation on his return early in August from a professional visit with Vaux to Vassar, where he had found "nothing but a miserable plan to be amended"[35]—a reflection of his disapproval of a single huge collegiate building set down in the middle of the country. At just the same time, Dorsheimer asked him to visit Buffalo and select a park site.[36]

Olmsted stopped at Buffalo on the way to Chicago and spent the afternoon of Sunday, August 16, driving about with Dorsheimer. Two possible city sites with fine views, Olmsted warned, would be too costly to develop as rural parks, although they certainly should be secured for small ones. Continuing into the countryside north of town, they came to an elevation from which an extended view of the city could be had. Olmsted stopped the horses. "Here," he said after a moment's pause, "is your park, almost ready made."[37]

The site that had recommended itself to his expert eye was rolling farm land. Traversed by a creek, which could be easily dammed to form a large lake, and dotted with trees whose fine form and foliage indicated favorable conditions of soil and climate, it was occupied only by a scattering of buildings of small value. Close enough to the city to be easily accessible, it had not yet been laid out in streets, and the one thoroughfare crossing it could be slightly diverted to follow the line of a natural depression and so be removed from sight of the pleasure drives of the park.[38]

Promising to stop for a more thorough examination on the way home, Olmsted left the next morning for Chicago. Arriving on Tuesday, he drove over the site of the proposed suburb, for which the promoter, E. E. Childs, fancied the banal name of Riverside. However banal the name, the land itself was easily the most attractive for its intended use of any near the city.[39]

While flat, miry prairie exposed to the harsh lake winds stretched bleakly for miles about it, the region bordering the Des Plaines River offered a promising contrast. Uneven in surface, it had river banks and low elevations covered with groves of thrifty native trees. Its lower parts were underlaid by a porous subsoil and, unlike the prairie back from it, drained well and rapidly.[40]

Since city dwellers desirous of the rural advantages of suburban life were generally reluctant to accept rural inconveniences with it, Olmsted's first advice to the Riverside Improvement Company was to provide frostproof, rainproof roads and walks on the property and thorough drainage. Roads should be laid out in easy curves to take advantage of the natural features of the land, and the houses should be built at least a specified minimum distance from them and approached by private drives. Two aspects of suburban life were to be accommodated: privacy for the indoor and outdoor domestic life of individual families in the community was to be secured by the placement of houses, in relation to each other and to walks and roads, and by planting; and the community interest of the residents, "the grand fact . . . that they are Christians, loving one another, and not Pagans, fearing one another," was to be recognized in "the completeness, and choiceness and beauty of the means they possess of coming together, of being together, and especially of recreating together on common ground." Therefore, Olmsted advised appropriating some of the company's best property for unfenced public grounds, raising the height of the mill dam to make the river wider for boating and skating, and running a public drive and walk along its bank, which should be furnished with boat landings, terraces, and rustic pavilions. He also advised the construction of a fine wide highway, with separated wheelways, bridle paths, and walks, well shaded, well drained, and comfortably passable in all seasons, to connect the suburb with the city of which it was a dependency.[41]

Having made his promised return visit to Buffalo and advocated the park site before a meeting of interested citizens presided over by former President Millard Fillmore,[42] Olmsted returned to New York. On September 1 his preliminary report on Riverside was ready, and he drafted an agreement between the improvement company and Olmsted, Vaux & Company providing that the firm should make a topographical survey of the property, perform the duties of landscape architects and architects, and superintend the work for seven and one-half percent of the cost of the improvements. Since this was estimated at a million-and-a-half dollars, the firm stood to make a commission of $112,500 or its equivalent in lots.[43] The company, on its part, estimated that it would have two hundred twenty-five thousand salable front feet, costing an average of $1.52 to buy and five dollars to improve and selling for forty to sixty dollars. Even after designating more than three million dollars of its anticipated profits to cover unexpected contingencies, it still expected to pay out to the investors some million dollars over a five-year period.[44]

Olmsted, not dazzled by profits in prospect, wrote Vaux, who had gone to Europe for a tour of parks and gardens in September, that "Chicago is a big speculation."[45] After his second trip to the property in November, however, his tone became more optimistic: he found that all ground near Chicago that might come into competition with Riverside presented "disadvantages for rural residences of an almost hopeless character," and he liked Riverside itself better than he had on first sight.[46]

Riverside, however, soon ran into difficulties. Although surveying, grading, and planning had advanced well by the end of 1868, Childs defaulted the following year on his cash payments to the landscape architects, who had to take lots.[47] Worse than that, he completely negated their plan, physically and ideologically, by deciding to build on the central open space, keynote of the whole design. He was restrained only by their vehement protest backed by the threats to resign and to state their case in the Chicago papers.[48] "A rather kite-flying affair," Vaux disgustedly concluded of the undertaking.[49] "Just a speculator," Dr. John H. Rauch, Chicago's chief health officer, said loftily of the promoter.[50] By April 1870, Frederick C. Withers, Vaux's architectural partner who was assisting in the supervision, reported from Riverside that the work was in such bad shape that it was losing business for the firm,[51] and two months later the partners resigned.[52] Finally, the Chicago fire of October 9, 1871, abruptly and completely paralyzed the sale of suburban real estate, and the Riverside Improvement Company had to suspend payment.[53]

Although Olmsted and Vaux had ended their connection with the company, their Riverside troubles were not over; they still held lots. Six years later Olmsted's four, which he had taken in lieu of seven thousand dollars, were worth only half that, and in 1882 the best offer he could get for one of them was one thousand dollars cash.[54]

Yet the suburb, however disappointing immediately as an investment, was a success as a place to live. The landscape architects had designed well, and the somewhat maligned promoter had conscientiously laid a durable foundation. Roads and walks were so well constructed that they required almost no upkeep. The waterworks were in full and satisfactory use. Drainage and sewerage systems—Waring's earth closets had been abandoned as "a complete failure for interior use"[55] in that climate after a few malodorous trials—met all demands.[56] By 1877 forty-five homes had been built and were occupied, public and private grounds were well kept, an efficient village organization run by a board of trustees was in operation, and speculators and home owners alike were holding their lots as good long-term investments.[57]

Even now, although it is surrounded by the city, Riverside retains much of its early attractiveness, and still illustrates, with "its close interlocking of planning, architecture and gardening, its rich invention, its breaking of the gridiron pattern . . . and its real concern with art in shaping the human environment," an early peak in suburban planning.[58]

While still involved with Riverside, Olmsted became engaged in another suburban problem more complex, less susceptible of solution, and nearer at hand: the effort to reverse the deteriorating trend of Staten Island and to make it the ideal suburb of New York. Since the end of the Civil War, land on Staten

Island had been selling slowly. Efforts to subdivide some of the large estates had failed, and in spite of the island's accessibility and the charm and variety of its scenery, its population growth from 1865 to 1870 had lagged far behind that of Westchester County and Long Island.[59] To popularize the island, its plain drawbacks had to be overcome first. The quarantine station was gone, but fever lingered to discourage suburban settlement. Ferry service was dangerously bad. Communication on the island was slow: the horse railroad between Mariners Harbor and Clifton, started in 1863, had been five years building; stages still, in 1869, connected inland towns with the ferries;[60] and the steam railway in which John Hull Olmsted had invested had gone bankrupt.[61] The fact that each village had its own government led to conflicts of interest and of jurisdiction, and to duplication—or neglect—of services. Improvements of a "comprehensive and continuous and permanent character" were required.[62]

In May 1870, the New York State Legislature appointed a commission to submit plans for the improvement of the island and communication between it and New York.[63] Olmsted, who believed Staten Island could be made one of the most desirable suburbs of the big city, in an open letter in the *World* addressed to the chairman of the Improvement Commission's committee on organization, suggested a method of laying out the work. Committees should be set up to determine the true prevalence, and if possible the cause, of malaria; to inquire into conditions of travel on ferries and main roads; to study the scenery and the by-roads and pleasure roads giving access to it; and to investigate the adequacy of the island's water supply and sewage disposal. Their inquiries complete, each committee should recommend specific measures for improvement within its field of investigation, and a fifth committee, composed of the four committee chairmen and the president, vice-president, and secretary of the commission, should digest the committee reports and recommend projects.[64]

Advice other than Olmsted's prevailed, and the investigations began ineffectually. Olmsted persuaded the commission to scrap the original organization and to appoint a "committee of experts," composed of himself, Dr. Elisha Harris, H. H. Richardson, and J. M. Trowbridge,* to do the entire job of conducting inquiries and drawing up recommendations.[65] In three months of intensive work they collected and analyzed a great mass of data. Their report, presented in January 1871, blamed the island's laggard development principally on its reputation for malaria and on its bad ferry service to New York. They offered a fourteen-point scheme of improvement, at an estimated cost of two to four million dollars, relating to ferries, roads, parks, and thorough drainage of low places.[66] Though neither the experts nor anyone else yet knew the connection between mosquitoes and malaria, drainage was a sound approach to the island's health problem. The conclusion, also sound, that the ferry service to New York

*Joseph Mott Trowbridge (1824–1901) was a civil engineer and graduate of West Point. He reentered the army during the Civil War; he was a resident of Staten Island.

needed improvement was horribly supported the following July, when the ferry-boat *Westfield* blew up at her Whitehall Street slip, killing one hundred and injuring two hundred persons.[67]

Whether from the reluctance of the villages to spend so much money, or from their inability to act in concert, or from resentment of the constitution of the reporting committee, no comprehensive and far-reaching plan to regulate the development of Staten Island was put into effect. Piecemeal improvements were undertaken, but a grand opportunity was lost. "If your solution of the great problem should be adopted and prove sound," one of Olmsted's colleagues had said to him at the beginning of the study, "Staten Island will be a nobler and far more enduring field of fame than has hitherto fallen to any landscape architect."[68] It turned out to be, instead, a vivid demonstration of the difficulty of devising an acceptable overall plan for a region composed for many autonomous village units and of the fact that it is easier to plan a community from the start than to manipulate the character of an established one.

Another suburban community designed by Olmsted, Vaux & Company soon after Riverside was Tarrytown Heights, a nine-hundred-acre tract of farm land in that romantic region made familiar through Washington Irving's *Sketch Book*. Twenty-five miles north of New York and accessible from it only by a bad road, it was in 1870 about to be brought within easy reach of the city by the new line of the New York, Boston, and Montreal Railroad. Accommodating roads and lots to the tract's hills, woods, streams, and views, the partners laid it out in one hundred fifty-nine villa sites ranging in size from two to fifteen acres and presented a report explaining the motive and the principles of the work.[69]

As the movement to the suburbs quickened, so did the park movement; while the more fortunate were adapting stretches of country to their residential use, something of the country was being transplanted with increasing frequency into the city for the benefit of the less fortunate. On April 14, 1869, the New York State Legislature passed the park bill for Buffalo;[70] in spite of some local opposition,[71] the recommended land was acquired; the topographical survey and map were begun in June 1870 under the direction of Olmsted, Vaux & Company; the firm's general plans were accepted; and ground was broken the following September.[72]

In 1871, San Francisco at last undertook a park. Using neither the site Olmsted had proposed nor the design he had prepared, the city instead assigned the planning and development of Golden Gate Park to a young engineer, William Hammond Hall, who at once turned to Olmsted for advice.[73]

During the same period Chicago's South Park got under way. The park bill, having failed in the referendum of 1867, passed in 1868; purchase of the land was almost completed by 1870; Olmsted, Vaux & Company presented their plan and report in March the following year, and after a delay caused by the fire, work began in 1873.[74]

The proposed Boston park was the subject of increasing discussion from

1869. The idea of a rural park for Boston went back at least as far as the decade before the Civil War, when the Boston landscape gardener Horace William Shaler Cleveland had proposed creating one on the Common, instead of treating it as an open field sprinkled with trees and crisscrossed by walks that were no more than shortcuts across it. At about the same time he had suggested setting aside Spot Pond and the surrounding region in Malden, a section of picturesque natural beauty, as a pleasure ground.[75]

In 1869 he made another proposal: Boston, surrounded on three sides by water and having seventy-five acres of open space in the Common and Public Garden in its midst, did not need a park for a breathing space and could not, indeed, acquire one within its limits except at prohibitive cost; the surrounding countryside, however, not only contained varied and beautiful scenery, but had been treated by private owners, whether wealthy or not, almost uniformly with judgment and taste. All the essential advantages of a park could be secured, Cleveland argued, at comparatively small expense, by finishing and planting in a suitable style the roads leading among these charming rural scenes. Boston could thus

> appropriate their beauty, and instead of adorning herself with a single costly bouquet, she may clothe herself with a garment of flowers which has been woven for her by the hands of her children. The expenditure of a comparatively small sum would make a park of the whole surrounding country, which would exert a higher and wider moral influence than could possibly be attained by the appropriation of any single tract to the purpose.[76]

Olmsted, who deplored the imprecise definition and connotation of the terms employed in landscape architecture, would hardly have subscribed to this use of the word "park," and he was probably not responsive to Cleveland's idea except as it recommended the enhancement of the unique character and merits of Boston's environs. A proposal more congenial to his way of thinking was Copeland's: to create, in cooperation with the surrounding suburbs, a "girdle" of parks about the city and outside its limits, which should stretch from Dorchester harbor on the south to Chelsea beach on the north and should be reached from Boston by radial roads and be connected with each other by a boulevard.[77] It was, in fact, a system of parks that Copeland proposed for Boston such as Olmsted and Vaux had shortly before proposed for the New York metropolitan area. Copeland and Cleveland, former partners in the practice of landscape architecture in Boston, were at one with each other and with Olmsted in holding that, whatever was done about its park, Boston ought to plan the city's expansion and not spill at random into the surrounding country.

Olmsted's principal contribution to the early discussion of a park for Boston was a paper, "Public Parks and the Enlargement of Towns," which he read before the American Social Science Association at the Lowell Institute in Boston the evening of February 25, 1870.[78]

327

The townward drift of populations everywhere in the civilized modern world was not, he said, some moral epidemic but the exercise, rather, of a rational choice of the advantages that the city offered over the country in society, comforts, diversions, service, leisure, and intellectual opportunities. It was a trend that would surely result in larger cities than the world had ever before known, cities whose size would greatly enhance both the peculiar advantages and the peculiar disadvantages of urban life.

When the crowded slum sections of a city burned over, he continued, an opportunity occurred to rebuild them on a more open plan and so reduce the crime, disease, and high death rate not only of those particular sections but of the city as a whole. The examples, however, of London after the great fire and of New York after the fire of 1835, when property owners could not be induced to accept proposed new plans that sacrificed certain individual interests to a more open and healthful street and building arrangement, showed that advantage was rarely taken of such opportunities. "The remedy for a bad plan, once built upon, being thus impracticable, . . . we are surely bound . . . to prevent mistakes in the construction of towns." Yet in the United States, where new towns were springing up by the hundreds, no care at all was being taken to avoid bad plans.

Boston, specifically, was sure to extend in the future over miles of country still thoroughly rural, in which farmers even then were laying out roads with an eye only to property lines and to shortening the hauling distance between, say, their woodlots and the railroad station, and in which speculators were staking off streets from plans formed with a ruler and pencil in a broker's office. By this piecemeal, haphazard, short-sighted manner of planning the extension of Boston, the lives of millions of future inhabitants of the enlarged city would be adversely affected.

The older downtown business parts of many cities were necessarily crowded and productive of the ill health and irritation traceable to congestion; but there was no reason, since towns were no longer walled and since their residential quarters were now distinct from their commercial quarters, that the same conditions should prevail everywhere in them. Streets laid out in the new parts of expanding cities should be wide and tree lined to allow liberal penetration of air and sunlight and to provide passages, refreshing in themselves, between the business and residential districts. Accommodations for recreation, pleasant and accessible enough to attract the great body of citizens regularly, ought also to be provided to give them pleasure and specifically to counteract the special ennervating conditions of the town.

> . . . We want a ground to which people may easily go after their day's work is done, and where they may stroll for an hour, seeing, hearing, and feeling nothing of the bustle and jar of the streets, where they shall, in effect, find the city put far away from them. We want the greatest possible contrast with the streets and the shops and the rooms of the town which will be consistent with convenience and the preservation of good order and

neatness. We want, especially, the greatest possible contrast with the restraining and confining conditions of the town, those conditions which compel us to walk circumspectly, watchfully, jealously, which compel us to look closely upon others without sympathy. Practically, what we most want is a simple, broad, open space of clean greensward, with sufficient play of surface and a sufficient number of trees about it to supply a variety of light and shade. This we want as a central feature. We want depth of wood enough about it not only for comfort in hot weather, but to completely shut out the city from our landscapes.

The word *park*, in town nomenclature, should, I think, be reserved for grounds of the character and purpose thus described.

Not only as being the most valuable of all possible forms of public places, but regarded simply as a large space which will seriously interrupt cross-town communication wherever it occurs, the question of the site and bounds of the park requires to be determined with much more deliberation and art than is often secured for any problem of distant and extended municipal interests.[79]

In spite of its vigorous backing, the Boston park bill passed by the Massachusetts Legislature failed to secure the necessary two-thirds majority in the general election of November 1870, but agitation for the park did not subside, and Olmsted did not cease to advise its proponents. "Better wait a few years," he philosophically advised, "than adopt a narrow local scheme."[80]

Meanwhile Central Park, the inspiration and example to the rest of the country and the cornerstone of the firm's reputation, was passing through a crisis, one which had been in the making since the election of November 1868, when two creatures of the Tweed Ring, John T. Hoffman and A. Oakey Hall, became, respectively, governor of New York State and mayor of New York City. The Ring already held the city comptrollership through Richard B. Connally, and Tweed himself was the power on the Board of Supervisors. On April 5, 1870, the Tweed charter, a "thoroughly delusive substitute for the promised scheme of local self-government" pledged to the city by the state Democratic party, passed the legislature.[81]

Under the new charter, Mayor Hall appointed Tweed head of the new Department of Public Works, and within a week of its passage he made their crony Peter B. Sweeney president of a new five-man Department of Public Parks, which replaced the old Board of Commissioners of Central Park.[82] Its members, besides Sweeney, were Robert J. Dillon, Thomas C. Fields, Andrew H. Green, and Judge Henry Hilton—"not a quintette we would have chosen," Vaux dryly observed to Olmsted. Everyone, he added, expected Olmsted, Vaux & Company to be summarily thrown out.[83]

In the new organization, a committee of three—Sweeney, Hilton, and Fields —assumed power over all appointments and over the execution of all orders. Green, frozen out of the treasury, was succeeded by Hilton; frozen also out of all participation in park affairs, he had to adjourn one after another stated meeting during the early part of 1871 because he was the only member of the board present. The committee meanwhile met and acted at will. Since the department controlled not only Central Park and the smaller parks and squares but the boulevards and street improvements of the west side and upper Manhattan, its opportunities for patronage and plunder were vast.[84] To a Bostonian who asked the reason for the change in Central Park's management, Olmsted replied: "The object of the change was, I believe, to give those who now hold what is called the patronage of the city, a larger amount of it. I have never heard any other reason assigned."[85]

Perhaps to disarm public opinion, the new board did not discharge Olmsted, Vaux & Company and passed a resolution continuing their employment. With this gesture, however, its concern with the landscape architects came to an end: by the time the nominal relationship between them expired the end of November 1870, the board had not once consulted the landscape architects, neither it nor its executive committee had once met with them, and it had regularly ignored their written communications.[86]

Worse than that, the department recklessly undertook to overhaul the park's landscape. Planting scheduled by the designers for the season was never ordered. Established planting was torn up: in parts where intricacy and low growth and picturesque obscurity had been the aim of the design, the new management grubbed out the undergrowth, smoothed the surface, and stripped the trees of branches to a height of ten and fifteen feet from the ground, complacently reporting that it was remedying previous "neglect," securing "circulation of air," and clearing out "tangled weeds."[87]

The meadows, whose single fault was that they were not as extensive as desirable, were in the eyes of the designers the critical, central features of the park; they had also been the most difficult and costly to form. The new board proposed establishing a zoo on the north meadow, thus obliterating the largest one in the park—the landscape value of which it held to be not worth mentioning—under a congeries of small buildings and their yards.[88] An opera house, a speedway, and a statue of the Boss himself were among the other constructions it proposed to introduce. The statue was to be erected, the *New York Times* sarcastically explained, "partly as a memento of the fact that the Central Park, once the pride of the city, has passed into the hands of the Tweed Ring, and partly because it is naturally supposed that a public which can allow a man like Tweed to arrive at his present position cannot possibly have too much of him."[89]

Ignorantly and arrogantly, the board set about perverting the design that had controlled the park's development for fourteen years. Green, loyal to the original plan, was a helpless minority of one on the board. The landscape architects, treated as if they were nonexistent, had no influence whatever on it. All they could do was appeal to the public through the newspapers.

It was not the activity of its friends that saved Central Park but the timely exposure and collapse of the Tweed Ring. The Park Department fell with the rest of the city government; on November 23, 1871, Sweeney and Hilton resigned, Colonel Henry G. Stebbins, one-time president of the old Board of Commissioners, became president and treasurer, Frederic E. Church, the landscape artist, became a member of the board, and Olmsted, Vaux & Company were appointed Landscape Architects Advisory, with power to pass on all structures proposed for the park and with the superintendence, on Olmsted's insistence, both of the planting and of the keeping of the park.[90]

Church's appointment, suggested by Vaux and pressed by both partners, was significant. "A quiet, retired man," Olmsted explained to a friend,

> a model of rank and file citizenship, but who in his special calling has earned the respect and regard of the Community—called on at last to serve the public in an office where his special training will be of value, in the place of a professional politician, is the more significant that the particular politician is one so much the opposite in his qualifications—Sweeney. (His appointment reads "in place of Peter B. Sweeney") . . . The appointment of Church signifies more,—that offices (for the present) are not for sale . . . but are to seek and draw in the best men. . . .[91]
>
> We were anxious as a matter of propriety that the art element should be recognized—that the public utility of devotion to art and the study of Nature in a public service of this kind should be recognized & Church seemed on the whole the most appropriate and respectable man to express this.[92]

SHAPING A PROFESSION; END OF A PARTNERSHIP
1871–1873

E ARLY in their association Vaux and Olmsted established a method of procedure that set a standard for the profession for which they were trying to win the standing accorded to law, medicine, and other disciplines. One of the partners paid a preliminary visit to study the ground of a proposed work and discussed with the client not a plan for laying it out but the general aims and ends that a plan should secure. For this advice the firm charged between fifty and five hundred dollars, depending on the size and difficulty of the work and its distance from New York. If their views were accepted and they agreed to undertake the job, the initial fee went on account; otherwise it was the end of the business for them.[1]

Their usual fee for the general plan of a suburban development, with supervision, was five to ten dollars an acre, payable in installments over a period of two or three years, although they might take part of their payment in stocks or lots, as with Tarrytown Heights, or agree to a percentage of the amount spent on improvement, as with Riverside. For a park or an estate, they charged ten to twenty dollars an acre, depending on the amount of study the plan required.[2] For South Park, an arrangement of land and water in a situation almost devoid by nature of any parklike features, they charged fifteen dollars; for the Buffalo park, a simpler piece of work, they charged ten dollars.[3] Only twice in almost forty years of practice did Olmsted have a serious difference with a client over his fee. In one case the amount was too small to justify litigation; in the other, when Andrew H. Green withheld his salary, Olmsted sued and secured judgment. In all other cases in which a client questioned his charges, an explanation produced payment.[4]

When the firm accepted a piece of work after the preliminary visit, they asked the client to furnish a topographical map of the ground prepared by a civil engineer familiar with local conditions. This survey was essential; they would never prepare a plan except from such a map, and they advised against the employment of anyone who would.[5]

The general plan based on the topographical survey was not final. It set forth the principles of the undertaking and the relation of the parts to each other and to the whole, but it was no more than a memorandum of the ideas in the designers' minds for the guidance of those who were personally in charge of the work. They never supplied a plan to be worked from except with additional instructions and under superintendence.[6] The final result was not a literal translation of the plan into landscape terms but was a matter of growth and adjustment.[7]

In most cases the firm agreed to organize the work. Olmsted or Vaux selected the men to direct it locally and took responsibility for purchase of materials, for employment, and for determination of financial methods.[8] The owner or an intelligent gardener might direct a small work with the advice given by one of the partners during occasional visits. When a larger work like a park was involved, they recommended or selected as resident superintendent a man in whom they had confidence and with whom they could work congenially. They installed George K. Radford, an English civil engineer who had done the topographical survey of South Park for them, as superintendent of the Buffalo Park, and when Radford fell out with the Common Council in 1873, they recommended as his replacement William McMillan, a nurseryman who had worked on Prospect Park and who then successfully managed the Buffalo park for many years. The superintendence of South Park and of the approach boulevards in Chicago was in the beginning placed under H. W. S. Cleveland, whom Curtis had introduced to Olmsted in 1868 and whom Olmsted had employed on Prospect Park.[9] It was customary for Olmsted, Vaux, or an associate to visit an important work several times a year, and the firm kept in close touch by correspondence with its progress.

The superintendent, the engineer, the architect, and the horticulturist in charge of the various phases of the work the firm was directing were not their employees but the client's. They submitted all their plans and drawings to Olmsted, Vaux & Company, however, and took their orders from them since the landscape architects had comprehensive charge of the work and final responsibility for the coherence and success of the result.[10]

Olmsted, Vaux & Company's own staff varied with the amount of their business. They used the same draughtsmen and clerical helpers that Vaux used in his architectural work, paying them as they employed them and thus avoiding the cost of maintaining a full-time staff. When especially busy, they engaged more helpers on a temporary basis. Their office, at 110 Broadway, was Vaux's architectural office, and they were able to rely for cooperation, when they needed it, on such of his associates as the English architect Frederick C. Withers.

Olmsted and Vaux regarded themselves as the agents of their client,[11] as much bound to his interest as a doctor is bound to that of his patient; they accepted payment only from him and declined payment or favors from nurserymen, contractors, and others whom they engaged in his behalf. The moderation of Olmsted's fees, even when, at the peak of his success, he could have demanded very large ones, was one expression of his regard for his clients' interest.

The standard of duty Olmsted and Vaux were setting for the profession was matched by its standard of dignity. Expert counselors in a difficult and little-understood specialty, they held that their business was to determine how the client's wishes could best be carried out and his purposes best served within the limits of his money and of topographical conditions.[12] If they could not bring the client to their point of view, or the client could not persuade them to his, they withdrew from the job. They declined orders to execute work they believed would be in the end unsatisfactory or unsound.[13] When Morris K. Jesup, genial and overbearing, flouted Olmsted's advice in an important particular of the laying out of his grounds and then put heavy pressure on him to withdraw his resignation, Olmsted courteously refused and explained why: Jesup considered of leading importance certain features of the property that Olmsted, taking account of the client's needs in the light of the whole topography, thought should be treated as secondary. If Jesup wanted those features emphasized, and subordinate elements geared to the major ones that he had determined on without considering the whole problem, there were men whose business it was to do such work; it was not Olmsted's, however, and he could not do it satisfactorily.[14] The firm usually refused to execute details of a design for which they did not have comprehensive responsibility, although they would advise established institutions on the placement of new buildings and roads.[15] Their position occasionally annoyed clients who failed to understand that they had engaged services of a different order from those offered by a nurseryman or gardener.

Olmsted and Vaux were not alone during these early years in their efforts to elevate their "unaccredited but important profession." Whatever the public thought—and the idea was undeniably prevalent that a landscape architect was a sort of gardener to be ordered to "embellish" grounds after land was graded, roads were built, and houses were erected—a handful of professional men regarded themselves not as the practitioners of a decorative and subsidiary art but of a basic one to which engineering, architecture, and horticulture were subordinate: "the art of arranging land so as to adapt it most conveniently, economically and gracefully to any of the varied wants of civilization."[16]

This inclusive definition was Cleveland's. Born in 1814 at Lancaster, Massachusetts, he had gone to school there under Jared Sparks, lived for a time as a boy in Havana while his father was minister to Cuba, and returned to the United States to study engineering and to take up farming. When he moved to the environs of Boston in 1854, he joined in a landscape gardening partnership with Robert Morris Copeland, who had submitted one of the unsuccessful plans in the Central Park competition. Cleveland and Olmsted, after their meeting in 1868, developed a solid friendship founded in part on a community of attitudes toward their profession. A man of vision, originality, and high professional competence, Cleveland was also a felicitous writer and a good speaker. He saw in the founding of new towns throughout the West a unique and beautiful opportunity to establish the principles of an art that should outrank all the fine arts, using scenery, architectural creations, and ornament, along with engineering skill, as "mere ingredients" and blending them by superior genius to form ideal cities.[17] Realizing the practical impossibility of changing a town plan once built upon, he was appalled by the thoughtless repetition of the gridiron street pattern, whether readily adaptable to the contour of the land or not, throughout the West. Some of his lectures, delivered in 1872 in Minneapolis, St. Paul, and Madison, on the scope and responsibility of landscape architecture in preparing the country for civilized living were immensely successful, he wrote Olmsted; he was very happy

not that he had made a hit but that the hit had been made.[18] Still, he recognized
it as an ominous portent for the future of urban life in the United States that
numbers of old surveyors, men without the least conception of landscape architecture as he and Vaux and Olmsted and a few others understood it, were setting
themselves up in the early 1870's as landscape architects.[19]

As the firm's business grew, it more and more took Olmsted out of town for
varying lengths of time. To a man whose ideal of happiness was domesticity, it
was a privation to be so much away from home; to one who suffered frequently
from indigestion and sleeplessness, eating at boardinghouses and hotels and
spending nights in strange beds and on trains was a hardship. His insomnia was
beginning to appear hopeless to him, a burden that could not be cast off, only
endured. When Edward Everett Hale, who regarded him as "one of the ablest
men living," urged him to read Dr. Hammond's monograph on sleep, Olmsted
answered: "Oh, I am under Dr. Hammond's personal care. The trouble is I will
not obey the rules which he lays down as essentials."[20] Small wonder: one of
them was to avoid mental overexertion, and Olmsted could not. Intense mental
effort and a great deal of worry went into all his work. Facility and virtuosity had
no place in his method. Careful mastery of the multitudinous details of each
piece of work was essential, and Olmsted was painstaking almost to the point of
perfectionism.

Whatever its hardships, travel had one compensation: it often took him
through or near Hartford so that he had many opportunities to spend a few
hours, or the night, at his father's home—not the one where he had grown up,
but the new one on Asylum Street to which John Olmsted had moved in November 1868.[21] Contact between the two Olmsted families was not confined to hasty
visits. Sometimes Olmsted's two boys would pass several weeks with their grandparents; sometimes Mary would spend a few days at Hartford with some of the
children on her way to or from summer visits with the Knapps, who had moved
to Sutton, Massachusetts; and John Olmsted almost every year took two or three
trips to New York, where his great interest was in visiting the parks and inspecting the firm's nearby works in progress.

Proud though the old man was of his son's accomplishment, he still retained something of his earlier skepticism about his capacity to earn a living.
When the default of Riverside's promoter on cash payments at the end of 1868
left Olmsted, Vaux & Company pressed for ready money, John Olmsted remarked that since Fred had no collateral to offer as security for a loan and "since
your firm is not known" he could see nothing to do but borrow three or four
thousand dollars on his own collateral and let the partners have it.[22] Typically,
he simultaneously underestimated and trusted his son; typically, too, he sent the
money promptly.

There was, in fact, some justification for John Olmsted's anxiety, and his
son, in moments of dejection, shared it. His fees were moderate, his expenses
high, and his eastern investments not particularly successful. He had bought

some Brooklyn lots of very dubious value,[23] he was part owner with Knapp and Thomas Hill, former president of Harvard, of a cranberry bog in Sutton that required frequent transfusions of money,[24] and only the *Sun* stock he held could be relied on to pay regular dividends.[25] From time to time Olmsted had to draw on his western capital to keep up with his expenses. Finally, at the beginning of 1871, he closed out his California investments for some ten thousand dollars gold.[26] On a brief professional visit to Bowles the following May, Olmsted voiced his discouragement with a bitterness that shocked his friend: he was, he said, working too hard, making too little money, and wearing his life out in poverty.[27]

Actually, Olmsted was not as unhappy as he led Bowles to believe. If his youthful buoyancy of spirits was gone, it had been replaced by an even-tempered composure that gave way rarely, and only under the strain of insomnia, illness, or such galling professional chagrin as he suffered throughout 1871, when the Tweed Ring was ravaging his beloved park. Bowles, however, found the pleasure of Olmsted's visit much qualified by his dismal revelation and with friendly sympathy tried to lift his spirits and make suggestions that might help him out of his predicament. Olmsted should practice alone, Bowles advised, not with a firm of architects that had many rivals. As for compensation, part of Olmsted's was the glory of doing for his generation what no other man was doing or could do.[28] Olmsted, who could pay no bills with his glory and who found it slighted where it should have been most appreciated, answered distractedly that even if he were not morally obligated to Vaux he had to have his assistance; if only he could get out of New York and do just enough work to insure an annual income of four thousand dollars and spend half his time in writing and consultation![29]

Bowles advised him to move at once to the country, set himself up as a consultant, and refuse detailed work. His own farm near Springfield, which he would not sell to any other man on earth for two or three times what he paid for it, he would sell to Olmsted for exactly its cost—it would be as good as money in his pocket to have Olmsted in the neighborhood. And in the country Olmsted would not drop from sight: his unique position insured his prominence no matter where he lived. He had given the park business a great impetus, and none could be established in the United States now without him. The press all over the country appreciated him, no one had more and better friends, and he could have fine publicity. His next five or ten years could be the most important in his professional life, Bowles urged.[30] This kind of thing was much pleasanter for Olmsted to hear, and much closer to the truth, than his father's dashing opinion: "Your firm is not known."

Olmsted as yet had little serious thought of leaving New York, where he was reasonably content in spite of political irritations and occasional depressions. His family life was full of interest for him, and the children, although "small of their age and none . . . quite strong," satisfactory. John, after spending the summer of 1869 in the West with Clarence King on the Survey of the Fortieth Parallel, was attending the new school that Knapp had started at Plymouth,

Mary Cleveland Olmsted

Above:
F.L.O. in Paris,
1878

Above:
Owen Frederick
Olmsted, circa
1878

Right:
Charlotte Olmsted,
circa 1876

Left:
John Charles
Olmsted, circa
1876

where, after earnest consultation with Olmsted, he had accepted a call to become minister of the First Congregational Church of New England.

"John stands high as a student," Olmsted proudly reported to Kingsbury, "and as a trusty fellow. He is building a steamboat, printing a newspaper and has a contract for clearing a wood lot. He had cut & split 3 cords with his own hands while bossing half a dozen other cutters." Owen, also one of Knapp's students, "is coming on very well also, but is still subject to singular fits of lethargy, ordinarily bright & sometimes very quick-minded." Charlotte, whose health gave her parents some anxiety, was attending Mrs. Handy's school in Boston, where study of the students' physical condition was the teachers' first duty. Only Marion was at home.[31]

The comparative childlessness of the Olmsted household was relieved on July 24, 1870, with the birth of a son, christened Henry Perkins and called Boy. Happily the baby, unlike Olmsted's other two infant sons, survived and grew hardy. Olmsted almost from the first planned that this one should continue his own work in landscape architecture and should continue it with advantages of training he himself had lacked. He was so determined that his only son should enter his profession that when the child was four, Olmsted changed his name to Frederick Law so that a Frederick Law Olmsted might be identified with the firm and the profession for a long generation after his death.[32]

Life in New York, not yet hopelessly poisoned by frustration over Central Park, had much to offer Olmsted. He went often, though irregularly, to the Union League Club. A member of the Century Association since 1859,[33] he spent an occasional Saturday evening at the clubhouse at 109 East Fifteenth Street, consorting with Bryant, Godwin, Richardson, Frederic Church, Mark Twain, and the old Sanitarians, and diligently avoiding Viele and Ben Butler. Out-of-town guests were not rare in the house on Amos Street, and none was more welcome than Bowles, who, after a night there in the spring of 1871, gave a lunch next day at the Brevoort House for Olmsted, Bret Harte, and several other men.[34] Olmsted kept in close touch with Godkin and contributed an occasional note to the *Nation*. Besides the squib already mentioned on the comparative viciousness of gossip and drunkenness, he wrote of the evolution and merits of boundary planting; the loss to science and learning incurred in the destruction by fire of the Chicago Academy of Sciences; the influence of the drought on the Chicago fire and of deforestation on the drought.[35] He concluded the last article prophetically:

> If the reduction of foliage in any considerable geographical division of the world tends to make its seasons capricious, as there is much evidence, the evils both of destructive drought and devastating floods are very likely to extend and increase until we have a government service which we dare trust with extensive remedial measures. It is not a matter which commerce can be expected to regulate.[36]

338

He reviewed in the *Nation* Cleveland's pamphlet, *Landscape Architecture as Applied to the Wants of the West, with an Essay on Forest Planting on the Great Plains*, which embodied, among other thoughts, the idea that treeless areas should be reforested to secure a climate more favorable to settlement;[37] and from time to time he contributed articles to other publications.

One of a committee to organize a permanent art gallery in New York, Olmsted worked with Samuel P. Avery, John La Farge, Joseph H. Choate, John Taylor Johnston, Frederic Church, Vaux, Curtis, Green, Potter, Stebbins, and a number of other men to found the Metropolitan Museum of Art and was a member of its first executive committee. Ironically, this excellent enterprise realized a threat to the physical integrity of Central Park, which Olmsted and Vaux were constantly having to defend against encroachments: in spite of opposition from Church and Johnston, a site in the park on Fifth Avenue at Eighty-sixth Street was selected for the museum's permanent building, with the cordial consent of most of the park commissioners. The legislature, responding to pressure by Tweed and Sweeney, authorized its placement there; and work on it was begun in 1874 according to a "rather Gothic" plan that had been prepared several years earlier by Vaux and J. Wrey Mould, an architect who had designed a number of the architectural features of Central Park.[38]

Olmsted saw old friends and made new. Now that he was a prominent man with a national reputation, half-forgotten ones renewed his acquaintance or boasted of it. Dr. D. T. Brown, director of the Bloomingdale Asylum, reported that Olmsted's old friend William Peet spoke eloquently and romantically of their boyhood days in Hartford and boasted that he had slept oftener with Olmsted than with anyone except his wife—"rather naïf for a man of fifty!"[39] Tom Beecher, once an object of Olmsted's youthful admiration and now a minister in Elmira, New York, took advantage of old acquaintance to inquire—not of "Dear Fred" but of "Dear Mr. Olmsted"—if he could recommend a landscape architect to do some work for the Elmira school board.[40]

Many of Olmsted's early friendships remained warm and constant. With Brace and Albert Henry Barnes and Kingsbury he exchanged letters and visits; but although there was the old affection, there was no longer the old unanimity of view among them. Olmsted had not realized how much he had changed, or how little they had, until he learned that Barnes was giving up writing for the *New York Times* because it published on Sunday, the day of rest on which, Barnes believed, all ordinary commerce should be dropped. Kingsbury, a well-to-do banker and railroad director, warmly approved the sacrifice to principle by Barnes, a poor minister who sorely needed the money he earned by journalism.[41] Olmsted found himself "quite taken aback" by their attitude.[42]

He saw no distinction between sacred and secular labor, he wrote Kingsbury. Because his office was so distracting during the week, he frequently worked on Sundays himself. What rest he took on that day was not the kind Sabbatarians would approve. He got up later than usual, ate a better breakfast than usual, read two newspapers, indulged himself with a cigar, and played with the children before setting to work. Late in the day he usually went out with his wife, taking the older children when they were home. In winter they skated on a nearby pond and in summer rowed on the bay or picnicked by a stream or on a hillside or—he was determined to spare Kingsbury nothing—drove to the brewery, where they sat in the garden and drank beer. Sunday evenings he read *Robinson Crusoe* to Marion, while Mary played cards with John and Owen and Charlotte. "And the truth is," he said, "I should be very angry with the man or men who prevented me from having my newspapers, my boat, my conveyances, my wine or my cigar. . . . If the *Times* should drop its Sunday edition, I should drop the *Times*, as I should drop my cook if she should drop my Sunday breakfast." Responsible for the temporal and spiritual welfare of five children whom he deeply loved, he was bringing them up to enjoy healthy pleasures in good company on Sunday ("I have taken the boys to a Beer Garden Concert. I never took them to a church"), and he thought they all were and would remain "honester and more conscientious" than if brought up as he had been. He was sorry that Kingsbury could not respect his views or even be amused by them, "but on proper occasions I must show my colors as well as I can." He supposed, he added, that he was not free "from the old man Adam" but hoped he had not crept into his letter.[43]

Olmsted's political opinions, like his religious, sometimes clashed with those of his best friends. Bowles in 1872 rather coolly supported Greeley for the presidency, because his nomination on both the Liberal Republican and the Democratic tickets indicated to him that *the war is really over.*"[44] Olmsted, on the contrary, could not think of "a worse thing to do, any possible thing, than for us to make the old humbug of a patriarch President." Greeley's alliance with the radical antislavery element, which harassed Lincoln during the war, and his advocacy of amnesty after it had been equally unpalatable to Olmsted. Greeley seemed to him nothing but a trader in the market of public opinion, ever in search of immediate advantage, a man who valued a principle "very much with reference to the sensational presentation of it and the demand which as so presented it can command among busy Touch and go minds. Just the worst habit possible for a President of the United States, who should be a balance wheel." More than that, Greeley was "the worst imposter who ever played upon the common people. He pretends to be a plain, careless, even rude farmer like man, simple and free of self-consciousness to the point of eccentricity—a just man, a generous compassionate man, temperate, unsophisticated, guileless. Now you know," he told Bowles, "that he is a fop, excessively self-conscious, studying effect with more elaboration and skill than any living actor or noted charlatan; that he is selfish, cruel, unjust, frantically passionate and self-willed. . . ." Worse than that, "there has not been a big scheme of political swindling going on here for years that this white hatted old patriarch has not been mooning round innocently while such dirty little steam tugs as Waldo Hutchings and John Cochrane were doing his work in them."[45]

340

Outraged that the Liberal Republicans had put forward such a man as a reform candidate in opposition to Grant, Olmsted believed the honest reformers had been sold out at their Cincinnati convention. When Bowles, who thought the slate had been drawn by a combination of political idiots and political buccaneers, half-heartedly protested that Greeley had done much for political reform and that Godkin probably favored him, too, Olmsted retorted that then "the damn'd infection of an excited rabble has made him crazy along with the rest . . . ." As a matter of fact, Godkin and the *Nation* came out for Grant, but Olmsted was disappointed at the magazine's "feeble tone" and had to take his comfort from the *Post*, which said Greeley's election would be a national calamity.[46]

Olmsted's dissatisfaction with the Liberal Republican convention was shared by some of the men who attended it. A group of them, led by Carl Schurz, held a conference at the Fifth Avenue Hotel in New York in late June 1872 to act on the reform nominee. Disappointingly, they endorsed him, on the theory that it was more important to defeat Grant than to replace Greeley, who seemed to have a chance of winning, with a cleaner candidate. A dissenting faction of the conference, which included J. Miller McKim, Edward Atkinson, and Robert Minturn, promptly held another meeting, drew up a platform and put up a "conscience ticket." The conscience ticket was probably the only one that could have been more distasteful to Olmsted than the Liberal Republican: the nominees were William Slocum Groesbeck, of Ohio, for president, and for vice-president— Olmsted.[47]

The second conference was too small to make a politically effective protest, and few took its nominations seriously. Some thought them embarrassing as well as ineffectual. Olmsted was one: he hid and was not to be found when reporters came to notify him of his selection,[48] and in a note to the *Post* of June 22 he sought to dissociate himself from the movement. Some of his friends tried to minimize the episode. McKim, however, an old abolitionist indifferent to contempt and inured to unpopularity, stoutly insisted to Olmsted that a conscience ticket put forward by such men as those who attended the second conference was not to be despised;[49] A. J. Bloor* advised Olmsted to let his name stand in nomination "to accustom the public to the association of high office and names of those other than political hacks";[50] and the *Nation* and *Post*, although conceding that the new slate was unlikely to have any effect on the November election, nevertheless said that its formation was "the one healthy and honorable incident thus far of the most shameful and paltry Presidential campaign in American history."[51]

Shortly before his admirers thrust this hollow honor on Olmsted, the political necessities of Central Park obliged him to accept a more substantial duty. On

---

*Alfred Janson Bloor (1828–1917) was a New York architect who had interrupted his practice during the Civil War to work for the Sanitary Commission in Washington. His relations with Olmsted were on the whole difficult.

May 28, 1872, he was elected president and treasurer of the Department of Parks, to fill the places vacated by Stebbins, who was going to Europe for a few months. So that Olmsted might accept the two offices, the firm of Olmsted, Vaux & Company resigned as landscape architects and general superintendents and Vaux was appointed landscape architect and superintendent at the same salary, six thousand dollars.[52]

Management of Central Park, after the havoc effected by the Tweed administration, was no sinecure. The Ring had done more than deface the landscape. It had left the Park Department with liabilities in excess of one-and-a-half-million dollars, a bank account overdrawn by almost one hundred ten thousand dollars, and accounts in chaos because funds applicable by law only to specified purposes had been put to unauthorized uses. It had, moreover, loaded the keepers' force with "deserving" job applicants who were largely ignorant, indifferent, and incompetent. A final blow, which could not be blamed on the Ring, was the destruction of almost eight thousand trees by the unusual cold during the winter of 1871–72.[53]

The rehabilitation of the park made headway under the new regime, but not with the smoothness and ease that the politically naïve might have expected. The reformers were almost as bald and insistent in their demands for patronage as the Ring had been.[54] The cost of maintaining the park, which had been a quarter of a million dollars during the first six months of the Ring's control, had to be reduced and was cut to one hundred seventy thousand dollars for the corresponding period of the new administration largely by reducing the work force.[55] Politicians and newspapers wrathfully protested the layoffs.[56] Olmsted's reorganization of the vitally important keepers' force provoked their special ire. The captain of the force was admittedly afraid to discharge even "regular deadbeats" who had "never performed one honest tour of duty since they were taken on." "Damn 'em," he complained to Olmsted, "they are every man laying wires to the Legislature, and they carry too many guns for me." The surgeon of the force, ordered by Olmsted to make a medical survey of the keepers, accepted his instructions with the remark that his head would surely roll for it. He was right: having reported that a full quarter of the men were unfit for active duty by reason of hernias, varicosities, rheumatism, partial blindness, and similar infirmities, he was dismissed by the board. Olmsted continued to press the reorganization. He was himself, despite the fact that he had studied the police systems of France, England, and Ireland and was one of the few men in America who had made it a business to be well informed on the subject of police organization and management, attacked in the press as a "silly, heartless, upstart, sophmorical theorist" whose "boyish experiments" were reducing the keepers' force to a state of rebellious demoralization.[57]

Olmsted's troubles included the worsening of his relations with Vaux. The partners had always argued intensely, at length, and to their mutual exhaustion. The misunderstanding that had arisen between them over Olmsted's assumption of the title architect-in-chief had been smoothed over, but it had exposed and aggravated a weak spot in their friendship. Vaux, resentful that too much credit for Central Park was habitually assigned to Olmsted and too little to himself, had become inordinately sensitive to the slight; although he knew that Olmsted had systematically striven to correct the injustice, he could not help blaming him for it. Whatever the specific causes of the dissolution of the firm, these frictions were probably contributory. On October 18, 1872, the partnership was terminated for "reasons of mutual convenience."[58] When Stebbins returned from Europe the next month to resume his duties with the park department, Olmsted and Vaux each resigned his position, one to be immediately appointed landscape architect with the duty of superintendence, the other to become consulting landscape architect.[59]

More poignantly than the end of the partnership, the death of his father on January 25, 1873, marked the close of a period in Olmsted's life.

Failing for some time and with the likelihood of death plainly before him, John Olmsted soon after Christmas summoned Fred and Allie to explain to them certain particulars they would need to know of his business and domestic affairs. "All with great cheerfulness, kindliness, and some pleasantry, . . . I felt the greatest respect for his character, meek, dignified, & sagacious," Olmsted told Kingsbury.[60]

On January 21, the old gentleman fell and broke his hip. His condition at first did not seem disquieting and Olmsted, who had hurried to Hartford as soon as he heard of the accident, returned next day to New York. The following morning, however, he received an alarming wire from Allie and hastened back to Hartford. It was midafternoon when he reached his father's house. Entering the sickroom, he found John Olmsted dozing and tossing feverishly. His doctor, who was at his bedside, did not expect him to live out the night. Yet when he woke, his mind was clear, and he greeted his son with cheerful surprise. Olmsted passed his remaining hours beside him, fanning him and occasionally moistening his lips. Soon after midnight, the dying man roused and exclaimed, "Air— give me all the air you can!" Olmsted hurried from the room to get Mary Ann Olmsted, his half-sister Mary, and Allie. Within a few minutes of their return, John Olmsted "breathed his last without a struggle, apparently conscious, & with his perfect senses until the end of life."

"He was a very good man and a kinder father never lived," was the just and simple tribute of his son.[61]

XXIX
FRICTION AND DISMISSAL
1873–1878

I T is strange how much of the world I feel has gone from me with him,"
Olmsted mourned on his father's death. "The value of my success in the
future is gone for me."[1]

But the real value of his success was gradually becoming plain, and he
could not remain indifferent to it. It rested on his perceptive and bold efforts to
control the urban environment so that, as the United States developed from a
nation of villages into one of cities, the advantages of urbanization should not be
outstripped by its drawbacks, and civilization and order rather than barbarism
and chaos should ensue.

It is hard to pinpoint the time when Olmsted's interest in urban problems
crystallized into a determination to contribute to their solution by deliberately
guiding the evolution of communities. The interest itself may have developed as
early as 1848, when his move to the island suburb of New York familiarized him
with various phases of metropolitan life. After that, his travels acquainted him
with many of the great and growing cities of Europe and America, where he observed the pathological and the healthy features of increasing urbanization and
its effects on people and their environment. Knowledge and interest crossfertilized
each other until, by the time the Central Park job opportunely offered, he was
equipped not merely technically to convert an unpromising tract into a recreation
area but philosophically to use the opportunity as the opening wedge in an
attack on peculiarly urban ills.

Olmsted's view that his profession was an instrument for shaping social development was explicitly stated many times, and it was central to all his large
undertakings. In the two useful decades that remained to him, he had a larger
opportunity than ever to demonstrate his professional capacities and their social
worth.

Not long before his father's death Olmsted had bought an English-basement
row house large enough to accommodate living quarters and office at 209 West
Forty-sixth Street in Manhattan. It was a typical New York brownstone, squeezed
onto a lot about sixteen feet wide and rising four stories above the street. In the
basement, at the south end next to the street, were the furnace with wood and
coal bins and the laundry facilities; at the other end was the kitchen with a
floor-to-ceiling icebox. On the ground floor, two or three steps above the sidewalk
level, the front door led into a long, narrow hall off which opened, to the right, a

small reception room used by both office and family callers, a bath room, and storage closets. At the end of the hall was Olmsted's office, originally the dining room, a room about twenty feet long and lit by two large windows at its north end. On the street side of the next floor was the parlor; the dining room, above the office, was connected with the kitchen below by the dumbwaiter shaft. Between parlor and dining room in the stair hallway lurked a small pantry and a closet. A front bedroom shared by Marion and Charlotte, a bathroom, and a back bedroom used by Olmsted and his wife occupied the next floor; and on the top were four small bedrooms, the two front for the boys and the two rear for servants. The dumbwaiter ran all the way to the fourth floor and afforded little Frederick, who was by then known as Rick, his personal means of transportation.[2]

The décor, as Frederick recalled it more than seventy years later, was "1860–1870 Victorian, some of it Bunthorne style." In the dining room stood an elaborate walnut sideboard, with incised carving. In the parlor, a pier glass filled the space between the two windows, and some of Watkins's Yosemite photographs, in jigsaw frames, hung on the other walls. Against one party wall stood an upright piano, much used by Mary Olmsted, who accompanied herself as she sang in a sweet, true voice. Opposite the piano and flanking the fireplace were tall, well-stocked bookcases, which gave a good idea of Olmsted's eclectic and avid reading habits.[3] Books were all over the house—Frederick estimated his father had a library of two thousand volumes—in entrance hall, office, reception room, and bedrooms as well as parlor. There were novels, both classic and contemporary; poetry, biography, and memoirs; books on government and politics, diplomacy, history, sociology, philosophy and religion, education, travel, and exploration; science and medicine; translations of Greek and Latin classics; series of governmental and institutional reports; fables and fairy tales and ballads; Bibles and cookbooks; guidebooks, foreign language dictionaries, and encyclopedias; sets of the *Nation*, the *Cultivator*, and *Household Words*; texts on mathematics, engineering, botany, and geology; and books on art, architecture, sculpture, seamanship, magic, and chess. A few old friends like Milton, Bunyan, Zimmermann, Gilpin, Emerson, Ruskin, and Mill Olmsted kept on his bedside table. In the office were park reports and volumes on landscape architecture, parks and gardens, agriculture, horticulture, trees, ferns, police organization, metropolitan improvement, model housing, and other facets of Olmsted's profession.[4]

Besides the books, the principal features of Olmsted's office were a large drafting table under the easterly window and a desk under the other. Over the table hung a big tray for drafting instruments, which, suspended by counterweighted cords, could be smoothly raised and lowered. Frederick could remember no decoration in the office other than photographs on the mantel of Vaux, Ruskin, and the French landscape architect Edouard André. He remembered, too, a large wall map of New York City hanging in the narrow hallway: late one night, when he was a very small boy, his brother John found him in his nightshirt scanning it; apparently he was sleepwalking and studying it to find his way back to bed.[5]

To a discerning observer, Olmsted's office could have given several clues to his personality. Its almost featureless simplicity suggested that self-expression had no place in his work. His business was the artistic solution of other people's problems; it was inappropriate to intrude his own personality into his executed works, irrelevant to express it in his workroom. This attitude was in clear contrast to that of his friend Richardson, who deliberately stamped his lavish and exuberant personality on his imposing office as plainly as he did on his architecture.[6]

It could rightly be inferred, too, that Olmsted was very little dependent on the facilities normally associated with a well-organized professional office. His creative work was done in the field, where he analyzed problems and reached decisions of design while directly observing the landscape he was shaping. His office was a place for maps, memorandums, the working out of technical detail, the drafting of reports—not for creativity. Equipment was serviceable, staff scant. Until his stepson John graduated from college and joined his office as draftsman in 1875, Olmsted, when he needed draftsmen, used those of Vaux or of some other associate. It was about 1885 before the first typewriter and stenographer appeared in his office; until then he drew up his reports in pencil on scratch paper, and his wife copied them neatly in ink.[7]

That his family helped in his office and that his office was in his home indicated the inseparability of his personal and professional life. Visitors were likely to look in on him before going upstairs. Among those Frederick recalled was William Cullen Bryant, the deep music of whose voice, as he read Homer to the assembled family in Greek, was unforgettable. Other guests were Clarence King, Vaux and his family, the William Emersons, Mary Olmsted's cousins Frank and Henry Perkins, Clarence Cook, the Braces, Richardson, John La Farge, and the then rare husband-and-wife medical team of Dr. Mary Putnam Jacobi and Dr. Abraham Jacobi.[8] Friends of the Olmsted children were always welcome. Olmsted, although rather silent and retiring in the presence of young people, took real pleasure in their company, and they were at ease in the cheerful and informal hospitality of his home.

Informal was certainly the word for it, John La Farge must have thought on one occasion. Late one afternoon, when Olmsted was out of town, La Farge came in and stayed so long that Mary Olmsted, who had provided a supper of corned beef and cabbage for herself and the children, felt obliged to ask him to stay. Accepting, he seemed disconcerted. It was not until her husband returned the next evening that she learned why: Olmsted had forgotten to mention that he had asked La Farge to come to dinner the previous night.[9]

Absentmindedness, fostered by deep absorption in professional problems, was characteristic of him. So was a certain even-tempered impersonality; he was interested in affairs rather than in persons. Frederick recalled that, when Mary Olmsted denounced someone as "a bad man," Olmsted replied: "Not a bad man, Mary. I don't know if there are any. Some men are more useful than others, and that man is comparatively useless."[10]

346

Still, he was capable of definite and sustained dislike. Beardless, he was occasionally mistaken for Ben Butler, whom he so despised that, when the general was running for governor of Massachusetts in 1881, Olmsted grew a beard. He wore it for the rest of his life to put an end to the resemblance and the confusion.[11] His impersonality failed him, too, when it came to Andrew H. Green. It extended, naturally, to his clients, whose problems, not personalities, concerned him.

Devoted to his children, Olmsted took his responsibility for their education and discipline seriously. When five-year-old Frederick, in a tantrum, threw a hammer at his mother, Olmsted set him on his knee and lectured him with such emotion on the naughtiness of his behavior that tears ran off his mustache. The child patted him kindly on the cheek and said, "Be quiet, Daddy, and let me talk."[12]

Feeling that his own education had been delegated to incompetents, Olmsted paid close attention to the children's and knew what they were studying and why. He advised frequently with Knapp about the boys' work, he encouraged them to develop a range of physical and mechanical skills, and he fostered their efforts in any direction that might educate them. He sent John west in the summer of 1869 and again in 1871 to work on the Survey of the Fortieth Parallel under Clarence King. Owen went to Maine in the summer of 1874, after he had passed his entrance examinations to the Columbia School of Mines, to serve under Frank Perkins on a United States Coast Survey party. Owen's technical skills were encouraged at home, too. He wired the house for call bells, and as soon as the telephone patents were published, he built and installed instruments in several rooms. For his nocturnal amusement, he made telegraph instruments and strung lines connecting his house and those of four classmates as far apart as Forty-sixth and Thirty-second streets. Owen, who poignantly resembled his dead father, was, of all the children, the one of whom Olmsted and his wife had the happiest expectations.[13]

Determined that neither John nor Owen should lose years in false starts as he had done, Olmsted brought John into his office as soon as he finished the Sheffield Scientific School at Yale. John soon became head draftsman; the office management in time devolved on him, and the household management, too, in the summers when his mother took the younger children to stay with the Braces at Lake Placid, with the Knapps at Plymouth, or in rented houses in Cambridge. From afar, Mary Olmsted spurred her eldest smartly: keep up the India ink work La Farge had recommended; have his father's room cleaned while he was out of town; be cheerful—too often his manner was that of a driven schoolboy, when it was not bumptious; and "take good care of your father and don't contradict him—he is not such a fool as you think him!"[14] John took to his training with wonderful ability and in a few years was Olmsted's mainstay. Forty years later his mother was able to say proudly that he had built up the business.[15]

It was already greatly increasing during the early 1870s. Not only did Olmsted have continuing responsibility for the New York and Brooklyn and Buffalo parks but he had professional interests all the way from the state of Washington to Washington, D.C.

The Northern Pacific Railroad, influenced by his old acquaintance Billings, employed him in 1873 to lay out its terminal city, Tacoma—and rejected his plan. In it the streets followed the contour of the land, which steeply descended to the bay; and the departure from customary usage was incomprehensible to town site promoters attuned to the familiar grid.[16] Early in 1874 he began work on the problem of arranging the grounds about the United States Capitol to form an appropriate setting for the massive, formal building. Late the same year he contracted with the park commissioners of Montreal to plan and supervise the building of a mountain park for that city.[17]

Meanwhile, the park movement in Boston was reviving, and he was called on by the Boston commissioners for plans and consultations. Lesser works carried on simultaneously included designs for the grounds of the Schuylkill Arsenal at Philadelphia; plans for the placement of new buildings and the extension of grounds for Amherst College, Trinity College at Hartford, and the Hartford Retreat; a plan for Niagara Square in Buffalo, in consultation with Richardson, who was designing a monument for it; a plan for a summer resort village at Chautauqua Point, New York; a plan for the Arnold Arboretum in Boston in collaboration with Charles Sprague Sargent; and designs for private grounds for John Crosby Brown at Orange Mountain, New Jersey, Charles A. Dana at Glen Cove, Long Island, Cyrus Field at Irvington on the Hudson, Henry B. Hyde at West Islip, Long Island, and a number of other clients.[18]

Much of Olmsted's new work, after the dissolution of his partnership with Vaux, was undertaken with Jacob Weidenmann. Born in Wintertur, Switzerland, in 1829, Weidenmann had studied architecture in Munich and come to the United States as a young man. After a short return home and an interlude in Peru, Weidenmann came back to the United States in 1856 and entered the practice of landscape architecture with Eugene Baumann, one of the creators of Llewelyn Park. In Hartford he designed Cedar Hill Cemetery, worked on city parks, and having met Olmsted in 1862, supervised the execution of Olmsted's early improvements at the Hartford Retreat. In 1874 Olmsted made a formal working arrangement with him.[19]

Until the end of 1877 Olmsted, as head of the New York park department's Bureau of Design and Superintendence, expended major efforts on the restoration of Central Park, the planning of Riverside Park, and plans for laying out the newly annexed twenty-third and twenty-fourth wards of New York. Over these harried years loomed the controversial figure of Andrew H. Green and the inescapable hazards of New York politics.

By 1873 Green was one of the most powerful politicians in the city. Samuel Tilden's law partner and trusted henchman, he had by then been a prominent figure in city government for twenty years. Shrewd and experienced, he had developed strong public support based on his impregnable reputation for honesty.

With the collapse of the Ring, he had been appointed deputy comptroller, and then comptroller, of New York City.[20] The city's finances were in Augean disorder, and with Herculean energy he set about policing them. Economy was his passion. Contractors and their laborers went unpaid while his auditors examined their bills for error and falsification; wages and salaries of city employees were withheld until verified; authorized public work went undone until its absolutely inescapable necessity was established to Green's satisfaction.[21] Both hated and admired for his conduct of his office, he seemed indifferent to popularity. Dedicated to economy, he delighted in power; his fiscal authority was the weapon he brandished in the service of both.

A reshuffle of the city's administrative structure, effected by the new charter of 1873, fortified Green's position, especially by requiring his signature on every municipal expenditure; he had, besides, the right to inquire into the expenses and to delay payment of the debts of every department.[22] Because of the diffusion of responsibility throughout the labyrinthine administrative structure, Green's power to get things done was limited, but his power to obstruct was almost absolute.

During the period of Green's comptrollership, which ended in November 1876, there was continuous conflict in City Hall. Green and the reformers wanted to reduce taxes, curtail the costly expansion plans authorized by the Ring, and concentrate on improving services in the built-up part of the city. The uptown real estate interests—allied with the laboring classes who benefited when jobs were plentiful—urged that the opening of new streets and the construction of sewers and parks would attract population and building uptown, relieve congestion downtown, broaden the tax base, and restore the plundered city treasury.[23]

Green's views were frequently represented in the Department of Public Parks, which at the time had the duty of planning the street system in upper New York, by Colonel Henry S. Stebbins, one of the four commissioners and one of the two strong and effective ones during the 1870s. Having been associated with Central Park either as member or president of the board of commissioners since 1859, except during the Tweed Ring interregnum, Stebbins was thoroughly conversant with the park and with all matters that fell within the jurisdiction of the department. He and Green, both anti-Tammany Democrats, often saw eye to eye. When they did not, Stebbins tended discreetly to yield to his powerful colleague.

The other strong member of the commission was William R. Martin, appointed in 1875 when Tammany recaptured the mayoralty. He did not shrink from collision with Green: he regarded him as his natural enemy. A lawyer affiliated with the "reformed" and reviving Tammany Hall, he had represented uptown property owners in suits against the city, and he was president of the West Side Improvement Association, which strongly advocated uptown development.[24] From 1874 to 1878 either Stebbins or Martin was president—the only paid officer—of the board of commissioners. Almost necessarily hostile to each other, each was a knowledgeable commissioner, and each had a respectful, even a cordial, regard for Olmsted.

The other commissioners who from term to term filled the remaining seats on the four-man board were comparative nonentities; some were conscientious and paid attention to expert advice; some were ignorant hacks.

The contention in the Department of Public Parks between the reformers and the Tammany men was scarcely a clash between the forces of light and the forces of darkness. It was, on the contrary, a struggle between politicians—one side having somewhat more respectable pretentions than the other—for control of park department patronage and policy. Tammany dealt frankly in patronage. Green professed that he did not; but like every other political leader in New York, he was anxious to place his supporters in departmental posts and to exclude those of his opponents. Although the stated policy of the Department of Public Parks was not to dispense patronage, patronage could often be wrung from it by someone with enough political muscle.

Green had muscle and used it. Sometimes it was insufficient, as when he tried and failed to force the removal of Olmsted's trusted chief clerk and friend, Howard A. Martin, whose offense was that he was the brother of William R. Martin.[25] Sometimes it was adequate, as when over Olmsted's repeated protests he replaced the bookkeeper with a candidate of his own—who then made a seventy-thousand-dollar mistake in his accounts, so bringing construction work on the park to an abrupt stop.[26]

In the patronage battle over the keepers' force it was, in the end, not so much the participants as Olmsted, who tried to stand clear and attend to his business, who was the loser. His effort to reconstitute the keepers' staff in its original form as a patronage-free body of specially trained men led both factions to turn on him. The commissioners removed the force from his control, and positions on it continued to be dispensed as rewards for political services almost as frankly as in Ring days. In protest, Olmsted offered his resignation in the middle of 1873 and was persuaded to withdraw it only when Stebbins begged him to do so as a personal favor and an act of friendship.[27]

After the Tammany candidate, William Wickham, became mayor in 1875 and appointed William R. Martin to equalize the commission between Tammany and reformers, Martin quarreled constantly with the comptroller. Stebbins warned Olmsted that, unless Green was "conciliated," Green would allow no bill favorable to the park to pass the legislature; he was the most powerful man in New York and would get the best of all opponents.[28] Olmsted was provoked to remark privately, and acidly, that the struggle in the board was not over whether patronage should be used or prevented from being used but over whether it should be used for the mayor's benefit or the comptroller's.[29]

Inadequate appropriations ranked with patronage as an obstacle to the park's restoration and as an irritant to its landscape architect. When the Board of Apportionment in 1874 sharply reduced the park department's estimate for the com-

350

ing year, Olmsted told an inquiring journalist that, while money could be saved with no detriment to the real value of the park, it would have to be saved on such nonessential items as ice-skating and music, but of course it would not be, because of their popularity. Instead, economies would be practiced just where they would do insidious and grave harm: woodwork, masonry, and drains already in need of repair would be further neglected, and planting and landscape effects, the maintenance of which required care and artistry, would become unsightly from negligent and inexpert treatment. "I tell you," he added bitterly,

> that I think the park is going to the devil and have grave doubt whether
> the undertaking to provide a *rural* recreation ground upon such a site
> in the midst of a city like this was not a mistake, was not doomed to
> failure because of the general ignorance of the conditions of success and the
> impossibility of getting proper care taken of it. . . . The Park can easily
> become a nuisance and a curse to the city.[30]

Such was the measure of Olmsted's discontent at the end of 1874. The fact that appropriations requested for 1876 and 1877 were similarly cut did nothing to relieve it.

During these two years disputes over patronage, wages paid to park department laborers, acts affecting the park pending in the legislature, and plans for the twenty-third and twenty-fourth wards kept antagonism seething between Green's friends and Martin's on the board of commissioners. Stebbins called Martin "a contemptible puppy" to his face.[31] Martin, under editorial attack by the *Times* (pro-Green) as "a sort of real estate speculator,"[32] wrote a letter to the *World* (anti-Green) defending his conduct on the board and assailing the comptroller's interference in the park department. Stebbins wailed that the department could do nothing without Green's support, which would never be forthcoming as long as he was so abused by Martin; and Olmsted noted that Martin's letter was a proper response to the *Times*'s editorial, which had misstated facts and imputed low motives to him.[33] Olmsted, however, wanted to keep out of the contention and, when Martin tried to enlist him on his side, declined to commit himself to either. Remembering Stebbins's frequent opposition to wrong and unjust courses on the park, and his personal considerateness toward himself, he wrote Martin that "I must remain his as I am your friend."[34]

The row between Green and Martin was merely an aspect of the dissension bubbling throughout the city administration. The aldermen, mostly Tammany men, early in 1875 recommended to the mayor that he prefer charges against Green and supplied a horrendous bill of particulars, ranging from personal vindictiveness through deceit to gross maladministration.[35] Fitz-John Porter, commissioner of public works that year, in a ferocious attack on Green in the *World*, accused him of brazen meddling in his, Porter's, department and of blocking works he could not control. For good measure, Porter quoted official records of the park department to indicate that Green, supporting resolutions offered by

Tom Fields (whom Green had since called "a cunning and corrupt representative and efficient aid of the Ring"), had made repeated salary grabs while he was on the park commission and that, on Fields's motion, he had in 1868 been voted, and as treasurer had paid himself, seventy-five hundred dollars for a history of Central Park of which he had produced not a page.[36] Green retaliated by writing long letters to the mayor and the press, defending himself and criticizing Martin, and by inspiring political moves. In 1876, after the fizzle of a Green-for-Mayor boom supported by contractors whom the city hired and Green paid, a bill—"Green's bill," Olmsted called it—was introduced into the legislature.[37] It would have reduced the four-man park board to one and extended the comptroller's expiring term by sixty days so that not Wickham, who had no intention of continuing Green in office, but Wickham's successor could make the appointment.[38] When this power play directed against the Tammany commissioners failed, they were assailed from another angle: a committee of citizens, supposedly put up to it by Green, petitioned the mayor to place charges of bad faith and official misconduct against them.[39]

These various maneuvers, and more, were covered in dogged and bewildering detail in the press. "Not a day passes," Olmsted observed in August 1876, "that some move intended to influence the public is not made in the quarrel between Green and Martin."[40]

Olmsted's own position in the department was delicate and unhappy. He wanted only to get on with the park department's business, but his efforts to do so without regard to partisan interests inevitably put him at odds with each side on particular issues. By repeatedly urging that the park laborers' wages be reduced to bring them into line with the prevailing wage and to husband the department's inadequate appropriation, he opposed Martin. By presenting a report recommending a reorganization of the gardeners' force to utilize better the insufficient maintenance fund, he offended Stebbins, who thought he detected in it a reflection on himself and Green. Olmsted's independent course, finally, made him an embarrassment to both sides and left him in a vulnerable position.[41]

The first open move to get rid of Olmsted came soon after his acceptance of an unpaid post on the New York Survey Commission on May 31, 1876. Dorsheimer, lieutenant governor and a member of the commission himself, assured Olmsted he could legally take the position. Nevertheless, the office of landscape architect to the park department was declared vacant, and Olmsted's salary was stopped on the advice of the corporation counsel, who said it was of dubious legality for Olmsted to hold both a city and a state post. Olmsted resigned from the survey and was reinstated as landscape architect to the park department by a resolution of July 26, which provided also that he should be paid in full from May 31, since he had continued to render his usual services. Stebbins, in the same meeting, offered a resolution, which was defeated, to discontinue Olmsted's services on the grounds of economy. Green then refused to pay Olmsted's back salary, and Olmsted, championed by Martin, sued and eventually collected his claim against the city.[42] Whether this harassment emanated from

Tammany or from Green, it was Martin, the Tammany man, who opposed it, and Stebbins and Green who contributed to it.

The hostility between Olmsted and Green did not prevent a limited agreement between them as to the future development of the city of New York. Both recognized that the great metropolitan complex was not a collection of separate communities but was functionally one. Green, however, was almost exclusively concerned with its physical and administrative development;[43] Olmsted was concerned with the social, human, and aesthetic problems arising from its growth. Green thought that, if the metropolitan area was to develop manageably, its street plan should be determined in advance of population and it should be administered as a unit; Olmsted believed that, if it was to develop humanely, the still unpopulous regions should be planned with a view to their probable future use and the well-being of their inhabitants. Here was a clear difference of emphasis, which led logically to a basic planning difference: Olmsted's view precluded, Green's did not preclude, the imposition of the conventional grid system of city streets on still undeveloped lands in the twenty-third and twenty-fourth wards.

In 1807, when New York was still a village without gas, running water, or sewer system, and with no more than premonitions of greatness, the street commissioners had adopted the grid system. (Olmsted thought there was some basis in fact for the tradition that one of them, picking up a mason's sieve that happened to be at hand, placed it over the map they were studying and asked, "What do you want better than that?") The plan provided for uniform blocks, two hundred feet deep, not one of which offered a better or a worse site than any other for whatever kind of building—church, school, butcher shop, blast furnace, or dwelling; and the extension of the grid plan as the city expanded northward had perpetuated the monotonous lack of choice and opportunity. Besides being monotonous, a street arrangement that disregarded topography could be expensive. Sometimes it necessitated costly excavations and fills that a less direct line would have avoided, and sometimes it squandered and destroyed advantages of site offered by a varied surface. The superiority of position that Rome gave to St. Peter's, London to St. Paul's, and Paris to the Madeleine nineteenth-century New York gave to nothing. Instead, it obliterated it under the grid.[44]

The system was calculated to insure overcrowding as well as monotony. The blocks had no alley down the middle, and every lot, regardless of use, was one hundred feet deep. Because of the price of New York real estate, buildings were economical of front footage and extended far back on their lots and high into the air. Individual houses on hundred-foot-deep lots for people of small means were unthinkable; for the well-to-do, they were uncomfortable. In the interiors of these narrow, deep boxes, there was necessarily some ill-ventilated and ill-lit space. Being the least desirable in the house, it was usually allotted to water closets, to which it was quite unsuitable. Kitchen odors wafted up the

353

same long flights of stairs that occupants toiled up. All waste—garbage, trash, ashes—instead of being carted off by way of the back alley as in other cities, had to be carried through the house and disposed of in the front.[45] As a result, wealthy neighborhoods suffered along with poor from untidy streets. In a one-family row house on a typical New York lot drawbacks were ameliorated by the occupants' adequate means; in the crowded tenements they were aggravated by poverty.

The drawbacks that afflicted residences also afflicted buildings for public and commercial use. There was the added disadvantage that streets serving commercial areas, traveled by heavy wagons, congested by delivery carts, and thronged with people, were laid out just like those in the less-frequented residential districts. The street system that had been intended to make all parts of the city equally convenient for all uses had instead, Olmsted argued, made all parts equally inconvenient.[46]

Olmsted and Vaux had tried to break the grip of convention in the late 1860s when they drew up a street plan for the rugged Riverside section on the upper west side of Manhattan. Green dismissed their "fanciful arrangements" as inappropriate to a commercial city and said that the grid had enabled the city "to accommodate a large prospective population" and had "sufficed up to this time."[47] The region was laid out, with difficulty and expense, on a somewhat modified grid approved by Green.

Olmsted's next opportunity, and his last, to supersede the mechanical street plan in the expanding city came after 1874, with the annexation to New York City—which until then had been limited to Manhattan Island—of the twenty-third and twenty-fourth wards, the region lying between the Harlem River and the southern boundary of Yonkers. Olmsted, as chief of the park department's Bureau of Design and Superintendence, and J. James R. Croes, civil and topographical engineer, were assigned the duty of providing plans for a street system and for the line of a rapid-transit steam railway to serve the annexed wards.

They were not the first to have been consulted. The park commissioners had already studied five sets of plans, all of which applied the grid to the largely hilly and refractory terrain, and had tentatively accepted one which Green had himself worked on and approved.[48] Martin's opposition to it had provoked Green to charge obstructionism. Martin had retorted that the annexed wards must be saved from being laid out on a modified grid plan made with the same disregard of cost as the one adopted for Riverside, which had impaired the value of property and crushed it under a load of needless assessments for uncompleted work; such abuses were not entitled to reverence because they were ancient or because Green originated and sustained them. It was on Martin's initiative that Olmsted and Croes, late in 1875, were ordered to prepare new plans.[49]

Their reports, presented in 1876 and 1877, bear the stamp of Olmsted's thought and style and appear to have been written largely by him. In them the authors gave their reasons for departing from the grid convention and made an alternative recommendation.

354

So far as the plan of New York remained to be formed, they argued, it would be inexcusable not to provide for all the requirements of a metropolis—not only those of commerce, but those of domesticity, art, science, religion, scholarship, and recreation. Just as a house had rooms and hallways adapted to different purposes, so a metropolis should be adapted at different points to different ends.[50] Yet it would be premature to plan in detail the use of every acre of ground in the new wards: before the population of New York should have doubled and they become populous, factors not yet operative—new motive powers and means of transit, improved methods of building, new professions and trades, scientific departures affecting heating, lighting, sanitation, communication—would come into being to influence in unforeseen ways the growth of the city.[51]

The first part of the new wards for which Olmsted and Croes offered a plan was the picturesque, hilly section between Riverdale Avenue and the Hudson River, which commanded a grand view of the water. Too rugged and wooded for farming, its only improvements were a number of villas and two religious institutions that had originally been private estates. Uncertainty as to how the region was to be laid out, and lack of good roads, had inhibited the development that pleasing scenery and fine views would otherwise have stimulated.[52]

The terrain did not lend itself to subdivision into conventional city lots; compact ranges of buildings could not be advantageously built upon it; nor could thoroughfares adapted either to heavy teaming or fast driving be readily laid out. Therefore, Olmsted and Croes argued, both industry and inexpensive housing had better be allowed to develop on more suitable ground, of which there was plenty elsewhere.[53]

The same conditions that made the region unsuitable for industry and low-priced houses made it admirable for residences for New Yorkers who could afford suburban homes. With its striking natural advantages, it could become the most attractive suburb in America, drawing and holding within the city limits wealthy families who would otherwise seek homes farther away. The gain to the city would be comparable to that which Central Park occasioned, with the difference that it would lie in conditions created at private, not public, expense.

To develop the region as a rural suburb meant regarding its picturesque character as a source of wealth and enhancing it, and adjusting its roads to a rather sparse population more concerned than the inhabitants of the built-up parts of the city with pleasure driving and walking. These were the leading ideas of the plan that Olmsted and Croes submitted for Riverdale; it was adapted specifically, and only, to rural suburban development.[54]

A few months later they presented the plan for a steam railway, with easy grades, that would afford moderately direct communication between desired points throughout the two new wards, would be easily accessible from points it did not directly touch, would nowhere cross streets or highways at the same level, and would interfere as little as possible with property divisions.[55]

Their final report, presented in November 1877, provided for the laying out of the central district of the annexed wards, where both business and residential use was contemplated.[56] Altogether, the plans provided for business sections in the Mill Brook and Cromwell's Creek sections; for a residential section on the high ground along the center of the district; for suburban homes along the western edge and at the northern end; for avenues of easy grade, which opened into occasional small parks, crossing the whole length and breadth of the two wards; and for routes for steam transportation so placed as not to interfere with other roads.

Again, Stebbins was displeased. Sharing Green's regard for the grid, he interpreted Olmsted's and Croes's analysis and rejection of it as an attack on earlier plans based on it, particularly the one in which Green had had a guiding hand; and he contended that the new plan sacrificed commerce and utility to aesthetic considerations.[57] Despite his opposition, the park commission adopted the new plans and, with them, a new and promising policy for directing the growth of that part of the city that remained to be developed.

The promise was soon scuttled, along with the architects of the policy.

During these same years, Olmsted was planning Riverside Park. To minimize the cost and at the same time retain the most desirable features of this unique territory, he had, with the help of an experienced engineer, studied and restudied and revised the plan. It had been reviewed and confirmed by successive park commissions under the presidencies of the Republican Salem Wales, Stebbins, and Martin; and Olmsted had himself twice taken the drawings for it to Albany and won legislative approval. A main feature of this carefully matured design was the terraced drive, three miles long, that overlooked the Hudson River. Its construction was to be the largest piece of contract work of its sort ever let by the city, and the letting of the contract, consequently, attracted wide attention. The respected trade paper, *Engineering News*, commented on the excellence of the specifications for the work, and some of the most reputable contractors in the country bid on it. The award went, as the city charter required, to the lowest bidder, whose bid was substantially below the average of the other bids.[58]

Olmsted took alarm. No well-informed man could suppose that certain parts of the work could be done at the estimated price except at a heavy loss to the contractor; nor could a rational man suppose that the contractor would voluntarily absorb the loss. Instead, he would try to evade the specifications. After construction was started, the experiences of the supervising engineer, James C. Aldrich, bore out Olmsted's fears. Aldrich repeatedly had to refuse to certify the contractor's work, or to insist that work be taken down, because it did not meet specifications. The contractor appealed to the park commissioners, and the commissioners several times withdrew Croes from his work uptown to run an independent inspection, and Aldrich's objections were every time sustained.[59]

Simultaneously, Olmsted was coping with an oppressive accumulation of reverses in connection with Mount Royal Park in Montreal. The site of the park was difficult, and quite unparklike in his sense of the word, a low hill not much more than seven hundred feet high, rising with moderate abruptness from the plain and water around. It fell naturally into several different sections, each of which Olmsted proposed to treat as its distinctive character suggested. Although he had been engaged late in 1874,[60] it was not until the summer of 1876 that work was begun. It was begun, at that, prematurely from Olmsted's point of view.

Well before they furnished him with the topographical map he always required before proceeding with a landscape design, the commissioners laid out a bridle road and asked him to furnish a plan for a carriage road to the top of the mountain. Over his urgent objections, they opened a road of sorts to the top by the end of February and asked him to designate the site and furnish the plan for a refectory there.[61] To his protests that nothing was so wasteful in landscape architecture as hasty and piecemeal work, the commissioners replied that, in the hard times then prevailing, they had to provide jobs for the city's unemployed.[62]

When the topographical map finally reached him in March, Olmsted learned from it that certain land specified earlier as owned by the city and to be included in the park's boundaries was in fact not owned by the city and had to be excluded,[63] and that a city street was already being extended to enter the park, although it was one of the more exacting parts of his function to provide a system of street connections and entrances to it.[64] Moreover, he was ordered by the park commissioners to put a reservoir in the place previously designated as an open glade; and he was confounded when the area of the reservoir was specified, successively, as five, twenty, and fifteen or sixteen acres. By the beginning of May 1876, he had three times recast the plan in important respects to adapt it to changing information, and he was by no means sure that his most recent instructions would prove to be final.[65]

When the finished road to the top of the mountain was opened, with ceremony and speeches, on the Queen's Birthday the end of May, Olmsted, although publicly polite about it,[66] was thoroughly unhappy. In a letter to the commissioners—which someone, to his further unhappiness, leaked to the press—he complained that it was such a road as, given its high and low points and the maximum grade allowed, anyone who had spent a year with a surveyor's party could have laid out and an intelligent farmer constructed; nothing could compensate him for the injury he must suffer from being supposed to be its designer.[67]

The main thrust of his complaint, however, was that a complex design, all the parts of which were dependent on each other and subordinate to the whole, which should be fully developed before any work at all was done on it, was being approached ignorantly and in fits and starts; that his overall plan was being ignored; and that no single competent person had full professional responsibility for carrying it out on the ground. He urged a "steadier, safer and more efficient system of administration"; and the commissioners, momentarily chastened, resolved to do better in the future.[68] Soon thereafter they offered suggestions, which Olmsted patiently rejected, for placing a smallpox hospital on the park and for planting a double row of evenly spaced trees along the road to the top of the mountain.[69]

The radical trouble, the one that underlay the hasty actions, the infirm decisions, and the inappropriate proposals, was that the park commissioners did not constitute a special body; they were members of the elected common council delegated to manage park affairs. They had no more expertise in them than any other members of the council; they might be turned out of office just as they were beginning to acquire some; and no continuity, either of men or of policy, could be assured. If the commissioners had no great knowledge of parks, the public had even less; Owen, who worked on Mount Royal in the summer of 1876, reported to Olmsted that there was much popular feeling against the park on the ground that it was a needless luxury.[70]

An important factor in the successful launching of the Buffalo park scheme had been the fact that, at its outset, Olmsted had gathered together in a small hall a group of philanthropic and civic-minded citizens and city officials, explained to them the advantages that flowed from a rural park in a big city, and gave them opportunity for questions and discussion.[71] In the hope that a similar public meeting would dispel some of the muddle that hampered the Montreal project, he proposed to give two lectures there in the summer of 1877, one on parks in general and the other on Mount Royal.[72] While the arrangements were still under discussion, the commissioners decisively rejected, on the ground of economy, Olmsted's strong advice that they recover at least part of the acreage first included in, and then excluded from, the park's boundaries; and they scrapped, without explanation, his design for laying out a parkway approach flanked by building lots.[73]

By midsummer 1877, Olmsted's New York and Montreal works were the source of such worry and irritation to him that his health began to break. The sweltering heat combined with anxiety to aggravate his insomnia, and he suffered from a recurrence of the malaria that sometimes troubled him, in addition to "the usual summer thing," which began with fainting and purging and ran into headache and neuralgia.[74]

He was remarkably cool, however, about the excitement that gripped New York the latter part of July, when the railroad strike exploded in Baltimore and spread all over the East. "There was a little row at Harrisburg last night," he wrote his wife at Lake Placid on the evening of the twenty-fourth, "very promptly and neatly put down by the citizens."

Whatever his sympathy for laboring men in general, he could not sympathize with the strike; he believed too deeply that justice in a democracy was obtainable by orderly means to countenance disorderly. Without excitement, he described the atmosphere of the city to his vacationing wife: the militia called up and waiting in the armories; the apprehension of riots; the falling off of the usual noise and bustle in the streets, "the transportation business having mainly ceased"; the sentinels and parades; the rising price of meat. He deprecated the alarm of a caller who "had evidently been among people who were a little panicky" but took his advice to wire Owen, who was at Harrisburg on a school project, to go to Phoenixville and stay there; and then, he added ironically, he "doubled the sentries and directed the armorer to load the individual mountain howitzers."[75]

For a few days he enjoyed the company of Richardson, who, caught in New York by the strike, stopped by Olmsted's home every evening. Together they walked to Fifth Avenue to get the *Post* and went on to French's hotel in Chatham Street for supper. By the twenty-seventh, the trains were running in and out of New York again, Owen was home, and Olmsted was planning business trips to Baltimore, Washington, and Montreal.[76] Altogether, the tenor of his life seems to have been little disturbed by the ominous flare-up.

Olmsted's trip to Montreal took place the end of September. For all the effect it had in educating public or official opinion there, he might as well have stayed at home. He had asked the park commissioners who were arranging the meeting to invite various influential men who had criticized his designs; and because he thought the park's educational, sanitary, and moral value needed to be better understood, he asked that personal invitations be sent to the teachers, doctors, and clergymen of the city. Later, in a report to the park commissioners, he described the meeting.

> . . . Half an hour after the time appointed, of a fine autumnal afternoon, in a hall for a thousand, in the heart of the city, time and place being selected by your commissioners with a view to the convenience of those invited, less than thirty persons (ladies, gentlemen and children) had come together. There was not, I believe, among them one teacher, one physician, or one clergyman; not one member of the City Council (the commissioners excepted) or of the executive departments of the city government. Nor was there one, as far as I have reason to suppose, of all those gentlemen as to whose propositions, demands and questions my judgment had during the three previous years been asked, and whose power to embarrass the undertaking I had been led to regard with concern.
>
> At the end my little audience kindly thanked me and asked for the publication of the papers read.[77]

The commissioners agreed with the request, making some suggestions about omissions; one admitted that he had not been able to follow Olmsted's argument and doubted any special good would come of publishing it.[78]

On his return, Olmsted was so unwell he could do no desk work. A month later, his doctors became so worried about him that they urged a complete change of scene and occupation. While he was still resisting the idea of asking the New York park commissioners for leave of absence, Olmsted became aware of an effort to drum him out of the park department. He realized that he was being systematically followed; when charges of misconduct against him—invented, he supposed, by his pursuers to hide their failure to find any damaging facts—were preferred before the commission, he was neither required nor invited to answer them: Martin himself rebutted them and scotched the scheme.[79]

The respite afforded Olmsted was only temporary. Martin was to leave the commission early in 1878, having been held over after the expiration of his term. Stebbins's term had expired in November 1877. Three Tammany men—a banker, a cotton broker, and a real-estate lawyer—composed a majority of the board at the end of the year. Without any knowledge of landscape architecture or any qualifications for park management, they seemed disinclined to gain any. In spite of Olmsted's several invitations, none of them once toured the park with him to be briefed on its aims, necessities, and problems.[80] They regarded it as a finished job requiring no further creative guidance. "The park is now completed and can with the aid of a few gardeners and laborers take care of itself," one of them told a *Herald* reporter.

> [Olmsted's] position is merely a sinecure and I believe in abolishing it and diverting the money thus saved to paying the poor laborers and policemen who make a living out of the work. We have to retrench somewhere and I think it would be infinitely better to cut off these high-toned fellows and help the poor laborers to work.[81]

John Kelly, the Tammany chief who succeeded Green as comptroller at the end of 1876, invoked Olmsted's outside work as pretext to stop his salary early in December and inquired of the commissioners if it was true, as alleged, that Olmsted's absences from his duties were "frequent and prolonged."[82] Before the matter could be resolved, Olmsted's doctors peremptorily insisted that he ask leave of absence. The commissioners granted him one, without pay, for three months beginning January first, and he engaged passage to Europe for the ninth.[83]

The board of commissioners snatched at the opening. Opposed only by Martin, it voted to abolish the Bureau of Design and Superintendence and all offices under it, adding a vacuous resolution appointing Olmsted "Consulting Landscape Architect," to be called in and paid as his services might be on occasion required. The following day it notified him that he could appear before it on the tenth to show cause why his office should not be abolished. Olmsted protested that by the tenth he would be well out to sea and requested that action on his removal be deferred and that Howard Martin, whose removal was encompassed with his own, be retained until his return.[84]

Both protest and suggestion went unheeded. Olmsted was out—out of Central Park, which he had cherished for twenty years, out of Riverside, where his vision was just beginning to take tangible form, and out of the annexed wards, where the promise of civilized planning for urban living flickered invitingly. Ill and heartsick, he sailed January 9 on the *Montana* for Liverpool, leaving instructions that his friends were not to exert themselves in his behalf and that no New York papers were to be sent to him.[85]

Olmsted's friends—among them Vaux, Godkin, Leopold Eidlitz, Waring, Potter, Dorsheimer, Parke Godwin, Miss Wormeley, Louisa Lee Schuyler, Bellows—and some of the newspapers—the *Post*, the *Tribune*, the *Herald*, the *World*, even the *Times*—strongly objected to his removal, however, and launched a campaign to have his dismissal rescinded. They were joined by one hundred eighty-five prominent men of both parties and various callings—architects, writers, doctors, publishers, scientists, artists, financiers, educators, businessmen, lawyers—who addressed a strongly worded petition to the board of commissioners. These protests were as ineffectual as Olmsted's own, and on January 24 the board reiterated its decision to abolish Olmsted's office.[86]

A melancholy consequence of the newspaper agitation was the public quarrel it precipitated between Vaux and Godkin and the strained relations it produced between Vaux and the Olmsted family. In all the published discussion arising out of Olmsted's dismissal, reference was nowhere made to Vaux's equal responsibility for the design of Central Park; it was as though Olmsted were its sole creator. Always touchy on the point, Vaux was especially stung by a letter of Godkin's in the *Tribune*, which, in urging Olmsted's reinstatement, entirely ignored Vaux's role.[87] After a personal protest to Mary Olmsted, in which his "chivvying" English manner irritated her and her "air of a successful buccaneer" outraged him,[88] Vaux wrote the *Tribune* an angry and excited reply, rebuking Godkin for his "greedy misrepresentations" on Olmsted's behalf.[89] Mary Olmsted, having spent the day in tears and in consultation with William Cullen Bryant and Judge John J. Monell, blue-penciled Godkin's proposed retort[90]—which when it appeared was still gratuitously cutting[91]—and had Owen publish in the *Tribune* a short note saying that no one had any authority to claim for Olmsted either more or less than an equal share with Vaux in the designs of Central Park and Prospect Park.[92] She also sent Vaux a stiff letter saying that she had written to the *Tribune* to gratify her husband's old partner's "injudicious desire for advertisement"—injudicious because, had Vaux waited for Olmsted to return and reply, his interests would have been better served—and warning him that she had heard that Viele was again advancing his claims to having designed the parks. "I trust you will not feel obliged to give him battle," she added, "until you can have the aid of Mr. Olmsted's sound judgment and practiced pen. I subscribe myself, though I own you have made it difficult for me to do so, Very sincerely your friend, Mary C. Olmsted."[93]

Then she bundled up the whole correspondence and sent it to John, who was traveling with Olmsted, to show to his father or not as he thought best, and gave herself over to fears that Olmsted would be much displeased that she had meddled in his professional affairs.[94]

Meanwhile, Olmsted was moving about Europe, scribbling memorandums in a pocket notebook on trees, avenues, gutters, street lighting, city government, zoos, parks, and anything else that caught his interest. Having landed at Liverpool, he had examined Birkenhead Park; in London he studied the zoo in Regent's Park. From London he went to Bruges, Brussels, Antwerp, The Hague, and Amsterdam. At Frankfort on the Main he saw an interesting palm garden and the best zoo, he thought, he had so far observed. Munich's English Garden pleased him, "a beautiful body of woodland scenery with large glades and some good meadows" and a branch of the Isar flowing through it. He was surprised to learn from an aged forester that no trees had been planted in it in his lifetime and many cut for fuel, which was a source of revenue.

In Venice Olmsted visited the botanic garden; around Florence he admired the rolling hills thick with young olive trees; at Pisa he found the botanic garden had a number of American trees, including a *Magnolia grandiflora,* planted in 1802, which was two feet thick. Camelias, palms, and subtropical plants flourished in Genoa's city garden, which swarmed with soldiers and sailors and children and nurses and had a gatekeeper wearing a London metropolitan policeman's uniform. The Villa Carlotta at Como had a magnificent *Mahonia japonica* twelve feet high; all its palms, yuccas, and conifers were covered with thatch supported by poles to protect them from snow. On March 2, he reached Mâcon in France, where he was pleased by the decorative use of plants and flowers at the Hôtel des Etrangers and by the price of the excellent local wine, one and a half francs per half-bottle. The park at Dijon, ascribed to Le Nôtre, drew noncommittal mention from him, but he liked the low, spreading box bushes, pleasingly grouped and massed on the stony hillsides between Mâcon and Dijon.[95]

From Dijon, Olmsted went to Paris. His stay there was unfortunate—he was sick, the weather was bad—and it would have been worse had it not been for the kindness of Edouard André. André, associated with his older colleague Adolphe Alphand in work on the Paris parks, had designed parks in England and Luxembourg and had been sent by his government to South America in 1875 to study certain wild grasses. Passing through New York in August 1876, he had met Olmsted, who had shown him over the New York parks, given a dinner party for him at Delmonico's, and told him what to see in the cities he was to visit. Renewed acquaintance with André somewhat redeemed the miserable stopover in Paris.[96]

When he reached home the end of April, Olmsted felt little better than when he had left.[97] It did nothing for his health and spirits to learn that Aldrich had been dismissed from the Riverside work; and his chagrin was aggravated when, in July, Croes, who was in the midst of laying out the new wards, was replaced as topographical engineer.[98]

XXX
TWO CAPITOLS; NIAGARA

1878–1881

DESPITE his reverses in the New York City park department, Olmsted could still consider the city itself dispassionately. In forecasting its future in the *Tribune* at the end of 1879, he referred to its assets and its drawbacks and discussed their effects on its standing as a metropolis.

Situated where its advantages for dealing with all parts of the country were matched by its advantages for dealing with Europe, New York had already established its commercial preeminence; and it was gaining rapidly in the intellectual and cultural prestige that distinctly advanced its claim to be considered a metropolis. Retarding it were its "slipshod, temporizing government of amateurs" and its "senseless" street plan.

> The tenement-house, which is the product of the uniform 200-foot-wide blocks, is beginning to be recognized as the primary cause of whatever is peculiarly disgraceful in New-York City politics, through the demoralization which it works on the more incapable class of working people. It is a calamity more to be deplored than the yellow fever at New-Orleans, because more impregnable; more than the fogs of London, the cold of St. Petersburg, or the malaria of Rome, because more constant in its tyranny.

Even the dwellings of comparatively wealthy men—the first-class, brownstone, high-stooped, fashionable modern houses—were a confession that it was impossible to build a convenient and comfortable residence, except at prohibitive cost, within the rigid grid: the family was lucky that had a slot twenty feet wide and five or six stories high, with two rooms out of three pleasingly proportioned and giving on the open air. And the worst of it was that the movement uptown was leading to nothing better: even half a dozen miles from the center of population, the grid was being repeated and new houses were being jammed side by side into it "as dark and noisome in their middle parts and as inconvenient throughout as if they were parts of a beseiged fortress." New York would have to offer extraordinary attractions to draw people to such quarters from the cheaper and more comfortable houses to be found in any other American city.

In speculating on the future of New York as a metropolis, Olmsted took account of areas far beyond its political boundaries. Newark, Newport, and Bridgeport were as essential parts of the metropolitan area as Brooklyn, Yonkers, and Jersey City; and Yale University, annexed for scholarly and scientific purposes to New York, was as important an element in its intellectual life as the colleges within its limits. "In fact, the railway, the telegraph, the telephone make a few miles more or less of so little consequence that a large part of the ideas of a city, which have been transmitted to us from the period when cities were walled and necessarily compact and crowded, must be put away."

Since new means of transportation and communication and new social usages had broken the mold of the city, an expanded idea of it, adapted to the changes, had to be substituted for the old. Prominent among the new realities was the two-pronged tendency toward concentration for business and social purposes and dispersion for domestic purposes. The first led toward closer and higher building in the business district; the other led to more open building in residential quarters, and to the demand for homes, combining rural and urban advantages and neither isolated, on the one hand, nor crowded solidly together, on the other, wherever they could be found in healthy, pleasing localities with ready access to business and cultural centers. Such suburbs were arising in attractive neighborhoods around London, Paris, Boston, Philadelphia, and western cities. New Yorkers, less than the people of any other large city, were following the suburban trend simply because so far there were no thoroughly healthy suburban neighborhoods in easy reach of New York. Whenever such suburbs were developed,

> the metropolitan advantages of New York, and the profits of its local trade must be greatly increased by constantly increasing accessions to its population of men who have accumulated means elsewhere, and who wish to engage in other than purely money-making occupations. Such men, living under favorable circumstances and with capital and energies economically directed to matters of general interest, are the most valuable constituents of a city; and it is by their numbers, wealth and influence, more than anything else, that a city takes its rank in the world as a metropolis.[1]

It is not surprising to find that the exponent of these advanced views was greatly attracted by the spacious, gracious suburbs of Boston.

The slow process of Olmsted's detachment from New York began in the summer of 1878 and was accomplished by 1881. The first summer he and his family shared a house on Kirkland Street in Cambridge with the Godkins, where Olmsted used a small upstairs room as office. The good company compensated for the tight squeeze, and proximity to important work justified the temporary move.[2] Olmsted was planning the Arnold Arboretum with Charles Sprague Sargent; he was engaged to lay out a hundred acres in park around the Back Bay fens, the first step in Boston's new park system, for which John, under his direction, was drafting plans; and he had begun work on the Connecticut capitol grounds at Hartford. Although he had other works including the new capitol at

Albany in hand besides, he spoke of himself as being not very active but better in health.[3]

In addition to Godkin, he could draw on Norton, Sargent, and Asa Gray in the neighborhood, Charles Francis Adams, Jr., in Quincy, and Richardson in Brookline for companionship to offset the attrition in his own family. Charlotte was soon to be married to a young Boston doctor, John Bryant; and Owen, early in the summer, had been sent to Wyoming to learn the cattle business on Clarence King's ranch near Cheyenne. An outdoor life seemed desirable to harden the never robust young mining engineer.[4]

The dispersion of adult children is in the course of nature; the severance of his friendship with Miss Wormeley is not easily explained. "Circumstances," she cryptically said, brought her correspondence with Olmsted to an end in 1878. There would seem to have been an emotional parting. *"Remember,"* she long after quoted him as saying, "whatever comes in life nothing can ever make me lose my perfect confidence in you."[5]

On her side the relationship had been ardent and confidential. She appealed for advice on personal and business matters. She indexed, as a convenience for him, the copy of William Robinson's *Wild Garden* he lent her. She confided in him the unhappiness of her childhood, blighted by the forbidding religiosity of the older sister who reared her, and the grief of her middle years when a friendship of seventeen years standing "that had nothing to do with marriage, but took the place of marriage" was brutally and gradually broken up so that she fled Newport for a time. She sympathized with Olmsted in his frustrations in the Sanitary Commission and the New York park department: while her griefs were personal, his were "griefs of purposes thwarted, worthy, *useful,* beautiful objects miscarried — high aims misunderstood — In short, dear friend, yours *is* a life, in a public and social sense, wasted and suffered to be lost. I have always felt this, and always resented it."[6]

For his part, Olmsted frankly valued her high regard and rarely hinted at its burdensome features; he seems to have concurred in her claim to be one of the very few who rightly understood and appreciated him; he responded solicitously to her various appeals; and he respected her excellent and cultivated mind. Her worshipful attitude may have embarrassed him; it irked his wife, who worshipped no one, not even Olmsted. Still, Mary Olmsted liked Miss Wormeley well enough to invite her, just before Olmsted left for Europe at the beginning of 1878, to spend January in New York with her[7]—and that must have been very well indeed, for Mary was notoriously loathe to waste her time on people who did not meet her exacting standards.

Nevertheless, the alienation occurred. A clue to it may lie in a remark of Waring's, who wrote Olmsted from Newport the next summer that Mrs. Olmsted must be a victim of Miss Wormeley's "insanity." So, he added flippantly, was Godkin—if he was not the cause of it: he was then visiting at Newport and was not as attentive as she would like. Not long after, Dr. Mary Putnam Jacobi wrote Olmsted that his description of Miss Wormeley suggested a type of hysteria—"pitiful, troublesome and dangerous"—not uncommon in women her age. Miss Wormeley was then fifty.[8]

Olmsted remembered her long and kindly: he drafted a friendly letter to her late in 1893, telling her of his work and travels. Whether he sent it or she received it, there is no way of knowing: she kept none of his letters.[9]

Olmsted's extraprofessional interests continued to be numerous. With Sargent and Gray, and in consultation with Ashburner, he discussed means of establishing a redwoods reservation on the West Coast and made recommendations to the secretary of the interior, Carl Schurz.[10] He advised on a proposal, which bore fruit only toward the end of the century, to establish a botanical society and garden, a zoological society, and a first-rate zoo in New York.[11] He had helped to draw up the *Handbook for Visitors to the Poorhouse* for the New York State Charities Aid Association in 1877, and he remained active on its executive committee.[12] As an expert witness he testified for H. H. Hunnewell, through whose beautifully landscaped estate near Wellesley the city of Boston had condemned a right of way, arguing that compensation should be based not on the value of the strip of land taken but on the value of the work of art destroyed.[13] He gave much time and thought to the Committee on Sites of the Citizens' Committee of the New York World's Fair proposed for 1883 to celebrate the hundredth anniversary of the treaty of peace between the United States and England. Beginning in 1879, zealous advocates, among them President Grant, insisted the fair should be held in Central Park, while the park's defenders vigorously opposed such an encroachment because of the devastation it would wreak on both scenery and site. The fair was first postponed to 1885 and eventually abandoned as the Columbian Exposition approached, but as late as September 1889, Olmsted warned a park commissioner not unfavorable to placing it on the park that he would do everything he could "publicly and privately, in New York, Albany, Washington and the country at large" to thwart the scheme.[14]

However busy, Olmsted had time and thought for his friends. Although he was no longer close to Vaux, he vigorously defended him in a chilly and extended exchange of letters with A. J. Bloor, who had been an associate of Vaux's for a short time, against Bloor's charges of bad faith;[15] and he had Bellows delete from his history of the Union League Club as unfair and offensive to Vaux a reference to Olmsted as "the originator" of Central Park.[16] Concerned for Knapp's health and morale, undermined by two years of agonizing neuralgia, Olmsted in 1880 planned and arranged a trip West for him, obtaining money to finance it and railroad passes mostly from old Sanitary friends of his own and Knapp's.[17] He was prompt and careful to advise Godkin, who was debating his future and the *Nation's*. In 1870 Olmsted had urged him not to give up the magazine for a professorship at Harvard; but in 1881, after Henry Villard bought the *Post* and proposed installing Carl Schurz, Horace White, and Godkin as editors and annexing the *Nation* to the newspaper, Olmsted advised Godkin, who was beginning to flag under the full responsibility for the weekly, to accept the offer.[18]

He found himself cast, too, in the thankless role of referee between his stepmother and his half-brother Allie. The aging lady and her youngest son, by then a prospering banker, quarreled at every opportunity, and each regularly appealed to Olmsted for support. They wrangled about Allie's management of John Olmsted's estate, about the need for improvements to her house, about moving her hedge and cutting her trees, about her intention to take another boarder, and about the custody of the neatly written four-volume daybook that John Olmsted had kept for half a century. Olmsted's ailing half-sister Mary, who lived with her mother, abetted the running fight until her death in 1875. Suspicion and resentment determined the relationship between mother and son, and there was little that Olmsted could do to restore a kindlier tone to it.[19]

During his first summer in Cambridge, Olmsted was putting the finishing touches on a labor that had occupied him off and on for two years: he was selecting decorative plants and pots for the new capitol at Albany. Although his wife later said he had little to do with the capitol "except back the others, and arrange the jardinieres,"[20] supporting the heretical proposals of Eidlitz and Richardson embroiled him in a nasty row between them and a number of their more conventional colleagues.

The new capitol had been started in 1867 after an Italian Renaissance plan by Thomas S. Fuller, designer of the Victorian Gothic capitol at Ottawa. Supposed to cost four million dollars, it had eight years later already consumed five million, and it was only two stories above ground. According to estimates, another seven million would be required to finish it.[21] The cost, and the suitability of the plan itself, came under such criticism that in 1875 the legislature appointed the New Capitol Commission, with Lieutenant Governor Dorsheimer as chairman, to determine if there had been fraud and whether the plans could be modified to reduce costs. To advise the commission, Dorsheimer appointed a board of three: Olmsted, Eidlitz, and Richardson.[22]

Eidlitz, whom Olmsted had known for years, was architect of the Academy of Music in Brooklyn and of the Produce Exchange and the Continental Bank in New York; independent and highly competent, he was preeminent for his ability to handle monumental design. Richardson, the younger of the two, was working on Trinity Church in Boston and was already recognized as unique among contemporary architects. He was a stylist who was breaking with the architectural convention of the day and forging his own idiom—picturesque, ebullient, solid. He loved the challenges that nineteenth-century America presented to architects and once said that what he most wanted to design was a grain elevator and the interior of a great river steamer.[23]

He was probably the most congenial architectural collaborator Olmsted ever had. At their first meeting, late in the 1860s, Richardson had spoken directly to

Olmsted's heart and to his experience when he remarked that for an architect the most valuable of all appliances were tracing paper and India rubber, and the spirit most to be cultivated and cherished was a willingness to discard drawings; never, until the building was "in stone beyond recovery," should there be any indisposition to reconsider and revise. Olmsted and Richardson shared, besides a passion for perfection, a profuse inventiveness, an enlightened concern to cope with aspects of contemporary life, each through his own art, and even something of the same reverence for scenery. When Richardson visited Niagara Falls with Olmsted, Olmsted, reversing the usual sightseeing procedure, drove him around for several hours before letting him even glimpse the falls. It was not until the next day that he fairly saw them. "When he did," Olmsted reported approvingly, "he had caught the idea of throwing curiosity aside and avoiding amazement, and was willing to sit for hours in one place contemplatively enjoying the beauty, saying little of what was before us . . . but taking quiet pleasure and laying up pleasure."[24]

When appointed to the board, Olmsted and Richardson were already experienced in working together: in 1871 Richardson had designed the buildings for the Buffalo State Hospital and determined their placement with the aid of Olmsted, who planned the grounds; and in 1874 they had collaborated on Niagara Square in Buffalo, where Olmsted was responsible for shaping and planting the ground and Richardson for designing the monumental arch—on which he had carefully provided uneven surfaces for Olmsted's climbing vines to grip.[25]

Olmsted owed his place on the board with the two architects to his experience as an administrator of large public works. Montgomery Schuyler, learned and witty critic of architecture, thought he was "a most valuable member of a body which was to undertake the reclamation of a less tractable wilderness than that out of which Central Park was made to blossom."[26]

There was nothing in the original plan, Schuyler said, to indicate that the architect had tried to design the buildings as a working whole with necessary and interdependent parts, or to designate in treatment portions superior in importance and portions subordinate to them, or to adapt structure to function in expression as well as in fact. The building as originally conceived would inevitably have been "huddled and confused," and much of the huddle and confusion would have been owing to "the wonderful wilderness of things into which it was meant to break out on top"—rows of round dormers in metal, eight little copper-covered towers in the style of Sir Christopher Wren, Greek pediments, Louis xiv pavilions hung with cast-iron festoons and crowned with iron balustrades, and crestings wherever they could be squeezed in.[27]

The interior indicated to Schuyler that not until he had designed the outside did the architect begin to consider how to accommodate the inside to it. His belated efforts were not very successful. The two legislative chambers were sixty feet off the ground and difficult to reach; corridors three hundred forty feet long were lighted by windows at either end; staircases were lighted only from the top; there was an enormous amount of waste space; a "great cavern" on the ground floor, lighted on but one side, was designated "art gallery"; and the finished decorative work was the subject "rather for wonder than for criticism." The huge Assembly Chamber, a hundred forty by eighty-five feet, was so badly planned that light from the windows would be entirely cut off on one side and obstructed on the opposite; and as for its proposed decorations, their rudeness held no hint of vigor, and their feebleness could never be mistaken for refinement.

These strictures appeared in *Scribner's Magazine* in December 1879; the twenty-eight-page report the advisory board submitted to Dorsheimer's committee in March 1876 anticipated them. Though damning, it was carefully factual and polite in tone. The board had found no gross fraud; the cost of the building so far had not been immoderate, considering the inadequate supervision of the work. The site, however, was ill chosen for a monumental building; some of the interior arrangements were inconvenient, and others were mean; an error of design had led to serious structural faults; and the exterior was banal and inexpressive.[28] These generalizations the authors persuasively documented. They could suggest few remedial measures. The cramped site could not be enlarged; and it was unthinkable to tear down five million dollars worth of building, even though nothing truly appropriate and convenient could possibly be created on the hollow rectangle of the established floor plan. The position and dimensions of every important room were already fixed, and the essential faults of the plan were permanently fastened upon the building.[29] Various interior changes could be made, however, to enhance dignity and convenience; the irregular and complex roof could be simplified in the interests of repose and economy; and the exterior could be given greater elegance and breadth by eliminating or altering some extraneous features.[30] Eidlitz and Richardson proposed dividing the work of redesigning between them, Richardson to take the inside and outside of the south side of the building, which included the Senate Chamber, and Eidlitz to take the interior and exterior of the north side, which included the Assembly Chamber and the proposed great tower.[31]

In a startling break with convention, as the drawings they presented with their report illustrated, the architects intended, also, to abandon Renaissance and finish the building in Romanesque, modifying features of the completed stories to make the transition as little jarring as possible. The break, though startling, was not arbitrary: while Romanesque had been the early love of Eidlitz and was particularly congenial to Richardson's talent, the change was not a matter of mere preference. It came about as the architects, trying to remedy the lack of repose and stateliness in the original plan, suppressed the pilasters and substituted in the masses containing the great rooms an unbroken field that could be emphasized as a feature.[32] The mixed treatment, however, was bound to arouse swarms of indignant critics in a period when many of the leading architects were reverent practitioners of Renaissance and Gothic. Olmsted was himself doubtful about the aesthetic propriety of switching styles in a partially finished building; but his faith in Richardson's instinct and Eidlitz's clear head overcame his misgivings. His own instinct, too, warned that in this case the more audacious course was also the safer. If the ill-designed building was to be in any way redeemed, not a cautious but a radical change had to be made.[33]

The first reaction to the new plan was favorable. After a summary of the advisory board's report and one of its perspective drawings appeared in *American Architect and Building News*, the magazine published a long article criticizing Fuller's design as inexpressive of the function and dignity of a capitol and asserting that the advisory board's success was proportionate to their disregard of the original design. Their modifications tended toward dignity, repose, expressiveness, and grace of detail.[34] This was almost the last kind word the advisory board got. The architectual fraternity, although it had uttered never a criticism of the manifest shortcomings of the original design, fell savagely upon the effort to improve it.[35]

Fuller launched the assault. Claiming that certain admittedly unfortunate features of his plan had been specified by the legislature, he blasted the new design and cited in his support a letter signed by three prominent New York architects, one of them Richard Morris Hunt, president of the New York chapter of the American Institute of Architects.[36] Then the chapter itself, through its secretary, Bloor, addressed a vehement remonstrance to the New York State Legislature, the gist of which was that the mingling of Renaissance and Romanesque was anathema to all good architects, and had it published in leading New York papers.[37] Richardson, offended that the chapter of which he and Eidlitz were members had publicly attacked their plan without first giving them a hearing, kept silent; but Olmsted, an honorary member, protested in a stiff and angry letter to Hunt that the remonstrance was couched in terms "apparently intended and certainly adapted to destroy all confidence in our taste and professional judgment."[38]

Notwithstanding Olmsted's protest, the chapter printed copies of the remonstrance and circulated it widely among architects; and Fuller applied to other chapters to help him. Rebuffed by Edward Cabot, president of the Boston chapter, he nevertheless got active support from several chapters and from some of the most popular architects of the day, among them Hunt, Richard Upjohn, James Renwick, and Alfred B. Mullet.[39]

Within a month of the publication of the Eidlitz and Richardson plans, the question of the comparative merits of the two designs had been lost from sight in the rancorous row over the style of the new one. Schuyler, dying to plunge into the middle of it, at first bottled his anger because of his friendship with some of the Institute members, then wrote a clever and devastating article for the *World*, which he showed to Olmsted. Olmsted dissuaded him from publishing it: the ill will already blazing hardly needed to be fanned.[40] Norton assured Olmsted, who anxiously sought his advice, that the mingling of styles was not necessarily antagonistic to "the received rules of art," although it might be to some building canons laid down by Renaissance builders, and he asserted that the advisory board had made the best modifications possible, considering the advanced state of the building, in "a structure radically vicious." He advised, however, that while Renaissance and Romanesque were not inharmonious, the upper stories ought to be brought into closer harmony with the lower since a change of style in a half-finished building might seem capricious unless clear utilitarian advantages or "a change in the national temper" dictated it.[41]

Olmsted replied that greater harmony would be sought, but at the expense of the building's Renaissance character: Eidlitz said he simply could not work in Renaissance and maintained that the inevitable jar between the lower and the upper stories would be a jar not between two styles but between bad architecture and good; and Richardson refused to revert to Renaissance. Two months later, after the advisory board had submitted revised designs, Olmsted feared that the whole thing still had "a patchwork character."[42]

As work proceeded according to the revised plan—"more Romanesque, but also, I hope, more coherent"—the purists increased their opposition. Testifying in March 1877 before a joint committee of Finance and Ways and Means, Hunt and Mullet agreed, Olmsted heard, that "our proposition is absurd and ridiculous"; Hunt had become "singularly excited and was near taking his coat off."[43] Hunt and four other architects* who had appeared at Albany recapitulated their testimony in a letter published in several New York papers and reprinted in *American Architect and Building News*. By stacking Romanesque on Renaissance, they declared, Eidlitz and Richardson implied one of two things: either the building could not be satisfactorily finished in Renaissance or they were incompetent to do it. Examples of monumental Renaissance buildings in Italy and elsewhere refuted the first proposition; if the second was accepted, Eidlitz and Richardson ought to resign—their narrow-mindedness and blind devotion to a favorite style had led them to neglect all considerations of aesthetic propriety.[44]

The truculent and insulting tone of the letter shocked the *American Architect* into commenting, "We doubt if any occurrence in this generation has done more to weaken the general confidence in architects as architects, among those who have witnessed it, than this unlucky quarrel." Norton concurred: the critical architects, by their bitterness, unfairness, and ignorant opposition were giving the whole profession a bad name.[45]

The clash of authorities was not confined to style. Eidlitz intended to replace the flat decorated iron ceiling originally designed for the Assembly Chamber with one of vaulted stone; his critics said the acoustics would be bad and the vault would come crashing down on the heads of the legislators.[46]

The lawmakers, buffeted and baffled by conflicting opinions, finally permitted the vaulted stone ceiling, supported by four massive marble columns and secured from above with concealed iron ties, and changed their minds several times about accepting the Romanesque style. Olmsted believed it was not their aesthetic convictions but their frustrated appetite for patronage that was responsible for much of their opposition to the new design. Dorsheimer agreed: there was not a single member, he said, who was not dissatisfied with the advisory

*George Post, Napoléon Le Brun, Henry Dudley, and Detlef Lienau.

board—"not because of our plans, that is only a pretext, not because of our administration that has been unprecedentedly economical and efficient and everybody knows it, but simply because no one thinks we have given him as much patronage as he ought to have."[47]

Romanesque arches began to rise upon the Renaissance like a new palace on the remains of an old. The legislature, however, after Eidlitz had finished the north façade in Romanesque, changed its mind a final time to favor Renaissance —Schuyler wished that each legislator had been required to record his definition of Renaissance along with his vote—and Richardson, when he came to complete the upper stories of the south facade, resorted to a sort of free Renaissance on the order of the chateau architecture of François I. Sixteenth-century French architecture had the advantage, Schuyler slyly remarked, of being a mixture of styles that, by lapse of time, had come to be recognized itself as a style; some minds were so constituted, or trained, as to be somehow soothed in the presence of a contemporary heresy by the reflection that the axial lines of openings are disregarded in the town hall at Beaugency and that Gothic niches are flanked by classical pilasters in the façade of the town hall of Orléans.[48]

Surprisingly, despite all the critical and legislative interference, the capitol in the end was not utterly botched, and the "monotonous huddle" of the lower stories was skillfully cleared up into a harmonious relationship with the parts above. When the unfinished building was ready for its gala opening in January 1879, the *American Architect* conceded that, although it had not the unity of a harmonious whole, "we have a work of vigor, individuality and artistic power which, in spite of a forced conformity to an original scheme that does not suit with it, and that involves many shortcomings in the final result, will give it a place of permanent honor."[49]

Olmsted's association with the work had not been happy. He was patching, not creating; the job had almost nothing to do with landscape architecture; even worse, he was operating in a field outside of his professional competence and, although ill qualified, had to take a vigorously partisan role in a dispute among experts.[50]

The quarrel had less drastic personal consequences than might have been expected, considering all the bad-tempered exchanges. Fuller was afterward on friendly terms with Eidlitz, and with Richardson, whose work he much admired;[51] and Olmsted, in spite of privately expressed strictures on Hunt, was later able to collaborate closely with him on a large and sustained work, the Biltmore Estate near Asheville, North Carolina. Still, it is no surprise not to find Hunt, or other prominent architects in opposition, listed among those Olmsted recommended in 1879 to a client as architects with whom he could work harmoniously. The list was headed by Eidlitz and Richardson, and it included, among a dozen others, Vaux and his associates Radford and Withers; McKim, Mead and Bigelow; and Farnsworth and Sullivan.[52]

The episode, although comparatively unimportant in Olmsted's career, is nevertheless illuminating. Architecture was a subject about which Olmsted had little to say, and that little bore rather on function than aesthetics. If a building was inconvenient for its use, exteriorly inexpressive of its purpose, or ill adapted to its surroundings, Olmsted could criticize it confidently. He lacked confidence in his own judgment, however, as he indicated by his anxious reliance on Richardson, Eidlitz, Norton, and Schuyler during the Albany capitol dispute. Yet, while his own taste was unsure and even undistinguished, it was rational and educable. It responded to well-reasoned novelty more sympathetically than it accepted fashionable convention. Probably Olmsted's association with Richardson, a great original like himself, influenced it in the direction of greater confidence and freedom and rather spoiled Olmsted for work with routinely competent architects and with talented and headstrong ones like Hunt.

Richardson was more than a stimulus to Olmsted; he was the ideal collaborator, being the foremost of the few architects who recognized in their practice "the inestimable advantage of a brotherly accord between [their] profession and that of the landscape architect."[53] When Richardson and Olmsted were engaged on the same work, it was a genuine collaboration from the start—the start being consultation about the site of the building and its approaches. Among the works they did jointly were the Crane Memorial Library at Quincy, where Richardson designed the building and Olmsted furnished plans for the grounds which Charles Francis Adams, Jr., executed under his direction; the Converse Memorial Library at Malden, Massachusetts; the library, station, and Ames Memorial Hall at North Easton, Massachusetts; two bridges in the Fenway; and a number of stations along the line of the Boston and Albany Railroad, among them Auburndale, Palmer, North Easton, Chestnut Hill, and Wellesley Hills.[54] With the proliferation of suburbs, and the concomitant need for improved commuter transportation, these last, especially, were a challenge to the architect and landscape architect who aimed to achieve sightly and convenient solutions of contemporary problems as they arose in their fields.

Of much more interest to Olmsted by the summer of 1878 was the work, begun four years earlier, on the Capitol grounds in Washington. The building, from the time of its inception, had been under the direction of talented architects, successively Dr. William Thornton, Benjamin Latrobe, Charles Bulfinch, Thomas U. Walter, and Edward Clark. The grounds, on the other hand, eighty years after having been set aside, documented Lord Bacon's observation that "when ages grow to civility and elegancie, men come to build stately, sooner than to garden finely." No plan for their improvement had been followed for long, and little of the work done had been permanently satisfactory. The soil was much to blame: a stiff clay that turned to powder in dry weather and to mortar in wet, it had in nature supported a scattering of scrub oak and still discouraged more pleasing and delicate vegetation.[55]

The grounds had been enclosed and encircled by a road a few years after George Washington's death. Whatever improvements may have been put upon them then were almost obliterated by the burning of the Capitol in 1814 and by subsequent building operations. By 1820 a wall and iron railing had been set around "Capitol Square," but six years later the commissioner of Public Buildings reported that the grounds were so encumbered with materials and shops that it was impossible to estimate the cost of improving them, especially since no improvement plan existed.

Bulfinch, however, applied himself to constructing a terrace to mask the exposed west basement wall of the Capitol and to making its western approach more presentable; because the city was expected to be built up east of the Capitol, the ground to the west, which sloped down to an alder swamp and Tiber Creek, had always been slighted despite the fact that it offered a splendid view up the Potomac Valley. John Foy, a gardener, was occupied during much of the period from 1825 to 1840 in carrying out a simple sort of enlarged dooryard design for the east grounds—flat rectangular grass plots bordered by trees and flowerbeds and separated by gravel walks, with a belt of close planting surrounding all. The scheme, according to Olmsted, was "pretty and becoming" as long as trees were young and turf and flowers well cared for; but as the trees grew, they robbed and dried the flower beds until they supported little but violets, periwinkle, and weeds. In the belt planting, fast growing deciduous trees, their thinning neglected, crowded and starved the finer conifers, magnolias, and hollies. Grass grew shabby. Appropriations were irregular and stingy.[56] When Olmsted first saw the grounds, on his visit to Congress with his father in 1839, they already must have been past their prime.

By the time of Andrew Jackson's presidency, it was plain that the principal part of the city would arise to the west of the Capitol, and about seven acres were added to the Capitol grounds on the western slope. Under the management of James Maher, said to have been a jovial and witty Irishman who owed his position to his friendship with Jackson, this section was planted with trees, many of them fast-growing, short-lived silver poplars and silver maples, which, after doing more or less harm to the more valuable growth, died out. The next enlargement of the grounds did not take place until 1873, when two squares were added, one south and one north of the new wings of the Capitol, bringing the grounds to about fifty acres. It was then that Olmsted was engaged to landscape the whole. He had been interested in the Capitol grounds ever since his residence in Washington during the war, and the Capitol was no doubt foremost among those fine buildings that, in their squalid settings, had reminded him of costly jewels on dirty hands. In summer the grassy terrace was dry and patchily barren and eroded; in all seasons it was an insufficient pedestal for so stately a building. On the grounds, the turf was shabby; there was but one really majestic tree—the "Washington elm," single survivor of a row of street trees east of the Capitol said to have been planted by Washington when he built a house there; and there remained but scatterings of Foy's and Maher's plantations.[57]

Early in May 1873, after Congress authorized the extension of the grounds, Senator Justin Morrill, of Vermont, chairman of the Senate Committee on Public Grounds, wrote Olmsted inviting him to Washington to confer with him and Edward Clark, architect of the Capitol, about landscaping the Capitol grounds.[58] Little can have been accomplished that summer: Olmsted was disabled for four months with a severe eye ailment. Although he was about recovered and could again read by the end of November, he could neither write nor draw by artificial light. Nor could he yet make outside engagements; the panic had forced changes of policy in the city works, and he was busy with plans to meet exigencies.[59] In any case, it was March 1874 before Congress made an appropriation of two hundred thousand dollars for the improvement of the Capitol grounds; Olmsted was then officially placed in charge of the work.[60]

Before the end of the month, Olmsted had visited Washington twice and made an urgent recommendation: the Capitol grounds should not be considered in themselves and separately but in connection with all contiguous public grounds, which reached as far as the White House.* In them or on their borders stood Capitol and executive mansion and the buildings occupied by the State, Justice, Treasury, War, Navy, and Agriculture departments and the Smithsonian Institution. Costly and elaborate, these buildings were designed to create in the minds of observers an impression of unity and grandeur. That they substantially failed was the fault of the numerous commonplace and inferior structures that intruded among them. The capital of the union manifested disunity; there was lacking a coordinating purpose, a "federal bond." Were the government buildings ranged around a single field of landscape, within which all other objects were not only beautiful but consistent and harmonious, a sustained and impressive effect could be had. If a space could now be introduced into the plan of the city by which such a result could be obtained, the capital could be transformed into a visual symbol of unity and dignity.[61]

And such a space was available: the canal district, most of it a dreary waste through which oozed the stinking waters of Tiber Creek, reached from the foot of the president's park to the base of Capitol Hill and beyond, and adjoined on their north side the public grounds where the Smithsonian Institution and the still unfinished Washington Monument stood. This section should be incorporated into the existing public grounds and the whole area placed under the control of a body so constituted that it would be likely to follow a sustained landscape policy year after year. As it was, sections of the grounds were held and managed by a dozen different congressional committees and other authorities, each with a different purpose; even should grounds so treated eventually be linked together, not landscape unity but its antithesis would be achieved.[62]

This proposal involved a question of policy so important, Olmsted thought, that a committe of American landscape architects, which ought to include

*The suggestion is reminiscent of Downing's intention for the Smithsonian grounds, which he regarded as "the first step in a scheme of planting to be extended in one connected design to the White House and the Potomac."

H. W. S. Cleveland and William Hammond Hall, should be appointed to pass on it, "it being one which in my judgment concerns the credit of the profession and the honor and dignity of the country." Congress, however, thought otherwise, and Olmsted had to go ahead with plans for the Capitol grounds only. He was to receive fifteen hundred dollars for the general design, with his traveling expenses and assistance on the ground in such work as setting stakes extra.[63]

The design problem hinged on the fact that these grounds were not their own justification; they were supportive to the Capitol building and subsidiary to it. Their motive could not be the usual one of securing breadth and repose of landscape effects; it must be, first, to facilitate the business of Congress by making the Capitol readily accessible from the twenty-one city streets that touched the boundaries of its grounds and, second, to display the great national monument advantageously. Olmsted provided forty-six foot and carriage entrances into the grounds; the roads and paths leading from them toward the building, traversing less than fifty acres of ground, necessarily cut it up into rather small pieces. He disposed the plantations so as to leave numerous clear spaces between the building and the outer part of the grounds to present the finer aspects of the Capitol to view; and he kept the openings and vistas as free as possible of roads and other constructions. Both the summer climate of Washington and the glaring whiteness of the building made a general impression of verdure and shadiness desirable; but provision had to be made to accommodate the traffic resulting from routine congressional business and from tourists and the huge throngs that overran the grounds on such occasions as inaugurations. A very large extent of paving and flagging, inimical to the effects of shade and greenery, thus had to be provided; and expedients had to be devised inoffensively to restrain the movements of visitors in certain directions and point them in others.[64]

No attempt to reconcile these more or less conflicting requirements could be made that would not result in a certain disjointedness of the plantations. To minimize it, Olmsted selected and arranged trees, not with a view to displaying individual or unusual qualities, but with a view to their growing together harmoniously in groups; he avoided distinct definition of the groups and tried to draw them into larger compositions; and he tried to produce an effect of depth and distance by obscuring minor objects. He used shrubbery rather profusely to offset the large extent of dead ground in walks and roads and adjacent streets that would otherwise have been conspicuous in views from the Capitol and across the grounds. While he sought variety and liveliness in the shrubbery, bloom was a minor consideration, and he preferred the simple to the showy, "the design being always not to make a lounging place or hold attention to details." Where he expected turf would be hard to maintain because of density of shade or for other reasons, Olmsted provided for ground cover of creepers and low perennials likely to stay green in summer. The low plantings would also serve to connect and merge the higher foliage with the verdure of the lawns and to increase the apparent perspective distance.[65]

The reason that Olmsted did not resort to the formal style of gardening in a situation so well adapted to it must be inferred: it was alien to his taste and habit; and it had no public acceptance in America at that time.

Besides designing the grounds, Olmsted had literally to create the soil to support turf and trees and shrubs. The eastern ground had to be stripped of all but a score of its six hundred trees and graded; it sloped eight feet from the Capitol up to the east boundary line, where the street had been graded seven feet down so that the building was invisible from it. Olmsted marked about a hundred of the thriftier trees in this area for transplanting, not very hopefully: their roots, having outgrown the small holes in which they had been planted, had been unable to penetrate the hard clay subsoil and had spread to form a flat network in the shallow topsoil accumulated through repeated dressings of Tiber mud and street manure.

To make soil, Olmsted proposed to deep plough, manure, harrow, and till; add whatever good soil he could obtain by paring vacant lots and old gardens; and use at least fifty cubic yards of fuel peat per acre in the subsoil and another fifty in the surface soil. He figured the cost, including draining, would be almost thirteen hundred dollars an acre; he figured, too, that his thrifty overlords would balk at the expense. "I should hardly like the Ways and Means to know that I meant to have $60,000 spent for the improvement of the soil," he confided to Waring when he asked his advice on the subject, "but I don't see how a tolerable condition can be hoped for at much less cost than that, do you?"[66]

Olmsted engaged as supervising engineer John Partridge, a Yankee "accustomed to hard work and to nice work, a methodical prudent man, precise and exacting," who was president of the Washington chapter of the National Association of Civil Engineers. His old friend Radford was employed to prepare working drawings for grading, sewer, gas, and water lines and other such work. Oliver Bullard was engaged for planting. Thomas Wisedell, a young Englishman who had designed theaters and worked successfully under Vaux on Prospect Park, was employed for the architectural work.[67]

In hiring contractors, Olmsted took the lowest bidder and the next three low bidders as well. The work began in the last few days of August,[68] and Olmsted made frequent trips from New York to Washington to supervise it in its critical early stages. He received, in addition, detailed reports from Partridge and sent him voluminous and minute instructions. One policy he repeatedly emphasized: no section of ground was to be brought near apparent completion unless it could be perfectly and finally finished within the remaining appropriation and before cold weather ended the outdoor working season.

> Besides the general objection that premature and incomplete finish always creates misconceptions and diminishes ultimate popularity, the more chaotic the ground looks until the rougher preliminary and foundation work is out of the way the better it will be thought of and the less will be the loss through damage and misuse of the final surfaces.

377

This was, he told Partridge, "the only *policy* I ever use and we must stand or fall by it. That is to say, we must leave our work in such shape that it will stand us in lieu of all lobbying."[69]

Work progressed so well that toward the end of November Olmsted reported to the public by means of a letter in the *New York Tribune* that the old park on the east ground was "swept away" and that grading there was almost finished. Where it was, the ground was being tilled, and the old sewer, gas, drainage, and water pipes were being taken up and replaced. Some of the old trees had been transplanted, some curbs and gutters were in, and some roads and walk foundations were laid. No work, he added, had yet been done on the west side, but the plan for it was well advanced and soon to be submitted.[70]

The promised design, when presented in January 1875, incorporated one of Olmsted's fine creative strokes: its leading feature was a splendid broad marble terrace, placed around the north, west, and south sides of the building, and approached on the west by a double flight of marble steps. Whereas the grassy earthwork it was to replace suggested rusticity and improvisation, the marble terrace would confer on the Capitol an air of stability, grandeur, and repose. It would form a transition, formal and elegant, between it and the adjoining grounds. It would elevate the neglected western approach to equal stateliness with the eastern. It would also, incidentally, permit substantial enlargement of the basement space of the already overcrowded Capitol.[71]

The aged Walter, former architect of the Capitol, declared that the terrace "would be the making of the building." The current architect, Clark, and other qualified critics agreed. The joint committee having oversight of the improvement studied the plan on the ground, where Olmsted had scaffolds set to indicate the dimensions of the terrace and to help them to visualize its effect, and they reported it favorably to Congress, which then adopted it.[72] It was, therefore, a disappointment to Olmsted when, in March, money for the terrace was deleted from the appropriation bill for the Capitol grounds, but with stoic optimism he put a good face on it: the more the proposal was discussed, the better it would be liked; and the next time he presented it, it could be in a more carefully matured and persuasive form.[73]

The appropriation for the terrace failed again in 1876 and 1877 and 1878. By then, work on the ground had to proceed without Olmsted's detailed oversight because he was in Europe. After he returned, still sick, he rather listlessly wrote the engineer in charge to let him know "from time to time" how things were going and to summon him when he was needed. By 1879, although he still considered the Capitol improvement his most important work, he was more interested in something else: the movement to restore the scenery around Niagara Falls to its early natural condition.[74]

Olmsted had been an occasional visitor to Niagara Falls ever since he first went there as a six-year-old boy in the course of a stay with his Uncle Owen at Geneseo. In 1834, when Olmsted made his second visit, two Scottish ministers, the Rev. Andrew Reed and the Rev. Thomas Mattheson, also visited the falls and were so impressed that in their account of their journey they made the exotic proposal that "such spots should be deemed the property of civilized mankind; and nothing should be allowed to weaken their efficacy on the tastes, the morals and the enjoyment of all mankind."[75]

The idea, of a piece with the one that three decades later motivated Olmsted's concern for the Yosemite Valley, was unproductive for a long time while mills, flumes, shops, icehouses, signboards, hotels, and fences gradually defaced and crowded the once natural riverbank and while visitors grew increasingly exasperated by the horde of peddlers, guides, photographers, gatekeepers, hack drivers, and assorted sharpers who importuned them at every step.

The degradation of the scenery and of the conditions for viewing it pained two visitors particularly: Frederic Edwin Church and Frederick Law Olmsted. Church, whose huge painting "Niagara Falls," first shown in 1857, had enraptured critics on both sides of the Atlantic, lectured some time before 1869 on the falls' impending ruin at the Century Club, where Vaux was one of his listeners; the idea that an international park should be reserved around the falls he discussed quietly with a few friends.[76] Olmsted, whose park work in Buffalo made it convenient for him to visit the falls from time to time, had Dorsheimer and Richardson meet him at Niagara Falls village early in August 1869 to discuss what might be done to preserve the falls scenery.[77] They rambled on Goat Island above the falls, and following the river bank on the American side downstream to Lewiston, they debated how much of the banks should be included in the reservation they proposed and considered means of securing state action. The following day Vaux and several other interested men joined them at the Cataract House, and the conversation continued. After this meeting, no tangible progress took place until late in 1878, when the governor general of Canada, the marquess of Dufferin and Ava, took a hand, allegedly at the instance of Church.[78]

Strangely, Olmsted seems to have been unaware of Church's activity. At the time of the Cataract House meeting neither he nor Dorsheimer, infrequent patrons of the Century Club house, had heard about Church's lecture there or realized that he entertained the idea of an international park; and it was more than a year and a half after the governor general's intervention that Olmsted was told by his erratic friend Hurlbert, by then editor of the *World*, that he and Church had called on Lord Dufferin and proposed to him that an international park should be established at Niagara Falls.[79] Lord Dufferin, to whom the idea may have occurred independently, in a meeting with Governor Lucius Robinson, of New York, mentioned the matter to him and then made the first official, public utterance on the subject: on September 26, 1878, in an address to the Ontario Society of Artists, he proposed that New York and Ontario combine to secure land for a public, international park at Niagara, which, he warned, "must not be desecrated, or in any way sophisticated, by the puny efforts of the art of the landscape gardener, but must be carefully preserved in the picturesque and unvulgarized condition in which it was originally laid out by the hand of Nature."[80]

Dufferin then, on October 1, wrote Robinson, recapitulating their conversation and saying that if New York would take the initiative, Canada would gladly cooperate.[81]

However jarring Lord Dufferin's derogation of the landscape architect's art may have been to Olmsted and Vaux, they could at least be glad that he had started the ball rolling. On January 7, 1879, Governor Robinson recommended to the legislature that a commission be appointed to devise, with representatives of the government of Ontario, a plan to protect Niagara; the legislature appropriated money for the commission's expenses; and the commissioners of the State Survey were selected to do the work.[82]

At least three of the six commissioners were already well known to Olmsted: Dorsheimer, George Geddes, and Frederick A. P. Barnard, president of Columbia College. The director of the State Survey was James T. Gardiner, who, with Clarence King, had surveyed and mapped the proposed Yosemite reservation for Olmsted in 1865. The commissioners ordered Gardiner to inspect the falls and prepare a report, and associated Olmsted with him in the work.[83]

On May 28, 1879, Olmsted and Gardiner made their first official inspection of Niagara,[84] and on September 27 they met with the Ontario and New York commissioners there. "The general outlines of a scheme which I presented was fully approved by all," Olmsted wrote Norton.[85] Oliver Mowat, prime minister of Ontario and one of the commissioners, reported on it to Lord Lorne, successor to Lord Dufferin. Only those arrangements were to be made that were necessary to restore and preserve the natural character of the scenery; it was not intended to make a park or artificial enclosures. The reservation was to include the islands above the falls and a strip on either side of the river, wide enough for planting to screen out the buildings behind it, from the head of the rapids downstream to the railroad suspension bridge. A modest fee, to defray expenses, would probably be levied on sightseers.[86]

The whole of the gorge below the falls, including the whirlpool, was excluded from the proposed park: Olmsted believed that the natural value of the scenery was in the most danger just about the falls and that the less ambitious proposal, being both more urgent and less costly, stood a better chance of enlisting public support.

In recommending the proposal, Mowat advised that the governments of the Dominion of Canada and of the United States should be regarded as the actual principals. While the rich state of New York could well afford to represent the United States's interest, Ontario had too limited revenues to assume a similar burden in connection with what was a national responsibility. That the preservation of the falls was such was surely clear from the fact that the Niagara River was navigable water under dominion control and an international boundary.[87]

At the September meeting the Ontario and New York commissioners agreed that a memorial with "weighty names" might favorably influence the governor general of Canada and the governor of New York. In the following months Olmsted directed the collecting of names, putting Dorsheimer, Church, Norton, and many others to work to secure the endorsement of notable men in several countries whose reputations could be expected to outlast their time so that it would be realized in the future as well as presently that the preservation of Niagara was a matter of profound and international concern.[88]

When the report appeared the end of March 1880, some seven hundred people, many of them internationally known, had signed the memorial appended to it. Scenes of natural beauty and grandeur like Niagara, they declared, were among the most valuable gifts of God to man. "The contemplation of them elevates and informs the human understanding. They are instruments of education. They conduce to the order of society. They address sentiments which are universal. They draw together men of all races, and thus contribute to the union and peace of nations." And it was the proper concern of the civilized world that Ontario and New York act to protect Niagara Falls.[89]

However axiomatic these affirmations seemed to the signatories, they were less than persuasive to the new governor of New York, Alonzo Cornell, who saw the international park scheme in terms of its cost to his state. Although the report had an encouraging reception from the press (Olmsted himself wrote leading notices for two New York papers), Cornell's "contemptuous opposition" left Olmsted by the end of May with no hope that the state would act to protect the falls. Nor was the proposal making much headway in Ontario against public apathy.[90]

The concern of an international elite obviously had to be reinforced by politically palpable local concern if the reservation was to succeed. Its proponents, Olmsted and Norton in their forefront, therefore organized a systematic campaign to publicize the danger to the falls, the remedy for it, and the reasons for applying it. Olmsted had already developed the rationale for securing to the public extraordinary passages of scenery in his long statement on Yosemite; suppressed, it had been without impact; so the thesis had to be presented again—in this instance briefly, simply, and repeatedly. The first impression on popular attention was to be followed by frequent statements, each complete in itself and clear in reiteration of the original appeal; and they were to be continuously varied and multiplied without long pause between until their cumulative effect should produce "a reverberation filling the air and compelling popular attention."[91]

The campaign opened with a couple of letters in the spring of 1880 by George Woodberry in the *Springfield Republican* and the *Boston Advertiser*,[92] but it did not gain momentum to persuade the New York State Legislature to act on the park bill during the current session. Olmsted had to admit to Mrs. Charles Darwin, whom he wrote in June, that the Niagara Falls project had failed "at every important point legislatively"[93] in New York and had apparently had no serious consideration in Canada.[94]

The initial failure notwithstanding, Olmsted and his associates continued to discuss means of acquiring the desired private properties on both sides of the border and plans for the management of the park once they were acquired.

381

Meanwhile, increasing manufacturing and increasing demand for water power sent the price of land around the falls edging rapidly upward; and sharp opposition to the park project was mounted by the *Niagara Falls Gazette* and by Hall and Murray, proprietors of a big wood-pulp mill, who owned seven hundred feet of the coveted shorefront.[95]

In the summer of 1881 the Bankers' Convention met at the falls; spurred by Howard Potter, it approved a resolution prepared by Norton and Olmsted endorsing the park plan; and late in the summer Henry Norman, a young Englishman recently graduated with honors from Harvard who had literary connections and promise, was employed by Olmsted and Norton to go to Niagara Falls and write a number of articles for New York, Boston, and Buffalo papers. They were printed and quoted extensively in the United States and Canada and were soon after issued in pamphlet form. The reverberations were beginning to fill the air.[96]

BROOKLINE; NIAGARA; THE STATE OF LANDSCAPE ARCHITECTURE

1881–1888

H AVING spent the summers in Brookline and the winters in New York for three years, Olmsted was ready by early 1881 for the permanent move. New York had become hateful to him; the Massachusetts countryside charmed him; and, the story goes, a significant trifle decided him. In Brookline on business during the winter, he was stopping for a few days with Richardson. One night a heavy snow fell, and Olmsted looked out the next morning to see a deeply whitened landscape—and a snowplow promptly, laboriously, clearing the street. "This," he said to his host, "is a civilized community. I'm going to live here."[1]

Early in the summer of 1881 he rented Mrs. Perrin's house on Walnut Street, improvised an office in it, and put his New York home up for lease.[2]

Olmsted could abandon New York, but he could not turn his back on Central Park. Still nominally consulting landscape architect, he was ignored officially, although Salem Wales, again on the commission by 1881, and Smith Lane, a Democratic commissioner, both wanted him back. They, Vaux, who became superintending architect in November 1881, and the veteran gardener W. L. Fischer all wrote him agitated and agitating letters about the progress of affairs on the park.[3] It was deplorable.

Four fully incompetent superintendents had held office since Olmsted's dismissal, and the job was again open.[4] Olmsted urged Weidenmann to apply for it, but a fifth incompetent was soon appointed and set diligently to "opening vistas." As a result, Fifth Avenue, which had been carefully screened out with plantations, was seen from within the park in all its architectural elegance; drab country to the northeast, laid out in blocks and sparsely occupied by market gardens and shanties, was overlooked from a high point; and interior views, supposed to steal beguilingly upon the eye, were fully exposed to it at a glance.[5] The world's fair promoters were urging their claims to the park, and there was a strong effort brewing to place a track for fast driving in it.[6] Olmsted did what he could to influence events by writing letters, some privately and some for publication, and during the fall of 1881 he wrote a long pamphlet, *The Spoils of the Park, with a Few Leaves from the Deep-Laden Note-Books of "A Wholly Unpractical Man."*[7]

In it he related the incessant pressures, first from Tammany, then from the "reformers," to which he had been subject as superintendent to give out jobs for reasons of political expediency and the failures and frustrations that ensued when nonprofessional considerations controlled. Charity toward some good and well-meaning commissioners restrained Olmsted from particularizing; so the account was disappointingly guarded and generalized, but he made his disappointment and the continuing danger to the park quite clear. Still hoping, more ardently than realistically, that the ruinous course might be reversed, he concluded *Spoils* by recommending, among other things, that the aims of the park's management be defined by law, that a board of directors with the usual duties of a commercial board be provided, and that the legislature take steps to safeguard the park's managers against "that form of tyranny known as advice or influence, and that form of bribery known as patronage."[8]

Press reaction to *Spoils* disappointed Olmsted: he felt that the papers slighted his point and tried to turn the pamphlet to partisan account, and many of his friends took it as a tract for civil-service reform rather than as a paper looking specifically to the rescue of Central Park. "I fear that its ruin is inevitable," Olmsted wrote Brace, "and it is very depressing to me. But my mind is pretty well made up to it, and this probably is my last blow."[9]

Not long before writing *Spoils*, Olmsted recast his Montreal lectures as a long report to the Mount Royal commissioners. (He was to sum it up later in the remark that the park showed bad blundering and offered fine panoramic views.)[10] He felt that much of his work there had been wasted in efforts to adjust a plan based on supposedly fixed conditions to capricious interpolations and deletions. After explaining in a didactic, patient way why the park's direction, by turns impulsive and desultory, had precluded a truly satisfactory result, Olmsted stated, as distinctly as in any report he made, the mystique of charming natural scenery as a curative influence, acting not through men's reason but on "the highest functions of the system, and through them upon all else below, tending, more than any single form of medication, to establish sound minds in sound bodies—the foundation of all wealth."[11]

If he could not really explain the process by which charming rural scenery healed, he was fully convinced that it did: his own case was in evidence. For three years or more his life had been a burden to him, how heavy a one he had not realized until the turning point, his departure from New York, was past and, living in Brookline, he at last began to mend. "I enjoy this suburban country beyond expression," he wrote Brace, "and the older I grow [the more] I find my capacity for enjoyment increasing."[12]

Spoils and the Mount Royal report documented and deplored projects that were partial failures. Two short reports on Buffalo and Boston, which Olmsted wrote late in 1881, made happier reading. By that time the Buffalo park system was one of his and Vaux's better-realized works; and the Boston system promised to be one of his most elaborate, beautiful, and useful.

Buffalo, founded in 1804, had begun with the advantage of a rational street plan. Laid out by Joseph Ellicott, younger brother and aide to Andrew Ellicott, who had been associated with L'Enfant in the planning of Washington, Buffalo's street plan combined broad radial ways with a number of distinct, rectangular street systems, each adjusted to the local topography. As a result the city, during its early development, had secured within its limits much of the hygienic advantage of a suburb. As commerce and population expanded, however, the threat arose of overcrowding within its boundaries and of the proliferation of unplanned, disconnected settlements with small lots on narrow streets in the bleak and scenically unprepossessing environs. It was in 1868 that Dorsheimer and other leading citizens, mindful of the danger, had sought the advice of Olmsted, Vaux & Company; by 1881 the city, working to their plan, had for the time at least largely averted the hazard by devoting some six hundred acres, both within and without its original limits, to parks and squares and parkways.[13]

The three-hundred-fifty-acre rural park, with picnic grove, and lake dredged out of what had been a sewage-filled swamp, lay three and a half miles north of the city hall and was surrounded and protected against close building by a privately developed rural suburb, a large cemetery, and the extensive grounds of a hospital. Two miles nearer town on a low bluff above Lake Erie was the fifty-acre Front, with a splendid view over the lake and the Niagara River to the Canadian shore. Across town to the east, the Parade offered some fifty-six acres, most of it in fairly level lawn, for games and military displays, besides a grove of trees and a refectory. Scattered about the city were eight more squares and places averaging five acres in size; and seven miles of one- and two-hundred-foot parkways, all of them turf bordered and planted with shade trees, connected the public grounds with each other and gave direct and pleasant passage from one sector of the city to another. These developments, in city outskirts subject to overflow, threaded by polluted watercourses and crisscrossed by railroad tracks, were surface- and thorough-drained; their soil was cultivated and enriched; thrifty vegetation was established on them; and the city's water and sewerage systems were extended to them.[14]

Thus the sophisticated planning of a system of complementary parks and parkways had secured to the city not only varied and frequent pleasure grounds but direct and pleasant roadways through environs, originally disagreeable and unhealthy, largely redeemed by the improvements.

The Boston report made it clear that the abatement of a nuisance was the primary aim of the Back Bay Fens improvement, the first feature of an extensive park and parkway system Olmsted conceived to protect and enhance the environs of Boston. The Fens was a pestilential swamp into which Muddy River and Stony Creek emptied the drainage of thousands of acres of suburban Boston. The Fens oozed in turn into the Charles River tidal basin. Besides being chronic menaces to health, the Fens's sluggish watercourses backed up when heavy rains and high tides coincided and flooded the lowlands they were supposed to drain.[15]

In his plan Olmsted ingeniously joined other purposes to that of abating a nuisance: to create a convenient passageway from the city to its suburbs across

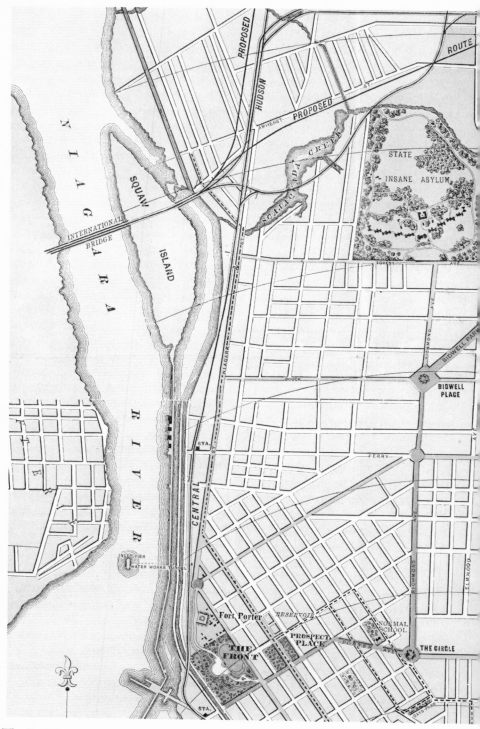

The Buffalo park plan, showing early use of parkways to connect pleasure grounds.

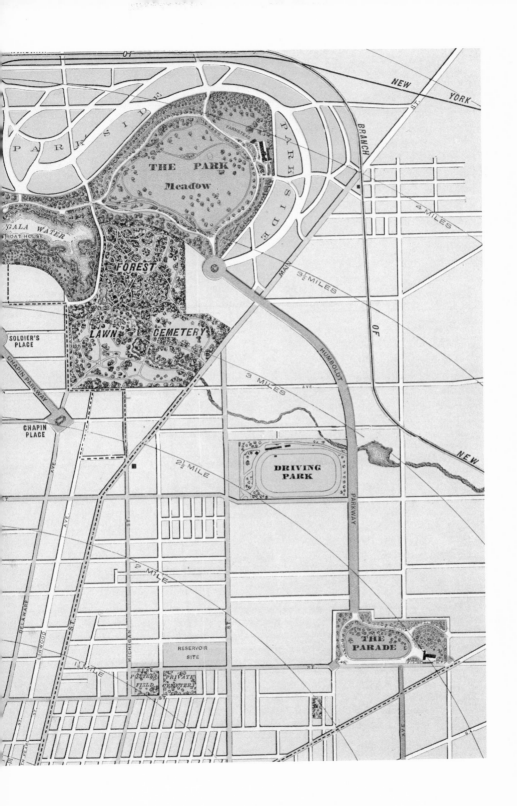

the Fens; to treat banks, bridges, basins, and causeways appropriately in relation to adjoining streets and the improvements that could be expected to be put upon them; and to turn all the work done for these purposes to account in the general plan of sylvan improvement of the metropolitan region.[16]

This scheme envisioned, at the end of 1881, a continuous system linking the Common and the Public Garden, Commonwealth Avenue, the Back Bay Fens, Muddy River and its upper valley, Jamaica Pond, the Arboretum,* and a rural park at West Roxbury.[17] It was a grand concept, the most sweeping Olmsted had yet devised; yet the idea was inherent in his and Vaux's first works, Central Park and Prospect Park, which they had intended as the opening features of a system of pleasure grounds and parkways to serve and refresh all of metropolitan New York.

The order of Olmsted's preoccupations was cruelly revised late in October 1881, when he received the completely unexpected news that Owen was gravely ill.[18]

Lured by prospects of health and wealth—Clarence King had spoken grandly of forty to fifty percent annual profit to be had by cattle ranching—Owen had spent almost two years learning the business on Owl Creek near Cheyenne under the supervision of King's manager, N. R. Davis.[19] His food had been coarse and his comforts scarce, and from one season to the next he had been exposed to unaccustomed heat, cold, snow, rain, dust, and fatigue. Nevertheless, he had been happy and rarely lonely. From the first winter, however, the cold had bothered him: "Although the thermometer does not stand very low, the cold wind blows right through one's body"; and he asked his brother John to send warm clothing from Brooks Brothers, the New York tailor where he had left his measurements. After a year in the open they remained the same: he still weighed a spare one hundred thirty-two pounds.[20]

Early in 1880, when King and Davis considered Owen adequately prepared

---

*It was desirable from the point of view of both Harvard College, which owned the Arboretum, and the city of Boston that the Arboretum should be incorporated into the city's park system. To accomplish that end, Olmsted suggested an ingenious legal arrangement that went into effect in 1882.

Under it, the Arboretum technically and practically constitutes part of the Boston park system, since the land was condemned for park purposes and is open to and used by the public for many of the same purposes as the other parts of the park system; but the land within the Arboretum, except for the roads constructed and maintained by the city, is leased to the college at a dollar a year for a thousand years for Arboretum purposes.

Thus the city taxpayers were relieved by the college of the expense of planting and maintaining a large area of park land and yet guaranteed perpetual access to it; and the college was relieved of the burden of building, maintaining, and policing the roads necessary for making the Arboretum's collections and landscape accessible to the public (Indenture between Harvard College and the City of Boston concerning the use of the Arnold Arboretum as a Public Park, 30 December 1882 [copy], LWR Files; FLO [son], memo, 9 April 1928, LWR Files).

to handle his own business, King raised thirty-five thousand dollars from friends in the East—among them Henry Lee, H. C. Lodge, and Abram Hewitt—for Owen to form the Rocky Mountain Cattle Company and buy a herd.[21] Owen looked about until he found one he could afford at the end of its journey from Oregon, bought fifty half-breed English bulls to improve its beef quality, and purchased the necessary horses and outfit. Meanwhile, he had prospected for suitable range and had hit on a ranch on Little Powder River in southeastern Montana west of the Black Hills. There he drove his fifteen hundred head of cattle and built his corrals, hay fences, and cabin with the aid of only three hired hands. Thriftily, he acted as his own foreman, and he worked alongside his hands in all weathers, sometimes spending sixteen or eighteen hours a day in the saddle.[22] He must have supposed the rugged outdoor life was invigorating; in any case, he did not know he was ill until he collapsed.[23]

Neither, it would seem, did anyone else. Even Olmsted, who saw him in October 1880, was totally unprepared for the bad news that came a year later. He had accompanied Charles Francis Adams, Jr., on one of Adams's annual railroad junkets west, stopping at Chicago and in Colorado before meeting Owen in Cheyenne.[24] Apparently nothing suggested to him that Owen, so touchingly the heir to his dead father's appearance and personality, was heir, too, to his fatal frailty.

At word of Owen's illness, John immediately went West.[25] Reaching Owen, he realized that he was desperately ill and resolved to bring him home. Olmsted and his wife, kept posted by John's wires and letters, spent three tormenting weeks prepared for word of Owen's death at any hour as he made his slow way home. He did not reach it. "My poor boy got no farther East than Albany, where his mother and I met him," Olmsted wrote a friend, "but he was already unconscious when taken from the train and breathed his last the following day."[26] It was November 21, 1881. Owen was twenty-four.

With practiced stoicism, Olmsted scarcely paused in his work. A fall from his horse early in December, however, broke his breastbone and inactivated him for a time; but by the middle of February he was well enough to go to Detroit for two weeks: Wales had told a Detroit park commissioner that Olmsted was the man to consult about laying out a park on Belle Isle in the Detroit River.[27]

Soon after his return, Olmsted received a letter from Wales, who had been studying *Spoils*, outlining a reorganization plan intended to remove Central Park from politics. Olmsted answered with rare heat: his life had been embittered and his health damaged by his late experience with Central Park; he had no confidence in Wales's reorganization scheme; and the recent park management was guilty of criminal breach of trust.[28]

Several days after loosing this blast, Olmsted received a letter from a rising young legislator at Albany, Theodore Roosevelt, who said he had read *Spoils* with "intense interest" and was preparing a bill naming such a board of directors for the park as Olmsted had suggested; he intended to propose for it Olmsted,

Vaux, Frederic Church, and Wales, among others, and he solicited Olmsted's advice.[29] His scheme, like Wales's, came to nothing.

While Wales, Vaux, William R. Martin, and Smith Lane all maneuvered for his restoration as architect-in-chief, Olmsted did nothing whatever to encourage them. The appointment early in 1883 of Viele, whom he held in low esteem both professionally and personally, as commissioner to succeed Lane made Olmsted's return even more unthinkable than it already was. He was shocked by the appointment and by the lack of public protest against it, he wrote Vaux, considering "the unquestionable fact that it has for twenty-five years been his principal public business to mutilate and damn the park."[30]

As though to justify Olmsted's not unprejudiced criticism, Viele immediately backed a proposal to move the menagerie onto the north meadow, thus negating one of the most critical features of the entire park. The *Tribune* roasted him editorially; and Olmsted regretted that Vaux, who had submitted his resignation as superintending architect, was leaving at a crisis when he might have blocked bad policies from the inside.[31] "For my part," he added, "for my personal health and welfare, it is everything not to be living in New York which would be hell to me."[32]

The hell would have been aggravated by the turn of events on Prospect Park. Work on it had been one of Olmsted's happiest professional experiences because the park commission had from its inception been under the enlightened guidance of James S. T. Stranahan.[33] Early in 1882, however, a new city administration moved to replace him. Hoping to alert the new mayor, Seth Low, and the new park commissioners to the urgency of keeping the park under expert and apolitical management, Stranahan asked Olmsted to send a copy of *Spoils* to each. If they read it, the lesson was wasted; early in July Stranahan, after twenty-two years of service, was removed.[34]

Not long before, Olmsted had remarked to Cleveland that every public work he had done, and left, was being despoiled by ignorant management.[35] He could expect that Prospect Park would be added to the list.

From temporary quarters in Brookline, Olmsted had been casting about for a place to establish his home and office permanently. Richardson, firmly bound to him by affection and shared works, wanted Olmsted to build on his lot on Cottage Street, close to his dignified old "Jamaica planter's" house and his sumptuous office. Olmsted, instead, was attracted by the Boylston farmhouse, set in a remnant of picturesque farmland at the corner of Dudley and Warren streets. Built in 1810, it was still owned by members of the Boylston family, the Misses Clark. They were unwilling to sell and quit their ancestral home. John worked out a formula to persuade them: Olmsted would build them a cottage on the property to be occupied rent free for their lives, and he would take house and land subject to a mortgage to give them a regular income.[36]

Olmsted took possession of the old frame house in the spring of 1883 and began repairs and alterations. The northeast ground floor room, the traditional funeral parlor of New England farmhouses, became his office. He extended it ten or twelve feet to the north to accommodate a long drafting table and to provide, overhead, for a sleeping porch opening from the bedroom above the office. Later, as they were needed, additional units of office space and a fireproof brick vault were added to the north and northwest in rambling structures on various levels, adjusted to topography and preserving the picturesque features of the site that had attracted Olmsted in the first place.[37]

His office always looked like what it was—part of his home comfortably adapted to office use. The fireplace on the west wall, converted in midcentury to burn coal and altered with a dark marble Victorian frame and mantel, blazed in winter with a fire that enhanced the pleasantly domestic air of the room. Its south and west walls, except over the fireplace, were lined with bookshelves filled with park reports and other professional works. Over the mantel and on the east wall between the windows hung photographs of Ruskin, Richardson, and Edouard André and a few framed reproductions of such notable works of Olmsted's firms as the United States Capitol grounds and Central Park. The desks by the windows were plain and the long table in the middle of the room was used primarily to spread plans for examination and discussion. The drafting itself took place in the attached drafting rooms, baldly simple wooden structures, well lighted and sheathed with cypress. Olmsted's bedroom, directly over the office, was lined with shelves full of books related to his profession, while his old favorites held their accustomed places on his bedside table.[38]

His three unmarried children lived at home. John, mainstay of the office, directed all the work done in it and kept it operating smoothly. Marion, delicate and subject to some sort of rheumatic trouble, was "just the nicest girl—little old maid—possible; patient, happy, indefatigable." Frederick, who had continued at boarding school in New York until Olmsted bought the Warren Street house, attended Miss Rideout's School in Brookline; at thirteen, he took after his father and was mischievous.[39]

Charlotte and her husband were living at Cohasset, where Richardson and Olmsted had designed house and grounds for them in 1880.[40] There had been early hints that Charlotte was unstable: in 1870 Miss Wormeley had offered Olmsted advice on how to deal with her "individuality";[41] and as late as October 1877, when Charlotte was twenty-two, Mrs. Knapp, who had taken her to inspect a kindergarten, besought Olmsted and his wife to allow her to open one herself—she was at a turning point in her life and could become happy and useful or disappointed and frivolous. "The most discouraging part of her character so far," Mrs. Knapp wrote, "has been a morbid lack of interest in everything, which almost seemed to amount to heartlessness."[42]

Her indifference had yielded to her interest in working with small children, but Charlotte did not pursue it: a year later, on October 15, 1878, she and Dr. Bryant were married in Trinity Church in Boston and set off on a long wedding trip in Europe. By April 1882, she had two little boys and had introduced her father, as he turned sixty, to the avocation of grandparent.

The idyll—if it was one—did not last. At the end of 1883, a few months after the birth of her third son, Charlotte became deranged. Friends tried to reassure Olmsted—"It is unscientific now to think of the mind as independent of the body," Vaux wrote encouragingly[43]—but their comfort was groundless. Charlotte never recovered.*

Olmsted was elected to the Saturday Club in March 1883.[44] The club, started in Boston in 1856, included among its early members such luminaries as Emerson, Agassiz, Judge Hoar, Richard Henry Dana, Jr., Lowell, Prescott, Motley, Benjamin Peirce, Sam Ward, Longfellow, Holmes, Whittier, and Hawthorne. Its distinguished quality had been effortlessly maintained, and at the time of Olmsted's election its membership included, besides the survivors from earlier days, Charles W. Eliot, president of Harvard, Norton, Charles Francis Adams, Jr., William James, William Dean Howells, Phillips Brooks, Charles Sprague Sargent, and Asa Gray. Its dinners, held once a month at the Palmer House, brought together for informal social exchange men of the best intellectual accomplishment in the locality—and, it could be argued, in the country.

Olmsted from youth had revered achievement and taken honors seriously. He still did. Neither iconoclast nor snob, he respected men and women who made a mark on their time through some contribution to society and country. To have his own acknowledged by election to the Saturday Club was an accolade by which he set great store.[45]

He was an acknowledged eminence, but he could hardly have posed as the model for one. He was too modest looking. His small frame, compact and always slender, towered over no one, and he had none of the little man's compensatory swagger. The expression of his blunt-featured face, with its quizzical blue eyes, was unself-conscious and kindly. His full beard, neatly trimmed, verged on the scraggly, and his hair, brushed back from his bald dome, fell during the 1870s in a loose wave to his collar; in the eighties and after, he wore it trimmed shorter. His manner was unassuming. He was fond of animals and children, cordial to the young, and respectful toward his subordinates, whom he selected with care for their expertise in special fields. Normally aloof in the office because he was preoccupied, he occasionally dropped into the drafting rooms to chat with the young men. Once, when one of them offered him a cigarette, he accepted it. It was the only time Frederick remembered seeing him smoke; he had stopped using cigars some time after the war.[46]

From his Warren Street home, Olmsted directed the work of his last dozen crowded years. "I keep working as close to my possibilities as ever," he wrote Brace in 1884,

---

*She died in a sanitarium in Norwood, Massachusetts, in 1908.

my possibilities, never large, growing perceptibly smaller with every year. John takes more & more off [me] and I have two good young men as "pupils," but the character of my business becomes smaller [sic]* & brings a great multitude of diverse concerns to me & I get very weary of turning so often from one thing to another and of so many long & short expeditions. Perhaps I all the more enjoy my house & place & the bits of quiet work I am able to do in it.[47]

He carried a heavy burden of professional works, some of staggering complexity. While he could decline work or drop it when his advice was ignored, he could not slight it; infinitely painstaking and exacting, he worried about doing his full duty to his clients and about the effect of the firm's performance on its reputation and on the profession's. There was a curious disparity between his passion for the contemplative enjoyment of scenery and his compulsion to work to his utmost limit. One can only speculate on its root: perhaps his anxiety for the future of the profession, growing intenser as his own shortened, was a factor.

In any case Olmsted, like Richardson in his last few years, assumed more work than he could attend to personally and to his own full satisfaction.[48] He drew continually, however, on unusually gifted assistants: John, whom he took into partnership in 1884, and the two apprentices he mentioned to Brace. One was Charles Eliot, son of President Eliot; the other was Henry Sargent Codman, a nephew of Charles Sprague Sargent.

Eliot, a Harvard graduate, after taking a few courses at Harvard's Bussey Institute, joined the office staff in the spring of 1883, when he was twenty-three. He stayed for two years, after which he studied parks and gardens in England and on the Continent. Returning to the United States, he opened his own office as a landscape architect in December 1886. Codman, graduated from Massachusetts Institute of Technology in 1884, when he was twenty, entered Olmsted's office almost immediately and worked there until the summer of 1887. Then he went abroad with Sargent and studied plant collections, nurseries, parks, and gardens in England, France, Germany, and Italy; worked under André in Paris for more than a year; and returned to be taken into partnership with Olmsted and John in 1889.†

During their apprenticeships, one or the other of the two young men accompanied Olmsted on the frequent travels he had come to dread. He could not sleep on overnight train trips; after longer journeys, he was likely to arrive sick and have to spend a day or two in bed before he could attend to business; and a hazard to his peace of mind was his forgetfulness, especially of names, which he thought was growing on him.[49] Eliot and Codman not only worked on a wide

---

*"Smaller" is apparently a slip for "larger."

†From 1884 to 1889, Olmsted's firm was F. L. & J. C. Olmsted; during Codman's partnership, from 1889 to 1893, it was F. L. Olmsted & Company.

range of professional problems under his direction but cushioned him as best they could against discomforts.

Olmsted still found his life, in the third decade of his practice and the seventh of his age, a wearying struggle against the common presumption that landscape architecture was not an art and was scarcely entitled to the standing of a trade.[50] Norton thought Olmsted expected too much of a people so uncultured that they could not appreciate beauty and preferred ugliness; Montreal's indifference to Mount Royal Park and New York's degradation of Central Park were only to be expected. "You are preaching truth above the comprehension of our generation," he told Olmsted, meaning to console.[51]

Cleveland took a more hopeful view. He had been practicing in Chicago since 1869, directing among other things the work Olmsted and Vaux had planned on South Park and Drexel Boulevard. He had all the business he could handle, at least until the fire, and yet he found little appreciation of his profession. But although in the West, he wrote Olmsted, scarcely an individual understood what landscape architecture was, a whole class appreciated it in the East.[52]

Mariana Griswold Van Rensselaer, a respected critic of architecture and landscape architecture, hardly agreed: the half-dozen skilled landscape gardeners (she preferred the term to landscape architects) in the country were little known except in large cities and little appreciated where known. "Until employers are themselves persons of culture, artists, when employed, are regarded as a kind of dilettanti whom it is necessary to employ rather to conform to the fashion than for such services as the employer is competent to appreciate and really enjoy the results of."[53]

If patrons and the public needed to be educated in landscape architecture, so did practitioners, but the only roads to competence for an aspirant were still the long, wasteful process of self-education such as Olmsted had pursued and apprenticeship in the office of one of the few practicing landscape architects. When Mrs. Van Rensselaer spoke of six she surely had in mind Olmsted and Cleveland, probably John C. Olmsted, and possibly three other men whose writings she recommended: Weidenmann, well known for his park and cemetery work, Francis Scott, a student of Downing's and author of *Suburban Home Grounds*, and M. A. Kern, landscape gardener of Forest Park in St. Louis.[54] (Most of them, not surprisingly, were or had been associated with Olmsted's firms.) The field, otherwise, was largely occupied by nurserymen, engineers, gardeners, surveyors, and architects who, however well qualified in their specialties, were qualified hardly at all in the more inclusive discipline.

Because of the scarcity of practitioners, landscape architecture could look to nothing but a barren future unless qualified young people were drawn to it. Olmsted was a careful counselor to those who asked his advice about training for it. Competent rivals were welcome; he viewed them as valuable recruits to the profession. As best he could from afar, he had given general advice to William Hammond Hall when Hall began Golden Gate Park.[55] In 1882, he counseled twenty-year-old George Kessler and referred him to Hunnewell, through whom Kessler got the job—laying out a railway excursion park near Kansas City for the Kansas City, Fort Scott and Gulf Railroad—that was the first step in his distinguished career of park making.[56]

That the public could be brought, in dramatic instances, to appreciate landscape values when the educational propaganda was steadily maintained was suggested by the ultimate success of the campaign to restore and reserve the scenery about Niagara Falls for public enjoyment. Unlike the reservation of Yosemite, which had been the work of a handful of men acting without popular support, the reservation of Niagara was finally brought about by widespread public interest and pressure, deliberately cultivated and applied. Woodberry's letters published in the spring of 1880 had opened the campaign. Norman's appeared the next year, and journals in New York and other eastern cities reprinted them and chimed in with editorials of their own.[57] In the summer of 1882 Jonathan Baxter Harrison, a young Unitarian minister recruited by Norton,[58] went to Niagara and wrote a series of letters first published in Boston and New York papers and then circulated in pamphlet form.[59] The following December Howard Potter, "bold, generous, sympathetic, and liberal" with both money and counsel,[60] called together a score of men, including Norton and Olmsted, who were active in the movement to preserve the falls. They decided to give up the international park idea because of the difficulty of meshing New York's moves with Canada's and to appeal instead for public backing of a plan to buy the land around the falls for a state reservation.[61] At Olmsted's request, they called a meeting on January 11, 1883, at Municipal Hall on Madison Avenue, at which the Niagara Falls Association was formed. Harrison, named secretary, was already blanketing New York State with circular letters, petitions, and pamphlets.[62]

Harrison traveled all over the state, addressing local groups to stir their interest and pride. His efforts secured wide journalistic support, and petitions and letters favoring the state reservation poured upon the legislature. The executive committee of the Niagara Falls Association drew up a bill providing for the selection and appropriation of land around the falls and for the appointment of five commissioners to manage the reservation.[63] Responding to the aroused public opinion, the Assembly passed the bill on March 14, 1883, and the Senate a month later. Governor Grover Cleveland signed it April 30 and named five commissioners: William Dorsheimer, J. Hampton Robb, of New York, Sherman Rogers, of Buffalo, Dr. Martin B. Anderson, of Rochester, and Andrew H. Green.[64]

The commissioners met in June and agreed—Green reluctantly—to adopt substantially the plan Olmsted and Gardiner had recommended. Assessors were appointed to determine the value of the lands they had designated to be included in the reservation; a proposal to extend it to take in the gorge below the falls and the whirlpool was rejected for fear the cost of the enlargement would lead to the defeat of the entire enterprise; and the assessors awarded $1,433,429.50 to the expropriated owners.[65]

The appropriation bill then ran into trouble in the legislature, and the Niagara Falls Association mobilized to save it. It circulated more petitions, issued addresses, got witnesses to testify before the appropriate committees, and again sent its tireless Secretary Harrison up and down the state on a speaking tour to get the cooperation of civic leaders and newspapers. Everywhere he enlisted support, the press took up the movement, and the whole country's interest was eventually engaged. The New York State Legislature and the state officers were swamped with letters, wires, and petitions; the bill for the bond issue to finance the purchase of the land was passed by both houses; and Governor David B. Hill, Cleveland's successor, signed it on April 30, 1885, just two years after the signing of the previous Niagara bill.[66]

Contemporaries intimately engaged in the movement gave Olmsted prime responsibility for its success. Potter, writing soon after the passage of the 1883 bill, said that if the Niagara scenery was saved the credit would be mostly Olmsted's. Norton agreed.[67] Ten years later, Harrison declared: "Success was obtained by the cooperation of multitudes; but the indispensable factor was Mr. Frederick Law Olmsted's thought. He was the real source, as he was the true director, of the movement, and but for him, there would be no State Reservation at Niagara today."[68]

Harrison modestly underplayed his own role, which had been to do most of the actual work. The campaign was as skillfully carried out as conceived. It was something of a landmark besides. It evolved, experimentally, a successful method of mobilizing public opinion to effect a reform; it engaged the backing of hundreds of public men in many fields and in several countries; it was conducted at small expense, Harrison's salary being the single substantial cost; it was untainted by any trace or suspicion of corruption; and it induced a state government to exercise its right of eminent domain to expropriate private property, not for any familiar and commonplace purpose, but for one lying in the realm of "elevated sentiment and spiritual emotion."[69]

While the public's interest had been assiduously directed to the movement, it had carefully not been invited to the friction within it. This arose from Green's appointment to the Niagara commission in 1883. On learning of it, Olmsted at once wrote Potter and Norton confidentially that it compelled him to "decline any responsibility that I might otherwise have henceforth to you or others in the matter and to escape my interest in it as fast and as far as I can without provoking inquiries frank answers to which would serve no good purpose."[70]

Potter, who considered Green "a public nuisance, an obstructionist and, I almost feel disposed to say, a 'Crank,'" also was disagreeably surprised by the appointment but hoped that the other commissioners could keep the peace and make the commission work. He thought that Green was coming to understand that people had lost confidence in him and regarded his connection with any public interest as objectionable; perhaps the realization would put him on his good behavior.[71]

Radford, however, reported to Olmsted that he had got the impression, in conversation with Green soon after his appointment, that Green expected to control three votes and the commission. If he did, and could prevent it from consulting Olmsted, would Olmsted want Radford and Vaux to incur Green's enmity by refusing to accept the appointment in Olmsted's place? Avoiding a direct answer, Olmsted emphatically replied that he would under no circumstances take a paying post under the commission.[72]

For a time it appeared that no landscape adviser would. Two members held that the commission's common sense would be an adequate guide to restoring the scenery around the falls and to managing the reservation. Dorsheimer, on the other hand, pressed strongly for a preliminary report from Olmsted, Gardiner, and Vaux; and Green, declaring that Olmsted was "particularly offensive" to him, insisted on consulting Vaux alone.[73] The year 1885 passed, and well into 1886 the commission was still muddling about without plan or professional advice and coming under editorial fire for its inaction.[74]

Responding to a feeler from Green in May 1886, Vaux said he would accept the work but preferred to do it with Olmsted. Olmsted, when Vaux told him of the overture, remained aloof. It was a big affair, and "unless I am called to I don't want to spend any more of myself upon it."[75]

When he was finally called, he responded. On October 6, 1886, the commission, unanimously persuaded at last of the need for professional supervision, directed the immediate employment of Olmsted and Vaux to prepare a plan for the state reservation. Green's motion the next month to rescind this action and employ Vaux alone was voted down; and Dorsheimer's motion confirming the previous employment of Olmsted and Vaux was carried four to one.[76]

In the report they presented in 1887, Olmsted and Vaux described their plan to restore the landscape around Niagara Falls, providing only such constructions as would forward the enjoyment of it, and touched on the changing public attitude toward natural scenery. No better illustration of it could be had, they said, than the fact that the recent legislation affecting Niagara had been enacted by popular demand, as contrasted with the fact that, when the state in 1806 sold the property around the falls which it had just repurchased, not a single person seemed to have thought the falls had any value except as water power.[77]

The extent of Olmsted's practice by the middle 1880s was evidence that landscape architecture was indeed increasingly in demand, whether or not it was more intelligently appreciated than formerly. Monied clients with country estates and Newport "cottages," people wanting suburban homes, administrators of colleges, hospitals, and schools, railroad companies with station grounds to be made sightly, promoters of real estate developments and summer resort sites, municipalities wanting parks designed, and federal and state agencies with arsenals and capitol grounds to be arranged—all consulted Olmsted's office.

A few clients, like Hunnewell, of Wellesley, themselves had a talent for the art; a few others, thinking landscape problems susceptible to common-sense solutions and mistaking their man, expected Olmsted to carry out their instructions. He resolutely declined to take orders from clients. In a deposition for Weidenmann, who was suing a cemetery company in Chicago that had employed him, flouted his advice, and refused to pay his salary, Olmsted set forth the position proper to a landscape architect: "When I am employed professionally, I do not serve under the direction of anyone. My business is to give advice in the form . . . of drawings and plans . . . and to see them executed. That was Mr. Weidenmann's position in all the work of designing and planning . . . so far as I know."[78]

Olmsted feelingly expressed his weariness with amateurs' equating their common sense with his experienced judgment after the Belle Isle commissioners proposed a major change in his plan for the Detroit park, which had been discussed thoroughly, accepted, paid for, and worked on for a year. "The planning of parks has been my profession for more than thirty years," he wrote.

> In every important case features of my plans have been asserted by what are called practical men to be in obvious conflict with common sense. . . . Under test, in every case I have had the good fortune to be vindicated and it has often happened that men who, for a time, had been strenuous in their opposition to my plans have come to me later with expressions of regret, explaining that they had not rightly seen what I was aiming at. . . . You may question if common sense is not liable to be at fault in the planning of parks. You may reflect that common sense would never have given the world a good many things the world values, and that if my plan for Belle Isle had been carried out the Detroit of the future might possibly have had a more valuable park than it is now likely to.[79]

He could also have pointed out that common sense had not shrunk from the proposal to insert into the nation's most famous rural park a large, incongruous, architectural feature to honor its foremost military hero. After President Grant's death in 1885, the suggestion was made to bury him and raise a big monument to him in Central Park. Work, meanwhile, was proceeding on Riverside Park, more or less according to the original plan of Olmsted and Vaux, and an alternate suggestion was made to build the sepulcher near its north end on the terrace that reached to the edge of a steep drop and commanded a superb view of the Hudson. The main work on the terrace was substantially done, a suitable terminal feature had not been decided on for the spectacular site, and the suggestion had a certain patriotic and common-sense appeal. When the ground was, in fact, designated for the tomb, Olmsted, without opposing the plan categorically, reminded the park commissioners that a large sum of money had already been spent to make provisions on Riverside Park "more favorable to gay, social, festive, active and sensational recreation" than was possible in Central Park. While the terrace was a fine site for a public monument, it will be extremely unfortunate if . . . the remains of the dead are brought into close association with the gayety of the promenade at this culminating point. . . .

The body of General Grant should lie in a place adapted to its permanent, undisturbed repose. . . . It should not be an incident to a festive promenade. It should have a distinctly solemn aspect.

It is not impossible that the two purposes, the festive and the funereal purpose, may both be successfully carried out in Claremont, but the problem is one that calls for more than native intelligence and horse sense.

With that *caveat*, Olmsted advised the commissioners to consult Vaux: "No man is better qualified to advise the city upon such a question as that which has thus suddenly arisen. . . ."[80]

Similarly, the plan for the Capitol terrace in Washington, having been studied and accepted by Congress, was abruptly subjected to a major change. An appropriation to start the terrace and stairways was at last made in 1884, and the work several times required Olmsted's presence in Washington before the end of the year.[81] As soon as it was fairly under way, Olmsted resigned so that responsibility should rest on Edward Clark, who, as architect of the Capitol, was the proper architectural agent of Congress.[82] Olmsted's responsibility for the Capitol grounds, unaffected by his resignation, continued; so did his interest in the terrace.

He protested with the full vigor of his strong conviction against the proposal, advanced as an afterthought early in 1886 and advocated by Senator Henry L. Dawes, of Massachusetts, to alter the accepted plan of the terrace by piercing its walls with windows so that the chambers within could be used for occupancy instead of for storage as designed. This was no minor alteration, Olmsted argued, but a major design change. The terrace was intended solely to create the impression that the Capitol, set at the peak of its slope, was held fast in place by a massive, solid base. It was not designed to reorganize the original design of the building or to make a more important feature of the subbasement or to light it or bring it out of the ground. To pierce its walls would be to negate its single intention. "Introduce windows then," he told Clark, who was lukewarm to his argument and seemed little impressed with Richardson's support of it, "and whatever infelicity there has been in the seat of the building will be aggravated and the purpose of the terrace subverted."[83] To Morrill he declared, "I would much rather the work were arrested for years than have it go on with that condition."[84] His protests availed somewhat: Congress had only the terrace wall on the west side between the stairs built with windows.

This was the last time that Olmsted was able to invoke Richardson's support: on April 27, 1886, after years of chronic illness growing gradually more severe, Richardson died.

Olmsted had seen him in Washington about two weeks before. Calling on him in his hotel room, Olmsted had found him weak, drowsy, and faint and slow of speech. During the visit, however, some question of a building came up that fired Richardson's interest; for an hour he talked with vivacity and humor about his office and work and methods so that Olmsted, on taking leave, said, "I shall have to report that I never saw you in better condition than you have been this evening."[85] Richardson returned to Brookline the next day and thereafter kept mostly to his bed; he cheerfully planned a trip to Nantucket to speed his recuperation; and he died so quietly in his sleep that no one in the room knew when his life ended.[86]

Olmsted grieved for his death and for its untimeliness. Not yet fifty, Richardson was just coming into the free and confident use of his remarkable powers. "He had never had so much to do; never had such assurance in his leadership and the public's grateful acceptance of it; never had been as ripely strong and happy in his art as in his last days," Olmsted mourned.[87]

Reflecting on his success, Olmsted concluded that it was in part independent of his genius as an architect. Much of it was due to his peculiar talent for winning "the interest of commonplace men in matters that would otherwise have been of no concern to them." He was able thus to create an atmosphere in which he was free to work in his unique, spontaneous way, sure of the confidence of his clients.[88] "I do believe that it was in his ability to secure from clients a proper footing more than anything else that his success is due," Olmsted told Mrs. Van Rensselaer.[89]

He and Sargent, thinking that a lavishly illustrated book on Richardson and his work should immediately be undertaken,[90] persuaded Mrs. Van Rensselaer to prepare it. Her handsome volume *Henry Hobson Richardson and His Works* came out in June 1888.[91] Olmsted's contribution to it took the form of advice and information. He warned the writer to avoid "the natural tendency to eulogy and partisanship"; he discussed the Albany Capitol dispute and refuted the charges of caprice and extravagance brought against the architects; and he explained the recent decision to take down Eidlitz's stone vault in the Assembly Chamber and replace it with a flat ceiling: the legislature's persistent neglect of the Eidlitz and Richardson firm's advice, offered yearly since 1882, to make "those slight repairs and adjustments such as it was no discredit to its architects that it should need" had resulted in such progress in dilapidation that the vault by 1888 had indeed become unsafe.*,[92]

The deaths, frequent during the decade, of old friends and associates from prewar and Sanitary Commission days, sometimes promoted a retrospective mood

---

*To another memorial that appeared about the same time, Olmsted contributed nothing at all: his early regard for Henry Ward Beecher had been eroded by the scandal of the minister's affair with the wife of a parishioner. Young Edward Bok, getting up a volume to memorialize Beecher, asked Olmsted for a eulogy of Beecher as a lover of nature. Refused, he tried again: would Olmsted write a tribute to Beecher as a humani-

in Olmsted. Dr. Bellows, Dr. Jenkins, Francis George Shaw, Dr. Van Buren, and George Geddes were among the friends to whom he was more than casually attached who died in the early 1880s. The year 1884 was deadly; Dr. Harris, John Hull Olmsted's old friend and mentor Dr. Parker, Olmsted's young architectural associate Wisedell, and his long-time English friend Alfred Field all died in the span of six months. In October, Olmsted saw Friedrich Kapp's obituary in the *Times* and wrote Brace, who had written it, that the social changes in their time had been so great that, while he still felt himself in the main current of contemporary life, the life they had shared in their youth seemed so different and distant that, instead of being shocked by the death of old friends, he wondered that they, and he, could have survived so long. "You decidedly have had the best & most worthily successful life of all whom I have known," he reflected. "The C. A.* is the most satisfactory of all the benevolent works of our time."[93] He had done some good work himself, he admitted,

> but it is constantly & everywhere arrested, wrenched, mangled and misused & it is not easy to get above intense personal disappointment & mortification. The politicians & the reporters & the editors don't torture me as they once did but still not a little and I am older and don't bear what comes as well—or without greater agitation—than I once did for I never bore it well. I think it comes harder to an old man to be grossly insulted.[94]

Times had indeed changed and he with them: he had no further interest in eternal mysteries ("I don't know and I don't care") but was concerned only to do faithfully what lay at hand.[95] "The most horrible waste in the world seems to me the waste of mind in what is called Theology and I repent of nothing more thoroughly than my own sin in superstitious maundering," he told Brace, who had shared his experience but not his deconversion.[96]

> I only think it is queer that I could ever have thought myself to have such ideas as I did, and queer that anyone else can continue to have them. I talk so much as this to no one but you and it is a mark of the amazing progress of New England that nobody else even invites me to. What a different, happier and better life I should have had, had it always been so.[97]

While among "Presbyterians, Baptists & some other clubs" the Pharisaical habit with its "delusions of inspired humility" still prevailed, he had no doubt that

---

tarian? The book appeared, made up of essays by illustrious contributors ranging from Grover Cleveland to—of all people—Anthony Comstock. Olmsted was not among them (Edward Bok to O, 24 March, 7 April 1887; *Beecher Memorial: Contemporaneous Tributes to the Memory of Henry Ward Beecher,* compiled and edited by Edward Bok [Brooklyn: privately printed, 1887]).

*Children's Aid Society.

there was a tremendous undercurrent sweeping it away. "And in spite of the growth of a wretched leisure class and its consequence in the spread of anarchy I can't think that in any half century before the world has advanced nearly as far as in the last. In the old language, I feel that we have been exceedingly blessed. Few men have more of the happy spirit of nunc dimitis."[98]

The happy spirit notwithstanding, Olmsted had no thought of laying down his arms. On the contrary, he thought of reentering the fray in New York. When Henry Beekman, president of the board of park commissioners in 1886, urged him and Vaux to take up management of the city's parks again, Olmsted took him seriously enough to draft a very long letter in reply.

He discussed three ways to treat Central Park. It could be managed, with little continuous regard to its general design, in a time-serving, desultory, piece-meal way, largely by compromising between different views. It could be managed, as Olmsted and Vaux would expect to manage it, with the steady purpose of pursuing its original ends. Finally, it ought to be considered whether, as the population of the city increased and the park became less a central than a downtown park, the difficulty of maintaining it in accord with its original design might become insuperable.[99]

This was a new and shocking suggestion, that Central Park as originally conceived might be becoming obsolete. It was new and shocking but as yet far-fetched: evidently Olmsted did not take it seriously, for the next year, again urged to return, he replied that he would assume no limited responsibility for the park but only for the city park system as a whole and only if Vaux was associated with him.[100]

These latest negotiations with the park commission, on which he kept Vaux posted, were the occasion for yet another unhappy misunderstanding with his former partner, who seemed to think that Olmsted was trying to snatch the lead in New York park affairs from him. Olmsted, protesting that he was considering Vaux's interests even more carefully than his own, declared that he could not understand the suspicious tone of Vaux's letters. "That after all these years we should be no better able to understand one another is one of strangest of life's experiences," he wrote.

> I still hope that what is best on the cards for you and Parsons will come out of this otherwise wasted time. Not that your interests are my primary object, of course. But I suppose that they lie right along with my primary object. I don't want to have to come back to New York but I am not sure that I should not even do that rather than lose all chance of bringing the parks back to original principles so far as that is now possible. To that end, with you or without you, I shall always do what seems to me best. There is nothing else that I care so much for.[101]

The emotional statement notwithstanding, Olmsted finally rejected the offer decisively. He would have accepted, he told William R. Martin, if there were any prospect of affecting the enterprise favorably, but there was not and could not be, New York being what it was.[102] At the end of 1887 Vaux was appointed landscape architect to the park department, while his younger associate, Samuel Parsons, Jr., who had been superintendent of planting and then superintendent of parks, continued in the latter capacity. Olmsted became an occasional consultant to the board.

After leaving New York, Olmsted had managed to visit Prospect Park about once a year, and during Stranahan's administration he found it, in all its upper part, in the East Woods, the Dairy District, and the Nethermead, thoroughly delightful. "I am prouder of it than of anything I have had to do with," he said.[103]

By the mid-1880s, however, it was faring little better than Central Park. It was the usual story: commissioners who understood nothing of the purpose or management of public parks not only failed through ignorance and negligence to realize landscape effects the designers had had in mind; they also made radical design changes without professional advice.[104] Alleging bad acoustics (on little evidence), they scrapped the music stand in the lake,* although shore, hedges, sculptured decorations, and pedestrian and carriage concourses had all been designed expressly to accommodate the crowds that would be drawn to the off-shore concerts.[105] They trimmed up a fine old natural wood, the sylvan character of which the designers had been at pains to preserve, and stuck a music stand in it where there was no provision at all for the convenience of listeners. They opened vistas through the trees on the borders of the park, which had been mounded and densely planted expressly to block out sight of the city beyond, to provide good views of it.[106] When it became known that the commissioners wanted also to turn the great oval at the entrance of Prospect Park into a sort of public garden—apparently having no idea that it had been designed to accommodate large gatherings and to facilitate the entrance of carriages into the park from six directions—*Garden and Forest* observed in its leading editorial of July 4, 1888, that every park in the country was suffering from the same causes then threatening Prospect Park: irresponsible commissioners and uneducated public intelligence.

To educate public intelligence was an important part of a landscape architect's professional obligation, Olmsted maintained.[107] Admittedly, he was not very good at it himself. The style of his professional papers was labored. Try as he might, he could not say just what he meant clearly and gracefully. More than that, he never wrote a systematic work on landscape architecture. The principles that guided him had to be mined from the pages of scores of his reports. He admired competent and more facile writers like Mrs. Van Rensselaer, Cleveland,

---

*Some years later it was restored (Clay Lancaster, *Prospect Park Handbook, with a Foreword by Marianne Moore* [New York: Walton H. Rawls, 1967], p. 112).

Samuel Parsons, father and son, and the journalist William A. Stiles even when they did not entirely satisfy him; one who did, the best of them all, was young Charles Eliot.

Eliot's letters from abroad, full of fresh and penetrating comments on the landscapes and gardens he was studying, delighted Olmsted and persuaded him that Eliot could serve the educative function of the profession better than any other English-speaking writer then being published. "I have seen no such justly critical notes as yours in Landscape Architecture matters from any traveler for a generation past," he wrote Eliot late in 1886. "You ought to make it a point of your scheme to write for the public, a little at a time, if you please, but methodically, systematically. It is a part of your professional duty to do so."[108]

In the course of his own professional duty Olmsted soon afterward helped Sargent to found *Garden and Forest*, a weekly magazine dealing with landscape architecture, forestry, horticulture, scenic preservation, and allied subjects. Sargent was the magazine's director and moving spirit; stockholders included such wealthy patrons of landscape architecture as Hunnewell and Frederick Lothrop Ames, a member of the Ames family for whom Richardson and Olmsted had worked at North Easton; and Stiles was the editor.[109]

Born in Essex County, New Jersey, and graduated from Yale in 1857, Stiles had been a surveyor, a teacher, and a journalist and was a scholarly amateur of mathematics, botany, and horticulture. As an editorial writer for the *New York Tribune*, he had raised an influential voice in the Niagara affair and in the defense of New York's parks.[110] In the new magazine, he planned to emphasize landscape architecture, although he thought hardly anybody cared to read about it. "It won't make a paper that will sell. But really it is the only feature of the paper that can make it different or better than any other garden paper."[111]

The magazine was supposed to be incorporated January 1, 1888, and to begin publishing soon after, but all arrangements were jeopardized in December by Sargent's sudden illness and by the consequent delay in the flow of funds from stockholders through him to Stiles. Olmsted threw five hundred dollars into the breach,[112] Stiles was able to meet preliminary expenses, and the first issue of the magazine, dated February 29, 1888, came out in good style. It marked an end as well as a beginning: on the front page were the picture and the obituary of the great botanist Asa Gray.

The beginning, Olmsted hoped, was to be that of a new era in gardening in which the concept of landscape would displace that of decoration. A "taste for organized beauty in gardening affairs," less common than it had been fifty years earlier, was about to revive, he predicted hopefully. "And it gives me satisfaction," he wrote Mrs. Van Rensselaer, "to think that though I seem to myself to have been all my life swimming against the tide I shall not sink before having seen it turn."[113]

Perhaps it was symptomatic of a turning tide that five young men, all of them referring to her articles on landscape in *Garden and Forest* and "none of them . . . very unpromising," had recently applied to Olmsted's office for advice about entering the profession.*,114

*For the next ten years *Garden and Forest* did its intelligent and literate best to educate the public to the value of landscape architecture. Within its chosen limits, it covered a wide range of topics, justifying the statement with which the *Century* greeted its first issue, that it would forward education in landscape architecture—so far as it could be forwarded by writing. Even before the appearance of the first issue, however, Weidenmann objected that Sargent, rather than start a magazine, ought to start a school that would train a body of qualified landscape architects and in due course freeze pretenders out of the profession. His point was well taken: aspiring professionals needed much more than a magazine to educate them; and the public interest in matters relating to landscape architecture was too small to sustain a magazine ("Landscape Gardening and Forestry," *Century Monthly Illustrated Magazine* 35 [March 1888]: 803; Jacob Weidenmann to JCO, 14 December 1887).

STANFORD UNIVERSITY; BILTMORE ESTATE
1886–1890

H IS last ten years of professional practice offered Olmsted three great opportunities. In 1886 he was employed to design the grounds of Leland Stanford, Jr., University at Palo Alto, California, in a region unaccommodating to the English style of landscape architecture. In 1888 he began work on George Washington Vanderbilt's estate, Biltmore, a vast acreage in the mountains of North Carolina near Asheville, which was intended to combine the functions of country retreat and paying enterprise. And in 1890 he began to create the grounds for the World's Columbian Exposition of 1893 at Chicago on low-lying swampland at the edge of Lake Michigan and to determine the physical arrangements, such as placement of buildings and lines and modes of transportation, connected with the fair.

During the same period his office was working on a number of public, private, and institutional grounds including Easton's Beach and the Frederick Vanderbilt place at Newport; Lawrenceville School, at Princeton; a series of parks for Rochester, New York; and Downing Park in Newburgh, for which Olmsted and Vaux, out of respect for Downing's memory and out of friendship for his widow, Mrs. Monell, furnished the plans without charge. Even before starting Biltmore and the Chicago fair, Olmsted told Brace that the firm had all the professional work they could do and that he would like to feel free to undertake less.[1] Why he did not feel free he did not explain; he hardly needed to, to the old friend who understood how he was dominated by his idea of duty.

Senator Leland Stanford of California and his wife, grieving for the untimely death of their young son* and wishing to do something in his memory to benefit the youth of California, planned to found a great university on a seven-thousand-acre site in the San Jose valley, not far from their Menlo Park home and thirty miles south of San Francisco. Except for the fact that the university was to be established at a distance from a population center, Stanford's plan was reminiscent of the college and community intended at Berkeley; but the grand scale of the senator's concept set it apart from Berkeley.

Harry Codman, who brought the work into the office, urged Olmsted to ask the unprecedented fee of ten thousand dollars for a preliminary plan. With mis-

---

*Leland Stanford, Jr., the Stanford's only child, died of typhoid fever in Florence on March 13, 1884, two months short of his sixteenth birthday.

givings, Olmsted did so; to his mild surprise, he got it.[2] He felt more serious qualms on another account: Senator Stanford was "bent on giving his University New England scenery, New England turf and trees," to be had only by the lavish use of water, which in those days was not obtainable in the region. "The landscape is said to be very fine in its way," Olmsted wrote Charles Eliot, whom he invited to work with him on the project, "but nobody thinks of anything in gardening that will not be thoroughly unnatural to it. What can be done I don't know, but it will be an interesting subject of study."[3] Eliot, on the point of opening his own office, did not accept Olmsted's invitation, and it was with Harry Codman and Frederick that Olmsted started for California late in August 1886.

Their first stop was in Minneapolis to see H. W. S. Cleveland, who had recently moved there to plan and direct work on the parks and parkways the city was starting. Cleveland, the one landscape architect in the country whose stature compared to Olmsted's, took his younger colleague on a long drive through the city and its environs to show progress and to describe plans. The president of the park commission, who accompanied them, asked Olmsted for a professional criticism of the works. Olmsted wrote him a letter, not of criticism, since he did not know enough of the local circumstances that determined what the park commissioners could expediently do, but of advice on their general duties: their overriding obligation was to create pleasing rural scenery; everything else—all buildings, roads, and other constructions—should be subordinate to the scenery and so far as possible unobtrusive; parsimony in the purchase of land should be strictly abjured since desirable tracts excluded for the sake of economy might well be required later when their price would have increased greatly. Olmsted mentioned, pointedly, that with "so experienced and so excellent a professional counselor" as Mr. Cleveland, the commission, if it listened to him, could expect to be safely guided past the pitfalls into which park commissions too often stumbled.[4]

The record of the rest of the trip is sketchy. The travelers reached Portland by the Northern Pacific Railroad and took the stage to San Francisco. Across the span of sixty years Frederick remembered the six-horse team laboring up and down long hills and an overnight stop at Yreka, near Mount Shasta whose snowy top glowed in sunlight all through the night.[5]

From San Francisco Olmsted and the young men traveled first by rail and then by stage—the dust in the stage as high as their shoe tops—to the Mariposa Big Tree Grove, where they spent the night with Galen Clark, who had been until the end of 1879 the official guardian of the Yosemite and the Big Trees. The two older men reminisced about their early association in the fabulous valley, and Clark probably brought Olmsted up to date on its troubled history.[6] Pinchpenny financing had been a leading cause of what the valley's friends plaintively called "Yo woe."[7] After 1880, however, a better rapport had developed between the legislature and a new set of Yosemite Valley commissioners, and funds had begun to flow more liberally from the one to the other. Rapidly increasing tourism made the arrangement and use of the valley floor an urgent

407

problem, and the commission had recently engaged William Hammond Hall, by then California state engineer, to survey the grant and make recommendations for its management. Hall urged the enlargement of the grant to include, and so protect, its watershed, judicious thinning and clearing of trees, and the allocation of a thousand acres of valley floor—that is to say, just about all of it not occupied by woods and rocky slopes and river—to fine forage crops for the use of tourists' horses.[8] The latter suggestion, if he heard of it, must have horrified Olmsted, who had always held that much of the valley's unique charm lay in the variety and delicacy of its native vegetation.

On this trip Olmsted made neither recommendations nor firsthand observation. For whatever reason, he did not enter the valley, although stage roads made access to it far easier than it had been when he was last there in 1865.[9]

Olmsted's visit to Senator Stanford at Menlo Park coincided with that of General Francis A. Walker, president of Massachusetts Institute of Technology, whom Stanford had met while consulting educators in the East and had brought West to advise on the building program. Another easterner to have a substantial say about the program was a young architect, Charles A. Coolidge. He had gone West to try to get the architectural part of the project for his firm, Shepley, Rutan, and Coolidge, successor firm to Richardson's, and had secured it.[10] Thus Olmsted again found himself engaged in a genuine collaboration; he was beginning a large landscape work by helping to select the site and decide on the placement of the buildings with the architect who was to design them.

The tract Stanford had designated for the university was mostly in parklike level ground sprinkled with oaks, which reached into rolling foothills where stood what remained of a forest of various conifers.[11] Olmsted favored the slope commanding the plain for the college buildings. Stanford, because young Leland had loved to ride over the plain, wanted the buildings placed there. Sympathetic to considerations of sentiment, Olmsted yielded the point. On September 29 he notified John, in Brookline, that the site had at last been settled, not as he wished, and that he had given instructions for a topographical survey of eight hundred acres. In keeping with his usual practice, he put a local engineer, J. G. McMillan, in charge of the field work. John was advised to prepare the office for a big job of plan drawing.[12]

With the main business of the trip dispatched, Olmsted indulged an interest of long standing: he visited Golden Gate Park in San Francisco. He had been following its development ever since Hall had written him, fifteen years before, introducing himself as chief engineer and superintendent of the park and asking him to recommend books and publications bearing on all phases of landscape architecture.[13] Olmsted had advised him to read such standard writers as Humphry Repton, Sir Uvedale Price, and John C. Loudon and had recommended *How To Lay Out a Garden*, by Edward Kemp, superintendent of construction of Birkenhead Park under its designer, Paxton. "As to general principles & spirit of design, all of Ruskin's art works are helpful," he had added.[14]

It was Hall's ambitious design to make a verdant landscape of the thousand acres of wind-whipped desert on the ocean side of San Francisco. Thoroughly familiar with the area from having mapped it for the army engineers during the Civil War, he knew that a copious supply of water was available not far beneath the surface. He intended to timber the shifting, largely barren sandhills, cover the valleys with shrubs and grasses, and devise such special features as picnic ground, open-air concert auditorium, garden, children's quarter, and lake. The long, narrow eastern panhandle he planned to shape and plant to provide a sheltered approach to the park proper in the teeth of the prevailing wind.[15] Each feature was to contribute to the intent of the whole, which was to provide relaxing and restful recreation in a rural setting for a varied population. When Hall sent Olmsted his design, Olmsted recognized many good elements in it but doubted that he could execute it on such a site and in such a climate.[16]

Hall, however, overcame the basic problem, that of holding the drifting sand, by establishing both native grasses and a European beach grass on the dunes. Within two years he had begun to shape the grounds, spread loam and street manure to make topsoil, set trees and shrubs and plant grass, and lay macadamized roads and walks. When he sent Olmsted his report of progress through 1873, Olmsted's misgivings gave way to optimism.[17] Two years later, when Olmsted received Hall's second biennial report, he wrote Hall that the results would far exceed anything that he had at first thought possible.*,[18]

In spite of his success, Hall had come under fire for cutting down trees— they were nurse trees and supposed to be thinned—and the legislature killed his budget. Charging political interference, Hall resigned in 1876 and took the job of state engineer. For ten years the plantations went unthinned, and Hall lamented to Olmsted that the design of the park was being perverted by commissioners who were trying to make a cross between an English meadow and a Dutch flower garden of it and who were yielding to the clamor for more walks, more roads, and more open spaces "for concerts, where beer may be had and dancing enjoyed. The idea of repose—the quietude if not the solitude—of natural like surroundings, appears to have been lost sight of entirely."[19]

With the installation of new commissioners in May 1886, Hall's advice was again solicited, and he emphatically urged that the plantations be thinned immediately before their deterioration ended in total ruin. Just as the commissioners were considering Hall's recommendations, they learned that Olmsted was visit-

*Meanwhile, Olmsted had encouraged Hall in another project. When Hall was put in charge of the Berkeley campus in 1874, he presented a plan and report to replace Olmsted's, which had been lost. Criticized for inserting too many artificial features, he appealed to Olmsted. Olmsted replied that Hall might well depart even further from nature because of the difficulty of doing landscape work in the English idiom in California, and he acknowledged that Hall knew better than he what could be accomplished in that climate (Hall to O, 12 March 1874; O to Hall, n.d. [after 12 March 1874], draft).

ing San Francisco. Sending him Hall's report, the president of the commission begged him to examine the park, tell them how the plantations should be treated, and comment on anything else that struck him.[20]

Olmsted, who was about to leave town, prepared a statement on the train on his way to Salt Lake City. Judiciously developed, Golden Gate Park would have a "unique and incomparable character," he said, because its design followed from "a thoroughly studious, inventive and scientific exercise of judgment" in grasping the opportunities and solving the problems presented by its site. The foundation was well laid, and the possibility of working to the design was demonstrated. He deprecated the ornamental grounds and flower garden as not compatible with territory to which the term *park* properly applied, and he categorically backed Hall on the need promptly to thin the plantations. Hall's practice of planting densely and thinning systematically to insure a sturdy and handsome growth to the remaining trees was sustained by experience the world over. Olmsted concluded with some axiomatic advice:

> The art of landscape architecture is a specialty which, in its exercise, peculiarly demands a forecast of the future. The materials of the work themselves grow and are progressive. To work with them demands sustained observation and intelligent making of deductions. I hope that Golden Gate Park may have these. It has been the ruination of many such grounds to have them pass rapidly under successive managements. The artistic direction of work on such grounds should, as far as possible, be continuous when once found fitting. . . .[21]

Olmsted's advice, fortified by that of Hall and of John McLaren, a Scottish gardener who had an extensive practice about San Mateo, prevailed, and his suggestion about continuous management was taken more literally than he could have anticipated: in 1887 the forty-year-old McLaren became superintendent of Golden Gate Park; he held the post until his death fifty-six years later.[22]

Home by October 18, Olmsted found that the firm had so much business that the overcrowded office had spilled over into the family dining room.[23] Of the major works—the far-flung Boston park system, a new zoological park for Washington D.C., the Niagara plan, and the new Stanford job—the Stanford problem was especially worrisome. The landscape treatment continued to be an issue between Olmsted and his client into the winter. In November Olmsted wrote the senator warning him against a tendency—from which, he guilefully alleged, he was himself not immune—to attempt a landscape work in a style inappropriate to its regional setting. The New England college campus with its green lawns and walks shaded by leafy trees was no suitable model for Stanford; it could not be satisfactorily transposed to California. "If we are to look for types of buildings and arrangements suitable to the climate of California it will rather be in those founded by the wiser men of Syria, Greece, Italy and Spain," he suggested.[24]

By then Olmsted had received an excellent topographical map from McMillan; and he had discussed with Walker the report in which Walker recommended to Stanford that he erect at once a nucleus of thirteen buildings—a memorial church and a dozen one-story buildings, stone and uniform in style, around a quadrangle; surrounding and adjacent to them could be added, as they were required, new series of buildings.[25] Stanford yielded to Olmsted's judgment on the style of landscape. For that of the buildings, he assumed some credit himself:

> When I suggested to Mr. Olmsted an adaptation of the adobe buildings of California with some higher form of architecture, he was greatly pleased with the idea and my Boston architects have skillfully carried out the idea, really creating for the first time an architecture distinctly Californian in character.[26]

The buildings Coolidge's firm designed incorporated both Olmsted's and Stanford's suggestions. Featuring short columns and low rounded arches with wide connecting arcades executed in the same style, they were reminiscent of California mission architecture, Mediterranean Romanesque, and Richardson. The quadrangle they were to surround, not grassed but paved, was to be planted with ornamental palms. Quadrangle and arcades together were planned to afford easy and comfortable passage in rain or blazing sun to classrooms, lecture rooms, and laboratories and to be at the same time conducive to sociability.

The consultants reached an understanding with each other more readily than with their client. The designs and the model, which Coolidge carried to California in April 1887, disappointed Stanford and his wife in several respects. They proposed alterations, one of them so radical that, Coolidge explained to them, it would change the grades and upset Olmsted's work. Stanford, according to Coolidge, replied that "a landscape Arch't and an Arch't might be disappointed but he was going to have the buildings the way he wanted them." Coolidge discreetly stopped objecting. "After this, we did the best we could to preserve your plan as intact as possible," he wrote Olmsted.[27] The conflict of taste over the entrance was yielded to the client, too. "Both Mr. and Mrs. S. think the main entrance should be a large memorial arch with an enormously large approach & in fact the very quietness and reserve which we like so much in it is what they want to get rid of," Coolidge reported.[28]

Since Stanford was eager to have the ground-breaking ceremony on May 14, which would have been his son's nineteenth birthday, there was no time to ship the amended plans east for Olmsted to approve.[29] Olmsted, however, accepted the changes philosophically. To Mrs. Van Rensselaer he observed, "There is a story to be told about the Stanford University. . . . The matter is not going well but not ruinously."[30]

Olmsted's relations with Stanford, which lasted pleasantly and in a tapering sort of way into the early 1890s, sometimes required him to draw on his reserves of patience. An early embarrassment occurred in June 1888 after he had arranged a meeting between Coolidge, the Stanfords, and Augustus Saint-Gaudens, whom Olmsted recommended to design the frieze of the big memorial arch. The sculptor, who had not yet achieved the full reputation that came with his later monumental works, recognized a great opportunity, and the Stanfords seemed impressed with him. About to go abroad, they asked him to have a sketch ready to show them on their return in October. Olmsted, who realized that neither the senator nor his wife seemed ever to have heard of the artist with whom they were dealing, quickly sent them a recent *Century* that carried an article about him and his work. Before they could have received it, Olmsted was mortified to get a note from Stanford saying that, on second thought, he felt "Mr. De Gordon" had better not try to do a model for the arch; they would come home with drawings "of about what we think we would like to have."[*,31]

It was part of Olmsted's plan to reforest the hills above the university and to establish on their lower slopes an arboretum featuring all the trees of California and of other parts of the world viable in that climate. Thomas H. Douglas, a Scottish forester whom Olmsted had engaged to supervise the planting, set up a nursery for propagating and experimenting, and Olmsted instructed him to keep full and careful records so that the history of every tree on the grounds could, if desired, be compiled from them a hundred years later "to aid investigation in schools of Dendrology, Horticulture and Botany."[32]

Although Stanford seemed to approve the scheme in principle, it went haltingly because he blew hot and cold. By the spring of 1889 he had vetoed two projects for the arboretum and the other planting, and Olmsted was at a loss to know what to propose next.[33] Codman, writing from Europe where he had gone to study, among other things, trees that flourished in climates like Palo Alto's, commiserated with Olmsted on the disheartening effect of the changes the senator, "a very uncertain man," kept suggesting.[34] Douglas, too, fretted under setbacks: he was allowed only Chinese helpers who, unable to read or understand English, set the plants at random if left to themselves.[35]

Work on buildings, roads, and planting proceeded notwithstanding occasional disconcerting changes of plan, and Olmsted several times traveled to California to give on-site advice. On his trips late in 1887 and 1888 Olmsted again visited Golden Gate Park, by then under the direction of McLaren. On the second occasion, the *San Francisco Examiner* quoted him as saying that he found the plantations strikingly improved, the tone of the decorative gardening quieter, and a "general gain of refinement and congruity in numerous points of detail" evident. The new children's quarter, concert ground, and deer glen were, he declared, the best of their kind in any park he knew of at home or abroad.

While Olmsted was happy to give an opinion on Golden Gate Park, he declined to join in the *Examiner*'s criticism of the Yosemite Valley commissioners,

---

*Saint-Gaudens got the commission and decorated the arch. It was wrecked in the earthquake of 1906.

whom it accused of mismanagement so gross that it was tantamount to vandalism. He had not been in the valley in more than twenty years, he said, and had no firsthand knowledge of conditions in it. Only when a reporter told him that the meadows, with their varied and beautiful vegetation, had been plowed for hay, did he exclaim, "That is very bad. Nothing can repair that injury."*,36

Olmsted probably visited the university site again in the summer of 1889, but it seems unlikely that he went after that. In 1890 he had a clash with Stanford's manager, Ariel Lathrop, over the control of the work. Olmsted, following his usual practice, had placed McMillan and Douglas in charge of their respective operations on the site. Employed and paid by Stanford, they took their orders from the firm, conducted their work under its direction, and made their frequent reports to it. McMillan and Douglas had warned Olmsted that Lathrop, although he had tolerated the arrangement for four years, had begun to act as though he felt it usurped his authority. As if to reassert it, Lathrop suddenly dismissed McMillan in the summer of 1890 without conferring with the landscape architects or notifying them of his intention or reasons and left them for weeks without progress reports. Olmsted, after rationalizing away his resentment, wrote Lathrop a long, polite letter hoping to clear up what he supposed was a misunderstanding between them. He explained that his professional procedures, including the one to which Lathrop had taken exception, had evolved in the course of thirty years of experience during which he had done scores of major works, public and private, and hundreds of smaller ones, which had earned him a reputation as a man who got good results. To get such results, he and his partners had to direct the execution of their designs through qualified men on the site who were subject to their orders. In no case was it enough for them to supply drawings and leave the carrying out of the work to agents not responsive to their instructions. Drawings were no more than memorandums the firm supplied to be referred to in getting on the ground a work of art requiring professional creativity and supervision. Aside from that, Olmsted added, Stanford, who had

*A thick sheaf of clippings testifies to the interest Olmsted continued to take in the controversy over the Yosemite commissioners, but his only published contribution to it was a privately printed memorandum dated March 8, 1890. In it Olmsted said that Robert Underwood Johnson, of the *Century*, had asked him the previous summer to write an article about the valley's management but that lack of firsthand information and of time to obtain it had prevented him. He criticized as ruinous to the scenery the proposal systematically to cut out all the young trees in the valley; nothing was more important to its charm than the constant renewal of its wood. He defended Johnson's good faith and good will in investigating the valley management and ridiculed the governor's published statement that Johnson had told him that, if he would employ his, Johnson's, "uncle" Frederick Law Olmsted as landscape architect for the valley, the *Century* would drop its inquiry. Finally he quoted, as directly applicable to Yosemite, the statement in the Niagara report that nothing of an artificial character should be placed on the property, no matter how valuable it was or how cheaply obtained, "the presence of which can be avoided consistently with the provision of necessary conditions for making the enjoyment of the natural scenery available" (Frederick Law Olmsted, "Governmental Preservation of Natural Scenery," 8 March 1890, printed circular, LWR Files).

not wanted a written contract with him, had verbally agreed to the stipulation in Olmsted's regular contract that the client should employ and pay engineers, foresters, and gardeners "to act cooperatively with, and under the general direction and supervision" of the landscape architects.[38]

Lathrop, in his reply, did not budge from the ground that the Olmsted firm had nothing to do with the university business except to supply drawings. This, Olmsted protested to Stanford, was as if a man wanting a fine statue should have an artist make a drawing and give it to a stone cutter, not a sculptor, to be executed.

> . . . Imagine a sculptor attempting to produce a statue, through workmen and by processes which a stone-cutter would use, throwing overboard all that he had learned of his profession beyond what a stone-cutter had learned; imagine this, and it may give you some idea of the position in which I feel that Mr. Lathrop demands that we shall place ourselves. We do not offer our services to be rendered under such conditions, and you have no right to put us, or let us be put, in such a position.[39]

Stanford sustained his manager. Olmsted, thereafter receiving neither reports nor requests for advice, felt that he had been frozen out of the work and resigned.[40] Nevertheless, on reading of the opening of the university in October 1891, he wrote congratulating Senator and Mrs. Stanford heartily, "None the less so, because it has been thought inexpedient that our connection should continue."[41]

Olmsted was already doing two pieces of work for George Vanderbilt—the grounds of his summer home at Bar Harbor and the lot of the family mausoleum in the Moravian Cemetery at New Dorp, Staten Island—when Vanderbilt asked him in 1888 to lay out the estate he was acquiring near Asheville, North Carolina.[42]

A grandson of Olmsted's one-time neighbor on Staten Island, William H. Vanderbilt, George Vanderbilt was a bachelor of twenty-six, "a delicate refined and bookish man, with considerable humor, but shrewd, sharp, exacting and resolute in matters of business." He had first begun buying the land after a visit to Asheville with his mother. He had found the air and climate invigorating, had admired the distant views, and had enjoyed long rides and drives through the hills and along the valleys. On one of his excursions he had come upon a spot that opened on the finest view he had seen in the region, and it occurred to him that he would like to have a house there. Deciding to buy the site and secure himself against near neighbors, he had by 1888 purchased through an agent and bit by bit about two thousand acres. He had had, to begin with, no very clear idea what to do with the place.[43]

Biltmore, in the form it eventually took, might have been considered a callous anomaly; it was a regal estate, with French Renaissance chateau, gardens, and dependencies, set down in a mountainous region of rural America, and of poor rural America at that. In its prime, it was the grandest country place in the United States. Yet it was more than a stately pleasure dome; a product of Olmsted's double-edged genius, it justified itself artistically as a superb piece of landscape design and socially as the first large experiment in America in practical forestry.

Forestry, the economical management of woodlands to produce a steady crop of timber and maintain at the same time a healthy and beautiful growth of trees, had been practiced in England and Europe for centuries. It did not yet exist in America. Where forests were so vast, there was no immediate incentive to husband and replenish them. It was easier to cut recklessly, abandon the deforested area, and move the lumbering operation to another stand of virgin growth. While the forests, especially in the East, were being substantially depleted, reforestation was not practiced. Investment in it would not have returned the large and quick profits that American businessmen wanted; for the first harvest, one had to look not months ahead as in agriculture but years.

Olmsted's concern for America's forests, though peripheral, was strong and of long standing. In 1871 he had drawn attention in the *Nation* to the relationship between forests and water supply. He agreed with H. W. S. Cleveland, who advocated the economical management of existing forests to perpetuate an invaluable natural resource and the reforestation of deforested regions to make their climate more favorable to settlement. Olmsted's close association with America's leading dendrologist, Charles Sprague Sargent, extended his knowledge of the subject. They had worked together to establish the Arnold Arboretum and to launch and support *Garden and Forest*; they had joined with Ashburner in a quest for means to protect the West Coast redwood forests; and together they were engaged in the long, and often frustrating, effort to protect the Adirondack forests from the ravages of lumbermen, railroads, squatters, and fires. Olmsted's plan for Stanford University, which provided for reforesting the slopes and setting up an arboretum, was evidence of the liveliness of his interest.

When Vanderbilt brought him to Asheville to examine his property and tell him if he had done anything "very foolish" in buying it, Olmsted assured him that if he had selected it for the air and the prospect, he had made no mistake. But Vanderbilt's supposition that he might make a park of the whole place was ill founded. The soil appeared poor; the woods had been repeatedly culled until nothing remained but runts and ruins and saplings; and the topography was so unsuitable for anything that might properly be called a park that even great expense would produce only unsatisfactory results.[44] "Such land in Europe," Olmsted suggested to his client,

> would be made a forest; partly, if it belonged to a gentleman of large
> means, as a hunting preserve for game, mainly with a view to crops of
> timber. That would be a suitable and dignified business for you to engage
> in; it would, in the long run, be probably a fair investment of capital and
> it would be of great value to the country to have a thoroughly well

organized and systematically conducted attempt in forestry made on a large scale. My advice would be to make a small park into which to look from your house; make a small pleasure ground and garden, farm your river bottom chiefly to keep and fatten live stock with a view to manure; and make the rest a forest, improving the existing woods and planting the old fields.[45]

Vanderbilt first intended building a large frame house,[46] but after a tour of the French chateau country with Richard Morris Hunt, he yielded to his architect's, and his own, predilection for palaces and decided on the extravagant chateau, to be built of limestone hauled six hundred miles from Indiana, that Hunt proposed.

Vanderbilt's lavish plans excited considerable interest, but in a young reporter for the *Sun* who heard Hunt describe them, they aroused something less than reverence. The size of the great house, its mass, its huge octagonal stone tower, especially its steep roof studded with an array of gables and little towers, were to be such, he wrote, that the "unthinking spectator, seeing it for the first time, might mistake it for a hotel, although people of education and taste would by no means fall into such an error."[47]

Olmsted, more respectful, told Hunt he liked the drawings when Hunt showed them to him in March 1889. Since the house site, open to the northwest, was bleak when the wind blew from that direction, he suggested that there should be a terrace on the southeast and provision below it for a sheltered ramble for outdoor exercise in blustery weather. To protect the great entrance court on the east side from the wind, a range of offices and stables might be extended eastward from the north end of the main house and partially concealed by a walled court. The value of the site was its outlook; soil and close scenery both needed the improving hand of man.[48]

Plans got under way rapidly. A road was built for the transport of building material to the house site, and the Brick House, one of the more substantial houses on the place, was cleaned and fitted so that Vanderbilt and his guests and Olmsted and Hunt and their assistants could stay there on their frequent visits. By early July stakes were in the ground to show the outline and dimensions of the house and scaffolds erected from which the views to be overlooked from windows and terraces could be seen;[49] and Olmsted had presented Vanderbilt with a plan elaborating on his first suggestions for laying out the entire property.

Since a fine natural forest existed not fifty miles from Vanderbilt's woodland and since the old fields, although taken over by scrub pine, had been exhausted only superficially by shallow cultivation, Olmsted thought that the land, when protected against grazing, fertilized, and deeply tilled, would sustain a flourishing variety of trees and shrubs and would be productive agriculturally as well. The whole estate, he advised, should rapidly be brought under cultivation as a forest, except for a park of about two hundred fifty acres around the house and the bottom lands along the French Broad River. Even before the forest became profitable, its management Olmsted felt would be an occupation "far more interesting to a man of poetic temperament than any of those commonly considered appropriate to a country-seat life." Vanderbilt would have, besides enjoyment, the satisfaction of knowing that he was doing his country an "inestimable service" by operating its first large-scale forestry experiment.[50]

Thwarted of his arboretum at Palo Alto, Olmsted proposed one for Biltmore to border roads that should be laid out from the house to the next valley south of it, along creeks to the French Broad bottoms, and circuitously back to the house. The picturesque waysides would offer a great variety of soils and exposures, and the arboretum was to be formed by cutting back and thinning the standing wood, leaving the best trees and bushes and making space for planting specimens of representative trees where they would grow and show to the best advantage.[51]

In devising the approach to the house, Olmsted calculated the emotional impact of a deliberately controlled visual experience. Abandoning the scantily timbered ridges where the road then ran, he designed the new road to follow along the ravines through a natural, wild, and sequestered way with a rich and varied border marked by incidents like pools, springs, and streams suggesting a deep and natural forest. No distant outlooks and no open spaces would break the seclusion of the passage "until the visitor passed with an abrupt transition into the enclosure of the trim, level, open, airy, spacious, thoroughly artificial Court, and the Residence, with its orderly dependencies, breaks suddenly and fully upon him." After this delightful shock he would enter the chateau, and from windows and terrace be struck by the grandeur of the mountains, the beauty of the valley, and the openness and tranquility of the park.[52]

Olmsted also proposed starting a nursery, supplemented by propagating house and trial garden, on the estate. Much of the plant material they would want could be gathered locally, set in the nursery for two or three years, and transplanted far more cheaply than it could be bought commercially.[*,53]

By the end of the year Olmsted and Vanderbilt were discussing plans for a village between Asheville and the estate and for a number of villas in the neighboring hills. As the scope of the work increased, so did Olmsted's enthusiasm for it, stimulated both by his conviction of its great public importance and by the "exacting yet frank, trustful, confiding and cordially friendly disposition toward all of us which Mr. Vanderbilt manifests."[54]

Except for the formal grounds around the house and the long eastward vista with its *rampe douce* suggestive of Vaux-le-Vicomte near Paris, the landscape work evolved gradually over a period of several years, one part after another,

---

*Olmsted enclosed with this report two pamphlets, Cleveland's *The Cultivation and Management of Our Native Forests for Development as Timber or Ornamental Wood* and his own and J. B. Harrison's collaborative *Observations on the Treatment of Public Plantations, More Especially Relating to the Use of the Axe.* The latter was the report of a study they had recently done at the request of a citizens' group exercised by what it had seen of tree-cutting in Central Park, which vindicated the thinning of the park's plantations as conducted under the direction of Vaux and Samuel Parsons, Jr.

usually on suggestions made by Olmsted and his associates in conversation with Vanderbilt. As each unit was developed and he liked the results, Vanderbilt told them to do more. "It was a very informal and pleasant personal relation that developed between father and George Vanderbilt," Frederick later wrote.[55]

Until his retirement in 1895, Olmsted went to Biltmore two or three times a year, often staying for weeks at a time. Occasionally he traveled with Vanderbilt in his private car. Sometimes he met Vanderbilt at Biltmore, where they stayed in the Brick House. Notwithstanding the house guests and the gaiety, the whist, and the long social evenings, Olmsted, with his client, engineer, and foremen, spent hours in the saddle planning and overseeing the multitude of operations involved in establishing a palace with its grounds and supporting outworks in the backwoods.

The lavishness of the operation overawed the local people. One of its most impressive single features was the private railway spur, nearly three miles long and costing $77,500, constructed to carry building materials from the main line to the house site. ". . . When he considers that the building of this road was a measure of economy . . . it is then that the Tar Heel begins to comprehend something of what it is to be a millionaire," remarked the same reporter who had poked fun at the fancy roof.[56]

Surveying, grading, roadmaking, the construction of bridges and culverts and drains and waterworks, the setting out of the nursery, the preparation ˙of fields, the planting of trees and shrubs, were done under the supervision of the engineers whom the Olmsted firm engaged and directed and whom Vanderbilt paid through his estate manager, Charles McNamee. As the nursery took shape, Chauncey D. Beadle, a Cornell graduate whose encyclopedic "tree-sharpness" was a source of wonder and admiration to Olmsted, took charge of it; and the forestry operations, toward the end of 1891, were entrusted to young Gifford Pinchot.

Pinchot, a wealthy New Yorker of French extraction, had decided to make a career of forestry on graduating from Yale in 1889, although there was then neither forestry nor a career to be had in it in the United States. To prepare, he had studied for a year at the Ecole Nationale Forestière at Nancy, cultivated acquaintance with the leading foresters of England, France, Germany, and Switzerland, and toured some of the most interesting of the European forests with Sir Dietrich Brandis, who had introduced systematic forestry to Burma and India and was acknowledged to be the foremost of living foresters. Of Pinchot's ambition to bring forestry to America, Brandis had said: "Nothing general can be done until some State or large individual owner makes the experiment and proves for America what is so well established in Europe, that forest management will pay."[57]

On his return to the United States, Pinchot had taken two long trips South and West to get some idea of the country and its forest resources. On the way home from one journey, he had stopped at Asheville, where he had been impressed by the unctuousness of the February mud, scandalized, although himself rich, by the contrast between the princely mansion rising on the Biltmore Estate and the one-room log cabins of the neighboring mountaineers, and intrigued by the estate just right for forest management on a large scale.[58]

Here was the "large individual owner" Brandis had posited on whose land the first persuasive American experiment in forest management was already being made. By then the estate, to which Vanderbilt was constantly adding, approached six thousand acres; forty thousand trees and shrubs were growing on forty acres of nursery and more in the propagating house; three hundred acres of old fields were planted in white pine; and Olmsted's "Project of Operations for Improving the Forest of Biltmore," which he had drawn up and submitted to Sargent for approval in the early summer of 1890, was in full swing.[59]

Pinchot met Olmsted for the first time the middle of October 1891 at Biltmore and was "much delighted" to learn that Olmsted had advised Vanderbilt to employ a forester. Olmsted interviewed him again the next month at Brookline and questioned him thoroughly about his experience and theories of forestry. On December 6, not quite a year after his return to the United States, Pinchot was appointed forester to the Biltmore Estate and took charge of the first large-scale example of practical forest management in the United States. "The conception," he later wrote, "was of course Mr. Olmsted's, but it was George Vanderbilt who put it through."[60]

Life in the Brick House, Olmsted's usual headquarters on the estate, was something less than luxurious, especially in winter. The house was draughty; the servants were "good, big, blundering, forgetful, thoughtless children"; and the cooking was simply demoralizing.[61] On arrival, Olmsted was usually sick for a couple of days from the train trip and the change of altitude.[62] Sometimes his acclimatizing illness was aggravated by insomnia, or sciatica, or facial neuralgia, or lumbago, or by something picked up from an associate. When he caught Hunt's grippe in October 1890, the "Confederate surgeon" who treated him dosed him with quinine, whiskey, and sleeping drugs so that his ears roared, his judgment wavered, and he wrote Mrs. William Dwight Whitney, whom as Miss Lizzie Baldwin he had worshipped long ago, a letter about which, when he recovered his wits, he was very uneasy.[63] He need not have worried: her sympathy was as quick and warm as formerly. Magically it lured the Fred Olmsted she had known, trusting and frank, out of the shell of his reticence just for a moment to confide in her again, as he had in his youth, his private reflections.*

As he grew old, he wrote her, he sometimes compared his accomplishments with his early ambitions and measured what he was against what he had hoped to become. He was, of course, disappointed. Yet,

---

*Olmsted's letter seems to have been in answer to a note from her prompted probably by Clarence Pullen's article in the September 27, 1890, *Harper's Weekly*, which described the Boston park system, gave some account of Olmsted's career, and spoke of his determining influence on the rural park movement.

I need not conceal from you that the result of what I have done is to be of much more consequence than anyone else but myself supposes. As I travel I see traces of influences spreading from it that no one else would detect—which, if given any attention by others, would be attributed to "fashion." There are, scattered through the country, seventeen large public parks, many more smaller ones, many more public or semi-public works, upon which, with sympathetic partners or pupils, I have been engaged. After we have left them they have in the majority of cases been more or less barbarously treated, yet as they stand, with perhaps a single exception, they are a hundred years ahead of any spontaneous public demand, or of the demand of any notable cultivated part of the people. And they are having an educative effect perfectly manifest to me—a manifest civilizing effect. I see much indirect and unconscious following of them. . . . I see in new works of late much evidence of efforts of invention—comprehensive design—not always happy but symptomatically pleasing. Then I know that I shall have helped to educate in a good American school a capital body of young men for my profession, all men of liberal education and cultivated minds. I know that in the minds of a large body of men of influence I have raised my calling from the rank of a trade, even of a handicraft, to that of a liberal profession—an Art, an Art of Design. I have been resolute in insisting that I am not to be dealt with as an agent of my clients but as a counselor—a trustee, on honor. I have always refused to take employment on other terms and when it appeared that I must do so or yield the point I have seven times already resigned the charge of important and interesting works. It is what I have done in these respects and what I see of the indirect effect on the standing of my profession and the progress of my art that leads me to write to you after so many years in the self-complacent way that I do; this, rather than anything you have seen or of which you have read.[64]

He recalled gratefully that she had persuaded him as a green young man that his rusticity and lack of education need not bar him from an intellectual life and that she had directed him to such sages as Ruskin and Emerson and Lowell, who encouraged him to respect and cultivate that instinctive, poetic love of scenery which later determined his profession. Still, he had been when she knew him and for another decade after merely an amateur, enthusiastic and undisciplined. How "such a loitering, self-indulgent, dilettante sort of a man as I was when you knew me and for ten years afterwards, could, at middle age, have turned into such a hard worker and *doer* as I then suddenly became and have been ever since" was a question to which he offered no answer.[65] He rarely referred to the terrible impact upon him of his brother's death, which had certainly been one element in his transformation.

Appropriately, it was to the woman he had so admired in youth that he expressed his nonchivalric regard for women, quite different from the conventional respect accorded them by Victorian mores. Just as he thought Sunday's activities should not be radically different from the weekday's, so he believed men's and women's roles should not be rigidly differentiated. He had himself taken an active part in the rearing of his children; now that women were beginning to make headway in the learned professions, he considered it a gain not simply for them but for civilization.[66] "I rejoice in it with you," he wrote Mrs. Whitney. "I think that hardly another man has as high an estimate of the possible capacities of women as compared with men in respect to organization, method and discipline in the management of affairs as I have as the result of my Sanitary Commission experience."[67] Mrs. Francis Bacon, Georgie Woolsey of hospital transport days, would, he believed, "upon orders, take command of the channel fleet, arm, equip, man, provision, sail and engage the enemy, better than any other landsman I know."[68]

Hypothesis and perhaps hyperbole entered into his estimate of Georgie Woolsey, but the case of Elizabeth Bullard showed that Olmsted meant what he said. Her father, Oliver, his long-time friend and occasional colleague, had been engaged at Olmsted's recommendation to carry out Olmsted's park design in Bridgeport. Elizabeth, a painter, had been her father's talented, though unofficial, collaborator. On Bullard's death in December 1890, the president of the park commission wondered whether Miss Bullard, familiar with her father's intentions for the Bridgeport parks, might not be a proper successor to him and asked Olmsted. Olmsted was delighted to urge her appointment. "There is some risk in it mainly because of difficulties of discipline, but my opinion is that it would have a wholesome effect on politics and patronage and stimulate the Commission to higher manliness," he explained, showing some residual chivalry after all.[69]

At about the same time he wrote Mrs. Whitney, Olmsted embarked on a flurry of correspondence with others of the little band of intimates who had been his confidants and her admirers. The epistolary impulse, a sort of clutch at the past, owed something to Brace's death in August 1890 and to Frederick's entering Harvard that fall: both events were ruthless reminders of time's swift flow.[70]

Brace had gone abroad for his health in May, and it was not until after his departure that Olmsted learned that his illness was serious. Word of his death in Switzerland reached Olmsted at Biltmore. It was a shock to him, a shock that, instead of subsiding, vibrated more painfully as he reflected on the friendship reaching back into youth that it ended. To Kingsbury, who sent him the obituary he wrote for the *Journal of the American Social Science Association,* Olmsted made some reticent reference to his feeling and then turned away from the sensitive subject to report on Biltmore and the firm's other work.[71] "Our business is constantly increasing," he wrote, "and in such a way that it is impossible to get the additional assistants for it, their being of a class of which there are but few accomplished in the world; so we are always personally under an agitating pressure and cloud of anxiety."[72]

There was, to be sure, "a little rush" of educated men wanting to become landscape architects who applied to the firm, but Olmsted could encourage only a few of them. The artistic inclination and fondness for gardens that some thought qualified them naturally for the profession, disqualified them in Olmsted's view, suggesting care more for beautiful objects and scenes than for scenery in composition. Nor could he encourage anyone to whom it would be a hardship to forego earning a fair living for some years. Graduate courses in architecture and engineering, freehand and mechanical drawing, botany, and horticulture; independent study of good pictures and fine architecture; two or three years of apprenticeship in his office, which would include drudgery, drafting, travel at the student's own expense, and extensive assigned reading; a tour of foreign study—all these prerequisites to beginning practice could consume eight years after college. Then the aspiring landscape architect would embark on a profession that was not a "staple" business and that offered no chance of making a fortune. There was still no such general, fairly steady demand for his services as there was for those of architects and engineers.[73] "Our people are ready to spend millions for skilled direction in building of houses or of railroads, where they yet grudge hundreds for the reconciliation of convenience with fitness and beauty of local scenery," Olmsted observed.[74]

One aspirant whose interest Olmsted systematically cultivated was his son. He looked forward to the day—distant by ten or more years, which he hardly expected to survive—when Frederick, bearer of his name and exponent of his school, should join the firm and become an acknowledged leader in the profession. This was no slight ambition to impose on a very young man. The accord and sympathy between them, however, was nearly perfect; it was their happy fortune that Frederick meant to be exactly what his father wanted him to be.

Frederick had been a good student, an active athlete, editor of the school paper, and a popular boy at Roxbury Latin School, which he had attended from 1888 to 1890. As he was about to enter Harvard, his father described him to Norton as

> still just a good healthy boy, keeping the boyish condition longer than
> most, but not puerile . . . he has himself under good discipline, is studious,
> patient, deferential, in that he receives advice gratefully and shapes his
> course reasonably by it. As to his education, not feeling myself to be a very
> competent adviser, I have given him the reins and he has chosen his
> advisers and made his plans, as far as I can judge, wisely. . . . I like him
> very much and he is affectionate and confiding, to me, more than boys
> generally to their fathers, I think.[75]

Although Olmsted refrained from advising Frederick on his college course, the Polonius in him would not be downed, and he advised him in detail on other subjects. Frederick was to spend at least five hours a week in extracurricular reading and thinking about landscape architecture. "I reckon that in four years you would thus have read everything not ephemeral in English, French and German and would be the best read man as to this Art in the world."[76]

He was to keep track of all that went on in the office to gain understanding of the bearing of practice and theory on each other. The firm's most important work was drawn to it by the name of Frederick Law Olmsted; when Olmsted dropped out, business could be expected to fall off; and Frederick's earning capacity would depend in considerable measure on the capital of knowledge he laid up by systematic reading during the next four years and on the insight he acquired into the conduct of business in the office.[77]

Having secured a more respectable standing for the profession than it could have attained without his efforts, Olmsted felt he had been

> rather grandly successful in this respect, and yet only successful in holding the fort as it were. It is as if the war had just begun and my part had been to keep the enemy in check until reinforcements could arrive. These young men, John and Harry, Eliot and Coolidge, with Sargent and Stiles and Mrs. Van Rensselaer, are the advance of the reinforcements. I want you to be prepared to be a leader of the van. How much abler should I have been had I had your education to this time of your education. How much more had I had that education that you may have ten years hence.[78]

Accustomed from the time he and Vaux began Central Park to look to distant results, Olmsted considered most of his work in the light of the credit it would reflect on Frederick in the future.

> How will it as a mature work of the Olmsted school affect Rick? . . . How is Rick to be best prepared to take advantage of what in reputation I have been earning? Reputation coming as the result of what I shall have done, but not coming in my time. How best prepared to carry on the war against ignorance and prejudice and meanness. How best to make L.A. respected as an Art and a liberal profession.[79]

The future of his son and of his profession were inseparably joined in his concern.

Like his own father, who had encouraged him to take dancing lessons, Olmsted set a high value on social grace as a lubricant in the dull or gritty situations of everyday life and as an aid to professional success. He urged Frederick to learn to make himself agreeable and interesting to cultivated people by being knowledgeable about current events, literature, art, and entertainment.

> Seek the best society. Seek to enjoy it. Seek to make yourself desirable in it. Make yourself well-informed on matters of conversation of the best and more fortunate sort of people. This is an essential element of your education. . . . You have disappointed me in not training yourself more to acquire social grace. It is entirely a matter of will. You have it in your power greatly to increase your value in this respect, your power to be

useful and through usefulness respectable to others and to yourself, which is the chief defense against misery in life. You have your defects and your weaknesses but on the whole you are in capital condition at the starting point of the University period of your life work.[80]

With scarcely a backward glance, Frederick took up the obligations his father laid on him.

XXXIII
THE CHICAGO FAIR; ENGLAND

1890–1892

NEW York had not wanted a world's fair, to celebrate the treaty concluding the Revolutionary War or anything else, if it was going to deface Central Park. Other cities snatched at the project, opportunely refurbished as an exposition hailing the four-hundredth anniversary of Columbus's discovery of America. Chicago, the successful candidate, was designated by Congress as host in April 1890.

The big international exhibitions of the second half of the nineteenth century have been called that period's "original form of group celebration" and "the great festivals in the life of nations."[1] Their practical aim was to bring together industrial products from all over the world and promote their exchange and use. Their ideal, which echoes faint and sad in the second half of the twentieth century, was to unite all mankind through industry. Queen Victoria's prince consort, Albert, patron of the first world's fair, had said that "the exhibition of 1851 shall give a vivid picture of the stage at which industry has arrived in the solution of that great task."[2]

In the notion of bringing together people from all countries in holiday throngs for enjoyment and instruction, there was something of Olmsted's ideal of communicativeness. By the fall of 1890, Olmsted was already a key man in the band of artists and architects whose collaboration was to produce the World's Columbian Exposition of 1893.

The exposition has been called an aesthetic disaster that set American architecture back fifty years:[3] it faithfully echoed the Beaux Arts style instead of exploiting the innovations of such talented Americans as Richardson, Louis Sullivan, or William LeBaron Jenney, whose original use of iron-and-steel skeleton construction in the Home Insurance Company Building in 1883 made possible and introduced the skyscraper. Nor did the exposition rival the five comparable European expositions in architectural originality: there was no light and soaring and inventive glass-wood-iron construction like the Crystal Palace in London in 1851 or any such audacious structures as the Eiffel Tower and the arched wrought-iron and glass and cast-iron and glass halls spanning thitherto unspannable spaces of the Paris expositions of 1855, 1867, 1878, and 1889. Although Chicago led America in bold and inventive commercial architecture,[4] the fair buildings, which were temporary and might have dared to be daring, were safely conventional in construction and soothingly classical in appearance. Only Louis Sullivan's Hall of Transportation escaped the coat of staff (a stucco-like preparation used on temporary buildings) and the white paint, which caused the classical mirage glittering on the shore of Lake Michigan to be known as the White City.

The Columbian Exposition undoubtedly encouraged a backward-harking disposition toward Beaux Arts classicism in American taste. But taste changes, and this penchant did not last; neither did it prevent the development of the new building techniques and their corollary styles then emerging. And the fair did do something positive and lasting. It persuasively demonstrated that architects and artists engaged together in creating such an entity as a great fair, which is much on the order of a city, could coordinate their plans so that every feature would stand in becoming relation to every other and to the whole affair. Conspicuous but superficial were the uniform whiteness of the buildings (unable to agree on color, the architects finally settled for white) and the uniform cornice line. Quite radical, on the other hand, was the intensive collaboration among architects, artists, and landscape architects in hammering out plans for all aspects of the fair: its layout, architectural style, grounds, waterways, transportation, statuary, fountains, and ornamentation.[5] In spite of some compromises and last-minute changes, they left no important feature to chance or impulse. "The efficient cooperation of these allied professions [architecture and landscape architecture] is one of the most happy results of the Exposition," Garden and Forest declared when it was all over. "It is greatly to the credit of both, and of excellent promise for the future of all art in this country."[6]

Olmsted's responsibility for the fair was large.* In the first place, he selected the site. Invited to Chicago in August 1890, when the fair commission could not agree on one, he hurried west with Harry Codman, whose three months' experience of the 1889 exposition in Paris was to make him a valuable collaborator.[7] After viewing seven possible sites, Olmsted and Codman recommended one that to the eye of common sense seemed quite unsuitable. Out of faith in their professional judgment, the commission accepted their advice.[8]

The four inland sites the landscape architects dismissed as having nothing, scenically, to compare with the one grand feature common to the other three, Lake Michigan. The most desirable and most distant from the city of the three shore sites had to be eliminated because the local railroads refused to extend their tracks and provide the facilities Olmsted and Codman thought necessary. They therefore fell back on a site closer to town called Jackson Park, no park at all but some five hundred acres of swampy land set aside for one twenty years earlier. Scarcely higher than the water level of the lake, subject to occasional overflow, divided by sandy ridges built up by the action of wind and flooding, it was hospitable to little but boggy, herbaceous vegetation and a sprinkling of scrub oak.

---

*According to a draft of articles of agreement between the exposition's directors and F. L. Olmsted & Company, the firm's fee for handling the work of landscape architecture at the fair was $22,500 (Draft of articles of agreement, [28 November 1890]).

It was familiar ground to Olmsted. He and Vaux had made a plan for Jackson Park in 1871.[9]

To help plan a world's fair was a new kind of undertaking for Olmsted: for the first time he was planning something ephemeral that would be dismantled in six months, not something lasting that would slowly come to fulfillment during decades. Still, the problem had one thing in common with that of the United States Capitol grounds: grounds were to be subsidiary to buildings; broad landscape effects were out of place and out of the question. The requirements of the scenery had to be accommodated to the requirements of the buildings with their need for easy access and free circulation.[10]

The fair grounds after the fair were to be turned into a park, as earlier planned. The first question was: to what extent might the general theory of the old plan for the site as pleasure ground be applicable to it as fair ground? The original design had featured a chain of interconnecting lagoons with natural shorelines; the sandy soil dredged out of the low places was to have been spread along the ridges to extend them and raise them well above the water level of the lake. The circular road system had included a long shore drive carried on a bridge over the single inlet that connected lake and lagoons, and a long pier extending into the lake was intended to protect the opening against silting and to accommodate boats.[11]

Olmsted concluded that the old design was, in general, appropriate and adaptable. The lagoons in the amended plan would in some instances have the character of canals with straight architectural shorelines in keeping with the buildings to which, in near perspective, they would form the foreground. Exhibition buildings would be disposed on the raised and extended sandbars and suitable approaches to them by land and water devised.[12] When they had a clear general idea of how to arrange the site, Olmsted and Codman conferred with Daniel H. Burnham and his partner, John Wellborn Root.

Burnham's part in the fair was decisive. One of the three or four most prominent architects in Chicago, he had been instrumental in securing the exposition for the city. His firm, Burnham and Root, were consulting architects to the fair, and for most of its duration he was director of works and chairman of the consulting board, which was composed of the architects, landscape architects, and engineers.

The landscape architects immediately put their impress on the fair by carrying their first disputed point, "that of tying the Fair to the Lake, and as it was a question chiefly of what people call taste and in which they hold that argument is out of place, and we carried it simply by argument, it is a triumph," Olmsted wrote John.[13]

After that critical determination was made, various arrangements of the site were discussed, and Root, finally, at a meeting of the design board, roughed out a preliminary plan on brown paper. On December 1, 1890, Root's sketch and a brief description were presented to the fair's national committee and accepted.[14]

The design provided for a great architectural court, by which everyone arriving by water, at its east end, and by rail at its west, should enter the grounds. The court held, besides the administration building in an open paved space, a large body of water with architectural banks, along the sides and east end of which some of the larger fair buildings were placed. A canal led out of the basin to the north into a series of lagoons, more or less parallel to the lake, on which faced other fair buildings. All important buildings were provided with both a land and a water approach. Near the middle of the lagoon system was an island of about fifteen acres. Clusters of trees, rather poor but the best on the fair grounds, already stood on it. It was meant, originally, to be kept free of noticeable buildings.[15] Two inlets, one at the south end of the fair grounds outside a long pier and the other at the north end inside a shorter pier, were to join the lake and the fair's internal waterways.

After the acceptance of the preliminary plan, Burnham was authorized to select architects outside of Chicago to design some of the main buildings. Among those he chose were McKim, Mead and White, Peabody and Stearns, and Van Brunt and Howe—all three firms with which, Olmsted had said a dozen years before, he could congenially work. Designated also were Hunt—his fashionable eminence made him an inevitable choice—with whom Olmsted was working fairly harmoniously at Biltmore and George B. Post, a highly successful New York architect who, with Hunt, had opposed the advisory board's plans for the Albany capitol. Several outstanding Chicago architects, including Jenney, whose association with Olmsted went back to the siege of Vicksburg, and Louis Sullivan, were invited to plan other major buildings.[16]

Just as the architects were holding their first meeting in Chicago in January, Root died unexpectedly of pneumonia. Their shock notwithstanding, the planners critically reviewed Olmsted's and Codman's general plan. Changes were suggested, counterproposals made, and advantages weighed; "the result was at length a cordial and unqualified approval of the plan as originally presented."[17] Individual buildings were assigned to the architects, and the dimensions of court, structures, and canals tentatively decided. Of this first session, Olmsted wrote Henry Van Brunt: "I feel with you warmly that the meeting at Chicago was a most happy, useful and promising occasion and I look forward with much pleasure to others to follow."[18]

More took place in February, at which the architects presented and discussed their preliminary sketches. Saint-Gaudens, summoned to advise on sculptural decoration and help select artists to execute it, proposed a colossal statue backed by thirteen columns, signifying the original thirteen states, for the east end of the court to hold it together architecturally. The sculptor was so moved, after one long session, by the congregation of such talent collaborating in so earnest and generous a spirit, that he made to Burnham the much-quoted remark: "Look here, old fellow, do you realize that this is the greatest meeting of artists since the fifteenth century?"[19]

Saint-Gaudens's proposal was debated in Chicago and again in Olmsted's Brookline office, where, to facilitate discussion, Olmsted had had set up a rough model of the fairgrounds. He, the sculptor, and several other collaborators one day were arguing whether the effect of statue and columns would be good or bad from within the grounds as obscuring the view over the lake. Frederick, who was present pursuant to his father's standing orders to seize all incidental opportunities of an educational sort, was sent to the barn for finishing nails and told to drive them into the model where the columns would be. When he had finished, the distinguished men all got down on their knees and squinted at the altered view and found the effect acceptable.[20]

The first difficulty Olmsted and Codman encountered was a familiar one to landscape architects accustomed to being answerable to committees. ". . . Among our hundreds of masters," Olmsted told a friend at the beginning of 1891,

> divided into several organizations, commissions, directors, committees, there is no one who will give us any exact instructions upon cardinal points, such as the extent of floor room there will be wanted for any department or subdepartment of the show. We keep making tentative plans, but the most liberal of these would not allow a tenth part of the aggregate space which we are unofficially advised will be wanted. For example, the Californians say that at least 20 acres will be wanted for their special state exhibit. We think two acres would be an extravagant allowance, etc. In general we are allowing 25% more space than was used at the last French Exposition.[21]

Another difficulty was the shore planting of the lagoons. In March, Olmsted wrote a long memorandum describing what he wanted and how it was to be obtained. The lagoon was to be made to look like a natural bayou, secluded and placid. Its low, barren shores were to be given a rich, affluent, and picturesque aspect by the profuse use of aquatic plants rooted partly below and partly above the surface of the water. The best of the trees on the island were to be retained and fertilized in the hope of improving their foliage. Between them and the water, plants, bushes, and young trees were to be set so that from a boat the island would appear a broad, dense bank of verdure.[22]

Except where architectural terraces were to be formed close to the water, the shore planting was to have three main objects: to make an agreeable low foreground over which the great buildings of the exposition would rise, gaining in apparent grandeur because they would seem more lofty and distant than they could otherwise appear; to establish some extent of broad and apparently natural scenery to counteract the theatricality and bustle of the rest of the exposition; and to secure, along with a general unity and continuity of shore, a mysterious, poetic effect through the intricate mingling of diverse kinds of foliage.[23] To obtain such results was a soluble professional problem; to secure them in only three short growing seasons and on shores where the water level varied from one year to the next by as much as four feet was one to tax ingenuity.

Olmsted intended that great numbers of plants native to the rivers and swamps of northern Illinois and of regions farther north should be collected and planted, along with a few mildly exotic ones selected to enhance the richness of the general effect. Trials of numerous plants were to be made in the summer of 1891; and large reserves of the hardiest were to be prepared for replanting on ground where other sorts had dried out or drowned out. To guard against the danger that shore planting established by the summer of 1892 might be torn out by the movement of ice during the winter, Olmsted proposed that the plantations be cut short in the fall and covered with litter and that the shore ice, when it formed, be cut free from the body of lake ice and held more or less in place with stakes, until the spring thaws dissolved it.[24]

Miles of lagoon shore were to be planted, the planting season would be very short, and the laborers would be working in icy water. The planting would be done by unskilled labor in a comparatively crude way; plants requiring delicate treatment and plants that would not root readily in wet, sandy soil could not be depended on; tough and hardy varieties, habituated to the prolonged cold of the lake water, would have to be set thickly, since there would be little opportunity to cultivate them after they were in.[25]

Olmsted was equally concerned about the kinds of boats that should be used at the exposition. Their use for transportation was incidental; their main purpose was decorative, to enhance the grace and gaiety of the scene. Water fowl, too, were to be established on the lagoons to lend animation and interest to the quieter stretches. Olmsted later explained:

> The effects of the boats and the water fowl as incidents of movement and life; the bridges with respect to their shadows and reflections, their effect in extending apparent perspectives and in connecting terraces and buildings, tying them together and thus creating unity of composition—all this was quite fully taken into account from the very first; and the style of boats best adapted to the purpose became at once, a topic of much anxiety and study.[26]

By March the fair was getting successfully under way and the landscape architects' work was well advanced, thanks in great part to Harry Codman. He was giving all his time to it and showing high ability on the social and diplomatic side as well as the executive. Olmsted was spending about half his time in Chicago and, between insomnia and the ailments induced by travel, he began by early June to feel about played out.[27]

At home the middle of June, he was worse than played out; he was seriously ill from arsenic poisoning contracted, it was thought, from the new bedroom wallpaper that was found to have arsenic in the Turkey red. In and out of bed for three weeks, he feared that he might be near the end of his career. In the circumstances, his concern to forward Frederick's found anxious expression.[28] From his sickbed Olmsted showered admonitions on Frederick, who was spending the summer in Chicago as aide-de-camp to Dion Geraldine, the superintendent of construction at the fair. Frederick should not outstay his welcome at the Glessner's, parents of his classmate George Glessner. Instead, he should look for a boardinghouse near the Rookery, Burnham's office, and take advantage of the opportunities Burnham promised to offer him to earn friends. He ought also to familiarize himself with good paintings in the art museum and in private collections and to work to improve his German by speaking it with Rudolf Ulrich, the German gardener whom Olmsted had lured from California to take charge of the fair's landscape department. He was to put himself immediately at the disposal of J. A. Campbell, a Paris-trained Scottish architect then visiting Chicago, who had been recommended to the Olmsteds by Julia Bryant. ("Do what you can for him promptly. He will be a good man for you to have known pleasantly when you go to Glasgow.")[29]

Frederick, who later said that working on the Chicago fair was one of the three most stimulating experiences of his professional life,[30] took to his duties as though born to them; by the end of July, Geraldine wanted to put him on the payroll. Olmsted, although pleased, would not permit it. "I am too old a public functionary to take any risks of being suspected of obtaining pecuniary favors for myself or any of my kin," he wrote Frederick. "I prefer that you pay for your schooling by doing such work as you are found up to, not be paid for going to school."[31]

Convalescent, Olmsted spent most of the summer in Brookline. His wife and Marion were in Maine, John was in and out of town on business, and the stenographers and other office staff were, one after the other, on holiday. The house was in the hands of charwomen and of carpenters, who were building an addition to the office.[32]

Olmsted passed some of the time in assembling his Sanitary Commission materials—publications, photographs, memorabilia—to deposit them in the Massachusetts Commandery of the Loyal Legion, an organization of Union officers and civilian loyalists. The Sanitary Commission by then, in spite of the evolution of the Red Cross from it, was little more than a half-forgotten footnote to the terrible drama of the Civil War, but it remained, in Olmsted's opinion, a memorable episode in the life of the nation, the record of which should be faithfully preserved.[33]

During the dog days Olmsted wrote to Frederick, as to his easiest confidant, several times a week. He warned against the malaria reported in Chicago and forbade him to gather swamp plants. He feared that the demands of his work were leaving him less time for "miscellaneous observation, reflection, imagination, inquiry and social experiences, than would be desirable." He told him about Lowell's funeral, which he attended along with Curtis, Norton, President Eliot, and other friends of his own generation. ("Dear me, how old they all looked!" he reflected.) Not wanting Frederick to be dependent, as he was, on the technical knowledge of horticulturists, he repeatedly exhorted him to pack his memory with the names, characteristics, and habitats of all the plants he came across.[34]

431

Frederick did his very best. Speaking as an old man of his efforts, he expressed interest not that as a young man he had so dutifully striven to do just what his father wanted but that his mind was constituted so like his father's that he, too, was never able to acquire a thoroughly satisfactory mastery of horticulture.[35]

Early in September Olmsted was again well enough to go to Chicago. He then made a quick trip to Marquette to advise on a private place, visited Louisville, where the firm was laying out Cherokee Park, and went on to Biltmore. Speechless with a bad cold, he kept indoors until it lifted and passed the time worrying about the estate and his client's departure from the original plan in favor of agricultural enterprises.[36] "I feel as always that I cannot afford to be away from here," he fretted to John.[37]

He stayed at Biltmore, conferring with Vanderbilt and directing work on the approach road, past the middle of the month. On the way home he stopped in Washington; the zoo did not need his personal attention, but he wanted to study a large project Senator Francis G. Newlands had invited him to consider— the laying out of the suburb that was to become Chevy Chase.*,[38]

In Brookline again, Olmsted heard from Codman of a contemplated plan to place the music hall on the wooded island at the fair. Feeling strongly that the isle should afford relief from "all the splendor and glory and noise and human multitudinousness of the great surrounding Babylon," Olmsted replied that, if he was overborne, he would yield with good grace, but his protest must be a matter of record.[39] At the same time, he was drawing up a circular for the state committees for the fair, telling them that treatment of their grounds should be simple and broad and warning them severely against "fussy, incongruous, meretricious, toy-like, grotesque or undignified effects."[40] By the beginning of December he was again in Chicago, worrying about the water shortage that was lowering the level of the lake and about the kinds of boats proposed for use on the canals.[41]

His vigorous letters to Burnham suggest that he had a hard time getting the point across that the boats were primarily for scenic effect, not for convenient transportation. The object of both waterways and boats was "poetic." If the boats were artistically becoming to the circumstances, they would be of ten times more value to the people on shore than to those aboard them, and unbecoming boats would be destructive of what would otherwise be the most valuable original feature of the exposition. Boats, birds, shores, waterways, were all design elements contributing to a coherent scenic effect; and the boats, to be appropriate in the landscape, should be small, nimble, light, quiet, and low. At the end of the month Olmsted was impatiently writing Burnham that not the slightest progress

---

*Nothing much came of Olmsted's conversation with Newlands. In the end, Chevy Chase was laid out by Nathan F. Barrett, a New York landscape architect who was afterward a charter member of the American Society of Landscape Architects (Edith Claude Jarvis, "Old Chevy Chase Village," *Montgomery County Story* 13 [November 1969]: 3).

had yet been made toward a sound conclusion in the boat matter, which, next to the selection of the site, was the most important single problem of the fair.[42]

Olmsted wound up the hectic year at Biltmore, arriving on New Year's Eve in Vanderbilt's private car, the *Swannanoa*, with, among others, Vanderbilt, Hunt and his son Dick, and Pinchot. In the first days of 1892 he initiated Pinchot into the workings of the estate, traveled over it with him, advised him on his duties, and discussed forming a library and collection of woods at Biltmore with a view to establishing a forestry school there. On the evening of January 6 the party again luxuriously embarked on the *Swannanoa*. The most interesting feature of the return trip was the stopover at Natural Bridge, where they hired a four-horse wagon and visited the grounds that H. W. S. Cleveland had arranged a few years before.[43]

When Olmsted reached home a few days later, he was unwell, bothered rather by chronic than by acute ailments. A comparatively recent one, very troublesome, was a constant ringing in his ears, through which he found it hard to follow general conversation. In the past few years, too, he had had a number of debilitating accidents—his wife estimated them at four or five a year—which ranged from being dumped out of a buggy into an eight-foot snowbank in Burlington, Vermont, to being in a train wreck on the Chicago, Burlington and Quincy, in which his lame leg was cruelly wrenched. (Interestingly, although he was laid up for ten days and lame for a month, he eventually had better use of the leg than at any time since the original accident, apparently because shortened tendons were forcibly stretched, or adhesions broken.)[44] An episode of heat prostration, the recent arsenic poisoning, neuralgia, sickness incidental to overnight train travel, his cruel, chronic insomnia, in addition to normal ageing, all took perceptible toll of his health. Less well able than ever before to stand up to strenuous demands, he had more of them to meet than at any previous time in his life.

Requests for guidance from young men interested in the profession were demands he always willingly met. In February he gave some characteristic advice to William Platt, who was to enter his office as a pupil after a trip to Italy with his brother Charles, a painter and etcher.* "I am afraid that I do not think much of the fine and costly gardening of Italy," Olmsted told him,

> and yet I am enthusiastic in my enjoyment of much roadside foreground
> scenery there, in which nature contends with and is gaining upon the
> art of man. I urge you again to hunt for beauty in commonplace and
> peasant conditions; rustic terraces, old footwalks with stairs and walls and
> gateways; rustic stables, sheds, wine-presses, tileries, mills pergolas and

---

*William Platt died in 1892, soon after his return to the United States. Charles, deeply impressed by his study of Italian villas and gardens, became a noted landscape architect.

> trellises, seats and resting places . . . and all of such things as are made
> lovely by growths that seem to be natural and spontaneous to the place,
> especially vines. Remember, too, that anything that can be done with vines
> in Italy, so far as concerns picturesque effect, can be done in the Atlantic
> states.[45]

Still feeling shaky in early March, Olmsted returned to Biltmore. Some of the work disappointed him, "but," he wrote John, "if I live another year and come here next spring, I can make adjustments and make the lower approach what we want, and a masterpiece."[46]

When he got back to New York soon after the middle of the month, his unique authority was at once enlisted in support of a strong popular movement to defend Central Park against another encroachment. A bill to construct a road for fast driving on the west side of the park had been quietly passed by the legislature on March 17 and immediately signed by the governor. The very next morning the commissioners of Central Park had met and, pointedly snubbing their landscape architect, Vaux, had directed their engineer to stake out the speedway.[47]

The haste of these peculiar official actions was matched by the swiftness of public outrage. Every newspaper in the city except the *Herald* went on the editorial offensive

> and threw hot shot not only at the race track law, as it was properly called,
> but at everybody who had anything to do with its passage. . . .
>   Popular feeling against the measure was not confined to any class of
> people. Everybody, or practically everybody except a few owners of fast
> trotting horses, declared that the law was an outrage. From the very start
> the demand was that the law must be repealed as speedily as it had been
> enacted. The city was alive with this sentiment.[48]

Olmsted was asked to send a statement to John Jay Chapman to be read at a mass protest meeting at Cooper Union on March 25. He responded:

> The earnings of the people of New York have been put into Central
> Park for an object. The question is whether the speed-track would be
> consistent with that object. If not, it would be as unreasonable, unjust and
> immoral a use of the Park as any other diversion of public property. . . .
>   As far as I have had a hand in determining to what object the Central
> Park should be adapted, my testimony is that the speed-track would be such
> a diversion, and that if not unconstitutional and illegal, it fails to be so
> only because those who give form to constitutions and laws are not in all
> technical points successful in accomplishing the objects with which they are
> charged.
>   The speed-track would thus, in my judgment, lessen the security of
> every man to the enjoyment of his earnings, and tend directly to anarchy.[49]

The park commissioners, startled by the public temper, rescinded the order to the engineer to stake out the speedway and set a public hearing for March 23. The hearing room was packed with business and professional men and delegates from labor organizations. The only advocates of the speedway were a scant dozen trotting-horse owners, with their lawyer, who had banded together, to the relish of their opponents, as "The Citizens' Association for the Preservation of the Park and the Safety of the People." After the mass meeting two days later, the commissioners decided to harken to the voice of those of the people who did not drive fast horses and voted, three to one, to ask the legislature to repeal the law and the governor to sign the repealer. Mayor Hugh J. Grant, a backer of the speedway, refused to join in their request but agreed not to oppose it.

The rest of the drama was played out in Albany. Near midnight April 14, after frantic last-minute maneuvers on both sides, the legislature repealed the race track law.[50]

Olmsted did not wait for the happy ending. On Monday, March 28, he summoned Frederick to dinner and told him to be prepared to sail for England with him and Marion the following Saturday.[51]

Afterward, Olmsted said that when he found that he could not meet the demands made upon him that spring, he "ran away to England."[52] He did himself less than justice: in both England and France he constantly studied means to enhance the fair's success; he wrote scores of pages of memorandums and recommendations to his office; and he studiously guided the professional education of Frederick and his companion, Phil Codman, who intended to become, like his brother Harry, a landscape architect.

Olmsted began the educational work on shipboard, discussing with Frederick Norton's statement, made in a lecture the boy had attended, that "the fine arts are the arts of beautiful expression." The definition dissatisfied Olmsted; it overemphasized the function of self-expression, when the artist's true job was less to express himself than to produce in others aesthetic experiences of an elevating nature. In Olmsted, the artistic and the social impulse were equally strong and indissolubly joined; he could not conceive of the first functioning independently of the second. The discussion profoundly impressed Frederick. Recalling it long after, he said: "Art as a means of self-expression was of no interest to my father, or only of academic interest. He was firmly convinced that the prime function of his own art, as of all the Fine Arts, was to bring inspiration and delight to *others* than [the] artists."[53]

The crossing was rough enough to make the young people seasick, but Olmsted did not miss a meal. He amused himself by planning the rest of the trip and by swapping such knowledgeable sea stories with the captain, at whose table he sat, that the captain thought he must be dealing with another seafaring man.[54]

The itinerary Olmsted made out was overambitious, but the little party made a brave start on it. In spite of the snow and hail that pursued them from their landing at Liverpool, they saw a number of public and private grounds, including Birkenhead Park and Chatsworth, by the time they reached Salisbury. "Gladstone's place in Cheshire, extremely simple and rural, really rustic in design," was one of the most successful.[55] They saw besides a good deal of English forestry and some water meadows, all suggestive for Biltmore. The weather notwithstanding, Olmsted was enchanted: "I find that as the result of forty years rumination of landscape that—much as I enjoyed it my first visit—I did not nearly understand the beauty and interest of the country."[56]

Henry Perkins and his wife Hannah came down from London to Salisbury to welcome their kinsmen. Perkins, undeterred by his adverse experience at Mariposa, had become a mining engineer. In the course of his adventurous and successful career he had married the daughter of a 'forty-niner and had her educated, been the chief engineer of a gold-mining property in Venezuela, settled at Chislehurst near London, and was just back from a camping trip with Lord Randolph Churchill in South Africa, where Churchill and a syndicate were interested in the Rand gold fields.[57] While the Perkinses gathered up the young people and took them off to Stonehenge, Olmsted stayed behind at the White Hart Hotel. Bundled up in his fur coat and ailing from a heavy cold picked up in another chilly inn, at Shrewsbury, he wrote his partners some of his thoughts on the fair.

He was pretty well satisfied with the general plan, but everything depended on how it was elaborated and on how the grounds, once brought to completion, were kept. There was the danger that the whole affair would turn out "too much disturbed, busy, fragmentary, incoherent, abounding in objects, lacking breadth & consistency and dignified sedateness," and that the wooded isle would be an insufficient corrective to the clutter; on the other hand, he was afraid of an "unfurnished effect." To overcome the conflicting hazards, they must emphasize undisturbed breadths of fine turf, graceful modeling of surfaces, and delicate play of light and shade and must press for originality of design, invention, simplicity, and elegance in the artificial objects on the grounds. The English landscape gardening he had so far seen was disappointing: he was struck with the constant adherence to a few aims and the consequent monotony of style and the meager variety of plant materials used. At the fair, they must take pains to avoid such an effect, which might follow from "too much similarity and repetition of terrace effects around the lagoons."[58]

Continuing cold, and a bitter east wind, quickly drove Olmsted out of England.[59] Leaving Marion with the Perkinses at Chislehurst, he went to Paris with the boys, and by the twenty-fourth was studying the grounds of the 1889 exposition. Although somewhat deteriorating, they had not been dismantled, and many of the buildings remained. Olmsted noted the condition of the staff on statuary and ornaments, the state of the walks, the turf, the fences and guardrails, and other particulars.[60]

The buildings themselves sharpened nagging doubts he had about the appropriateness of the grandiose neoclassicism and fake solidity of those intended for Chicago.

> The buildings (as they now appear) have much more color and much more ornament in color, but less in moulding and sculpture than I had supposed. They show, I think, more fitness for their purposes, seem more designed for the occasion and to be less like grand permanent architectural monuments than ours are to be. I question if ours are not at fault in this respect and if they are not going to look too assuming of architectural stateliness and to be overburdened with sculptural and other efforts for grandeur and grandiloquent pomp. I mean to express a doubting apprehension only.[61]

More than ever he thought that the picturesque wooded isle should be made the most notable landscape feature of the fair.[62]

During his week in Paris Olmsted was frequently with Edouard André, who, since their last meeting in 1878, had published his notable *L'Art des Jardins* and furnished plans for reconstructing the old part of the city of Montevideo. He was concluding his twenty years' work of transforming the old fortifications around Paris into public gardens, and he was about to be named professor of architecture and gardens at the horticultural school at Versailles, the first official chair of the sort in France. André told Olmsted what chateaux and nurseries to visit on his journey along the Loire, and out of his experience with the Paris exposition, he advised Olmsted that the terraces around the large buildings tended to have a barren air unless liberally furnished with palms, well-grown hollies, and similar trees in tubs and that vases filled with plants should ornament the parapets.[63]

Olmsted and the boys left Paris on April 30 for Orléans. After visiting a nursery there, they went on the same day to Blois, where they "chanced upon an interesting old French inn, with a courtyard and smell of the stables and a fine view of the Loire." Although the weather was cold and damp and his Shrewsbury cold still clung to him, Olmsted was enchanted with the journey along the serene, finely cultivated Loire valley. The chateaux, especially Amboise, were interesting even apart from their historical and monumental appeal. More interesting was what he saw of peasants, farms, and rustic hamlets. "But as to landscape and gardening," he commented, "it is chiefly what to avoid."[64]

His own observation of stately French buildings bore out André's warning: "I am much impressed with what we have seen at Chantilly, Blois and Chambord, at the dreary effect of very large buildings, with large grounds, not generously garnished with foliage."[65]

Olmsted and his young companions returned to England by way of the Isle of Guernsey, where "a little farm with a little park, very wild," struck him as one of the finest things he had seen.[66] Another delight was the New Forest, which they visited the middle of May, making a pilgrimage to the church of Boldre of which Gilpin, author of *Forest Scenery*, had been vicar. Frederick's and Phil's responses to the scenic fare being put in their way consistently pleased Olmsted.

> Both are learning more incidentally and unconsciously, without effort, than otherwise. Much more so than they think, I believe, consequently they value less than I do for them constant opportunities to be used without intention or effort. . . . I don't think that either Phil or Rick realizes the value which close observation (but observation which is not recordable, or even to be given form to verbally) may come to have in future practice, in aiding inventive design.[67]

He had himself a strong conviction, based on experience,

> of the value of what may be caught and stored in this way; which may become confused and lost to distinct remembrance, and yet, by some subtle process, consciously affect, long afterwards, essentially original inventive action of the intellect, and important convictions. I don't think the seeds of thought, their germination and conditions of growth, are sufficiently regarded in our current theories of education and metaphysics. Nor are all the injuries that result from cramming and didactic processes.[68]

Olmsted was inclined to put reliance on precedent in the didactic category. In reply to a suggestion tossed off in one of John's letters that they might design a "manufacturing village," Olmsted replied:

> There are few things I had rather do, provided I could do it well. . . . I know of nothing good of the kind in England, but will enquire. I have lost modesty a good deal, however, since I left home and think that perhaps we should not find much to help us. There is such a thing as checking invention, and perhaps, if we take up such a problem at the roots without assistance from the work of others we shall do better.[69]

Although he was finding no "unexpected things in design of much value," Olmsted felt that he was learning more than he ever had before in traveling, in the sense of making positive what before had been conjectural and doubtful. A conjecture sustained was that ornamental planting at the fair would have to be handled with great discretion. He had not seen a single square yard in England or France that pleased him so far. Everything in the way of bedding planting at the Paris fair, so far as he could judge by what was left, must have been

438

extremely disquieting, gaudy and childish if not savage, and an injury to the Exposition, through its disturbance of dignity, and injury to breadth, unity and composure. I do not mean to suggest any change of our plans or limitations on their development; I only hope that in elaborating them simplicity and reserve will be practiced, and petty effects and frippery avoided.[70]

In the course of the trip Olmsted several times remarked, not very convincingly, that he thought he was getting the better of his insomnia, but by the time he was again with the Perkinses at Chislehurst, his nights were a torment of sleeplessness, his days a misery of fatigue. Dr. Henry Rayner undertook to cure him. Rayner was a specialist in nervous diseases, a son-in-law of Olmsted's old friend Alfred Field, and once a guest of the Olmsteds in Brookline. Calling on Olmsted at Henry Perkins's, he saw how wretched he was and proposed carrying him off to his own home at Hampstead Heath, where he could supervise a treatment.[71]

Gratefully and submissively, Olmsted put himself in Rayner's hands. Rayner could find nothing much wrong with him physically and told him that, under favorable circumstances, he could expect to keep at work for several years to come. For a while, Rayner kept Olmsted "practically in prison," so closely did he supervise him. Carefully protected against excitement, Olmsted was, however, driven out daily with Marion or Frederick by the doctor or his wife Rosa. Phil came often to see him, and after Phil left for home, George Glessner, who had joined Frederick, came. Olmsted sent the boys to see Olmsted Hall and laid out cycle tours and camera work for them. He tried to be cheerful, and credulous, too, when the Rayners told him he was looking better and gaining weight, but his progress was uncertain and prone to setbacks. One of the worst of these came as a result of a call from Radford, who bore ill news of Vaux.[72]

Letters from Stiles had already familiarized Olmsted with the background. The Commissioners of Accounts of New York City, after the speedway defeat, had begun an investigation of the park department. Interrogating Vaux, they had baited him—asking him, among other things, the botanical names of flowers he did not know—until he lost his temper and made a show of himself.[73] The investigating commissioners then reported to Mayor Grant that Vaux had admitted his incompetence on the witness stand and recommended his dismissal and that of Samuel Parsons, Jr., too. The mayor referred the matter to the park department, which referred it for decision to Commissioner Paul Dana.*,[74] The Times angrily charged that all investigations of the Commissioners of Accounts were "necessarily shams—conclusions reached before enquiry begun" and that the spirit of the investigation suggested that they were seeking to create and fill

---

*Paul Dana, son of Olmsted's old friend Charles A. Dana, was generally sympathetic to Olmsted's and Vaux's views on Central Park.

vacancies. Vaux and Parsons were "the two representatives of civilization in the department" and would be "displaced for the representatives of Tammany. This is a very cheerful state of things, but we deserve it for electing Mr. Grant mayor."[75]

While the *Times* had rushed to Vaux's defense, Stiles had privately invoked Olmsted's aid. He wrote that the mayor was "furious" with Vaux for his part in frustrating the speedway and wanted to replace him with a more malleable landscape architect. Stiles had begged Olmsted to see Paul Dana, who would soon be in London, and speak to him in Vaux's behalf.[76] Radford supplemented Stiles's report one July evening, coming late to Rayner's house and staying for two endless hours. His account of Vaux's exhibition and humiliation was

> told in a very bad way, without apparent sympathy. . . . just the bad, contentious, English shop-keeping way. He said plainly that Vaux had been good for nothing, even architecturally, for a long time past; that he, Radford, had been the architect. (Vaux had only been in the way and a marplot) that in the final flurry with the Park Department, Vaux had acted against the advice of all his friends, etc.

Radford left Olmsted with the impression that Vaux had retired, probably for good, to Rondout, his country place up the Hudson, to eke out his life in poverty.[77]

Radford's version of Vaux's affairs so agitated Olmsted that for forty-eight hours he had no useful sleep. Toward Radford he tried to be charitable—"He meant no harm. It was only his unfortunate way."—but he was indignant with himself that he had, for the moment, fallen in with Radford's view of Vaux's character and failings, and exceedingly sorry for Vaux and grieved that he could do nothing for him and his family. Besides self-reproach, there was a new problem to occupy his wakefulness: if Vaux was definitely retired, ought not the Olmsted firm to open a strong branch in New York, where there were three thousand acres of new parks to be laid out—and Tammany to be fought? "Of course one of us would have to live there. . . . I can't say that I have any appetite for the fight that would be inevitable."[78]

Better by the middle of July, Olmsted, with Frederick and George, cruised for a week or so on the Thames in electric launches from Richmond to Oxford and back to observe the kinds of boats in use. He wrote his partners a detailed account of the electric boats he favored for the fair, describing their various seating arrangements, their different styles of awnings, and their finish, color, furnishings, and decorations.[79]

He found a fertile source of inspiration in the vegetation along the Thames banks, especially the willows. Their variety of age and size and color, their intermingling with sedge and rushes and other common native water plants, their different growing positions—sometimes horizontal where a bank undercut by the current had dropped over, sometimes growing in water, sometimes overhanging reedy plants growing on water-covered shoals in front of them—all were suggestive of various ways the lagoons at the fair might be treated.[80]

While the riverbanks gave him ideas about what to do, the waterside lawns and gardens furnished fine examples of what to avoid. Most of them were ruined by bedding plants and fussy decorations—"out of place, impertinent, offensive to the genius loci, misplaced, tawdry, vulgar finery."[81]

Olmsted's long-standing distaste for bedding-out, carpet-bedding, and allied practices was shared by William Robinson, then England's premier gardener and writer on garden subjects. Since the early 1870s Robinson had been campaigning against such floral formalities, against glass-houses, glittering and conspicuous, that were their necessary adjuncts, and against topiary work. His eloquent advocacy, in his books and in the magazines he published, of the native plants of England and of Alpine and Rocky Mountains wildflowers, of old-fashioned cottage gardens, and of herbaceous borders had been instrumental in promoting a natural style and a new taste, antithetical to the formal, in English gardening. The formalists persisted, however, some mutely tenacious like the unknown creators of the Thames-side gardens Olmsted criticized, some articulate and contentious like the architect Sir Reginald Blomfield, who asserted that the garden, merely the setting and adjunct of the house, should be architectural in design and planned by the architect, from whom the gardener should take his orders.[82] Blomfield had just published *The Formal Garden in England*, Robinson was counterattacking with *Garden Design and Architects' Gardens*, and Olmsted was following the dispute, which was acrimonious, without much sympathy for either side. He was interested in gardens primarily as elements in landscape design, and it seemed to him that neither the disputants nor anyone else in England had "landscape sense" or made other than piecemeal criticism that aimed only at details and ignored the basic matters of landscape composition and architectural propriety.[83] "I am sure," he wrote his partners, "that a complete return to the old formal gardening is to be desired rather than that the present confused contradictory hash of formal-natural gardening should continue. The tendency to formality is very strong here, and as for a true natural style, I see nothing of it."[84]

There was, in fact, less of the art of landscape design in France and England than in Brookline, he thought. "Almost everywhere, and most in the newest work, the landscape end is confused with and subordinated to other ends, Japanese ends." (And in Japan, so far as he could judge, there was no landscape work at all, "using the word landscape in any useful sense.") He added:

> in spite of this, such is the advantage of a temperate and moist climate, there is nothing in America to be compared with the pastoral or with the picturesque beauty that is common property in England. I cannot go out without being delighted. . . . Sometimes the question comes to me, whether,

even on the Atlantic slopes, we are not so far removed in climatic condition from those on which this pastoral beauty depends, that it is futile to contend with our difficulties. But when I ask what is the alternative, I always conclude that we must be only more fertile in expedients to make the most of our opportunities. The absurdity of seeking good pastoral beauty in the far West is more and more manifest.[85]

Returning, little improved, to the Perkinses at Chislehurst toward the end of July, Olmsted set about calling on some of the professional people his illness had kept him from seeing earlier. He and his children spent a day with Robinson at Gravetye, Robinson's home near East Grinstead, south of London. Robinson had bought the manorial seat, with about two hundred acres of land, in 1884 and was "judiciously revising," Olmsted approvingly noted, the stone manor house that was already three centuries old. It could hardly have surprised Olmsted, who had known Robinson more than twenty years, to find that the anti-formalist gardener, whose vigorous personality shrank neither from contention nor inconsistency, maintained around the old manor house a delightful terraced garden, its plan geometrical and formal, its detail spontaneous and irregular.[86] The reunion of the old friends, whatever their theoretical differences, was cordial; Robinson gave Olmsted a fine pair of antique cast-iron firedogs as a memento and told him he might visit the fair.[87]

Olmsted also met Henry Ernest Milner, successor to the extensive landscape business established by his father Edward, who had originally worked for Paxton. A few years earlier, Olmsted had heard derogatory reports ascribing "thoroughly speculative, brokerish, shopkeeperish" business methods to Milner. He had disbelieved them, but he had wondered whether there might not be "too much of trade and too little of art in his great business. But it is a difficult question," he had admitted, "and [William] Morris's success in combining art and commercial profit is to be reflected upon."[88] Meeting Milner, Olmsted found him "a nice fellow in every way," and, he wrote John, he thought Milner would do "anything we think best for the profession. He makes the highest claims for L. G. as a fine art."[89]

The fair's classification committee, less enlightened, had not recognized landscape architecture as a division of the fine arts and had not asked the profession to mount a display. Milner's attitude encouraged Olmsted to hope that landscape architects might arrange a semiofficial exhibit in the landscape architects' office at the fair. "Milner and no doubt André would join us in protest against the existing prepared classification, and help us to make a considerable exhibition."[90]

Olmsted also saw Paul Dana in London and got a quite different account of Vaux's affairs than Radford had given. Vaux had indeed gone to Rondout sick, angry, and humiliated, but he had gone for a vacation; he had not been dismissed and was not going to be, Dana thought. Dana hinted, also, that Olmsted's firm might be invited to plan one of the new New York parks.[91]

Having already stayed abroad much longer than he had at first intended, Olmsted and his children made their way slowly back to Liverpool. They spent a week at Oxford, where the private garden of the Warden of Wadham College was, Olmsted remarked, "the most pleasing we have seen" and made an excursion to nearby Blenheim. They stopped a night in the Cotswolds.[92] After a trip, again following in Gilpin's tracks, by carriage and boat along the River Wye into Wales, they traveled north into Shakespeare country and stopped for a week at Stratford-on-Avon, calling on Alfred Field's widow at Leamington Spa and sightseeing at Kenilworth Castle. At Derby they toured the arboretum, and Olmsted made a note to look up Downing's article on it in the *Horticulturist* "to see how it has miscarried." Moving northward into Nottinghamshire, they drove through Sherwood Forest and visited Thoresby Hall, where Olmsted admired the very little, very good, formal planting of the terrace. "Block pattern of golden yew, aucuba, laurel, etc., cut square, solid. Best formal terrace geometric planting we have seen." Nearby, he saw a fine house with its pleasure ground the despised "hash" of "formal informal. Flat turf, trees scattered in natural forms naturally disposed, with many circular beds, bedding plants formally arranged generally with a high standard geranium in the middle."[93]

They passed through the region of great places—Chatsworth, Haddon Hall, Kettleston Hall, Melbourne Hall—but Olmsted indicated no change in the opinion he had earlier expressed, that the best ornamental grounds they saw were those in which the vines and creepers were outwitting the gardener.[94]

At Liverpool the travelers embarked on the Inman Line's *City of New York*. The passage was rough. Throughout, Frederick was queasy with seasickness, Marion was prostrate, and Olmsted suffered from insomnia and facial neuralgia. When he reached New York, he doggedly insisted that he was not sick. Still, he had to admit that he was scarcely as well as when he had set out six months before in the hope of recovering his health.[95]

B Y the first of October, Olmsted was in Chicago. He found the progress of the fair just about what he expected: well behindhand. Worse than that, Harry Codman, the incomparable supervisor of the firm's complex business on the site, was sick with some recurring intestinal complaint. While he was there, Olmsted finished his study of the island planting and took time to write a long letter to Stiles spiking a suggestion submitted to *Garden and Forest* that the southern part of the fair site, around the basin and canals, be made into a formal garden with appropriate permanent architectural structures after the fair closed.[1]

Garden and Forest's editorial, appearing in October, elaborated on Olmsted's points. The suggestion that the grand basin would be "wasted" if not preserved overlooked the crucial fact that its walls, like the other structures on the grounds —even the grounds themselves—were temporary. Canals, basin, and terraces were covered with staff applied on walls made of very slender piles and planking, strong enough to last about a year. It was anticipated, indeed planned, that the staff would peel and break and the timbers rot and crumble so that in a few years' time, by the action of natural forces, an irregular shoreline suitable to a park in the natural style would be established. Even the apparently firm high ground was an illusion: it was nothing but ridges enclosing great craters covered, for the time, by buildings and terraces. There was not an acre of such ground on which a good formal garden could be made without an enormous outlay for grading, masonry, and building. It would be far less expensive and more satisfactory to provide agreeable natural scenery. Echoing Olmsted's impatience and his language, the editorial observed: "This makeshift propensity to force things to answer some end for which they were not designed and for which they are therefore imperfectly adapted, seems to have become one of the acquired vices of our national character."[2]

Quick trips afield took Olmsted to Milwaukee, Kansas City, and St. Louis. He was back in Chicago in time for the dedication ceremonies on October 21. It was an unfortunate time to see the grounds, with buildings and landscaping unfinished, and he expected the proceedings in Post's Manufactures and Liberal Arts building to be a bore.[3] His apprehension was apparently not widely shared: a crowd of some hundred thirty thousand thronged the building for the occasion.[4]

Notwithstanding the disorder of the site, Olmsted's experienced eye took satisfaction in its promise. In the great collaboration in which he was participating, he took more than satisfaction. "The general fervor of the artists was delightful to witness and more delightful to fall into," he wrote Mrs. Van Rensselaer from Brookline early in November.

> If people generally get to understand that our contribution to the under-
> taking is that of the framing of the scheme rather than the disposition of
> flower beds and other matters of gardening decoration—as to which those
> familiar with European exhibitions will be disappointed—it will be a great
> lift to the profession—will really give it a better standing than it has in
> Europe. I was exceedingly pleased to find how fully the architects
> recognized our service in this respect.[5]

Olmsted's visit to Biltmore, in November and December, was the first he or anyone else from the firm had made to the estate in nine months. In that time, several things Olmsted did not like had been done, the blame for which he laid to his firm's insufficient supervision. Disturbed about their performance at Biltmore, Olmsted was uneasy, too, about Franklin Park, to which he thought John, largely responsible for the execution of the plan, was giving too little attention.[6]

Both worries were thrown abruptly into the background when on January 13, 1893, twenty-nine-year-old Harry Codman, apparently recuperating from an appendectomy, unexpectedly died. His death was a multiple blow: to Olmsted's affections, to the fair's smooth progress, and to the profession. Olmsted had groomed him and loved him and relied heavily on him; at the fair he stood "for the one uniting element and represented among the various professions and crafts the general design in its comprehensiveness and consistency"; and no man at his age had accomplished more in the profession or shown brighter promise.[7]

Age and ailments notwithstanding, Olmsted went to Chicago the beginning of February to shoulder Codman's work. Phil Codman traveled with him, and Charles Eliot, asked to pitch in and help, followed early in the month.* When Olmsted and Phil reached Chicago, it was eight degrees below zero, and the ground, frozen three feet deep, had to be blasted with dynamite where earth was still to be moved. There was an appalling amount to be done, but after a few days Olmsted began to see daylight and was confident enough of progress to make a hasty excursion with Eliot to see the Milwaukee parks—first sending home for the names of the Milwaukee commissioners, not one of which he could remember.[8]

---

*Eliot had moved quickly into the front rank of landscape architects through his brilliant campaign, begun in 1890, to bring into being the Boston region's Metropolitan Parks Commission. In March 1893 he accepted Olmsted's and John's invitation to become a partner in the firm; the firm name was changed to Olmsted, Olmsted and Eliot; and after the legislature passed the Metropolitan Parks Commission bill in June, the firm was appointed landscape architects to the commission (Norman T. Newton, *Design on the Land: The Development of Landscape Architecture* [Cambridge: Harvard University Press, 1971], p. 330).

Back in Chicago on February 17, he kept to his hotel on doctor's orders, rebelliously asserting that he would have gone to the exposition's office anyway, "but for a small blizzard's coming." Inactive, he had time for some concentrated worrying, which he poured out upon John. His health was so uncertain, he wrote, that he could no longer be counted on to carry his share of the firm's work. Eliot, who had "a weak constitution with proclivities to lung trouble," already had too much to do; and John, consequently too hurried, was forced to run the unacceptable risk of doing less than creditable work just as his father was being forced to relinquish some of his responsibility. "You should above all things aim to keep up and advance the reputation and character of the House," the anxious old man warned. "Better make little money and live low for a while rather [than] fail in that."

John should inform the Kirkwood Land Company in Atlanta that, in the crisis into which Codman's death and Olmsted's illness had thrown them, the firm would prefer to be relieved of its obligation to lay out their residential suburb. And could they not cut loose from American University, in Washington, whose unsuitable site promised a forbidding amount of work for the firm and expense for the institution?[9]

With the approach of spring, Olmsted made another trip to Biltmore and to Atlanta,[10] but with the opening date of the fair looming close, his most urgent concern was finishing the fair grounds. Codman's death and his own infirmity had forced him to rely overmuch on Ulrich, who tended fussily to concern himself with work that others could oversee, instead of confining himself to the operations that he alone was competent to do. Exhorting him to keep *landscape* in mind, Olmsted voiced again his uneasiness about the architectural aspect of the fair: the architects intended to make the White City whiter by far than he would choose to have it. The blue lake, the bright sky, the hot sunlight, the white buildings, the sparkling water—the ensemble would be overpowering. All the relief possible would be wanted of the dark green foliage, in which red and yellow should be seen only in glints. Ulrich was to strive for expanses of fine turf, to minimize decorative planting and set out only what could be maintained perfectly, and to subordinate what there was of it firmly and deliberately to foliage, which was the landscape element that would redeem the White City from its own overwhelming whiteness.[11] Here showed a trace of Olmsted's feeling that, despite the comradely ambience of the fair, landscape architecture, already slighted by the classification committee, was receiving somewhat less consideration than was its due.

Landscape architecture went unmentioned, too, in the invitation to the gala banquet for some two hundred fifty eminences in honor of the fair's director of works, Burnham, held on March 25 at the Madison Square Concert Hall in New York. A twelve-page brochure elaborately printed and illustrated, the invitation featured on its cover, in laurel wreaths, *Painting, Architecture,* and *Sculp-*

ture. At the banquet itself, however, landscape architecture, in the person of its leading practitioner, was handsomely recognized.

In his toast to the friend he had admired for twenty years, Charles Eliot Norton said: "Of all American artists, Frederick Law Olmsted, who gave the design for the laying out of the grounds of the World's Fair, stands first in the production of great works which answer the needs and give expression to the life of our immense and miscellaneous democracy."[12] Burnham declared to the distinguished diners:

> Each of you knows the name and genius of him who stands first in the heart and confidence of American artists, the creator of your own parks and many other city parks. He it is who has been our best adviser and common mentor. In the highest sense he is the planner of the Exposition— Frederick Law Olmsted. No word of his has fallen to the ground among us since he first joined us some thirty months ago. As artist, he paints with lakes and wooded slopes; with lawns and banks and forest-covered hills; with mountainsides and ocean views. He should stand where I do tonight, not for his deeds of later years alone, but for what his brain has wrought and his pen has taught for half a century.[13]

Olmsted missed these tributes; he was making a tour of the firm's southern works.[14] On his return, he went to Chicago, where he found a strike, unfinished business, and confusion but thought he detected some underlying method.[15] Although the time specified for the arrival of exhibits had been November, the temporary transportation tracks to the exhibit buildings had not been laid until January; few exhibits had arrived before March, and of those many could not be installed because of the unfinished state of the buildings.[16] Much of the landscape architects' work could not even be started until the temporary tracks and roads were taken up. Olmsted predicted that their work would not be half done by the opening date because of the tardiness of others; the most important part of it would have to be done at night after the first of May.[17]

Toward the end of April Olmsted was in bed with a sore throat and ulcerated tooth, but although he was sick and complaining of having to eat slops, his spirits were hesitantly rising: the planting was coming out well, the white ducks on the lagoon looked nice, the electric launches were "capital," and the work was visibly advancing.[18]

In the next few days heavy rains made a vast puddle of the site and doused Olmsted's rising spirits. He lamented that they would have to fall back on temporary expedients to make even a poor showing at the opening and would have to make their final adaptations later. He touched a strange note of plaintiveness in remarking that his nasty diet and the noise and scurry were all very distressing to "a dilapidated old man."[19]

At the end of the month he was sounding desperate. He was sick—or sicker

—from having sloshed about in the rain; he was having a row with the Horticulture Department and the French museum men; continuing rain and cold were holding up planting; even Burnham was critical of the unfinished appearance of the grounds; he was determined to keep them disorderly where necessary, however, so that there could be no mistaking their incomplete condition.[20]

When May 1 came, the ceremonies, even in the unfinished setting, were imposing. They began at nine in the morning with a procession of carriages escorted by cavalry from the city to the fair site, where the president of the United States, the duke of Veragua—guest of honor by reason of his descent from Columbus—and the chief members of the exposition took their seats at the front of a raised platform accommodating about two thousand invited guests at the east end of Hunt's Administration Building facing the lake. A crowd estimated at three to four hundred thousand was packed in front of the platform and along the shores of the great basin, over which gondolas and electric launches silently glided, and aggressive little steam launches outrageously scooted with raucous whistles. Olmsted stayed away from the dignitaries' stand and with the architects McKim and Post moved about during the music and prayers and speeches, turning a critical eye on arrangements.[21]

The fair's requirements kept Olmsted in Chicago until the middle of the month. The grounds were still far from ready, even the best of the walks were unsatisfactorily rough, Burnham as Olmsted had foreseen was not insisting on a decent standard of maintenance, and Olmsted was unwilling to leave important questions, coming up daily, to be determined by Ulrich and Phil.[22]

Although he went to New York the middle of May to consult with Professor William R. Ware, of Columbia University, about plans for the college's new site on Morningside Heights,[23] Olmsted was not yet through with the fair. Returning to Chicago for a few days in June, he observed it in full swing and from Biltmore, his next stop, wrote a number of recommendations to Burnham.

The walks, rough and inferior, should be watered and rolled nightly. The force employed to pick up litter and trash ought to be doubled. The abominable steamboats, graceless, noisy, and as out of place in the lagoons as a cow in a flower garden, constituted so intolerable an injury to the exposition that the contract for them should be broken. Colored awnings should be placed on stairways and terraces, and seats under the awnings, to reduce heat and fatigue and to mitigate the white glare of the buildings. Water closets needed more careful supervision. "Incidents of vital human gaiety," apparently spontaneous, should be introduced—small parties of singers, strolling banjo players, lemonade peddlers in picturesque dress, musicians on the boats—to lighten the rather too sober mien of the crowds.[24]

Some flaws of course were irreversible. Nothing could remedy the occupation of the wooded island by the Japanese temple and the display of horticultural exhibits. Nor was it possible to eliminate the too numerous small pavilions and concession buildings that intercepted vistas and disturbed spaces intended to serve for the relief of the eye from the too constant demands upon it of the

John Charles, Marion,
and young Frederick in
tobogganing costume

Above: F.L.O. at
Chislehurst, 1892

Above:
F.L.O., circa 1890,
from a photograph
by his son Frederick

Right:
Marion Olmsted,
circa 1890

Left: Frederick
Law Olmsted (son)
in the early 1890s

exposition buildings. Nor could the width of the lagoon between the wooded island and the Horticulture Building be restored once it had been narrowed to make room for a branch railroad, which finally was not built; the cramping of the water at that point and the flattening out of the leafy recesses of the island irrevocably diminished picturesqueness of effect.[25]

Nevertheless, taking into account the uncertainties and reverses that had plagued the great enterprise, Olmsted was not dissatisfied with the results. Above all, the "happy comradeship" among the planners had been significant.[26] "Really," he reflected,

> I think that it is a most satisfactory and encouraging circumstance that it could be found feasible for so many men of technical education and ability to be recruited and suitably organized so quickly, and made to work together so well in so short a time. . . . Too high an estimate cannot be placed on the industry, skill and tact with which this result was secured by the master of us all, yet I venture to say that, considering the impromptu way in which Mr. Burnham had to go to work, and the extremely varied antecedents in the matter of education, custom and habit of those through whom he had to operate, equal success would have been possible only in a country which was in a high degree, socially as well as politically, a republic.[27]

Writing to Burnham soon after, Olmsted developed the point along the lines of the barbarism and civilization thesis he had found useful in discussing Mariposa. The chief interest of the exposition lay, he thought, in its demonstration of the specialization and cooperation characteristic of a cultivated society, as opposed to the makeshift arrangements that were the rule in a pioneer society. The fair had been a glowing illustration of civilization and communicativeness.[28]

The Chicago fair set the capstone on Olmsted's contemporary reputation. *Garden and Forest* declared that the harmony of the scene and the perfection and convenience of the arrangements were due to the genius of one man, Frederick Law Olmsted.

> Many others have brought to this great enterprise their gifts of labor, devotion, artistic training and the enthusiasm born of a great opportunity, but the spark of genius which has produced a single and consistent work of art, changing the sandy and uninviting waste of Jackson Park into a marvel of beauty, sprang from his brain. . . .[29]

Charles Sprague Sargent affectionately dedicated the fifth volume of his monumental *Silva of North America* to "Frederick Law Olmsted, the great artist whose love for Nature has been a priceless benefit to his fellow-countrymen." Mrs. Van Rensselaer published an appreciative account of Olmsted's career in the *Century*.[30] Yale and Harvard, both of which had given him an honorary Master of Arts degree in 1864, conferred the honorary degree of Doctor of Letters on him.[*,31]

Characteristically, Olmsted was glad of his honorary degrees because of the attention they focused on his profession. Characteristically, too, when Mrs. Van Rensselaer consulted him about her article, he advised her to write on scenery making, not on him as an individual.[32] Finding that her assignment was specifically biographical, he talked to her freely: if he was to be brought before the public, it should be as an articulate exponent of landscape architecture. He asked her to emphasize the definitive influence on his taste and style of his early exposure and responsiveness to the scenery of the Connecticut valley, New England, and New York State, not grand or spectacular scenery, but rural, domestic, and conducive to pensive moods and poetic fancies.[†] The principal aim of her article should, of course, be to increase the respect of the American public for the art.

> The main question is, should Landscape Architecture be regarded as an art and a profession or as a matter of common sense in which one man's ideas are of equal weight with another's. The less you make of me except as a text, the more of the essence of the art and the need of the profession in American society & civilization the better.[33]

When Mrs. Van Rensselaer asked him about his early work on Central Park, Olmsted was specific but discreet. He urged her to do justice to Vaux and to bring out his indebtedness to his architectural partner. He asked her not to detail his collisions with Viele and Green and successive park commissioners. He could look back benevolently by then, from his eminence, on the early commissioners, "really, as a whole, a superior body of men; they gained the public con-

---

*Their commencement exercises fell on the same day, and Olmsted, having received Harvard's invitation first, was in Cambridge on June 28 to receive the citation which read: "Fredericum Law Olmsted, qui ruris specie in urbes introducta casas pauperum, domus feliciorum, aedificia publica exornavit, aeque saluti et delectationi civium omnia consuluit" (To Frederick Law Olmsted, who, having introduced the aspect of the country into the city, has made beautiful the cottages of the poor, the homes of the more fortunate and public buildings, and has equal regard for the welfare and pleasure of all citizens [Theodora Kimball, memo, n.d. LWR Files]).

Burnham was honored with a Litt. D. at the same commencement, and Hunt was awarded the Queen's Gold Medal by the Royal Institute of British Architects for his work on the fair (O to MGVR, [June 1893]; *Dictionary of American Biography*, s.v. "Hunt, Richard Morris").

†"I have often thought," he said incidentally, "there was less regard for scenery and consequently for landscape architecture now than then and have been inclined to trace the loss to modern methods of travel. A man in a hurry, a man moving fast, cannot enjoy scenery contemplatively. . . . Modern means of travel are most unfavorable to the enjoyment of scenery" (O to MGVR, [June 1893]).

fidence and, taken altogether, they deserved it more than bodies of public servants in our cities often do."[34]

Of the early commissioners he spoke charitably; of the park he spoke
ardently. It had given him the opportunity to use resources he had accumulated,
almost unwittingly, in the course of his "somewhat vagabondish somewhat poeti-
cal life." More than that, he had reasons aside from his love of landscape and
scenery-making for seizing the occasion with an almost desperate enthusiasm:
his despair at his brother's death, his mortification at his publishing failure, and
finally—to this he referred in such obscure terms that Mrs. Van Rensselaer cannot have known what he meant—his shock that Emily Perkins had jilted him.
The trauma of all these reverses he had submerged in his passion for the park.

> The sum is that I put into Central Park, and so did Vaux and others,
> a degree of devotion that no greed and no selfish ambition would have
> induced. Why—how I came to—does not concern the public. It is not
> necessary that you should fully understand it. The fact is that there was
> an artistic devotion in the early Central Park work such as a political work,
> short of war, seldom engages, and something of this fact it may be well the
> public should recognize.[35]

When Mrs. Van Rensselaer's article appeared, Olmsted wrote her that it
was a "feat." She professed to be not satisfied with it: the editors had restricted
her to biographical material so that she had not been able to promote the "cause"
as openly as Olmsted had wished. Nevertheless, the article was the most comprehensive that had appeared until that time on Olmsted and his work.[36]

After the opening of the Columbian Exposition, Olmsted turned his attention to the firm's other business. The Boston and metropolitan parks system were
by far their most important current public works.[37] He was also particularly interested in their operations in the South. These included Cherokee Park, one of
three parks being built for Louisville; the Kirkwood land development project
and the Cotton Exposition grounds in Atlanta; and the grounds of the United
States military reservation at Hot Springs, Arkansas. Biltmore was, of course,
their most spectacular southern work.

Olmsted's concern for comparatively small southern projects arose from his
conviction that landscape architecture had a promising future in the South.
Soon, he reasoned, the major northern cities would all have been provided with
parks. "Future business in park designing," he told John.

> will be in the south and, as I have said to you, in the arid regions; con-
> cerning both of which regions our firm and the art of Landscape
> Architecture has nothing to show and is very ignorant and unprepared. I
> want you to be making way in the sub-tropical and the arid cities before
> I go. I want the firm to have an established "good will" at the south.[38]

Olmsted's prophecy was not borne out. It was true that the climatic and related natural conditions in the South and Southwest presented a challenge, which, if adequately met by landscape architects, might have resulted in very distinctive and admirable and peculiarly American developments in the art. Both challenge and solutions were much on Olmsted's mind; yet, as he knew, any greatly original development in landscape architecture, as in other arts, required a favorable background of sensibility and wealth among its potential clients. Such a background scarcely then existed in the South and Southwest.[39]

Concerning the Boston parks, Olmsted's forecast had more validity. Work on the Boston system was proceeding under city authority; and the Metropolitan Parks Commission, promoted by Eliot and the editor and journalist Sylvester Baxter and established by the state legislature in 1893, was acquiring appropriate lands in outlying locations so that municipalities in the metropolitan region could combine to preserve and use their scenic and recreational resources. Olmsted recognized the unique significance of Boston's regional undertaking, both to the development of its suburbs and to the standing of the firm and the profession. "I am of the opinion," he wrote his partners,

> that with regard to the protection of the good will capital, nothing else compares in importance to us with the Boston work, meaning the Metropolitan quite equally with the city work. The two together will be the most important work of our profession now in hand anywhere in the world. They will be more important historically; more important educationally, and, well done, as they may be, will, before the end of your probable lives, have done more than any other now in hand to build up the profession. The time will come when if the possibilities of the situation are realized, they will be the seed of as good crops in general suburban improvement as the Central Park has been in respect to public urban parks.[40]

Confident of the firm's preeminence in park design, Olmsted was less than satisfied with its work on private places. With these, he felt they had been unfortunate, having had no conspicuous successes and several near failures. Hence the importance of making a striking success at Biltmore, "the most distinguished private place, not only of America, but of the world, forming at this *period*."[41]

Too unwell to work during the summer of 1893, Olmsted in August spent, for the first time, a week at the cottage on Deer Isle, in Penobscot Bay, where his wife and Marion, and sometimes the boys, had been going for several summers.*[42] Toward the end of October he went to Biltmore for a month. Although

---

*Deer Isle was the setting of an amiable literary hoax, *Studies in Early American History: A Notable Lawsuit*, by Franklin H. Head, who cooked it up after talking with Marion, at a dinner party, about Deer Isle, Penobscot Bay, legends of Captain Kidd, and other more or less related subjects. The substance of the yarn was that an early Olmsted had befriended an Indian chief who, in gratitude, gave him a deed to Deer Isle in 1699.

bothered by neuralgia and the roaring in his ears, he could still, on rare days, spend six hours in the saddle overseeing planting or, with a gang of assistants bearing maps, going over the main lines of the arboretum. It fascinated and absorbed him, and it would be, he predicted, "a great work."[43]

As grievous as his infirmities was his tormenting worry that the firm had taken on more jobs than it could satisfactorily handle. "I am sure," he wrote his partners,

> that on general principles we ought to attend personally to the progress
> of affairs at Atlanta, Louisville, Kansas City, Chicago [where the fair was
> to be dismantled and the South Park Commission advised on the adaptation
> of the grounds], Detroit, Buffalo and Rochester before winter. . . . Of
> course, I shrink greatly from these western journeys but more from the
> possible consequences of omitting them. You cannot afford to take the risk
> to your professional reputation which you seem to be ready to, and,
> remember, in any broad organizing view of the situation, you cannot rely
> on my help. My health is extremely frail and I may be tipped out any
> day.[44]

Olmsted blamed age for another hindrance besides frailty: a weakened ability to deal urbanely with stupid suggestions. When Boston's mayor and park commissioners, toward the end of the year, instructed John to adjust the road system of Franklin Park so as to squeeze in two more miles of bridlepath, Olmsted found he could not oppose their afterthought politely. Boston was already being lavishly provided with bridleroads. If the landscape architects had thought still more necessary, they would have designed the park quite differently in the first place with a view to them; and John's altered plan, reluctantly amended to provide them, was as good a botch as could be contrived but still a botch and ought to be presented as such. It would be injurious to the park and costly, and the result would not begin to justify the expense. "To do any justice to the proposition," Olmsted complained to John, "one must put himself in a position of sympathy with the attitude of the Mayor. I cannot do it. That I cannot do.

In 1892, the story continued, evidence was found in a cave on the island that a heavy, nail-studded chest had been removed from it, presumably about 1807, by a trapper working for John Jacob Astor—who, by coincidence, just about that time began to show signs of being wealthy. More coincidences opportunely followed, suggesting, finally, that the foundation of the Astor fortune had been treasure in that nail-studded box, buried by Captain Kidd and wrongfully abstracted from Olmsted property by an Astor minion. Olmsted, therefore, was suing the Astor family for five million dollars, and legal luminaries of the highest candlepower were engaged on either side of the litigation.

Head read his little fantasy before a Chicago literary club of which he was a member and had it privately printed. It got into the papers as early as 1894 and gained considerable circulation and credence, which its inventor, who had strewn it with give-aways, had not anticipated. The Olmsteds received so many inquiries about their "lawsuit," that, in self-defense, Frederick drew up a circular to be mailed in answer, explaining the circumstances of the invention (FLO [son] printed circular, LWR Files).

. . . I suppose it is old age that unfits me to deal with problems that are instinctively hateful to me."[45] Still, he urged upon John the diplomacy he could not himself muster, and concluded:

> I agree that it is not as bad as several projects for bridle roads in Central Park but I have never been in an attitude toward them but one of resistance and now at last after thirty years of fighting them the victory seems to have been finally secured.
>
> This folly is the same and it makes me sick to begin over again, with an issue so poor. I can only say that as I am situated here I plainly cannot do it.[46]

Olmsted was reluctant, so long as he was at Biltmore, to let other problems intrude.[47] The estate, which by then covered some hundred thousand acres of mountain land, was of consuming interest to him because of its potential importance. It was unique in America as a large-scale demonstration of economical forest management; he intended to start the first national school of forestry on it; the arboretum, for which more thousands of species and varieties had been collected than were shown even at Kew, was to be an experiment station and dendrological museum of large practical and scientific interest; and as the finest country place in the United States and one already much visited, Biltmore would have through its landscape design an impact on rural taste that would strongly influence it in the naturalistic direction.*,[48] Finally, Biltmore would be his last work, his last profession of faith and art. Olmsted never quite said as much but in his letters mentioned, cooly enough, the unlikelihood of his making many more visits there.[49]

Olmsted, who spoke warmly of Vanderbilt's "capital qualities," nevertheless found his client occasionally difficult. With some of Olmsted's proposals Vanderbilt was not in sympathy and toward some he was lukewarm so that it took "constant vigilance" to keep him in line; and he sometimes ordered things done before the landscape architects had thoroughly studied them.[50] "When Mr. Vanderbilt comes here by himself," Olmsted commented,

> he is liable to act, especially under suggestion of McNamee and Gall,† with a certain degree of willful abruptness, being no more than laymen in

---

*Vanderbilt usually traveled to Biltmore in the *Swannanoa* with a carload of friends. In February 1894 he brought, among others, "Mrs. and Miss Jones who," as Olmsted grumpily put it, "were at the Sargents' last week and who are supposed to be in some way inclined to dabble in Landscape Architecture." The slight was comically off the mark: "Miss Jones" was Beatrix, later Mrs. Max Farrand; in the course of her "dabbling" she became one of the eleven founders of the American Society of Landscape Architects, an eminent practitioner, and eventually the *grande dame* of the profession (O to JCO, 25 February 1894; Newton, *Design on the Land*, pp. 387–88).

†James C. Gall was an engineer who had worked on the drainage of Central Park and on various government works before Olmsted brought him to Biltmore as superintendent of landscape construction (O to G. W. Vanderbilt, 26 March 1889).

general able to realize the manner in which one element of a big scheme reticulates in its details with others and the amount and kind of study necessary to make it harmonize with all others.[51]

Vanderbilt's disinclination to methodical planning was matched by his cavalier method of financing the work. He was spending about a quarter of a million dollars annually for the improvements and maintenance carried out under the direction of the Olmsted firm through Gall, superintendent of landscape work, Beadle, superintendent of the nursery, and Bottomly, the head gardener. Except in rare and minor instances, no part of this large expenditure was either made through the firm or audited by it. The firm gave instructions to the three superintendents and their subordinates as to how to accomplish what Vanderbilt said he wanted done and submitted an estimate of the cost of the operation to Vanderbilt before he finally authorized it. But he rarely made a specific appropriation for a specific operation; he ordered it done and then paid whatever expense the three department heads incurred in doing it. "It was a very loose and casual way of doing business on his part," Frederick later commented,

> but that was the way he wanted the work done, conforming to his impulsive decisions from time to time. The Olmsted firm would have preferred a systematic budgeting of the expenditures on Biltmore Estate work under their guidance, such as the firm often helped to set up and administer for more businesslike clients, especially public agencies. . . . the worst feature of this casual and informal fiscal control was that inevitably much that was done proved to be wasteful, and disappointing in the long run, when [Vanderbilt] found himself unable to maintain, in a really satisfactory manner, indefinitely, what had been accomplished.*,[52]

Olmsted visited Biltmore in February 1894 in the course of a six-week tour made with Phil Codman.† Stopping first in Brooklyn, Olmsted visited Prospect Park and saw the commissioners, who wanted to engage him again as consulting landscape architect. He agreed that the firm should pay twelve visits a year for a fee of two thousand dollars and traveling expenses. The business would probably be difficult and unpleasant and would involve a political fight, he warned his office, but it was their professional duty to take it and get the development of the park back on course.[53]

---

*It is worth noting, however, that Biltmore, alone of Olmsted's major works, is now being maintained in the spirit of the original. It is owned by George W. Vanderbilt's heirs, who have opened it to the public.

†On March 6, Olmsted's stepmother, Mary Ann (Bull) Olmsted, died at Hartford. Olmsted wrote John from Chicago on March 11 that he would have to leave "Hartford Affairs" to his wife Mary; discrimination in the distribution of heirlooms was important. Allie received John Olmsted's four-volume daybook, which had long been a cause of friction between him and his mother (O to JCO, 11 March 1894).

Biltmore: the vista and *rampe douce,* one of Olmsted's rare designs in the formal style (courtesy Biltmore House and Gardens, Asheville, North Carolina).

After a short stay at Biltmore, Olmsted and Phil set off to Chicago, Milwaukee, Louisville, and Atlanta. At Atlanta Olmsted met the promoters of the Cotton Exposition and inspected the proposed site. It was small, covering less than two hundred acres, and from the landscape point of view, unpromising. Compared to the Chicago exposition, this one would be a modest affair; thousands of dollars were to be used on it as millions had been at Chicago. Olmsted, nevertheless, was eager to take the work, both to demonstrate that old sectional rancors were losing their potency and because it was "very desirable to make the firm favorably known at the South and 'extend its connection' as the merchants say."[54]

The weather at Louisville and Atlanta was unseasonably sultry, and by late March, when Olmsted got back to New York for further dealings with the Prospect Park commissioners, he was feeling "disordered."[55] Scarcely recovered, he set out on another long journey, with John, in June. They went first to Chicago, then on to St. Paul. There Olmsted had to go to bed for a week while John dealt with all business in his stead. Olmsted's attending doctor sternly warned that he must give up train travel. To get home, Olmsted went to Duluth and through the Great Lakes and the St. Lawrence River by boat, so reaching Brookline with a minimum of railroading.[56]

He at once began to plan how to get as close as possible to Biltmore by water and wrote Gall to find out whether he could, after arriving by steamer at Wilmington, North Carolina, take a boat on the Cape Fear River and get within a day's railroad ride of the estate. "If I can do this, I may be able to get to Biltmore once or twice more than I would if obliged to go wholly by rail," he explained.[57]

Olmsted was at Deer Isle in July. Frederick, having been graduated magna cum laude from Harvard, was in Colorado with a Coast and Geodetic Survey party under the direction of his cousin Frank Perkins. John, on whom Olmsted's illness had thrown a heavy burden, suddenly decided to take advantage of the slack summer season and left, with no opportunity to consult with his father, for six weeks in Europe. Olmsted was disconcerted by his departure and found himself at sea in some matters of business.[58]

Eliot, left in charge of the office, tried to calm his anxiety. He and John both realized, he wrote, that the business was chiefly Olmsted's creation; they felt that his share of the firm income should continue to be much the largest and that, so long as he was feeling ill, he should neither work nor worry. "You have so long relied upon John," he went on,

> that I can easily imagine how it must feel to have him slip away. But I hope you will not allow any small affairs to worry you. We shall be able to look after those here; and you may rest assured that nothing radical or of uncommon importance will be undertaken without consultation with you. The fact that you stand in the background as head of the firm is, of course, of great value to our joint business and neither John nor I would

wish to have you formally withdraw one day before fate may compel that event.[59]

The letter, however kindly meant, must have suggested to the old man that his young partners already considered him as being "in the background" and were facing the prospect of his retirement.

Concern for Frederick's future and the profession's continued to be a dominant theme of Olmsted's letters to his son. From Deer Isle he wrote:

> In guiding your education, more especially your out-of-school education, through traveling and social influences, I have had the fact much in mind that most of the men who have thus far been at all notable in the practice of our art, have jumped into it, as I did, without adequate special education, and I have wanted as far as I could to make you exceptional. . . . I have used my best judgment to have you trained from the start as a Landscape Architect with a liberal general education to base your special training on.

Frederick's summer with the Coast and Geodetic Survey, although something of an "excursus," would sharpen certain incidental but important skills—the ability to estimate heights and angles and rates of grade, to pace accurately, to keep his direction in timber and on devious courses, to follow trails, to locate springs and judge the lines of watercourses and natural drainage, and so forth. More important, it would allow him to study local botanical conditions in a mountainous region where extensive greensward was not natural and to reflect on the question Olmsted thought crucial to the future: how, in such areas, could the profession make satisfactory foregrounds of domestic landscapes consistent with convenience and economical expenditure? Olmsted knew of no such work, unless their recent efforts at Perry Park, a residential neighborhood near Denver, had come out well. He asked Frederick to visit it and take pictures of the improved parts, especially the lake and lake shores.

> It is an essay—our design is—to apply sound principles to the situation in a small way, but I am almost certain that it has been badly botched and that the result would be most unsatisfactory to me.* It is the only work that we have done, except at Palo Alto, in which we have attempted to wrestle at all with the class of conditions in question; and at Palo Alto, you know how we were served, were forced to resign to avoid responsibility for what was done.

*A report on Perry Park, dated September 8 and apparently written by Frederick, said that, although work had been brought to a halt by the depression, the little landscaping so far done was pleasing and promising.

459

He was eager to set Frederick to work on the Biltmore arboretum, both for the prestige and the experience he would gain. If it realized Olmsted's hopes, its planting would be regarded as a historic event. "I would like to have you assist at the planting of the first tree," he wrote his son. "I shall get Professor Sargent to hold it if I can."[60]

He had already told Gall, "To do what I can in elaborating the design of the Arboretum after it has been accomplished is the most important duty that I look forward to; and you cannot overrate my desire to be able to do it."[61]

Before he got back to Biltmore, Olmsted had to go to Brooklyn to see the Prospect Park commissioners. The firm's principal duty on the park, he reported to Vaux, was to scotch operations further superseding the original design and to get the concert ground and the plantations, which through neglect were "wholly ruined," returned to their original concept. With perceptible dissatisfaction he commented: "This last week under instructions I defined a site for a house for tennis players which I suppose White is to plan. (Though White has been referred to as if he was the Architect of the Park, we have not seen him nor been brought into communication with him.)"[62]

Olmsted wanted no reflection of the White City in Prospect Park.

Olmsted was at Biltmore with his wife and Marion and Frederick by the beginning of November, settled in one of the estate houses, the Rivercliff Cottage on the French Broad River.[63] Rumblings from New York, which he could not ignore, disturbed him there. A year previously the park board, ignoring a report drawn up by its landscape architect, Vaux, had ordered its engineer to prepare a design for a speedway along the Harlem River. The plan, no more attractive than if made for a street railway line, would have excluded both pedestrians and boats from the river bank and was contrary to a legislative prohibition against building a road for fast driving without providing a pedestrian walk between it and the river. Contracts were nevertheless let, and Paul Dana resigned from the board in protest, at the same time deploring its "crude and spiteful line" toward Vaux. To criticism that the road was being built without any consultation with a landscape architect or any regard for artistic values, the remaining board members had stated that they would consult the department's landscape architect "at the proper time."[64] "This inability to appreciate the value of artistic training is the essence of vulgarity," *Garden and Forest* editorialized scathingly in August 1894. "It is worse than simple ignorance; it is the complacent belief that nothing is better than ignorance."[65]

In October the board gracelessly yielded an inch: it resolved to appoint a landscape architect to review the speedway plans, with the insulting provision that all landscape architects applying must file testimonials of competence.[66] Olmsted, at Biltmore, then received word from the board that he was the landscape architect they wanted to review the plans.

He replied that, having done a study for a trotting course along the Harlem River thirty years before, he was familiar with the ground and had no doubt that he would give the board the same advice as its regular adviser; he must decline to serve them. He sent a copy of his letter to Stiles, and wrote Eliot:

> I hope that you will agree with me that it was my duty to take the course I have. It was only last year that one of them said "the woods are full of landscape architects": his real thought being, "if Mr. Vaux will not advise what we want we can easily find a landscape architect who will."[67]

In New York on his way home from Biltmore, Olmsted agreed to see the commissioners, who formally requested him to report on the landscape treatment of the speedway. Olmsted wrote them a letter vindicating Vaux.[68]

This was another skirmish in an old war, and to Olmsted it was wearisome and distracting. The focus of his concerns was narrowing; the two things of importance to him were Biltmore and Frederick's preparation for his life's work. From Brookline that winter he wrote often to his son at Biltmore, reiterating in a dozen ways the advice that he should constantly observe and question Bottomly, Beadle, and Pinchot and then review and organize the knowledge he had freshly acquired. Nowhere but at Biltmore could Frederick so well advance this critical phase of his education and make himself the most learned man in the office and in the profession about plants and shrubs and trees.[69]

Frederick was staggered by the difficulty of the learning task Olmsted so insistently set him. The son had inherited from the father certain traits of mind that made it almost impossible to become highly expert in the scientific classification of plants. Although the field was not completely barred to Frederick's intelligence, it was one he could penetrate only with distressing labor. Like his father, he was not greatly interested in plants as plants; both were alert to their qualities of form, color, and texture and interested in them as elements in landscape composition.[70] Disheartened by the difficulty of making himself into the human botanical encyclopedia that his father wanted him to become, Frederick toyed with the notion of dropping landscape architecture for zoology.

Olmsted, remembering his own father's long indulgence toward him as he skipped from one calling to another (he currently saw it as overindulgence), told Frederick to think the question over very carefully and present his reasons in writing. He promised to review them without any prejudice except, perhaps, a prejudice in favor of giving him his head. But, he added:

> It will take a good deal to overcome this one consideration with me, the consideration that I can bequeath you as a Landscape Architect, fairly well fitted as you easily may be, an inheritance many times the value (in the form of prestige and the commercial good-will of my business) than I otherwise can.[71]

Frederick's answering letter was "full, clear and sensible." To it Olmsted replied:

> If you are weak in what you have led me to believe that you consider
> yourself weak, with reference to our profession, such weakness would, in
> my judgment, be much more destructive to your success as a Zoologist. . . .
> The difficulties which would, in this respect, stand before you in one case,
> would not probably be less; they would probably be greater, in the other. I
> am pretty confident that if you realize the importance of overcoming them,
> you will be able to do so. . . . There is not another man in the world who,
> at your age, has been as well-prepared as you are for the practical study of
> our profession in all respects, *except* those of which you are learning in the
> Biltmore School and under the guidance of Beadle and Pinchot and their
> assistants, and with the use of the nursery and the forest and the con-
> servatory and gardens and the library of the Vanderbilt undertaking. . . .[72]

Frederick was persuaded. He dropped all thought of zoology. The crisis passed,
and he wholeheartedly embraced his father's profession and made it his own.

At the start of the new year, Olmsted admitted to Frederick that he was
greatly oppressed and confused; he wondered if his memory might be getting a
little weak. Never before had he so felt his age. He mustered energy, however, to
begin to plan a systematic course of training in every branch of landscape architecture to be given in the office. "We are gradually preparing a grand professional post-graduate school here," he wrote Frederick.[73] Before his return to Biltmore with his wife and Marion late in February, the winter gloom was relieved
by occasional bright spots. Charlotte's sons, "good but unremarkable," visited for
a time, and Olmsted found in himself "a natural affection" for them.[74] Good
news came from his old friend Waring: in announcing that William L. Strong,
the new mayor of New York, had made him street-cleaning commissioner,
Waring spoke with affectionate gratitude of Olmsted's early influence on him.[75]
The happy prospect glimmered that Pinchot, about to resign his Biltmore post,
might accept an appointment as New York park commissioner. Olmsted urged
him to:* although trained as a forester, Pinchot understood that forests, gardens,
and parks were managed on distinctly different principles.

> And, confidentially, I will say that no one in the service of the Park
> Commission is nearly as much inclined to make this distinction as, in my
> judgment, is desirable. I think Central Park is, for this reason, a much less
> valuable property than it might have been, or than even now it might be
> made.[76]

Vaux, of course, was in the service of the park commission; so was Samuel
Parsons, Jr. The park suffered, Olmsted thought, from the disposition, which

---

*Pinchot did not accept.

Vaux had to some degree and Parsons had more than Vaux, to aim at garden as distinguished from landscape effects.[77] Olmsted, although sometimes privately critical of Vaux's park work, backed him without reservation in his continuing imbroglio with the park commission.

This reached a crisis the last of February 1895, when the newly appointed board of park commissioners abruptly passed a resolution placing all landscape and architectural work on the Harlem River driveway in charge of their landscape architect—subject to the supervision and control of an advisory committee made up of Olmsted, Stanford White, Saint-Gaudens, Post, Hunt, Stiles, and Charles W. Clinton.[*,78] Stiles, completely outraged, fired off a barrage of letters to Olmsted, which overtook him as he reached Biltmore. Olmsted would not consider, would he, associating himself with nonlandscape architects to criticize Vaux's work? Certainly he, Stiles, would not. White would accept and thought they all should out of courtesy to the board and then reorganize as a committee, not to oversee Vaux, but to advise the board. Stiles scorned White's scheme: if the board would accept that arrangement after their acceptance, it would before, he told White; and its appointment of a supervising committee to pass on Vaux's design degraded both the design office and its occupant. The resolution setting up the committee had almost broken Vaux's heart; he was old and poor, and it was cruel to give him the alternative of swallowing an indignity or being thrown into want. Olmsted could do as he pleased, but he, Stiles, would have no part of the committee.[79]

Olmsted would have no part of it either. He wrote the secretary of the park commission:

> One method of obtaining advice on matters of design has been consistently and successfully followed by almost every park board in the country. It is the employment of a paid, professional Landscape Architect, directly and solely responsible under the Board for the ultimate result to be attained. To introduce between the Board and this adviser a number of men who can not be held directly accountable for this result by the public, would be a departure from this well tried system for which I can see no justification. I must therefore respectfully decline the position offered me.[80]

His words were measured, but he seethed. "It makes me grind my teeth," he wrote Stiles, "to see how Vaux is treated. But the harder it is, the more expedient it is, to keep one's temper in anything that is to come before the public."[81]

By the time Olmsted's refusal reached the board, both it and the prospective committee members were backing water; Paul Dana had worked on them. The president in an interview with the Sun explained that the committee's function would be to advise the board and announced that Vaux's original report had been accepted and Vaux ordered to prepare new plans for the drive to supersede the

---

*Clinton was a New York architect and a charter member of the American Institute of Architects.

engineer's. These were the two points Stiles had stood on. Having gained them, he decided to accept appointment to the committee: he heard Vaux hoped he would since, except for Olmsted, he would be the only true friend of landscape architecture on it.[82]

The consideration that the committee, if he declined to join it, would be essentially packed against natural landscape and against Vaux had, in fact, made Olmsted worry over his own refusal of the appointment.[83] He could not willingly see the management of New York's rural parks pass into the even partial control of such architecture-oriented strong men as Hunt and White. The battle was already joined, notably in Prospect Park, between the proponents of natural, rural landscape and

> those who are disposed to revise every body of public land that has been laid out regardfully of natural beauty with the object of transforming it as far as possible into a field of architectural beauty. . . . Stanford White has been and is trying to establish the rule of motives that are at war with those that rule in the original laying out of Brooklyn Park. He distinctly hates those older motives. He would at least, now that so much has been established in the spirit of the original design, get the Commissioner to make the Park an incongruous hybrid between that which was aimed at in this design and that which would be aimed at in such a design as a French architect would have made early in the century, introducing sentimental passages of "Nature" like that attempted at Petit Trianon, but making them secondary, and as interludes of efforts approaching the ruling Versailles character.[84]

This was conjecture about White, Olmsted admitted. Even so, it was time for those who were essentially of one mind to close ranks against an enemy who was organized, able, proud, and enthusiastic.

> They have struck down Vaux and are doing their best to kill him in the name of the Lord and of France. They are strong; they are sincere; they are confident; they are mostly cultivated gentlemen to be dealt with courteously, but they are doctrinaires and fanatics and essentially cockneys, with no more knowledge of nor interest in rurality than most men of Parisian training and associations.[85]

If Olmsted was harsh toward White, he was also prophetic. The unobtrusive mode of park architecture he and Vaux had installed on Prospect Park was on its way out; in its place, for better or worse, the firm of McKim, Mead and White and their likeminded associates fastened on the park conspicuous classicism and imposing monumentality.

Through professional association, the "men of the enemy" had become Olmsted's friends, and at Chicago and Biltmore he had worked with them in "hearty, active, friendly cooperation." The reason, he said, was simple: there was a place for everything. The Chicago fair and Biltmore in its immediate surroundings were places essentially architectural.

> At Chicago we sought for a site, first, that would be favorable to formality and architectural gardening. There was none available. Taking the site that in all other respects was most suitable we tried to reconcile a picturesque motive with the formal stateliness that our architectural associates were determined to have in the buildings, and we succeeded to their satisfaction. Here, again, at Biltmore we have managed to reconcile the requirements of Hunt in his Renaissance buildings with a generally picturesque natural character in the approaches, and in the main landscape features, introducing more or less formal spurs and outworks of architectural motive and purpose. And Hunt has accepted our way of doing it, and even, at my request, has aided in marrying the two motives, extending, modifying and altering the architectural outworks at my suggestion. . . . There has not been the slightest break of harmony between us.[86]

But Olmsted was apprehensive that the harmony might dissolve; he rather expected discord over the Biltmore Village. The firm's English plan for it and Hunt's French were irreconcilable. Vanderbilt leaned toward Hunt's. He was expected at Biltmore late in April, and Olmsted intended to explain the firm's plan to him in person, being unwilling, he said, to leave him to Hunt, who was "earnest, tempestuous and used to having his own way."[87]

Meanwhile, he was troubled by the lack of good soil for planting and feared a contrast between the magnificence of the house and its immediate grounds and the poverty of the grounds beyond. Moreover, the plans for the arboretum were going awry: Beadle and Pinchot thought the planting list had not been properly worked out by Warren H. Manning, the firm's horticulture expert and director of planting.*[88] One difficulty lay in drawing up the list. In an arboretum not exclusively scientific, there was considerable latitude for the exercise of the list-maker's taste or fancy; and the nonuniformity of nomenclature among English, French, German, and American botanists and nurserymen with whom orders would be placed almost insured confusion and duplication.[89]

Olmsted asked Sargent, who had been consulting on the arboretum from the beginning, if he thought that a botanist of unquestionable authority should be employed to compile the list. It would, of course, be very desirable to secure

---

*Manning was going through European and American catalogs and ordering almost everything, not only natural varieties, but a number of horticultural varieties, at which Beadle poked fun, ridiculous both as to their nomenclature and their value in an arboretum. He collected a fine variety, notwithstanding (FLO [son], interview).

such a man as curator, with the list his first duty. "But it must be borne in mind," he added,

> that Mr. Vanderbilt has not yet so great an interest in this Arboretum nor so clear an appreciation of its value that it would now be expedient to urge upon him the permanent employment of such a man. His interest in the Arboretum is, as yet, mainly interest in a pleasure ground, but with judicious advice he may give this pleasure ground great permanent value as an Arboretum.[90]

Sargent replied that a scientific arboretum, like the Arnold and Kew collections, was valuable only when run by scientific men; its value depended on its permanence and on such adjuncts as library and herbarium. Permanence could not be expected in one dependent on an individual's interest, which might flag, or fortune, which might wane. Ideally, the arboretum should be generously endowed to assure its upkeep, and the money placed in the hands of a board of trustees to whom the grounds should be deeded. Sure that Vanderbilt would not consider such an arrangement, Sargent advised Olmsted to drop the idea of a scientific arboretum and plan instead one of a more popular, ornamental, and picturesque character.[91]

Olmsted was dashed and confused that Sargent, who had seemed to approve the original plan, should propose this radical modification of it. The arboretum had come to be to him, of all Biltmore projects, the most cherished. It loomed in his mind as one of great national importance, and he was not willing to negate that importance by scrapping its scientific aspect.

It was during March and April, while Olmsted was grappling with the arboretum and other Biltmore questions, that it began to dawn on Frederick that his father was losing his grip on professional problems.[92] For some time past Olmsted had had to be reminded of the names of the park commissioners he was going to meet—not surprisingly, for his habit of impersonality had become second nature—and sometimes he had to be briefed on their business before he saw them. Occasionally he complained that he had lost track of the particulars of important work. None of this appeared unnatural in the elderly head of a firm dealing with scores of park commissioners and other clients and having dozens of projects, ranging from huge to modest, simultaneously in hand. During the spring at Biltmore, however, he was becoming repetitious and noticeably forgetful; unable to hold in mind the particulars of problems, he found it increasingly hard to reach solutions. Frederick began unobtrusively to assume responsibilities that seemed to baffle his father and to make decisions in his name, all the time prompting him discreetly and covering for him as well as he could.[93]

Olmsted himself seemed to sense that something was amiss. Intending to go North about May 10, he wrote his office the week before that he wanted John to

466

meet him in Washington and help him there and in New York and Brooklyn: he felt out of touch with works in those cities and was afraid to deal with them alone.[94] A week later, he faced, or almost faced, the frightening truth. "It has today, for the first time, become evident to me that my memory for recent occurrences is no longer to be trusted," he wrote John. The firm had to be protected; he should not be entrusted with important business. But it was too much for him to accept all the implications of the failure he could feel approaching: he believed, or said he believed, that, although he forgot verbal instructions, he had not lost his capacity in invention, design, and reasoning.[95]

Even as he started on his long decline, Olmsted seemed to a stranger both impressive and endearing. Carl Alwin Schenck, the young forester whom Pinchot, departing from Biltmore, had recruited in Germany and brought to the estate, arrived the end of April and spent several weeks with the Olmsteds in the Rivercliff Cottage while his own quarters were being made ready. He recognized Olmsted as "not merely *the* great authority on all landscapism and indeed the creator of landscape architecture in the U. S. A.; he was also *the* inspirer of American forestry. And he was more: he was the loveliest and most loveable old man whom I have ever met."[96]

As Olmsted's mental condition deteriorated, it became evident not only in his forgetfulness but also in a faint bewilderment and vacancy of facial expression. John Singer Sargent, imported by Vanderbilt the middle of May to paint Olmsted's and Hunt's portraits to hang in the great house, could not have failed to spot it with his portraitist's eye, and Olmsted's family feared that it would be ruthlessly recorded.[97] But the artist saw more than the old man's recent affliction: he saw and suggested his wise and humane spirit.

Sargent posed Olmsted against the northerly side of a mass of trees and undergrowth on the east side of the approach road, about half a mile from the house, where planting done under his direction merged into the native woodland. The Kalmia was just coming into flower, and a few unusually late blossoms lingered on the dogwood. There was a light overcast when Sargent began to work; it held during several sittings, in the course of which he blocked out the figure and the background and began work on the head. Then followed clear and sunny days, with bright light and sharp shadow, so that the lighting on the face was wrong. Sargent left the Olmsted portrait and turned to Hunt, whom he posed on the east terrace against the background of the house. When he finished Hunt's portrait, and the weather persisted brightly fair, he continued work on Olmsted's in his improvised studio in an unfinished west room of the big house where he had blanked off all openings except one to the northwest.[98] Frederick often watched Sargent at work and vividly remembered his manner.

> . . . He would stand off, some twenty feet or so from his subject and the canvas, very deliberately but very alertly looking back and forth from one to the other and mixing a brush full of paint on his palette, then at last

467

give a little lift of his shoulders and with a very springy motion for so heavy a man walk forward swiftly to the canvas and make a brush-stroke like an arrow going to the bullseye.[99]

When the head was finished to Sargent's satisfaction, it was still sunny and the outdoor light still unsuitable. Olmsted, restless and anxious to be off, would wait no longer on the weather. He summoned John to escort him north, on his last round of professional visits, and with no doubt unconscious symbolism he left his clothes and his son, the young Frederick Law Olmsted, to wear them and pose in his place.[100]

OLMSTED and John left Biltmore about the first of June and, after a stop in Washington, reached Brookline on the tenth.[1] Olmsted realized that his memory was going, but as best he could he applied his mind to Biltmore. He wrote a detailed, sensible letter of instructions to Beadle about planting the lower approach road, another to Gall on the need to find gravel beds for roadmaking on the estate, and three in a single day, almost identically worded, to Vanderbilt on some other matter.[2] Uncertain of what had been done and fearful of duplicating orders, he appealed to Frederick to make "any confusion in my mind as little conspicuous as you conveniently can."[3]

His fixed habit of industry had not begun to slacken, and he looked forward to the possibility of laying out a manufacturing village near Pittsburgh. It was "the sort of work that I would like best, as being more comprehensive and more fully touching social problems on a large scale than others coming to us."[4]

He inspected the Boston work and was not dissatisfied: "As a general thing, the comprehensive improvement of Boston suburbs, which is by far our most important work, is in a healthy state of development. I hope that in time you will have the leading pilotage of it," he wrote Frederick.[5]

He was failing, nevertheless, and he knew it. During June and July the combination of oppressive heat, insomnia, and spotty memory almost undid him. "I have rarely felt so little master of myself," he lamented to Frederick.[6]

Later, at Deer Isle, he was no better. Ravaged by sleeplessness and anxieties, he consoled himself during the long, unhappy nights by writing to Frederick. He fretted lengthily that he might have left undone something that he could have done for his education; he urged him repeatedly to make himself the most knowledgeable man in the profession in botany and horticulture; he worried that, if Beadle's and Pinchot's criticisms of Manning's list were right, the arboretum would be the worst professional blunder of his life; he begged Frederick for detailed progress reports on Biltmore. His letters labored the same points over and over.[7]

After John wrote him that his failing memory would make necessary "some slight readjustments of firm matters,"[8] Olmsted fell prey to suspicions: he felt he had been "set aside" by his partners, and he fancied that John, his talented, devoted, indispensable right hand for almost twenty years, had executed a "coup" that jeopardized Frederick's interest in the firm.*,[9] As his mind and world slowly darkened, a fixed point of light for a time remained: Frederick, his dearest, brightest hope. "I love you and take joy in you with all my heart," he ended one letter; and of one of Frederick's, which he kept beside him and read repeatedly during the night, he said: ". . . Nothing goes so far to lift me out of the feeling of desolation. It is not childishness. It is the assurance that you are taking up what I am dropping."[10]

In the middle of October Olmsted returned to Brookline to see doctors. Rayner was consulted by letter. The consensus was that a mild, damp climate would be good for him. He was horrified to find that he was to be "taken out to England to die by Mother and Marion," as he despairingly put it to Frederick, and he begged him to send snapshots showing the progress of work at Biltmore. "I suppose it will be some months before the advance of my illness will make these of no use to me."[11]

Mentally failing though he was, Olmsted saw through his doctors' pretense that he was to be cured; and he rightly suspected that one purpose of the trip to England was to get him away from the office.[12] The prospect of leaving Frederick desolated him.

> I try every night to find some excuse that will serve to insist on your being with us. . . . If I live till spring I shall try hard to get them to send for you. I do so want to guide you in Italy or anywhere in the South of Europe. I do so want to educate you, start your education for the South. But you can write to me. Your letters are excellent. I enjoy them more than anything else. Tell me all about Biltmore. Don't assume that "the office" tells me anything. You understand this sets me out of the office. I don't suppose they will let you come, but if I live I shall try.[13]

Although the firm had put Frederick on salary, twelve hundred dollars a year, the first of November and had notified Vanderbilt that he was officially its representative,[14] John withdrew him from the work and recalled him to Brookline to say goodbye to their father, who was sailing the sixteenth. When Frederick got home, he found his mother, whose pluck in crises was legendary, had in this protracted one lost heart. She begged him to sail with them and get them settled in England. So Frederick, with his parents and sister, sailed on the *Cephalonia* from East Boston the morning of November 16.[15]

Sharing a stateroom with his father, Frederick recognized, as a measure of his decline, his reversion to preoccupations discarded long ago: memories of his early discipline under various ministers cropped up, he worried about the state

---

*Queried about the "coup" long afterward, Frederick said there had been no ground whatever for his father's suspicions. John had always treated him generously and, on Eliot's death in 1897, took him into the firm as a full partner without requiring him to put up a cent of capital (FLO [son] to LWR, 10 October 1948, LWR Files).

of his soul, and for the first time in Frederick's memory he spent hours reading the Bible.[16]

The *Cephalonia* docked at Liverpool Tuesday morning, November 26, and by the following evening the Olmsted party had reached Exmouth and taken lodgings. Frederick spent the next several days scouting the region, and at nearby Lympston he found and rented Crossway, a modern, two-story villa. Standing in four acres of ground, it featured, luxuriously, eleven bedrooms, steam heat, electric light, hot and cold running water, pretty furnishings, and a fine view of the sea—all for three pounds a week.[17] Frederick moved his charges into it and went to London to visit Kew Gardens.

Olmsted could still produce a lucid letter. He wrote instructing Frederick whom to see at Kew, and how to approach them. He was to get from Sir Joseph Hooker and other Kew officials all possible details—down to where they bought their plant labels—about the operation of the arboretum; and he was to elicit their remarks on the plans for the Biltmore arboretum. "Take such course as you best can to draw them out and get their comments and criticisms," he ordered, "always giving emphasis to the fact that here is a very rich man who for his own pleasure can be drawn to serve Art and Science and popular education in a rarely good way."[18]

Olmsted had to interrupt his next letter to Frederick because "my keeper, who under Dr. Rainer's [sic] direction is always after me with a sharp stick, is calling and I must close." In it he had been urging Frederick to get the direction of the Biltmore arboretum into his own hands. It was the broken old man's last coherent advice to his son.*,[19]

Frederick sailed for home just before Christmas. He might have hoped that the household he left behind him, placed amid the sort of scenery they all appreciated, could maintain at least tranquility. The Devon landscape was pure Constable, the sunsets were gorgeous, the moonlit nights mild and beautiful. There was a pretty garden about the house, a gardener to tend it, the gardener's wife to "accommodate," and a cook they had brought with them from home. Short trips, and friends nearby, provided the changes of scene and cast without which Mary's spirit parched and her wit turned acid. Yet the scenic charm, the domestic comfort, the available variety, all were ineffective. Olmsted's piteous condition was scarcely bearable to his wife and daughter; by early January they could no longer stand being in the same house with him and for relief went to London. There they stayed until Mr. Bridge, Olmsted's "keeper," whom Frederick summed up as "a useless ex-curate," verged on a breakdown and called them back the middle of the month.[20]

Again at Crossway, Marion became so nervous and excitable that her mother feared she might "go off" like Charlotte. Because of Mr. Bridge's incapacity, the two women had to take turns driving the demented old man in the chaise behind an irritating pony named Peggy who could not be got out of a

*See Appendix A.

471

walk. Mary, homesick, took out an exile's spite on the host country: she disliked the English and couldn't understand the language, but she tried to be nice to them; she always assured them that the American attitude toward them, since they backed the slaveholders in the war, was not hatred but "good-natured contempt."[21]

The members of the tense and incompatible household spent much of the winter being sick and getting on each other's nerves. Mr. Bridge, dour and shaggy in his undefined breakdown, reminded Mary of a Scotch terrier. Olmsted was so confused and agitated that business papers and journals had to be withheld from him and his wife had to keep out of his way; in addition, he had influenza. Marion had bronchitis, Mary laryngitis. In early February Mary wrote Frederick that she did not expect to get back alive: she was tired out at last.[22]

In these straits, Rayner acted as *deus ex machina*. He invited Marion, whose list of complaints by then included gout, to London and so got her off her mother's hands. Mary wrote Frederick that she was going to send Marion home: she could not take care of two invalids. She had had an attack of angina herself, and if she was going to die, she preferred to do it with her daughter on the other side of the ocean. Rayner soon terminated the impossible situation by engaging board for Olmsted at Dr. Pott's sanatarium at Amersham, in Buckinghamshire.[23]

Olmsted, meanwhile, was having occasional lucid, or at least docile, intervals. He longed to go to Kew, but when his wife told him he could not "make an exposure of himself," he accepted her decision with pathetic meekness. The news of Vaux's death, which was finally broken to him late in February, some three months after it occurred,* quite animated him: he said briskly that he must write something about it.[24]

Olmsted, still in the charge of Mr. Bridge, was transferred to Amersham early in March. He went protesting that he would rather go home and that nothing ailed him except the noise in his head. His wife and daughter, liberated, set out to see the south of England. When they reached London March 31, Mary at once called on Rayner and the same day went to Bromley, in Kent, to look at Dr. Madden's sanitarium, to which Rayner wanted Olmsted moved. Rayner thought he had had a slight stroke, the effects of which were passing, and that he might live to be a very old man, essentially witless.[25]

Mary was dejected by the prospect and alarmed about Marion. She was dis-

---

*Vaux's troubled life came to an end, so far as anyone could tell, late on Tuesday, November 19, 1895. He left his Bensonhurst home, was seen and greeted by an acquaintance on a pier in Gravesend Bay in the afternoon, and his body was found in the water at the foot of Bay Seventeenth Street the next Thursday morning. His hat, glasses, and one shoe were missing, and he had a bruise and a slight cut over one eye, according to newspaper reports, but there was no indication of such violence as to cause death. So dense a fog had enveloped the whole harbor on the day he disappeared that the pilots of ferryboats, unable to see twenty feet ahead, were docking in the wrong slips at Manhattan's South Ferry. It was thought possible that Vaux might have blundered off the pier in the fog. His total estate was valued at twenty-five hundred dollars (*New York Times*, 20, 22, 27 November 1895).

appointed but not surprised, she wrote her sons, that Marion had proved unequal to the strain of the recent painful months: she was a dear, sweet soul but had never grown up. After two weeks in London, Mary carried out her earlier decision: she took Marion to Liverpool by easy sightseeing stages and on April 23 sent her off to the States, sick with a cold and heartbroken over her father's condition. Alone, Mary returned to London.[26]

Olmsted by then had been moved to Bromley and was making it known that he was wild to get back to his office. Depressed and for once indecisive, Mary felt quite unequal to figuring out a scheme of life for herself and a husband whose future was an indefinite term of mental blankness. Frederick and John had not responded to her one proposal, which she said had originated with Rayner and Marion. She had asked her sons to build a year-round cottage at Deer Isle for Olmsted's retirement on a forty-six acre tract that she had bought without consulting them some time before leaving for England. She had no idea what ought to be done, or was going to be done, by whom; and, in rare helplessness, she wrote John and Frederick that they would have to take charge.[27] Then she went to Paris.

Paris was wonderfully curative. Julia Bryant was there; so were other friends, and theater, opera, galleries, shops, and dressmakers, all restorative to the brisk little woman who loathed melancholy and loved activity. There were memories, too, of her first happy visit as John Hull Olmsted's bride, and she looked up the apartment they had had on the rue Duphot. She stayed in Paris almost a month, taking a week out to go to Nice to visit John's grave and order repairs on it, and to Geneva, and she returned to Bromley and her duty with spirit and wardrobe well refreshed.[28]

Meanwhile her son John, resigned to the fact that "Mother is bound to have her own way," had authorized building the cottage on her Deer Isle land. He instructed Frederick to engage the architect, William Ralph Emerson, to design a cottage, "not too cheap," and to arrange that some small work, especially landscape work, be always in progress to occupy their father. As for their mother, John grumbled that she would find the place unbearable in winter, with only a deranged old man and stupid nurses and servants for company; but, of course, she would not take advice.[29] So Mary got "her own way"—or somebody's: she insisted throughout that the project was Rayner's and Marion's.

On July 2 Mary, Olmsted, Mr. Bridge, and Miss Rüdiger, a German woman Mary had engaged in Paris as a companion, sailed from Liverpool on the *Pavonia*. Ten days later they reached Boston, where Frederick met them and escorted them home. The next day they left for Deer Isle. Olmsted was thus whisked in and out of town to keep him away from his office and to hide his senility, so far as it was possible to do so, from notice outside a small circle of familiars.[30]

Living in a rented cottage at Deer Isle, the various members of the household tried for the next two months to keep Olmsted occupied with picnics, sailing, drives, walks, rowing, and visits to the building site of the new cottage, Felsted. Friends and neighbors visited, and Frederick came up for weekends. The summer passed not badly; soon it was gone. Southeasterly storms came in September; then the Maine winter set in. Mary suffered from rheumatism and loneliness. Olmsted's memory was quite gone, and he had to be constantly watched. Matters did not much improve when, after the first of the year, they were able to move into Felsted. Olmsted was sometimes melancholy, often agitated, and occasionally violent. Usually he turned his violence on inanimate objects, but he was capable of seizing and shaking Miss Rüdiger, beating the horse, and hurling the woodbox at Mr. Bridge. Mr. Bridge resigned and was replaced by another attendant who, suspected of doping his patient to make him docile, was soon dismissed. When spring came, Olmsted ignored the puttering work Frederick and John had hoped would keep him interested; instead, he took long walks and was unhappy.[31]

After a long, fair trial, which was a trial indeed to all participants, the Deer Isle experiment was abandoned. Frederick was appointed his father's legal guardian, and in September 1898 Olmsted was committed to the McLean Hospital at Waverley, Massachusetts, and installed in a cottage on the grounds he had long before designed.

The grounds displeased him ("They didn't carry out my plan, confound them!"),[32] and he fiercely hated the place. Groping in the limbo of senile dementia, he could find nothing to cheer him. He bitterly complained of neglect, and loneliness, and toothache, and treatment en masse and wrote vehement, disconnected, piteous letters made especially heartrending by an occasional flash of good sense. He could find nothing to cheer him, that is, unless a sense of Frederick's love and fidelity sometimes penetrated the chaos of his darkened mind.

During the five years of his father's confinement, Frederick often stayed with him in his cottage. He was at his bedside at two in the morning of August 28, 1903, as he lay dying. Watching the old man's life ebb, the son fancied that his uppermost feeling was relief: he was not losing his father; he had lost him, and poignantly realized the loss, long ago when his mind failed. But at the instant of death, there suddenly came over Frederick the feeling that the alien personality, which for so long had occupied his father's body and stood between him and all who cared for him, had fled without a trace, and it was as though, after an eight-year separation, he stood at the deathbed of his beloved father's real, old self.[33]

A private funeral service was held the following Monday morning at Olmsted's Warren Street home. Later, his ashes were deposited, without ceremony and without mourners, in the family vault in the Old North Cemetery at Hartford: Olmsted had never cared for pomp, and he had thought cremation the only decent way to dispose of the dead.*,[34]

*See Appendix B.

AFTERWORD

THE 1890s was a decade of staggering reverses for the emerging profession of landscape architecture. Olmsted retired, senile. Codman's death in 1893 and Eliot's in 1897 removed two of the best of the few young practitioners. Cleveland, aged and disabled, lingered until 1900. And *Garden and Forest*, the profession's most effective journalistic champion, gave up the ghost at the end of 1897, two months after the death of its talented editor, Stiles.

It was symptomatic of the trend of American life that the magazine had never achieved the audience or the influence that Downing's *Horticulturist*, addressing the people of a nation largely rural, had had forty years earlier. While a sophisticated, small, and on the whole wealthy minority realized that by engaging the services of a landscape architect they could secure the best use of their land, popular interest in the role that landscape architecture might play in directing and civilizing America's physical development was lacking—just as a substantial corps of landscape architects was lacking, either to propagate the faith or practice the art.

Notwithstanding their meager numbers and the small appreciation they commanded, the sturdy remnant of the profession rallied from its setbacks. On January 4, 1899, eleven landscape architects, including Samuel Parsons, Jr., Warren H. Manning, Beatrix Jones, the Olmsted brothers, and Downing Vaux, son of Calvert Vaux, met to form the first professional association of landscape architects, the American Society of Landscape Architects. The following year Harvard established the first university curriculum of professional training in landscape architecture as a memorial to Charles Eliot; and President Eliot, his father, chose the young Frederick Law Olmsted to head it. Thus the profession closed ranks and entered the twentieth century.[1]

More than any other one man, Frederick Law Olmsted had defined the character and role of landscape architecture in the nineteenth century, and his influence on it reached far into the twentieth. But it would diminish him to sum him up in the context of landscape architecture. He transcended his profession. In a career that spanned half a century of headlong social change, he left his clear mark on movements that helped to reshape American society. Sensitive in a rare degree to their drift and direction, he posted himself in the forefront of his time and from his intellectual lookout alerted his contemporaries to, and sug-

475

gested solutions for, problems they scarcely yet recognized. The educated foresight that made him a public figure of singular effectiveness in his own day makes him a historic personage whose failures and success speak suggestively to ours.

From the peak of his years Olmsted looked back on his life and warned his son, "You will find it is what you have *been* and not what you have done that you care for."[2] He implied more than once that he had too much sacrificed being to doing. Seen from the vantage point of the late twentieth century, both his being and his doing appear as uniquely admirable achievements of the American genius.

APPENDIX A: THE BILTMORE ARBORETUM

AFTER Olmsted's retirement, the arboretum plan was carried forward under Beadle's management, and the school of forestry established under Schenck's. The latter, continuing until 1909 when Schenck had a falling-out with Vanderbilt, successfully trained a number of talented young men who pioneered the new field.[1] The arboretum, on the other hand, fizzled. Olmsted had been right in his assessment of Vanderbilt's interest in it, and Sargent had been correct in saying that it should be immunized to shifts of personal predilection and private fortune. Soon after the turn of the century, Vanderbilt suffered financial reverses; the arboretum was an early casualty, and estate expenditures for improvements and, more importantly, for maintenance were reduced from about a quarter of a million dollars a year to seventy thousand.[2]

Frederick, to whom it had never been intimated that Vanderbilt might be spending more than he could afford, was incensed when Vanderbilt's financial adviser, Hamilton McKown Twombly, reproached him for letting Vanderbilt go into landscape over his head. "The trouble with you landscape architects," Twombly accused, "is that you don't protect your clients from their own ignorant impulsiveness about matters in which they rely on your experienced judgment."

Frederick, as sensitive as his father to the good name of his profession, retorted with some bitterness that the accusation came with ill grace from the very man who had earlier dismissed the elder Olmsted from a large work for insisting that, in his opinion, what Twombly wanted to do was contrary to his best interests.

"If we had known earlier," Frederick afterwards wrote regretfully, "that George Vanderbilt was spending more than his income on the Biltmore Estate and eating seriously into his capital, we could, and would, have urged methods of economizing—to any desirable degree—much more satisfactory in the net results, and less wasteful, than [what] inevitably happened when the annual expenditure was suddenly and arbitrarily cut to about a quarter of what it had been running."[3]

APPENDIX B: MARY

MARY Cleveland Bryant Perkins Olmsted survived her husband by eighteen years, active and tart to the day of her death. Shuttling between Brookline and Deer Isle, and occasionally wintering in the Caribbean and passing the spring in Washington, she managed to secure the degree of movement and change necessary to her contentment. She continued to be intolerant of static situations, and she still moved bores along with a flick of the tongue. When she was not in motion, she read voraciously, preferring English and French novels; she researched the family history; and she reminisced, interestingly. At Christmas time 1909, she recalled that the first Christmas tree she had ever seen was at William Cullen Bryant's home in 1844, when they were still a novelty: "I believe I am the only survivor of that party, and how the trees have spread!"[1] She knitted, too, until World War I, when everyone began to knit; then she took up tatting.

Her son John married Sophia White in January 1899; and in March 1911 Frederick married Sarah Sharples. Frederick and Sarah lived, like Mary, at 99 Warren Street. Mary found the couple, neither of them in their first youth, rather too staid for her taste and from time to time pressed them to "move things around." Their little girl Charlotte, when she became conversable, amused her. "She's a funny child," the old lady said. "She talks to me as if I were her age."[2]

By then there were few people her age left for Mary to talk to. After John's death in February 1920, she became dependent, in her independent way and not ungratefully, on Frederick. In her will she left him everything that was hers "in consideration of his unfailing devotion and care for my comfort since the death of his father . . ."[3]

On the morning of April 23, 1921, as she was reading the *Boston Transcript* in her room, without warning and without complaint Mary died. She had lived ninety-one years and lived them with curiosity and zest; and death came to her with the grace of surprise that she had always welcomed in life.

NOTES

FOREWORD

1. Frederick Law Olmsted, *A Journey in the Seaboard Slave States, with Remarks on Their Economy* (New York: Dix & Edwards, 1856), pp. 214–15.
2. *Garden and Forest: A Journal of Horticulture, Landscape Art, and Forestry* 6 (3 May 1893): 192.

CHAPTER I

1. Henry K. Olmsted and George K. Ward, comps., *Genealogy of the Olmsted Family in America Embracing the Descendants of James and Richard Olmsted and Covering a Period of nearly Three Centuries 1632–1912* (New York: A. T. de la Mare, 1912), pp. xv–xviii, 6–7.
2. *Ibid.*, pp. 7–12.
3. *Ibid.*, pp. 12–15.
4. *Ibid.*, pp. 16, 18, 23.
5. *Ibid.*, pp. 23–36, 60; Gideon Olmsted, *Journal of an Intended Voyage from New London to Guadalupe in the Sloop "Sea Flower"* (copy), Laura Wood Roper Files, Washington, D.C. (hereafter cited as LWR Files).
6. Elihu Geer, *Hartford City Directory for the Year Commencing July 18, 1876, with a reprint of the entire Business Directory of Hartford for 1825* (Hartford: privately printed, 1876), pp. 314–19.
7. Edward A. Lawrence, *The Life of Reverend Joel Hawes, D.D.* (Hartford: Hammersley & Co., 1871), p. 55.
8. H. K. Olmsted and G. K. Ward, *Genealogy*, pp. 36, 60.
9. [Mariana Griswold Van Rensselaer], "Sketch of the Life of Frederick Law Olmsted," (unpublished manuscript), LWR Files.
10. Geer, *Hartford Directory*, pp. 314, 320.
11. John Olmsted's Journal 1825–1835, Frederick Law Olmsted Papers, Library of Congress, Washington, D.C. (hereafter cited as JO Jnl.).
12. *The 70th Annual Report of the Officers of the Retreat for the Insane at Hartford, Connecticut* (Hartford: Case, Lockwood and Brainard, 1894), pp. 15, 19, 41; JO Jnl., 1 June 1840.
13. Isaac N. Bolles, *Directory and Guidebook for the City of Hartford, 1844* (Hartford: Republican Courier, 1844), p. 100.
14. *Historic Documents and Notes: Genesis and Development of the Connecticut Historical Society and Associated Institutions in the Wadsworth Atheneum* (Hartford: Connecticut Historical Society, 1889), pp. 32, 48.
15. Frederick Law Olmsted, Jr., and Theodora Kimball, eds., *Forty Years of Landscape Architecture: Frederick Law Olmsted, Senior*, 2 vols. (New York and London: G. P. Putnam's Sons, 1922, 1928), 1: 45.
16. MCO, manuscript fragment, LWR Files.

17. H. K. Olmsted and G. K. Ward, *Genealogy*, p. 60; "Hull Family," manuscript notebook, LWR Files.

18. F. L. Olmsted, Jr., and T. Kimball, *Forty Years*, 1: 46.

19. O, autobiographical fragment, n.d.

20. JO Jnl., March 1826–April 1827.

21. H. K. Olmsted and G. K. Ward, *Genealogy*, p. 60.

22. MAO to JHO, 14 April 1846; JO Jnl., 3 June 1827.

23. F. L. Olmsted, Jr., and T. Kimball, *Forty Years*, 1: 47.

24. *Ibid.*, 1: 54; JO Jnl., 20 April 1828.

25. JO Jnl., July 1828.

26. F. L. Olmsted, Jr., and T. Kimball, *Forty Years*, 1: 46–47.

27. *Ibid.*, 1: 51–52.

28. JO Jnl., 11 August 1828.

29. *Ibid.*, August 1828.

30. MCO, manuscript fragment, LWR Files.

31. F. L. Olmsted, Jr., and T. Kimball, *Forty Years*, 1: 47–48.

32. *Ibid.*, 1: 48.

33. JO Jnl., 9 November 1829–21 May 1836.

34. Edwin Stanley Welles, ed., *Letters of Rev. Dr. Joab Brace 1781–1861* (Newington, Conn.: privately printed, 1942), p. 7.

35. MCO manuscript fragment, LWR Files.

36. F. L. Olmsted, Jr., and T. Kimball, *Forty Years*, 1: 57.

37. *Ibid.*, 1: 56–57.

38. Joab Brace, *Half-Century Discourses: History of the Church in Newington* (Hartford: Ecclesiastical Society, 1855), p. 41.

39. JO Jnl., 21 May 1836.

40. F. L. Olmsted, Jr., and T. Kimball, *Forty Years*, 1: 61; JO Jnl., 1 July 1836–20 November 1837.

41. F. L. Olmsted, Jr., and T. Kimball, *Forty Years*, 1: 61.

42. [Van Rensselaer], "Sketch."

43. F. L. Olmsted, Jr., and T. Kimball, *Forty Years*, 1: 48–50.

44. *Ibid.*, 1: 48–50.

45. *Ibid.*, 1: 59.

46. O to MGVR, 17 February 1893.

47. F. L. Olmsted, Jr., and T. Kimball, *Forty Years*, 1: 60.

48. *Ibid.*, 1: 65.

49. G. Olmsted, *Journal of an Intended Voyage.*

50. O to MGVR, 17 June 1893.

51. *Ibid.*

52. *Ibid.*; F. L. Olmsted, Jr., and T. Kimball, *Forty Years*, 1: 59–60.

53. O to MGVR, 17 June 1893; F. L. Olmsted, Jr., and T. Kimball, *Forty Years*, 1: 56, 61.

54. O to Mrs. William Dwight Whitney, 16 December 1890; *Historic Documents and Notes*, p. 48.

55. JO Jnl., 27 January 1831–19 October 1833.

56. *Ibid.*, 24 October 1837, 1 July 1835.

57. *Ibid.*, 10, 13 January 1834, 9 November 1835, 25 March 1839.

58. *Ibid.*, 20 January 1838, 14 March 1842.

59. [Van Rensselaer], "Sketch"; JO Jnl., 1 January 1827, 22 December 1831, 16 January 1832, 28 November 1836, 6 March 1840.

60. JO Jnl., 8 June 1842.

61. F. L. Olmsted, Jr., and T. Kimball, *Forty Years*, 1: 47.

62. JO Jnl.
63. *Ibid.*, 20 January 1830.
64. *Ibid.*, 28 May–3 June 1832.
65. *Ibid.*, 25 January 1832, 17 August, 10 October 1835, 4 September 1838, 12 July 1839.
66. JO to O, 4 September 1838.
67. JO Jnl., 20 April, 28 May, 10 June 1836.
68. FJK to O, 31 January 1873.
69. JO Jnl., 11 August 1836.
70. *Ibid.*, 18 August–5 September 1834.
71. *Ibid.*, 17 June 1833.
72. *Ibid.*, 14 June 1837.
73. *Ibid.*, 17 June 1837.
74. *Ibid.*, 18–25 August 1838.
75. O to Thomas Hill, 3 November 1875.
76. JO Jnl., 18–25 August, 29 August–4 September 1838.
77. JO to O, 27 September 1838.
78. *Ibid.*, 7 October 1838.
79. JO Jnl., 9–24 December 1839.
80. *National Intelligencer*, 16, 20 December 1839.
81. Constance McLaughlin Green, *Washington, Village and Capital 1800–1878* (Princeton: Princeton University Press, 1962), p. 21.
82. JO Jnl., 9–24 December 1839; *National Intelligencer*, 3, 11, 17 December 1839.
83. *National Intelligencer*, 16, 17, 19, 23 December 1839.
84. JO Jnl., 9–24 December 1839.
85. *Ibid.*, 1 February, 21 February–6 March, 6 April 1840.

CHAPTER II

1. JO Jnl., 9 May 1840.
2. O to JHO, 5 June 1840.
3. *Ibid.*, July 1840.
4. JO Jnl., 18 August 1840, 4 January 1841.
5. *Ibid.*, 3, 16, 23 November 1840, 15–19 January, 1–15 March 1841.
6. O to MAO, 20 March 1841.
7. O to JHO, 29 March 1840.
8. JO Jnl., March 1842.
9. *Ibid.*, 9 March, 18, 31 May, 14 June, 8 August 1842.
10. *Ibid.*, 5, 28 September, 28 October 1842.
11. Emma Brace, ed., *The Life of Charles Loring Brace, Chiefly Told in His Own Letters* (New York: Charles Scribner's Sons, 1894), pp. 9–10.
12. *Dictionary of American Biography*, s.v. "Brace, Charles Loring."
13. Frederick J. Kingsbury, "Charles Loring Brace," *Journal of the American Social Science Association* 27 (October 1890): 50–52.
14. JO Jnl., 28 September 1842.
15. E. Brace, *Brace*, pp. 9–10.
16. O to JHO, 3 October 1842.
17. O to JO, 24 September 1842.
18. Tyler Dennett, *Americans in Eastern Asia: A Critical Study of the Policy of the United States with Reference to China, Japan and Korea in the Nineteenth Century* (New York: Macmillan Company, 1922), pp. 113–26.

19. John Robert Morrison, *A Chinese Commercial Guide, consisting of a collection of details and regulations respecting foreign trade with China*, 2nd ed. (Macao: S. Wells Williams, 1844), p. 84.

20. JO Jnl., 26 October, 27 November 1842; 4 January, 10, 15 February 1843.

21. O to JHO, 11 December 1842.

22. JO Jnl., 18, 22, 27 December 1842; 19 January, 20 February, 5, 6, 27 March 1843.

23. Richard Henry Dana, Jr., *The Seaman's Friend* (Boston: Charles C. Little & James Brown & Benj. Loring & Co., 1841), pp. 158–59.

24. O to JHO, 8 April 1843.

25. *Ibid.*

26. *New York Journal of Commerce*, 23 February 1843.

27. O to JHO, 8 April 1843.

28. *Ibid.*, [9–10 April 1843]; JO Jnl., 14, 20, 26 April, 24 July 1843.

29. JO Jnl., 20–24 April 1843.

30. O, log of voyage, 24 April 1843.

31. *Ibid.*

32. O to JO, 24 September 1843; O to parents, 6 August 1843.

33. O, log of voyage, 24, 27 April 1843.

34. *Ibid.*, 27 April 1843.

35. *Ibid.*, 8 May 1843.

36. O to parents, 6 August 1843.

37. *Ibid.*

38. O to JHO, 10 December 1843.

39. *Ibid.*

40. [Frederick Law Olmsted], "Real China" (fragment copy), n.d., LWR Files.

41. [Frederick Law Olmsted], "A Voice from the Sea," *American Whig Review* 14 (December 1851): 525–35; O to JHO, 10 December 1843.

42. Morrison, *Chinese Commercial Guide*, p. 272; O to JO, 24 September 1843.

43. O to JHO, 8 [October], 10 December 1843.

44. O, log of voyage; O to parents, 6 August 1843.

45. O, log of voyage, 4 July 1843.

46. *Ibid.*, 7–8 July 1843; O to parents, 6 August 1843; O to JHO, 10 December 1843.

47. O to JHO, 10 December 1843; O to parents, 6 August 1843.

48. O, log of voyage, 3 August 1843; O to parents, 6 August 1843; O to JHO, 10 December 1843.

49. O to parents, 6 August 1843, postscript by Dr. Green.

50. O, log of voyage, 8–9 August 1843; O to parents, 6 August 1843; O to parents, 5 September 1843; O to JHO, 10 December 1843.

51. O to JO, 24 September 1843; O to parents, 5 September 1843.

52. *Ibid.*

53. O to JO, 24 September 1843.

54. *Dictionary of National Biography*, s.v. "Morrison, John Robert."

55. Morrison, *Chinese Commercial Guide*, pp. 85–87.

56. Dennett, *Americans in Eastern Asia*, p. 49.

57. Morrison, *Chinese Commercial Guide*, p. 162.

58. Dennett, *Americans in Eastern Asia*, p. 49.

59. Morrison, *Chinese Commercial Guide*, pp. 161–62.

60. Dennett, *Americans in Eastern Asia*, p. 49.

61. O to JO, 24 September 1843.

62. O to Maria Olmsted, Thanksgiving, 1843.

63. [F. L. Olmsted], "Real China."

64. O to JO, 24 September 1843.
65. O to JHO, 8 [October], 10 December 1843.
66. [F. L. Olmsted], "Real China."
67. O to parents, 20 November 1843.
68. George B. Stevens, *Life, Letters and Journals of the Reverend and Honorable Peter Parker, M.D.* (Boston and Chicago: Congregational Sunday-School and Publishing Society, 1896), p. 238.
69. O to parents, 20 November 1843.
70. Morrison, *Chinese Commercial Guide*, p. 89.
71. O to parents, 20 November 1843; Stevens, *Peter Parker*, p. 229.
72. *Dictionary of American Biography*, s.v. "Parker, Peter"; Stevens, *Peter Parker*, pp. 238–39; O to parents, 20 November 1843.
73. O to JHO, 10 December 1843.
74. O to parents, 20 November 1843; O to William James, 8 July 1891.
75. O to parents, 20 November 1843; O to Maria Olmsted, Thanksgiving, 1843.
76. O to Maria Olmsted, Thanksgiving, 1843.
77. JO Jnl., 30 November 1843.
78. O to Maria Olmsted, Thanksgiving, 1843.
79. *Ibid.*
80. [F. L. Olmsted], "Real China."
81. O to JHO, 10 December 1843; O to JO, 3 December 1843; O to Maria Olmsted, Thanksgiving, 1843.
82. O to JHO, 10 December 1843; O to JO, 27 December 1843.
83. O to JO, 27 December 1843.
84. O to JHO, 10 December 1843.
85. O to Maria Olmsted, Thanksgiving, 1843; *New York Journal of Commerce*, 16 April 1844.
86. O to JO, 27 December 1843.
87. O to William James, 8 July 1891 (copy).
88. MCO, undated memo, LWR Files.
89. JO Jnl., 27 January 1844.

CHAPTER III

1. JO Jnl., 23, 30 April 1844.
2. O to JHO, [June] 1844.
3. *Ibid.*, 19 June 1844; JO Jnl., 18–26 July, 19 August 1844; MAO to JO, 8 August 1844.
4. MAO to JO, 8 August 1844.
5. JO Jnl., 30 October 1844; O to JO, 2 February 1845.
6. O to CLB, 25 February 1845.
7. JO Jnl., 1 January, 12 February 1845; O to JHO, "April something," 1845.
8. O to CLB, [June] 1845.
9. O to JHO, 27 May, 18 June 1845.
10. JO Jnl., 28 May, 6 June 1845.
11. O to JO, 10 June 1845.
12. JO Jnl., 20 June 1845.
13. O to CLB, 22 June 1845.
14. O to JHO, 23 June 1845; O to CLB, 22 June 1845.
15. O to JHO, 23 June 1845.
16. JO Jnl., 6, 28 August 1845.
17. *Ibid.*, 13 August 1845; O to FJK, 1 September 1845.

18. JO to O and JHO, 6 October 1845.
19. *Ibid.*, 9 October, 30 December 1845; JO to O, 8 November 1845.
20. JO to O and JHO, 30 December 1845.
21. O to Mrs. William Dwight Whitney, 10 December 1890.
22. O to FJK, [end March] 1846.
23. JO to JHO, 3 February 1846.
24. O to JHO, 3 February 1846; O to CLB, 5 February 1846.
25. JO to JHO, 3 February 1846; O to JHO, 3, 11 February 1846.
26. O to JHO, [16] February 1846.
27. Emma Brace, ed., *The Life of Charles Loring Brace, Chiefly Told in His Own Letters* (New York: Charles Scribner's Sons, 1894), pp. 43–53.
28. O to JHO, 13 March 1846.
29. O to CLB, 22 February 1846; O to JHO, 28 March 1846.
30. JO to JHO, 18 March 1846; MAO to JHO, [March], 1846; O to CLB, [March] 1846.
31. O to JHO, 22 March 1846.
32. O to CLB, [March] 1846.
33. MAO to JHO, 2 April 1846; O to JHO, 3 April 1846.
34. O to JHO, 3 April 1846; MAO to JHO, 3 April 1846; Owen Pitkin Olmsted to JHO, 5 April 1846.
35. MAO to JHO, 7 June 1846.
36. O to CLB, 15 March 1887; O to JHO, 7 April 1846:
37. JO to JHO and O, 6 October 1845; O to JHO, 13 March 1846.
38. JO Jnl., 10 April 1846.
39. O to JHO, 16 April 1846.
40. *Ibid.*
41. [Mariana Griswold Van Rensselaer], "Sketch of the Life of Frederick Law Olmsted," unpublished manuscript, LWR Files, Washington, D.C.
42. George Tatum, "The Beautiful and the Picturesque," *American Quarterly* 3 (Spring 1951): 36–51.
43. [Van Rensselaer], "Sketch."
44. *Dictionary of American Biography*, s.v. "Geddes, James"; *National Cyclopaedia of American Biography*, s.v. "Geddes, George."
45. O to JO and JHO, 4 May 1846; O to JHO, 19 June 1846.
46. O to FJK, 29 April 1846.
47. O to JHO, 11, 19 June 1846; O to JO, 16 June 1846.
48. O to JO, 4 May, 16 June 1846.
49. O to JHO, 26 June, 12 August 1846; O to FJK, 14 July 1846; O to JO, August 12, 1846.
50. O to FJK, 14 July 1846.
51. O to JO, 16 June 1846; O to JHO, 19, 26 June 1846.
52. O to FJK, 15 May 1846; O to JO, 16 June 1846.
53. O to JHO, 19 June 1846.
54. *Ibid.*, 12 August 1846.
55. O to JO, 1 July 1846.
56. O to CLB, 30 July 1846.
57. *Ibid.*, 27 May 1846.
58. JO Jnl., 24 August–11 September 1846.
59. O to JO, 18 September 1846.
60. JO to JHO, 26 July 1846.
61. O to JO, 23 July 1846; O to JHO, 28 September 1846.
62. JO to JHO, 9 November 1846.

CHAPTER IV

1. O to JHO, 26 October 1846; O to CLB, 27 January 1847.
2. MAO to JHO, 12 November 1846.
3. JO to JHO, 7 February 1847.
4. O to JHO, 16 February 1847.
5. O to FJK 19 February 1847; O to JHO, 16 February 1847.
6. O to FJK, 19 February 1847; O to JHO, 23 March 1847; O to CLB, 23 March 1847.
7. JHO to FJK, 12 March 1847.
8. *Ibid.*, [May] 1847.
9. FJK to JHO, 8 May 1847.
10. JO to JHO, 16 February 1847; JHO to FJK, 12 March 1847; JHO to FJK, 18 June 1847.
11. O to JHO, 11 May 1847; JHO to FJK, 18 June 1847.
12. JHO to FJK, 18 June 1847; O to CLB, 26 July 1847; JHO to Clinton Collins, 8 December 1847 (Mrs. Ruth Allan Wolkowska Collection, East Hampton, New York).
13. JHO to FJK, 18 June 1847; O to JHO, 16 February 1847.
14. JO to O and JHO, 8 June 1847.
15. JO Jnl., 12–23 July 1847; JO and JHO to O, 6 July 1847.
16. O to CLB, 26 July 1847; JHO to FJK, 18 June 1847.
17. O to JHO, 9 September 1847.
18. *National Cyclopaedia of American Biography*, s.v. "Bronson, Greene C."; *Dictionary of American Biography*, s.v. "Bushnell, Horace."
19. O to JHO, 9 September 1847.
20. O to CLB, 27 July 1847.
21. *Ibid.*, 20 September 1847; O to FJK, 23 September 1847.
22. JHO to Collins, 8 December 1847 (Wolkowska Coll.).
23. JHO to FJK, 7 October 1847.
24. O to JO, 27 October 1847; O to JHO, 10 November 1847.
25. JO to JHO, 2 November 1847.
26. O to JHO, 9 September, 10 November 1847.
27. Maria Olmsted to JHO, 18 October 1847.
28. JO Jnl., 21 December 1847; JO to O, 16, 18 December 1847.
29. JO Jnl., 27, 28 December 1847.

CHAPTER V

1. Undated clipping from *New York Daily Tribune* in JO Jnl., 1847.
2. O to JHO, 6 March 1848.
3. JO to O and JHO, 29 January 1849.
4. O to CLB, 9 March 1848.
5. Margaret Boyle Cullen, unpublished manuscript (copy), LWR Coll.
6. MCO, undated memo.
7. Frederick Law Olmsted, Jr., and Theodora Kimball, eds., *Forty Years of Landscape Architecture: Frederick Law Olmsted, Senior*, 2 vols. (New York and London: G. P. Putnam's Sons, 1922, 1928), 1: 85–86.
8. *Ibid.*
9. O to JHO, 22 March 1848; MCO, undated memo.
10. O to JO, 9, 20 March 1848; JO Jnl., 13 April 1848.
11. O to JHO, 16 March 1848.
12. FLO (son), interview.

13. MCO, undated memo; O to CLB, 25 March 1848.

14. MCO undated memo.

15. O to JHO, 19 January 1848; O to JO, 24 March 1848.

16. O to CLB, 25 March, 28 May 1848.

17. Emma Brace, ed., *The Life of Charles Loring Brace, Chiefly Told in His Own Letters* (New York: Charles Scribner's Sons, 1894), pp. 61–62; O to CLB, 7 January 1849.

18. JO Jnl., 18 July 1848.

19. Fanny Olmsted to JHO, 8 September 1848.

20. MCO, undated memo.

21. O to JHO, 16 March 1848.

22. O to JO, 25 September 1848.

23. JO to JHO, 20 October 1848.

24. O to JHO, 19 January 1848.

25. JO to JHO, 15 September, 11 October 1848.

26. JHO to FJK, 30 October 1848; JO Jnl., 30 October, 21 December 1848; O to JHO, 6 January 1849.

27. JO Jnl., 6 February 1849; O to JHO, 10 February 1849.

28. JHO to FJK, 10 February 1849.

29. *Ibid.*, 16 March 1849; JO Jnl., 8 May 1849.

30. JO Jnl., 16 July–8 September 1849; JHO to FJK, 7 July 1849.

31. JHO to FJK, 16 August 1849.

32. O to FJK, [31 August 1849]; JO Jnl., 11 September 1849; Maria Olmsted to Mary Olmsted, 30 September 1849.

33. O to JO, 7 November 1849.

34. *Ibid.*, 3 October, 17 November 1849.

35. *Ibid.*, 17, 21 November 1849.

36. JHO to FJK, 6 October 1849; O to JO, 7 November 1849; JHO to FJK, 9 January 1850.

37. O to JO, 4 January 1850.

38. *Ibid.*, 12 December 1849, 26 January 1850.

39. [Frederick Law Olmsted], "Appeal to the Citizens of Staten Island," [1850].

40. O to JO, 7 November 1849.

41. JHO to FJK, 9 January 1850.

42. *Ibid.*, 6 October, 24 November 1849, 9 January 1850.

43. O to JO, 29 February 1850.

44. *Ibid.*

45. *Ibid.*

46. *Ibid.*, 10 March 1850; JHO to FJK, 16 March 1850.

47. JHO to FJK, 16 March 1850.

48. O to JO, 29 February, 14, 17 March 1850.

49. JO Jnl., April 1850; [Frederick Law Olmsted], *Walks and Talks of an American Farmer in England*, 2 vols. (New York: G. P. Putnam, 1852), 1: 6.

CHAPTER VI

1. JHO to Bertha Olmsted, 27 April 1850.

2. [Frederick Law Olmsted], *Walks and Talks of an American Farmer in England*, 2 vols. (New York: G. P. Putnam, 1852), 1: 10–13.

3. JHO to Bertha Olmsted, 27 April 1850.

4. [F. L. Olmsted], *Walks and Talks*, 1: 11–46.

5. *Ibid.*, pp. 41–46.

6. *Ibid.*, pp. 46–49.

7. O to JO, 11 August 1850.

8. [F. L. Olmsted], *Walks and Talks*, 2: 30.

9. *Ibid.*, 1: 99.

10. *Ibid.*, 1: 217–21; 2: 48.

11. *Ibid.*, 1: 213–14.

12. *Ibid.*, 2: 103.

13. *Ibid.*, 2: 104–6.

14. *Ibid.*, 1: 71.

15. *Ibid.*, 2: 53–63.

16. *Ibid.*, 2: 189–92.

17. *Ibid.*, 2: 88–91.

18. W. G. Hoskins, "The Anatomy of the English Countryside: the Road between," *Listener*, 13 (May 1954): 819–21.

19. Frederick Law Olmsted, *Walks and Talks of an American Farmer in England* Columbus, Ohio: Jos. H. Riley and Co., 1859), pp. 263–64.

20. [F. L. Olmsted], *Walks and Talks*, 2: 154.

21. *Ibid.*, 2: 67.

22. *Ibid.*, 1: 133.

23. Dorothy Stroud, *Capability Brown* (London: Country Life Limited, 1950), pp. 124, 173–74.

24. JHO to Mary Olmsted, 4–5 July 1850.

25. *Ibid.*

26. *Ibid.*

27. *Ibid.*

28. *Ibid.*

29. *Ibid.*

30. Jane Loring Gray, ed., *Letters of Asa Gray*, 2 vols. (Boston: Houghton Mifflin and Co., 1893), 2: 371.

31. O to Andrew Jackson Downing, 23 November 1850 (copy), LWR Coll.

32. JHO to Mary Olmsted, 4–5 July 1850.

33. "F" [Frederick Law Olmsted], "The House of Commons: A Ministerial Crisis Night," *Hartford Daily Courant*, 25 July 1850.

34. *Times* (London), 29 June, 1 July 1850.

35. *Hartford Daily Courant*, 25 July 1850.

36. *Times* (London), 1 July 1850.

37. *Hartford Daily Courant*, 25 July 1850.

38. *Ibid.*

39. JHO to Mary Olmsted, 4–5 July 1850.

40. *Ibid.*

41. O to Downing, 23 November 1850.

42. O to JO, 11 August 1850.

43. *Ibid.*

44. *Ibid.*

45. Edmund Berks to JHO, 11 August 1850.

46. JHO to Mary Olmsted, 9 September 1850.

47. Emma Brace, ed., *The Life of Charles Loring Brace, Chiefly Told in His Own Letters* (New York: Charles Scribner's Sons, 1894), pp. 90, 197.

48. JHO to FJK, October 1850.

49. *New York Daily Tribune*, 24 October 1850.

50. JHO to FJK, October 1850.

51. *New York Daily Tribune*, 24 October 1850.

52. JHO to FJK, October 1850.

CHAPTER VII

1. JHO to JO, October 1850.
2. O to CLB, 11 January 1850.
3. *Ibid.*
4. JHO to FJK, 1 December 1850.
5. O to FJK, 21 December 1850.
6. O to CLB, 12 November 1850.
7. O to FJK, 21 December 1850; Emma Brace, ed., *The Life of Charles Loring Brace, Chiefly Told in His Own Letters* (New York: Charles Scribner's Sons, 1894), pp. 103, 112–13.
8. O to CLB, 11 January 1851; JHO to FJK, 28 January, 10 March 1851.
9. E. Brace, *Brace*, p. 141.
10. O to FJK, 5 August 1851.
11. *Ibid.*, 21 December 1850.
12. O to CLB, 8 April 1851; O to FJK, 5 August 1851.
13. JHO to FJK, 12 September 1851; O to CLB, 27 May 1851; JHO to FJK, 11 August 1851.
14. JHO to FJK, 11 August 1851.
15. O to FJK, 5 August 1851.
16. JHO to FJK, 12 September 1851.
17. JO to Sophie Hitchcock, 28 October 1851, Letters of Mrs. Page, Archives of American Art, Detroit, Michigan.
18. JO Jnl., 15, 24 October 1851.
19. O to JO, 21 November 1851, with postscript by Maria Olmsted; O to JO, 26 November 1851.
20. *New York Daily Tribune*, 5 December 1851.
21. O to JO, 8 December 1851.
22. *New York Daily Tribune*, 6 December 1851.
23. O to JO, 4 December 1851.
24. [Frederick Law Olmsted], "A Voice From the Sea," *American Whig Review* 14: (December 1851): 525–35.
25. O to George Palmer Putnam, 6 November 1851, New York Public Library.
26. Advertisement printed inside back cover of *Walks and Talks of an American Farmer in England* (New York: G. P. Putnam, 1852), vol. 1.
27. O to JO, 17 January 1851.
28. *Horticulturist* 7 (March 1852): 135–41; *American Whig Review* 15 (March 1852): 282; O to JO, 24 February 1852.
29. George Haven Putnam, *A Memoir of George Palmer Putnam, Together with a Record of the Publishing House Founded by Him*, 2 vols. (New York and London: G. P. Putnam's Sons, 1903), 1: 248–49, 361; O to JO, 19 May 1852.
30. O to FJK, 17 October 1852.
31. O to Letitia Brace, 22 January 1892.
32. *New York Daily Times*, 13 February 1853.
33. [Frederick Law Olmsted], *Walks and Talks*, 2: 106.
34. O to JO, 12 August 1846.
35. O to JHO, 5 June 1840; [F. L. Olmsted], *Walks and Talks*, 2: 106.
36. [F. L. Olmsted], *Walks and Talks*, 2: 104–5.

CHAPTER VIII

1. JO Jnl., 11 December 1852, 6 April 1853.
2. "Yeoman" [F. L. Olmsted], *New York Daily Times*, 19 February 1853.

3. *Ibid.*, 13 February 1854.

4. *Ibid.*, 10 March, 13 August 1853.

5. *Ibid.*, 30 June 1853.

6. *Ibid.*, 13 August 1853.

7. *Ibid.*, 13 February 1854.

8. *Ibid.*, 30 March 1853, 26 January 1854.

9. *Ibid.*, 12, 26 January 1854.

10. *Ibid.*, 21, 30 June, 21 July 1853.

11. *Ibid.*, 30 March, 28 April 1853; 26 January, 25 February 1854.

12. *Ibid.*, 12 January 1854.

13. *Ibid.*, 13 February 1854.

14. Laura Wood Roper, "Frederick Law Olmsted in the 'Literary Republic,'" *Mississippi Historical Review* 39 (December 1952): 462.

15. *Ibid.*, p. 463.

16. *Ibid.*, p. 463.

17. *Ibid.*, pp. 463–64.

18. *Ibid.*, pp. 464–65.

19. *Ibid.*, p. 465.

20. O to JO, [spring, 1853]; 18, 19, 26 May 1853.

21. O to JO, 16 June 1853; JO Jnl., 30 September 1852.

22. Frederick Law Olmsted, *A Journey through Texas; or, a Saddle-Trip on the Southwestern Frontier; with a Statistical Appendix* (New York: Dix, Edwards and Co., 1857), preface, note by the editor.

23. *Ibid.*, pp. 1–11, 17–18.

24. "Yeoman," *New York Daily Times*, 12 January 1854.

25. O to CLB and Charles W. Elliott, 1 December 1854.

26. *Ibid.*

27. "Yeoman," "The Nebraska Question in Texas," *New York Daily Times*, 13 May 1854.

28. "Yeoman," *New York Daily Times*, 21 March 1854; F. L. Olmsted, *A Journey through Texas*, p. 132.

29. F. L. Olmsted, *A Journey through Texas*, pp. 172–77. For further data on the German settlements in Texas, see Rudolf Leopold Biesele, *History of the German Settlements in Texas, 1831–1861* (Austin: Press of Von Boeckmann-Jones, 1930); Albert Bernhardt Faust, *The German Element in the United States, with Special Reference to Its Political, Moral, Social and Educational Influence*, 2 vols. (Boston and New York: Houghton Mifflin Co., 1907); and Moritz Tiling, *History of the German Element in Texas from 1820 to 1850* (Houston: privately printed, 1913).

30. F. L. Olmsted, *A Journey through Texas*, p. 132.

31. *Ibid.*, pp. 142–46.

32. *New York Daily Times*, 3 March 1854.

33. Laura Wood Roper, "Frederick Law Olmsted and the Western Texas Free-Soil Movement," *American Historical Review* 56 (October 1950): 58–64.

34. O or JHO, "A Few Dollars Wanted To Help the Cause of Future Freedom in Texas," [October 1854]; Selma Metzenthin Raunick, "A Survey of German Literature in Texas," *Southwestern Historical Quarterly* 33 (October 1929): 150.

35. F. L. Olmsted, *A Journey through Texas*, p. 133.

36. *Ibid.*, p. 167; JO, [Appeal for money for Douai], 4 October 1854, Mrs. Ruth Allan Wolkowska Collection, East Hampton, New York.

37. Biesele, *German Settlements in Texas*, p. 171; Tiling, *German Element in Texas*, p. 122; Schem's *Conversations-lexicon*, s.v. "Degener, Edward."

38. F. L. Olmsted, *A Journey through Texas*, pp. 196–99.

39. *Ibid.*, pp. 271, 303.

40. *Ibid.*, p. 325.
41. *Ibid.*, pp. 45–46, 379, 407.

CHAPTER IX

1. JHO to O, 13, 15 June, 3 July 1854.
2. JO Jnl., 1 August–2 September 1854.
3. *New York Daily Times*, 11, 13 October 1854.
4. *Ibid.*, 20, 21 October 1854.
5. *Ibid.*, 24 October 1854.
6. *Ibid.*, 28 March 1854.
7. Frederick Law Olmsted, "Work and Wages," *New York Daily Times*, 3 February 1855.
8. *Ibid.*
9. O to JO, [?] February 1855.
10. F. L. Olmsted, "Labor," *New York Daily Times*, 19 February 1855.
11. Adolf Douai to JHO, 4 September 1854.
12. JHO to JO, 31 October 1854.
13. Charles N. Riotte to O and JHO, 14 October 1854.
14. "Outrages in Texas Other Than Indian," *New York Daily Times*, 12 January 1855; "Emigrants and Texas," *New York Daily Times*, 19 January 1855; Friedrich Kapp, *Die Sklavenfrage in den Vereinigten Staaten* (New York: L. W. Schmidt, 1854), reviewed in *New York Daily Times*, 15 January 1855.
15. *New York Daily Tribune*, 20 January 1855.
16. Edward Degener to JHO, 2 November 1854.
17. "York" [F. L. Olmsted], "Correspondence of the S. A. Z.," *San Antonio Zeitung*, 23 December 1854; Douai to O and JHO, 10 December 1854; JHO to JO, 28 January 1855.
18. Laura Wood Roper, "Frederick Law Olmsted and the Western Texas Free-Soil Movement," *American Historical Review* 56 (October 1950): 60.
19. Douai to O, 4, 26 August 1855.
20. Riotte to O, 19 August, 23 October 1855.
21. O to Edward Everett Hale, 23 August 1855, 17 January 1856, New England Emigrant Aid Co. Papers, Kansas Historical Society, Topeka; *New York Daily Times*, 31 January 1856; Riotte to O, 25 January 1856; JHO to O, 4 May 1856.
22. Kansas State Historical Society, "Selections from the Hyatt Manuscripts," *Transactions*, vols. 1 and 2 (Topeka: George W. Martin, Kansas Publishing House, 1881), p. 221.
23. *Ibid.*, p. 223.
24. *Ibid.*
25. *Topeka Daily Capital*, 8 January 1884.
26. Kansas State Historical Society, "Hyatt Manuscripts," p. 224.
27. *Ibid.*, p. 224.
28. *Ibid.*
29. *Topeka Daily Capital*, 8 January 1884.
30. Kansas State Historical Society, "Hyatt Manuscripts," pp. 215–16.
31. O to JHO, 31 December 1854.
32. *Ibid.*, [?] February, 11 July 1855.
33. O to JO, 31 December 1854.
34. JHO to JO, 17 December 1854.
35. O to JO, [?] February 1855, 7 November 1854; JHO to JO, 5 December 1854.
36. JHO to Bertha Olmsted, 28 January 1855.
37. JHO to JO, 9 March 1855.

38. *Ibid.*, 9, 19 March 1855.
39. *Ibid.*, 20 March 1855.
40. JHO to Bertha Olmsted, 6 May 1855.

CHAPTER X

1. JHO to Bertha Olmsted, 6 May 1855.
2. George Palmer Putnam to Arthur T. Edwards, 1 February 1855, Dix & Edwards Papers, Houghton Library, Harvard University, Cambridge, Massachusetts.
3. JHO to Bertha Olmsted, 6 May 1855.
4. *Ibid.*
5. Memo of Agreement between Dix & Edwards and Frederick Law Olmsted, 2 April 1855.
6. JHO to JO, 9 March 1855.
7. O to JO, 13 March 1855.
8. JHO to Bertha Olmsted, 6 May 1855.
9. Laura Wood Roper, " 'Mr. Law' and *Putnam's Monthly Magazine*: A Note on a Phase in the Career of Frederick Law Olmsted," *American Literature* 26 (March 1954): 88–93.
10. *Ibid.*, p. 90.
11. *Ibid.*, p. 92.
12. Copy of lease, 6 April 1855.
13. Memo of Agreement between Dix & Edwards and Frederick Law Olmsted, 2 April 1855.
14. O to JO, 13 April 1855.
15. *Ibid.*, 27 April 1855.
16. *Ibid.*, 23 November 1855.
17. O to FLO (son), 15 August 1891.
18. O to JO, 13 March, 7 July 1855.
19. Edwards to O, 6 August 1855; O to Edwards, 7 August 1855.
20. O to JHO, 19 August 1855, Dix & Edwards Papers.
21. O to JO, 28 May, 8 November 1855.
22. *Ibid.*, 28 May 1855.
23. *Ibid.*, 7, 13 July, 8 November 1855.
24. *Ibid.*, 8, 23 November 1855.
25. Laura Wood Roper, "Frederick Law Olmsted in the 'Literary Republic,' " *Mississippi Valley Historical Review* 39 (December 1952): 469.
26. *Ibid.*, pp. 469–72.
27. *Ibid.*, p. 473.
28. JHO to Bertha Olmsted, 7 February 1856.
29. O to Bertha Olmsted, 19 July 1856.
30. "Yeoman" [F. L. Olmsted], "Perilous Voyage of the 'Arabia,' " *New York Daily Times*, 17 March 1856.
31. O to JHO, 11 March 1856.
32. O to Dix & Edwards, 19 March 1856.
33. Document signed "James Buchanan," 12 March 1856.
34. O to JO, [before 27 March 1856], 27 March 1856.
35. JHO to O, 28 May 1856.
36. O to JO, 23 May 1856; JO Jnl., 1 July 1856.
37. O to JO, 27 March 1856.
38. *Ibid.*, [before 27 March 1856]; O to Dix & Edwards, 19 March 1856; O to JO, 27 March 1856.

39. O to Charles Eliot, 4 March 1886.

40. O to JO, 23 May 1856; O to Dix & Edwards, 3 August 1856, Dix & Edwards Papers.

41. *New York Daily Times*, 10 July 1856.

42. Roper, "Olmsted in the 'Literary Republic,'" pp. 472–73.

43. O to Bertha Olmsted and Mary Olmsted, 19 July 1856; O to Dix & Edwards, 19 March 1856.

44. Bayard Taylor, "Writers for *Punch*," *At Home and Abroad*, 2nd ser. (New York: G. P. Putnam, 1862), pp. 416–21.

45. O to Dix & Edwards, 3 August 1856, Dix & Edwards Papers.

46. FLO (son), interview.

47. JO to JHO, 21 July, 1 August 1856; JO to Owen Pitkin Olmsted, 19 August 1856.

48. J. A. Dix to O., [rec'd 4 September 1856].

49. JHO to O, 20 April 1856.

50. Edwards to O, 30 April 1856; JHO to O, 4 May 1856.

51. Edwards to O, 4 May 1856.

52. *Ibid.*, 16 May, 17 June 1856; JHO to JO, 19 June 1856.

53. O to Dix, 3 August 1856, Dix & Edwards Papers.

54. JHO to O, 10 July 1856.

55. *Ibid.*, 27 July 1856.

56. Dix to O, 29 July 1856; O to JHO, 19 August 1856, Dix & Edwards Papers.

57. Dix to O, 6 August 1856.

58. O to Dix, 29 August 1856, Dix & Edwards Papers.

59. Dix to O, [rec'd 4 September 1856].

60. Edwards to O, 8 August 1856.

61. O to Dix, 4–5 September 1856, Dix & Edwards Papers.

62. *Ibid.*

63. Rollo Ogden, ed., *The Life and Letters of Edwin Lawrence Godkin*, 2 vols. (New York: Macmillan Co., 1907), 1: 112–14, 170.

64. O to his partners, 27 October 1856, Dix & Edwards Papers.

65. O to Edwards (draft), 25 December 1856.

66. O to JO, 7–17 February 1857; O memo, 10 February 1857.

67. O to JO, 7–17 February 1857; *New York Daily Times*, 10 June 1857.

68. JHO to Owen Pitkin Olmsted, 6 January 1857; O to Owen Pitkin Olmsted, 3 January 1857; Power of Attorney, 5 January 1857; JO Jnl., 8 January 1857.

69. O to Hale, 10 January 1857, New England Emigrant Aid Co. Papers, Kansas State Historical Society, Topeka, Kansas.

70. Frederick Law Olmsted, *A Journey through Texas; or, a Saddle-Trip on the Southwestern Frontier; with a Statistical Appendix* (New York: Dix, Edwards & Co., 1857), preface.

71. Laura Wood Roper, "Frederick Law Olmsted and the Western Texas Free-Soil Movement," *American Historical Review* 56 (October 1950): pp. 61–64.

72. Roper, "Olmsted in the 'Literary Republic,'" pp. 473–76.

73. O to JHO, 16 February 1857.

74. O to JO, 7–17 February 1857.

75. *Ibid.*; O to JHO, 16 February 1857; O memo, 10 February 1857.

76. Roper, "'Mr. Law' and *Putnam's*," p. 93.

77. GWC to CEN, 19 August 1857, George W. Curtis Papers, Houghton Library, Harvard University, Cambridge, Massachusetts.

78. O to JO, 7–17 February 1857.

79. *New York Daily Times*, 19 January 1857.

80. Roper, "'Mr. Law' and *Putnam's*," p. 92.

81. GWC to O, 6, 18 August 1857.
82. JHO to O, 6 July 1857; *New York Daily Times*, 13 July 1857.
83. JHO to O, 18 January, 15 February, 6 July, 11 August 1857.

CHAPTER XI

1. Frederick Law Olmsted, Jr., and Theodora Kimball, eds., *Forty Years of Landscape Architecture: Frederick Law Olmsted, Senior*, 2 vols. (New York and London: G. P. Putnam's Sons, 1922, 1928), 2: 34–35.
2. *Ibid.*, pp. 3–17.
3. *Ibid.*, p. 14.
4. *Ibid.*, pp. 18–24.
5. *Ibid.*, pp. 24–28.
6. *Ibid.*, pp. 28–29.
7. *Ibid.*, p. 30.
8. *Ibid.*, pp. 31–32, 32n.
9. *Ibid.*, pp. 32–33.
10. *New York Daily Times*, 3 March 1857.
11. F. L. Olmsted, Jr., and T. Kimball, *Forty Years*, 2: 32–33.
12. O to JHO, 11 September 1857.
13. Asa Gray to president, board of commissioners of Central Park, 24 August 1857; James Hamilton petition, September 1857; petition of president, board of commissioners of the New York Park, 24 September 1857; O to Commissioners of Central Park, 12 August 1857.
14. O to JHO, 11 September 1857.
15. F. L. Olmsted, Jr., and T. Kimball, *Forty Years*, 2: 36.
16. O to JHO, 11 September 1857.
17. F. L. Olmsted, Jr., and T. Kimball, *Forty Years*, 2: 38–40.
18. O to JO, 9 October 1857.
19. *New York Times*, 6, 17, 21, 25 November 1857.
20. *New York Evening Post*, 15 August 1857; *New York Daily Times*, 17 August 1857.
21. O to JO, 9 October 1857.
22. *Ibid.*
23. JHO to O, 11 August 1857.
24. JO to O, 27–28 September 1857.
25. JHO to JO, 15, 16 September, 8 October 1857.
26. *Ibid.*, 19 October 1857.
27. MCO to JO, 8 November 1857.
28. JHO to O, 13 November 1857.
29. JO to Mary Olmsted, 24 November 1857; JO to O, 28 November 1857.

CHAPTER XII

1. Anonymous, "Calvert Vaux, Designer of Parks," *Park International* 1 (September 1920): 139–43.
2. CV, memo, November 1894, Marion Vaux Hendrickson Collection, New York, N.Y.
3. *Ibid.*
4. *Ibid.*
5. JHO to O, 4 May 1856.
6. CV, memo, November 1894, Marion Vaux Hendrickson Collection.

7. Frederick Law Olmsted, Jr., and Theodora Kimball, eds. *Forty Years of Landscape Architecture: Frederick Law Olmsted, Senior*, 2 vols. (New York and London: G. P. Putnam's Sons, 1922, 1928), 2: 42.

8. O to JO, 14 January 1858.

9. Board of Commissioners of Central Park, *Documents for the Year Ending April 30, 1858* (New York: Wm. C. Bryant & Co., 1858), doc. 8, 11 September 1857.

10. *Ibid.*

11. CV, memo., November 1894, Marion Vaux Hendrickson Collection; F. L. Olmsted, Jr., and T. Kimball, *Forty Years*, 2: 43.

12. *New York Times*, 21 April 1858.

13. *Ibid.*, 23 March 1858.

14. *Ibid.*, 21 April 1858.

15. *Ibid.*, 30 April 1858.

16. F. L. Olmsted, Jr., and T. Kimball, *Forty Years*, 2: 214–32.

17. Board of Commissioners of Central Park, *Minutes of Proceedings for the Year Ending April 30, 1859* (New York: Wm. C. Bryant & Co., 1859), pp. 26–34.

18. F. L. Olmsted, Jr., and T. Kimball, *Forty Years*, 2: 554–55.

19. Robert J. Dillon and August Belmont, "A Card to the Public," *New York Times*, 7 June 1858; *New York Times*, 8, 10 June 1858.

20. *New York Times*, 14 December 1857.

21. *New York Daily Tribune*, 8 June 1858.

22. F. L. Olmsted, Jr., and T. Kimball, *Forty Years*, 2: 42.

23. *Ibid.*, 2: 51–52.

24. *New York Times*, 11 November 1858.

25. Charles W. Elliott to O, 6 June 1859.

26. O to Parke Godwin, 1 August 1858.

27. *New York Times*, 6, 7, 17, 18 August 1858.

28. *Ibid.*, 2, 3 September 1858.

29. *Ibid.*, 6, 21 September, 3 November 1858.

30. George Templeton Strong, *The Diary of George Templeton Strong*, ed. Allan Nevins and Milton Halsey Thomas, 4 vols. (New York: Macmillan Company, 1952), 2: 412.

31. GEW to O, 12 April 1858; Indenture, MCO and Andrew Hadley, 17 March 1860.

32. Lease, 5 October 1858.

33. F. L. Olmsted, Jr., and T. Kimball, *Forty Years*, 1: 7.

CHAPTER XIII

1. Andrew Jackson Downing, *A Treatise on the Theory and Practice of Landscape Gardening Adapted to North America* . . . , 8th ed., enlarged revised and newly illustrated, with a supplement by Henry Winthrop Sargent (New York: O. Judd & Co., 1859), pp. 24–25.

2. J. E. Spingarn, "Henry Winthrop Sargent and the Early History of Landscape Gardening and Ornamental Horticulture in Dutchess County, New York," *Year Book, Dutchess County Historical Society*, 1937 (n.p.), p. 39.

3. Downing, *Landscape Gardening*, p. 25.

4. Frederick Law Olmsted, Jr., and Theodora Kimball, eds., *Forty Years of Landscape Architecture: Frederick Law Olmsted, Senior*, 2 vols. (New York and London: G. P. Putnam's Sons, 1922, 1928), 1: 123–24.

5. *Ibid.*, p. 124.

6. Downing, *Landscape Gardening*, p. 34.

7. *Ibid.*, p. 427.

8. O to Parke Godwin, 1 August 1858.

9. F. L. Olmsted, Jr., and T. Kimball, *Forty Years*, 2: 65–66.

10. *Ibid.*, 1: 125.

11. O to JO, 6 February, 22 July 1860; D. J. Brown to O, 9 March 1861.

12. O to CLB, 8 December 1860.

13. *Ibid.*

14. F. L. Olmsted, Jr., and T. Kimball, *Forty Years*, 2: 58–61.

15. John Foord, *The Life and Public Services of Andrew Haswell Green* (Garden City, N.Y.: Doubleday, Page & Co., 1913), p. 43.

16. *Dictionary of American Biography*, s.v. "Green, Andrew Haswell."

17. George Mazaraki, "The Public Career of Andrew Haswell Green" (Ph.D. dissertation, New York University, 1966), p. 10.

18. AHG to O, 9 August 1859.

19. O to JO, 23 September 1859.

20. *Ibid.*

21. CV to O, 29 September 1859.

22. AHG to O, 1 October 1859.

23. O to MCO, 6 October 1859.

24. F. L. Olmsted, Jr., and T. Kimball, *Forty Years*, 2: 54–56.

25. Sarah Agnes Wallace and Frances Elma Gillespie, eds., *The Journal of Benjamin Moran, 1857–1865*, 2 vols. (Chicago: University of Chicago Press, 1948–49), p. 598.

26. F. L. Olmsted, Jr., and T. Kimball, *Forty Years*, 2: 55–56.

27. *Ibid.*, pp. 56–57.

28. AHG to O, 21 October 1859.

29. A. J. Dallas to O, 3, 11 October 1859; MCO to O, 10 October 1859.

30. GEW to O, 17 October 1859.

31. MCO to O, 10, 18 October 1859.

32. O to JO, 23 September 1859, 6 February 1860; MCO to O, 2 October 1859.

33. Charges and Specifications preferred by Thomas Hogg and others against Central Park Commission (n.d.) (copy), LWR Files; F. L. Olmsted, Jr., and T. Kimball, *Forty Years*, 2: 62; O to JO, 12 March 1860.

34. AHG to O, 10 February, 26 July 1860.

35. O to AHG, 21, 28 December 1860.

36. William Emerson to MCO, 12 June, 25 July 1860.

37. F. G. Shaw to O, 22 May 1860; Contract between Mason Brothers and Shaw, 22 May 1860.

38. O to JO, 14 June 1860.

39. FLO (son), interview; O to Mrs. William Dwight Whitney, 16 December 1890.

40. O to JO, 21 October 1860.

41. JO Jnl., 14 August 1860.

42. FLO (son), interview.

43. O to JO, 21 October 1860.

44. O to MCO, 14 November 1860.

45. O to JO, 15 November 1860.

46. HWB to O, 3 November 1860.

47. O to James T. Fields, 21 October 1860, Fields Papers, Huntington Library, San Marino, California.

48. O to HWB, 30 October 1860, Bellows Papers, Massachusetts Historical Society, Boston, Massachusetts.

49. HWB to O, 3 November 1860.

50. *Ibid.*
51. Laura Wood Roper, "Frederick Law Olmsted in the 'Literary Republic,'" *Mississippi Valley Historical Review* 39 (December 1952): 479.
52. *Ibid.*, pp. 459, 478–79.
53. *Ibid.*, pp. 478–79.
54. O to CLB, 8 December 1860.
55. Preston King to O, 28 January 1861.
56. George Templeton Strong, *The Diary of George Templeton Strong*, ed. Allan Nevins and Milton Halsey Thomas, 4 vols. (New York: Macmillan Company, 1952), 89, 90, 90n; William M. Browne to O, 14 June, 10 December 1860.
57. Roper, "Olmsted in the 'Literary Republic,'" pp. 479–80.
58. John Bigelow, *Retrospections of an Active Life*, 5 vols. (New York: Baker & Taylor Co., 1909–13), 1: 325–26.
59. *Ibid.*, pp. 340–44.
60. *Ibid.*
61. *Ibid.*
62. O to Board of Commissioners of Central Park, 22 January 1861 (draft).
63. Bigelow, *Retrospections*, 1: 340–44.
64. O to JO, 22 March 1861.
65. Board of Commissioners of Central Park, *Fourth Annual Report, January 1861* (New York: Wm. C. Bryant & Co., 1861), pp. 61–105.
66. O to Board of Commissioners of Central Park, 22 January 1861 (draft).
67. Bigelow, *Retrospections*, 1: 340–44.

CHAPTER XIV

1. MCO to JO, 22 March 1861.
2. Frederick Law Olmsted, *The Cotton Kingdom: A Traveller's Observations on Cotton and Slavery in the American Slave States*, 2 vols. (New York and London: Mason Brothers and Sampson Low, Son & Co., 1861), 1: 4.
3. John Delane to O, 21 February 1861.
4. William H. Russell, *My Diary North and South* (Boston: T. O. H. P. Burnham, 1863), pp. 19–28.
5. *Ibid.*, p. 66.
6. F. L. Olmsted, *Cotton Kingdom*, 1: 8n.
7. George Templeton Strong, *The Diary of George Templeton Strong*, ed. Allan Nevins and Milton Halsey Thomas, 4 vols. (New York: Macmillan Co., 1952), 3: 114–16.
8. W. H. Russell to O, 11 April 1861.
9. Strong, *Diary*, 3: 123–27.
10. Alfred Field to Lottie Field, 14 May 1861, Errington Letters (copies), LWR Files.
11. O to JO, 17 April 1861.
12. Sampson Low, Son & Co. to O, 29 June 1861.
13. HWB to O, 29 April 1861.
14. O to HWB, 1 June 1861, Bellows Papers, Massachusetts Historical Society, Boston, Massachusetts.
15. Charles J. Stillé, *History of the United States Sanitary Commission, Being the General Report of Its Work during the War of the Rebellion* (Philadelphia: J. B. Lippincott & Co., 1866), p. 33.
16. William Quentin Maxwell, *Lincoln's Fifth Wheel: The Political History of the United States Sanitary Commission* (New York: Longmans, Green & Co., 1956), p. 5.
17. *Ibid.*, pp. 2–3; Stillé, *Sanitary Commission*, p. 46.

18. Maxwell, *Lincoln's Fifth Wheel*, p. 4.

19. *Ibid.*, p. 6.

20. Stillé, *Sanitary Commission*, pp. 48–50, 58.

21. *Ibid.*, p. 58.

22. *Ibid.*, p. 53.

23. *The Sanitary Commission of the United States Army: A Succinct Narrative of Its Works and Purposes* (New York: published for the benefit of the United States Sanitary Commission, 1864), pp. 3–6.

24. Stillé, *Sanitary Commission*, p. 59.

25. Maxwell, *Lincoln's Fifth Wheel*, p. 8.

26. Oliver Otis Howard, *Autobiography*, 2 vols. (New York: Baker & Taylor, 1907), 2: 168–69.

27. O to HWB, 1 June 1861, Bellows Papers.

28. HWB to O, 5 June 1861.

29. GEW to O, 31 October 1861.

30. A. J. Dallas to O, 22 April, 5 May 1861.

31. GEW to O, 13 May 1861.

32. O to JO, 26 June 1861.

33. Strong, *Diary*, 3: 159–62.

34. O to JO, 26 June 1861; O to MCO, 2 July 1861.

35. MCO to O, 4 August 1861.

36. O to MCO, 28 June 1861.

37. Maxwell, *Lincoln's Fifth Wheel*, pp. 14–15.

38. Russell, *Diary*, p. 67.

39. O to MCO, 28 June 1861.

40. Pass, signed Drake DeKaye, 28 June 1861.

41. O to MCO, 28 June 1861.

42. [Frederick Law Olmsted], Report of a Preliminary Survey of the Camps of a Portion of the Volunteer Forces near Washington [Washington, 1861], United States Sanitary Commission Doc. 17.

43. O to MCO, 2 July 1861.

44. *Ibid.*

45. Russell, *Diary*, pp. 395, 403–4.

46. *Ibid.*, pp. 390–91; O to MCO, 9 July 1861.

47. O to MCO, 2 July 1861.

48. Strong, *Diary*, 3: 164–65.

49. O to HWB, 14 July 1861, United States Sanitary Commission Papers, Public Library, New York, N. Y.

50. HWB to O, 18 July 1861, United States Sanitary Commission Papers.

CHAPTER XV

1. George Templeton Strong, *The Diary of George Templeton Strong*, ed. Allan Nevins and Milton Halsey Thomas, 4 vols. (New York: Macmillan Co., 1952), 3: 170.

2. Charles J. Stillé, *History of the United States Sanitary Commission, Being the General Report of Its Work during the War of the Rebellion* (Philadelphia; J. B. Lippincott & Co., 1866), p. 91; O to MCO, 29 July 1861.

3. O to JO, 3 August 1861.

4. Stillé, *Sanitary Commission*, pp. 88–89.

5. O to MCO, 29 July 1861.

6. *The Sanitary Commission of the United States Army: A Succinct Narrative of Its Works and Purposes* (New York: published for the benefit of the United States Sanitary Commission, 1864), p. 14.

7. O to JO, 3 August 1861.

8. *Ibid.*

9. O to HWB, 9 August 1861, United States Sanitary Commission Papers, Public Library, New York, N. Y.

10. Stillé, *Sanitary Commission*, p. 110.

11. *Ibid.*, pp. 290–94.

12. *Ibid.*, pp. 93–94.

13. *Ibid.*, pp. 249–50.

14. [Frederick Law Olmsted], *Sanitary Commission No. 60: An Account of the Executive Organization of the Sanitary Commission, and the Reasons for It* . . . (Washington, D.C.: McGill & Witherow, 1862), p. 57; Stillé, *Sanitary Commission*, pp. 189–90.

15. O to MCO, [14 August 1861].

16. *Ibid.*, 29 July 1861.

17. Eliza H. Schuyler to HWB, 10 September 1861, Bellows Papers, Massachusetts Historical Society, Boston, Massachusetts.

18. [Frederick Law Olmsted], Report of the Secretary with Regard to the Probable Origin of the Recent Demoralization of the Volunteer Army at Washington . . . (Washington, D.C.: McGill & Witherow, 1861), United States Sanitary Commission Doc. 28.

19. O to MCO, [6 September 1861].

20. Strong, *Diary*, 3: 180.

21. O to MCO, [6 September 1861].

22. O to JO, 12 September 1861.

23. Stillé, *Sanitary Commission*, pp. 114–15, 120–21.

24. Strong, *Diary*, 3: 180–81.

25. O to JO, 12 September 1861.

26. *Ibid.*

27. *Ibid.*

28. William Quentin Maxwell, *Lincoln's Fifth Wheel: The Political History of the United States Sanitary Commission* (New York: Longmans, Green & Co., 1956), p. 96.

29. Strong, *Diary*, 3: 178.

30. O to HWB, 19 September 1861, United States Sanitary Commission Papers; Maxwell, *Lincoln's Fifth Wheel*, pp. 96–97.

31. O to HWB, 25 September 1861, United States Sanitary Commission Papers.

32. *Ibid.*, 3 October 1861.

33. Maxwell, *Lincoln's Fifth Wheel*, p. 54.

34. O to HWB, 19 September 1861, United States Sanitary Commission Papers.

35. *Ibid.*

36. Maxwell, *Lincoln's Fifth Wheel*, p. 71.

37. Strong, *Diary*, 3: 196.

38. O to HWB, 25 September 1861, United States Sanitary Commission Papers.

39. Strong, *Diary*, 3: 183.

40. O to HWB, 29 September 1861, United States Sanitary Commission Papers.

41. O to MCO, 28 September 1861.

42. *Ibid.*

43. O to MCO, 19 October 1861.

44. HWB to his wife, 17 October 1861, Bellows Papers.

45. Maxwell, *Lincoln's Fifth Wheel*, pp. 98–102.

46. Charlotte Channing Stearns Eliot, *William Greenleaf Eliot, Minister, Educator, Philanthropist* (Boston and New York: Houghton, Mifflin & Co., 1904), pp. 167–72.

47. Strong, *Diary*, 3: 188–89.

48. Maxwell, *Lincoln's Fifth Wheel*, p. 104.

49. Strong, *Diary*, 3: 165.

50. *Ibid.*, p. 174.

51. O to Dorothea Dix, 24 October 1861, United States Sanitary Commission Papers.

52. United States Sanitary Commission, "To the Loyal Women of America," [1 October 1861].

53. O to Dorothea Dix, 24 October 1861, United States Sanitary Commission Papers.

54. Eliza H. Schuyler to O, 9 September 1861, United States Sanitary Commission Papers.

CHAPTER XVI

1. J. H. Douglas and Frederick Newman Knapp, "Report on Ball's Bluff," 28 October 1861, United States Sanitary Commission Papers, Public Library, New York, N.Y.

2. FNK to HWB, 29 October 1861, United States Sanitary Commission Papers.

3. William Quentin Maxwell, *Lincoln's Fifth Wheel: The Political History of the United States Sanitary Commission* (New York: Longmans, Green & Co., 1956), pp. 76–77.

4. George Templeton Strong, *The Diary of George Templeton Strong*, ed. Allan Nevins and Milton Halsey Thomas, 4 vols. (New York: Macmillan Co., 1952), 3: 187; O to HWB, 30 October 1861, United States Sanitary Commission Papers.

5. O to CLB, 18 November 1861.

6. O to Mary Olmsted, 6 November 1861; O to CLB, 18 November 1861.

7. O to Charles H. Russell, 12 November 1861 (draft).

8. Strong, *Diary*, 3: 191–92.

9. Laura Wood Roper, "Frederick Law Olmsted in the 'Literary Republic,'" *Mississippi Valley Historical Review* 39 (December 1952): 480–81.

10. *Ibid.*, p. 481.

11. *Ibid.*, p. 480.

12. O to MCO, 19 November 1861.

13. William Howard Russell, *My Diary North and South* (Boston: T. O. H. P. Burnham, 1863), pp. 589–90.

14. O to Alfred Field, 30 January 1862 (copy).

15. *Ibid.*

16. O to CLB, 18 November 1861.

17. *Ibid.*

18. "Yeoman" [F. L. Olmsted], "The Rebellion. How to Reason with the South. How to Deal with the Slavery Question," *New York Times*, 4 December 1861.

19. O to CLB, 18 November 1861.

20. Laura Wood Roper, "Frederick Law Olmsted and the Port Royal Experiment," *Journal of Southern History* 31 (August 1965): 272–84.

21. O to JO, 19 April 1862.

22. *New York Times*, 25 November 1861.

23. *New York World*, 27 November 1861.

24. *New York Daily Tribune*, 10 December 1861; Strong, *Diary*, 3: 198.

25. Maxwell, *Lincoln's Fifth Wheel*, p. 109; *New York Times*, 25 November, 4, 6, 14 December 1861.

26. O to HWB, 20 December 1861, United States Sanitary Commission Papers.

27. [Henry Whitney Bellows], "Memo To Be Left with Major-General George B. McClellan by the President of the Sanitary Commission," [7 December 1861], National Archives, War Records, Headquarters, Army of the Potomac, Letters Rec'd from Misc. Branches, book 32.

28. Maxwell, *Lincoln's Fifth Wheel*, pp. 107–8.

29. *Ibid.*, pp. 108, 113.

30. O to MCO, 8 December 1861.

31. O to HWB, 20 December 1861, United States Sanitary Commission Papers.

32. [Frederick Law Olmsted], "Report to the Secretary of War of the Operations of the Sanitary Commission, and upon the Sanitary Condition of the Volunteer Army . . . December 1861" (Washington, D.C.: McGill & Witherow, 1861).

33. O to HWB, 20 December 1861, United States Sanitary Commission Papers.

34. Maxwell, *Lincoln's Fifth Wheel*, p. 115.

35. *Ibid.*, p. 118; Charles J. Stillé, *History of the United States Sanitary Commission, Being the General Report of Its Work during the War of the Rebellion* (Philadelphia: J. B. Lippincott & Co., 1866), p. 125; O to Bertha Olmsted, 25 January 1862; O to HWB, 11 January, 25 February 1862, United States Sanitary Commission Papers.

36. Maxwell, *Lincoln's Fifth Wheel*, pp. 122, 126.

37. *Ibid.*, pp. 126–27; C. A. Finley to Abraham Lincoln, 11 April 1862, Robert Todd Lincoln Papers, Library of Congress, Washington, D.C.

38. United States Statutes at Large, 37th Congress, Second Session, 16 April 1862, "An Act to Reorganize and Increase the Efficiency of the Medical Department of the Army."

39. Stillé, *Sanitary Commission*, pp. 128–30.

40. *Ibid.*, p. 131; Maxwell, *Lincoln's Fifth Wheel*, p. 137.

41. Strong, *Diary*, 3: 218.

42. O to JO, 19 April 1862.

43. Journal of General Samuel P. Heintzelman, Manuscripts Division, Library of Congress, Washington, D.C.; Strong, *Diary*, 3: 218.

CHAPTER XVII

1. George Templeton Strong, *The Diary of George Templeton Strong*, ed. Allan Nevins and Milton Halsey Thomas, 4 vols. (New York: Macmillan Co., 1952), 3: 215.

2. George Opdyke to O, 19 March 1862; O to JO, [25 March 1862].

3. O to JO, 19 April 1862.

4. Charles J. Stillé, *History of the United States Sanitary Commission, Being the General Report of Its Work during the War of the Rebellion* (Philadelphia: J. B. Lippincott & Co., 1866), pp. 143–50.

5. O to JO, 19 April 1862.

6. *Hospital Transports: A Memoir of the Embarkation of the Sick and Wounded from the Peninsula of Virginia in the Summer of 1862* (Boston: Ticknor & Fields, 1863), p. xiii.

7. *Ibid.*, p. 17.

8. Strong, *Diary*, 3: 220–21.

9. *Ibid.*, p. 221; *Hospital Transports*, pp. 18–20; Georgeanna Woolsey Bacon and Eliza Woolsey Howland, eds., *Letters of a Family during the War for the Union 1861–1865*, 2 vols. (printed for private distribution, 1899), 1: 314.

10. *Hospital Transports*, pp. 18–19.

11. *Ibid.*, pp. 20–21.

12. *Ibid.*, pp. 21–22.

13. Joseph K. Barnes et al., eds, *The Medical and Surgical History of the War of the Rebellion*, 1861–1865, 12 vols. (Washington: Government Printing Office, 1870–88), appendix to part 1; Strong, *Diary*, 3: 222.

14. Bacon and Howland, *Letters*, 1: 326.

15. *Hospital Transports*, pp. 25–26.

16. *Ibid.*, p. 30.

17. *Ibid.*, pp. 30–31.

18. *Ibid.*, pp. 31–33.

19. *Ibid.*, pp. 33–34.
20. *Ibid.*, p. 35.
21. *Ibid.*
22. *Ibid.*, pp. 36–37.
23. *Ibid.*, p. 37.
24. *Medical and Surgical History*, appendix to part 1.
25. *Hospital Transports*, pp. 23, 139–42.
26. *Ibid.*, p. 47; [Katherine Prescott Wormeley], *The United States Sanitary Commission: A Sketch of Its Purposes and Its Works Compiled from Documents and Private Papers* (Boston: Little, Brown & Co., 1863), p. 677.
27. *Hospital Transports*, p. 88.
28. *Ibid.*, p. 85.
29. Bacon and Howland, *Letters*, 1: 344, 2: 373.
30. Katherine Prescott Wormeley, *The Other Side of War with the Army of the Potomac. Letters from the Headquarters of the United States Sanitary Commission during the Peninsula Campaign in Virginia in 1862* (Boston: Ticknor & Company, 1889), pp. 205–6.
31. Bacon and Howland, *Letters*, 2: 423.
32. *Hospital Transports*, p. 69.
33. Bacon and Howland, *Letters*, 1: 348.
34. *Hospital Transports*, pp. 46, 64.
35. *Ibid.*, p. 73.
36. *Ibid.*, pp. 73–75.
37. *Ibid.*, pp. 77–78.
38. *Ibid.*, pp. 78–80.
39. *Ibid.*, pp. 98–106.
40. O to Hammond, 17 June 1862, private letter book, p. 6.
41. *Hospital Transports*, pp. 104, 152.
42. *Ibid.*, p. 111.
43. O to MCO, 11 June 1862.
44. Bacon and Howland, *Letters*, 2: 395–96.
45. William Quentin Maxwell, *Lincoln's Fifth Wheel: The Political History of the United States Sanitary Commission* (New York: Longmans, Green & Co., 1956), p. 156.
46. Stillé, *Sanitary Commission*, p. 135; Hammond to O, 17 June 1862, National Archives, War Records, Surgeon General's Office, letter book 31.
47. *Hospital Transports*, pp. 155–59; O to HWB, 22 June 1862, private book, p. 8, official book, p. 13.
48. *Hospital Transports*, pp. 132–36.
49. *Ibid.*, p. 162.
50. O to CLB, [29 June 1862].
51. *Ibid.*
52. O to MCO, 3 July 1862.
53. O to HWB, 4 July 1862, private book, p. 48.
54. *Medical and Surgical History*, appendix to part 1.
55. O to HWB, 4 July 1862, private book, p. 48.
56. *Ibid.*
57. *Ibid.*
58. *Hospital Transports*, pp. 160–61.
59. O to HWB, 4 July 1862, private book, p. 48.
60. O to Lincoln, 6 July 1862, private book, p. 58.
61. *Ibid*; O to Alexander Dallas Bache, 8 July 1862, R. H. 1930, Huntington Library, San Marino, California; O to Preston King, 9 July 1862, Nicolay Papers, Library of Congress, Washington, D.C.; Bache to O, 11 July 1862.

62. Bache to O.
63. O to Bache, 8 July 1862, R.H. 1930, Huntington Library.
64. O to HWB, 13 July 1862, private book, p. 28.
65. *Ibid.*, p. 24.
66. Bacon and Howland, *Letters*, 2: 458; Maxwell, *Lincoln's Fifth Wheel*, p. 161.
67. Bacon and Howland, *Letters*, 2: 458–59; HWB to CV, 12 July 1862.
68. Wormeley, *The Other Side of War*, p. 206.

CHAPTER XVIII

1. Charles J. Stillé, *History of the United States Sanitary Commission, Being the General Report of Its Work during the War of the Rebellion* (Philadelphia: J. B. Lippincott & Co., 1866), pp. 475–77.
2. O to MCO, 12, 20 August 1862.
3. O to John S. Newberry, 21 August 1862, private book, p. 35.
4. John D. Defries to Edwin Stanton, 22 August 1862, and D. H. Watson to Defries, 23 August 1862, National Archives, War Department, Secretary, p. 763.
5. HWB to Salmon P. Chase, 25 November 1862, Chase Papers, Library of Congress, Washington, D.C.
6. O to CLB, 25 August 1862.
7. *Ibid.*
8. *Ibid.*
9. O to MCO, 20 August 1862.
10. George Worthington Adams, *Doctors in Blue: The Medical History of the Union Army in the Civil War* (New York: Henry Schuman, 1952), pp. 73–76; George Templeton Strong, *The Diary of George Templeton Strong*, ed. Allan Nevins and Milton Halsey Thomas, 4 vols. (New York: Macmillan Co., 1952), 3: 253–54.
11. Strong, *Diary*, 3: 253.
12. O to MCO, 28 August 1862, "Saturday, August 1862."
13. *Ibid.*, 1 September 1862.
14. *Ibid.*, 13, 15 September 1862.
15. O to CV, 23 August 1862; O to JO, 15 September 1862.
16. O to MCO, 13, 21 September 1862.
17. Adams, *Doctors in Blue*, pp. 77–78.
18. O to MCO, 21 September 1862; Strong, *Diary*, 3: 257.
19. O to MCO, 26, 29 September 1862.
20. CLB to O, 12 September 1862.
21. O to CLB, 30 September 1862.
22. CLB to O, 1 October 1862.
23. O to CLB, 4 October 1862.
24. CLB to O, 1 October 1862.
25. O to CLB, 4 October 1862.
26. O to HWB, 7 October 1862, private book, p. 83; John Bowne to Dr. Lewis H. Steiner, 3 August 1865, Lewis Henry Steiner Papers, Maryland Historical Society, Baltimore, Maryland.
27. GWC to O, 29 September 1862.
28. David Dudley Field to O, 29 September 1862.
29. HWB to O, 1 October 1862, United States Sanitary Commission Papers, Public Library, New York, N.Y.
30. O to HWB, 3 October 1862, Bellows Papers, Massachusetts Historical Society, Boston, Massachusetts.

31. O to MCO, 21 September 1862.

32. HWB to O, 1 October 1862, United States Sanitary Commission Papers.

33. O to HWB, 2, 3, 4, 7 October 1862, private book, pp. 46, 56, 68, 83.

34. HWB to O, 8 October 1862, United States Sanitary Commission Papers.

35. O to HWB, 2 November 1862, private book, p. 102; HWB to O, 29 November 1862, United States Sanitary Commission Papers.

36. GTS to O, 6 December 1862, United States Sanitary Commission Papers.

37. Strong, *Diary*, 3: 276, 291.

38. William Quentin Maxwell, *Lincoln's Fifth Wheel: The Political History of the United States Sanitary Commission* (New York: Longmans, Green & Co., 1956), pp. 186–87; O to HWB, 2 November 1862, private book, p. 102.

39. [Frederick Law Olmsted], The General Secretary of the Sanitary Commission, *Sanitary Commission No. 60: An Account of the Executive Organization of the Sanitary Commission, and the Reasons of It, Suggested by the Criticisms of a Committee of the "Cincinnati Branch of the Sanitary Commission"* (Washington, D.C.: McGill & Witherow, 1862).

40. O to Dr. Samuel Gridley Howe, Dr. Agnew, et al., 3 January 1863, private book, p. 195.

41. Maxwell, *Lincoln's Fifth Wheel*, pp. 185, 188; O to HWB, 2 January 1862, private book, p. 172; O to Newberry, 10 January 1862, private book, p. 205.

42. HWB to O, 9 December 1862, United States Sanitary Commission Papers.

43. O to MAO, 26, 27 January 1862, private book, pp. 210, 219.

44. Maxwell, *Lincoln's Fifth Wheel*, pp. 191–93; Lemuel Moss, *Annals of the United States Christian Commission* (Philadelphia, J. B. Lippincott & Co., 1868), pp. 567–68.

45. *Sanitary Commission Bulletin* 1 (12 January 1863): 87.

46. O to GTS, 26 December 1862, private book, p. 156.

47. O to Newberry, 10 January 1863, private book, p. 205.

48. [Henry Whitney Bellows], "A Sketch of the Origin and History of the Union League Club of New York, Prepared at the Request of the Committee on the Library and Publications, by One of Its Founders" (draft, ca. 1876–77), LWR Files.

49. *Ibid.*

CHAPTER XIX

1. O to MCO, 13 November 1862.

2. *Ibid.*, 11 October 1862.

3. KPW to O, 8, 9, 10 October 1862.

4. O to MCO, 11 October 1962.

5. KPW to FLO (son), 4 July 1903.

6. HWB to O, 11 February 1863.

7. O to HWB, 13 January 1863, United States Sanitary Commission Papers, Public Library, New York, N.Y.

8. O to CV, 16 February 1863, private book, p. 249.

9. O to ELG, 4 April 1865, Godkin Papers, Houghton Library, Harvard University, Cambridge, Massachusetts.

10. O, journal, 18 February–4 April 1863.

11. *Ibid.*

12. *Ibid*; FNK to HWB, 11 March 1863, Bellows Papers, Massachusetts Historical Society, Boston, Massachusetts.

13. O to ELG, 4 April 1863, Godkin Papers.

14. O, journal, 18 February–4 April 1863.

15. O to MCO, 8 March 1863.

16. John S. Newberry to HWB, 11 March 1863, United States Sanitary Commission Papers.

17. HWB to John H. Heywood, 10 March 1863, United States Sanitary Commission Papers.

18. HWB to Newberry, 10 March 1863, United States Sanitary Commission Papers.

19. George Templeton Strong, *The Diary of George Templeton Strong*, ed. Allan Nevins and Milton Halsey Thomas, 4 vols. (New York: Macmillan Co., 1952), 3: 304–5.

20. O, journal, 18 February–4 April 1863.

21. *Ibid.*

22. *Ibid.*

23. *Ibid.*

24. O to JO, 1 April 1863.

25. *Ibid.*

26. *Ibid.*

27. *Ibid.*

28. O to HWB, 1 April 1863, private book.

29. *Ibid.*, 12 February 1863, private book, p. 244.

30. O to MAO, 11 October 1862.

31. [Frederick Law Olmsted], "The Genesis of a Rumor," *Nation*, 6 (23 April 1868): 328–29.

32. O to ELG, 4 April 1863, Godkin Papers.

33. O to JO, 1 April 1863.

34. O to HWB, 1 April 1863, private book; O to Newberry, 31 March 1863, United States Sanitary Commission Papers.

35. O to ELG, 4 April 1863, Godkin Papers.

36. ELG to O, 9 May 1863.

CHAPTER XX

1. O to [James Yeatman], 21 April 1863 (copy).

2. C. R. Agnew to O, 24 April 1863.

3. O to JO, 18 April 1863.

4. O to HWB, 25 April 1863, private book, p. 259.

5. O to JO, 18 April 1863.

6. *Ibid.*, 25 April 1863.

7. *Ibid.*, 2 May 1863.

8. O to HWB, 20 May 1863, private book, p. 271.

9. CV to O, 12 May 1863; O to JO, 22 May 1863.

10. O to ELG, 4 April 1863, Godkin Papers, Houghton Library, Harvard University, Cambridge, Massachusetts.

11. O to MCO, 26 June 1863.

12. "Prospectus for a Weekly Review," [ca. 1 July 1863].

13. O to MCO, 26 June 1863.

14. *Ibid.*

15. George Templeton Strong, *The Diary of George Templeton Strong*, ed. Allan Nevins and Milton Halsey Thomas, 4 vols. (New York: Macmillan Co., 1952), 3: 326.

16. O to MCO, 29 June 1863.

17. *Ibid.*, 2 July 1863.

18. *Ibid.*, 7 July 1863.

19. Strong, *Diary*, 3: 329.

20. O to MCO, 7 July 1863; Georgeanna Woolsey Bacon and Eliza Woolsey Howland, eds., *Letters of A Family during the War for the Union, 1861–1865*, 2 vols. (printed for private distribution, 1899), 2: 526–27.

21. O to MCO, 7 July 1863.

22. *Ibid.*, 15 July 1863.

23. *Ibid.*

24. O to ELG, 15 July 1863, Godkin Papers.

25. *Ibid.*, 19 July 1863, Godkin Papers.

26. *Ibid.*, 15 July 1863, Godkin Papers.

27. William Q. Maxwell, *Lincoln's Fifth Wheel: The Political History of the United States Sanitary Commission* (New York: Longmans, Green & Co., 1956), p. 212.

28. O to MCO, 20 July 1863.

29. O to ELG, 15 July 1863, Godkin Papers.

30. *Ibid.*

31. O to HWB, 28 July 1863, Bellows Papers, Massachusetts Historical Society, Boston, Massachusetts.

32. *Ibid*; O to ELG, 1 August 1863, Godkin Papers.

33. O to MCO, 27 July 1863.

34. O to HWB, 28 July 1863, Bellows Papers.

35. O to MCO, 20 July 1863.

36. *Ibid.*, 27, 29 July 1863.

37. O to JO, 2 August 1863.

38. *Ibid.*, [ca. 5 August 1863]; Rollo Ogden, ed., *The Life and Letters of Edwin Lawrence Godkin*, 2 vols. (New York: Macmillan Co., 1907), 1: 225–26.

39. Charles A. Dana to O, 7 August 1863.

CHAPTER XXI

1. Las Mariposas Estate, Mariposa County, California (map), Max Strobel, engineer; lithograph by Sarony, Major and Knapp, 449 Broadway, New York (LWR Files, Washington, D.C.).

2. O to JO, 11 February 1864.

3. Las Mariposas Estate (map).

4. [Frederick Law Olmsted], *Mariposa Estate, the Manager's General Report, January 1, 1864* (New York: Wm. C. Bryant & Co., 1864), p. 48; Benjamin Silliman, Jr., *A Report of an Examination of the Mariposa Estate in California, Made in May, 1864* (New York: Wm. C. Bryant & Co., 1864), p. 21.

5. O to JO, 11 February 1864.

6. Newell Chamberlain, *The Call of Gold: True Tales on the Gold Road to Yosemite* (Mariposa, Calif.: Gazette Press, 1936), p. 111.

7. Silliman, *Report of the Mariposa Estate*, p. 5.

8. [Benjamin M. Stillwell], Chairman of the Late Committee of Investigation, *The Mariposa Estate: Its Past, Present and Future Comprising the Official Report of J. Ross Browne . . . and Other Documents* (New York: Russell's American Steam Printing House, 1868), pp. 5–10, 42–52.

9. *Ibid.*, pp. 34–41; O to G. W. Farlee, 30 October 1863, Mariposa letter book, p. 45.

10. Morris Ketcham to O, 5 December 1863.

11. [F. L. Olmsted], *Mariposa Estate, Manager's Report*, p. 32.

12. Silliman, *Report of the Mariposa Estate*, p. 21.

13. O to Morris Ketchum, 2 November 1863 (draft).

14. *The Mariposas Estate* (London, 1861), p. 6.

15. O to HWB, 10 August 1863, Bellows Papers, Massachusetts Historical Society, Boston, Massachusetts.

16. O to MCO, 12 August 1863.

17. O to JO, 20 August 1863.

18. *Ibid.*, 10, 12, 13 August 1863; O to MCO, 11, 13 August 1863; O to HWB, 13 August 1863.

19. O to JO, 12 August 1863.

20. *Ibid.*, 13 August 1863.

21. HWB to O, 13 August 1863.

22. *Ibid.*

23. O to HWB, 19 August 1863, Bellows Papers.

24. HWB to O, 20 August 1865.

25. O to HWB, 19 August 1865, Bellows Papers.

26. Extract from the minutes of the board of trustees of the Mariposa Company, 20 August 1863.

27. George Templeton Strong, *The Diary of George Templeton Strong*, ed. Allan Nevins and Milton Halsey Thomas, 4 vols. (New York: Macmillan Co., 1952), 3: 350.

28. KPW to O, 2 September 1863.

29. Louisa L. Schuyler to O, 26 August, 1 September 1863.

30. KPW to O, 2 September 1863.

31. Charles Eliot Norton, *Letters of Charles Eliot Norton*, ed. Sara Norton and Mark Anthony De Wolfe Howe, 2 vols. (Boston: Houghton Mifflin Co., 1913), 1: 264.

32. FNK to O, 15 September 1863.

33. *New York Times*, 14 September 1863.

34. A. D. Bache to O, 15 September 1863.

35. MCO to FJK, 30 August 1863.

36. [Frederick Law Olmsted], "New York to San Francisco, 14 September–12 October 1863."

37. O to MCO, 25 September 1863.

38. *Ibid.*

39. O to MCO, 10–12 October 1863.

40. *Ibid.*

41. *Ibid.*; O to MCO, 12 October 1863.

42. O to MCO, 13 October 1863.

43. Adolph Knopf, "The Mother Lode System of California," *United States Geological Survey Professional Paper No. 157* (Washington, D.C.: Government Printing Office, 1929), p. 83.

44. O to MCO, 14–15 October 1863.

45. *Ibid.*

46. *Ibid.*

47. *Ibid.*; O to MCO, 30 October 1863.

48. O to MCO, 14–15 October 1863.

49. *Ibid.*

50. O to MCO, 15–18 October 1863.

51. *Ibid.*

52. O to MCO, 14–15 October 1863.

53. O to MCO, 15–18 October 1863.

54. *Ibid.*

55. O to James Hoy, 19 October 1863, Mariposa letter book, p. 1.

56. *Ibid.*

57. *Ibid.*

58. *Ibid.*

59. O to MCO, 15–18 October 1863.

60. O to Hoy, 19 October 1863, Mariposa letter book, p. 1.
61. *Ibid.*
62. O to MCO, 15–18 October 1863.

CHAPTER XXII

1. O to James Hoy, 19 October 1861, Mariposa letter book, p. 1; O to George W. Farlee, 29 October 1863, Mariposa letter book, p. 27.
2. O to Farlee, 29 October 1863, Mariposa letter book, p. 27.
3. O to JO, 20 October 1863.
4. [Frederick Law Olmsted], *Mariposa Estate, the Manager's General Report, January 1, 1864* (New York: Wm. C. Bryant & Co., 1864), pp. 19–26, 31.
5. *Ibid.*, pp. 33–39.
6. *Ibid.*, p. 32; O to FNK, 21 November 1863.
7. [F. L. Olmsted], *Mariposa Estate, Manager's Report*, pp. 23–31.
8. O to MCO, [ca. 20 October 1863].
9. O to Morris Ketchum, 2 November 1863 (draft); O to Farlee, 30 October 1863, Mariposa letter book, p. 45.
10. O to Ketchum, 2, 6 November 1863 (draft).
11. *Ibid.*; O to Farlee, 30 October 1863, Mariposa letter book, p. 45; [F. L. Olmsted], *Mariposa Estate, Manager's Report*, pp. 32, 58–59.
12. O to Farlee, 29 October, 14 November 1863, Mariposa letter book, pp. 27, 103.
13. O to JO, 30 November 1863.
14. O to MCO, 15–18 October 1863.
15. O to JO, 27 November 1863, 11 February 1864; O to MCO, 20 November 1863.
16. O to JO, 30 October 1863.
17. O to MCO, 31 October 1863.
18. O to Farlee, 14 November 1863, Mariposa letter book, p. 103.
19. O to MCO, 31 October 1863.
20. O to JO, 20 November 1863.
21. O to Farlee, 14 November 1863, Mariposa letter book, p. 103.
22. O to MCO, 20 November 1863.
23. *Ibid.*
24. O to ELG, fragment, [ca. 15 May 1865], Godkin Papers, Houghton Library, Harvard University, Cambridge, Massachusetts; Frederick Law Olmsted, "History of Civilization in the Last Fifty Years"; Frederick Law Olmsted, "A Pioneer Community of the Present Day."
25. O to ELG, 4 April 1865, Godkin Papers.
26. O to Knapp, 21 November 1863.

CHAPTER XXIII

1. O to MCO, [ca. 20 October 1863].
2. *Ibid.*, 31 October 1863.
3. O to FNK, 21 November 1863; O to ELG, 25 December 1863, Godkin Papers, Houghton Library, Harvard University, Cambridge, Massachusetts; O to A. D. Bache, [n.d], RH 1929, Huntington Library, San Marino, California.
4. O to FNK, 21 November 1863.
5. J. D. Whitney to O, 23 November 1863; O to JO, 27 November 1863.
6. *Mariposa Gazette*, 5 December 1863.

7. Morris Ketchum to O, 5 December 1863.

8. Ketchum to O, 13 December 1863.

9. O to Ketchum, 10 December 1863, Mariposa letter book, p. 121.

10. O to MCO, 17 December 1863.

11. O to G. W. Farlee, 2, 16 January 1864, Mariposa letter book, pp. 145, 151; O to Ketchum, 18 February 1864, private letter book, p. 67.

12. O to Farlee, 1 March 1864, Mariposa letter book, p. 175; O to FNK, 11 November 1863.

13. O to James Hoy, 1 January 1864, Mariposa letter book, p. 153.

14. O to Farlee, 1 March 1864, Mariposa letter book, p. 175.

15. O to HWB, 5 March 1864, Bellows Papers, Massachusetts Historical Society, Boston, Massachusetts.

16. O to Hoy, 5 March 1864, private letter book, p. 70.

17. Howard A. Martin to O, 11 March 1864.

18. O to MCO, 6 December 1863; O to JO, 11 February 1864; O to HWB, 5 March 1864, Bellows Papers.

19. [Frederick Law Olmsted], *Mariposa Estate, the Manager's General Report, January 1, 1864* (New York: Wm. C. Bryant & Co., 1864).

20. O to Ketchum, 18 February 1864, private letter book, p. 67.

21. O to T. Starr King, 17 December 1863, private letter book, p. 24.

22. O to MCO, 17 December 1863.

23. O to JO, 30 October 1863.

24. O to William Ashburner, 3 January 1864, private letter book, p. 49.

25. O to ELG, 4 April 1864, private letter book, p. 106.

26. Ketchum to O, 10 December 1863; O to Ketchum, [January 1864], private letter book, p. 54.

27. KPW to O, 10 January 1864; Starr King to O, 31 December 1863; *Mariposa Gazette*, 16 January 1864.

28. KPW to O, 7 December 1863, 10 January 1864; FNK to O, 11 March 1864; J. H. Douglas to O, 3 January 1864; A. J. Bloor to O, 1 December 1863; A. D. Bache to O, 26 February 1863.

29. Frederick Law Olmsted, Jr., and Theodora Kimball, eds. *Forty Years of Landscape Architecture: Frederick Law Olmsted, Senior*, 2 vols. (New York and London: G. P. Putnam's Sons, 1922, 1928), 2: 554–60.

30. CV to O, 30 January 1864.

31. F. L. Olmsted, Jr., and T. Kimball, *Forty Years*, 2: 555.

32. CV to O, 30 January, 25 February 1864.

33. *Ibid.*, 19 October 1863.

34. O to CV, 26 November 1863, private letter book, p. 17.

35. *Ibid.*

36. O to CV, 25 March 1864.

37. CV to O, 18, 30 January, 5 February 1864.

38. O to JO, 11 March 1864.

39. *Ibid.*

40. O to J. H. Brayton, 26, 29 March 1864, private letter book, pp. 79, 92; O to JO, 16 October 1864.

41. Harriet Errington to Lottie [Mrs. Alfred] Field, 17 March 1864, Errington Letters (copies), LWR Files, Washington, D.C.

42. MCO, memo, [ca. May 1864].

43. H. Errington to Rosa [Field], 7 May 1864, Errington Letters.

44. Georgiana Errington to Lottie Field, 8 May 1864, Errington Letters; H. Errington to Lottie Field, 20 June 1864, Errington Letters.

45. O to JO, 25 June 1864.
46. *Ibid.*
47. FLO (son), interview.
48. MCO to JO, 7 April 1864.
49. *Ibid.*
50. George W. Curtis to O, 30 March 1864; O to Francis G. Shaw, 5 May 1864.
51. O to Ketchum, 1 April 1864, private letter book, p. 98.
52. *Ibid.*, 10 May 1864, private letter book, p. 163.
53. O to JO, 25 June 1864.
54. *Mariposa Gazette*, 18 June 1864.
55. O to ELG, 2 April 1864, Godkin Papers.
56. O to Ketchum, 28 May 1864, Mariposa letter book, p. 174; Benjamin Silliman, Jr., *A Report of an Examination of the Mariposa Estate in California, Made in May, 1864* (New York: Wm. C. Bryant & Co., 1864), p. 33.
57. O to HWB, 28 April 1864, Bellows Papers.
58. HWB to O, 4 May 1864.
59. H. Errington to Lottie Field, 20 June 1864, Errington Letters.
60. O to Hoy, 13 July 1864, Mariposa letter book, p. 222.
61. H. Errington, journal, 4 July to 16 August 1864, Errington Letters.
62. *Ibid.*; Frederick Law Olmsted, "A Pioneer Community of the Present Day."
63. Albert D. Richardson, *Beyond the Mississippi, from the Great River to the Great Ocean: Life and Adventure on the Prairies, Mountains and Pacific Coast . . . 1857–1867* (Hartford: American Publishing Co., 1867), p. 431.
64. H. Errington, journal, Errington Letters.
65. *Ibid.*
66. *Ibid.*
67. F. L. Olmsted, "Pioneer Community of the Present Day."
68. O to ELG, 24 July 1864, Godkin Papers.
69. O to Farlee, 7 August 1864, Mariposa letter book, p. 225.
70. O to HWB, 8 August 1864, Bellows Papers.
71. O to E. L. Miller, 8 August 1864, private letter book, p. 229.
72. O to JO, August 1864; Frederick Law Olmsted, "Plan of Narrative for Clark's and Yosemite," August 1864.
73. Frederick Law Olmsted, "The Yosemite Valley and the Mariposa Big Trees: A Preliminary Report (1865)," with an introductory note by Laura Wood Roper, *Landscape Architecture* 43 (October 1952): 16.
74. O to JO, August 1864.
75. H. Errington to Frank Errington, 20 August 1864, Errington Letters.
76. F. L. Olmsted, "Plan of Narrative."
77. Carl P. Russell, *One Hundred Years in Yosemite: The Story of a Great Park and Its Friends* (Berkeley and Los Angeles: University of California Press, 1947), pp. 147–48.
78. Russell, *One Hundred Years in Yosemite*, pp. 48–50.
79. *Ibid.*, p. 96; F. L. Olmsted, "Plan of Narrative."
80. Russell, *One Hundred Years in Yosemite*, p. 92; Alexander Deering to O, 15, 27 August 1868.
81. O to JO, 14 September 1864.
82. *Ibid.*
83. *Ibid.*
84. William Henry Brewer, *Up and Down California in 1860–1864: The Journal of William Henry Brewer*, ed. Francis P. Farquar (New Haven: Yale University Press; London: Oxford University Press, 1930), pp. 547, 549n.
85. O to JO, 14 September 1864.

CHAPTER XXIV

1. O to G. W. Farlee, 1 September 1864, Mariposa letter book, p. 227.
2. O to JO, 19 September 1864.
3. James Hoy to O, 12 September 1864.
4. O to Hoy, 19 September 1864, Mariposa letter book, p. 236.
5. William Henry Brewer, *Up and Down California in 1860–1864: The Journal of William Henry Brewer*, ed. Francis P. Farquar (New Haven: Yale University Press; London: Oxford University Press, 1930), pp. 547–48; O to Hoy, 24 October 1864, Mariposa letter book, p. 243.
6. O to Hoy, 3 October 1864, Mariposa letter book, pp. 236, 238.
7. O to FNK, 28 September 1864.
8. O to Hoy, 8 October 1864, Mariposa letter book, p. 238.
9. *Ibid.*, 24 October 1864, Mariposa letter book, p. 243; 29 October 1864, private letter book, p. 324.
10. O to William Ashburner, 4 November 1864, private letter book, p. 304.
11. O to Farlee, 9 November 1864, Mariposa letter book, p. 251.
12. O to Hoy, 24 October 1864, Mariposa letter book, p. 243; O to Farlee, 31 October 1864, Mariposa letter book, p. 247; O to Hoy, 31 October 1864, private letter book, p. 310.
13. O to JO, 16 October 1864; O to J. G. McCullough, 31 October 1864, private letter book, p. 302.
14. O to FNK, 1 January 1865; O to McCullough, 31 October 1864, private letter book, p. 302.
15. O to JO, 16 October 1864.
16. *Mariposa Gazette*, 15 October 1864; O to Colonel James, 20 October 1864, private letter book, p. 249.
17. O to Clarence King, [ca. 23 October 1864], private letter book, p. 294.
18. *Mariposa Gazette*, 5 November 1864.
19. O to Farlee, 9 November 1864, Mariposa letter book, p. 251; *Mariposa Gazette*, 12 November 1864; O to ELG, 29 November 1864, Godkin Papers, Houghton Library, Harvard University, Cambridge, Massachusetts.
20. *Mariposa Gazette*, 12 November 1864.
21. O to Ketchum, Son & Co., 16 November 1864, private letter book, p. 332; O to Samuel H. Willey, 21 November 1864, S. H. Willey letter book, University of California Archives, University of California, Berkeley, California; Ketchum, Son & Co. to O, 27 October 1864.
22. Ketchum to O, 27 August 1864.
23. O to JO, 29 November 1864.
24. O to Hoy, 24 November 1864, Mariposa letter book, p. 253.
25. O to JO, 29 November 1864.
26. *Ibid.*
27. O to Farlee, 29 December 1864, Mariposa letter book, p. 261.
28. O to Hoy, 12 December 1864, Mariposa letter book, p. 258; O to Farlee, 9 December 1864, Mariposa letter book, p. 261.
29. O to Farlee, 29 December 1864, Mariposa letter book, p. 261.
30. ELG to O, 25 December 1864–5 January 1865, Godkin Papers.
31. *Ibid.*
32. O to ELG, 9 January 1865, Godkin Papers; O to MCO, 8 January 1865.
33. O to ELG, 10 January 1865, Godkin Papers.
34. *Ibid.*, 9, 10 January 1865, Godkin Papers.
35. *Daily Alta California*, 13 January 1865; *Mariposa Gazette*, 21 January 1865.

36. O to JO, 11 February 1865.

37. O to MCO, 13 January 1865.

38. O to ELG, 22 January 1865, Godkin Papers.

39. O to MCO, 12 February 1865.

40. O to Hoy, 13 February 1865, Mariposa letter book, p. 275.

41. O to MCO, 12 February 1865.

42. O to JO, 30 January 1865.

43. O to Hoy, 13 February 1865, Mariposa letter book, p. 275.

44. O to MCO, 25, 30 January, 3 February, 2 March 1865; O to HWB, 18 January 1865, Bellows Papers, Massachusetts Historical Society, Boston, Massachusetts.

45. O to HWB, 18 January 1865, Bellows Papers.

46. O to ELG, 20 February 1865, Godkin Papers.

47. O to MCO, 13, 28 January 1865; O to ELG, 26–30 January 1865, Godkin Papers.

48. O to JO, 30 January 1865.

49. O to MCO, 6 April 1865.

50. *The Production of Wine in California: Particularly Referring to the Establishment of the Buena Vista Vinicultural Society* (San Francisco: Towne and Bacon, 1865).

51. O to MCO, 10 February 1865.

52. O to ELG, 2 March 1865, Godkin Papers.

53. O to MCO, 28 January 1865.

54. O to CV, 12 March 1865; O to JO, 11 February 1865.

55. *Ibid.*

56. O to MCO, 6 February 1865.

57. *Ibid.*, 1 March 1865.

58. O to JO, 16 March 1865.

59. CV to O, 9 January 1865; O to MCO, 27 February 1865.

60. O to ELG, [ca. end of March 1865], Godkin Papers.

61. MCO to Grandmama [Mrs. Cyrus Perkins], 31 March 1865.

62. O to ElG, [ca. end of March 1865], Godkin Papers.

63. O to MCO, 5 April 1865.

64. *Ibid.*, 11 April 1865

65. *Ibid.*, 16 April 1865.

66. O to ELG, 27 May 1865, Godkin Papers.

67. O to MCO, 16 April 1865.

68. O to JO, 29 April 1865.

69. O to MCO, 16 April 1865.

70. *Ibid.*

71. Agreement between Dodge Brothers and Mariposa Co., 27 April 1865; O to JO, 29 April 1865.

72. O to Ketchum, Son & Co., 29 April 1865, private letter book, p. 386.

73. H. Errington to Rosa Field, 7 May 1865, Errington Letters (copies), LWR Files.

74. *Ibid.*

75. O to ELG, 10 June 1865, Godkin Papers.

76. ELG to O, 23 July 1865 (copy).

77. *Ibid.*

78. O to ELG, 10 June 1865, Godkin Papers.

79. John Bowne to Dr. Lewis H. Steiner, 3 August 1865, Lewis Henry Steiner Collection, Maryland Historical Society, Baltimore, Maryland.

80. Ashburner to O, 14 June 1865; Hans Huth, "Yosemite, the Story of an Idea," *Sierra Club Bulletin* 33 (March 1948): 65.

81. O to JO, 5 July 1865; Frederick Law Olmsted, "The Yosemite Valley and the Mariposa Big Trees: A Preliminary Report (1865)," with an introductory note by Laura Wood Roper, *Landscape Architecture* 43 (October 1952): 16.

82. O to JO, 5 July 1865.

83. Ketchum, Son & Co. to O, 21 July 1865; O to JO, 5 July 1865.

84. O to MCO, 11 July 1865.

85. O to S. H. Willey, 26 June 1865, private letter book, p. 414.

86. O to JO, 24 July 1865.

87. Board of Park Commissioners to O, 26 July 1865; ELG to O, 23 July 1865, Godkin Papers.

88. O to CV, 1 August 1865.

89. Huth, "Yosemite," p. 68.

90. *Ibid.*, p. 67.

91. *Ibid.*, p. 65.

92. O to C. King, October 1864, private letter book, p. 294; O to James T. Gardiner, 23 October 1864, private letter book, p. 292; MCO memo to Theodora Kimball, n.d., LWR Files.

93. F. L. Olmsted, "Yosemite and Mariposa Big Trees," pp. 12–13.

94. *Ibid.*, pp. 13–25.

95. Thomas Jefferson to William Caruthers, 15 March 1815, Thomas Jefferson Papers, vol. 203, Library of Congress, Washington, D.C.

96. Huth, "Yosemite," p. 52.

97. *Ibid.*, p. 52; F. L. Olmsted, "Yosemite Valley and Mariposa Big Trees," pp. 12–13.

98. Minutes of the Yosemite Commission, 7–9 August 1865.

99. Albert D. Richardson, *Beyond the Mississippi: From the Great River to the Great Ocean, Life and Adventure on the Prairies, Mountains and Pacific Coast . . . 1857–1867* (Hartford: American Publishing Co., 1867), p. 240.

100. Minutes of the Yosemite Commission, 9 August 1865.

101. Alexander Deering to O, 15 August 1868; Galen Clark to O, 1 March 1868.

102. Samuel Bowles, *Across the Continent: A Summer's Journey by the Rocky Mountains, the Mormons and the Pacific States* (Springfield, Mass.: S. Bowles & Co., 1866), p. 231.

103. Bowles to O, 9 September 1865; O to Bowles, 20 September 1865.

104. H. Errington to Lottie Field, 10 August 1865, Errington Letters.

105. O to Williams, Hill and Watkins, 9 August 1865, Vaux Papers, Public Library, New York, N.Y.; O to CV, 19 September 1865, Vaux Papers.

106. Minutes of the Yosemite Commission, 7–9 August 1865.

107. H. Errington to Lottie Field, 10 August 1865, Errington Letters.

108. O to MCO, 23 August 1865.

109. *Ibid.*

110. J. M. McKim to O, 26 July 1865; O to McKim, 9 September 1865, private letter book, p. 447.

111. O to MCO, 23 August 1865.

112. Olmsted, Vaux & Co., *Report upon a Projected Improvement of the Estate of the College of California at Berkeley, near Oakland* (San Francisco: Towne and Bacon, 1866), p. 14.

113. O to Willey, 31 August 1865, S. H. Willey letter book; Willey to O, 22 September 1865.

114. O to Willey, 25 July 1865 (copy).

115. Samuel Hopkins Willey, *Thirty Years in California: A Contribution to the History of the State from 1849 to 1879* (San Francisco: A. L. Bancroft & Co., 1879), p. 69.

116. O to Edward Dugdale, 15, 29 September 1865, Mariposa letter book, pp. 308, 310; O to Bowles, 20 September 1865; O to CV, 19 September 1865, Vaux Papers.
117. O to CV, 19 September 1865, Vaux Papers.
118. O to JO, 28 September 1865.
119. Bowles, *Across the Continent*, p. 302.
120. *Mariposa Gazette*, 7 October 1865; L. F. Jones to O, 9 October 1865.

CHAPTER XXV

1. [Daniel C. Gilman], "Our National Schools of Science," *North American Review* 105 (October 1867): 495–520.
2. O to MGVR, 11 June 1893.
3. CV to O, 20, 22 May 1865.
4. *Ibid.*, 6 July 1865.
5. *Ibid.*, 10 May 1865.
6. O to CV, 1 August 1865 (copy).
7. CV to O, 3 June 1865.
8. *Ibid.*, 20 May 1865.
9. *Ibid.*, 22 May 1865.
10. *Ibid.*, 3 June 1865.
11. *Ibid.*, 22, 30 May 1865.
12. O to Board of Trustees, Mariposa Co. (draft), 30 November 1865; O to Edward Dugdale, 25 November 1865 (draft); Howard Potter to O, 22 September 1865; Howard A. Martin to O, 13 November 1865; D. O. Mills to Lee & Waller, 11 October 1865.
13. E. Neely to O, [ca. 5 May 1866].
14. Calvert Vaux, "Fifth Annual Report, 1865," *Annual Reports of the Brooklyn Park Commissioners 1861–1873. Reprinted by Order of the Board . . . January 1873* (n.p.), pp. 78–82.
15. Egbert Viele, "First Annual Report, 1861," *Annual Reports of the Brooklyn Park Commissioners*, pp. 28, 32.
16. Vaux, "Fifth Annual Report, 1865," *Annual Reports of the Brooklyn Park Commissioners*, pp. 80–85; CV to O, 17 September 1864, 20 May 1865.
17. Olmsted, Vaux & Company, "Sixth Annual Report, 1866," *Reports of the Brooklyn Park Commissioners*, pp. 92–94.
18. Rollo Ogden, ed., *The Life and Letters of Edwin Lawrence Godkin*, 2 vols. (New York: Macmillan Co., 1907), 1: 224.
19. Royal Cortissoz, *Life of Whitelaw Reid*, 2 vols. (New York: Charles Scribner's Sons, 1921), 1: 137; E. L. Godkin, "The *Nation* and the Boston Recruiting Fund," *Boston Advertiser*, 20 November 1868.
20. *Nation* 1 (6 July 1865): 1.
21. Frank Preston Stearns, *The Life and Public Services of George Luther Stearns* (Philadelphia: J. B. Lippincott & Co., 1907), pp. 295–96.
22. Ogden, *Life and Letters*, 1: 241–42.
23. Godkin, "*Nation* and Boston Recruiting Fund."
24. Bowles to O, 8 December [1868]; *Springfield* (Mass.) *Republican*, 30 November 1868.
25. O to CEN, 22 December 1865, Norton Papers, Houghton Library, Harvard University, Cambridge, Massachusetts.
26. Stearns, *Life and Public Services*, p. 366.
27. *Ibid.*
28. Ogden, *Life and Letters*, 1: 242.

29. *Ibid.*, 1: 242–44; Gustav Pollack, *Fifty Years of American Idealism: The New York Nation, 1865–1915* (Boston: Houghton, Mifflin Co., 1915), p. 32; J. M. McKim to ELG, 3 December 1869.

30. FLO (son), interview.

31. George Spring Merriam, *Life and Times of Samuel Bowles*, 2 vols. (New York: Century Co., 1885), 2: 50–57.

32. *Nation* 4 (27 June 1867): 520–22; 3 (10 August 1866): 122; 3 (20 December 1866): 498–99; 1 (28 September 1865): 410–12; 3 (27 September 1866): 255–56; 2 (8 March 1866): 297; 2 (15 March 1866): 329; 3 (8 October 1866): 310–11; 6 (27 February 1868): 162; 3 (19 July 1866): 52–55.

33. O to CEN, 23 February 1866, Norton Papers.

34. Ashburner to MCO, 11 October 1865.

35. Duncan, Sherman & Co. to O, 21 April 1866.

36. W. C. Anderson to J. H. Headley, 3 July 1866.

37. E. Neely to O, [ca. 5 May 1866]; MCO memo, [ca. 5 May 1866].

38. Resolution of Board of Commissioners of Prospect Park, 29 May 1866.

39. O to CEN, 15 July 1866, Norton Papers.

40. O to CEN, 15 July, 26 August 1866, Norton Papers.

41. O to CEN, 26 August 1866, Norton Papers; GWC to O, 26 September 1866.

42. GWC to O, 6 September 1866; *New York Evening Post*, 6 September 1866.

43. "Mr. Beecher's Magnanimity," *Nation* 3 (6 September 1866): 192–93; "One Excuse for Conservatives," *Nation* 3 (13 September 1866): 210; "Mr. Beecher's General Laws," *Nation* 3 (20 September 1866): 230; "The Week," *Nation* 3 (27 September 1866): 241; "Work for Conservative Republicans," *Nation* 3 (27 September 1866): 250; "Terms of Reconstruction," *Nation* 3 (4 October 1866): 270.

44. GWC to O, 6 September 1866; *New York Evening Post*, 6 September 1866.

45. O to CEN, 12 September 1866, Norton Papers.

46. CEN to O, 2 September 1866; *Nation* 3 (6 September 1866): 181, 190.

47. O to CEN, 12 September 1866, Norton Papers.

48. *Ibid.*

49. CEN to O, 16 September 1866, Norton Papers; *Nation* 3 (1 November 1866): 351.

50. Francis Lieber to O, 8 November 1866; *Nation* 3 (1, 8 November 1866): 341, 361.

51. JO Jnl.; O to CEN, 11 January 1867, Norton Papers.

52. Ashburner to O, 27 February 1866.

53. Whitney, Ashburner, and Raymond to Low, 29 November 1865, California State Archives, Sacramento, California; F. F. Low, Governor's Biennial Message, 4 December 1865 (copy), LWR Files.

54. Bowles to O, 8 July [1866].

55. Deering to O, 4 January 1867, 15 August 1868; Galen Clark to O, 1 March 1868.

56. O to Low, 23 October 1866, California State Archives.

57. Galen Clark to O, 18 July 1868.

58. California, State Geologist [Josiah Dwight Whitney], *Yosemite Guide Book: A Description of the Yosemite Valley and the Adjacent Regions of the Sierra Nevada, and of the Big Trees of California* (Cambridge: University Press, Welch, Bigelow & Company, 1870), p. 20.

59. *Nation* 6 (27 February 1868): 163; *Congressional Globe* 82 (3 June 1868): 2817.

60. Edwin T. Brewster, *Life and Letters of Josiah Dwight Whitney* (Boston: Houghton, Mifflin Co., 1909), pp. 263–64.

61. Whitney to O, 8 March 1869.

62. *New York Evening Post*, 9 March 1870.

63. Carl Parcher Russell, *One Hundred Years in Yosemite: The Story of a Great Park and Its Friends* (Berkeley and Los Angeles: University of California Press, 1947), p. 151.

64. *Ibid.*

CHAPTER XXVI

1. O to CEN, 12 September 1866, Norton Papers, Houghton Library, Harvard University, Cambridge, Massachusetts.

2. Olmsted, Vaux & Co., *Preliminary Report in Regard to a Plan of Public Pleasure Grounds for the City of San Francisco* (New York: Wm. C. Bryant & Co., 1868).

3. O to CV, 19 September 1865 (*San Francisco Bulletin* clipping, n.d., enclosed), Vaux Papers, Public Library, New York, N.Y.; Ashburner to O, 4 November 1865; H. P. Coon et al. to O, 17 November 1865.

4. O, V & Co., *Report for San Francisco*, p. 5; Coon to O, 29 December 1865, 27 February 1866.

5. O, V & Co., *Report for San Francisco*, p. 8.

6. *Ibid.*, p. 17.

7. *Ibid.*, p. 19.

8. *Ibid.*, pp. 19–20.

9. *Ibid.*, pp. 20–21.

10. *Ibid.*, p. 23.

11. *Ibid.*, pp. 22, 24.

12. *Ibid.*, p. 22.

13. Coon to O, 29 June 1866; *Daily Alta California*, 11 May 1866.

14. Olmsted, Vaux & Co., *Report upon a Projected Improvement of the Estate of the College of California at Berkeley, near Oakland* (San Francisco: Towne and Bacon, 1866).

15. *Ibid.*, pp. 4–5.

16. *Ibid.*, pp. 6–7.

17. *Ibid.*, pp. 8–11.

18. *Ibid.*, p. 24.

19. *Ibid.*, p. 12.

20. *Ibid.*, p. 17.

21. *Ibid.*, p. 26.

22. *Ibid.*, pp. 24–25.

23. Frederick Billings to O, 12 June 1866.

24. S. H. Willey to O, 9 June 1867.

25. William Ashburner to O, 20 May 1870.

26. Ashburner to O, 1 June 1870.

27. Daniel C. Gilman to O, 18 December 1872.

28. Olmsted, Vaux & Co., *A Few Things To Be Thought Of Before Proceeding To Plan Buildings for the National Agricultural Colleges* (New York: American News Company, 1866).

29. [D. C. Gilman], "Our National Schools of Science," *North American Review* 105 (October 1867): 498–501.

30. Lilley Brewer Caswell, *A Brief History of the Massachusetts Agricultural College* (Springfield, Mass.: F. A. Bassette Co., 1917), pp. 3, 5.

31. Frank Prentice Rand, *Yesterdays at Massachusetts State College 1863–1933* (Published by Associate Alumni, Massachusetts State College, 1933), p. 75.

32. [Charles W. Eliot], "Science," *Nation* 2 (8 January 1866): 88; O to CEN, 26 April 1866, Norton Papers.

33. O to CEN, 26 April 1866, Norton Papers.

34. *Proceedings of the Massachusetts Historical Society* (Boston), 50: (January 1917) 168–70.

35. JO Jnl., 24 May 1866.

36. O, V & Co., *A Few Things*, pp. 5–9.

37. *Ibid.*

38. *Ibid.*, pp. 9–11.

39. *Ibid.*, pp. 12–17.

40. *Ibid.*, pp. 17–22.

41. *Ibid.*, p. 23.

42. H. F. French to O, 23 June 1866; D. W. Lincoln to O, 28 June 1866; O to Lincoln, 3 July 1866.

43. *Springfield* (Mass.) *Republican*, 14 July 1866.

44. French to O, 30 July 1866.

45. *Boston Advertiser*, 30 July 1866; Rand, *Yesterdays*, p. 15.

46. French to O, 3 August 1866; O to CEN, 26 August 1866, Norton Papers.

47. Edward Dickinson to O, 22 October 1866; *Springfield* (Mass.) *Republican*, 17 October 1866.

48. "How Not To Establish an Agricultural College," *Nation* 3 (25 October 1866): 335–36.

49. O to CEN, 26 August 1866, Norton Papers; [D. C. Gilman], "Our National Schools of Science"; [D. C. Gilman], "Educational," *Nation* 3 (27 December 1866): 513.

50. W. C. Flagg to O, 21 November 1866; J. B. Turner to O, 21 December 1866.

51. W. H. Brewer to O, 23 November 1866.

52. French to O, 24 November 1866; *Cultivator and Country Gentleman* 28 (6 December 1866): 386.

53. French to O, 1 June 1868.

54. W. A. P. Dillingham to O, 22 November 1866.

55. Merritt Caldwell Fernald, *History of the Maine State College and the University of Maine* (Orono, Maine: University of Maine, 1916), p. 23.

56. *An Act To Establish the State College of Agriculture and the Mechanic Arts, Passed, February 1865*, Printed by Direction of the Trustees (Portland: Press of Brown Thurston, 1865), p. 7.

57. Maine, Forty-sixth Legislature, *Annual Report of the State College of Agriculture and the Mechanic Arts* (n.p., n.d.), House No. 57, pp. 15, 29.

58. *Ibid.*, pp. 18, 24.

59. Dillingham to O, 9 February 1867; S. L. Goodale to O, 20 April 1867; Fernald, *History of Maine State College and University*, pp. 28–29.

CHAPTER XXVII

1. American Social Science Association, *Document Published by the Association, with Abridgement of Its Transactions* (Boston: Wright and Potter, 1866), Part 1, p. 3; Part 2, p. 73.

2. "Eighth Annual Report, 1868," *Annual Reports of the Brooklyn Park Commissioners 1861–1873, Reprinted by Order of the Board . . . January 1873* (n.p.), pp. 155, 162.

3. A. H. Barnes to O, 16 February 1869; Ulysses Prentiss Hedrick, *A History of Horticulture in America to 1860* (New York: Oxford University Press, 1950), p. 260.

4. Alfred Theodore Andreas, *History of Chicago*, 3 vols. (Chicago: A. T. Andreas, 1884), 2: 478–79.

5. Frederick Law Olmsted, *A Consideration of the Justifying Value of a Public Park* . . . (Boston: Tolman & White, 1881), pp. 8, 18–19.

6. Frederick Law Olmsted, *Public Parks and the Enlargement of Towns* . . . (Cambridge, Mass.: Riverside Press, 1870), p. 11.

7. *Ibid.*, p. 18.

8. William Bross to O, 28 April 1866; William Dorsheimer to O, 23 July 1866; Montgomery Meigs to O, 23 June 1866.

9. George G. Meade to O, 7 June 1867; Olmsted, Vaux & Co. to New Britain Park Commissioners, April 1870; *Report of the Park Commissioners Appointed by an Act of the Legislature Entitled "An Act To Authorize the Selection and Location of Certain Grounds for a Public Park for the City of Newark," Approved April 9, 1867* (Trenton, N. J.: True American Office, 1868).

10. Olmsted, Vaux & Co., *Report on the Proposed City Park* (Albany, N.Y.: J. Munsell, 1868); John H. Rauch to O, 13 April 1869.

11. HWSC to O, 8 April 1869; James T. Fields to O, 15 November 1869; R. M. Copeland to O, 3 December 1869; Henry Villard to O, 8 December 1869.

12. Henry P. Phelps, *The Albany Handbook* (Albany, N.Y.: Brandow & Barton, 1884), pp. 159–60.

13. Alonzo Church, *Newark Sunday Call*, 12 May 1912.

14. F. T. Stanley to O, 12 January 1869.

15. Commissioners of Fairmont Park, *Annual Reports 1 through 4* (Philadelphia, 1869–72), pp. 26, 57.

16. GEW to O, 22 August 1869; A. J. Bloor to O, 5 February 1867; H. Janin to O, 30 March 1866.

17. Peter Melendy to O, 31 December 1867; William Warren Ferrier, *Origin and Development of the University of California* (Berkeley: Sathergate Book Shop, 1930), p. 301; E. S. Dwight to O, 11 July 1867.

18. Caroline E. Monell to O, 5 March 1867; Charles Scribner to O, 29 July 1868; Ford, Olmstead & Co. to O, 1 November 1867.

19. Fred C. Withers to O, 25 October 1867; F. B. Sanborn to O, 18 October 1866.

20. KPW to O, 13 August 1867.

21. HHR to O, 13 October 1868.

22. CEN to O, 13 February 1868; ELG to O, 8 August 1870.

23. J. C. Derby to O, 4 August 1866.

24. John Bowne to O, 20 February, 22 November 1867.

25. L. L. Schuyler to O, 27 August, 8 November 1869.

26. E. M. Gallaudet to O, 10 March, 23 April 1866; FNK to O, 9 July, 13 August, 12 October 1866.

27. Howard Potter to O, 20 June 1866, 5 October 1867.

28. Francis Fowler to O, 9 March 1867.

29. Abby H. Woolsey to O, 5 August 1867; Edith Armstrong Talbot, *Samuel Chapman Armstrong: A Biographical Study* (New York: Doubleday, Page & Company, 1904), p. 172.

30. W. A. Dickinson to O, March 1870.

31. A. D. White to O, 20 May, 22 June 1867, 14 June 1873; Ezra Cornell to O, 26 August 1867.

32. Olmsted, Vaux & Co., *Preliminary Report upon the Proposed Suburban Village at Riverside, near Chicago* (New York: Sutton, Bowne & Co., 1868), pp. 4–5.

33. Andrew Jackson Downing, *A Treatise on the Theory and Practice of Landscape Gardening Adapted to North America* . . . , 8th ed., enlarged, revised and newly illustrated, with a supplement by Henry Winthrop Sargent (New York: O. Judd & Co., 1859), pp. 568–72.

34. O to MCO, 23 August [1868].

35. *Ibid.*, 4 August 1868.

36. Buffalo Park Commission, *Preliminary Report Respecting a Public Park in Buffalo, and a Copy of the Act of the Legislature Authorizing Its Establishment* (Buffalo: Matthews & Warren, 1869), p. 11.

37. *Buffalo Courier*, 26 November 1869.

38. Buffalo Park Commission, *Preliminary Report*, pp. 21–23.

39. O to MCO, 23 August [1868]; O, V & Co., *Preliminary Report upon Riverside*, p. 4.

40. *Ibid.*, pp. 14–15.

41. *Ibid.*, pp. 10–11, 20, 23, 26–28.

42. *Buffalo Courier*, 26 August 1868.

43. Draft of a Proposed Agreement between the Development Company and the Landscape Architects [September 1868] (copy), LWR Files.

44. Prospectus of the Riverside Improvement Enterprise (n.p., n.d.), LWR Files.

45. O to CV, 29 August 1868.

46. Prospectus of Riverside.

47. CV to O, 18 June 1869, [ca. October 1869].

48. O to E. E. Childs, 28 October 1869.

49. CV to O, 15 June 1869.

50. John H. Rauch to O, 21 April 1869.

51. CV to O, 11 April 1870.

52. C. H. Hueller to O, 15 June 1870.

53. George Skinner to O, 25 February 1872; C. H. Hueller to O, 25 November 1871.

54. O to E. B. McCagg, 26 January 1877; A. J. Cross to O, 9 October 1882.

55. W. L. B. Jenney to O, 20 December 1870.

56. L. Y. Schermerhorn to O, 13 April 1877.

57. *Ibid.*

58. Christopher Tunnard, *The City of Man* (New York: Charles Scribner's Sons, 1953), p. 202.

59. Henry George Steinmeyer, *Staten Island 1524–1898* (Richmond, N.Y.: Staten Island Historical Society, 1950), pp. 67–68.

60. Charles William Leng and William T. Davis, *Staten Island and Its People, a History 1609–1929*, 4 vols. (New York: Lewis Historical Publishing Co., Inc., 1930), 1: 302.

61. Steinmeyer, *Staten Island*, p. 67.

62. George Bowman to O, 29 July 1870.

63. Leng and Davis, *Staten Island*, 1: 303.

64. *New York World*, 20 July 1870.

65. O to W. B. Duncan, 22 September 1870; N. C. Miller to O, 14 October 1870.

66. Staten Island Improvement Commission, *Report of a Preliminary Scheme of Improvements, Presented January 12th, 1871* (New York: James Sutton & Co., 1871).

67. Leng and Davis, *Staten Island*, 1: 305.

68. George Bowman to O, 21 July 1870.

69. Tarrytown Heights Land Company, *Prospectus of the New Suburban District of Tarrytown Heights, with Plan and Report of Messrs. Olmsted, Vaux & Co., Landscape Architects . . .* (n.p., n.d.), pp. 14–20.

70. Buffalo Park Commission, *Preliminary Report*, pp. 28–49.

71. *Buffalo Courier*, 26 November 1869.

72. Buffalo Park Commission, *First Annual Report January 1871* (Buffalo: Warren, Johnson & Co., 1871), p. 14.

73. William H. Hall to O, 22 August, 29 November 1871, 15 January 1872.

74. Everett Chamberlain, *Chicago and Its Suburbs* (Chicago: T. A. Hungerford & Co., 1874), pp. 313, 316, 320; Chicago South Park Commission, *Report Accompanying Plan for Laying out the South Park, Olmsted, Vaux & Co. Landscape Architects* (Chicago: Evening Journal, 1871).

75. H. W. S. Cleveland, "Landscape Gardening," *Christian Examiner* 58 (May 1855): 384; HWSC to O, 12 February 1881.

76. [Cleveland], *The Public Grounds of Chicago. How To Give Them Character and Expression* (Chicago: Charles D. Lakey, 1869), pp. 8–10.

77. [Robert Morris Copeland], "The New Park," *Boston Daily Advertiser* (supplement), 12 March 1870; "The Park Question," *Boston Daily Advertiser*, 2 December 1869.

78. *Boston Advertiser*, 26 February 1870.

79. F. L. Olmsted, *Public Parks*, pp. 13, 22–23.

80. James Haughton to O, 15 October 1870, 13 January 1871; O to Charles G. Loring, 21 January 1871 (copy).

81. Frederick Law Olmsted, Jr., and Theodora Kimball, eds., *Forty Years of Landscape Architecture: Frederick Law Olmsted, Senior*, 2 vols. (New York and London: G. P. Putnam's Sons, 1922, 1928), 2: 86.

82. *Ibid.*

83. CV to O, 11 April 1870.

84. F. L. Olmsted, Jr., and T. Kimball, *Forty Years*, 2: 87.

85. O to Charles G. Loring, 21 January 1871 (copy).

86. F. L. Olmsted, Jr., and T. Kimball, *Forty Years*, 2: 88.

87. *Ibid.*, p. 90.

88. *Ibid.*, pp. 90, 504–5.

89. *New York Times*, 30 December 1870.

90. F. L. Olmsted, Jr., and T. Kimball, *Forty Years*, 2: 92–93.

91. O to CLB, 24 November 1871.

92. *Ibid.*

CHAPTER XXVIII

1. O to H. G. DeForest, 25 June 1881.

2. Memo of Schedule of Charges [1873].

3. O to William McMillan, 26 January 1889.

4. Frederick Law Olmsted, Jr., and Theodora Kimball eds., *Forty Years of Landscape Architecture: Frederick Law Olmsted, Senior*, 2 vols. (New York and London: G. P. Putnam's Sons, 1922, 1928), 2: 109.

5. O to J. M. Drill, 8 May 1882.

6. O to Ariel Lathrop, 7 July 1890 (draft).

7. O to Sidney Stratton, 2 May 1889.

8. O to Ariel Lathrop, 7 July 1890 (draft).

9. GWC to O, 30 March 1868.

10. O to JCO, 15 March 1894; O to J. J. Albright, 31 May 1892.

11. O to Douglass, 2 May 1887 (copy).

12. O to Charles Eliot, 28 October 1886.

13. O to E. T. Slocum, 15 March 1887 (copy); O to C. A. Roberts, 5 October 1889 (copy).

14. O to Morris K. Jesup, 22, 31 January, 11 February 1889 (copies).

15. O to Henry Beekman, 20 May 1886 (draft); O to Albert Wright, 1 February 1889 (copy).

16. H. W. S. Cleveland, *Landscape Architecture as Applied to the Wants of the West, with an Essay on Forest Planting on the Great Plains* (Chicago: Jansen, McClurg & Co., 1873), p. 17.

17. *Ibid.*, p. 80.

18. HWSC to O, 26 February 1872.

19. *Ibid.*, 7 September 1870.

20. Edward Everett Hale, Jr., *Life and Letters of Edward Everett Hale*, 2 vols. (Boston: Little, Brown and Co., 1917), 2: 147.

21. JO Jnl., 23 November 1868.

22. JO to O, 29 October 1868.

23. C. C. Martin to O, 21 February 1870, 29 March 1871.

24. FNK to O, 24 October, 11 December 1868, 6 January 1869; J. W. Stockwell to O, 8 June 1871.

25. C. A. Dana to O, 1 July 1869, 6 January [1870], 15 September 1870.

26. William Ashburner to O, 10 January 1871; L. S. Pease to O, 12 January 1871.

27. Bowles to O, 3 May 1871.

28. *Ibid.*

29. O to Bowles, 2 June 1871.

30. Bowles to O, 14 June 1871.

31. O to FJK, 23 December 1869.

32. JO Jnl.; FLO (son), interview.

33. The Century Association, *The Century 1847–1946* (New York: The Century Association, 1947).

34. George Spring Merriam, *Life and Times of Samuel Bowles*, 2 vols. (New York: Century Co., 1885), 2: 170.

35. [Frederick Law Olmsted], "Genesis of a Rumor," *Nation* 6 (23 April 1868): 328–29; "Suburban Home Grounds," *Nation* 13 (26 October 1871): 275–77; "Chicago Academy of Sciences," *Nation* 13 (7 December 1871): 367; "Chicago in Distress," *Nation* 13 (9 November 1871): 305.

36. [F. L. Olmsted], "Chicago in Distress," p. 305.

37. HWSC to O, 2 February 1874.

38. Winifred Eva Howe, *A History of the Metropolitan Museum of Art, with a Chapter on Early Institutions of Art in New York* (New York: [Printed at the Gillis Press], 1913), pp. 116–17, 123, 139–53.

39. D. T. Brown to O, 16 July 1873.

40. T. K. Beecher to O, 28 April 1873.

41. A. H. Barnes to CLB, 31 October 1870; FJK to O, 24 March 1871.

42. O to FJK, 20 April 1871.

43. *Ibid.*

44. Bowles to O, 15 May 1872.

45. O to Bowles, 11, 14, 16 May 1872.

46. *Ibid.; New York Post*, 14 May 1872.

47. *New York Post*, 22 June 1872; *Nation* 14 (27 June 1872): 413.

48. MCO, memo, n.d.

49. J. M. McKim to O, 24 June [1872].

50. A. J. Bloor to O, 23 June 1872.

51. *Nation* 14 (27 June 1872): 413; *New York Post*, 22 June 1872.

52. F. L. Olmsted, Jr., and T. Kimball, *Forty Years*, 2: 93.

53. *Ibid.*, pp. 94–98.

54. *Ibid.*, pp. 126–27.

55. *Ibid.*, p. 94.

56. *Ibid.*, p. 101.

57. *Ibid.*, pp. 130–31.

58. *Ibid.*, 1: 16.
59. *Ibid.*, 2: 94.
60. O to FJK, 28 January 1873.
61. *Ibid.*

CHAPTER XXIX

1. O to FJK, 28 January 1873.
2. FLO (son), "Random Notes on FLO's Office at 209 West 46th Street," June 1952, LWR Files.
3. FLO (son), interview.
4. "List of Books Belonging to F. L. Olmsted, December 1882," LWR Files.
5. FLO (son), interview.
6. FLO (son) to LWR, 16 June 1952, LWR Files.
7. FLO (son) to LWR, 7 June 1952, LWR Files.
8. FLO (son), "Random Notes on FLO's Office at 209 West 46th Street."
9. *Ibid.*
10. FLO (son), interview.
11. *Ibid.*
12. *Ibid.*
13. O to FNK, 8 October 1866, 20 June 1870.
14. MCO to JCO, 25 June, 6 July, 17 August, 12 September 1876, 16 July 1879.
15. MCO, memo, n.d., LWR Files.
16. Frederick Billings to O, 19, 25, 26 September 1873; John W. Reps, *The Making of Urban America: A History of City Planning in the United States* (Princeton: Princeton University Press, 1965), p. 410.
17. O to Justin Morrill [1 January 1874?] (draft).
18. FNK to O, 28 September 1874; Montgomery Meigs to O, 6 May 1875; William A. Dickinson to O, March 1870; A. Jackson to O, 5 April 1873; G. W. Russell to O, 10 June 1874; Buffalo Park Commissioners, *Fifth Annual Report, January 1875* (Buffalo: Warren Johnson & Co., 1875), pp. 13–16; O to Rev. J. R. Miller, 18 January 1876; Charles Sprague Sargent to O, 13 October 1873; Charles A. Dana to O, 27 May 1874; Cyrus Field to O, 30 October 1874; Henry B. Hyde to O, 17 August 1874.
19. Marguerite Weidenmann, interview, 1 August 1950; O to Jacob Weidenmann, 19 May 1874 (draft of proposed agreement).
20. Seymour Mandelbaum, *Boss Tweed's New York* (New York: John Wiley & Sons, 1965), pp. 83–86.
21. *Ibid.*, p. 90.
22. *Ibid.*, pp. 106–7.
23. *Ibid.*, pp. 95, 115.
24. *Ibid.*, p. 114.
25. O, memo, 10 March 1874, Box 30.
26. O, memo, 25 March 1875, Box 30.
27. Frederick Law Olmsted, *The Spoils of the Park, with a Few Leaves from the Deep-Laden Note-Books of "A Wholly Impractical Man"* . . . (February 1882), p. 24.
28. O, memo, 1 May 1875, Box 30.
29. O, memo, 28 April 1875, Box 30.
30. O to Junius Henri Browne, 12 November 1874 (draft), Box 29.
31. O, memo, 28 April 1875, Box 30.
32. *New York Times*, 28 April 1875.
33. O, memo, 29 April 1875.
34. O to William R. Martin, 25 May 1875.

35. *New York Post*, 3 June 1875.

36. *New York World*, 3 December 1875.

37. *Ibid.*, 1 October 1876; O, memo, 6 May 1876, Box 30.

38. *New York World*, 26 November 1876.

39. *Ibid.*, 24 November 1876; *New York Times*, 24 November 1876.

40. O, memo, 7 August 1876, Box 30.

41. O, memos, 27 April, 1 May 1875, Box 30.

42. Frederick Law Olmsted, Jr., and Theodora Kimball, *Forty Years of Landscape Architecture: Frederick Law Olmsted, Senior*, 2 vols. (New York and London: G. P. Putnam's Sons, 1922, 1928), 2: 108–9; Howard A. Martin to W. M. Pritchard, 29 July 1876, Box 30.

43. George Mazaraki, "The Public Career of Andrew Haswell Green" (Ph.D. dissertation, New York University, 1966).

44. Frederick Law Olmsted and J. James R. Croes, *Preliminary Report of the Landscape Architect and the Civil and Topographical Engineer, upon the Laying Out of the Twenty-third and Twenty-fourth Wards, and Report of the Landscape Architect and the Civil and Topographical Engineer, Accompanying a Plan for Laying out That Part of the Twenty-fourth Ward, Lying West of Riverdale Road* ([New York]: Board of the Department of Public Parks, December 20, 1876), document 72, p. 5.

45. *Ibid.*, pp. 6–8.

46. *Ibid.*, pp. 9–10.

47. Albert Fein, *Landscape into Cityscape: Frederick Law Olmsted's Plans for a Greater New York City* (Ithaca: Cornell University Press, 1968), p. 329.

48. F. L. Olmsted and J. J. R. Croes, *Preliminary Report*, document 72, p. 11.

49. O, memo, 29 April 1875, Box 30; Mandelbaum, *Boss Tweed's New York*, p. 116; W. R. Martin to H. A. Martin, n.d., LWR Files.

50. F. L. Olmsted and J. J. R. Croes, *Preliminary Report*, document 72, p. 4.

51. *Ibid.*, p. 10.

52. *Ibid.*, p. 13.

53. *Ibid.*, p. 14.

54. *Ibid.*, p. 18.

55. Frederick Law Olmsted and J. James R. Croes, *Report of the Civil and Topographical Engineer and the Landscape Architect, Accompanying a Plan for Local Steam Transit Routes in the Twenty-third and Twenty-fourth Wards* ([New York]: Board of the Department of Public Parks, March 21, 1877), document 75.

56. Frederick Law Olmsted and J. James R. Croes, *Communication from the Landscape Architect and the Civil and Topographical Engineer, in Relation to the Proposed Plan for Laying out the Central District of the Twenty-third and Twenty-fourth Wards, Lying East of Jerome Avenue and West of Third Avenue and the Harlem Railroad* ([New York]: Board of the Department of Public Works, November 7, 1877), document 76.

57. [O] to W. R. Martin, 2 April 1877 (copy), Box 31.

58. Frederick Law Olmsted, untitled galley proof, 8 January 1879, LWR Files.

59. *Ibid.*

60. O to Commissioners of Mt. Royal Park, 23 November 1874; P. O'Meara to O, 31 December 1874 (telegram).

61. H. A. Nelson to O, 9 March 1876, LWR Files.

62. O to Nelson, 6 January 1876 (draft), LWR Files.

63. *Ibid.*, 8 April, 3 November 1876 (drafts), LWR Files.

64. *Ibid.*, 10 April 1876 (draft), LWR Files.

65. *Ibid.*, 11, 29 April, 16 June 1876 (drafts), LWR Files.

66. *Montreal Evening Star*, 25 May 1876; *Montreal Gazette*, 25 May 1876.

67. *Montreal Evening Mail*, 10 June 1876; O to Montreal Park Commissioners, 13 June 1876 (draft).

68. *Montreal Evening Mail*, 13 June 1876.
69. O to Nelson, 15, 20 March 1876 (drafts), LWR Files.
70. Owen F. Olmsted to O, 22 August 1876.
71. O to Nelson, 24 July 1876 (draft), LWR Files.
72. Nelson to O, 7 September 1877, LWR Files.
73. *Ibid.*, 26 May 1877, LWR Files.
74. O to MCO, 3 August 1877.
75. *Ibid.*, 24, 25 July 1877.
76. *Ibid.*, 27 July 1877.
77. Frederick Law Olmsted, *Mount Royal, Montreal* (New York: G. P. Putnam's Sons, 1881), p. 6.
78. *Ibid.*
79. F. L. Olmsted, untitled galley proof, 8 January 1879, LWR Files.
80. F. L. Olmsted, *Spoils of the Park*, p. 30.
81. *New York Herald*, 10 January 1878.
82. F. L. Olmsted, Jr., and T. Kimball, *Forty Years*, 2: 110.
83. *Ibid.*, 2: 111; *New York World*, 10 January 1878.
84. F. L. Olmsted, Jr., and T. Kimball, *Forty Years*, 2: 111.
85. Theodora Kimball, memo quoting MCO, n.d.
86. F. L. Olmsted, Jr., and T. Kimball, *Forty Years*, 2: 112.
87. *New York Tribune*, 11 January 1878.
88. MCO to JCO, 24 February 1878; CV to ELG, March 1878.
89. *New York Tribune*, 19 February 1878.
90. MCO to JCO, 24, 25 February 1878.
91. *New York Tribune*, 20 February 1878.
92. *Ibid.*, 21 February 1878.
93. MCO to CV, 21 February 1878 (draft).
94. MCO to JCO, 25 February 1878.
95. O, notebook, Box 48.
96. O to Edouard André, August (draft), 3 November 1876, 29 July 1878.
97. Oliver Bullard to O, 29 April 1878.
98. F. L. Olmsted, untitled galley proof, 8 January 1879, LWR Files; O to Leopold Eidlitz, 19 July 1878 (draft); J. J. R. Croes to O, 28 July 1881, LWR Files.

CHAPTER XXX

1. Frederick Law Olmsted, "The Future of New York," *New York Tribune*, 28 December 1879.
2. FLO (son), interview.
3. O to Edouard André, 29 July 1878.
4. Clarence King to O, 15 October 1878.
5. KPW to Emma Brace, 20 February 1904.
6. KPW to O, 9 July, 17 August 1873, 22 August 1870, 29 December [1871], 15 January 1874, 29 February 1876.
7. KPW to O, 22 November 1877.
8. GEW to O, 4 August 1879; Mary P. Jacobi, 1 February [1880?].
9. O to KPW, 10 December 1893 (letter press copy); KPW to Emma Brace, 20 February 1904.
10. O to Charles Sprague Sargent, 29 November 1878; William Ashburner to O, 4 January 1879; Asa Gray to O, 22 January 1879.
11. Albert S. Bickmore to O, 8 March 1876, 2 August 1877; Howard A. Martin to O, 25 May 1878; O to Board of Commissioners, Department of Public Parks, 2 January 1878; O to JCO, 25 February 1894.

12. Louisa L. Schuyler to O, 12 February [1877]; Susan M. Van Ameringe to O, 7 January 1880, 19 November 1881.

13. O to George Shattuck, 31 December [1877] (draft).

14. W. H. C. Price to O, 21 June 1879; O to J. D. Crimmins, 28 November 1889; O to CV, 3, 5 January 1881, Vaux Papers, Public Library, New York, N.Y.

15. O to A. J. Bloor, 20, 23 September, 4 October 1882.

16. O to HWB, 24 October 1879, Bellows Papers, Massachusetts Historical Society, Boston, Massachusetts.

17. E. Thurber to O, 9 May 1880; Francis L. Lee to O, 4 May 1880; Howard Potter to O, 29 May 1880; FNK to O, 20, 21, 25 June, 5, 23, 25 July, 8 August, 1 September 1880.

18. O to ELG, 25 April 1881 (draft).

19. MAO to O, 18 August 1873, 11 April 1875, 27 April, 14 July, 15 October 1879, 6 September 1883; Albert Henry Olmsted to O, 17, 26 February, 5, 26 March 1873, 13 October 1879.

20. Theodora Kimball, memo, n.d., LWR Files.

21. Henry-Russell Hitchcock, *The Architecture of Henry Hobson Richardson* (Hamden, Conn.: Archon Books, 1961), p. 167; Frederick Law Olmsted, Leopold Eidlitz, and Henry Hobson Richardson, *Report of the New Capitol Commission Relative to the Plans Submitted by Messrs. Frederick Law Olmstead* [sic], *Leopold Eidlitz and H. H. Richardson* (State of New York, Senate, March 3, 1876), no. 49, p. 4.

22. Hitchcock, *Richardson*, p. 168.

23. Mariana Griswold Van Rensselaer, *Henry Hobson Richardson and His Works* (Boston and New York: Houghton, Mifflin Co., 1888), p. 22.

24. *Ibid.*, pp. 27, 118.

25. Hitchcock, *Richardson*, pp. 118–19; H. H. Richardson to O, 6 December 1874.

26. Montgomery Schuyler, "The Capitol of New York," *Scribner's Monthly Magazine* 19 (December 1879): 161–78.

27. *Ibid.*, pp. 161–63.

28. F. L. Olmsted, L. Eidlitz, and H. H. Richardson, *Report of the New Capitol Commission*, pp. 6, 14–15.

29. Schuyler, "The Capitol of New York," p. 164.

30. F. L. Olmsted, L. Eidlitz, and H. H. Richardson, *Report of the New Capitol Commission*, pp. 23–26.

31. Hitchcock, *Richardson*, pp. 169–70.

32. Schuyler, "The Capitol of New York," p. 167.

33. O to CEN, 22 April 1876, Norton Papers, Houghton Library, Cambridge, Massachusetts.

34. *American Architect and Building News* 1 (11, 18 March 1876): 82, 91.

35. O to CEN, 2 April 1876, Norton Papers; Schuyler, "The Capitol of New York," p. 166.

36. *American Architect and Building News* 1 (1 April 1876): 106–10.

37. *Ibid.*, p. 114; O to William Dorsheimer, 20 April 1876 (draft).

38. Van Rensselaer, *Richardson*, p. 75; O to William M. Hunt, 4 April 1876 (draft).

39. O to CEN, 13 April 1876, Norton Papers; Schuyler, "The Capitol of New York," p. 166.

40. Schuyler to O, 5 April [1876]; CEN to O, 18 April 1876, Norton Papers.

41. CEN to O, 4, 18 April 1876 (typed copies).

42. O to CEN, 22 April, 7 June 1876, Norton Papers.

43. *Ibid.*, 27 December 1876, 28 March 1877, Norton Papers.

44. *American Architect and Building News* 2 (17 March 1877): 85.

45. *Ibid.*, 91; CEN to O, 25 March 1877 (typed copy).

46. O to CEN, 15 February 1877, Norton Papers.

47. O, memo on patronage at Albany Capitol, n.d.
48. Schuyler, "The Capitol of New York," pp. 167–69.
49. *American Architect and Building News* 5 (18 January 1879): 29.
50. O to CEN, 7 June 1876, Norton Papers.
51. O to MGVR, 19 August 1886.
52. O to H. Y. Attrill, 8 July 1879 (draft).
53. "The World's Fair and Landscape Architecture," *Century Illustrated Monthly Magazine* 6 (April 1893): 952.
54. Charles F. Adams, Jr., to O, 17 November 1881, 31 March 1882; E. S. Converse to O, 15 April 1884; O. A. Ames to O, 13 July 1881; F. L. Ames to O, 29 April 1884; C. E. Stuart to O, 13 October 1882; J. H. Russell to O, 1, 3, 5 April 1884; JCO to G. R. Hardy, 3 May 1884.
55. John Nolen, "Frederick Law Olmsted and His Work. II: The Terraces and Landscape Work of the United States Capitol at Washington," *House and Garden* 9 (March 1906): 117–28; *Annual Report of the Architect of the United States Capitol for the Fiscal Year Ending June 30, 1882, Edward Clark, Architect, with a Paper Relating to the Trees, Shrubs and Plants in the United States Capitol Ground, Together with Some Observations upon the Planting and Care of Trees in the District of Columbia by Frederick Law Olmsted, Landscape Architect* (Washington: Government Printing Office, 1882), p. 13.
56. *Ibid.*, pp. 13–14.
57. *Ibid.*, pp. 14–15.
58. Justin Morrill to Henry G. Stebbins, 10 May 1873.
59. Albert Henry Olmsted to O, 28 May 1873; O to Morrill, 26 November 1873, Morrill letter book pp. 5262–63, Olmsted Associates Papers, Library of Congress, Washington, D.C.
60. Ihna Thayer Frary, *They Built the Capitol* (Richmond: Garrett and Massie, 1940), p. 307.
61. O to William H. Hall, 28 March 1874 (draft), Box 35; O to Morrill, [1 January 1874?] (draft), Box 35.
62. O to Morrill, [1 January 1874?] (draft), Box 35.
63. O to Hall, 28 March 1874 (draft), Box 35; Morrill to O, 27 March 1874, Olmsted Associates Papers.
64. *Annual Report of the Architect of the Capitol for the Year Ending June 30, 1882*, pp. 15–16.
65. *Ibid.*
66. *Ibid.*, p. 15; O to GEW, 19 July 1874 (draft).
67. O to Morrill, 16 August 1874, Morrill letter book, p. 5481, Olmsted Associates Papers.
68. *Ibid.*
69. O to J. Partridge, 5 October 1874, 18 June 1875 (copies).
70. *New York Tribune*, 28 November 1874.
71. *Annual Report of the Architect of the United States Capitol for the Fiscal Year Ending June 30, 1881. Edward Clark Architect* (Washington: Government Printing Office, 1881), pp. 14–15.
72. *Ibid.*, p. 14; O to Perry, 20 March 1885, letter book, June 1884–September 1887, pp. 178–81.
73. Edward Clark to O, 6 March 1875, Architect of the Capitol's Office letter press 18: 179; O to Morrill, 11 March 1875, Morrill letter book, pp. 5710–11.
74. O to F. H. Cobb, 11 June 1878, Architect of the Capitol's Office; O to André, 6 June 1879 (draft).
75. Charles M. Dow, *The State Reservation at Niagara, a History* (Albany: J. B. Lyon Company, 1914), p. 9.

76. *Ibid.*, p. 12; O to Thomas V. Welch, 16 February 1889 (copy).
77. Dow, *Niagara*, pp. 10–11.
78. O to Welch, 16 February 1889 (copy).
79. *Ibid.*
80. Calvert Vaux, letter in *New York Tribune*, 6 October 1878.
81. O. Mowat, Report to [Lord Lorne], 9 December 1879 (copy), Box 31.
82. *Special Report of the New York State Survey on the Preservation of the Scenery of Niagara Falls, and Fourth Annual Report on the Triangulation of the State. For the Year 1879. James T. Gardner, Director* (Albany: Charles Van Benthuysen & Sons, 1880), p. 7.
83. *Ibid.*, p. 7; J. B. Harrison, "Charles Eliot Norton and Niagara Falls," Norton Papers, Library of Congress, Washington, D. C.
84. *Special Report on Niagara Falls*, p. 19.
85. O to CEN, 10 October 1879, Norton Papers, Houghton Library.
86. O. Mowat to [Lord Lorne], 9 December 1879 (copy), Box 31.
87. *Ibid.*
88. O to CEN, 10 October 1879, Norton Papers, Houghton Library.
89. *Special Report on Niagara Falls*, pp. 31–39.
90. O to CEN, 20 April 1880, Norton Papers, Houghton Library; Harrison, "Norton and Niagara."
91. J. B. Harrison, "The Movement for the Redemption of Niagara," *New Princeton Review* 1 (March 1886): 235.
92. CEN to O, 28 May 1880 (copy), Box 31.
93. O to Mrs. Charles Darwin, 11 June 1880 (draft), Box 31.
94. W. O. Buchanan to O, 30 March 1880, Box 31.
95. Buchanan to O, 17 April, 12 June, 9 August 1880, Box 31.
96. O to Howard Potter, 4 July 1881 (draft), Box 31; Potter to O, 18 July 1881, Box 31; Harrison, "Norton and Niagara"; CEN to O, 24 July 1881 (copy), Box 31.

CHAPTER XXXI

1. FLO (son), interview.
2. *Ibid.*
3. Salem Wales to O, 7 February, 27 October 1881, 28 January 1882; Smith Lane to O, 12 February 1881; CV to O, 20 October, 16, 20 November 1881.
4. O to *New York Herald*, 2 February 1881 (copy).
5. J. Weidenmann to O, 12 January, 9 June, 5 November 1881, 10 March 1882; O to W. L. Fischer, 19 October 1881; Fischer to O, 7 November 1881; *New York Sun*, 22 October 1882.
6. O to CV, 1, 3, 5 January 1881, Vaux Papers, Public Library, New York, N.Y.
7. Frederick Law Olmsted, *The Spoils of the Park, with a Few Leaves from the Deep-Laden Note-Books of "A Wholly Unpractical Man ..."* (February 1882).
8. *Ibid.*, pp. 56–57.
9. O to CLB, 7 March 1882.
10. O to MGVR, 23 September 1893.
11. Frederick Law Olmsted, *Mount Royal, Montreal* (New York: G. P. Putnam's Sons, 1881), p. 23.
12. O to CLB, 7 March 1882.
13. [Frederick Law Olmsted], *The Buffalo Park System, September 1881* (Buffalo: Matthews, Northrup & Co., 1881), pp. 3–7.
14. *Ibid.*, pp. 7–11.

15. Board of Commissioners of the Department of Parks for the City of Boston, *Seventh Annual Report, for the Year 1881* (Boston: Rockwell and Churchill, 1882), p. 27.

16. *Ibid.*, pp. 27–28.

17. *Ibid.*, pp. 26–27.

18. MCO to Henry Perkins, 25 November 1881, LWR Files.

19. Clarence King to O, 15 October 1878.

20. Owen Frederick Olmsted to JCO, 17 November 1878, 27 March 1879.

21. King to O, 26 March 1880.

22. Class of 1878 School of Mines, Columbia College, *In Memoriam: Owen Frederick Olmsted, C.E.*, p. 13.

23. MCO to Ruth [Tomkins], 17 March 1882.

24. Charles Francis Adams, Jr., to O, 19 October, 5 December 1881; J. Wrey Mould to O, 20 October 1880; HWSC to O, 14 February 1881.

25. O to CEN, 19 October 1881, Norton Papers, Houghton Library, Harvard University, Cambridge, Massachusetts.

26. O to F. H. Cobb, 22 November 1881, Architect of the Capitol's Office, Washington, D. C.

27. CV to O, 9 December 1881; F. L. Ames to O, 16 February 1882; Salem Wales to O, 21 January 1882.

28. Wales to O, 14 March 1882; O to Wales, 15 March 1882.

29. Theodore Roosevelt to O, 19 March 1882 (copy).

30. CV to O, 9 January 1883, Box 30; O to CV, 11 January 1883, Vaux Papers, Public Library, New York, N.Y.

31. *New York Tribune*, 13 February 1883; O to CV, 11 January 1883.

32. O to CV, 11 January 1883.

33. O to Sylvester Baxter, 24 November 1881.

34. James S. T. Stranahan to O, 16 March, 7 July 1882.

35. O to HWSC, 9 February 1881.

36. FLO (son) to LWR, June 1952, LWR Files.

37. *Ibid.*

38. *Ibid.*

39. O to FJK, 6 September, 1893; C. F. Ware to O, 1 November 1881.

40. John Bryant to O, 20 August 1880; Anthony Waterer to O, 29 March 1881; Henry-Russell Hitchcock, *The Architecture of Henry Hobson Richardson and His Times* (Hamden, Conn.: Archon Books, 1961), pp. 205–8.

41. KPW to O, 22 August 1870.

42. Lucia Knapp to O, 3 October 1877.

43. CV to O, 7 October 1883.

44. O to CEN, 11 March 1883, Norton Papers.

45. *Ibid.*

46. FLO (son), interview.

47. O to CLB, 1 November 1884.

48. FLO (son), interview.

49. O to JCO, 9 November 1882.

50. O to HWSC, 9 February 1881.

51. CEN to O, 23 October 1881 (copy).

52. HWSC to O, 12 February 1881.

53. Mariana Griswold Van Rensselaer, "Landscape Gardening, I," *American Architect and Building News* 22 (4 October 1887): 157.

54. Mariana Griswold Van Rensselaer, "Landscape Gardening, III," *American Architect and Building News* 23 (7 January 1888): 3–5.

55. O to William H. Hall, 5 October 1871, 20 February 1872.

56. O to George Kessler, 5 March 1822; Kessler to O, 22 January, 15 February, 12, 18, 23 March, 26 April, 7 October 1882; Mel Scott, *American City Planning since 1890* (Berkeley and Los Angeles: University of California Press, 1969), pp. 13–17.

57. Henry Norman, *The Preservation of Niagara Falls, Letters to the Boston Daily Advertiser, the New York Evening Post, Herald and Tribune in August and September 1881* (New York, 1881).

58. CEN to O, 2 November 1881 (copy).

59. J[onathan] B[axter] Harrison, *The Condition of Niagara Falls and the Measures Needed To Preserve Them: Eight Letters Published in the New York Evening Post, the New York Tribune and the Boston Daily Advertiser* (New York, 1882).

60. O to CLB, 7 March 1882.

61. O to CEN, 3 December 1882, Norton Papers; Jonathan Baxter Harrison, "Charles Eliot Norton and Niagara Falls," Norton Papers, Library of Congress, Washington, D.C.

62. Howard Potter, printed invitation, 4 January 1883, Box 31; Harrison to O, 9 January 1883, Box 31.

63. Charles M. Dow, *The State Reservation at Niagara: A History* (Albany: J. B. Lyon Company, 1914), p. 23.

64. *Ibid.*, pp. 23–25.

65. *Ibid.*, p. 31.

66. *Ibid.*, p. 35.

67. Potter to O, 19 May 1883; CEN to O, 25 March 1885 (copy).

68. Harrison, "Charles Eliot Norton and Niagara Falls," Norton Papers, Library of Congress.

69. J. B. Harrison, "The Movement for the Redemption of Niagara," *New Princeton Review* 1 (March 1886): 245.

70. O to Potter, 9 May 1883 (draft), Box 31; O to CEN, 11 May 1883, Norton Papers, Houghton Library.

71. Potter to O, 19 May 1883, Box 31.

72. O to CEN, 11 May 1883, Norton Papers, Houghton Library.

73. *Ibid.*, 4 August 1885, Norton Papers, Houghton Library.

74. *New York Tribune*, 10 March 1886.

75. CV to O, 21 May 1886, Box 31; O to CV, 24 May 1886 (draft), Box 31.

76. Memos, 6 October, 3 November 1886, Box 31.

77. Frederick Law Olmsted and Calvert Vaux, *General Plan for the Improvement of the Niagara Reservation: Supplemental Report of the Commissioners of the State Reservation at Niagara, Transmitted to the Legislature Jan. 31, 1887* (Albany: The Argus Co., 1887), pp. 11, 21.

78. O, Deposition for J. Weidenmann, 20–28 February 1888.

79. O to C. A. Roberts, [after] 11 July 1889 (copy).

80. O to J. Crimmins, *New York Times*, 8 August 1885.

81. O to JCO, 1 September 1884.

82. Edward Clark to O, 17 June 1885, Office of the Architect of the Capitol, letter book 28, p. 276.

83. O to Charles Eliot, 20 July 1886; O to Clark, 21 March 1886 (copy).

84. O to Justin Morrill, 18 February 1886, Office of the Architect of the Capitol.

85. O to MGVR, 2 May 1886.

86. *Ibid.*

87. *Ibid.*

88. *Ibid.*, 11 August 1886.

89. *Ibid.*

90. O to MGVR, 6 [May] 1886.

91. Mariana Griswold Van Rensselaer, *Henry Hobson Richardson and His Works* (Boston and New York: Houghton Mifflin Co., 1888).

92. O to MGVR, 11, 19 August, 21 December 1886, 9 April 1887.

93. O to CLB, 1 November 1884.

94. *Ibid.*

95. O to CLB, 15 March 1887.

96. *Ibid.*

97. *Ibid.*

98. *Ibid.*

99. O to Henry Beekman, 10 June 1886 (draft).

100. O to J. D. Crimmins, 2 July 1887 (copy).

101. O to CV, 5, 9 July 1887 (copies).

102. O to William R. Martin, 9 June 1888 (copy).

103. O to A. A. Smith, 18 October 1886; O to Stranahan, n.d., Box 25.

104. J. Y. Culyer to O, 11, 18 December 1886, Box 25.

105. *Garden and Forest: A Journal of Horticulture, Landscape Art, and Forestry* 1 (4 July 1888): 217–18.

106. C. C. Martin to O, 1 June 1888, Box 25.

107. O to Eliot, 28 October 1886.

108. *Ibid.*

109. William A. Stiles to O, 25 December 1887, Box 23.

110. *Garden and Forest* 10 (13 October 1897): 399–400.

111. Stiles to O, 13 December 1887, Box 23.

112. *Ibid.*, 27, 28 Decembeor 1887, Box 23.

113. O to MGVR, 9 April 1888.

114. *Ibid.*

CHAPTER XXXII

1. Frederick Law Olmsted, *City of Newport, Improvement of Easton's Beach, Preliminary Report* (Boston: Franklin Press, 1883); O to Frederick Vanderbilt, 2 August 1888; O to E. M. Moore, 26 January 1889; CV to Newburgh Park Commission, 27 June 1889 (copy), LWR Files; O to CLB, 15 March 1887.

2. FLO (son), interview.

3. O to Charles Eliot, 20 July 1886.

4. Frederick Law Olmsted, "Letter of Professor Olmsted. Relative to the General Duties of Park Commissioners and Incidental Matters," *Fourth Annual Report of the Board of Park Commissioners of the City of Minneapolis for the Year Ending March 14, 1887* (Minneapolis: Tribune Job Printing Co., 1887), pp. 15–25.

5. FLO (son), interview.

6. *Ibid.*

7. [William Ashburner], *Biennial Report of the Commissioners to Manage the Yosemite Valley and the Mariposa Big Tree Grove* (Sacramento: State Office, 1877), p. 15.

8. [William Hammond Hall], "Report of the State Engineer. To Preserve from Defacement and Promote the Use of the Yosemite Valley," *Appendix to the Journals of the Senate and Assembly of the 27th Session of the Legislature of the State of California* (Sacramento; 1887), 1: 13–37.

9. Frederick Law Olmsted, "Governmental Preservation of Natural Scenery," 8 March 1890, printed circular, LWR Files; [Ashburner], *Biennial Report*, p. 13.

10. George T. Clark, *Leland Stanford, War Governor of California, Railroad Builder and Founder of Stanford University* (Stanford: Stanford University Press, 1931), pp. 401–3.

11. *Garden and Forest: A Journal of Horticulture, Landscape Art, and Forestry* 1 (9 December 1888): 507.

12. O to JCO, 29 September 1886, Box 36; O to JCO, 24 September 1886.

13. William Hammond Hall to O, 22 August 1871.

14. O to Hall, 5 October 1871 (copy).

15. "Report of William Hammond Hall, Consulting Engineer," *The Development of Golden Gate Park and Particularly the Management and Thinning of Its Forest Tree Plantations* (San Francisco: Bacon & Company, 1886), p. 9.

16. O to Hall, 20 February 1872 (copy).

17. Guy and Helen Giffen, *The Story of Golden Gate Park (Illustrated)* (San Francisco: Phelps & Van Orden Co., 1949), p. 20.

18. O to Hall, 21 January 1876 (draft).

19. Harold Gilliam and Michael Bry, *The Natural World of San Francisco* (Garden City, N.Y.: Doubleday, 1967), pp. 120–25.

20. Statement of the Park Commissioners," *Development of Golden Gate Park*, p. 4.

21. "Communication from Hon. Fred Law Olmsted," *Development of Golden Gate Park*, pp. 22–26.

22. Giffen, *Story of Golden Gate Park*, pp. 63–66.

23. FLO (son), interview.

24. O to Leland Stanford, 27 November 1886 (copy), Box 36.

25. *Ibid.*

26. Hubert Howe Bancroft, *History of the Life of Leland Stanford: A Character Study* (Oakland, California: Biobooks, 1952), p. 117.

27. Charles A. Coolidge to O, 3 May 1887.

28. *Ibid.*

29. *Ibid.*

30. O to MGVR, 17 May 1887 (copy).

31. *Ibid.*, 14 June 1888.

32. Diane Kostal McGuire, "Early Site Planning on the West Coast: Frederick Law Olmsted's Plan for Stanford University," *Landscape Architecture* 47 (January 1957): 349.

33. O to Thomas H. Douglas, 23 May 1889 (copy), Box 36.

34. Henry S. Codman to O, 20 March 1888.

35. O to Stanford, 16 March 1889 (copy).

36. *San Francisco Examiner*, 22 December 1888.

37. O to GEW, 10 June 1889 (copy).

38. O to Ariel Lathrop, 7 July 1890 (copy).

39. O to Stanford, 7 August 1890 (copy).

40. O to FLO (son), 1 August 1894; FLO (son) to LWR, 16 June 1952, LWR Files.

41. McGuire, "Early Site Planning," p. 349.

42. O to FJK, 20 January 1891.

43. *Ibid.*

44. *Ibid.*

45. *Ibid.*

46. FLO (son) to LWR, 21 November 1952, LWR Files.

47. *New York Sun*, 29 June 1890, LWR Files.

48. O to Hunt, 2 March 1889 (copy), Box 33.

49. O to Charles McNamee, 31 May 1889 (copy).

50. O to George W. Vanderbilt, 12 July 1889 (draft), Box 33.

51. *Ibid.*

52. *Ibid.*

53. *Ibid.*

54. *Ibid.*, 11 December 1889 (copy); O to W. H. Thompson, 6 November 1889 (copy).

55. FLO (son) to LWR, 21 November 1952, LWR Files.

56. *New York Sun,* 29 June 1890, LWR Files.

57. Gifford Pinchot, *Breaking New Ground* (New York: Harcourt, Brace and Company, 1947), p. 15.

58. *Ibid.*, p. 48.

59. Gifford Pinchot's Diary, 2 February 1891, Gifford Pinchot Papers, Library of Congress, Washington, D.C.; O to FJK, 20 January 1891; O to G. W. Vanderbilt, 16 June 1890 (copy).

60. Pinchot's Diary, 14 October, 12 November 1891; Pinchot, *Breaking New Ground,* pp. 48–49.

61. O to JCO, 29 October 1890.

62. *Ibid.*, 31 October 1890, 17 March 1893; O to partners, 1 November 1893.

63. O to Mrs. William Dwight Whitney, 16 December 1890 (copy).

64. *Ibid.*

65. *Ibid.*

66. *Ibid.*

67. *Ibid.*

68. *Ibid.*

69. *Ibid.*

70. O to FJK, 20 January 1891.

71. *Ibid.*

72. *Ibid.*

73. O to GWC, 22 January 1891 (copy).

74. *Ibid.*

75. O to CEN, 24 September 1890, Norton Papers, Houghton Library, Harvard University, Cambridge, Massachusetts.

76. O to FLO (son), 5 September 1890.

77. *Ibid.*

78. *Ibid.*

79. *Ibid.*

80. *Ibid.*

CHAPTER XXXIII

1. Sigfried Giedion, *Space, Time and Architecture: The Growth of a New Tradition* (Cambridge: Harvard University Press, 1941), p. 182.

2. C. B. Norton, *World's Fairs from London 1851 to Chicago 1893* (Chicago: Published for the World's Columbian Exposition 1893, Milton Weston Company, 1890), p. 12.

3. Giedion, *Space, Time and Architecture,* p. 210.

4. *Ibid.*, p. 209.

5. Christopher Tunnard, *The City of Man* (New York: Charles Scribner's Sons, 1953), p. 304.

6. "Landscape Gardening at the Columbian Fair," *Garden and Forest: A Journal of Horticulture, Landscape Art, and Forestry* 6 (6 December 1893): 501.

7. O to FLO (son), 7 August 1890.

8. Frederick Law Olmsted, "A Report upon the Landscape Architecture of the Columbian Exposition to the American Institute of Architects," p. 6 (typed copy), LWR Files.

9. *Ibid.*, pp. 7, 9.

10. *Ibid.*, p. 4.

11. *Ibid.*, p. 11; Chicago South Park Commission, *Report Accompanying a Plan for Laying out the South Park, Olmsted, Vaux & Co., Landscape Architects* (Chicago: Evening Journal, 1871), frontispiece design.

12. F. L. Olmsted, "Report upon the Landscape Architecture," p. 11.

13. O to JCO, 24 November 1890, Box 38.

14. F. L. Olmsted, "Report upon the Landscape Architecture," pp. 12–13.

15. *Ibid.*

16. Norman T. Newton, *Design on the Land: The Development of Landscape Architecture* (Cambridge: Harvard University Press, 1971), p. 360.

17. F. L. Olmsted, "Report upon the Landscape Architecture," p. 14.

18. O to Henry Van Brunt, 22 January 1891 (copy).

19. Charles Moore, *Daniel Hudson Burnham, Architect, Planner of Cities* (Boston and New York: Houghton Mifflin Co., 1921), 1: 47.

20. FLO (son), interview.

21. O to FJK, 20 January 1891.

22. [Frederick Law Olmsted], "Memorandum as to What is to be Aimed at in the Planting of the Lagoon District of the Chicago Exposition, as Proposed March, 1891," *American Florist* 11 (11 January 1896): 602–4.

23. *Ibid.*

24. *Ibid.*

25. *Ibid.*

26. F. L. Olmsted, "Report upon the Landscape Architecture," p. 14.

27. O to JCO, 14 March 1891, Box 38.

28. Edward S. Wood to O, 13 June 1891; O to FLO (son), 28 June, [July] 1891.

29. O to FLO (son), [July], 7 July 1891.

30. FLO (son), draft of autobiographical article for *Harvard Class of 1894, Twenty-fifth Anniversary Report*, LWR Files.

31. O to FLO (son), 29 July 1891.

32. *Ibid.*, 11 August 1891.

33. Charles J. Stillé to O, 1 June 1891.

34. O to FLO (son), 2, 11, 15, 17 August 1891.

35. FLO (son), interview.

36. O to JCO, 12, 15, 25 September, 1 October 1891.

37. *Ibid.*, 28 September 1891, Box 33.

38. *Ibid.*, 12 September 1891.

39. O to Henry S. Codman, 4 November 1891, Box 38.

40. [Frederick Law Olmsted], "Draft of a Circular Proposed To Be Issued to State Committees," [ca. November 1891], Box 38.

41. O to JCO, 1 December 1891.

42. O to Daniel H. Burnham, 23, 28 December 1891 (copy).

43. Pinchot's Diary, 30, 31 December 1890, 1–9 January 1892, Gifford Pinchot Papers, Library of Congress, Washington, D.C.; HWSC to O, 5 August 1881.

44. O to partners, 31 October 1890; MCO to FJK, 25 February [1886?]; FLO (son), interview.

45. O to William Platt, 1 February 1892 (copy).

46. O to JCO, 5 March 1892, Box 33.

47. *The Central Park Race Track Law Was Repealed by Public Sentiment* (New York: Albert B. King, 1892), p. 6.

48. *Ibid.*

49. O to John J. Chapman, 24 March 1892 (copy), LWR Files.

50. *Central Park Race Track Law*, pp. 8–9, 14, 19.

51. O to FLO (son), 28 March 1892 (telegram).

52. O to FJK, 6 September 1893.

53. FLO (son), interview; FLO (son) to LWR, June 1952, LWR Files.

54. O to JCO, n.d. [written on *S. S. Pavonia*], Box 38.

55. *Ibid.*, 15 May 1892.

56. *Ibid.*, 20 April 1892, Box 21.

57. *Ibid.*; FLO (son), interview.

58. O to H. S. Codman, 20 April 1892.

59. O to H. S. Codman, 21 April 1892.

60. O to partners, Report, April 1892.

61. *Ibid.*

62. *Ibid.*

63. Edouard André to O, 29 April 1892; Phil Codman (writing at O's dictation) to H. S. Codman, 1 May 1892.

64. O to MCO, 3 May 1892.

65. P. Codman to H. S. Codman, 1 May 1892.

66. O to JCO, 15 May 1892.

67. *Ibid.*

68. *Ibid.*

69. *Ibid.*

70. *Ibid.*

71. R. Percy Smith, "Henry Rayner, M.D. Aberd., M.R.C.P. Edin.," *Journal of Mental Science* 72 (April 1926): 171–79; O to FJK, 6 September 1892.

72. O to H. S. Codman, 16 June 1892; O to JCO, 27 June 1892; O to partners, July 1892, Box 21.

73. W. A. Stiles to O, 18 April 1892.

74. *New York Times*, 13 April 1892.

75. *Ibid.*, 16 April, 10 June 1892.

76. Stiles to O, 18 April 1892.

77. O to partners, July 1892.

78. *Ibid.*

79. *Ibid.*, 17 July 1892.

80. *Ibid.*

81. *Ibid.*

82. Geoffrey Taylor, *Some Nineteenth Century Gardeners* (Tiptree, Essex, England: Skeffington, 1951), p. 82.

83. O to JCO, 27 June 1892, Box 21.

84. O to partners, July 1892.

85. O to H. S. Codman, 30 July 1892.

86. O to MGVR, 7 November 1892; FLO (son), interview.

87. William Robinson to O, 15 August, 7 December 1892.

88. O to Charles Eliot, 4 March 1886.

89. O to JCO, 6 August 1892.

90. *Ibid.*

91. *Ibid.*

92. O, notebook, Box 48; O to FJK, 6 September 1893; O to JCO, 25 August 1892.

93. O, notebook, Box 48.

94. O to JCO, 19 May 1892.
95. O to MCO, [ca. 1 September 1892]; O to FJK, 6 September 1893.

CHAPTER XXXIV

1. O to JCO, [1 October 1892?]; O to W. A. Stiles, 7 October 1892.
2. "The Future of the Fair Grounds," *Garden and Forest: A Journal of Horticulture, Landscape Art, and Forestry* 5 (19 October 1892): 501–2.
3. O to JCO, 11 October 1892.
4. Foreign Office, 1893, Miscellaneous Series, *No. 292. Reports on Subjects of General and Commercial Interest. United States. Report on the Inauguration and Condition of the World's Columbian Exposition* (London: Printed for Her Majesty's Stationery Office, Harrison and Sons, 1893), p. 3.
5. O to MGVR, 7 November 1892.
6. O to JCO, 11 October, 27 November 1892.
7. "Henry Sargent Codman," *Garden and Forest: A Journal of Horticulture, Landscape Art, and Forestry* 6 (18 January 1893): 36.
8. O to JCO, 4, 6 February 1893.
9. *Ibid.*, 17 February 1893.
10. *Ibid.*, 17 March 1893.
11. O to Rudolph Ulrich, 11 March 1893, Box 38.
12. Charles Moore, *Daniel Hudson Burnham, Architect, Planner of Cities* (Boston and New York: Houghton Mifflin Co., 1921), 1: 74.
13. *Ibid.*, pp. 78–79.
14. O to JCO, 23 March 1893.
15. *Ibid.*, 10, 13 April 1893.
16. Foregin Office, *No. 292*, p. 6.
17. O to JCO, 13 April 1893.
18. *Ibid.*, 23 April 1893.
19. *Ibid.*, 27 April 1893.
20. *Ibid.*, 28 April 1893.
21. Foreign Office, *No. 292*, p. 2; O to JCO, 3 May 1893.
22. O to JCO, 10, [15] May 1893.
23. *Ibid.*, [15 May] 1893; William R. Ware and Frederick Law Olmsted, *Columbia College in the City of New York. Report of Professor William R. Ware and Mr. Frederick Law Olmsted on the Occupation of the New Site* (26 May 1893).
24. O to D. H. Burnham, 20 June 1893 (draft), Box 38.
25. Frederick Law Olmsted, "A Report upon the Landscape Architecture of the Columbian Exposition to the American Institute of Architects," pp. 17–19 (typed copy), LWR Files.
26. O to KPW, 10 December 1893 (draft).
27. F. L. Olmsted, "Report upon the Landscape Architecture," p. 20.
28. O to D. H. Burnham, 2 October 1893 (draft).
29. *Garden and Forest* 6 (3 May 1893): 192.
30. Mariana Griswold Van Rensselaer, "Frederick Law Olmsted," *Century Illustrated Monthly Magazine*, 46 (October 1893): 860–67.
31. Timothy Dwight to O, 25 June 1893; C. W. Eliot to O, 31 May 1893.
32. O to MGVR, 22 May, 17 June 1893.
33. *Ibid.*, [June 1893].
34. *Ibid.*, 11 June 1893.
35. *Ibid.*
36. O to MGVR, 23 September 1893; MGVR to O, 27 August 1893.

37. O to partners, 28 October 1893.
38. O to JCO [13 March 1894].
39. FLO (son) to LWR, 30 November 1951, LWR Files.
40. O to partners, 28 October 1893, Box 32.
41. *Ibid.*, 1 November 1893.
42. O to FJK, 6 September 1893.
43. O to JCO, 27 October 1893.
44. O to partners, 28 October 1893.
45. O to JCO, 27 October 1893.
46. *Ibid.*
47. *Ibid.*
48. Frederick Law Olmsted, "George W. Vanderbilt's Nursery," *Asheville Lyceum* (December 1891), pp. 5–7; O to G. W. Vanderbilt, 30 December 1893 (copy); O to Charles Eliot, 29 April 1895.
49. O to James C. Gall, 7 July 1894 (copy).
50. O to partners, 8 November, 3 May 1893.
51. O to JCO, 25 February 1894.
52. FLO (son) to LWR, 1 November 1951, LWR Files.
53. [O] to JCO and C. Eliot, [before 21 February 1894]; O to Olmsted, Olmsted & Eliot, 18 February 1894.
54. O to JCO, 11, [13], 15 March 1894.
55. O to partners, 15 March 1894; O to C. Eliot, 20 March 1894.
56. O to Gall, 7 July 1894 (copy).
57. *Ibid.*
58. O to FLO (son), 1 August 1894.
59. C. Eliot to O, 25 July 1894.
60. O to FLO (son), 1 August 1894.
61. O to Gall, 7 July 1894 (copy).
62. O to CV, [summer 1894] (draft).
63. MCO [?] to Theodora Kimball, memo, n.d., Box 21.
64. "New York's Proposed Speed Road," *Garden and Forest* 6 (18 October 1893): 431; "The Harlem Speedway," *Garden and Forest* 7 (8 August 1894): 311; Paul Dana to O, 30 October 1894.
65. "The Harlem Speedway," *Garden and Forest* 7 (8 August 1894): 311.
66. "Landscape Art and the Harlem Speedway," *Garden and Forest* 7 (10 October 1894): 414.
67. O to C. Eliot, 10 November 1894.
68. O to FLO (son), 23–26 December 1894, Box 21.
69. *Ibid.*
70. FLO (son) to LWR, 10 October 1951.
71. O to FLO (son), 1 January [1895], fragment, LWR files.
72. *Ibid.*, 3 February 1895, LWR Files.
73. *Ibid.*, 7 January, 3, 15 February 1895.
74. *Ibid.*, 10 February 1895.
75. GEW to O, 6 January 1895, Box 22.
76. O to Gifford Pinchot, 9 January 1895 (copy), LWR Files.
77. O to FLO (son), 5 October 1895.
78. Secretary, New York Department of Public Parks to O, 28 February 1895.
79. Stiles to O, 1, 5, 7 March 1895; [Stanford White] to Stiles, 5 March 1895 (copy).
80. O to C. deF. Burns, 9 March 1895 (copy), Box 22.
81. O to Stiles, 10 March 1895 (copy).
82. Stiles to O, 9, 13 March 1895; *New York Sun*, 10 March 1895.
83. O to Stiles, 10 March 1895 (copy).

84. *Ibid.*
85. *Ibid.*
86. *Ibid.*
87. O to C. Eliot, 29 April 1895.
88. O to partners, 3 April, 21 [March] 1895.
89. JCO to FLO (son), 31 January 1895.
90. O to Charles S. Sargent, 25 April 1895 (copy), Box 34.
91. Sargent to O, 4 May 1895 (copy).
92. FLO (son) to LWR, 29 September 1951, LWR Files.
93. *Ibid.*
94. O to C. Eliot, 3 May 1895.
95. O to JCO, 10 May 1895.
96. Carl A. Schenck to Stella Obst, 24 August 1950 (copy), LWR Files.
97. FLO (son), interview.
98. FLO (son) to Thomas A. Fox, 13 September 1933 (carbon), LWR Files.
99. *Ibid.*
100. O to C. Eliot, 10, 19 May 1895; JCO to MCO, 24 May 1895; FLO (son) to LWR, 29 September 1951, LWR Files.

CHAPTER XXXV

1. Charles Eliot to JCO, 3, 6, June 1895.
2. O to C. D. Beadle, 27 July 1895; O to James Gall, 29 July 1895 (copy); Theodora Kimball, memo, n. d.
3. O to FLO (son), [July 1895], LWR Files.
4. *Ibid.*, 23 July 1895, LWR Files.
5. *Ibid.*
6. O to FLO (son), [July 1895], LWR Files.
7. *Ibid.*, 31 July, 8 August 1895, LWR Files; O to FLO (son), 2 September 1895.
8. JCO to O, 2 September 1895.
9. O to FLO (son), 5 October 1895; O to FLO (son), [after 5 October 1895], LWR Files.
10. O to FLO (son), n.d. [after 5 October 1895], 14 October 1895, LWR Files.
11. *Ibid.*, 15 October 1895, LWR Files.
12. *Ibid.*, 7 November 1895, LWR Files.
13. *Ibid.*, n.d., LWR Files.
14. JCO to FLO (son), 6 November 1895.
15. FLO (son), interview; Marion Olmsted, Diary, 16 November 1895, LWR Files.
16. FLO (son), interview.
17. Marion Olmsted, Diary, 26 November–1 December 1895, LWR Files.
18. O to FLO (son), 5 December [1895], LWR Files.
19. *Ibid.*, 10 December 1895 (copy).
20. Marion Olmsted, Diary, 6, 7 December 1895, LWR Files; MCO to FLO (son), 18 January 1896.
21. MCO to FLO (son), 18, 19, 23–27 January 1896.
22. *Ibid.*, 18, 23–27, 28 January, 5 February 1896.
23. *Ibid.*, 20, 23 February 1896.
24. *Ibid.*, 23 February 1896.
25. MCO to sons, 2–5, 15 March 1896; MCO, Diary, 31 March 1896, LWR Files; MCO to JCO, 2 April 1896.
26. MCO to FLO (son), 2 April 1896; MCO, Diary, 23 April 1896, LWR Files.

27. MCO to sons, 25–26 April 1896; MCO to JCO, 2, 12 April, 10 May 1896; MCO to FLO (son), 18 January, 10 May 1896.

28. MCO, Diary, 28 April–26 May 1896, LWR Files; MCO to FLO (son), 10, 22 May 1896; MCO to JCO, 10 May 1896.

29. JCO to FLO (son), 16, 19, 24 April 1896.

30. FLO (son), interview; MCO, Diary, 2–15 July 1896, LWR Files.

31. MCO, Diary, July–December 1896, LWR Files; FLO (son), interview.

32. O to "Folks at home," 20 January 1900, Medical Records, McLean Hospital, Waverley, Massachusetts.

33. FLO (son) to CEN, 5 September 1903, Charles Eliot Norton Papers, Houghton Library, Harvard University, Cambridge, Massachusetts; FLO (son), interview.

34. W. H. Manning, memo, 26 November 1910, LWR Files; FLO (son), interview.

AFTERWORD

1. Norman T. Newton, *Design on the Land: The Development of Landscape Architecture* (Cambridge: Harvard University Press, 1971), pp. 336, 387–89.

2. O to FLO (son), [after 5 October 1895], LWR Files.

APPENDIX A: THE BILTMORE ARBORETUM

1. Carl Alwin Schenck, *The Biltmore Story: Recollections of the Beginning of Forestry in the United States* (St. Paul: American Forest History Foundation, Minnesota Historical Society, 1955), pp. 173, 202; Gifford Pinchot, *Breaking New Ground* (New York: Harcourt Brace and Company, 1947), p. 65.

2. FLO (son) to LWR, 29 September 1951, LWR Files.

3. *Ibid.*

APPENDIX B: MARY

1. MCO to Ruth Tompkins, 22 December 1909, Box 22.

2. Sarah Sharples Olmsted, interview.

3. Theodora Kimball, memo, n.d., LWR Files.

INDEX

Note: For full forms of abbreviated names, see Key to Correspondents, p. xvii.